The Complete Guide to ADHD: Nature, Diagnosis, and Treatment is a welcome addition to the voluminous literature on clinical care of children and adults with ADHD. It provides a comprehensive range of the most important topics on ADHD guided by a developmental approach to the disorder and a critical eye for the most useful research findings of which clinicians need to be aware. I highly recommend this book to clinicians, students in training to be clinicians, and other educated readers desiring a state-of-the-science review of information about ADHD and the evidence-based approaches to its assessment and management.

Russell A. Barkley, PhD, Clinical Professor of Psychiatry,
Virginia Treatment Center for Children and
Virginia Commonwealth University Medical Center, Richmond, VA, USA

The Complete Guide to ADHD: Nature, Diagnosis, and Treatment is a state-of-the-art comprehensive resource for clinicians, researchers, and mental health trainees working with individuals with ADHD throughout the lifespan. Maniadaki and Kakouros have nicely weaved their considerable clinical expertise with cutting edge empirical research to provide readers with critical background information on ADHD as well as clear, concise recommendations for assessment and treatment of this disorder from a developmental perspective. Their multilevel approach to assessment and intervention offers a unique, systems-based context to providing services for the ADHD population. This book is an important resource that is a must-read for all professionals working with children, adolescents, and adults with ADHD.

George J. DuPaul, PhD, Professor of School Psychology,
Lehigh University, Bethlehem, PA, USA

The Complete Guide to ADHD: Nature, Diagnosis, and Treatment is a crowning achievement that comprehensively reviews the history, course, diagnosis, and treatment of ADHD. It includes practical evidence-based approaches as well as clinically-rich case examples across the developmental spectrum. The book is a great resource for practitioners and students alike.

Gregory A. Fabiano, PhD, Professor of Counseling, School, and
Educational Psychology, University at Buffalo, NY, USA

Katerina Maniadaki and Efthymios Kakouros provide a masterly integration of historic, neuroscientific, neurodevelopmental, and clinical perspectives of ADHD. The inclusion of case studies highlights its complexity and broad array of functional impairments. Their insightful and highly readable interpretation of current advances in ADHD, together with their comprehensive, multi-level systemic approach to assessment, diagnosis, and intervention, makes this book an essential resource for clinicians, researchers, educators and other professionals who wish to better understand, help and support, individuals with ADHD.

Rosemary Tannock, PhD, Senior Scientist, Neurosciences & Mental Health Program of the Research Institute, The Hospital for Sick Children & Professor Emerita, University of Toronto (Special Education, Psychiatry), Canada

The Complete Guide to ADHD: Nature, Diagnosis, and Treatment is an excellent addition to the field that skillfully blends together its comprehensive coverage of ADHD theory, research, and practice within a developmental framework. Particularly helpful are the numerous case examples and clinical insights that appear throughout the text, bringing to life how ADHD and its associated features unfold across the life span and deviate from typical development.

Arthur D. Anastopoulos, PhD, Professor of Human Development and Family Studies, University of North Carolina at Greensboro, NC, USA

The Complete Guide to ADHD: Nature, Diagnosis, and Treatment is an exemplary professional guidebook and must-read for students, educators, and clinicians. Clearly the product of seasoned clinicians and scholars, this remarkable book distills the voluminous research on ADHD into a highly accessible and usable form. Their multilevel approach to clinical care across the lifespan is an invaluable resource for all professionals helping those affected by ADHD.

Linda Pfiffner, PhD, Professor, Department of Psychiatry, University of California, San Francisco, CA, USA

The Complete Guide to ADHD

This exciting new resource offers a comprehensive guide to ADHD, the most frequently diagnosed neurodevelopmental disorder and one of the most researched areas in child mental health. It brings together high-level research with the latest scholarship and applies them to practice, providing a unique and innovative perspective. Inside readers will find a critical presentation of current scientific knowledge regarding the nature, etiology, diagnosis, and management of the disorder. The book covers ADHD from infancy to adulthood and presents the whole range of possible comorbidities. The authors explore the topic from the perspective of researchers, academics, and clinicians while also offering a structured assessment procedure and a complete early intervention and treatment program, as well as illuminative case studies and practical tools for educators.

Katerina Maniadaki is a Professor of Developmental Psychopathology and the Head of the Department of Social Work at the Athens University of Applied Sciences. She has been working as a clinical child psychologist with children with ADHD and other developmental disabilities since 1997.

Efthymios Kakouros is a Professor of Developmental Psychopathology and the Head of the Department of Early Childhood Education at the Athens University of Applied Sciences. He has been working as a psychologist in child mental health services since 1983.

The Complete Guide to ADHD

Nature, Diagnosis, and Treatment

Katerina Maniadaki and
Efthymios Kakouros

Routledge
Taylor & Francis Group
NEW YORK AND LONDON

First edition published 2018
By Routledge
711 Third Avenue, New York, NY 10017

and by Routledge
2 Park Square, Milton Park, Abingdon, Oxon, OX14 4RN

Routledge is an imprint of the Taylor & Francis Group, an informa business

Library of Congress Cataloging-in-Publication Data
Names: Maniadaki, Katerina, author.
Title: The complete guide to ADHD : nature, diagnosis, and treatment / by Katerina Maniadaki and Efthymios Kakouros.
Description: First edition. | New York, NY : Routledge, 2018. | Includes bibliographical references and index.
Identifiers: LCCN 2017047160 (print) | LCCN 2017048337 (ebook) | ISBN 9781315316048 (ebk) | ISBN 9781138231085 (hbk) | ISBN 9781138231092 (pbk)
Subjects: LCSH: Attention-deficit hyperactivity disorder—Diagnosis. | Attention-deficit hyperactivity disorder—Treatment.
Classification: LCC RJ506.H9 (ebook) | LCC RJ506.H9 M36 2018 (print) | DDC 618.92/8589—dc23
LC record available at https://lccn.loc.gov/2017047160

ISBN: 978-1-138-23108-5 (hbk)
ISBN: 978-1-138-23109-2 (pbk)
ISBN: 978-1-315-31604-8 (ebk)

Typeset in Galliard
By Apex CoVantage, LLC

Contents

About the Authors

Katerina Maniadaki, PhD, is Professor of Developmental Psychopathology and Head of the Department of Social Work at the Athens University of Applied Sciences. She received her undergraduate degree in Philosophy, Pedagogy, and Psychology from the University of Athens, her undergraduate degree in Psychology from the Université Louis Pasteur, her master's degree (D.E.S.S.) in Developmental Psychology from the Université René Descartes, and her PhD in Developmental Psychopathology on the subject of ADHD from the University of Southampton. Since 1996, she has been working as a clinical child psychologist at the Psychological Center "ARSI" in Athens. Her clinical and research interests include developmental psychopathology issues, mainly early identification, secondary prevention, and treatment of neurodevelopmental disorders. The main body of her work is on ADHD. She has published scientific books, edited collections, book chapters, and papers in Greek and international journals. She has presented more than 100 papers in scientific conferences and she is the coordinator of numerous training programs on ADHD for mental health professionals and educators. Her contribution in scientific research, culture, and humanity has been also recognized with the Universum Donna 2016 award from the international organization Universum Academy Switzerland.

Efthymios Kakouros, PhD, is Professor of Developmental Psychopathology and Head of the Department of Early Childhood Education at the Athens University of Applied Sciences. He has been working as a psychologist in mental health services for children and adolescents in Greece and other European countries since 1983. His clinical and research interests include mainly childhood developmental disorders. In 1990, he founded the Psychological Center of Developmental and Learning Disabilities "ARSI" and he has been its scientific director since then. He has published scientific books, edited collections, book chapters, and papers in scientific journals. He has presented more than 150 papers in conferences and he has been an invited lecturer in many training programs for professionals.

Foreword

The sheer scope and range of the ADHD-related research literature and the rate at which new findings are published is now truly quite overpowering; it is difficult for even the specialist researcher to keep up and stay well-informed of all the important new developments—let alone the interested clinician, committed student, or concerned parent. The field is also getting more and more technical and sophisticated, with crucial developments in areas such as genetics and neurobiology, more and more difficult for the layperson to understand. What is required is a guide to scientific developments that synthesizes the literature in a way that is both comprehensive and compact and that communicates sophisticated ideas in a straightforward way without any sense of dumbing down.

In their book *The Complete Guide to ADHD: Nature, Diagnosis, and Treatment*, Katerina Maniadaki and Efthymios Kakouros have achieved this fine balance to great effect. Furthermore, by taking an explicitly developmental perspective, they have achieved a sense of coherence while, at the same time, they are moving the field forward to consider different perspectives and possibilities. I warmly recommend this impressive book.

Edmund Sonuga-Barke, PhD, FMedSci
Professor of Developmental Psychology,
Psychiatry and Neuroscience
Kings College London

'comorbid' may be less helpful in clinical case conceptualization and in parent communication than describing more general mechanisms that may unite putatively distinct disorders.

For this reason, some researchers suggest that comorbidity may be an artifact of current classification systems imposing categorical distinctions that do not really exist (Angold, Costello, & Erkanli, 1999; Achenbach, Conners, Quay, Verhulst, & Howell, 1989; Maj, 2005). This artifact possibly results from the way in which different symptoms are lumped together or split apart by these systems. In this case, there is a bias that can give a false impression of comorbidity. In other words, a child may suffer from *a single underlying condition* that displays features of *two or more* arbitrarily defined and differentiated disorders (Bradshaw, 2001). Therefore, sometimes comorbidity may refer to an overlap in symptoms rather than to co-occurrence of different disorders.

This view is strengthened by a current trend in psychiatry according to which mental disorders should not be regarded as distinct clinical entities but as syndromes, namely collections of interrelated clinical phenotypes resulting from pleiotropic genes. According to Nasrallah (2013),

> given the extensive structural and neurochemical interconnectedness of brain cells, regions, and circuits, it is surprising that we have not approached psychiatric disorders in this fashion long ago, instead of falling in the trap of manufacturing artificially isolated mental disorders and then inventing the concept of common comorbidity to explain what we are seeing instead of seeking a genetic linkage between them.

The two major classification systems, DSM-5 and ICD-10, follow different approaches to the issue of comorbidity. DSM-5 promotes the use of multiple diagnoses and does not classify cases with two co-occurring disorders separately. In contrast, ICD-10 includes some diagnostic categories that correspond to mixed disorders, with a combination code, for example *hyperkinetic conduct disorder*. This fact suggests that, in some cases, comorbidity justifies the establishment of separate diagnostic categories. DSM-5 now recognizes that ADHD can be comorbid with even more disorders than before, including ASD. This change in perspective renders the concept of comorbidity even more significant.

Therefore, we consider that the use of the term comorbidity in developmental psychopathology is often problematic—even misleading—because it implies that there are distinctly different etiologies and pathogenic processes for each disorder, but this does not depict the reality in clinical practice. In order to overcome these problems, Kaplan, Crawford, Cantell, Kooistra, and Dewey (2006) suggest viewing some frequently comorbid neurodevelopmental disorders as the phenotypic expression of the *atypical brain development* that affects multiple areas of behavior simultaneously. This term does not refer to a distinct disorder, but rather, it is an integrative concept of etiology, the expression of which leads to varying symptoms across individuals. Powell and Bishop (1992) summarized as follows:

> It seems more likely that a wide range of learning disabilities can be caused when early development of the brain is disrupted, but the specific pattern of cognitive deficits will depend on the extent and the location of the underlying neurological abnormality.
> (p. 762)

Atypical brain development, then, is a term that can be used to address the full range of developmental problems that are found to be overlapping much of the time in any sample of children (Dewey, Kaplan, Crawford, & Wilson, 2002).

One of the implications of this conceptual framework is a shift from diagnostic categorization to etiology and functional analysis of the child's difficulties. As a consequence, improved matching of intervention strategies to a child's deficiencies could result in clinical settings. For example, in a setting where functional analyses supersede categorization in importance, a child would probably receive treatment for his individual difficulties "in reading, self-control, attention, auditory discrimination, motor coordination, self-esteem, peer relationships," rather than for "ADHD" or any other disorder in general (Dewey et al., 2002).

Following the same line of reasoning, Gillberg (2010) argues that there are some symptoms of neurological nature that prompt many parents of preschoolers (3 to 5 years of age) to seek out developmental evaluation in mental health services. These symptoms may be present in one or (usually) more of the following domains: (a) general development, (b) communication and language, (c) social interrelatedness, (d) motor coordination, (e) attention, (f) activity, (g) behavior, (h) mood, and/or (i) sleep. Gillberg (2010) suggests that these symptoms should be regarded as early indicators of some neurodevelopmental disorder that affects the child in various areas. Therefore, the term comorbidity is not considered to be appropriate for describing this kind of difficulties, as these difficulties do not represent distinct disorders but neurodevelopmental problems due to atypical brain development. Consequently, in developmental psychopathology, diagnosis of a disorder cannot fully describe the person's clinical presentation if the effects of brain dysfunction on other areas are not taken into account.

Very often, these difficulties are not considered significant at such young ages and children do not undergo an overall developmental evaluation. However, the presence of major problems in at least one of the aforementioned domains before the age of 5 signals major problems in the same or overlapping domains long after their clinical surfacing in the first few years of life. Therefore, both evaluation from a multidisciplinary clinical team and subsequent intervention before the age of 5 years are essential and should not be limited in only one domain but follow a holistic approach (Gillberg, 2010).

Taking all the aforementioned discussion into consideration, we would like to express our doubts about the adequacy of the term comorbidity when it comes to describing and delineating the reality of mental—and more specifically developmental—disorders. As Gillberg (2010) points out, "in actual fact, when we talk about comorbidity, what we are usually referring to is 'coexistence,' 'association,' 'overlap,' 'additional problems' or suchlike" (pp. 6–7). Nonetheless, because the use of this term has been established in the literature, we chose to use it in the present text despite our reservations.

7.1.2 Comorbidity in the Case of ADHD

Comorbidity has come to the forefront as one of the most important aspects of ADHD because this disorder presents the highest comorbidity rates in psychopathology. ADHD is associated with at least one other disorder at a rate of 60% to 100%, depending on the sample (Biederman, Faraone, Keenan, Steingard, & Tsuang, 1991; Ishii, Takahashi, Kawamura, & Ohta, 2003; Kadesjo, 2000; Spencer, 2006). Indeed, 67% to 80% of clinic-referred children and 80% of clinic-referred adults with ADHD exhibit at least one comorbid disorder, whereas almost half of them exhibit two comorbid disorders (Barkley, Murphy & Fischer, 2008). Even in community based samples, as many as two in three of all individuals with ADHD meet criteria for at least two additional disorders (Gillberg, 2004). Some studies reveal that comorbidity rates are higher in the case of ADHD, combined type (Cumyn, French, & Hechtman, 2009; Wilens et al., 2009).

These high comorbidity rates do not allow the attribution of co-occurring disorders to chance and point out that clinical evaluation and treatment of people with ADHD should not be restricted merely to ADHD symptoms but include a broad range of emotional, developmental, and behavioral problems. Appropriate case management involves addressing the full range of clinical problems displayed. Therefore, when clinicians make a diagnosis of ADHD in any individual, they have to always consider a whole range of possible comorbid disorders.

ADHD is frequently comorbid with ODD, CD, ADs, Obsessive Compulsive Disorder (OCD), TDs, and ASD, among others. At the same time, a wide range of learning disabilities may accompany the presence of ADHD and need to be also addressed both as regards assessment and intervention (Gillberg, 2010). These problems are usually at least as important as ADHD in contributing to the impairment and to the longer term outcome in the individual (Wehmeier, Schacht, & Barkley, 2010). Comorbidity complicates treatment and significantly increases the morbidity and burden of ADHD.

In order to truly understand the nature of comorbidity of ADHD with different disorders, clinicians should be able to discriminate the way in which ADHD is related to each comorbid disorder, depending on its kind. For example, comorbidity of ADHD with ASD is more likely to be attributed to common etiological mechanisms, because there is very strong evidence that complex genetic and neurobiological factors underlie both conditions. However, in the case of ADHD and CD, comorbidity seems more likely to result from an epigenetic process through which new problems arise on the basis of the interaction between an individual's symptoms, which are neurobiological in nature, and environmental factors, for example, parenting practices.

Therefore, a clinician's interpretation of comorbidity of ADHD with different disorders is of utmost importance. For instance, if clinicians follow the line of reasoning presented before, once a diagnosis of ADHD has been made in a child, they can design a treatment plan in order to *prevent* the development of CD. In this case, they will target not only the ADHD symptomatology but parent and teacher behavior as well. Consequently, behavior modification techniques for the treatment of child inappropriate behaviors will be combined with parent and teacher training in effective coping strategies so that the escalation of behavior problems inherent in ADHD to the full range of symptoms of CD is avoided.

A recent relevant study, carried out by Takeda, Ambrosini, deBerardinis, and Elia (2012), revealed that comorbidity of ADHD with other disorders is not associated either with the intellectual capacity of individuals with ADHD or the socioeconomic status of the family. However, it was found that comorbidity rates were clearly more elevated among older children. This finding can be explained through the epigenesis of problems in older children on the basis of the presence of ADHD.

In our view, if comorbidity of ADHD is the result of epigenesis, as is possibly the case in CD or ODD, it is reasonable that prevalence is higher among individuals of older age. However, in case ADHD shares similar genetic and neurobiological substrate with another disorder, as is possibly the case in ASD, comorbidity is expected to be present at a very early stage and no difference in frequency depending on the child's age should exist.

It is generally accepted that comorbid cases of ADHD are associated with greater impairment in daily life and have a poorer prognosis (Shaywitz & Shaywitz, 1991). As Goldstein & Goldstein (1998) note, ADHD likely acts as a catalyst. ADHD symptoms alone may not cause serious problems to the individual, but if combined with negative life events or other risk factors, they appear to dramatically worsen those events and exacerbate the impact they have on the individual's current and future functioning. Therefore, comorbidity of ADHD with other disorders sometimes reflects at a behavioral level the result of the interplay between ADHD symptomatology and the environment's response to it.

Comorbidity alone does not determine the outcome of ADHD. For example, in case ADHD co-occurs with ASD, prognosis is definitely poorer relative to cases in which ADHD co-occurs with speech-sound disorder. Furthermore, the level of severity of the comorbid disorder plays a decisive role in the prognosis of ADHD.

We believe that it is essential for the clinician not only to recognize comorbidity but also to distinguish the predominant problem in each case, namely the one that causes more severe impairment in the individual's functioning and usually leads to the epigenesis of other problems. At the same time, the clinician should comprehend the process of epigenesis itself. Besides, current trends in intervention for mental disorders put an emphasis on targeting treatment at the primary diagnosis and continuing until secondary symptoms interfere with treatment or become primary (Modular Therapy; Weisz et al., 2012).

A clinician should comprehend the way in which new problems arise on the basis of the predominant problem and how comorbidities impact functional impairment. New problems affect the symptoms of the predominant disorder, leading to the emergence of a new pattern of behavior that gives the impression that different disorders co-occur. This approach may help the clinician target which presenting disorders are causing the most distress, impairment in functioning, or interference with the treatment of the primary disorder (Reid, Graziano, McNamar, Paneto, & Geffken, 2015). Due to the process of epigenesis, this kind of intervention seems to effectively reduce secondary co-occurring symptoms, as well.

7.2 ADHD and Speech and Language Problems (SLPs)

7.2.1 Epidemiology

Language disorder and *speech-sound disorder*, along with *childhood onset fluency disorder* and *social (pragmatic) communication disorder*, are classified into the broader category of *communication disorders* in DSM-5. Language disorder now incorporates the DSM-IV *expressive language disorder* and *mixed receptive-expressive language disorder*. Speech-sound disorder was formerly known as *phonological disorder*. *Speech* is the expressive production of sounds and includes an individual's articulation, fluency, voice, and resonance quality. *Language* includes the form, function, and use of a conventional system of symbols in a rule-governed manner for communication. *Communication* includes any verbal or nonverbal behavior that influences the behavior, ideas, or attitudes of another individual (APA, 2013).

In this chapter, childhood onset fluency disorder (stuttering) will be excluded from presentation, as the authors believe that its nature is completely different from the other communication disorders and should be better regarded as an anxiety disorder (Maniadaki & Kakouros, 2007). In addition, studies that investigate language deficits in children with ADHD rarely include stuttering. The other three disorders will be addressed collectively as Speech and Language Problems (SLPs) through this section.

Deficits in language development during preschool years seem to be the main reason for referral of children with ADHD to mental health services. Furthermore, it has been found that more than half of the children with ADHD were in contact with speech/language services during their preschool years (Bruce, Thernlund, & Nettelbladt, 2006; Hagberg, Miniscalco, & Gillberg, 2010). Additionally, language deficits during this developmental period may predispose children toward the development of academic problems (Gremillion & Martel, 2014). It has been found that SLPs in children with ADHD are associated with markedly poorer academic functioning relative to children with ADHD but without language problems (Sciberras et al., 2014). Moreover, it seems that some SLPs in individuals with ADHD persist into adulthood, because adults with ADHD are twice more likely to meet the diagnostic criteria for a DSM-IV language disorder than normal controls (Biederman, Monuteaux, Mick, Spencer, Wilens, Silva et al., 2006).

A recent study (Sciberras et al., 2014) showed that the risk of SLPs for children with ADHD is nearly three times higher relative to typically developing children. In this study, ADHD status was a unique predictor for SLPs. Forty percent of children in the ADHD group had SLPs. These problems were more common for ADHD, combined type (47%), followed by ADHD, hyperactive/impulsive (36%), and ADHD, inattentive type (33%). It seems that children with ADHD exhibit problems in all domains of language development at a rate of almost 50% and have speech delays at a rate of 20% (Baird, Stevenson, & Williams, 2000; Bruce, Thernlund, & Nettelbladt, 2006; Oram, Fine, Okamoto, & Tannock, 1999).

7.2.2 Description of SLPs in Children With ADHD

Children with ADHD and SLPs are a heterogeneous group linguistically, with impairments ranging from mild to severe (Goldstein & Goldstein, 1998). Even in cases in which a comorbid SLP has not been diagnosed, children with ADHD may have many kinds of language and/or communication difficulties compared to their typically developing peers (Väisänen, Loukusa, Moilanen, & Yliherva, 2014).

Language functions that have been found to be deficient in individuals with ADHD include all language domains but mainly pragmatics, grammatical and syntactic complexity, verbal fluency, and verbal intelligence (Wassenberg et al., 2010). So far, research on language development in children with ADHD has mainly focused on pragmatics, which refers to language use within the communicative context. Research in other language domains, namely phonology, semantics, syntax, and morphology, are relatively limited. Furthermore, studies on expressive language exceed the number of studies on receptive language among children with ADHD.

In regard to receptive language, research findings are inconsistent. Some researchers claim that children with ADHD do not usually encounter more difficulties relative to typically developing children (Cohen et al., 2000). Other studies, however, reveal mild difficulties in this domain among children with ADHD (Bruce et al., 2006). According to Wassenberg and colleagues (2010), the speed of the complex sentence comprehension is impaired in children and adolescents with ADHD. In other words, children with ADHD comprehend language at a slower rate than children without ADHD. This may be explained in the context of a more general deficit in information processing speed (Cardy, Tannock, Johnson, & Johnson, 2010). Furthermore, it has been demonstrated that children with ADHD have difficulties in tasks that involve the identification of central or main ideas in a narrative (Papaeliou, Maniadaki, & Kakouros, 2015).

Individuals with ADHD exhibit various pragmatic deficits and consistently perform less well than typically developing children on pragmatic language uses even when their linguistic comprehension is normal (Bruce et al., 2006; Kim & Kaiser, 2000). For instance, these children have difficulties in initiating a conversation, taking turns, and maintaining or changing topics during conversations (Staikova, Gomes, Tartter, McCabe, & Halperin, 2013). Furthermore, they have difficulties in the appropriate timing and quantity of language within social contexts. In other words, these children may talk excessively and at inappropriate moments, which negatively affects both learning process and social interaction (Tannock, 2002). They also face difficulties while adapting their communication strategies according to the needs of the listener or the situation, and they fail to adjust the formality level of language according to the person they interact with (Lorch, Milich, Flake, Ohlendorf, & Little, 2010; Tannock & Schachar, 1996).

Children with ADHD are usually more talkative during spontaneous conversations and play settings relative to typically developing children. However, when confronted with tasks that require planning and organization of verbal responses, they usually have decreased verbal output and more dysfluencies (Tannock, 2002). More specifically, children with ADHD often have difficulty when asked to narrate a story or a fact, give a definition, give instructions, or answer specific questions. In such cases, they produce utterances that lack cohesion, and they use significantly more and longer mazes than typically developing children. These mazes include pauses, false starts, fillers, revisions, and repetitions (Redmond, 2004).

Children with ADHD may interrupt their interlocutor and have difficulty focusing on the topic of conversation. These difficulties indicate that children with ADHD do not have merely problems in their language development but deficits in higher cognitive functions that are required for organizing thought and behavior.

Another language domain in which children with ADHD may encounter difficulties in preschool years is the phonological domain. Preschoolers with ADHD often exhibit articulation and other phonological problems that significantly impact intelligibility, such as phoneme addition, omission, distortion, or substitution (Lewis et al., 2012; Shriberg, 2003). An important factor that accounts for these deficits in phonological acquisition is the presence of deficits in auditory discrimination (Oliveira & Costa, 2012). Through our clinical practice, we have observed that children with ADHD often face difficulties in their capacity for auditory discrimination, particularly when it comes to some specific phonemic combinations. Children with ADHD often mispronounce or omit some phonemes (particularly the voiceless and continuant phonemes /ð /, /θ/, and /f/) have difficulty pronouncing difficult words at a regular rate, may reverse phonemes or whole syllables, and have difficulty articulating consonant clusters and multisyllable words. As a consequence, their speech is not always easily comprehensible, which can cause them great frustration.

As research findings suggest, older children with ADHD have much less difficulty in speech relative to younger children (Grodzinsky & Diamond, 1992; Fischer, Barkley, Edelbrock, & Smallish, 1990). This can be attributed to the fact that articulation problems may subside with the passage of time even when children with such difficulties do not attend speech therapy. In school-age years, articulation problems usually seem to subside, but difficulties in auditory discrimination persist and are often manifested in written speech, as well. These difficulties may be associated with "dyslexic type" difficulties, which are very often observed among these children (Agapitou & Andreou, 2008; Beitchmann et al., 1996). However, parents and educators very often fail to identify these difficulties because children are usually aware of the words that they cannot easily articulate and they tend to avoid their use. Cohen and colleagues (1998) carried out a study based on a clinical sample of 380 children, 7 to 14 years of age, and they concluded that 40% of these children had difficulties in language development that had not been recognized before.

Children with ADHD usually feel frustrated when communicating with others, especially with other children, due to their SLPs. Obviously, these difficulties have a negative impact on their social interactions, including the forming of positive peer relationships (Staikova et al., 2013). However, there is a bidirectional association between speech and social interaction. Difficulties with language development in children with ADHD may lead to limited social interaction, which in turn further minimizes opportunities for language skills development (Gremillion & Martel, 2014).

For the aforementioned reasons, we strongly believe that early treatment of these problems is of paramount importance. Besides the obvious benefit of eliminating speech and language difficulties, early treatment can limit the epigenesis of new problems that usually arise on the basis of the comorbidity of ADHD and SLPs. Early treatment can also be conducive to preventing or reducing the severity of learning difficulties that usually arise in the framework of the preceding comorbidity (see Section 12.5.2).

7.2.3 Nature of the Relationship Between ADHD and SLPs

Although the high prevalence of comorbidity of ADHD with SLPs has been adequately acknowledged and substantiated, its precise nature remains inconclusive. The mechanisms underlying the relationship between these two disorders are complex, and debate continues regarding the direction of the influence. Various theories have been proposed to explain this association.

Hinshaw, Lahey, and Hart (1993) argue that ADHD and SLPs share a common underlying etiology, as comorbidity of these disorders is already present in early childhood. Tannock and Schachar (1996) claim that this shared biological etiology concerns deficits in executive functions at least as far as pragmatic difficulties are concerned. According to this approach, deficits in executive functions cause simultaneously both the core symptoms of ADHD and difficulties in pragmatics. They are also considered to cause difficulties in planning, organizing, and manipulating extensive forms of language behavior, including the cases of narration and conversation.

Speech and language skills are not only a dimension of language development but also a prerequisite for the development of other cognitive functions, including perception, attention, and short-term memory (Marchand & Fernald, 2008). For example, it has been found that delayed language development may hinder the development of sustained attention and voluntary control that, in turn, can lead to poorer and more slowly developing receptive and expressive language (Gartstein, Crawford, & Robertson, 2008; Ruf, Schmidt, Lemery-Chalfant, & Goldsmith, 2008). In addition, language facilitates the organization and planning of behavior. For example, it is important for the development of "self-talk," which constitutes a fundamental element in behavioral control as well as for communication in social contexts (Bruce et al., 2006). In this sense, the association between language development and higher cognitive functions seems to be bidirectional (Gremillion & Martel, 2014).

On the other hand, it is evident that cognitive skills affect language development in all domains. For example, the impact of attention and intellectual functions widely determines language development. There is considerable evidence that some difficulties in language development may derive from the primary ADHD symptoms and the cognitive deficits that often define this disorder (Papaeliou et al., 2015). It is claimed that symptoms of impulsivity may account mainly for difficulties in describing and narrating facts or events, along with difficulties in pragmatics, which are often observed among children with ADHD. In contrast, symptoms of inattention may have a closer association with vocabulary development (Geurts, 2008; Gremillion & Martel, 2014).

Language develops within a social context where children verbally interact with their parents (Yoder & Warren, 1993). Based on this fact, Camarata and Gibson (1999) proposed a theoretical model that attempts to associate primary ADHD symptoms with difficulties in language development of these children. According to this model, during infancy, attention deficits may disrupt joint attention activities between infant and parents, so that parental language expansions or extensions are less effective in developing the child's language.

In preschool years, both inattention and impulsivity of children with ADHD may interact with the language learning transactions between toddler and parents during communication. As a consequence, the social context that supports language acquisition may be disrupted. For example, the child's difficulties in sustained attention along with distractibility and difficulty following rules render verbal transactions brief and intermittent. Furthermore, the caregiver may quickly abandon activities that are based on verbal communication because the child seems to get easily bored. Alternatively, due to the child's impulsivity, the adult may adopt a more directive and less interactional and supportive verbal style of communication. As a result, the focus of adult–child interactions may shift from playing and positive exchanges to attempts to manage the child's behavior. Therefore, the difficulties of children with ADHD in language development, and particularly in pragmatics, can be interpreted as the outcome of limited learning opportunities, resulting from the primary ADHD symptoms and their impact on adult responses toward the child.

Impaired attention also plays a prominent role in vocabulary and grammatical development. As Mueller and Tomblin (2012) explain, in order to acquire language skills, the infant must be able to selectively focus on relevant linguistic input and ignore irrelevant input. Simultaneously, the infant must sustain this focus in order to form an association between an object and a label in the process of lexical learning. When the source of language input shifts, the infant must also be able to shift attention to avoid missing relevant input. As language develops, the infant must also attend to linguistic sequences for the development of grammatical skills. Therefore, attentional deficits may be a cause of disruption in the process of language learning.

Longitudinal studies also corroborate the potential impact of core ADHD symptoms on language development. These studies verify continuity in the slow rate of language development from infancy to school-age years, and they reveal the importance of working memory in this process. More specifically, it seems that vocabulary size in infancy is strongly related to early lexical and grammatical development (Bates, Bretherton & Snyder, 1988) and to linguistic and cognitive skills at age 4 years (Feldman et al., 2005). Individual differences in rapid auditory processing, phonological awareness, and segmentation abilities in the first year of life are related to lexical development in the second and third years because the ability to rapidly process speech sounds is central to understanding language in real time (Kuhl, Conboy, Padden, Nelson & Pruitt, 2005; Newman, Ratner, Jusczyk, & Dow, 2006). Furthermore, higher speed in word recognition at early stages of language development may facilitate children both in inducing the meaning of novel words from their linguistic and nonlinguistic context and also in tracking morphosyntactic regularities that are critical for lexical, grammatical, and syntactic development (Marchand & Ferland, 2008).

Early efficiency in speech processing and vocabulary learning can affect language development in many ways. Infants who can more quickly identify the referent of a word are more capable of processing secondary aspects of the referential context that could support more complex lexical representations. Faster lexical access could enable the child to attend to subsequent information in the speech stream, facilitating tracking of distributional cues that are crucial for "building" grammar rules. On the other hand, children who are less capable of processing oral speech need greater exposure to the same word in order to reach the same degree of representational detail with typically developing children. Consequently, they have a slower rate of vocabulary growth and weaker systems of relations across phonological and lexical forms (Marchman & Bates, 1994).

According to more recent longitudinal studies (Marchand & Ferland, 2008), speed of spoken language understanding and vocabulary size at 2 years of age predict cognitive and language skills not only in preschool years but also in later childhood. These skills are strongly related to working memory and, therefore, to children's expressive language. Consequently, individual differences in working memory in school-age years can be tracked back to indices of processing speed and vocabulary knowledge in infancy. These individual differences are the outcome of endogenous differences in the neurological mechanisms guiding early perceptual, attentional, or motor development, combined with children's early language experiences (Colombo, 2004; Marchand & Ferland, 2008). This conclusion suggests that (a) difficulties in the aforementioned domains are highly likely to be related to primary ADHD symptoms as the cognitive function of attention is involved, (b) there is room for considerable improvement as these skills are also affected by the children's language experiences, and (c) intervention for language difficulties is completely justified as early as the age of 2 years (see Section 12.5.2).

All the previously discussed hypotheses about the nature of the association between ADHD and SLPs are based on their alleged comorbidity, as they are classified as independent and distinct clinical entities in DSM-5. In our view, however, delays in language development, as well as speech and language problems in general, are manifested in the context of another disorder or neurological dysfunction that affects language development in one of the ways that have been described so far, alone or in combination. As Hagberg, Miniscalco, & Gillberg, (2010) claim, language difficulties are not usually isolated phenomena but closely associated to other neurodevelopmental disorders. Based on this line of reasoning, we do not adopt the concept of comorbidity for SLPs and ADHD. To the contrary, we consider that speech and language problems should be evaluated as *symptoms* of another disorder and not as ***a distinct disorder***. In the case of ADHD, our clinical experience corroborates this view.

In conclusion, SLPs of children with ADHD seem to be strongly related to the neurological background, the primary symptoms, and the cognitive deficits that define the disorder. Furthermore, they seem to be early signs of SLD, which is present in the majority of these children. They can also be an early indicator for the identification of children at high risk for developing ADHD and learning problems (Gremillion & Martel, 2012). For this reason, as we will discuss subsequently (Section 12.5.2), targeted early intervention for SLPs within the framework of ADHD is of prime importance not only for language development but also for the cognitive development and learning course of these children. Contrariwise, treatment of SLPs in preschoolers without awareness of the existence of ADHD and intervention at this level as well leaves the functionally most impairing symptoms in children with language difficulties unrecognized and untreated.

7.3 ADHD and Specific Learning Disorder (SLD)

7.3.1 SLD in DSM-5

One of the most robust findings regarding ADHD is that children and adolescents with this disorder are at a higher than average risk for academic underachievement and learning disabilities. In order to better understand this important area of impairment among individuals with ADHD, it is of paramount importance to conceptually define the terms "learning" and "learning disabilities."

From an etymological standpoint, learning disabilities refer to a difficulty that generally concerns an individual's ability to learn. Learning is not restricted to academic knowledge but also includes almost all acquired knowledge that shapes human behavior. According to this line of reasoning, we suggest that learning disabilities can be defined as "failure or inability of the individual to acquire knowledge or skills that are necessary for effectively adapting to the environmental demands."

Historically, learning disabilities were conceptualized as difficulties in learning despite normal intelligence (Shaywitz & Shaywitz, 1993). The discrepancy model has served as the fundamental conceptualization of learning disabilities for decades, despite robust evidence that it is conceptually and statistically flawed (Tannock, 2013). Nowadays, the education sector in the United States has already reduced or eliminated the dependency on an IQ-achievement discrepancy for identification of students with SLD. This change has been mandated by U.S.

federal law (Individuals with Disabilities Education Improvement Act, 2004), which defines SLD as

> a disorder in one or more of the basic psychological processes involved in understanding or in using language, spoken or written, that may manifest itself in the imperfect ability to listen, think, speak, read, write, spell, or do arithmetical calculations.

Depending on their etiology, learning disabilities can be attributed to (a) poor effort, which may include a nonsystematic participation in the educational process, lack of interest and motivation, and limited opportunities for learning; (b) some kind of neurological dysfunction; or (c) a combination of these. The first case may be described as "general learning disabilities" because academic underachievement can be attributed to environmental and not to biological causes. The second case may be referred to as "specific learning disabilities" (SLD in DSM-5) because academic underachievement is supposed to derive primarily from biological underlying factors. This distinction may lead to differential intervention, depending on the speculated cause of learning disabilities.

According to DSM-5, SLD is one of the neurodevelopmental disorders with a biological origin that includes genetic, epigenetic, and environmental factors. The way in which these factors interact affects the individual's ability to perceive and process verbal and nonverbal information efficiently and accurately. SLD incorporates deficits that negatively impact academic achievement and impede the ability to learn and use certain academic skills, such as reading accuracy, fluency and comprehension, spelling and written expression, arithmetic calculation, and mathematical reasoning. As a result of deficits in keystone academic skills, difficulties arise in learning more complex subjects and cause the students' academic achievement to lag far behind what is expected for their age and intellectual ability. SLD is a clinical diagnosis that is not synonymous with "learning disabilities" in general. That is, not all children with learning disabilities who might be detected within the education system necessarily meet the criteria for the diagnosis of SLD. By contrast, those who meet the criteria for the diagnosis of SLD can be characterized as children with learning disabilities (Tannock, 2013).

SLD has become the umbrella term for mathematics, reading, and written expression disorders in the updated DSM-5. DSM-IV previously classified these as separate diagnoses. Instead, these disorders are now housed under one overarching category with added specifiers (e.g., *SLD with impaired reading, writing or mathematics*).

Three subcomponents of the Reading Disorder (RD) are expressly differentiated: word reading accuracy (which includes decoding), reading rate and fluency, and reading comprehension. Impaired subskills of the SLD with impairment in written expression are spelling accuracy, grammar and punctuation accuracy, and clarity or organization of written expression. Four subskills are found in the MD: number sense, memorization of arithmetic facts, accurate or fluent calculation, and accurate math reasoning. Each impaired academic domain and subskill should be recorded. It is also noted that the term *dyslexia* can be alternatively used to describe difficulties in reading, whereas the term *dyscalculia* can be alternatively used to describe difficulties in mathematics. For this reason, these terms will be used interchangeably henceforth. A description of the severity degree must also be included, namely mild, moderate, or severe.

Furthermore, the IQ-achievement discrepancy criterion is eliminated and replaced with four new diagnostic criteria, all of which should be met. Thus, intellectual assessment will no longer be required for a DSM5 diagnosis of SLD, except when Intellectual Disability (ID) is suspected.

The first criterion refers to the main characteristics of SLD, where six symptoms are described. At least one of these symptoms must have persisted for at least six months despite the provision of extra help or targeted instruction. The second one refers to the measurement of these characteristics and determines that the affected academic skills should be substantially and quantifiably below levels expected for the individual's age and cause impairment in academic, occupational, or everyday activities, as confirmed by individually administered standardized achievement measures and comprehensive clinical assessment. The third criterion refers to the age of onset, which has also been modified by specifying that although onset of difficulties is during school-age years, they may not fully manifest themselves until later, when academic demands become more intense and surpass the child's innate intelligence or compensatory strategies. Finally, the fourth criterion specifies which disorders or adverse conditions must be ruled out before a diagnosis of SLD can be made. These are ID, uncorrected auditory or visual acuity problems, other mental or neurological disorders, psychosocial adversity, lack of proficiency in the language of instruction, and inadequate instruction.

Therefore, SLD is presented as a distinct diagnostic category, and its differential diagnosis versus ADHD is suggested. It seems that in DSM-5 no etiological association between SLD and ADHD is recognized, despite the fact that comorbidity rates are so high that they are unlikely to be attributed to chance. More specifically, in DSM-5 it is pointed out that SLD should be distinguished from the poor academic performance associated with ADHD, because in the latter condition the problems may not necessarily reflect specific difficulties in learning academic skills but rather difficulties in performing these skills.

With respect to differential diagnosis between ADHD and SLD, DSM-5 states that children with SLD may seem inattentive because of the frustration that they may be experiencing and also because of their poor motivation and poor skills. It is noted that in children with SLD without ADHD, inattention does not cause any other difficulties apart from those that have to do with their school work. At this point, we would like to emphasize that this statement contradicts our clinical experience, according to which there are not two qualitatively distinct kinds of inattention that distinguish ADHD from SLD.

7.3.2 Epidemiology

In a recent meta-analysis of 17 studies on comorbidity of ADHD and learning disabilities, comorbidity rate was estimated at 45%, which is higher than reported by previous research (DuPaul, Gormley, & Laracy, 2013). This rate increases considerably in clinic-referred samples, as it has been estimated that approximately 70% to 80% of children with diagnosed ADHD experience academic underachievement and approximately one-third have SLD (DuPaul & Volpe, 2009; Mayes & Calhoun, 2006). It is therefore evident that even children with ADHD who do not meet the criteria for the diagnosis of an SLD appear to have learning difficulties in a variety of fields (Mayes, Calhoun, & Crowell, 2000).

The most commonly co-occurring SLD with ADHD is RD,[1] and this is the reason why it has sparked a consuming interest among researchers (Pham & Riviere, 2015; Sexton, Gelhron, Bell, & Classi, 2012). In studies with community-based samples, comorbidity of ADHD and RD ranges from 18.9% to 44% (Carroll, Maughan, Goodman, & Meltzer, 2005; Pastor & Reuben, 2008). Moreover, 33% to 80% of the children who meet the criteria for the diagnosis of dyslexia manifest ADHD symptoms as well (McGee & Share, 1988; Shaywitz & Shaywitz, 1988).

However, it has been argued that review articles erroneously report that the most common SLD is RD, and that this happens because disorder of written expression is often overlooked in research (Mayes & Calhoun, 2006). In large school-based epidemiologic studies, the percentage of children with a significant weakness in written expression (Hooper et al., 1993) is far greater than in reading (Shaywitz, Shaywitz, Fletcher, & Escobar, 1990). Similar results have been found in clinical samples, with the disorder of written expression being the most frequent SLD among children with ADHD (Mayes & Calhoun, 2006). Comorbidity between ADHD and disorder of written expression is estimated at 55% to 64% (Yoshimasu et al., 2011). According to our clinical view, children who have difficulties in reading usually encounter similar difficulties in writing of less, equal, or greater severity.

With regard to comorbidity between ADHD and MD, considerably fewer studies have been conducted relative to RD. It is estimated that 11% to 30% of children with ADHD have comorbid MD (Capano, Minden, Chen, Schachar, & Ickowicz, 2008; Geary, 2004). Furthermore, almost 25% of children with MD also exhibit ADHD and RD (Shalev, 2004).

In case ADHD co-occurs with an SLD, prognosis is poorer because behavioral problems are more commonly displayed, and children are more likely to drop out of school (Willcutt et al., 2001). Furthermore, there is evidence that these children have more serious cognitive deficits (Willcutt et al., 2005).

7.3.3 Nature of the Relationship Between ADHD and Dyslexia

The core difficulty among children with dyslexia concerns their ability to fully develop their reading skills. Dyslexia is characterized by "difficulties with accurate and/or fluent word recognition and poor spelling and decoding abilities" (Lyon, Shaywitz, & Shaywitz, 2003, p. 2). These difficulties cannot be explained by problems in intellectual development, sensory deficits, or poor efforts (Sireteanu, Goertz, Bachert, & Wandert, 2005). Poor reading skills inevitably affect reading comprehension and negatively influence academic performance. These difficulties often persist into adulthood (Miranda, Mercader, Fernández, & Colomer, 2017).

Historically, since the development of phonetic writing, there has always been a minority of children with normal intelligence and intact vision who struggle to master reading skills. Numerous researchers have investigated the causes of this impairment. The first detailed account of a child who had inexplicable difficulties in learning to read was by the British physician Pringle Morgan (1896), who coined the term *congenital word blindness*. Dr. Morgan observed that one of his patients, 14-year-old Percy F., was not able to learn to read fluently despite his teachers' painstaking efforts, his high intelligence, and his acute vision. Morgan deduced that this was due to a congenital defect that resulted in difficulties storing the visual impressions of words. Nowadays, this kind of difficulties is usually attributed to the presence of dyslexia (Lyon, Shaywitz, & Shaywitz, 2003).

In the 1960s, dyslexia was frequently conceptualized as a visual perceptual disorder. However, over the past years, there has been growing recognition that it is characterized by a core deficit in phonological processing, namely categorizing phonemes and associating them with the corresponding written symbols (White et al., 2006). Recent evidence, however, questions the assumption that reading processes require only phonological mechanisms. Difficulties in other domains of language development, including semantics, syntax, and discourse, also seem to affect the literacy acquisition (Bishop & Snowling, 2004).

As reading and writing skills are inextricably linked, individuals with dyslexia may also have difficulties in writing. Their written text is often characterized by bad handwriting quality, untidiness, and smudges (Re et al., 2007). Oftentimes, they do not use spaces between words, or spacing is uneven. Additionally, they may make poor use of lines on paper. Other features that are noted in writing include poor alignment of words, instability and slanted letters, bad use of punctuation, absence of uppercase letters or insertion of uppercase letters between lowercase letters, and spelling mistakes, as well as omissions, additions, transpositions, and replacements of letters, syllables, or words.

More important, they usually have difficulty in written expression, which can be attributed both to impaired language development and to cognitive deficits in organization, planning, and other executive functions (Cornoldi, Del Prete, Gallani, Sella, & Re, 2010). All these difficulties escalate when the child is required to write fast, namely automatically. However, in case the child is highly motivated or is given unlimited time to finish their task, all the aforementioned mistakes decrease substantially. In general, dyslexia typically encompasses far more difficulties than those related to decoding and spelling words.

Early signs of dyslexia may appear in the preschool years, for example difficulty learning names of letters, counting objects, or learning the correspondence between letters and sounds in order to decode words accurately. It is obvious that children who have imprecise representations at the phonological level will have difficulty establishing mappings between phonology and orthography. During the scribbling period and early stages of learning to write, these children often use mirror writing. According to our clinical experience, children with dyslexia often write some numbers and/or letters reversely as early as the age of 4.

Various interpretations have been proposed to account for the high comorbidity rates of ADHD with dyslexia. Initially, it was suggested that ADHD is a secondary outcome of dyslexia (Stanovich, 1986; Pennington, 1991). Following this line of causality, the child with dyslexia is unable to complete successfully academic tasks, becomes frustrated or overwhelmed by the academic demands, and as a result, appears inattentive and distractible, possibly demonstrating behavioral problems as well (Frith, 1995).

However, this hypothesis is not consistent with evidence for phenotypic and genetic correlations between inattention symptoms and prereading skills in preschool children before the onset of formal reading instruction (Willcutt et al., 2007). In addition, ADHD symptom ratings before school entry predict scholastic achievement in later years (Fantuzzo et al., 2003; Merrell and Tymms, 2001). Besides, if this argument was valid, ADHD symptoms could not appear before school entry and would deteriorate as the child grows up. This is incompatible with the developmental course of ADHD, which usually progresses gradually from hyperactivity and inattention into academic failure and maybe ODD or even CD (see Chapter 3). Finally, the aforementioned hypothesis is inconsistent with the prevailing view that ADHD is a neurodevelopmental disorder that appears at an early stage of development.

In a longitudinal study, Fergusson & Horwood (1992) concluded that the exact opposite happens. In other words, early attention problems have been suggested as a possible causal factor in reading difficulties upon entry to formal schooling and even earlier (Shaywitz & Shaywitz, 2008). This view is in line with our clinical experience. Children with ADHD who experience learning difficulties may find it challenging to master reading, but they usually achieve it quite early. However, they are usually slow readers, as they try to avoid mistakes, and oftentimes they do not succeed in reading accurately, thus having difficulties in reading comprehension. While typically developing children manage easily to acquire automatic reading skills through practice, children with ADHD do not.

According to Logan (1997), an automatic process is fast, effortless, autonomous, and unconscious. The most important requirement for the development of automatic reading and writing skills is for the individual to recognize very rapidly the sounds that are represented by letters, to encode the relevant items in memory, and to retrieve them in a subsequent encounter. For both encoding and retrieval, attention is central as it is integral for translating print into speech (Reynolds & Besner, 2006). Therefore, there is accumulating evidence that attentional mechanisms play a critical role in reading and that disruption of these attentional mechanisms plays a causal role in reading difficulties (Shaywitz & Shaywitz, 2008). In fact, in cases of children with the inattentive subtype of ADHD, the presence of dyslexia is an even more common phenomenon (Willcutt & Pennington, 2000; Mayes & Calhoun, 2007).

Children with ADHD face difficulties in acquiring reading fluency due to deficits both in attention and verbal processing speed, which constitutes a predictive factor in reading fluency (Jacobson et al., 2011; Semrud-Clikeman, Guy, Griffin, & Hynd, 2000; Willcutt, Pennington, Olson, Chhabildas, & Hulslander, 2005). These difficulties become more prominent in cases where attention deficits are accompanied by impulsive behavior. For these reasons, when children with ADHD have the opportunity to read a text silently first and then aloud, their reading performance improves markedly.

High comorbidity rates between ADHD and dyslexia, along with the great impact of attention on the development of automatic reading skills, have led several researchers to conclude that these two disorders share, at least partially, a common etiological mechanism with neurological underpinnings and genetic basis (Eden & Vaidy, 2008; Gayan et al., 2005). This hypothesis is substantiated by studies that detected deficits in some common cognitive mechanisms, including processing speed, rapid naming, working memory, and attention. In addition, findings from twin studies have shown that common genetic influences on processing speed increase susceptibility to both dyslexia and ADHD (McGrath et al., 2011; Willcutt et al., 2010). There is also accumulating molecular evidence for a partial genetic overlap between dyslexia and ADHD, with the genetic correlation being stronger between dyslexia and inattention (Boada, Willcutt, & Pennington, 2012; Pham & Hasson, 2014; Rosenberg, Pennington, Willcutt, & Olson, 2012).

To date, a possible causal relationship between ADHD and learning disabilities (and vice versa) remains unclear, and future studies are required to elucidate the nature of this relationship. Better understanding of the mechanisms by which ADHD is associated with both reading and mathematics underachievement is critical for the development of early targeted interventions that might be able to circumvent the later academic underachievement frequently associated with ADHD (Gremillion & Martel, 2012).

7.3.4 Nature of the Relationship Between ADHD and Dyscalculia

A substantial proportion of individuals with ADHD manifest problems in mathematics that cause impairments in academic achievement and daily functioning, with estimates ranging from 10% to 60% (Capano et al., 2008; Mayes et al., 2000). Common difficulties concern either calculations or mathematical reasoning and problem solving (Pham & Riviere, 2015). Children with ADHD often do not read the instruction of a problem carefully, do not copy the numbers correctly, omit carries and borrows, and make mistakes in calculations.

These difficulties are often attributed to general cognitive deficits, such as impaired attention (Lindsay, Tomazic, Levine, & Accardo, 2001) or working memory (Rosselli, Matute, Pinto, & Ardila, 2006), and not to specific deficits related to mathematics. Findings of a recent study corroborate this view and reveal a significant association between difficulties in mathematics and inattention (Greven, Kovas, Willcutt, Petrill, & Plomin, 2014). This mirrors the pattern of relationship between ADHD symptoms and dyslexia, where there is also larger phenotypic and genetic association with inattention.

However, some subgroups of children with ADHD may encounter more specific deficits in basic numerical processing, including, for example, the ability to process quantity or to automatically associate quantities with written numbers (Rubinsten, Bedard, & Tannock, 2008). In these cases, difficulties are detected in visuospatial working memory (Capano et al., 2008).

An area of growing scientific interest is the association between reading and mathematics, in order to determine the factors contributing to individual differences in these domains and to better understand comorbidity between MD and dyslexia, which co-occur at a rate of 20% to

60% (Dirks, Spyer, van Lieshout, & de Sonneville, 2008; Mayes & Calhoun, 2006). The overlap between these two disorders has typically been attributed to similar kind of deficits, namely in language and working memory processes, that are required for both effective reading and mathematical reasoning (Landerl, Bevan, & Butterworth, 2004; Rousselle & Noel, 2007).

For example, it has been found that children with comorbid dyscalculia and dyslexia have difficulty in reading comprehension. Good understanding of a text reflects the importance of executive function skills such as working memory, inhibition, planning, and goal-directed behavior (Locascio, Mahone, Eason, & Cutting, 2010; Sesma, Mahone, Levine, Eason & Cutting, 2009). In addition, it requires the strategic allocation of attention (Pennington & Ozonoff, 1996). Similarly, these executive function skills are also necessary for mathematical reasoning (Best, Miller, & Naglieri, 2011; Harlaar, Kovas, Dale, Petrill, & Plomin, 2012). Generally, verbal working memory abilities predict both later mathematical ability and reading comprehension (Martinussen & Tannock, 2006; Passolunghi & Siegel, 2004).

In the attempt of seeking common cognitive deficits between dyslexia and dyscalculia, the role of language deficits as mediator in the manifestation of difficulties in mathematics has also been investigated, similarly to the role that these deficits play in reading difficulties. It is argued that language may act as a restrictive factor against some aspects of mathematics, regardless of basic mathematical skills, because children need language to comprehend, express, and learn mathematics (Pimperton & Nation, 2010). Different aspects of language may affect certain mathematical skills in a different way. For example, it has been found that children with poor semantic language skills are less likely to succeed both in reading comprehension and mathematics (Ouellette, 2006; Young et al., 2002). Furthermore, general verbal ability seems to be involved in how children reason numerically, whereas phonological skills are involved in executing arithmetic problems (Vukovic & Lesaux, 2013).

The importance of language for mathematics is particularly relevant in elementary school, where mathematical learning is principally concerned with developing mathematical reasoning skills and mastering complex mathematical procedures. The delivery of mathematics curriculum often occurs via written texts that pose several challenges (Harlaar, Kovas, Dale, Petrill, & Plomin, 2012). First, they are very concise, because each word and symbol should be read and understood with precision. Second, they use a specialized vocabulary in which everyday words such as ***volume, product, plot,*** and ***odd*** have different meanings in mathematical contexts. Third, mathematical texts often contain more concepts per sentence than other texts, and complex grammatical processes are often used to compress complex ideas into just a few words. All these characteristics require good language skills in order to be understood by the student as the verbal number system is linguistically structured. Thus, it appears that the overall level of language development is related to the development of mathematical reasoning (Vukovic & Lesaux, 2013). According to LeFevre and colleagues (2010), mathematical cognition might actually reflect language-related skills and processes.

A growing body of studies indicate that aspects of language development such as phonological processing and, particularly, phonological decoding constitute underlying processes that are important for both reading and mathematics (Fuchs et al., 2005; Hecht, Torgesen, Wagner, & Rashotte, 2001; Simmons & Singleton, 2008). It has been confirmed that phonological processing directly affects learning, understanding, and manipulating numbers (Vukovic & Lesaux, 2013). For example, the ability to make a connection between quantity and a written number seems to be based on the same cognitive skill that allows associating phonemes with corresponding letters, which is called phonological processing of speech (Rubinsten & Henik, 2006). Phonological decoding, which is known to have a primary role in reading, also seems to be closely associated with converting phonological representations of numbers into numerical symbols (Lopes-Silva, Moura, Costa, Haase, & Wood, 2014).

Empirical studies have identified a relationship between phonological processing and arithmetic attainment. Phonological loop function has been found to predict addition accuracy and more mature addition performance in 6-year-old children (Noel, Seron, & Trovarelli, 2004). Addition problem solving has been correlated with phonological memory in both preschool and school-aged children (Rasmussen & Bisanz, 2005). Phonological awareness at 5 years has been recognized as a significant predictor of both reading and mathematics 1 year later (Simmons et al., 2008). Similarly, phonological processing at 8 years has been identified as a significant predictor of arithmetic computation skills at 11 years. It can be hypothesized, therefore, that phonological processing and mathematical attainment share common cognitive mechanisms (Hecht, Torgesen, Wagner & Rashotte, 2001).

This supposition is further substantiated by neuroimaging studies showing that number processing shares a common neural network with phonological processing and reading, suggesting that there is a linguistic basis for some aspects of mathematics (Dehaene, Molko, Cohen, & Wilson, 2004; Dehaene, Piazza, Pinel, & Cohen, 2005). In addition, some molecular genetic studies provide evidence for genetic overlap among language skills and mathematics (Docherty, Kovas, Petrill, & Plomin, 2010; Hart, Petrill, & Thompson, 2010; Marino et al., 2011). It has been argued that a network of highly pleiotropic genes contributes to this overlap, influencing executive functions that are common in processing both speech and mathematical tasks (Harlaar et al., 2012).

We would like to highlight that these general cognitive impairments are considered to be integral features of ADHD, as it has been documented so far. In the section that follows, we make an attempt to reveal the interconnection among ADHD, SLPs, and all three kinds of SLD.

7.3.5 Interconnection Between ADHD, SLPs, and SLD

In our view, SLPs and SLD[2] could be perceived along a continuum, under the "umbrella" of ADHD, and not as distinct diagnostic categories in classification systems. An integrated and holistic approach of these problems is required for a number of reasons. First, high comorbidity rates of SLPs, dyslexia, and dyscalculia have been reported not only with ADHD but also among each other. Second, common genetic and cognitive mechanisms have been found underlying all three disorders. Third, the impact of executive functions, and particularly working memory and attention, on language development and academic learning has been widely acknowledged. Separating SLPs, SLD, and ADHD into distinct disorders and merely relating them by using the concept of comorbidity impedes the understanding of the real nature of their association and poses insurmountable obstacles both in research and clinical practice.

In research, studies on SLPs are usually carried out by speech and language pathologists, whereas SLD is the focus of psychologists and special educators. Thus, research on these disorders follows different paths, and research findings are rarely interconnected within a common theoretical framework (Bishop & Snowling, 2004). For example, rather than investigating the potential impact of attention deficits on SLD, given their frequent comorbidity, most studies analyzing the cognitive profiles of dyslexia and dyscalculia have excluded children with ADHD (Moll, Göbel, Gooch, Landerl, & Snowling, 2016). This approach is at odds with the growing consensus that neurodevelopmental disorders are caused by multiple risk factors that accumulate to produce a continuous distribution of behavioral outcomes, with some children reaching a diagnostic threshold for "affectedness" (Hulme & Snowling, 2009; Pennington, 2006).

In clinical practice, this approach leads to a plethora of professionals of different specialties working on the diagnosis and treatment of ADHD by focusing on only a small part of the individual's difficulties, which is treated in isolation, according to each professional's perspective.

As far as diagnosis is concerned, even when the child has difficulties in more than one area of development, as is often the case in neurodevelopmental disorders, emphasis is usually placed on *one* of them, depending on the predominant concern expressed by parents and the specialty of the person who is evaluating the child (Gillberg, 2010).

With regards to treatment, speech and language pathologists may work toward improving children's speech, without considering deficits in executive functions, difficulties resulting from the primary ADHD symptoms, and difficulties in self-regulation, which cause major problems in everyday functioning. Special educators may use specific teaching techniques for the improvement of academic skills and school performance of these children, without considering the etiological mechanisms that are responsible for poor academic performance and difficulties in acquiring rudimentary academic skills. They may also fail to associate these difficulties both with the core symptoms and cognitive deficits that define ADHD and with early problems in the area of language development. Finally, psychologists may be concerned with the child's behavior, self-esteem, or parent and teacher counseling, overlooking difficulties in language, and considering that learning difficulties do not fall into their area of expertise and "are not their job" to deal with.

Taking into consideration the areas in which a child with ADHD may have deficits, the fact that professionals fail to grasp these difficulties within a common framework leads to a fragmentary treatment of these problems, depending on the specialty of the therapist. The relationship among difficulties of children with ADHD in different domains of development is so complex that practitioners who expect direct routes between one specific intervention focusing on a single target and general outcomes certainly follow a wrong pathway. For example, it has been found that traditional academic interventions designed to promote the development of initial reading skills among preschool children at high risk of experiencing reading difficulties do not prove beneficial if attention problems are not addressed simultaneously (Rabiner, Malone, and Conduct Problems Prevention Research Group, 2004).

To buttress what we have discussed so far, we refer to a study of 25 children of 2.5 years of age with a diagnosis of *specific language disorder*, given by speech and language pathologists (Miniscalco, Nygren, Hagberg, Kadesjo, & Gillberg, 2006). A multidisciplinary clinical team, blind of the initial diagnosis, reassessed these children at age 7.5 years. They concluded that 70% had ADHD, ASD, ID, SLD, or a combination of two or more of these disorders. However, no child was suspected of having any of these disorders during initial assessment, and the only treatment that they had received up to that point was speech therapy.

We believe that, from a clinician's perspective, it is more informative to consider both SLPs and SLD as categories of symptoms manifested within the framework of ADHD. SLPs predispose children to develop learning difficulties in reading, writing, and mathematics as soon as they begin formal schooling. We argue that SLPs, dyslexia, and dyscalculia are etiologically associated, at least partially, influence each other, and are also influenced by cognitive deficits that characterize ADHD, such as deficits in attention and working memory. Therefore, specific difficulties in language and learning are interrelated clinical dimensions of the presentation of a neurodevelopmental disorder, like ADHD, at different developmental stages. The diagnosis that a child with these difficulties may receive is largely dependent on their age at the time of evaluation and, as we mentioned before, the specialty of the professional assessing the child (Bishop & Snowling, 2004).

This point of view coincides partially with the illusory recovery model proposed by Scarborough and Dobrich (1990). This model regards language impairment and dyslexia as different manifestations of the same underlying disorder. In other words, the problems of a child in oral language appear to resolve as the child enters elementary school, only to be replaced by literacy problems. Consequently, age determines whether oral or written language problems are more apparent.

Moreover, this point of view is in line with the contemporary view that in order to understand disorders fully, we need to consider the relationships between them, both cognitive and etiological. Studies focusing on "pure" groups simply follow the wrong approach (Pennington & Bishop, 2009).

If we review altogether the research findings presented so far, this view is adequately corroborated. First, it is widely accepted that dyslexia is closely associated with problems in language development that many of these children experience during preschool years and seem to persist over time (Biederman, Monuteaux, Mick, Spencer, Wilens, Silva et al., 2006). It has been found that problems in language development during preschool years adversely affect the emerging literacy skills as well as the development of basic mathematical skills (Pennington & Lefly, 2001; Snowling, Gallagher, & Frith, 2003; Vukovic & Lesaux, 2013). Furthermore, academic achievement is directly affected by deficits in phonological awareness, proper use of grammar and syntax, language processing speed, language comprehension, and narrative skills. All of these, which verify a link between language development and the development of main academic skills, are impaired in many children with ADHD, resulting in learning difficulties, especially in subjects that are based on language processing (Wassenberg et al., 2010).

Attention and other executive functions that are impaired in children with ADHD have been found to play a prominent role in all the aforementioned areas, including several areas of language development, learning, reading, writing, and mathematical reasoning (Shaywitz, & Shaywitz, 2008). In other words, the same endophenotypes have been associated with reading difficulties, mathematical difficulties, and ADHD. Coupled with this is these children's difficulty modifying and adjusting their verbal expression in order to successfully respond to a specific task's requirements. It becomes therefore understandable why difficulties in language development may become a hindrance to the efforts of children with ADHD to successfully respond to school demands, especially within the Western education system, which places a particular emphasis on language skills (Mathers, 2006; Wassenberg et al., 2010). Therefore, it is possible that both language problems and deficits in executive functions are synergistically related to SLD *and* ADHD, providing a mechanistic explanation of this association (Gremillion & Martel, 2012).

In conclusion, genetics and cognitive overlap of dyslexia and dyscalculia seem to be associated on the one hand with SLPs and on the other hand with deficits in executive functions. However, both SLPs and impaired executive functions are present in the majority of individuals with ADHD. Therefore, if we consider high comorbidity rates of dyslexia and dyscalculia both with ADHD and between them, overlaps on a genetic and neurological level, and common endophenotypes, we can formulate an alternative hypothesis in order to understand the nature of their relationship: dyslexia and dyscalculia may in some cases be part of the wider ADHD symptomatology, and their manifestation is triggered by impaired executive functions and SLPs on the basis of a common genetic background affected by pleiotropic genes. Given the well-established heterogeneity of ADHD, it cannot be argued that the aforementioned approach applies in all cases of people with the disorder but in a substantial part of them.

7.4 ADHD and Intellectual Disability (ID)

7.4.1 Intellectual Level of Children With ADHD

Up until recently, scientific research on ADHD and intelligence focused on defining the intellectual capacity of children with ADHD and investigating possible effects of ADHD on intellectual development. According to Barkley (1995), ADHD has a unidirectional effect on intellectual development in two ways. First, to a smaller degree, it affects the acquisition of cognitive skills. Second, to a larger degree, it affects the successful and effective use of already possessed skills.

Children with ADHD are reported to score on average 7–15 points below their typically developing peers on standardized intelligence tests (Faraone et al., 1993; Fischer et al., 1990). According to a recent meta-analysis, this difference is estimated at 9 points on average (Frazier, Demaree, & Youngstrom, 2004). Findings suggest that these children have particular difficulty in the verbal scales of intelligence tests (Andreou et al., 2005). However, we should not hastily conclude that children with ADHD have lower intelligence than typically developing children. It is acknowledged that the most popular intelligence tests, such as WISC-V and Stanford-Binet, assess to a great extent the child's academic knowledge (Bohline, 1985). It is possible that this difference reflects the children's learning difficulties given that children with learning disabilities, even if they do not have ADHD, usually score lower on intelligence scales (Barkley, DuPaul, & McMurray, 1990). Furthermore, it might merely represent differences in test-taking behavior, for example inattentive behavior (Barkley, 1990). Therefore, relatively lower performance of children with ADHD on intelligence tests seems to be associated on the one hand with their difficulties in responding to specific subscales that require good attention skills and, on the other hand, with their difficulties in learning.

However, intelligence is a protective factor that can promote both the progress and the adaptive behavior of children with ADHD. Sometimes, intelligence can serve as an equalizer. High intelligence may help the child to develop coping strategies and insight into their problems (Goldstein & Goldstein, 1998). Maybe this is one of the main reasons why some children may meet all the criteria for the diagnosis of ADHD but have no particular difficulty in daily functioning.

7.4.2 Validity of the ADHD Diagnosis in Children With ID

Very little is known about the presence of ADHD in children with ID because few researchers have investigated this issue so far. The reason why researchers did not focus on comorbidity between ADHD and ID is that individuals with ID were generally excluded from ADHD research projects (Lindsey, 2002).

In DSM-5, ID replaced the diagnostic label *mental retardation*. It describes individuals with an IQ score lower than or equal to 70 and significant impairments of general mental abilities that impact adaptive functioning in three domains, namely conceptual, social, and practical. ID is classified as a neurodevelopmental disorder that appears for the first time during the developmental period. DSM-5 emphasizes the need to use both clinical assessment and standardized testing of intelligence when diagnosing ID, with the severity of impairment based on adaptive functioning rather than IQ test scores alone. This new approach derives from the conclusion that impairment in adaptive behavior is eventually what determines the kind of support that each individual with ID needs. Moreover, it has been confirmed that reliability of the IQ score is extremely poor, especially if the IQ score is low.

Many researchers question the validity of the diagnosis of ADHD among individuals with ID and argue that symptoms of inattention, hyperactivity, and impulsivity do not justify the diagnosis of ADHD in this population but constitute a secondary problem of intellectual incapacity. This phenomenon is called *diagnostic overshadowing* and constitutes a salient concern in the case of individuals with ID. It refers to the tendency of clinicians to attribute every problematic behavior of these people solely to their low intellectual capacity rather than to a diagnosable comorbid disorder that warrants specific treatment (Jopp & Keys, 2001; Mason & Scior,

2004). The presumption that ADHD symptoms are inherent to ID has promoted a diagnostic stance that has generally discouraged identification of the disorder in this population. Indeed, in earlier editions of DSM, low IQ was a rule out for ADHD (Antshel et al., 2006).

In DSM-IV, it was stated that an additional diagnosis of ADHD should be given to children with mental retardation only if the symptoms of hyperactivity, impulsivity, and inattention are excessive for the child's mental age. However, in clinical practice, in most cases that a child received the diagnosis of mental retardation, no further evaluation for a potential comorbidity with ADHD took place (Antshel et al., 2006). Therefore, even if the criteria for the diagnosis of ADHD in children with ID are met, in practice professionals are still hesitant to acknowledge comorbidity between these two disorders. As a result, ADHD remains largely underdiagnosed and insufficiently treated within this population (Fuller & Sabatino, 1998).

However, available evidence does not justify this practice. First, behavior problems and/or psychiatric disorders are four to five times higher in children with ID compared to typically developing children (Koller, Richardson, Katz, & McLaren, 1983; Rutter, Tizard, Yule, Graham, & Whitmore, 1976). Furthermore, the prevalence of ADHD within populations with ID ranges from 18% to 40% (Pearson & Aman, 1994). In a study that was carried out on a community sample with the aim of investigating behavioral disorders in children with ID, it was found that ADHD was the most frequently manifested disorder within the population of these children (Strømme & Diseth, 2000). Furthermore, research on children who had borderline intelligence or ID of mild severity highlighted that ADHD was present in up to 39% of the cases (Baker, Neece, Fenning, Crnic, & Blacher, 2010; Dekker & Koot, 2003; Emerson, 2003). A secondary analysis of the results of a community-based study with a sample of 10,000 children and adolescents in the United Kingdom revealed that ID was associated with a tenfold increase in the risk for ADHD (Emerson, 2003). In other words, ADHD has been found to be more likely to occur in the context of developmental delay, such as borderline-to-mild ID (Voigt, Barbaresi, Colligan, Weaver, & Katusic, 2006).

On a theoretical level, this evidence can be explained by the neurodevelopmental model proposed by Accardo, Accardo, & Capute (2008). This model postulates that developmental delay (significant lag in the attainment of developmental milestones), dissociation (significant difference between the developmental rates of two streams of development), and deviance (behavior that is atypical at any age) reflect underlying dysfunction in the CNS. Consequently, dissociation and deviance should occur more commonly in association with more significant delays. ADHD, conceptualized in this model by both dissociation and deviance, should therefore be more commonly recognized in children with ID than in those without.

There is also evidence that the manifestation of ADHD in the population of individuals with mild ID is not differentiated from its manifestation in individuals without ID (Neece, Baker, Crnic, & Blacher, 2013). Furthermore, ADHD symptoms in children with ID persist over extended periods of time (Aman, Armstrong, Buican, & Sillick, 2002).

Therefore, a crucial question arises about the extent to which the difficulties observed among children with both disorders differ from the difficulties observed among children who have only one of them. In an attempt to answer this question, Ahuja, Martin, Langley, & Thapar (2013) used a clinical sample that consisted of three groups of children presenting (a) ADHD and ID of mild severity, (b) ADHD without ID, and (c) ID of mild severity without ADHD. It was concluded that children with ADHD and mild ID had more behavioral problems relative to children who had ADHD or mild ID alone.

Other studies have found that more severe neuropsychological deficits are exhibited in individuals with ID and comorbid ADHD in comparison with those who have ADHD alone, particularly with regard to executive impairment (Seidman, Biederman, Monuteaux, Doyle, &

Faraone, 2001; Seidman et al., 2006). In addition, it has been suggested that the combined effects of ADHD and ID have a greater detriment on these domains than either condition alone (Robins, 1992). In sum, these findings indicate that co-occurrence of ADHD with ID constitutes a more severe form of psychopathology. This finding extends to adults as well (Rose, Bramham, Young, Paliokostas, Xenitidis, 2009).

In conclusion, despite the fact that professionals do not often give the diagnosis of ADHD to individuals with ID, this population is at an increased risk for ADHD over and above that associated with their developmental delays (Hastings et al., 2005). Therefore, ADHD should not be rejected as a diagnosis simply because a child has ID. Rather, ADHD seems to be a valid diagnosis in the context of ID (Antshel et al., 2006; Hastings, Beck, Daley, & Hill, 2005).

7.5 ADHD and Anxiety Disorders (ADs)

7.5.1 Epidemiology

ADs are marked by excessive fear or worry, behavioral avoidance, attentional biases toward threatening stimuli, and a high degree of distress and impairment (APA, 2000). ADs are distinguished from each other depending on the stimulus or the situation that may trigger them, along with the content of thoughts and beliefs that are associated with them. Many of the ADs appear for the first time during childhood and tend to accompany the individual by adulthood, unless they are timely treated. The main ADs described in DSM-5 are *separation anxiety disorder, selective mutism,*[3] *specific phobia, social phobia, agoraphobia, panic disorder*, and *generalized anxiety disorder*. The majority of them manifest twice more often in women than men.

Empirical data concerning comorbidity of ADHD with ADs in children are limited and oftentimes inconsistent. This fact can be attributed to the difficulty recognizing symptoms of anxiety in childhood, as children seem to express a wide spectrum of emotional problems (Achenbach & Edelbrock, 1991).

According to epidemiological studies, ADHD co-occurs with ADs in approximately 25% of children in the general population and around 30% to 40% of clinic-referred children (Larson, Russ, Kahn, & Halfon, 2011; Schatz & Rostain, 2006; Tannock, 2009). These rates seem to increase when ADHD also co-occurs with ODD or CD (Abikoff et al., 2002). Moreover, 15% to 30% of the children with ADs meet the criteria for the diagnosis of ADHD (Tannock, 2009). Given that ADs are more common within female populations, they are also more common among girls with ADHD relative to boys (Gershon, 2002). Adults with ADHD also manifest increased rates of ADs relative to the general population (Biederman et al., 1993). Finally, according to a recent study in Norway, elevated anxiety was found in 33% of 3- to 4-year-old children with ADHD.

The magnitude of increase in ADs among individuals with ADHD is larger than among those without ADHD. The population-wide prevalence of at least one AD among individuals with ADHD is approximately 4% among preschoolers, 18% among school-aged children, and 47% among adults (Krone & Newcorn, 2015). The occurrence of comorbidity between ADHD and ADs seems to increase during development and is particularly high in adolescence, probably due to the inherent developmental stressors of adolescence, combined with impairments in daily functioning deriving from ADHD.

Some studies suggest that comorbidity rates between ADs and ADHD are higher among children with the inattentive subtype of ADHD (Russo & Biedel, 1994), whereas others consider that comorbidity with ADs is higher in the combined subtype (Tsang et al., 2015). Finally, other studies have reported no statistical difference in comorbid ADs across ADHD subtypes (Lubke, Hudziak, Derks, van Bijsterveldt, & Boomsma, 2009).

7.5.2 Nature of the Relationship Between ADHD and ADs

Rates of comorbid ADHD and ADs are greater than would be expected by chance. However, the nature of their association is not entirely clear, and it has been suggested that ADHD with comorbid ADs may be a distinct entity (Jensen et al., 2001). It has been found that severity of ADHD symptomatology is positively correlated with the comorbidity of ADHD with ADs (Tsang et al., 2015).

Some researchers argue that comorbidity between ADHD and ADs constitutes a more severe form of psychopathology than either of these disorders alone, and that children with a dual diagnosis evidence greater impairment (Jensen et al., 1993; 2001; Tsang et al., 2015). That is, when compared to children with either ADHD or ADs alone, children in the comorbid group may present with great symptom severity, attentional problems, and school fears (Bowen, Chavira, Bailey, Stein, & Stein, 2008). Some studies have revealed that children with comorbid ADHD and ADs show worse social functioning compared to peers with just solely ADHD (Hoza et al., 2005; Mikami, Ransone, & Calhoun, 2011). Moreover, in addition to their ADHD symptoms, these children may also manifest behaviors such as moodiness, excessive worry, difficulty shifting attention, and inflexibility (Reynolds & Lane, 2009).

However, other studies do not verify this finding (Lee, Falk, & Aguirre, 2012), and some researchers suggest that, when controlling for ODD, children with ADHD and ADs do not differ in social functioning compared to peers solely with ADHD (Newcorn et al., 2004). In general, studies to date have provided support for both the no effect and exacerbation hypotheses (Becker et al., 2012).

Some studies have found that children who have both disorders tend to perform better on tasks measuring inhibitory control (Manassis, Tannock, & Barbosa, 2000), whereas other studies have not supported this finding (Sorensen, Plessen, Nicholas, & Lundervold, 2011). Another study has shown that children with this type of comorbidity perform better on tasks measuring sustained and selective attention (Vloet, Konrad, Herpetz-Dahlmann, Polier, & Gunther, 2010). There is also some evidence that children with ADHD and ADs show greater working memory impairments (Jarrett, Wolff, Davis, Cowart, & Ollendick, 2016; Skirbekk, Hansen, Oerbeck, & Kristensen, 2011). According to Tannock (2009), these inconsistent findings are open to interpretation depending on the level of difficulty of the task. More specifically, children with ADHD and ADs may perform better on cognitively easier tasks and worse on more complex and mentally effortful tasks. For example, anxiety at moderate levels may enhance vigilance and regulate impulsivity but disrupt more complex cognitive processes, such as working memory.

On the other hand, studies reveal that symptoms of anxiety in children with ADHD may attenuate externalizing ADHD symptoms and minimize the effects of impulsivity (Schatz & Rostain, 2006). For example, it has been theorized that the presence of comorbid ADs is associated with less impulsivity and aggression among children with ADHD (Pliszka, 1992; Tannock, 2000).

It has been argued that ADHD may lead to the development of ADs owing to the fact that children undergo negative experiences in various areas, including peer interactions, academic failure, bad parenting strategies, and failure in sports activities (Lilienfeld, 2003). According to this line of reasoning and our clinical viewpoint, we consider that ADs are the outcome of an epigenetic process. Children with ADHD experience elevated levels of stress on account of the fact that they have difficulties in fulfilling the expectations held by their environment. Besides, children with ADHD and ADs are usually characterized by a generalized feeling of worry that stems from their grave concern to effectively respond to everyday social demands. For this reason, they often seem to be unwilling to get involved in new activities and avoid taking risks.

They usually keep these concerns to themselves, but they have no difficulty expressing them when they are prompted to do so (Tannock, 2009). This fact also indicates that children with ADHD and ADs often have low self-esteem.

There is also some evidence that shared neurobiological features may account for some cases of comorbidity between ADHD and ADs, namely dysregulation of the temporal lobes and the noradrenergic system, which occur in both ADs and ADHD (Krone & Newcorn, 2015).

Understanding anxiety in ADHD may ultimately assist in tailoring treatment decisions and advance treatment choices. For example, there is evidence that stimulant medications may be less effective and produce greater side effects in case ADHD is comorbid with ADs (March et al., 2000; Tannock et al., 1995). In contrast, nonstimulant medications, such as ATX, can be recommended when anxiety is present in ADHD (Geller et al., 2007; Pliszka et al., 2006).

Moreover, it seems that comorbid ADHD may interfere with mechanisms necessary for successful CBT, possibly due to impaired attention and other cognitive deficits that define ADHD (Halldorsdottir & Ollendick, 2014). For example, inattention and/or overactivity may interfere with habituation and decrease the efficacy of exposure treatments (Benito, Conelea, Garcia, & Freeman, 2012). Furthermore, working memory deficits in individuals with ADHD may hamper changes in maladaptive cognitions and coping self-talk, which have been found to predict successful outcomes in interventions for ADs (Hedtke et al., 2009). Therefore, recognizing comorbidity may lead to adapting traditional cognitive techniques according to the needs of these individuals.

7.6 ADHD, Depressive Disorders (DDs), and Bipolar Disorders (BDs)

7.6.1 DDs and BDs in DSM-5

In DSM-5, the former *mood disorders* chapter is now divided into two separate and distinct chapters, *bipolar and related disorders* and *depressive disorders.* With the addition of two new disorders, there are now four main DDs: (a) *major depressive disorder*, (b) *persistent depressive disorder*, (c) *Disruptive Mood Dysregulation Disorder* (DMDD), and (d) *premenstrual dysphoric disorder.* There are also three main BDs that are differentiated by a possible predominance of manic episodes (bipolar I disorder), depressive episodes (bipolar II disorder), or hypomanic episodes (cyclothymic disorder).

Specific reference should be made to DMDD that concerns mainly children previously diagnosed with BDs. This disorder refers to children with persistent irritability and frequent episodes of extreme behavioral dyscontrol (APA, 2013). The addition of this disorder was in response to growing concern that children have been overmedicated due to the premature overdiagnosis of BDs (Moreno et al., 2007; Olfson, Blanco, Liu, Moreno, & Laje, 2006). In the United States, in less than a decade, the rates of BDs diagnosis in children and adolescents showed a 40-fold increase (Blader & Carlson, 2007; Moreno et al., 2007). Furthermore, it was found that many children who received this diagnosis did not have distinct mood cycles considered to be the hallmark of BDs (Brotman et al., 2006; Carlson, 2009). Therefore, DSM-5 has provided "a diagnostic home for children whose rages do not otherwise satisfactorily fit into the current concepts of ADHD or ODD and have thus been called 'bipolar' to signal the severity of the problem and its mood-related nature" (Margulies et al., 2012, p. 489).

The concept of DMDD derived from a syndrome called severe mood dysregulation, which was described by a research group in the intramural program of the NIMH (Leibenluft, Charney, Towbin, Bhangoo, & Pine, 2003). The discerning difference from BD was that the symptoms characterizing this syndrome were chronic and did not manifest during clearly distinct episodes.

According to DSM-5, DMDD is characterized by severe recurrent temper outbursts, manifested verbally and/or behaviorally, which are inconsistent with the child's developmental level and out of proportion in intensity or duration to the situation or provocation. They must occur, on average, three or more times per week. Additionally, the mood between temper outbursts must be persistently irritable or angry most of the day, nearly every day, and be observable by others. These symptoms must have been present for at least 12 months with no more than 3 consecutive months of symptom-free period. Furthermore, they must be present at least in two of three settings and to a severe degree at least in one setting. The diagnosis should not be made for the first time before the age of 6 or after the age of 18. The age at onset is before 10 years. Finally, the individual must not have a history of either a manic or a hypomanic episode, and symptoms cannot be attributed to the use of any substance or to any other medical or neurological condition.

It is noted that DMDD *cannot* coexist with ODD or bipolar I disorder, but *can* coexist with ADHD and CD. Children who also meet the criteria for the diagnosis of ODD should only be given the diagnosis of DMDD. Therefore, a child with ADHD and aggressive behavior that also manifests chronic irritability between aggressive episodes can additionally receive the diagnosis of DMDD. In conclusion, differential diagnosis must be made among DMDD,[4] bipolar I disorder, and ADHD with comorbid ODD (Pliszka, 2015).

As opposed to other disruptive disorders, DMDD was set in the chapter of DDs. This choice was based on some evidence that, with the passage of time, these children tend to progress into depression (Sobanski et al., 2010; Stringaris & Goodman, 2009). In our opinion, however, the inclusion of DMDD to DDs is somehow problematic. As Harwood (2015) notes, "the inclusion of this new 'disruptive' and 'energetic' disorder as a form of 'depression' has yet to meet with substantive critique" (p. 191). We argue that it would be more suitable for this disorder to be classified within Disruptive, Impulse-Control, and Conduct Disorders, because poor self-regulation seems to be its core symptom. Other researchers have also raised their concern about the appropriateness of this classification (Copeland, Angold, MRCPsych, Costello, & Egger, 2013).

7.6.2 Epidemiology

Studies have revealed that ADHD very often co-occurs with DDs (Barkley et al., 2008; Kessler et al., 2006). A national survey of the health of 61,779 children aged 6–17 years reported depression in 14% of children with ADHD versus 1% of those without ADHD (Larson et al., 2011). Chronis-Tuscano and colleagues (2010) found that 18.4% of children diagnosed with ADHD at age 4–6 years experienced recurrent depression by age 18, compared to only 1.6% of a matched control group. Evidently, the risk for major depression among children and adolescents with ADHD is 5.5 times higher relative to the general population, with rates ranging from 12% to 50% (Angold, Costello, & Erkanli, 1999).

Prevalence estimates of major DD in samples of adults with ADHD range from 16% to 31% (Wilens, Nierenberg, Rostain, & Spencer, 2008). Conversely, a substantial number of adults with DDs also meet the criteria for ADHD. More specifically, 9.4% of adults with major DD and 22.6% of adults with dysthymic disorder also meet the criteria for ADHD (Kessler et al., 2006). A recent study confirmed that DMDD co-occurs with ADHD, combined presentation, at a rate of 39% and with ADHD, inattentive presentation, at a rate of 12% (Mayes et al., 2015).

Comorbidity between ADHD and BDs seems to be more complex. Clinical studies have revealed that 22% to 61% of children and adolescents with BDs also suffer from ADHD (Birmaher et al., 2010; Patel et al., 2006), whereas rates of BDs among children with ADHD range from 7% to 21% (Biederman, Faraone, & Mick, 1996; DonFrancesco et al., 2011). In adulthood, a systematic review of clinical studies reported comorbidity between ADHD and BDs in around 5% to 20% of cases (Wingo & Ghaemi, 2007). Prevalence is greater in men compared to women. For example, a study on adults with BDs carried out by McIntyre and colleagues (2010) revealed that 14.7% of men and 5.8% of women also had ADHD. In this group, BDs were manifested at a younger age than expected and the outcome of BDs was poorer.

According to these findings, it seems that co-occurrence of ADHD and BD is not a rare phenomenon. However, Werry (1997) notes that these rates are extremely low among the general population and, therefore, interpretation of findings that come from clinic-referred samples should be made with great caution.

7.6.3 Nature of the Relationship Between ADHD and DDs

Understanding the nature of the association between ADHD and DDs is a crucial issue, as individuals with this comorbidity seem to display greater levels of psychosocial impairment, poorer outcome, and higher suicide rates than individuals with either ADHD or DDs alone (Barkley et al., 2008; Daviss, 2008; Miller, Nigg, & Miller, 2007). In adolescents, this comorbidity leads to a greater degree of domestic conflict and more negative life events relative to ADHD alone. Female patients with both depression and ADHD have earlier age of onset of depression, longer duration of depressive episodes, and higher rates of suicidality and hospitalizations than those with depression alone (Biederman, Ball et al., 2008). After successful treatment, these patients have higher rates of depressive recurrence (Rohde, Clarke, Lewinsohn, Seeley, & Kaufman, 2001).

A common notion is that the cumulative effects of ADHD-related impairments in conjunction with adverse environmental circumstances triggered by them may lead some children and adolescents to eventually develop depression (Ostrander, Crystal, & August, 2006; Herman, Lambert, Ialongo, & Ostrander, 2007). According to Cantwell (1987), children with ADHD and learning disabilities may have what Weiss & Hechtman (1993) termed "demoralization syndrome." In other words, they may express feelings of frustration and believe that they are worthless, mainly because of their poor academic performance. These children are likely to give the impression that they suffer from depression when they are at school, but they do not give the same impression in different settings.

A well-articulated theory regarding heterotypic development between behavioral disorders and DDs is the "failure model," which suggests that conduct problems result in conflict with others, rejection, a lack of support, poor skill development, and being difficult to teach, which in turn lead to failure experiences that influence subsequent depression (Capaldi, 1991; 1992; Patterson & Capaldi, 1990). It has been found that peer rejection and frequent conflicts between the child with ADHD and their parents are mediating factors between ADHD and DDs (Humphreys, Eng, & Lee, 2013), especially among girls (Roy, Hartman, Veenstra, & Oldehinkel, 2015). This finding may be attributed to the fact that girls are generally more sensitive to peers' opinions, and thus may be affected more by peer dislike and victimization (Bakker, Ormel, Verhulst, & Oldehinkel, 2010).

Another view highlights that there are some common genetic factors between these two disorders. This view relies on family studies that show that individuals with ADHD have relatives with a DD at a higher rate than expected and, conversely, individuals with a DD have relatives with ADHD at a rate that is higher than expected (Faraone & Biederman, 1997). Evidence from multigeneration studies shows that the incidence of ADHD in offspring of adults with recurrent depression is higher than in the general population (Biederman, Faraone, Keenan, & Tsuang, 1991).

Another theory explaining comorbidity between ADHD and DDs is the one referring to the co-occurrence of three disorders. According to this theory, when two disorders co-occur (A and B), and the second one usually co-occurs with a third disorder (C), the first one will also co-occur with this third disorder, resulting in comorbidity of three disorders (A, B, and C) (Angold, Costello, Farmer, Burns, & Erkanli, 1999; Burke, Loeber, Lahey, & Rathouz, 2005). For example, both ADHD and CD have high comorbidity rates with DDs. Co-occurrence of ADHD and DDs may merely be the result of co-occurrence of ADHD and CD. This interpretation seems logical if we consider that children with ADHD and CD have negative interpersonal interactions and often view others' responses toward them as hostile. Moreover, they have poor academic performance and often receive criticism and punishment for their behavior. All these experiences are high-risk factors for the development of depression (Capaldi, 1992).

7.6.4 Nature of the Relationship Between ADHD and BDs

There is a long-standing debate regarding the nature of the relationship between ADHD and BDs because certain symptoms of mania, which is the distinctive feature of BD, are predominant symptoms of ADHD. These symptoms are distractibility, motor restlessness, and over-talkativeness (Kent & Craddock, 2003; Klassen, Katzman, & Chokka, 2010). Furthermore, flight of ideas or racing thoughts seen in mania may also be difficult to distinguish from ceaseless distractible thought processes seen in many adults with ADHD (Asherson, 2005). Moreover, predominant mood characteristics of mania are chronic irritability, aggression, and mood lability. These characteristics are also common in individuals with ADHD and probably contribute to the increase of rates of comorbidity between these two disorders (Skirrow, Hosang, Farmer, & Asherson, 2012).

It was proposed that there might be a separate clinical phenotype incorporating features of both ADHD and BDs (Faraone, Biederman, Mennin et al., 1997; Faraone, Biederman, & Monuteaux, 2001). This viewpoint was supported by evidence that this phenotype involves a strong genetic predisposition, emerges earlier in life, is associated with more severe symptoms and impairment, and has a higher rate of comorbidity with other disorders (Arnold et al., 2011; Tamam et al., 2008).

Some researchers estimate that ADHD might be a risk factor for the manifestation of BDs, especially among boys (Arnold et al., 2011; Biederman, Monuteaux, Mick, Spencer, Wilens, Silva et al., 2006). According to a recent study, children with comorbid diagnoses of ADHD and DDs have an increased risk of diagnostic conversion from DDs to BDs in adolescence and adulthood (Chen et al., 2015). Nevertheless, longitudinal studies provide very little evidence that ADHD is a reliable antecedent to the development of BDs that continues into adulthood (Duffy, 2012).

In conclusion, to date there is insufficient evidence to infer the nature of the relationship between ADHD and BDs. Future studies may shed light on this issue, given the fact that many children with a former diagnosis of BDs would now receive the diagnosis of DMDD. This transition will possibly create new dynamics in the samples chosen to be included in research groups.

7.6.5 Treatment in Case of Comorbidity of ADHD, DDs, and BDs

Treatment of comorbid ADHD and DDs is a complicated issue (Biederman, Ball et al., 2008; Wilens et al., 2008). Symptoms of ADHD might be expected to interfere with both structured psychosocial treatments for depression and antidepressant medication adherence (Ruf et al., 2008). Thus, comprehensive treatment approaches for this comorbidity are needed (Knouse, Zvorsky, & Safren, 2013).

It is still not clear how comorbid DDs impact the response of children with ADHD to pharmacological treatments for ADHD. A common clinical practice is to begin with a single medication to target the more severe disorder, usually depression, before resorting to medication combinations, because improvements in one disorder may coincide with improvements in the other (Daviss, 2008; Pliszka et al., 2006).

Maladaptive cognitions play a critical role in the development, maintenance, and treatment of depression and are directly targeted in cognitive-behavioral approaches (Beck, 2008). Therefore, one of the primary targets of CBT for depression is modification of these automatic negative thoughts, maladaptive attitudes, and core beliefs. Drawing upon the cognitive developmental model of depression, several researchers have adopted the view that a lifetime of perceived failure experiences among individuals with ADHD might lead to the development of negative patterns of thinking, thus increasing vulnerability to depression (Murphy, 2006; Ramsay & Rostain, 2003).

In a relatively recent study investigating the difficulties of a group of 81 adults diagnosed with ADHD, Mitchell, Benson, Knouse, Kimbrel, and Anastopoulos (2013) found that inattentive symptoms were associated with the development of negative automatic thoughts even after accounting for depression symptom severity, although adults with comorbid ADHD and depression showed higher levels of negative automatic thoughts than patients with ADHD alone.

Behavioral avoidance has also been implicated in the development and maintenance of depression and is targeted by CBT. Depressed people engage in a high frequency of avoidance and escape from aversive internal and external stimuli with such behaviors as withdrawing or complaining. Avoidance leads to a narrowing of the individual's behavioral repertoire and supports passivity, as opposed to initiative or action (Ottenbreit & Dobson, 2004; Martell, Addis, & Jacobson, 2001). Adults with ADHD often rely on avoidant coping because of difficulties with executive functioning, which underlies planning and problem solving (Boonstra, Oosterlaan, Sergeant, & Buitelaar, 2005). Consequently, behavioral avoidance is highly likely to be associated with the development of DDs among individuals with ADHD (Knouse et al., 2013).

Comorbidity of ADHD with BDs is similarly complicated. Research suggests that incorrect treatment of this comorbidity could lead to nonresponse or exacerbation of symptoms (Skirrow, Hosang, Farmer, & Asherson, 2012). Mood stabilizing agents and atypical antipsychotics may be beneficial for children with early-onset BDs but are unlikely to enhance attention in children with ADHD and can be associated with serious side effects (Dols et al., 2013; Young, Taylor, & Lawrie, 2015). On the other hand, stimulants have been shown to be ineffective in the treatment of BDs and may cause disruption of sleep and circadian rhythms, thus exacerbating BD symptoms (Clavenna & Bonati, 2014; Goldsmith, Singh, & Chang, 2011).

In the case of comorbidity of ADHD and BDs, a combination of treatments is often required. It is recommended to consider BDs as the initial and primary target of treatment for two reasons: (a) the greater severity and more sinister prognosis of BDs, and (b) the risk that medications for ADHD may exacerbate bipolar symptoms if the patient is not first "covered" by a mood stabilizer (Youngstrom, Arnold, & Frazier, 2010).

7.7 ADHD and Obsessive-Compulsive Disorder (OCD)

7.7.1 OCD in DSM-5

In DSM-IV, OCD was classified as a subcategory of ADs because anxiety was considered the core symptom of the disorder. In DSM-5, OCD is newly classified into a separate diagnostic category termed ***obsessive-compulsive and related disorders***, including ***body dysmorphic disorder***, ***hoarding disorder***, and ***hair-pulling disorder*** (trichotillomania). The emphasis is now put on obsessive preoccupation and repetitive behaviors.

According to DSM-5, OCD is typically characterized by the presence of obsessions and/or compulsions. Obsessions are recurrent and persistent thoughts, urges, or images that are experienced as intrusive and unwanted. Compulsions are repetitive behaviors or mental acts that an individual feels driven to perform in response to an obsession or according to rules that must be applied rigidly. Obsessions and compulsions preoccupy the individual for at least one hour per day and cause acute distress and impairment in functioning. Children usually report obsessions that are related to either fears about various infections or issues of religion and sexuality.

For the diagnosis of OCD in adults, clinicians must determine whether the individual shows insight into the senselessness of the obsessive behavior. This insight is one of the key criteria to differentiate OCD from psychosis. Clinicians must also specify the degree of insight into the symptomatology (good/fair, poor, or absent insight) and whether the patient has a current or past history of a TD. In this case, the diagnosis is *Tic-Related OCD* (APA, 2013; Thomsen, 2013). It is noted that young children may not be able to articulate the aims of obsessions or compulsions.

Comorbidity of OCD with other mental disorders is extremely high. Individuals with OCD also exhibit some other kind of ADs at a rate of 76%, whereas 30% of them have a TD. Furthermore, co-occurrence of OCD, TD, and ADHD is very often encountered among the population of children (APA, 2013).

7.7.2 Epidemiology and the Nature of the Relationship Between ADHD and OCD

Studies of referred and nonreferred children have consistently documented elevated rates of ADHD in children with OCD and, conversely, high rates of OCD in children with ADHD. Presence of ADHD among children with OCD, particularly boys with an early onset, ranges from 0% to 25% (Farrell & Barrett, 2006; Ivarsson, Melin, & Wallin, 2008; Masi et al., 2006). The rate of OCD among children with ADHD is estimated to be 8% to 10% (Geller et al., 2007) and is considerably higher than the estimated population prevalence of 2% to 3%. In similar studies on young adults with ADHD, OCD rates ranged from 0% to 6% (Biederman, Faraone et al., 2006; Skirbekk, Hansen, Oerbeck, & Kristensen, 2011).

ADHD is reported as the most common comorbidity in early-onset OCD when TDs and Tourette's disorder are excluded (Walitza et al., 2008). Comorbidity of ADHD in early-onset OCD also seems to predict a higher severity of OCD and a higher grade of persistence of OCD (Walitza et al., 2008).

Finally, recent studies have revealed elevated rates of ADHD in children with OCD who present hoarding behavior (Frank et al., 2014; Hacker et al., 2016; Hamblin et al., 2015; Park et al., 2016; Storch et al., 2016). In an epidemiological study of 2,693 adults, lifetime hoarding symptoms were associated with childhood ADHD, specifically inattention symptoms (Fullana et al., 2013).

Despite considerable evidence for the frequent comorbidity of these two conditions, however, the reasons behind this overlap have yet to be fully understood. There is little evidence that ADHD and OCD co-occur in families. It has been found that first-degree relatives of individuals with TDs display increased rates of both OCD and ADHD (Pauls, Alsobrook, Goodman, Rasmussen, & Leckman, 1995). Furthermore, a more recent study concerning the relationship between OCD and ADHD in children and adolescents using familial risk analysis provided evidence of a familial relationship in addition to unique etiological factors for both OCD and ADHD (Geller et al., 2007).

Neuroimaging studies revealed abnormal activation of the cortico-striato-thalamo-cortical circuits responsible for cognitive control and performance monitoring, although the specific brain regions activated differ between ADHD and OCD (Brem, Grünblatt, Drechsler, Riederer, & Walitza, 2014; Bush, Valera, & Seidman, 2005; Harrison et al., 2009). In line with structural findings, the results of neuropsychological tests and corresponding brain activation studies showed deficits in response inhibition common to both disorders. Abnormal inhibitory processes may therefore be responsible for both the perseverative, compulsive symptoms characterizing individuals with OCD and the disinhibited, impulsive behaviors seen in ADHD (Brem et al., 2014).

Moreover, Palumbo and colleagues (1997) argued that ADHD, OCD, and ASD share a common etiological mechanism, which is the reason why these three disorders very often co-occur. Additionally, according to a study carried out by Ivarsson and Melin (2008), the presence of ASD symptoms among children with OCD is associated with the fact that these disorders are comorbid with ADHD. Findings suggest that these three disorders are related, but the nature of this relationship has not yet been clarified.

From a clinical perspective, it is important to know the prevalence and clinical features of comorbid ADHD and obsessive-compulsive behaviors because the comorbid group may have increased morbidity and pose unique treatment challenges to clinicians (Arnold, Ickowicz, Chen, & Schachar, 2005). Comorbidity of ADHD and OCD is accompanied by major difficulties in psychosocial functioning and increases the risk for developing BDs, TDs, and CD (Masi et al., 2006). Furthermore, a study on adaptive, emotional, and family functioning of children with OCD and comorbid ADHD revealed that OCD and ADHD have additive contributions to social disability (Sukhodolsky et al., 2005). As far as treatment is concerned, stimulants used for ADHD are ineffective in treating OCD and may exacerbate obsessions or compulsions in some cases. On the other hand, serotonin reuptake inhibitors effectively treat OCD but are ineffective for ADHD and may worsen ADHD symptoms by causing behavioral activation in some children (Arnold et al., 2005).

7.8 ADHD and Tic Disorders (TDs)

7.8.1 TDs in DSM-5

In DSM-5, TDs are included in *motor disorders*, along with *DCD* and *stereotypic movement disorder*. Motor disorders are classified into the broader category of neurodevelopmental disorders. TDs include *Tourette's disorder, persistent (chronic) motor* or *vocal tic disorder*, and *provisional tic disorder*.

The aforementioned disorders differ from each other depending on the type of tics (motor, vocal, or a combination of the two) and the duration of the symptoms. In Tourette's disorder, both types of tics are present for at least one year. In persistent motor or vocal tic disorder, one of the two types of tics is present for at least one year. In provisional tic disorder, either one or both types of tics are present for less than a year. The age of onset is before the age of 18. It is noted that these symptoms should not be attributable to the physiological effects of a substance (e.g., cocaine) or another medical condition (e.g., Huntington's disease).

Tics are defined as rapid, recurrent, nonrhythmic motor movements or vocalizations. An individual may have various tic symptoms over time, but at any point in time, the tic repertoire recurs in a characteristic fashion. Although tics can include almost any muscle group or vocalization, certain tic symptoms, such as eye blinking or throat clearing, are more common. Tics are usually worsened by anxiety, excitement, and exhaustion and are better during calm, focused activities. Tics are generally experienced as involuntary but can be voluntarily suppressed for varying lengths of time. Onset of tics is typically between ages 4 and 6 years. Peak severity occurs between ages 10 and 12 years, with a decline in severity during adolescence (APA, 2013).

7.8.2 Epidemiology and the Nature of the Relationship Between ADHD and TDs

Tics are common in childhood but transient in most cases. Simple and provisional tics are manifested at a rate of 6% to 20% (Swain, Scahill, Lombroso, King, & Leckman, 2007). Only 20% of these children will continue having tics in adulthood (Bloch et al., 2006). In contrast, prevalence of chronic motor tics and Tourette's disorder is lower and ranges from 0.6% to 3.8% (Khalifa & von Knorring, 2005). ADHD and TDs commonly co-occur. Children with ADHD have high rates (8% to 20%) of concurrent TDs (Biederman et al., 2005; Gillberg et al., 2004), and around 35% to 50% of children with TDs also present with ADHD (Kurlan et al., 2002; Rothenberger, Roessner, Banaschewski, & Leckman, 2007).

Tourette's disorder very often co-occurs with OCD as well. Nearly 90% of clinic-referred individuals with Tourette's disorder have at least one comorbid psychiatric condition, the most common being OCD and/or ADHD (Freeman et al., 2000). Therefore, co-occurrence of the three disorders, namely Tourette's disorder, OCD, and ADHD, is a common phenomenon that occurs at a rate of 34% (Mathews & Grados, 2011).

The high co-occurrence of these disorders has raised significant clinical attention. Although many studies have tried to clarify their overlap with regard to psychopathological, psychophysiological, and neuropsychological aspects, the pathophysiological mechanism underlying this comorbidity is still unclear (Brand et al., 2002; Banaschewski, Neale, Rothenberger, & Roessner, 2007).

Some researchers contended that this high rate of comorbidity may be due to Berkson's bias[5] or various other referral biases, whereby subjects with more than one disorder are more likely to be part of a clinical sample (Pauls et al., 1986; Spessot, & Peterson, 2006). However, research on epidemiological samples is indicating that the comorbidity of TDs and ADHD is not restricted to clinic-referred samples (Banaschewski, Neale, Rothenberger, & Roessner, 2007).

Comings and Comings (1990) proposed that a wide range of psychiatric and behavioral disorders, including OCD and ADHD, represent variant genetic forms of Tourette's disorder. However, research findings are inconclusive and do not provide sufficient substantiation to this hypothesis. On the one hand, neuroimaging studies consistently point to involvement of cortico-striato-thalamo-cortico circuits in all three disorders, suggesting that disturbances in these structures contribute to behavioral outcomes such as impulsivity, hyperactivity, compulsions, and tics (Brem et al., 2014; Marsh, Maia, & Peterson, 2009). On the other hand, an extensive review of clinical and neuropsychological studies did not confirm that these disorders constitute different phenotypes of a common etiological mechanism (Rothenberger et al.,

2007). It is likely, however, that Tourette's disorder and some forms of ADHD share common pathways of expression (O'Rourke et al., 2011).

There is serious evidence suggesting an increased genetic burden influencing the risk of Tourette's disorder and comorbid disorders. In a prospective study of children at risk for Tourette's disorder, children whose parents had both Tourette's disorder faced a three times greater risk of developing ADHD compared to the children whose only one parent had Tourette's disorder, and two times greater risk of developing either tics, ADHD, or OCD (McMahon et al., 2003). Moreover, it has been shown that children with Tourette's disorder very often have siblings who manifest ADHD without tics at a higher and statistically significant rate relative to the control group (Knell & Comings, 1993; Pauls, Leckman, & Cohen, 1993).

A latent class analysis of 952 individuals from 222 families has shown that 34% of all Tourette's disorder affected individuals had comorbid OCD and ADHD, while only 10% had comorbid ADHD without OCD (Grados, Mathews, and The Tourette Syndrome Association International Consortium for Genetics, 2008). It is therefore estimated that the association between Tourette's disorder and ADHD is partially mediated through the genetic relationships between ADHD and OCD, and OCD and Tourette's disorder (Mathews & Grados, 2011).

Research on the effects of the comorbidity between ADHD and TDs on the individual's functioning has led to inconsistent findings. Some studies have shown that the presence of TDs leads to the aggravation of ADHD symptoms. These studies have also shown that Tourette's disorder symptoms are greater in severity in the context of ADHD relative to Tourette's disorder alone (Banaschewski, Neale, Rothenberger, & Roessner, 2007; Spencer et al., 1998). Other studies, however, have shown that the presence of TDs does not add more cognitive dysfunctions or more difficulties in interpersonal relations, nor does it increase the severity of symptoms among children with ADHD (Lin, Lai, & Gau, 2012; Rothenberger et al., 2007). Studies on both children (Spencer et al., 1998) and adults (Spencer et al., 2001) have shown that TDs have a mostly remitting course and their presence does not adversely affect the course of ADHD.

However, comorbidity between ADHD and TDs significantly imposes an additional risk for ADs among children with ADHD (Carter et al., 2000; Roessner, Becker, Banaschewski, & Rothenberger, 2007). In line with this observation, children with comorbid ADHD and TDs display fewer hyperactive/impulsive symptoms than children with solely ADHD but have comparable levels of inattentive symptoms. In parallel, children with comorbid ADHD and TDs seem to have less peer/interpersonal difficulties. A possible explanation for these differential comorbid patterns is that TDs may possess a "counter-effect" to interpersonal problems at school, mediated by the presence of ADs or by its influences on ADHD core symptoms (Lin et al., 2012).

7.9 ADHD and Developmental Coordination Disorder (DCD)

7.9.1 DCD in DSM-5

The interest of the scientific community in mild and moderate impairments in motor control grew out mainly out of the study of Minimal Brain Dysfunction. This diagnostic term was previously used for children having normal (or near-normal) intelligence but varying degrees of learning and behavior problems associated with brain dysfunction (Clements, 1966b; see Section 1.4.1). The diagnosis of this disorder relied mainly on the presence of "soft neurological signs" or motor deficits that were believed to reflect brain dysfunction but for which structural neurological correlates had not been identified (Tupper, 1987). Therefore, clumsiness and problems in motor coordination were evaluated as clear signs of neurological dysfunction (Denckla & Rudel, 1978). Motor coordination problems have previously been labelled *clumsy child syndrome, non-cerebral palsy, motor-perception dysfunction, minor neurological dysfunction*, or *dyspraxia of childhood.*

In DSM-5, DCD is classified into *motor disorders*, which belong to the broader category of neurodevelopmental disorders. The acquisition and execution of coordinated motor skills is substantially below that expected given the individual's chronological age and opportunities for skill learning and use. Motor clumsiness persistently interferes with their functioning and impacts academic/school productivity, prevocational and vocational activities, leisure, and play. Because of these difficulties, people with DCD are likely to avoid participating in activities that they consider to be challenging. Onset of symptoms is in the early developmental period. However, the disorder is not usually diagnosed before the age of 5. Additionally, the motor skills deficits must not be attributable to ID, vision impairment, or a neurological condition affecting movement, such as cerebral palsy, muscular dystrophy, or some degenerative disorder (APA, 2013).

Children with motor coordination problems show a heterogeneous phenotype, with some of them being mainly disturbed in fine and others in gross motor performance (Green, Chambers, & Sugden, 2008; Polatajko & Cantin, 2005). Coordination problems are usually apparent from a very young age. Children with such problems oftentimes delay in achieving motor milestones, such as sitting, crawling, and walking. Furthermore, these children have difficulty processing visuospatial information and they experience numerous functional difficulties related to their motor skills (Wilson & McKenzie, 1998).

The limitations in daily life caused by poor motor performance vary with age. Evidence suggests that these problems persist into adolescence and adulthood, confirming that they represent deviations from normal behavior and not a mere developmental delay (Cantell, Smyth, Ahonen, 2003; Cousins & Smyth, 2003). At age 4 to 6 years, children with this disorder have difficulty mainly in getting dressed, drawing, tying shoelaces, buttoning shirts, using scissors, zippers, forks, and knives, pedaling, negotiating stairs, and completing puzzles (Missiuna, Gaines, Soucie, & McLean, 2006). Even when the skill is achieved, movement execution may appear awkward, slow, or less precise than that of peers. Children of 7 to 10 years old still have difficulty getting dressed and may display slow speed or inaccuracy with motor aspects of activities such as handwriting, swimming, doing crafts, playing ball games, and doing sports activities. Adolescents of 11 to 19 years old face problems with clumsiness in writing and drawing, building models, eating meals with age-appropriate utensils and without mess, and participating in team exercise activities. Young adults find it difficult to acquire new skills that involve complex/automatic motor skills, including using tools and driving (APA, 2013; Fliers et al., 2008).

As a result of the aforementioned difficulties, individuals with motor problems tend to avoid social and physical activities in which they assume they will fail (Chen & Cohn, 2003). These difficulties may have a negative impact on academic performance, mainly because of difficulties in speed but also in the quality of writing, thus leading to an illegible written text. Children with such difficulties also experience a host of secondary psychosocial issues, including problems with social and peer relationships (Dewey, Kaplan, Crawford, & Wilson, 2002; Miyahara & Piek, 2006) and low self-esteem (Missiuna, Moll, King, Law, & King, 2006; Piek, Baynam, & Barrett, 2006; Piek, Dawson, Smith, & Gasson, 2008; Polatajko & Cantin, 2005). Moreover, research has revealed that adolescents with DCD are at a greater risk for developing obesity and vascular problems due to limited physical activity (Cairney, Hay, Faught, & Hawes, 2005).

7.9.2 Epidemiology and the Nature of the Relationship Between ADHD and DCD

Comorbidity of ADHD and DCD has received little attention in research. As a result, the effect that it may have on children's development has been rather neglected (Gillberg, & Kadesjo, 2009). This can be attributed to the fact that the difficulties associated with this disorder usually fall within the sphere of interest of child neurology, developmental pediatrics, physiotherapy, and occupational therapy, whereas ADHD is usually studied within the fields of psychology and child psychiatry. However, recent clinical and experimental evidence suggests a greater role of motor factors in ADHD than was considered before (Fliers et al., 2008).

The prevalence of DCD in children aged 5 to 11 years is 5% to 6%. Boys are more often affected than girls, with a male-female ratio between 2:1 and 7:1 (APA, 2013; Lingam, Hunt, Golding, Jongmans, & Emond, 2009; Missiuna et al., 2008). Comorbidity rates between ADHD and DCD range between 30% and 50% (Gillberg et al., 2004; Fliers et al., 2008).

High comorbidity rates between these disorders are expected given their joint evolution from the Minimal Brain Dysfunction classification (Pick, Pitcher, & Hay, 1999). In the Scandinavian countries, the combination of ADHD and motor coordination problems has led to a special term, *Deficits of Attention and Motor Perception* (DAMP), to describe children with this comorbid condition without serious learning difficulties or cerebral palsy (Gillberg, 2003). According to Gillberg, & Kadesjo, 2003), "there is a widespread realization that ADHD is so often associated with motor control problems that a term acknowledging both types of deficit is needed in clinical practice" (p. 65).

According to currently available empirical data, children with ADHD encounter a variety of difficulties both in gross and fine motor skills. These include repetitive movements, fine motor difficulties, deficient coordination, poor balancing, and excessive overflow movements (Sergeant, Piek, & Oosterlaan, 2006). The majority of studies find a closer association between ADHD and problems in fine motor skills, but there are also some studies that conclude that problems in gross motor skills are more significant (Fliers et al., 2008). It has been argued that the inattentive subtype of ADHD is more strongly linked with problems in fine motor skills, whereas the combined subtype is more often associated with problems in gross motor skills (Piek et al., 1999).

Initially, it was argued that fine motor difficulties in children with ADHD were caused by inattention, but more recent findings demonstrated that motor coordination problems are rather linked to a motor deficit as a separate entity from ADHD symptomatology (Miyahara, Piek, & Barrett, 2006; Pitcher, Piek, & Hay, 2003). However, the exact pathophysiological mechanisms implicated remain unspecified.

DCD is considered a multifactorial disorder influenced by both genetic and environmental factors (Pearsall-Jones et al., 2009). The genetic component appears polygenic, with many genes of small effect thought to cause the disorder in unfavorable environmental circumstances (Fliers et al., 2012). Studies on the familiality of ADHD and DCD identified a possible shared etiological background due to genetic factors and/or shared environmental factors (Fliers et al., 2009; Kaplan, Wilson, Dewey, & Crawford, 1998; Martin, Piek, & Hay, 2006). Converging evidence points into the direction of an overlapping etiology with a strong shared heritability as well as unique contributors. However, little is known about the specific genetic factors involved.

It has been argued that these two disorders may share a common underlying neurocognitive mechanism. Delay of brain maturation as well as functional deficits in basal ganglia, parietal lobe, and cerebellum have been suggested as the dominant source of neuropathology in motor coordination problems (Zwicker et al., 2009). Neuroimaging studies in children with

ADHD have also revealed abnormalities in these areas that are integral to sensory-motor control (Kaplan & Stevens, 2002; Kim, Lee, Shin, Cho, & Lee, 2002; Valera et al., 2007) (see Section 5.3.1). These factors may underlie the suboptimal motor performance previously reported in some children with ADHD.

It is speculated that a dopamine-induced imbalance of basal ganglia neurocircuits may be an important neurobiological component in both ADHD and DCD (Archer & Beninger, 2007; Arnsten & Li, 2006). Moreover, the role of lateralization and interaction between the two cerebral hemispheres are factors that must be taken into consideration when these two disorders are comorbid (Roessner, Banaschewski, Uebel, Becker, & Rothenberger, 2004). It seems that more encompassing areas of the cerebellum may be affected when there is a dual diagnosis of ADHD and DCD (Zwicker et al., 2009).

Besides, there is evidence to suggest that impairments in DCD can be accounted for by deficits in executive functions. Motor skills are the outcome of many different processes, such as perceptual, feedback, and learning processes, motor preparation, and movement execution processes. These processes rely on the visual system, memory, attention, the balance system, the kinesthetic system, and the motor effector system (Geuze, 2005; Smits-Engelsman, Westenberg, & Duysens, 2008). Any defect in one of these processes or systems may lead to motor coordination problems. As children with ADHD have been identified with a deficit in visuospatial organization, problems with processing kinesthetic information, and working memory impairments, comorbidity of these two disorders is expected (Parush, Sohmer, Steinberg, & Kaitz, 1997; Yochman, Parush, & Ornoy, 2004). Therefore, the overlap of ADHD and motor coordination problems could be understood as the result of an aberrant brain development, probably affecting complex neuronal networks.

It is of particular interest that SLD, particularly in reading, is more commonly manifested among children with comorbid ADHD and DCD relative to children who have only ADHD (Watemberg, Waiserberg, Lerman-Sagie, 2007). SLPs also occur frequently in individuals with DCD, probably on the basis of a dyspraxic deficit (Dewey, Kaplan, Crawford, & Wilson, 2002). Furthermore, DCD often coexists with ASD, which in turn often coexists with ADHD. In clinical practice this means that clinicians dealing with DCD must be aware of its strong link with ADHD and ASD, and conversely, specialists of ADHD and ASD have to know about the very strong association with motor impairment and be able to diagnose such problems in their clinical population (Gillberg, 2003).

Findings indicate the existence of a strong genetic relation among all these disorders and once again highlight the difficulties arising due to our limited understanding of their co-occurrence, which leads to multiple diagnoses according to current classification systems. We think that the view of Kaplan and colleagues (Gilger & Kaplan, 2001; Kaplan et al., 2001) is of great interest, as they suggest that ADHD, DCD and other childhood developmental disorders (such as RD) show high comorbidity because they all reflect a generalized heterogeneous neurodevelopmental condition known as atypical brain development (see Section 7.1.1). This term refers to the general underlying impairment of development that occurs in some children, and manifests in many ways in the behavioral, academic, and emotional domains. Therefore, impairments in attention, motor skills, and other developmental tasks are caused when the early development of the brain is disrupted. In a similar vein, the overlap between DCD and SLPs has also been attributed to neuromaturational delay, and it has been suggested that the behavioral expression of each is dependent on timing and severity of disruption in brain development (Hill, 2001).

Atypical brain development results from polygenic etiology affecting complex neuronal networks and can be manifested in various ways through behavior, learning, and emotional development depending on the degree and exact location of the neurological dysfunction. This term can be used to describe the set of developmental problems that very often overlap, as it has been clearly stated so far.

It has been suggested that comorbidity between ADHD and DCD constitutes a predictive factor for poorer outcomes of ADHD (Pitcher et al., 2003; Visser, 2003). A Scandinavian study has shown that adults with comorbid ADHD and DCD have a poorer outcome than adults with ADHD only with regard to social functioning, work career, psychiatric problems, and substance abuse (Rasmussen & Gillberg, 2000). These findings suggest that the association between ADHD and motor coordination problems is an important predictive feature and highlight the necessity of treating motor problems among individuals with ADHD as part of the intervention.

7.10 ADHD and Autism Spectrum Disorder (ASD)

7.10.1 Epidemiology and Common Characteristics of ADHD and ASD

In the 1960s, autism was considered a rare disorder that affected 1 in 10,000 children. Nowadays it is estimated that it affects at least 1 in 100 children (APA, 2013). In DSM-I and II, autism did not exist as an independent disorder but was classified under the label of *schizophrenic reaction, childhood type.* In the next editions of DSM, autism was renamed into *autistic disorder* and was included in a class of *pervasive developmental disorders*, along with *Asperger's disorder, Rett disorder, childhood disintegrative disorder*, and *pervasive developmental disorder not otherwise specified.*

The changes introduced in DSM-5 reflect a significant departure from the diagnostic criteria that have been used in past decades. The most salient change is a conceptualization of autism and related disorders as a continuum rather than a group of related but taxonomically distinct diagnoses (McPartland & Dawson, 2014). Four of the aforementioned disorders are merged into the single category *ASD*, included in the broader category of neurodevelopmental disorders. Rett disorder is no longer included in DSM. Three levels of symptom severity and the intensity of the support needed are specified.

A second major change reflected in the current diagnostic criteria is the collapsing of the traditional "triad of impairments" into two symptom domains. The category "social communication deficits" now combines social *and* communication problems. A further change is that the diagnostic criterion of onset before 36 months of age used in DSM-IV is replaced with the following "open" definition in DSM-5: "Symptoms must be present in early childhood, but may not become fully manifest until social demands exceed limited capacities" (APA, 2013).

Until the publication of DSM-5, a dual diagnosis of ADHD and ASD was not allowed as the diagnosis of any of these two disorders precluded the other. ADHD symptoms among individuals with ASD were regarded as secondary ASD symptoms (APA, 2000). However, over the last years, there is increased empirical and clinical evidence that ADHD and ASD often coexist (Simonoff et al., 2008). For this reason, DSM-5 allows, for the first time, a comorbid diagnosis of ADHD with ASD as these two disorders are no longer mutually exclusive.

This new attitude is a significant sign of progress, as it provides clinicians with an opportunity to acknowledge both the converging and discrete symptom presentations of ASD and ADHD and allows for more efficient clinical management of this comorbid condition. On the other hand, it underscores the importance of better understanding the boundaries and overlaps between these disorders (Ronald, Larsson, Anckarsäter, & Lichtenstein, 2014). Diagnostic constraints have limited the scope of past research on co-occurring ADHD and ASD because many studies have excluded individuals with any co-occurring symptoms to establish homogeneous samples. As a result, research samples rarely represented the clinical reality, and findings of these studies could not be generalized (Davis & Kollins, 2012). Therefore, research specifically focusing on co-occurring ADHD and ASD has only recently evolved.

Comorbidity rates between ADHD and ASD are high. A review of 35 ASD and ADHD co-occurrence studies yielded estimates ranging from 37% to 85% in clinical samples (Leitner, 2014). Moreover, estimates suggest that 30% to 50% of individuals with ASD also display ADHD symptoms, and similarly, two-thirds of individuals with ADHD exhibit features of ASD (Davis & Kollins, 2012; Hattori et al., 2006; Mulligan et al., 2009; Nijmeijer et al., 2009). A recent study investigated the presence of ADHD in children with ASD, aged 6 to 17, using data from the *Survey of Pathways to Diagnosis and Services*, a community-based, nationally representative survey in the United States (Stevens, Peng, & Barnard-Brak, 2016). The comorbid presence of ADHD was estimated at around 59%. Finally, in children with a primary diagnosis of ADHD, the level of autistic symptomatology seems to correspond to the severity of the ADHD subtype, that is, children with the combined type of ADHD tend to demonstrate the most autistic symptoms (Reiersen et al., 2007).

A subgroup of individuals with ASD also have deficits in executive functions and difficulties associated with attention and self-control, whereas another subgroup of individuals with ADHD encounter difficulties in pragmatics and social interaction (Arnold et al., 2003; Gadow, DeVincent, & Pomeroy, 2006; Leyfer et al., 2006). Furthermore, it has been shown that individuals with ADHD who also have motor and language problems have higher autism symptom scores than those with ADHD alone (Mulligan et al., 2009; Reiersen, Constantino, & Todd, 2008). Knowledge of these facts is of major practical importance for professionals who implement interventions for ADHD.

The two disorders have many common characteristics in cognitive, behavioral, and social domains (APA, 2000; Mayes, Calhoun, Mayes, & Molitoris, 2012). Furthermore, both disorders are more common in boys than girls, are manifested in preschool years, have a genetic predisposition, and are often comorbid within the same individual and across family members. Presence of this comorbidity increases the chance of developing SLPs, learning disabilities, and motor coordination problems. Finally, both disorders cause significant academic, emotional, and adaptive problems (Rao & Landa, 2013).

Individuals with ADHD seem to have pragmatic language difficulties similar to individuals in the ASD spectrum (Bishop & Baird, 2001). However, these difficulties are usually milder among individuals with ADHD than among individuals with ASD (Geurts et al., 2004). Furthermore, individuals with ADHD have difficulties with reference to empathy, facial affect recognition, social perspective taking, and other communication skills, although these are milder than in ASD (Dyck, Ferguson, & Shochet, 2001; Hattori et al., 2006; Marton, Wiener, Rogers, Moore, & Tannock, 2009; Nijmeijer et al., 2008).

Another domain in which ADHD and ASD share common characteristics is motor development. Evidence suggests that delays in motor milestones may be a common feature of early ASD (Bolton et al., 2012) and ADHD (e.g., Gurevitz et al., 2012), although evidence in the latter case is more limited. Motor deficits may be associated with shared risk for ASD and ADHD, as similar levels of motor impairment and similar deficits in visuomotor integration have been found in both disorders (Reiersen et al., 2008). Besides, as has been mentioned before, both disorders have high comorbidity rates with DCD.

Neuroimaging and neuropsychological studies have shown that executive functioning deficits are common in both ADHD and ASD, with slightly different areas of impairment observed (Gargaro, Rinehart, Bradshaw, Tonge, & Sheppard, 2011). With respect to ASD, impaired performance is typically observed in tasks that require planning and cognitive flexibility. Individuals with ASD also display difficulties in disengaging and shifting their attention within and between sensory modalities (Elsabbagh, Fernandes et al., 2013; Elsabbagh, Gliga et al., 2013).

On the other hand, ADHD is mainly associated with impairments in response inhibition and sustained attention (Barkley, 1997c). It has been suggested that attention difficulties common to ASD and ADHD are responsible for language delays in both groups, as well as other language impaired populations (Kelly, Walker, & Norbury, 2013).

Research comparing individuals with both diagnoses to individuals with a single diagnosis suggest that co-occurring symptoms are associated with greater impairment than a single diagnosis. Comorbidity of ADHD and ASD is associated with lower quality of life, more impairment in everyday life, and poorer adaptive functioning than any of these conditions alone (Rao & Landa, 2013; Yerys et al., 2009). According to a study conducted by Mulligan and colleagues (2009) in 12 European countries, comorbidity between ASD and ADHD increases the risk for the occurrence of ODD or CD. Furthermore, response to stimulants might be poorer when ASD co-occurs with ADHD (Arnold et al., 2012), even though some studies do not verify such differences (Santosh, Baird, Pityaratstian, Tavare, & Gringras, 2006). Other studies have shown that co-occurring ADHD and ASD may be less responsive to standard treatments for either disorder than individuals with "pure" forms of the disorders (Antshel et al., 2011).

7.10.2 The Nature of the Relationship Between ADHD and ASD

High comorbidity rates and common features between ADHD and ASD have raised the intriguing possibility that ASD and ADHD may share developmental pathways and risk factors (Reiersen & Todd, 2008). A range of emerging evidence for common ASD and ADHD endophenotypes (Rommelse et al., 2011), and genetic (Ronald, Edelson, Asherson, & Saudino, 2010) and environmental risk factors (Ronald, Pennell, & Whitehouse, 2011), has led some researchers to suggest that these two disorders represent different manifestations of a common underlying disorder—in other words, different aspects of an underlying continuum of impairment. More specifically, it has been hypothesized that ADHD and ASD constitute a spectrum disorder, which in its milder form is manifested as ADHD and in its more severe form is manifested as ASD (Gargaro, Rinehart, Bradshaw, Tonge, & Sheppard, 2011; Van der Meer et al., 2012).

However, research findings do not provide support for this view. Despite the presence of common characteristics, early signs of the two disorders differ significantly (Johnson, Gliga, Jones, & Charman, 2015). Furthermore, in studies based on samples of twins, correlation of genetic effects on the manifestation of these two disorders was modest (Reiersen, Constantino, Volk, & Todd, 2007; Ronald et al., 2010). Moreover, a recent GWAS did not find any significant genetic correlation between the two disorders (Cross-Disorder Group of the Psychiatric Genomics Consortium, 2013). Some of the risk alleles seem to demonstrate a pleiotropic effect, resulting either in an ASD or ADHD phenotype. However, other alleles seem to be disorder-specific risk factors (Taurines et al., 2012). Finally, in ASD, as opposed to ADHD, anatomical studies found larger total brain and white matter volumes in most cortical brain regions and in the cerebellum, caudate, and globus pallidum (Piven et al., 1996).

Another explanation is that ADHD and ASD are distinct disorders that share common endophenotypes (Gottesman & Gould, 2003). This view was based on findings revealing similar performance in measures of empathy, sensory responsiveness, or emotional regulation (Rommelse et al., 2011). Other findings supporting this view emerged from twin studies showing that more children with one condition show features of the other condition than complete comorbidity (Ronald, Larsson, Anckarsäter, & Lichtenstein, 2014). In addition, 50% to 70% of the covariance of ASD and ADHD symptoms may be explained by shared additive genetic factors (Reiersen et al., 2008). Finally, family-based studies have shown increased ASD symptoms in affected and nonaffected siblings of individuals with ADHD, which indicates familiality of the co-occurrence of ASD and ADHD symptoms (Mulligan et al., 2009).

Finally, according to a recent theory, common early signs of these two disorders reflect common mechanisms of brain adaptation in the face of mild but widespread disturbances to early brain function (Dennis et al., 2013; Johnson, 2012; Johnson, Jones, & Gliga, 2015). Under this view, the diagnostic features of ADHD differ from those in ASD by virtue of the time in the life course when the adaptation processes begin. In ASD this process starts earlier than in ADHD. For example, social withdrawal in toddlers with emerging ASD may be the result of their inefficient processing of complex spatial-temporal information. When the same information processing difficulties emerge later in development, they may lead to slightly different adaptive responses. For example, they may lead to behavioral problems, indicating the clinical symptomatology of ADHD. Therefore, comorbidity of the two disorders is likely to emerge in case adaptation processes last for a longer time period.

A future research trend is conducting prospective studies of infants at high risk for developmental impairments, in order to examine brain development prior to symptom emergence, namely before the age of 2. In this way, shared or unique variance in causal paths to symptomatology of ADHD and ASD can be detected (Johnson et al., 2015). Symptoms of both ADHD and ASD emerge through a complex interaction between neurodevelopmental vulnerabilities and aspects of the child's prenatal and postnatal environment. After the clear emergence of symptoms, it becomes hard to untangle these factors. On a clinical level, professionals are restricted to treat the symptoms rather than the primary pathological processes that cause the disorder. Therefore, mapping the course of these disorders from birth is of utmost importance for understanding the chain of causal mechanisms leading to symptoms emergence and their overlap (Johnson et al., 2015).

7.11 ADHD, Oppositional Defiant Disorder (ODD), and Conduct Disorder (CD)

7.11.1 Epidemiology and Diagnostic Criteria in DSM-5

Children with ADHD are particularly vulnerable to developing conduct problems, such as oppositional, disruptive, hostile, and defiant behavior, as well as overt and covert aggression (Danforth, Connor, & Doerfler, 2016). A pattern of angry/irritable mood, argumentative/defiant behavior, or vindictiveness lasting at least six months and exhibited during interaction with at least one individual who is not a sibling leads to the diagnosis of ODD. Three categories of symptoms are provided: (a) angry/irritable mood, (b) argumentative and defiant behavior, and (c) vindictiveness. Three levels of severity are proposed, based on the number of settings the symptoms are present (APA, 2013).

In case the person manifests a repetitive and persistent pattern of behavior in which the basic rights of others or major age-appropriate societal norms or rules are violated for at least 12 months, a diagnosis of CD, beginning either in childhood (below 10 years) or in adolescence, may be established. Four categories of symptoms are provided: (a) aggression to people and animals, (b) destruction of property, (c) deceitfulness or theft, and (c) serious violations of rules. In DSM-5, it is suggested that the clinician specifies whether the individual is characterized with "limited prosocial emotions," that is callous or unemotional traits that may be expressed through a lack of remorse or guilt and disregard for the feelings, wishes, and well-being of others. Three levels of severity are proposed, based on the number of symptoms that exceed those necessary for the diagnosis (APA, 2013).

In DSM-IV, ODD and CD were classified into the category of *attention deficit and disruptive behavior disorders*, along with ADHD. However, in DSM-5 their classification changed because the broad category to which they belonged was eliminated. ADHD moved to neurodevelopmental disorders, whereas ODD and CD are now classified into the category of *disruptive, impulse-control, and conduct disorders. Antisocial personality disorder, pyromania, kleptomania*, and *intermittent explosive disorder* are also classified into this group. This different classification represents current notions that differentiate the etiological background of ADHD from that of the aforementioned disorders. Furthermore, DSM-5 acknowledges for the first time comorbidity of CD with ODD.

Comorbidity of ADHD with ODD/CD seems to be quite common. Research findings suggest that 35% to 60% of clinical samples of children with ADHD also meet the criteria for the diagnosis of ODD up to the age of 7, whereas approximately 20% meet the criteria for the diagnosis of CD (Elia, Ambrosini, & Berrettini, 2008; Posner et al., 2007; Wilens, Biederman et al., 2002). Moreover, comorbidity between symptoms of ADHD and ODD is evident even during the early preschool years (Harvey, Friedman-Weieneth, Goldstein, & Sherman, 2007).

Among older ages, comorbidity between ADHD and CD is more prevalent. In adolescence, comorbidity between ADHD and CD lies between 40% and 60% (Barkley, Fischer et al., 1990). Furthermore, 15% to 25% of these children may meet the criteria for the diagnosis of *antisocial personality disorder* (Biederman et al., 1992; Weiss & Hechtman, 1993). These rates are similar or slightly lower in epidemiological studies carried out in the general population (Wichstrom et al., 2012).

ADHD seems to be one of the earliest and most reliable predictors of the manifestation of these disorders (Fischer, Barkley, Edelbrock, & Smallish, 1993; Mannuzza & Klein, 1992). Furthermore, comorbidity between ADHD and these disorders is significantly more prevalent among boys than girls (Kutcher et al., 2004). Comorbidity is usually higher in the case of children with the combined subtype of ADHD and much lower among children with the inattentive subtype. ODD has been demonstrated to be particularly associated with symptoms of hyperactivity and impulsivity (Rabiner & Coie, 2000; Massetti et al., 2008). Finally, a meta-analysis found that children with ADHD are 11 times more likely to develop ODD or CD relative to typically developing children (Robison et al., 2005).

These high levels of comorbidity among supposedly different domains of externalizing problems, such as inattention, hyperactivity, aggression, and defiance, make these conditions complex and particularly hard to treat (Tuvblad, Raine, Zheng, & Baker, 2009). Children with comorbid ADHD and ODD/CD present more severe symptomatology and poorer outcomes relative to children with a single diagnosis (Satterfield & Schell, 1997). A strong inclination to lie, aggression, argumentative behavior, and acts of theft are more commonly observed among these children (Barkley, 1990; Kuhne, Schachar, & Tannock, 1997). Prognosis is even poorer in case the second disorder appears before the age of 10 (McGee & Share, 1988). These children experience peer rejection more frequently (Carlson, Tamm, & Gaub, 1997; Fletcher, Fischer, Barkley, & Smallish, 1996), manifest more intense ADHD symptoms (Waschbusch, 2002), and have more pronounced neurocognitive deficits (Moffitt, 1990). In this group, antisocial behavior might be manifested early and in a more persistent and stable form during development (Biederman et al., 2011; Tandon, Si, & Luby, 2011).

Furthermore, there is evidence that children with ADHD and aggressive behavior exhibited at a very young age are more likely to develop delinquent behavior in adolescence and adulthood relative to their peers (Barkley et al., 2004; Mannuzza, Gittelman-Klein, Bessler, Malloy, & LaPadula, 1993; Satterfield et al., 2007). These children manifest more severe forms of juvenile delinquency at a younger age relative to children with conduct problems alone (Sibley et al., 2011).

Retrospective studies show that a great number of young adults with delinquent behavior have a history of problems related to ADHD in their childhood (Moffitt, 1990). In one of our studies based on a sample of 93 male inmates in juvenile detention centers, we found that 66.7% met the criteria for the diagnosis of CD, whereas 25.8% displayed ADHD symptomatology (Maniadaki & Kakouros, 2008).

It should be highlighted that not all children with ADHD manifest such problems or end up being involved with the criminal justice system. ADHD may indirectly lead to delinquent behavior through family disruption and learning difficulties, which may deprive the adolescents of the opportunity to experience success at school and at home, and push them to seek acceptance and recognition by delinquent peer groups (Maniadaki et al., 2009; 2010).

Studies on adults have revealed that comorbidity of ADHD and ODD/CD in childhood is associated with increased risk for BDs, multiple ADs, and Substance Use Disorder (SUD) (Harpold et al., 2007). Therefore, lifetime conduct problems are associated with a higher burden of psychopathology in adults with ADHD (Vitola et al., 2012).

In conclusion, we could infer that comorbidity between ADHD and ODD/CD, as well as the age at which this comorbidity appears, seem to be more reliable predictive factors for these children's developmental course than the severity of ADHD symptoms (Barkley, Fischer et al., 1990). Some researchers have claimed that comorbid ADHD and CD may constitute a genetically distinct or a more severe subtype of ADHD (Christiansen et al., 2008; Thapar, Harrington, & McGuffin, 2001). This view is based on findings that indicate higher rates of antisocial behavior, substance abuse, and psychiatric problems among parents of children with comorbid ADHD and CD relative to parents of children with only ADHD (Faraone, Biederman, Jetton et al., 1997).

7.11.2 The Nature of the Relationship Between ADHD, ODD, and CD

ODD usually appears a little later in development than ADHD, and CD often develops later than ODD, typically in early adolescence (Barkley, 1990). Some researchers argue that ODD and CD are discrete disorders and follow a divergent developmental course, with the former having a more positive prognosis (Biederman, Faraone, Milberger et al., 1996; Diamantopoulou, Verhulst, van der Ende, 2011). Others consider that the two disorders are hierarchically related, with ODD being a developmental precursor or a milder form of CD and only a proportion of ODD cases progressing to CD (Cohen, 1998; Rowe, Costello, Angold, Copeland, & Maughan, 2010). The analysis that will follow adopts this latter explanation and, therefore, for reasons of briefness, the term Conduct Problems (CPs) will stand for both ODD and CD.

A number of models have been proposed to explain high comorbidity between ADHD and CPs. According to the *correlated risk factors model*, comorbidity may be due to shared risk factors (Rhee et al., 2008). According to the *developmental precursor model*, ADHD may lead to the development of CPs through the stress it places on the family and the disruption of family functioning, which in turn places children at risk for CPs (Beauchaine, Hinshaw, & Pang, 2010; Johnston & Jassy, 2007). However, recent findings suggest that comorbidity between ADHD and CPs may be better explained by integrating the preceding models, as multiple mechanisms seem to be involved (Harvey, Breaux, & Lugo-Candelas, 2016). Therefore, understanding the nature of the relationship among these disorders requires a comprehensive approach to a series of factors and their interactions (Danforth et al., 2016). We will make an attempt to describe this approach using the developmental paradigm in psychopathology.

Behavioral genetics studies indicate that comorbidity among externalizing disorders results largely from heritable mechanisms. A converging literature documents that the combination of ADHD and CPs has a stronger genetic base relative to ADHD alone (Faraone, Biederman, &

Monuteaux, 2000). Across several large twin studies, a common latent factor accounts for much of the covariation among ADHD and CPs (Krueger et al., 2002; Tuvblad, Zheng, Raine, & Baker, 2009).

In addition, many other behavioral and personality traits that commonly occur in individuals with ADHD and facilitate the development of CPs, such as low self-control and emotion dysregulation, have substantial genetic effects on the expression of their behavioral trait phenotype (Bezdjian, Baker, & Tuvblad, 2011; Biederman et al., 2012; Nemoda, Szekely, & Sasvari-Szekely, 2011). Among them, a behavioral trait of key importance in ADHD is impulsivity. This is a multidimensional trait including a sense of urgency, lack of planning, lack of persistence, and novelty seeking. Novelty seeking includes frequent risk-taking behaviors, exploration, and sensation seeking (Danforth et al., 2016). Obviously, these characteristics facilitate the development of CPs. A meta-analysis of 41 twin, family, and adoption studies shows that about half the variance in impulsivity is explained by genetic factors (Bezdjian, Baker, & Tuvblad, 2011).

To date, over 15 candidate genes with risk alleles important for CPs and ADHD have been identified in human and animal studies. Most of them are involved in the process of encoding for proteins that are important for the CNS monoaminergic neurotransmission (Niv & Baker, 2013).

However, genetic risk factors express their phenotypic properties most strongly in environments characterized by adverse and stressful conditions. In other words, the development of CPs in individuals with ADHD depends considerably on exposure to potentiating environmental risk factors. For example, children with ADHD possessing a specific Catechol-*O*-methyltransferase (COMT, an enzyme that functions to metabolize catecholamines in the CNS prefrontal cortex) gene variant were more likely to develop CPs if they also had low birth weight relative to children with ADHD who had the same variant but normal birth weight (Thapar et al., 2005). In other words, the genetic risk expressed itself most strongly in an adverse environment characterized by low birth weight and not in other types of environments. Furthermore, adolescents with ADHD who had a polymorphism in the dopamine transporter gene and grew up in adverse family conditions developed more severe ADHD symptomatology than adolescents with ADHD who had a different genotype or were raised in less adverse family conditions (Laucht et al., 2007).

Therefore, gene-by-environment research reveals that genetic risk factors phenotypically express themselves more powerfully in certain adverse environments, which explains why some children with ADHD develop CPs and others do not (Danforth et al., 2016). Furthermore, numerous studies, including many with longitudinal designs, have demonstrated that children who experience early family dysfunction are more likely to show CPs (Burke, Loeber, & Birmaher, 2002). It seems that accumulating environmental risk exposure facilitates progression along the externalizing spectrum among trait-impulsive, genetically vulnerable individuals, such as individuals with ADHD (Beauchaine et al., 2010).

Negative parent–child interactions are one of the main risk factors that often render the environment adverse and, therefore, favorable for the development of CPs among children with ADHD. A basic element of these interactions is negative reinforcement, whereby a child or parent response functions to allow them to avoid or escape an aversive stimulus. Because of this contingency, the response is strengthened. This process has been thoroughly described by Patterson (1982) in his model of *coercive interaction.*

For example, in the case of lax parenting, the parent may give the child a direction and the child may obstinately refuse to follow it and defiantly yell. Eventually, the parent may acquiesce or withdraw the direction so that the child stops yelling. In this case, defiant child yelling and disobedience is reinforced and strengthened because it functions to allow the child to avoid doing the task described in the parent's direction. On the other hand, parent acquiescence in similar situations is reinforced and strengthened because it allows the parent to escape defiant child yelling (Danforth et al., 2016). Given that children with ADHD and their parents frequently manifest behaviors that are aversive to the other party, coercive interaction constitutes a common way of communication. Children with comorbid ADHD and CPs are particularly sensitive to this process (Luman et al., 2009).

Parents of children with ADHD give frequent attention to maladaptive child behaviors, thus issuing commands and verbal reprimands and inflicting punishments. In addition, they usually attend less to appropriate behavior and give fewer rewards for compliance. Oftentimes, they are inconsistent in strategies they employ to manage their children's negative behavior. These parents are also more directive, negative, and rejecting. Furthermore, they sometimes use lax and other times excessively harsh parenting practices. Although the two styles seem incompatible, research suggests that parents of children with ADHD often use both styles (Seipp & Johnston, 2005). These practices usually evoke strong feelings of deprivation in children, reinforcing their oppositional and defiant behavior (Maniadaki, Sonuga-Barke, Kakouros, & Karaba, 2006b). Although most studies refer to mothers, similar findings were revealed by the limited studies that were conducted with fathers of children with ADHD (Romirowsky & Chronis-Tuscano, 2014).

Parents' interpretations of the child's negative behavior also influence their reactions to this behavior. In case parents perceive the child's misbehavior as intentional or willful, they are more distressed and they are more likely to use harsh, coercive, or other power assertive discipline strategies (Bugental & Johnston, 2000; Johnston, Chen, & Ohan, 2006). There is strong evidence that parents of children with ADHD tend to report negative, blame-oriented attributions for their child's negative behaviors, to which they are likely to respond with harsh discipline tactics, exacerbating the coercive cycle (Johnston & Ohan, 2005). To conclude, the data support the relevance of coercion in the development of CPs in children with ADHD (Johnston & Mash, 2001).

In sum, genetically influenced neurodevelopmental deficits and core ADHD symptoms introduced early into the parent–child interactions sometimes trigger permissive and other times harsh responses. They also lead to lack of attention and absence of positive reinforcement when desirable behavior is exhibited. Consequently, harsh punishment, coupled with inattention and lack of reinforcement for appropriate or prosocial behavior, increases the risk for escalation of coercive interaction between parent and child, which potentiates the development of CPs, thus aggravating already existing developmental difficulties (Granic & Patterson, 2006). According to Patterson, DeGarmo, and Knutson (2000), ADHD represents the first stage in the development of CPs and antisocial behavior the second stage, with coercion serving as a shared mechanism.

This pattern of communication further exacerbates the child's inherent failure to develop effective self-speech for behavioral self-control. Parents of children with ADHD are less likely to engage in conversation that constructively teaches the child the parameters of self-directed speech, which is important in the development of verbal working memory and self-control (Danforth et al., 2016). However, these children are in pressing need of their parents' contribution to developing self-control because their deficient impulse inhibition forms the basis for many behavioral problems. These children delay in the development of internalization of self-speech because verbal working memory that supports internalized speech is deficient.

An advantage of the rule-governed behavior component of verbal working memory is that the description of the contingency provided by the internal self-rule helps the child bridge the gap between current behavior and delayed outcomes. Self-rules allow a typical child to behave toward future goals rather than being influenced by the immediate consequences of behavior. However, given the deficits previously mentioned, children with ADHD are more heavily influenced by immediate rather than delayed reinforcement. It should be reminded that negative reinforcement within a coercive communication is a form of immediate reinforcement. Therefore, it is conducive to shaping the behavior exhibited by children with ADHD toward a negative direction (Danforth et al., 2016).

Parental stress is another risk factor for the development of CPs among children with ADHD. This kind of stress occurs when a parent's perception of the demands of parenting exceeds the parent's capacity to cope with them. Parents who experience heightened stress tend to be more authoritarian, harsh, and negative in their parenting and get involved in less positive forms of communication with their child (Deater-Deckard, 1998; Theule et al., 2013).

The effect of these practices on the development of CPs in children was described earlier (see Section 2.4). Therefore, it is evident that parenting stress coupled with harsh or/and lax parenting strategies create an environment characterized by psychosocial adversity that, in turn, intensifies stress and facilitates the expression of genetic risk, adding further to the cyclical impact on the development of CPs among children with ADHD.

To conclude, it seems that children with ADHD have a genetic risk to exhibit negative behaviors that simultaneously interact with parental cognitive and behavioral variables in a transactional manner to exacerbate the disruptive behavior of the child. Genetic predisposition is expressed more strongly in environments characterized by psychological adversity and stress. On the other hand, genetically defined neuropsychological deficits and ADHD symptomatology affect the way in which parents perceive their child's behavior and, accordingly, respond to it. Consequently, a pattern of coercive interaction between them is likely to develop, or parents may disengage altogether when the child is well-behaved. Moreover, this kind of interaction is incompatible with a parenting style that teaches a child to control their behavior with self-directed and eventually private speech. Elevated parental stress, caused by perceived inability to effectively respond to the demanding role of parenting a child with ADHD, and blame-oriented attributions for the child's misbehavior further enhance the risk for harsh parenting and coercive interactions, leading to the development of CPs.

As development progresses, high-risk environments extend to deviant peer group affiliations, neighborhood violence, and exposure to criminality and drug use. Individuals confronted with these accumulating risk factors are prone to develop comorbidity of ADHD and early-onset CPs in childhood, with an increased likelihood of emerging antisocial personality traits later in life (Beauchaine et al., 2010).

Therefore, understanding the process of epigenesis of ODD and CD in a child with ADHD, along with the factors that facilitate their development, is particularly significant for the prevention of CPs. The clinician must be able to comprehend and prevent factors that increase the risk for the development of these disorders among children with ADHD, as they bring numerous negative outcomes in their developmental course.

7.12 ADHD and Substance-Related and Addictive Disorders

7.12.1 ADHD and Substance Use Disorder (SUD)

SUD and *Gambling Disorder* (GD), which is discussed in the next section, are classified into the broad category of *substance-related and addictive disorders* in DSM-5. SUD combines the DSM-IV categories of *substance abuse* and *substance dependence* into a single disorder measured on a continuum from mild to severe. Each specific substance (apart from caffeine) is addressed as a separate use disorder (e.g., *alcohol use disorder, stimulant use disorder*, etc.), but in almost all cases the same overarching diagnostic criteria are used. These criteria have increased relative to the previous DSM editions (APA, 2013).

Findings from a great number of studies point to the conclusion that ADHD co-occurs with SUD, mainly alcohol and toxic substances, at a rate that cannot be attributed to chance. Studies on individuals with ADHD reveal increased rates of SUD that range from 35% to 71% (Wilens, 2004). Furthermore, studies on individuals with SUD also reveal heightened ADHD rates, even though they vary significantly across studies (Wilens, 2009). These rates range from 2% in Iceland (Hannesdottir, Tyrfingsson, & Piha, 2001) to 83% in Japan (Matsumoto, Kamijo, Yamaguchi, Iseki, & Hirayasu, 2005).

A meta-analysis of 12 studies, based on a sample of adults seeking treatment for SUD, reported a 23% overall prevalence of ADHD (van Emmerik-van Oortmerssen et al., 2012). Moreover, in a recent study applying the same assessment methods in all participants from treatment centers in 10 countries, the prevalence of ADHD in adults seeking treatment for SUD ranged from 6% to 33%, with an average of 14% (van de Glind et al., 2013).

However, ADHD is speculated to be underdiagnosed in the population of adults seeking aid in detoxification. For example, in a study carried out in an addiction treatment center, while 3% of patients were noted in the records as having ADHD, systematic assessment using a standardized screener identified a rate of 44% (McAweeney, Rogers, Huddleston, & Moore, 2010). Another study has shown that only 12% of patients with SUD and ADHD had been identified as having ADHD in childhood, and only 4% of them had received appropriate treatment (Skutle et al., 2015).

The most frequently used substances among individuals with ADHD are alcohol and cannabis (Faraone et al., 2007), followed by lower rates of cocaine and amphetamines (Charach, Yeung, Climans, & Lillie, 2011; Sullivan & Rudnik-Levin, 2001). One of the hypotheses that have been put forward in order to understand the relationship between ADHD and substance use is that, for some individuals with ADHD, use of such substances constitutes some sort of self-medication in an unsuccessful attempt of self-treatment (Skutle et al., 2015). It has been suggested that cannabis might reduce anxiety and internal restlessness (Vorspan, Mehtelli, Dupuy, Bloch, & Lépine, 2015) but is unlikely to help with concentration (Bidwell, Henry, Willcutt, Kinnear, & Ito, 2014). Therefore, it is possible that these users are not detected for the presence of ADHD because cannabis may have reduced some of its symptoms and associated characteristics. In addition, many users mention a significant relief from ADHD symptoms during cocaine use, which is probably attributed to the dopamine release and its concentration in the synapses (Volkow et al., 2003). As far as alcohol is concerned, it seems to have a different effect, offering calmness and reducing insomnia, from which some people with ADHD often suffer (Ohlmeier et al., 2008).

Problems with substance use usually appear for the first time in adolescence or during the first years of adulthood (Gillberg et al., 2004). Adolescents who have school failure experiences and low self-esteem are more susceptible to the systematic substance use during adolescence (Marshal et al., 2003; Townsend, Flisher, & King, 2007). It seems that failure to engage in activities that promote future goal attainment, such as academic success, creates vulnerability to alcohol misuse. Therefore, one potential ADHD-related pathway to substance use is through school failure.

Some parenting practices, including lack of monitoring of these adolescents, also play a major role (Molina et al., 2012; Walther et al., 2012). It has been shown that clear limit setting and consistent rule enforcement act as protective factors for adolescents with ADHD against the negative social influences of deviant peers who may be involved in substance use. To this end, it is useful for parents to be aware of their child's activities, friendships, and whereabouts (Molina et al., 2012). Vigilant parenting, however, reflects only one side of the parent–teen dynamic. Recent literature recognizes that parental awareness of their teens' activities and whereabouts may reflect teen disclosure in the context of a warm and supportive relationship rather than active parental effort to supervise (Kerr, Stattin, & Burk, 2010).

There is converging evidence that ADHD may constitute the first step in a social deviance pathway leading to SUD in adolescence through adverse family functioning and affiliation with deviant peers (Marshal et al., 2003; Mason, Walker, Wine, Knoper, & Tercyak, 2007). However, a second pathway has been proposed, suggesting a paradoxical *suppression effect*, such that childhood ADHD leads to adolescent social impairment, withdrawal, and social isolation, which in turn leads to *decreased* substance use. It has been argued that adolescents with ADHD who have few friends may have more restricted social access to substances, as substance use primarily occurs in social contexts (Molina et al., 2012; 2014; Sibley et al., 2014).

High comorbidity rates between ADHD and CD, which is closely related to SUD, have led to the suggestion that CD holds a key role in the emergence of substance use in individuals diagnosed with ADHD (Flory & Lyman, 2003). Some studies have shown an association between ADHD and increased substance use over and above the risk posed by CD (Burke, Loeber, Lahey, 2001; Elkins, McGue, & Iacono, 2007), whereas others have proposed that CD mediates the relationship between ADHD and later substance use (Brook, Brook, Zhang, & Koppel, 2010; Fergusson, Horwood, & Ridder, 2007). It may be that ADHD and CD together generate a greater risk for later substance use than either disorder alone. Alternatively, ADHD and SUD relate in a complicated manner, perhaps involving comorbid CD under some circumstances but not others (Zucker, 2006a).

From our point of view, if the association between ADHD and CD is conceptualized within the developmental perspective described in the previous section, this debate is meaningless. Such debates usually derive from our failure to conceive the nature of overlapping symptoms in developmental psychopathology, generated by the comorbidity concept per se and the categorical approach of current classification systems. In most cases, there is not *one* deficit or disorder that can account for the development of SUD, but rather a combination of overlapping and dynamic factors that can often trace their roots back to ADHD (Carrellas, Wilens, & Anselmo, 2016).

In another series of studies, an attempt was made to associate some main ADHD characteristics with the possibility of developing SUD, apart from the potential comorbidity with CD. Impulsivity is a core component of the ADHD phenotype as well as a correlate for substance use (Iacono, Malone, & McGue, 2008; Verdejo-Garcia, Lawrence, & Clark, 2008). This trait overlap supports arguments that impulsivity contributes to the association between ADHD and substance use to a great extent (Roberts, Peters, Adams, Lynam, & Milich, 2014; Rooney, Chronis-Tuscano, & Huggins, 2015).

In a study investigating rates of alcohol use among college students diagnosed with ADHD, impulsivity was found to account for heightened rates of alcohol use among this population (Rooney, Chronis-Tuscano, & Huggins, 2015). In addition, it has been found that several facets of impulsivity appear to differentially contribute to substance use among adults with ADHD (Roberts et al., 2014). Two of these facets are lack of premeditation and negative urgency. Lack of foresight and poor planning that characterize individuals with ADHD may contribute to their heightened rates of alcohol use. In addition, negative urgency, conceptualized as a failure to inhibit strong impulses while experiencing strong negative emotion, may account for tobacco and marijuana use.

Finally, some researchers have formulated the hypothesis that a neurobiological link between the two disorders exists at some level, because they share similar deficits in anterior cingulate activation and the frontosubcortical systems (Frodl, 2010). According to the results of neuroimaging studies, diminished reward anticipation was associated with reduced activation in the striatum among individuals with ADHD. Individuals with SUD have also shown alterations in fronto-striatal circuits during craving (Frodl, 2010).

Changes in the dopaminergic system also play an important role in both disorders (Bédard et al., 2010; Volkow, Fowler, Wang, Baler, & Telang, 2009). The role of dopaminergic system in the perception of reward and the individual's concomitant motivation has been thoroughly discussed in Section 6.5. This system constitutes the principal neuronal background for the functioning of drugs that act on it and lead to the release of dopamine, which creates the feeling of pleasure. Transmission of dopamine in the cerebral cortex is involved in the processing of sensory information associated with emotions (Xu & Zhang, 2004). A review of relevant studies (Le Foll, Gallo, Le Strat, Lu, & Gorwood, 2009) has shown that different aspects of the phenotype of addiction are significantly influenced by the dysfunction of dopaminergic receptors that results from genetic factors.

A continuing debate among researchers is the extent to which pharmacological treatment of ADHD in childhood confers a risk of subsequent SUD. The current literature appears to contain conflicting data and divergent opinions. Some authors have suggested that children treated with stimulant medication were at greater risk for substance use (Brandon, Marinelli, Baker, & White, 2001; Lambert, 2005). Others indicated that childhood stimulant treatment does not increase the risk for later development of SUD (Barkley, Fischer, Smallish, & Fletcher, 2004; Mannuzza, Klein, & Moulton, 2003). In addition, some studies have shown that stimulant treatment may have protective effects, reducing the propensity toward substance use (Biederman, Wilens, Mick, Spencer, & Faraone, 1999; Whalen, Jamner, Henker, Gehricke, & King, 2003). This debate is presented in detail in Section 11.4.

Comorbidity between ADHD and SUD is associated with poor prognosis for both disorders (Wilens & Fusillo, 2007) and greater morbidity, including earlier onset of the SUD (Arias et al., 2008) and shorter transition from use to dependence (Biederman et al., 1997). A substantial overrepresentation of all childhood and adolescent problems has been found in the comorbid SUD/ADHD group, especially more episodes with temperamental outburst, along with poor school performance (Skutle et al., 2015). Furthermore, this group is more likely to develop other psychiatric disorders (Kessler et al., 2005; Wilens et al., 2005) and presents a high risk for suicide attempts (Huntley et al., 2012). Comorbid ADHD and SUD produce significant and unique treatment challenges, including less likelihood of successful treatment completion, a longer time to recovery, and earlier relapse (Kolpe & Carlson, 2007; Miranda, Colomer, Berenguer, Roselló, & Roselló, 2016).

Some studies make an attempt to differentiate the study on comorbidity between ADHD and SUD depending on the specific substance used, based on the assumption that different etiological mechanisms may cause, for example, the use of toxic substances as opposed to alcohol. However, it is highlighted that there is considerable room for further investigation in order to gain insight into the way in which pharmacological properties and social roles of various substances may differentiate the use patterns among individuals with and without ADHD (Sibley et al., 2014).

Regarding alcohol use, it is estimated that ADHD is present in at least 20% of excessive alcohol users. Among adolescents who use mental health services for this reason, ADHD prevalence is estimated at 35% (Molina et al., 2002). Moreover, adolescents with ADHD seem to have an earlier onset of alcohol use. Early initiation of alcohol use is associated with driving while intoxicated and unintentional injury (Hingson & Zha, 2009; Sibley et al., 2014). Moreover, initiation of alcohol use among children with ADHD at a younger age may form part of the etiological chain of events that characterizes the relationship between alcoholism and criminality in adulthood (Zucker, Donovan, Masten, Mattson, & Moss, 2008). According to a recent meta-analysis, ADHD is mainly associated with increased risk for developing Alcohol Use Disorder in adulthood (Lee, Humphreys, Flory, Liu, & Glass, 2011).

Parental drinking is the most important predictor of alcohol use in ADHD adolescents (Biederman, Faraone et al., 2000). Alcohol use is more commonly observed in parents of children with ADHD (Knopik et al., 2006), possibly in an attempt to reduce parental stress (Pelham et al., 1998). This fact has a deleterious effect on parental practices and increases youth access to alcohol (Komro, Maldonado-Molina, Tobler, Bonds, & Muller, 2007). It is also likely that adolescents with alcohol abusing parents possess the strongest genetic risks for early alcohol use (Sher et al., 2005, Zucker, 2006b). It has been suggested that shared genetic risk factors explain 64% of the overlap between ADHD and alcohol use (Capusan et al., 2015).

In addition, an increasing body of literature shows an interesting association between ADHD and cigarette smoking. ADHD is a significant predictor for early initiation of cigarette use after adjusting for potential confounding variables (Ercan et al., 2003; Wilens, 2004). Adolescents with ADHD are three times more likely to become smokers relative to the general population (Tercyak, Lerman & Audrain, 2002). From the moment adolescents with ADHD initiate smoking, they are five times more likely to escalate to heavy use than typically developing peers (Sibley et al., 2014). Elevated cigarette use among adolescents with ADHD is particularly concerning, as it increases the risk for developing later SUD (Palmer et al., 2009). Furthermore, individuals with ADHD report greater difficulty quitting smoking (Pomerleau, Downey, Stelson, & Pomerleau, 1995).

7.12.2 ADHD and Gambling Disorder (GD)

In DSM-IV, pathological gambling was classified into the category of *impulse control disorders not elsewhere classified.* In DSM-5 it was moved into the category of substance-related and addictive disorders and is the sole condition in the new category of behavioral addictions. This revision was based on a substantial amount of research findings according to which pathological gambling is similar to substance-related disorders in terms of clinical expression, brain origin, comorbidity, physiology, and treatment (APA, 2013).

Neuroimaging and neurochemical studies suggest that gambling behaviors activate reward systems similar to those activated by drugs and produce some behavioral symptoms that appear comparable to those produced by the SUDs (APA, 2013). For example, pathological gamblers are often unwilling to quit gambling despite its negative consequences. In addition, they continue to bet more money than they can afford and then chase their losses by returning to gambling (Black et al., 2013). Therefore, nonoptimal arousal states and an increased need for rewarding activity, such as those found in individuals with ADHD, increase the chances that a person will become hooked by the powerful stimulating effect of gambling (Blasczynski, 1998).

Individuals with GD report ADHD symptoms at a rate ranging from 20% to 30% in childhood (Clark, Nower, & Walker, 2013; Rodriguez-Jimenez et al., 2006) or in adulthood (Aymamí et al., 2015). Reports of childhood ADHD symptomatology also correspond with increased severity of adult problem gambling (Breyer et al., 2009; Grall-Bronnec et al., 2011). According to a recent meta-analysis, the mean prevalence of ADHD in individuals with problem gambling was 18.46% and the mean prevalence of problem gambling in individuals with ADHD was 11.75% (Theule, Hurl, Cheung, Ward, & Henrikson, 2016). Individuals with problem gambling were 4.18 times more likely to have ADHD than controls. Individuals with ADHD were 2.85 times more likely to experience problem gambling than individuals without ADHD.

ADHD is associated with a younger age of onset of gambling behavior (Aymamí et al., 2015; Chamberlain, Derbyshire, Leppink, & Grant, 2015). This finding is particularly important, because earlier onset of gambling behavior has been linked to greater severity of the problem, as well as to more severe consequences in the individual's life (Granero et al., 2014; Jiménez-Murcia et al., 2010). For example, Breyer and colleagues (2009) have shown that young adults who reported childhood ADHD symptoms persisting into adulthood presented a more severe gambling problem than those with nonpersistent or no ADHD symptoms. Individuals in the former group were more frequently involved with the law and had problems with their job.

The relationship between ADHD and pathological gambling can be explained by similar interpretations with those presented in the previous section regarding ADHD and SUD. One of these interpretations, which has been particularly investigated in relation with pathological gambling, is its connection with some personality traits, mainly impulsivity, which is both a key behavioral feature of ADHD and a hallmark of GD (Black, Monahan, Temkit, & Shaw, 2006; Black et al., 2013; Forbush et al., 2008).

Impulsive individuals are more likely to engage in risk-taking or sensation-seeking activities to alleviate a state of recurrent psychological underarousal, as is typically present in ADHD (Liu et al., 2013). Gambling is one such risk-taking activity. Moreover, a recent meta-analysis has found strong support for decision-making deficits in individuals with ADHD (Mowinckel, Pedersen, Eilertsen, & Biele, 2015). Problem gambling also represents a deficit in decision making (Vitaro, Arseneault, & Tremblay, 1997).

Impulsivity has also been viewed in terms of a discounting framework for probabilistic choice, according to which the value of a choice outcome decreases as a function of its delay or probability of receipt (Green & Myerson, 2004). For example, an individual who discounts delayed outcomes is likely to choose a smaller, more immediate reward over a larger, more delayed reward (Dai et al., 2016). It has been found that individuals with GD respond more positively to immediate reward than to greater but delayed reward, therefore they are particularly susceptible to gambling, which provides immediate reward (Reynolds, 2006; Vitaro, Arseneault, & Tremblay, 1997). Thus, inability to delay gratification and/or engage in reasoned decision making in the face of mounting losses could lead to gambling problems. All the aforementioned characteristics directly refer to the way individuals with ADHD perceive reward (see Section 6.5).

High levels of impulsivity among children in kindergarten forecast a significantly higher propensity toward gambling involvement in the sixth grade, for example involvement in games of chance (Pagani, Derevensky, & Japel, 2009). Moreover, high levels of impulsivity among adolescents predict the development of problem gambling in adulthood (Slutske, Caspi, Moffitt, & Poulton, 2005). Finally, it has been found that problem gamblers have higher levels of impulsivity than controls (Castellani & Rugle, 1995; Forbush et al., 2008), and that impulsivity may predict gambling behavior (Clarke, 2004).

It has also been shown that individuals with GD have deficits in various executive functions, similarly to individuals with ADHD. For example, a characteristic of these individuals is their inability to divide their attention among competing stimuli, leading them to ignore internal perceptions of self-restraint (McCown & Chamberlain, 2000). This deficit has been described as "myopia of the future" (Bechara, 2003).

Additionally, beyond impulsivity, other personality traits that have been described among pathological gamblers is novelty seeking (as described in Section 7.10.2), risk-taking, negative emotionality (LaBrie et al., 2003; Slutske et al., 2005), poor self-directedness, and exceeding limits (Black, Shaw, & Allen, 2008; Forbush et al., 2008). All these characteristics, however, are also observed among individuals with ADHD, as it has been described in previous chapters.

Pagani and colleagues (2009) summarize the pathway from ADHD to GD as follows:

> Children with ADHD show significant aberrations in the neural substrates associated with decision making and reward processing during guessing and gambling, to the extent that they experience enhanced sensitivity to unfavorable outcomes. In turn, their greater vulnerability to a negative affective reaction to incorrect guessing and unexpected losses influences less insightful subsequent estimations in guessing and gambling. This creates a vicious circle of ineffective self-assessment and self-regulation processes. These characteristics are noted in adult pathological gamblers with a confirmed childhood history of ADHD.
>
> (p. 241)

In conclusion, pathological gambling may form part of a spectrum of risky behaviors that also include substance use and delinquent behavior. These behaviors are linked among them with several characteristics that are fundamental in the clinical presentation of individuals with ADHD. Once more, understanding of the complex pathways that originate from the neurodevelopmental deficits characterizing ADHD and may end up to risky behaviors like the ones described earlier is far more informative for the clinician than establishing a multmorbid diagnosis of ADHD, ODD, CD, SUD, and GD, which might often be the case among adolescents and adults with ADHD.

7.13 ADHD and Sleep-Wake Disorders (SWDs)

7.13.1 The Process of Sleep and SWDs in DSM-5

Sleep is a complex process described as a rapidly reversible state of reduced responsiveness to the environment. For the advent of sleep, brain activity in the area that is responsible for alertness must be reduced. Sleep and wakefulness are regulated by mutual inhibition between sleep- and arousal-promoting circuitry (Fuller, Gooley, & Saper, 2006). Several neurotransmitters, particularly noradrenaline, norepinephrine, dopamine, and acetylcholine, are involved in this process.

Sleep architecture refers to the basic structural organization of normal sleep, namely the cyclical pattern of sleep, as it shifts between the different sleep stages (Kirov & Brand, 2014). In order to enhance comprehension of this process and related disturbances, and fully appreciate the intricate relationships among sleep, wakefulness, attention, and arousal, we will briefly review the mechanisms involved in the neurobiology of sleep.

Sleep has two qualitatively distinct stages: Non-rapid Eye Movement (NREM) and Rapid Eye Movement (REM), which are both active processes. NREM sleep is a period of relatively low brain activity, although the brain's regulatory capacity is still active and body movements are preserved. REM sleep is a period of desynchronized cortical activity, high metabolic rate, lack of muscle tone, and episodic bursts of rapid eye movements (Mindell & Owens, 2010). NREM sleep and REM sleep alternate in cycles through the night. First occurs NREM sleep, which lasts for approximately 80 minutes, and then REM sleep, which lasts for approximately 10 minutes. This sleep cycle of a total duration of 90 minutes is repeated three to six times every night. During these successive cycles, duration of NREM sleep decreases whereas duration of REM sleep increases. This process is governed by the endogenous *circadian rhythm* that influences the internal organization of sleep and timing and duration of daily sleep-wake cycles.

The relationship between ADHD and SWDs has been well-documented in systematic reviews (Barrett, Tracy, & Giaroli, 2013; Cortese et al., 2013; Hysing, 2014) and meta-analyses (Cortese, Faraone, Konofal, & Lecendreux, 2009; Sedky, Bennett, & Carvalho, 2014). The first references to sleep disturbances associated with ADHD were made in 1957 by Laufer and Denhoff, who noted: "Generally, the parents of hyperkinetic children are so desperate over the night problems that the daytime ones pale in significance." In 1973 Wender reported that "children with minimal brain dysfunction had an increased frequency of sleep difficulties: difficulty falling asleep and remaining asleep, and early awakening." Nevertheless, after these initial observations, researchers' interest in sleep difficulties waned and started to revive approximately 15 years ago, leading to major progress over the last 5 years.

Restless sleep has been used as a diagnostic criterion for ADHD in DSM-III, although it was eliminated from subsequent and current DSM editions, which likely contributed to a certain neglect of the relationship between sleep and ADHD (Cortese, 2015). Moreover, rating scales for ADHD included items related to sleep disturbances (Conners, Sitarenios, Parker, & Epstein, 1998b). Some researchers have called ADHD "a 24-hour disorder" because sleep disruption caused by increased nocturnal activity may contribute to daytime symptomatology (Corkum, Moldofsky, Hogg-Johnson, Humphries, & Tannock, 1999).

In DSM-5, SWDs encompass ten disorders or disorder groups. The core features of each disorder relate to the patient's dissatisfaction regarding the quality, timing, and amount of sleep, with resulting daytime distress and impairment. These disorders constitute a wide spectrum, on the one side of which we find difficulties in falling asleep and on the other side difficulties in awakening and getting into a state of alertness in order to respond to daily activities (APA, 2013).

7.13.2 Subjective Studies of Sleep in Individuals With ADHD

Researchers have analyzed sleep and alertness in individuals with ADHD using both subjective and objective studies. The former have been based on questionnaires and sleep diaries filled out by the children or their parents. Rates of sleep problems among individuals with ADHD vary depending on demographics and the type of measurement (e.g., subjective vs. objective), and have been reported as high as 70% (Engelhardt, Mazurek, & Sohl, 2013). Sleep disturbance is by far one of the most reported problems by parents of children with ADHD, who commonly recount restless, inadequate, and often delayed and/or fragmented sleep in their children (Silvestri & Aricò, 2012).

In a nationally representative study of approximately 5,000 Australian preschoolers, it was found that 52% of children with ADHD aged 4 to 5 years also encountered sleep difficulties (Hiscock, Canterford, Ukoumunne, & Wake, 2007). In the same study, it was found that children with more severe sleep difficulties were 12 times more likely to receive the diagnosis of ADHD. This finding seems to be associated with the fact that systematic lack of sleep may cause or aggravate learning and behavioral problems, including some symptoms that mimic those of ADHD (Fallone, Owens, & Deane, 2002). In this case, due to the manifestation of ADHD-like symptoms in individuals with primary sleep disorders, misdiagnosis may occur (Huang et al., 2007; Walters et al., 2000).

The developmental course of sleep disturbances in individuals with ADHD is consistent with the notion that these disturbances persist throughout the life span (Cassoff, Wiebe, & Gruber, 2012), at least in cases ADHD symptomatology persists as well (Gregory, Agnew-Blais, Matthews, Moffitt, Arseneault, 2016). Furthermore, it has been shown that sleep disturbances among children with ADHD can already be detected in infancy (Ball et al., 1997). O'Callaghan and colleagues (2010) report that sleep problems between the ages of 2 and 4 predict attention deficits at age 5 years, suggesting that sleep disturbances in early childhood may be an initial symptom of later ADHD. Further evidence has been provided by Scott and colleagues (2013), who found that age-specific reduction in sleep duration of a standard deviation or more across a 1-year time interval in preschoolers was a significant predictor of ADHD diagnosis.

Children with ADHD often present bedtime resistance, sleep-onset difficulties, long sleep latency, difficulties with morning awakenings, shorter duration of sleep, and daytime sleepiness. Additionally, they have poor sleep efficiency, frequent motor movements during sleep, and frequent night awakenings (Corkum, Tannock, Moldofsky, Hogg-Johnson, & Humphries, 2001; Owens, 2005).

In contrast to many studies in children and adolescents with ADHD, there is only a handful of studies examining sleep disturbances in adults with ADHD, so available empirical data are limited. Nonetheless, it has been reported that adults with ADHD experience considerable subjective and objective impairment in sleep, such as bad quality of sleep, insomnia, restless sleep, and daytime sleepiness (Gau et al., 2007; Schredl, Alm, & Sobanski, 2007; Surman, 2006). In summary, sleep disturbances among adults with ADHD seem to resemble those found in children.

In some cases, individuals with ADHD report that they experience daytime somnolence even after a good night sleep (Golan, Shahar, Ravid, & Pillar, 2004). They also have higher rates of *obstructive sleeping apnea*, which is usually accompanied by snoring (O'Brien et al., 2003; Cortese, Faraone et al., 2009; Golan et al., 2004), *periodic limb movement disorder* (nocturnal myoclonus), and *restless legs syndrome* (Picchietti et al., 2007). It seems that these problems are more intense in case ADHD co-occurs with other disorders, especially ADs and DDs (Mayes et al., 2009).

Possible differences of sleep disturbances depending on ADHD subtype have also been investigated. Children with the inattentive subtype display fewer nighttime sleep problems but more hypersomnia, excessive daytime sleepiness, and increased duration of sleep relative to children with the combined subtype. On the other hand, children with the combined subtype have more sleep problems such as insomnia, frequent night awakenings, nightmares, and walking during sleep (LeBourgeois, Avis, Mixon, Olmi, & Harsh, 2004; Mayes et al., 2009). Similar findings were found in a research based on a sample of adults with ADHD. It has been proposed that a problem of underarousal in the inattentive subtype may be accountable for the excessive daytime sleepiness and hypersomnia, whereas symptoms of inattention do not affect either the duration or the quality of sleep (Mahajan, Hong, Wigal, & Gehricke, 2010). On the other hand, a problem of hyperarousal in the combined subtype may be accountable for difficulties in initiating or maintaining sleep (Mahajan et al., 2010; Silvestri et al., 2009).

7.13.3 Objective Studies of Sleep in Individuals With ADHD

Objective studies have used techniques such as polysomnography, actigraphy, infrared video camera, and the Multiple Sleep Latency Test (MSLT; Cortese, Konofal, Yateman, Mouren, & Lecendreux, 2006). There is little agreement in the literature regarding objective differences in sleep among children with ADHD, as studies have usually used small samples and report conflicting results (Hastings & Felt, 2012). Several reviews have pointed out that objective measures have not largely confirmed subjective parental reports of sleep disturbances (Cohen-Zion & Ancoli-Israel, 2004; Corkum et al., 2001).

Some researchers hypothesized that this inconsistency between parental subjective reports and objective measurements may be attributed to the fact that the difficulties reported as significantly higher in children with ADHD refer to inappropriate behavior in the context of problematic parent–child interaction. In other words, it has been suggested that parents of children with ADHD may overreport high levels of daytime and sleep-related problematic behaviors in a sort of negative halo effect, as a result of increased sensitivity to behavioral problems in these children (Konofal, Lecendreux, & Samuele Cortese, 2010). Therefore, sleep disturbances reported by parents may represent decreased cooperation with the child in establishing a sleep routine and the child's defiant and dilatory behavior with reference to sleep (Corkum et al., 2001; Wiggs, Montgomery, & Stores, 2005). However, other research findings suggest that parents can effectively differentiate between child "unwillingness" (bedtime refusal) versus "inability" (sleep-onset delay) to fall asleep (Gruber et al., 2012).

It has also been argued that this phenomenon might be explained by night-to-night variability in sleep patterns, which would be captured subjectively but would not be evident on testing in a sleep laboratory (Cohen-Zion, & Ancoli-Israel, 2004; Gruber, Sadeh, & Raviv, 2000). Furthermore, studies conducted in a laboratory environment cannot measure environmental factors, including noise at home or anxiety related to school subjects. Finally, subjective studies address sleep-related behaviors, whereas objective studies focus on sleep physiopathology. Consequently, a perfect correlation between these two types of variables seems unlikely (Konofal et al., 2010).

However, it has been reported that although no differences are found in sleep architecture by macro-structure standards (number of awakenings/arousals) between ADHD and control groups, abnormalities were traced in the micro-structure of sleep. Cyclic alternating pattern rates are lower in the ADHD group, suggesting a condition of hypoarousal (Akinci et al., 2015; Gruber et al., 2007; Miano et al., 2006; Parrino et al., 2004).

Finally, abnormalities were found with reference to REM sleep whose duration was sometimes increased and sometimes decreased (Cohen-Zion, & Ancoli-Israel, 2004; Sadeh, Pergamin, & Bar-Haim, 2006). Moreover, a delay in the onset of REM sleep was noted (Silvestri et al., 2009; Owens, 2005). These findings should be investigated further, mainly because REM sleep may serve important adaptive functions, such as implicit learning and consolidation of procedural memory (Diekelmann, & Born, 2010), emotional processing and regulation (Walker, 2009), and incorporation of recent memories into a broader vital context (Kirov, 2013).

A new method that has become a major assessment tool in sleep research is actigraphy, a noninvasive method for recording motor activity and sleep parameters by means of an electronic device worn on the body. The actigraph allows a patient's activity information to be obtained either in an experimental setting or in a natural setting for a prolonged and continuous period (De Crescenzo et al., 2016). According to studies that use this method, children with ADHD are demonstrated to have sleep onset latency, lower sleep efficiency, and less total sleep time (Moreau, Rouleau, & Morin, 2014; Radek, 2013). A recent meta-analysis of 24 studies comprising 2,179 children has shown that children with ADHD present a higher mean activity during structured sessions and a moderately altered sleep pattern compared to typically developing children (De Crescenzo et al., 2016).

7.13.4 *The Nature of the Relationship Between ADHD and SWDs*

The relationship between sleep and ADHD is a highly complex and multifactorial one. From a clinical perspective, it is very important as it relates to ADHD management. From a research perspective, it can contribute to the potential elucidation of basic mechanisms regulating attention, vigilance, arousal, and alertness, which are key aspects associated with ADHD (Owens et al., 2013).

Previous research has examined the relationship between sleep disturbances and ADHD, and a bidirectional association has been suggested such that sleep contributes to increased manifestation of ADHD symptoms and ADHD contributes to worsened sleep (Alfano & Gamble, 2009; Owens, 2005). In line with this view, ADHD and sleep are not just comorbid but the day and night manifestations of underlying physiological and developmental deficits. Several mechanisms have been proposed that are not mutually exclusive.

Neurobiological mechanisms that are responsible for the development of both ADHD and SWDs seem to have a lot of common characteristics. From a structural point of view, the reticular activating system and prefrontal cortex have been implicated in the regulation of attention and arousal. Attention and arousal, in turn, are properties that define the wake state. Cycling through the wake and sleep states reflects changes in brain arousal (Muzur, Pace-Schott, & Hobson, 2002). In addition, the thalamus is thought to play a role in working memory and behavioral inhibition abnormalities in ADHD, and in the regulation of NREM sleep (Owens, 2005). Thus, both problems with attention/alertness and sleep may be the results of abnormal cortex arousal function.

Additionally, aberrations in dopaminergic and noradrenergic functions seem to play a major role both in ADHD and in the alternation of NREM-REM sleep (Monti & Monti, 2007; Pace-Schott & Hobson, 2002). The same conclusions are drawn regarding the function of serotonin (Monti & Monti, 2007).

Furthermore, serotonin is a precursor for melatonin (a hormone that is produced by the pineal gland), and its deficiency may result in deficient melatonin synthesis and in a delayed sleep phase syndrome, respectively. Melatonin regulates circadian rhythms and increases during sleep. It also helps our body to know when it is time to go to bed and when it is time to wake up. Synthesis and release of melatonin in the brain are activated by darkness and are deactivated by light. Concentration of melatonin in the blood reaches the highest levels shortly before bedtime at night (Van Veen, Kooij, Boonstra, Gordijn, & Van Someren, 2010). Individuals with ADHD and sleep problems were demonstrated to have delayed evening increase in endogenous melatonin levels (Nováková et al., 2011).

Therefore, it seems that ADHD is likely to affect the capacity for self-regulation and the developmental characteristics that are essential in the training of circadian rhythms (Gruber, 2009). Findings suggest that among adults with ADHD, severity of the disorder is closely related to a circadian rhythm disorder and long sleep latency at night (Rybak, McNeely, Mackenzie, Jain, & Levitan, 2006). Such a delay in the endogenous circadian system may disrupt the sleep-alertness cycle and may account for fatigue and daytime sleepiness (Van der Heijden, Smits, Someren, & Boudewijn Gunning, 2005). Furthermore, this may underlie and contribute to symptoms of bedtime discomfort with secondary resistance to go to bed, which may be erroneously considered as the expression of oppositional behavior (Cortese et al., 2006).

Moreover, in many ADHD cases, sleep problems are the result of procrastination, where the individual's poor time management problems lead to the extension of work hours into the sleep hours, thus perpetuating chronic sleep disturbances (Yoon, Jain, & Shapiro, 2012). In addition, descent into sleep requires disengagement of cortical functioning from the environment, which may be particularly challenging for individuals with ADHD. Sleep propensity is also affected by environmental sleep facilitators and inhibitors to which individuals with ADHD may be differentially sensitive. For example, external factors that inhibit sleep, such as TV or social interactions, may function as competing priorities for sleep or as relatively more reinforcing (Owens et al., 2013).

A group of researchers have focused on the potential role of iron because it affects dopamine synthesis and dopaminergic signaling, and both ADHD and some SWDs are associated with lower ferritin levels (Oner, Dirik, Taner, Caykoylu, & Anlar, 2007). Ferritin is a protein that carries iron inside the cells and is used as a measure of iron levels. Low iron levels may result in reduced dopamine synthesis and abnormal dopaminergic signaling, thus accounting for comorbidity between ADHD and SWDs. This hypothesis is based on the fact that children with ADHD and low ferritin levels seem to display a more severe ADHD symptomatology and problems with sleep-wake transitions (Cortese, Konofal, Dalla Bernardina, Mouren, & Lecendreux, 2009). However, more experimentally driven data are needed to confirm the iron deficiency hypothesis.

Another hypothesized factor that has been proposed as causing sleeping disturbances in individuals with ADHD is stimulant medication. Findings of relevant studies are inconsistent. Some studies have supported that the use of stimulants is related to increased sleep disturbances, mainly insomnia and short duration of sleep (Galland, Tripp, & Taylor, 2010; Mick, Biederman, Jetton, & Faraone, 2000), whereas others have shown no change in sleep in children and adolescents treated with stimulant medication (O'Brien et al., 2003; Kim et al., 2010; Giblin & Strobel, 2011). In addition, well-controlled studies have demonstrated that sleep problems exist in medication-free individuals with ADHD (Gruber, & Sadeh, 2004; Hvolby, Jorgensen, & Bilenberg, 2008; Sobanski, Schredl, Kettler, & Alm, 2008). The increased reported difficulties with sleep in some children with ADHD treated with stimulants have been explained as a result of the stimulant medication wearing off and/or causing a *rebound effect*, leading to an apparent increased arousal and hyperactivity (Hastings & Felt, 2012).

Finally, it has been proposed that sleep disturbances in ADHD may be attributed to comorbid disorders, such as ODD, ADs and DDs (Mayes & Calhoun, 2009; Mick et al., 2000). However, this issue is controversial. Strong evidence of a cross-sectional association between internalizing problems and sleep problems has been found in children with ADHD. However, the association between sleep and externalizing problems is less clear, with some studies finding a link, while others have not (Mulraney, Giallo, Lycett, Mensah, & Sciberras, 2016).

7.13.5 Impact and Treatment of SWDs in Individuals With ADHD

Any sleep disorder that results in inadequate sleep duration, disrupted sleep, or excessive daytime sleepiness may have extremely negative effects on every person, but these effects might be cumulative for individuals with ADHD (Gruber et al., 2012). The most obvious outcomes are excessive daytime fatigue, cognitive impairment, and probably mood lability. Short duration of sleep among children with ADHD has been demonstrated to be greatly associated with poor academic performance, as well as with behavioral problems (Fallone, Owens, & Deane, 2002; Langberg, Dvorsky, Marshall, & Evans, 2013; Owens, 2008).

With regard to attention, it seems that children with ADHD are more seriously affected by sleep difficulties relative to typically developing children (Waldon, Vriend, Davidson, & Corkum, 2015). A study compared children with ADHD and sleep difficulties to children with ADHD without sleep difficulties and a control group, and has shown that the first group had more deficits both in reaction times and selective attention (Gruber et al., 2007). Another study has revealed that poor quality of sleep in these children was associated with lower performance on the WISC-III verbal scales and an overall lower verbal IQ (Andreou, Karapetsas, Agapitou, & Gourgoulianis, 2003).

Sleep disturbances in children with ADHD may be a burden for the whole family. Parents of children with ADHD report that sleep problems are a particularly challenging feature of looking after their child (Cortese, 2015). In addition, it has been demonstrated that sleep problems may be associated with poorer family functioning (Sung et al., 2008).

The findings presented so far have prompted researchers to recommend baseline assessment of sleep problems during initial evaluation of childhood ADHD (Sadeh, Pergamin, &

Bar-Haim, 2006), and continued assessment of sleep disturbance as part of ongoing ADHD treatment (Cortese et al., 2013). During this assessment, the clinician must distinguish a physiological sleep problem from a behavioral condition of which the sleep problem is but one of the symptoms (Gruber et al., 2012). Successful management of sleep disturbances in children with ADHD may significantly reduce behavioral symptom severity, improve the quality of life of these children and their family members, and support cognitive development (Kirov & Brand, 2014; Weiss, Craig, Davies, Schibuk, & Stein, 2015).

When developing a treatment plan for sleep disturbances in children with ADHD, the implementation of a sleep hygiene program is of the utmost importance. In case this intervention proves to be inefficient, administration of melatonin is the next preferred treatment (Owens et al., 2013; Weiss et al., 2006). Within the framework of a behavioral program, turning off stimuli like TVs or computers at least an hour prior to bedtime and adopting a regular bedtime routine, which allows the patient to relax, are highly recommended. These practices may be complemented with sleep diaries to keep track of bedtimes and rising times, as well as logs of activities done prior to bedtime (Yoon et al., 2012).

The first randomized controlled study of a manualized behavioral intervention specifically targeting sleep in children with ADHD has established that the sleep intervention was associated with substantial and sustained benefits by not only reducing sleep disturbances but also improving health-related quality of life, behavior, and daily functioning (Hiscock et al., 2015; Sciberras, Fulton, Efron, Oberklaid, & Hiscock, 2011). Moreover, a review of relevant studies proved the efficacy of melatonin in the treatment of sleep disturbances (Bendz & Scates, 2010; Weiss, Wasdell, Bomben, Rea, & Freeman, 2006).

7.14 ADHD, Feeding and Eating Disorders (FEDs), and Obesity

7.14.1 Epidemiology and Diagnostic Criteria in DSM-5

FEDs encompass *anorexia nervosa* and *bulimia nervosa* (two disorders previously included in the chapter of *eating disorders* in DSM-IV), along with *binge eating disorder* (now recognized as its own category), *pica, rumination*, and *avoidant/restrictive food intake disorder*. DSM-IV listed the latter three among disorders usually first diagnosed in infancy, childhood, or adolescence, a chapter that does not exist in DSM-5. These disorders are characterized by a persistent disturbance of eating or eating-related behavior that results in the altered consumption or absorption of food and significant impairment in physical health or psychosocial functioning (APA, 2013).

In DSM-5, it is noted that obesity, resulting from the long-term excess of energy intake relative to energy expenditure, is not included as a mental disorder. However, the robust associations between obesity and a number of mental disorders (e.g., binge eating disorder, DDs, BDs, schizophrenia) are highlighted. Therefore, obesity is conceptualized as a general medical condition of multiple etiologies with psychological and psychiatric factors being of major importance (Nazar et al., 2016).

Among the behavioral dysfunctions associated with ADHD, recent research points to less well-recognized dysregulated eating behaviors in a subset of individuals with ADHD. It has been established that individuals with ADHD are at high risk for pathological eating throughout development. Emerging evidence suggests that ADHD and FEDs, specifically those involving binge eating/purging (e.g., anorexia nervosa, binge-purge subtype; bulimia nervosa; and binge eating disorder) may coexist, resulting in increased severity of associated health issues (Bleck, DeBate, Levin, & Baldwin, 2016). However, findings are not always consistent across studies.

In addition, growing evidence for an association between obesity and ADHD has emerged (Alfonsson, Parling, & Ghaderi, 2012; Cortese et al., 2015; Cortese et al., 2013), although this may appear to be counterintuitive when hyperactivity is present, given the increased energy that it requires (Reinblatt et al., 2015). This association suggests that factors associated with ADHD may increase the risk for weight gain, as it has been confirmed by both epidemiological and clinical studies (Racicka, Hanć, Giertuga, Bryńska, & Wolańczyk, 2015).

These studies reveal a new trend in psychopathology research. While comorbidity between ADHD and psychiatric disorders has been extensively investigated, the possible association with somatic conditions has received less attention (Cortese & Castellanos, 2014). However, it has become evident that many conditions classically conceptualized as disorders of the CNS include alterations in other physiological systems as well (Qureshi & Mehler, 2013).

Adults with ADHD have been reported to present bulimia nervosa at a rate of 11.2% (Surman, Randall, & Biederman, 2006), in contrast to 1.5% in the general population (Hudson, Hiripi, Pope, & Kessler, 2007). In addition, two prospective studies suggest that childhood ADHD may play a role in the development of bulimia nervosa in young adults (Biederman et al., 2007; Mikami, Hinshaw, Patterson, & Lee, 2008). Regarding binge eating disorder, a prevalence of 8.1% has been found in adults with ADHD, in contrast to the expected 3.5% for the general population (Hudson et al., 2007; Mattos et al., 2004).

However, relatively little is known about the relationship between ADHD and binge eating in children. In a retrospective study of two pediatric community mental health centers, 27% of preadolescent children with ADHD also presented binge eating disorder, compared to 2% of controls (Reinblatt et al., 2015). In other words, a child with ADHD had 14 times the odds of presenting binge eating disorder than a child without ADHD.

Regarding obesity, a recent meta-analysis reported an approximately 70% increased pooled prevalence of obesity in adults and 40% in children with ADHD compared with controls (Cortese et al., 2015). Additionally, studies have demonstrated greater ADHD symptomatology in overweight/obese children, with one large prospective study of 8,106 children (7–8 years old at baseline) showing that childhood ADHD symptomatology significantly predicted obesity in adolescence (Khalife et al., 2014). Finally, the odds of being overweight/obese are at least 1.5 to 2 times greater in children with ADHD than typically developing children (Halfon, Larson, & Slusser, 2013; Waring & Lapane, 2008).

There is some evidence that the association between ADHD and obesity may depend on the individual's sex. Byrd, Curtin, and Anderson (2013) found that the prevalence of obesity in treated girls compared with untreated boys with ADHD was lower. Similarly, in the study of Kim, Mutyala, Agiovlasitis, and Fernhall (2011), prevalence of obesity was higher in men than in women. A prospective follow-up study of 6 to 12-year-old boys has shown that at 33-year follow-up, men diagnosed with ADHD in childhood had a significantly higher Body Mass Index (BMI) and obesity rates than those without childhood ADHD (Agranat-Meged et al., 2005). However, in a recent review and meta-analysis, it was argued that neither sex nor age group seem to influence the association between ADHD and obesity, suggesting that the relationship is already present in childhood in both sexes (Cortese et al., 2016).

7.14.2 The Nature of the Relationship Between ADHD, FEDs, and Obesity

At present, contributing factors underlying the relationship between ADHD, FEDs, and obesity are being investigated. A better insight into this association is important for two reasons. First, it may contribute to the understanding of possible causal mechanisms underlying ADHD, FEDs, and obesity. Second, it might have important implications for the management of these disorders, given the enormous personal, family, and social burden associated with these comorbid conditions (Cortese & Vincenzi, 2012).

As mentioned earlier, among FEDs, those involving binge eating have been specifically linked to ADHD and have received the most research attention. Binge eating is defined as eating significantly more food in a short period of time than most people would eat under similar circumstances, with episodes marked by feelings of lack of control (APA, 2013). This kind of disordered eating has been found to partially mediate the ADHD symptom—weight status association—because loss of control and excessive food intake are important determiners of weight gain (Lourenço et al., 2008; Pagoto et al., 2009). Similarly, controlling for binge eating seems to attenuate the relationship between ADHD and BMI among overweight/obese children with ADHD (Reinblatt et al., 2015). Therefore, mechanisms that might explain the occurrence of binge eating in individuals with ADHD also account for the relationship between ADHD and obesity. As there is a paucity of research data regarding the rest of FEDs in relation to ADHD, this section will focus on binge eating disorder and obesity under the general nomination ***problematic eating behavior*** to encompass both of them.

Several hypotheses have been proposed with respect to underlying mechanisms of these associations. First, it has been argued that ADHD and problematic eating behavior may be the expression of a common neurobiological dysfunction or may share common biological underpinnings, at least in a subset of individuals. Neurochemical mechanisms that have been proposed to underpin these associations include altered reinforcement mechanisms, brain-derived neurotropic disorder, and melanocortin-4-receptor (MC4-R) deficiency (Cortese & Vincenzi, 2012). Given the limited and inconsistent findings regarding the latter neurobiological dysfunctions, we will describe the first one, which is the most studied until today.

Recent evidence indicates that binge eating, obesity, and ADHD are characterized by suboptimal dopamine levels (Albayrak et al., 2013; Choudhry et al., 2013; Cortese, Dalla Bernardina, & Mouren, 2007). More specifically, genetic variation in the responsiveness of the dopamine mesolimbic system, namely alterations in the dopamine D2 receptor (DRD2) and, to a lesser extent, DRD4, may link ADHD and problematic eating behavior through its role in maladaptive reward perceptions. The role of deficits in rewarding activity has been well-documented in ADHD (see Section 6.5). However, it has also been a major target for research on vulnerability to problematic eating behavior, due to its involvement in the motivation and reinforcement of food-seeking behavior (Berridge, Ho, Richard, & DiFeliceantonio, 2010) because food, particularly hyperpalatable high-fat and high-sugar food, constitutes a primary reward (Seymour, Reinblatt, Benson, & Carnell, 2015).

Research support largely comes from neuroimaging studies indicating reductions in dopamine receptors in the striatum of individuals with problematic eating behavior (Volkow, Wang, Fowler, & Telang, 2008; Wang et al., 2001). However, scientists now generally agree that these findings reflect neuroadaptations that occur in response to abnormally prolonged stimulation of the dopamine system due to chronic overconsumption of highly palatable foods rather than as a casual factor of problematic eating behavior (Berridge et al., 2010; Davis, 2013). Moreover, accumulating evidence indicates that an amplified dopamine signal increases the risk for problematic eating behavior due to a stronger appetitive response to food cues (Davis, Strachan, & Berkson, 2004; Tomasi et al., 2015). Cortese and Vincenzi (2012) have called this condition a ***reward deficiency syndrome*** that is characterized by insufficient dopamine-related natural reinforcement that leads to "unnatural" immediate rewards, such as inappropriate eating.

A second hypothesis is that psychopathological factors common to both problematic eating behavior and ADHD may mediate the association between these two conditions (Cortese, Dalla Bernardina et al., 2007). These factors include social and familial support and personality traits. Peer rejection and negative parent–child relationships (e.g., punitive parenting) have been separately theorized as associated with both ADHD and problematic eating behavior (Mikami et al., 2008). Additionally, several personality traits have been linked to this comorbidity, including novelty seeking, self-directedness, obsessive compulsiveness, low levels of effortful control, and perfectionism (Fernández-Aranda et al., 2013).

Furthermore, two of the core symptoms of ADHD, impulsivity and inattention, may increase the risk of irregular and dysregulated eating patterns and lifestyle through separate but related means (Cortese, Faraone, Bernardi, Wang, & Blanco, 2013).

Impulsivity has been demonstrated to contribute to problematic eating behavior in children through disordered eating patterns, both in quantity and quality of foods consumed (Van Egmond-Fröhlich, Weghuber, & de Zwaan, 2012) and through limited physical activity as well (Thamotharan, Lange, Zale, Huffhines, & Fields, 2013). Dysregulation of dopamine may mediate consumption of high-caloric, low-nutrient foods (Tanofsky-Kraff & Yanovski, 2004) as well as impulsivity, leading to problematic eating behavior (Davis et al., 2006).

It has also been argued that the choice of pleasurable, high-caloric foods may sometimes result from a tendency to use food in order to "medicate" the low mood (Davis et al., 2004; Wang et al., 2004), as individuals with ADHD tend to have more mood lability than normal controls (Oliver, Nigg, Cassavaugh, & Backs, 2012). This tendency has been called *hedonic* or *emotional eating*—that is, eating to soothe negative emotions rather than to satisfy physiological need—and it may mediate the link between ADHD symptoms and problematic eating behavior (Davis et al., 2006; Patte et al., 2016). ADHD-related symptoms appear to interfere with individuals' abilities to withhold urges to binge or eat for emotional reasons and, consequently, can lead to weight gain. From an evolutionary perspective, impulsivity was likely advantageous during other eras in fostering high-calorie eating when food was available, but has become maladaptive in today's environment where high-calorie food is highly accessible (Patte et al., 2016).

The role of impulsivity in problematic eating behavior has been further substantiated by studies revealing that higher reward sensitivity was predictive of greater palatable food intake and weight gain but only among participants with diminished inhibitory control, which is a key characteristic of ADHD (Appelhans et al., 2011; Nederkoorn et al., 2010). Therefore, problematic eating behavior among ADHD individuals can be explained by the joint action of impulsivity and higher reward sensitivity, in other words, by an imbalance between the drive to consume and the diminished ability to delay gratification (Carr, Daniel, Lin, & Epstein, 2011).

Inattention and associated deficits in executive functions may play a role in problematic eating behavior by diminishing an individual's receptivity to internal satiation cues and lack of awareness of food intake (Cortese & Vincenzi, 2012). Therefore, these individuals may forget about eating when they are engaged in interesting activities but are more likely to eat when less stimulated. In addition, poor planning and organizational abilities may contribute to difficulty maintaining regular eating patterns that promote healthy weight, thus leading to disordered consumption habits and raising the odds of becoming overweight (Davis et al., 2006). It has been revealed that children with ADHD skip meals, especially breakfast and dinner, significantly more often than controls, eat more often than five times a day, eat fewer fruits and vegetables, and drink more sweetened beverages (Ptacek et al., 2014).

Another mediating factor that has been suggested between ADHD and problematic eating behavior is body dissatisfaction. It has been found that body dissatisfaction moderates the relationship between ADHD and disordered eating attitudes and behaviors in children who are overweight or obese (Gowey, Stromberg, Lim, & Janicke, 2017).

Disordered sleep should also be taken into account as a possible contributing factor in the complex relationship between ADHD and problematic eating behavior (Cortese & Castellanos,

2014; Cortese, Maffeis et al., 2007). For example, sleep-disordered breathing is a common problem in ADHD but has also been shown to produce both FEDs and obesity (Cortese et al., 2008). Sleep-disordered breathing may cause sleep fragmentation, leading to excessive daytime sleepiness. In a study conducted on a sample of 70 obese children, excessive daytime sleepiness was associated with symptoms of inattention, hyperactivity, and impulsivity (Cortese, Maffeis et al., 2007).

In addition, it has recently been demonstrated that young children who do not get enough sleep are at increased risk of becoming overweight, as each fewer hour a child sleeps raises the BMI by a factor of 0.5. (Cortese, Faraone, Konofal, & Lecendreux, 2009). The obesogenic effect of reduced sleep is thought to be mediated by both behavioral and hormonal factors. It has been suggested that, at least in some patients, problematic eating behavior may be related to a metabolic and/or circadian abnormality (Vgontzas et al., 2006). Animal models have shown that dysregulated circadian rhythm may lead to metabolic dysfunctions (Arble, Ramsey, Bass, & Turek, 2010). In addition, sleep deprivation reduces leptin and raises ghrelin levels, which increases appetite. A lack of sleep may additionally cause fatigue during the day, reducing activity levels (Fliers et al., 2013).

Finally, it has been hypothesized that an underlying mental health condition, such as DDS, BDS, ADs, and SUD, may mediate the relationship between ADHD and problematic eating behavior (Cortese, Dalla Bernardina et al., 2007). Biederman and colleagues (2007) conducted a stratified analysis that examined comorbidities among adolescents with ADHD with and without FEDs, and found that those with co-occurring DDs, ADs, and CPs were more likely to have a FED. Moreover, in a recent meta-analysis (Nigg et al., 2016), it has been found that the association of ADHD with overweight and obese status is larger in adolescence than in childhood and is more reliable in girls than in boys during adolescence. However, the association was accounted for by those with comorbid DDs and CD, suggesting that problematic eating behavior might be associated with particular subpopulations of ADHD rather than with ADHD globally.

Based on the potential contribution of ADHD in the development of problematic eating behavior, it has been suggested that the treatment of ADHD, either pharmaceutical or psychosocial, might be expected to prevent disordered eating because stimulants improve ADHD and restore normal eating behaviors in patients with both conditions (Levy et al., 2009; Sokol et al., 1999). ADHD medications could act on both the brain pathways involved in ADHD and those that mediate abnormal eating behaviors. For example, a trial reported the efficacy of ATX in weight reduction in obese women (Gadde et al., 2006). In addition, it has been argued that the treatment of impulsivity and inattention in the framework of ADHD could improve abnormal eating behaviors as well (Surman et al., 2006). However, the tolerability of stimulants in individuals with ADHD and problematic eating behavior has not been examined, and there are no randomized control trials assessing the effects of behavioral therapies targeting ADHD symptoms on weight and eating-related outcomes (Cortese & Castellanos, 2014). Others (Stulz et al., 2013) suggest that both conditions require equal clinical attention, and that focusing primarily on ADHD symptoms and expecting that problematic eating behavior will be automatically alleviated might result in disappointing outcomes.

7.15 Commentary

In this chapter, we have thoroughly discussed comorbidity of ADHD with 13 different disorders or groups of disorders, according to the nomenclature of DSM-5. Although we expressed our reservations regarding the concept of comorbidity in the beginning of the chapter, we chose to use it in order to be in line with current scientific literature. Now that this chapter has come to an end, existing evidence has been presented, and hypothesized mechanisms explaining several comorbidities have been discussed, we would like to close with a brief commentary, illustrating some thoughts that the elaboration of this chapter has elicited.

In clinical practice, "pure" ADHD cases are almost nonexistent. However, the whole diagnostic and treatment system in developmental psychopathology is based on a clear distinction among disorders, corroborated by research findings provided by studies that, in their majority, include pure samples and exclude cases in which comorbid conditions are present. As clinicians, we wonder how such numbers of pure cases can be found in research, whereas they rarely exist in clinical practice. It could be argued that the most severe cases, among which comorbid cases may present more often in mental health services. Although this explanation is rational, we truly doubt that researchers usually screen for all 13 possible comorbid disorders presented in this chapter during their sample selection procedures. Thus, theoretically, co-existence of difficulties other than those inherent in ADHD symptomatology in research samples, at least at some level, seems to be the rule rather than the exception. However, this co-existence is not taken into account in the discussion of the findings in studies whose authors claim that their samples consist of pure ADHD cases.

On the other hand, we wonder how research findings based on pure—or claimed to be pure—samples can be of benefit to clinicians, whose patients usually exhibit much more complex and multifaceted conditions. How do current diagnostic systems really contribute to the establishment of a clinically meaningful diagnosis? More importantly, how do they help treatment planning? If mechanisms leading to the appearance of symptoms or common etiological factors underlying symptoms are not profoundly understood and made explicit in the diagnostic manuals, how can individuals with ADHD be addressed holistically, with all their deficits taken into account and all their needs met? From our point of view, such a framework largely lacks in developmental psychopathology. Pennington and Bishop (2009) are in line with this viewpoint.

Through the evidence presented in this chapter, it has become clear that many causal factors underlying several disorders are not disorder specific. A relevant example is the joint action of impulsivity and higher reward sensitivity, two central characteristics of ADHD that have been implicated as mediating factors in the relationship between ADHD and four other disorders: FEDs involving binge eating, SUD, CD, and GD. It is obvious that this deficiency seems to play a central role in the association of ADHD with a number of maladaptive behaviors that are listed as distinct disorders in current classification systems. If impulsivity alone is taken into account, it seems present in a much larger number of the disorders presented so far.

We really wonder whether inability to inhibit responses, to delay aversion, or to correctly perceive rewards that are related to food, games of chance, several substances, or risky behaviors, substantially differ in each one of these cases or is the same inability just referring to a different object. In other words, we argue that the impaired function (response inhibition, ability to delay aversion, reward sensitivity) is more important than its object (food, games of chance, substances, or risky behaviors).

We suggest that when the aforementioned disorders, which are mainly characterized by behaviors inherent in ADHD, namely impulsivity (or response disinhibition) and higher reward sensitivity, are present in individuals with ADHD, they may not be distinct disorders but etiologically linked to ADHD. We argue that as it does not make a big difference whether a phobia concerns spiders, blood, or clowns, or whether OCD behaviors concern counting, checking, or cleaning, similarly it does not make a big difference whether response disinhibition and high reward sensitivity lead to overeating, gambling, using substances, or engaging in deviant behaviors. The appearance may change, but the nuclear deficiency underneath is similar.

Following this orientation, we find particularly interesting the conceptualization of mental disorders and their symptoms as a network, within which comorbidity reflects direct relations between symptoms of multiple disorders (Cramer et al., 2010; see Section 7.1.1). The understanding of these relationships, the factors that influence them, and the mechanisms that are implicated may be more insightful and meaningful for the clinician than the simple acknowledgement of their comorbidity.

A second example refers to the case of a child who presents ADHD combined with ADs, DDs, and CPs. All three latter disorders are thought to be mediated by adverse environmental circumstances triggered by the cumulative effects of ADHD-related impairments. We believe that a child with ADHD has similar chances of developing either ADs/DDs or CPs, depending on their genetic predisposition, personality, intelligence level, sex, and so forth, as a response to negative life experiences that may stem from the core ADHD symptomatology and complicate as a result of environmental responses to it. The way in which the individual will interpret this core ADHD symptomatology resulting in inability to respond to environmental demands may determine whether emotional experience will be internalized or externalized, that is turn out as anxiety, depression, defiance, or aggression. Therefore, understanding of the factors that influence these interpretations may be more useful for the clinician than separating anxiety from depression, and depression from defiance and aggression.

Finally, a third example concerns the case of a child with the main characteristics of ADHD who also presents learning difficulties preceded by speech and language problems, motor clumsiness, oppositional behavior that escalates within coercive interactions, anxiety in the face of stressful situations, difficulties in pragmatics, provisional tics, and disordered sleep and eating. Data presented in this chapter make it evident that such a phenotype is absolutely expectable in a child with ADHD. Rather than attributing numerous different diagnostic labels to this child, it is much more helpful to conceive these difficulties as manifestations of one clinical disorder of greater severity, resulting from genetic, neuropsychological, but also environmental factors, along a continuum, according to the dimensional approach in psychopathology.

To strengthen this point of view, we reproduce an extract from Section 7.9.2 (after elimination of citations):

> SLD, particularly in Reading, is more commonly manifested among children with comorbid ADHD and DCD relative to children who have only ADHD. SLPs also occur frequently in individuals with DCD. Furthermore, DCD often coexists with ASD which in turn often coexists with ADHD.

How is all this complicated research information relevant in clinical practice if we consider all these disorders as distinct entities and cannot conceive how they are related to genetic and epigenetic processes?

The concept of atypical brain development that affects multiple areas of behavior simultaneously is also of particular interest (Kaplan et al., 2006; see Sections 7.1.1 and 7.9). In all "comorbid" disorders described so far, structural and neurochemical abnormalities have been found at greatly overlapping brain regions across disorders. Abnormal activation of the cortico-striato-thalamo-cortical circuits has been found in almost all of them! In addition, aberrations in dopaminergic and noradrenergic functions seem to play a major role in most of them. It seems very logical that such abnormalities, resulting from pleiotropic genes, may cause different but interrelated symptoms across individuals as a result of the extent and the location of the underlying neurological abnormality. This point of view, coupled with the recent theory of brain adaptation (Johnson, Jones, & Gliga, 2015), according to which differences in early signs of neurodevelopmental disorders may reflect the time in the life course when brain adaptation processes begin in the face of mild but widespread disturbances to early brain function, can shed light to our comprehension of the subject. Furthermore, it can aid clinicians to implement early intervention programs that target the primary pathological processes underlying these disorders instead of treating the symptoms of full-blown disorders.

The exact nomination of these phenotypes, which largely depends on the age of the individual at the time of assessment and the professional specialties involved, seems to us as much less important than the acknowledgement of this atypical brain development and the functional analysis of the individual's impairments in several domains. In some cases, this nomination even makes things worse, for example when a speech therapist establishes the diagnosis of a Language Disorder in a 3-year-old child who is actually a child with ADHD and ASD (see Section 7.3.5).

In sum, we hold the view that conceptualizing successive manifestations of several disorders as secondary to ADHD symptomatology might better reflect reality than specify different comorbid disorders based on successive, cross-sectional topographies of symptoms. When development is considered explicitly, there is more continuity and overlap between the supposedly differentiable disorders than would be assumed from the current diagnostic nomenclature. We would like to conclude with the following remark of Beauchaine, Hinshaw, & Pang (2010), which is in line with our own reasoning:

> Future models of comorbidity need to consider far more than symptom overlap or independence per se. To understand etiology, maintenance, and life trajectories toward psychopathology, a broader and more conceptually based understanding of "comorbidity" is required.
>
> (p. 334)

Notes

1 DSM-IV terminology is used because studies cited were based on it.
2 In this section, we do not make a special reference to difficulties in written expression, because we consider that the views expressed about dyslexia apply to the disorder of written expression as well.
3 Selective mutism was recently classified into the category of ADs, because anxiety has been recognized as the predominant problem of children with this disorder.
4 A recent study concluded that almost 91% of the children with DMDD meet the criteria for the diagnosis of ODD (Mayes et al., 2015).
5 The Berksonian bias is the higher mathematical chance to be referred: referral rate for disorder A + referral rate for disorder B. Referral bias mostly reflects the higher rate of referral due to higher impairment in case of two disorders (A + B).

Part II

Clinical Assessment of ADHD

8 Clinical Assessment in Developmental Psychopathology

8.1 Parental Causal Attributions and the Role of Diagnosis

People are usually informally evaluated in their daily social interactions. Their appearance, character, and behavior are assessed according to other people's values and expectations. Children often receive such evaluations from parents, siblings, teachers, and other people with whom they interact. Depending on their kind of relationship with the child, they shape their views about the child's development, personality, intelligence, school performance, and behavior in general. Their attitudes and responses toward the child usually result from these views.

Sometimes, it is likely that parents or teachers realize that the child's development or behavior deviates from what they consider developmentally appropriate. In case this deviation is attributed to the child's immaturity or poor upbringing, it does not usually cause great concern. In case it is considered abnormal, the child might be referred for clinical assessment.

When parents worry about their child's development, initially they usually make their own causal inferences. For example, if a child presents speech delay, parents may think that the child is just like them, if they also had such a developmental history. In other cases, a child's learning difficulties may be attributed to poor effort or laziness. Hyperactivity and impulsivity may be characterized as liveliness or disobedience depending on the adult's level of tolerance.

The way in which parents respond to the child's behavior is consistent with their causal attributions. If speech delay is attributed to the child's resemblance to parents, then it may be considered "hereditary" and expected to dissipate as the child grows up. Furthermore, depending on whether a child's hyperactivity and impulsivity are interpreted as liveliness or disobedience, these behaviors may please parents or discontent them. According to the attribution theory, whether people react to failure with anger or sympathy depends on causal controllability, a concept closely linked to responsibility (Weiner, 1993). Causal beliefs of responsibility for misbehavior promote anger, while causal beliefs of nonresponsibility promote sympathy. Therefore, diagnosis of the problem can lead to therapeutic advantages through its link to increased sympathy and decreased criticism. The following example is typical of the way in which causal attributions may influence parental responses toward the child.

> Andrew is a 10-year-old boy, referred to our clinic by his father, who requested an IQ test in order to find out whether his son was mentally disabled. When we asked him how he was led to this request, he answered: "Depending on the test's results, I will decide on the most appropriate way to treat my son, namely continue punishing him or not. This child has been confusing me so far. Sometimes he gives me the impression that he is very intelligent, and then I punish him because I cannot justify his low academic performance. Other times, he gives me the impression that he is mentally disabled, and then I feel guilty because I conclude that the child is not lazy but simply cannot perform any better."

It becomes evident that clinicians usually have to deal with several causal attributions about children's difficulties, many of which may be false or contradictory (Maniadaki, Sonuga-Barke, & Kakouros, 2005). The diagnosis of a certain problem may be the first step in the treatment process because it can help parents to form realistic interpretations about the child's difficulties, based on clinical assessment. Consequently, this is the most important step toward modification of their maladaptive beliefs, which lead to negative responses to children's behavior.

Oftentimes, parents are profoundly disappointed with their child's behavior. Prior to diagnosis, the child may be seen as naughty, lazy, or even socially deviant. Blame and accusations may lead parents to feel guilty and believe that they are not fulfilling their roles. Diagnosis removes the responsibility from both child and parents. Therefore, parents may feel extremely relieved when their definition of the reality of their child's problem are confirmed and legitimated by a professional (Klasen, 2000). Even though diagnosis may also bring ambivalent feelings for some parents, it can generally offer a more optimistic outlook for the future.

Finally, diagnosis is empowering when it helps individuals understand themselves or make healthy changes (Surman, 2013). Therefore, it can help children understand the causes of their difficulties, recognize their strengths, and change negative self-views. For adults, it can offer explanations for a lifetime of struggles, which can replace self-blame.

8.2 Definition and Purposes of Diagnosis and Assessment

According to Achenbach (1985), the term *diagnosis* has acquired two meanings. The first views diagnosis and classification as equivalent, and focuses on the formal assignment of a case to specific categories drawn from a system of classification, such as DSM or ICD. The second meaning is broader and considers diagnosis to be a process of collecting detailed information directed at understanding the nature of the problem, its possible causes, treatment options, and outcomes. In this sense, the term *diagnosis* equals the term *assessment.*

For reasons of clarity, we will use the term *assessment* when referring to screening, documenting impairment, intervention development, and outcome evaluation, and the term *diagnosis* with the narrower meaning proposed by Achenbach. We consider diagnosis as one of the goals of assessment, namely an approximation of the underlying problem, based on a functional description of the symptoms observed and described by the individual or a collateral informant (Posserud et al., 2014).

Assessment is a flexible and ongoing process of hypothesis testing regarding the nature and etiology of a person's difficulties. The clinician systematically tests the hypotheses formulated about the individual's functioning in relation to empirical data. This process begins with the first session and continues until the end of treatment, during which hypotheses are retained, revised, or discarded (Weis, 2014).

There are several purposes for which child assessments are conducted. First, assessment can be conducted to screen children for possible behavior problems or developmental delays. Second, assessment can be used to reach a diagnosis and determine the nature or cause of the problem. Third, assessment can be conducted to make a prognosis about the outcome of the child's difficulties. Prognosis is based on knowledge of risk and protective factors that affect child behavior, and on the findings of longitudinal studies of long-term outcomes for different types of disorders. A fourth purpose of assessment is to determine the need for treatment, specify treatment goals, and develop treatment targets. Finally, assessment can be used to monitor progress and evaluate treatment efficacy (Mash & Terdal, 1988; Weis, 2014). Progress monitoring is essential to determine the implementation integrity of interventions. Evaluation of treatment efficacy determines whether treatment objectives are met, whether changes are attributable to specific interventions, whether the outcomes are long-lasting and generalizable across settings, and whether treatment outcomes are acceptable to the participants.

Clinicians should be aware that children depend on evaluations by other people, and it is only if others perceive a mental health problem that they will be evaluated by a professional (Yeh & Weisz, 2001). Despite the recent advances made in the last decades in neuroscience, both with regard to neuroimaging techniques and genetics, the precise underlying pathologic processes for each individual often remains obscure, even if a certain diagnosis is given (Posserud et al., 2014). Therefore, assigning a name to a set of difficulties is not identical with fully understanding these difficulties. Finally, because children are changing and continue developing after the diagnosis, it is important that assessment be periodically repeated, reviewed, and maybe revised (Parritz & Troy, 2014).

8.3 Multilevel Approach

The way in which clinicians perceive diagnosis is part of a broader, empirically founded theoretical context, which guides their reasoning and clinical decisions. This theoretical context includes the clinicians' views about the main principles that govern human behavior and psychopathology. It also determines the aspects on which they will focus during assessment.

Multilevel approach to assessment and treatment of developmental disorders is based on the principles of cognitive-behavioral theory and is systems oriented. Reaching a diagnosis is considered a multifaceted endeavor that involves multiple factors. In the case of ADHD, consideration of empirically driven conceptual models of ADHD serves as the basis for organizing and implementing assessment.

Within this framework, assessment is considered a comprehensive and multidimensional process, which does not have a narrow focus on assessing symptoms, but constitutes an effort to achieve sufficient understanding of the child and the child's broader life context. Whole-family variables are also being assessed. The child is viewed as part of a larger network of interacting social systems and subsystems. The interrelated influences of child and family cognitions, affects, and behavior within the context of ongoing social interactions are systematically investigated. Behaviors are placed in the contexts in which they occur, and functional relationships that may contribute to their development and preservation are examined. Not only difficulties but strengths and positive aspects are also assessed in order to be used as a starting point for treatment.

Clinicians adopting a multilevel approach should have a wide range of knowledge in order to incorporate all these factors into assessment. Among others, they should have extensive knowledge of general theories and tools of psychological assessment in order to choose the suitable methods for each case. They should also be aware of the main principles of developmental psychology in order to be able to distinguish between developmentally appropriate and inappropriate behaviors. Basic knowledge of social psychology is essential for clinicians in order to understand the process of attitude formation and change, the way in which attitudes affect behavior, and the impact of the group on individual behavior. Finally, clinicians need to have deep knowledge of psychopathology in general and developmental psychopathology in particular in order to reach diagnosis, including differential diagnosis and assessment of comorbidity.

Assessment relies on the use of various methods, including rating scales, interviews, psychometric tests, functional behavioral analysis, and clinical observation. The choice of assessment methods depends on the purpose of the assessment, the nature of the problem, child and family characteristics, and reliability and validity of the assessment measures. The selection of assessment targets, methods, and measures must be based on deep knowledge of theoretical models and research findings in psychopathology (Hunsley & Mash, 2007). Evidence-based assessments need to be sensitive to key characteristics of the individual, including age, gender, ethnicity, and culture. In addition, clinicians need to be aware of the incremental validity of different measures. Incremental validity refers to the issue of whether more information (informants and/or methods) contributes unique information to decision making and whether this information improves diagnostic accuracy or treatment planning (Sowerby & Tripp, 2009).

Diagnosis is reached within a multidisciplinary team and is based on the cooperation of scientists of different specialties. Collection of information is carried out with the participation of multiple informants, namely the child and several adults knowledgeable about the child's functioning, especially parents and teachers. Consequently, information regarding the child's behavior in different settings (home, school, neighborhood, etc.) is gathered. This information elucidates different people's views about child behavior, and actual differences in child behavior across settings and raters. For example, parents and teachers tend to report more behavioral problems than do children, whereas children tend to report more anxiety and mood problems than do parents and teachers (Kamphaus & Frick, 2002).

Developmental considerations are incorporated into the interpretation of the assessment. The developmental psychopathology perspective emphasizes that normative development provides a crucial and necessary comparison for determining whether youth behavior is atypical or problematic (Rutter & Sroufe, 2000). Children's age and gender are taken into account. Following a developmental perspective, children's levels of functioning within different developmental domains and their patterns of coping in relation to different developmental tasks are being evaluated. Norm-references data are used to evaluate developmentally appropriate and inappropriate behaviors. The use of such data assists clinicians in comparing results from different measures and assessing the outcomes of treatment in relation to socially acceptable behavior. For example, it has been shown that although children with ADHD and CD improve with treatment, their behavior does not completely normalize (Barkley & Guevremont, 1992).

Finally, assessment is oriented to the collection of information that will lead to effective interventions. Therefore, assessment data are translated into a workable treatment plan and continues throughout treatment. Multilevel assessment is a flexible and dynamic process, which constantly reviews and revises the goals of treatment.

9 The Diagnostic Criteria of ADHD

9.1 Issues Regarding the Conceptualization of DSM and ICD

The use of classification systems of mental disorders, such as DSM and ICD, is controversial. It has been suggested that *labeling* and *classifying* behaviors may negatively affect self-perceptions and lead to stigma. Stigmatization may cause a sense of shame that decreases self-esteem and lowers self-worth. On the other hand, it can lead to self-fulfilling prophecies (Baum & Olenchak, 2002). In other words, some individuals may alter their behavior to fit the diagnostic label or use the diagnosis to excuse deviant behavior (Weis, 2014).

However, the use of diagnostic criteria assists in organizing the results of psychological assessment, facilitates communication among professionals, allows prognosis on the basis of the existing research literature, contributes to setting realistic expectations regarding an individual's future, sets the main goals of treatment, and facilitates scientific research (First et al., 2004). In addition, we believe that the impact of diagnosis based on these criteria does not stem from the diagnosis itself but from the interpretation that individuals may put on it. Clinicians hold a crucial role regarding the direction that this interpretation will take.

Since they first appeared, DSM and ICD remain cornerstones of clinical practice. However, despite their significant contribution to research and clinical practice, these categorical classification systems share many weaknesses. In every revision, options are considered for improving their utility. Some points of criticism concern the general conceptualization of these systems and others concern the diagnostic criteria of particular disorders.

The major shortcomings of these systems lie in their categorical nature, lack of developmental perspective (undifferentiated approach with reference to the individual's gender and age), phenomenological approach (emphasis on the description of the symptoms), failure to focus on the etiology of the disorders, and overlap of symptoms among disorders (Beauchaine, Klein, Erickson, & Norris, 2013). In other words, these systems are static, focus exclusively on the individual, and ignore developmental and contextual factors.

More specifically, the utility of employing categorical models for diagnosing mental disorders has been questioned. It has been postulated that mental disorders, particularly those that refer to children and adolescents, should not be viewed as distinct nosological entities, qualitatively different from "normal" (categorical classification), but as behaviors or traits varying along a continuum and differing quantitatively from those encountered in the general population (dimensional classification) (Hudziak et al., 2007; Krueger & Bezdjian, 2009; Sonuga-Barke, 1998). Categorical models fail to account for important sources of variance. Dimensional models introduce quantitative variation and graded transition between forms of disorder by age and gender. Dimensions assume continuity between normality and psychopathology, whereas categories suppose discontinuity (Rutter, 2011). Therefore, dimensional models can facilitate acquisition of complementary information regarding risk, resilience, etiology, prevention, and intervention (Rutter & Sroufe, 2000).

As a result, there is growing support for a dimensional view of mental disorders. In the case of ADHD, a dimensional view proposes that deficits that characterize ADHD represent "delay in the acquisition of certain skills" compared to normal developmental expectancies, and not complete "lack of skill" (Barkley, 1997a; Levy et al., 1997). It is suggested that attention, self-control, and motor activity be viewed as continuous dimensions of behavior. Therefore, an individual's experience with ADHD would be conceptualized not as part of a distinct category but rather along a continuum of increasing symptoms and severity (Bell, 2011).

However, most researchers concur that the current categorical model of classification should not be abandoned entirely (Brown & Barlow, 2005). Switch to a purely dimensional approach would reduce the information of the traditional diagnostic categories with all their current implications concerning etiology, prognosis, and treatment (Moller, 2009). The challenge is to determine at what level dimensional features can best be incorporated in current taxonomies in order to complement their categorical aspects. The addition of dimensional components could be useful as an indicator of symptom severity and as an indicator of the individual's level of functioning (Brown & Barlow, 2005; First & Westen, 2007). Joint consideration of categorical and dimensional models would facilitate our understanding of the development, maintenance, and course of mental disorders, as well as the development of co-occurring problems (Drabick & Kendall, 2010). As children are constantly undergoing development and interacting with their environment, disorders are best conceptualized as sharing both categorical and dimensional aspects (Carrey & Gregson, 2008).

The second point of criticism concerns the lack of developmental perspective (Hudziak et al., 2007; Regier, Narrow, Kuhl, & Kupfer, 2009). DSM is not norm-referenced, and fails to provide a mechanism for determining the severity of symptoms in relation to children of similar age and gender. The same criteria are used irrespective of chronological age, and adjustment is not made for age-appropriate behavioral change (Stefanatos, & Baron, 2007). ADHD is viewed as a static condition in which the symptoms remain essentially the same regardless of age (Barkley, 2003).

Developmental psychopathology differs from adult psychopathology in many ways. The most significant difference is that the expression of psychopathology in children often changes both qualitatively and quantitatively throughout development. Therefore, behaviors that are considered normal and adaptive at one age may be considered pathological at another age and vice versa. According to Hudziak and colleagues (2007), a classification system that takes into account developmental differences in the expression of psychopathology should consider the following: (a) variations in both typical and atypical development across age; (b) gender differences in the expression of psychopathology; (c) differences among sources of information; and (d) tendencies for children to manifest multiple kinds of problems.

9.2 Weaknesses of the DSM-IV Diagnostic Criteria for ADHD

Few disorders have undergone as many changes in name and diagnostic criteria as ADHD, perhaps because few disorders have been the subject of as much taxonomic study (Willcutt, 2006). In surveying empirical literature, the DSM-IV diagnostic criteria for ADHD have received various criticisms, leading to proposals for changes and modifications in DSM-5. The most important concerns were the following.

9.2.1 The Validity of the Three Subtypes of ADHD

The subtyping of the disorder in DSM-IV implied that ADHD comprises three different and clearly distinct subtypes with discrete presentation and outcomes. This subtyping was developed in an attempt to capture the heterogeneity of the disorder.

However, it has been shown that about one-third of children with ADHD will change from one subtype to another at least once during an 8-year period (Lahey et al., 2005; Todd, Huang, & Henderson, 2008). Therefore, whether a child is diagnosed with the one or the other subtype of ADHD may reflect the developmental stage at which symptoms become evident (Stefanatos & Baron, 2007). It seems that the three subtypes of ADHD are characterized by instability over time, a fact that questions the usefulness of their existence (Hinshaw, 2001; Milich, Balentine & Lynam, 2001). Furthermore, the findings of recent studies incorporating genetics and imaging data do not find clear evidence to support these subtypes as clinical entities (Baeyens, Roeyers, & Walle, 2006; Lubke et al., 2007).

Over the last years, a considerable amount of research has scrutinized the accuracy of the three ADHD subtypes, and some researchers believe that ADHD, predominantly inattentive type should be considered a separable disorder with an alternative underlying neurobiology (Hinshaw, 2001; Milich et al., 2001). Children in this group seem to differ from the other two subtypes with reference to their clinical presentation, associated problems, outcomes, and response to medication. These children are characterized by sluggish cognitive tempo, daydreaming, and mental spaciness along with hypoactive and slow-moving motor function (Carlson & Mann, 2002; McBurnett, Pfiffner, & Frick, 2001). Socially, they are withdrawn, shy, and less prone to initiate social interactions (Bauermeister et al., 2005). Disobedience and defiance that usually characterize the other two subtypes are rare in these children, whereas comorbidity with ADs and DDs is more frequent (Gadow, Sprafkin, & Weiss, 2004). Furthermore, a meta-analysis suggests that the DAT1 gene, which has been implicated in ADHD, is more closely associated with ADHD, combined type, than ADHD, inattentive type (Waldman & Faraone, 2002).

9.2.2 The Age of Onset Criterion

DSM-IV asserted that impairment due to some ADHD symptoms must be present before the age of 7 for a valid diagnosis. However, this choice was not empirically validated, and research suggests that many children with ADHD do not show symptoms causing functional impairment until after this age. According to Barkley (2003), "the age of onset for ADHD symptoms [. . .] is not justifiable on any historical, empirical, and pragmatic grounds" (p. 80).

An examination of the DSM-IV field trials revealed that the ADHD subtypes had different ages at onset, with later onset for ADHD, inattentive type (43%). In all, 75% did not manifest functional impairment before 7 years of age (Applegate et al., 1997). Willoughby and colleagues (2000) suggested that this criterion was too restrictive for ADHD, inattentive type. A systematic review about the age of onset criterion for ADHD failed to find any clinical difference between children identified as onset by age 7 versus later in terms of clinical presentation, course, comorbidity, severity, impairment, outcome, or treatment response (Kieling et al., 2010).

Furthermore, adult with symptoms of ADHD often find it difficult to retroactively and accurately recall the onset of impairment related to symptoms (Barkley & Biederman, 1997; McGee, Williams, & Feehan, 1992; Todd et al., 2008). An adult population study revealed that only 50% of individuals with ADHD retrospectively recalled an onset before 7 years, whereas 95% recalled an onset before age 12 (Kessler et al., 2005).

Finally, in clinical practice we often encounter children with ADHD whose impairments were not noticed until late elementary or middle school, due to protective factors, including high intelligence, well-structured and supportive family, and/or school environment (Sibley, Waxmonsky, Robb, & Pelham, 2013).

It has also been suggested that the presence of ***impairment*** be removed from the age of onset of the symptoms because symptom impairment depends upon several factors that are not exclusively associated with the individual (Polanczyk et al., 2010).

9.2.3 The Presence of Unitary Diagnostic Criteria for All Ages

The DSM-IV criteria did not apply equally well to different ages and did not take into consideration the *heterotypic continuity* of ADHD, which represents two phases or alternative presentations of the disorder. The symptom list for ADHD in DSM-IV was developed and field tested on predominantly school-aged male children. Therefore, these criteria failed to reflect developmental expression through the age range. The utility of extending that list to preschoolers and adults was seriously questioned (Barkley & Murphy, 2006; Narrow, First, Sirovatka, & Regier, 2007).

Converging evidence suggests that ADHD is identifiable and clinically meaningful in preschoolers (Keenan & Wakschlag, 2002). The level of the recognition and treatment of preschool ADHD has increased rapidly over recent years. Early identification can lead to the implementation of preventative interventions that minimize the expression of the disorder. However, it was suggested that DSM-IV diagnostic items and thresholds might not be appropriate for preschoolers and some adjustment might be needed to take account of the developmental relevance of the items (Sonuga-Barke, Daley, Thompson, & Swanson, 2003).

For example, many of the items for inattention were written in a way that referred to school work and might have a wider developmental applicability across school-age ranges of childhood, leading to underdiagnosis in preschoolers (Wakschlag, Leventhal, Thomas, & Pine, 2007). Furthermore, ADHD, inattentive type is rare during preschool years, and ADHD subtypes exhibit moderate stability (Egger & Angold, 2006; Lahey et al., 2005).

Some researchers suggest that ADHD, hyperactive-impulsive type and ADHD, inattentive type may constitute different developmental stages of the same disorder, with the hyperactive-impulsive behavior first being present at age 2–4 years and attention disorder following during school-age years (Hart et al., 1995; Loeber et al., 1992). In addition, some symptoms may not be discriminative in preschool children due to normative variation in the acquisition of regulatory skills. For example, the symptom "often interrupts or intrudes" is endorsed for nearly half of typically developing preschoolers (Byrne, Bawden, Beattie, & Dewolfe, 2000; Egger & Angold, 2006). Finally, a number of behaviors described in DSM-IV occur normatively in preschoolers, but it is the accrual of a constellation of such behaviors that indicates psychopathology (Wakschlag et al., 2007).

Similar concerns have also been raised regarding the clinical utility of the criteria set in diagnosing ADHD in adults. The DSM-IV diagnostic criteria for ADHD were not tested in field trials with adults, leading to age-inappropriate descriptors for adults (e.g., "often runs about or climbs excessively") (Matte et al., 2012). Thus, it has been recommended that DSM-IV criteria be reworded to improve adult symptomatic presentation.

9.2.4 The Failure to Acknowledge Gender Differences

Girls with ADHD usually manifest less overt symptoms than the disruptive behaviors typically seen among boys. For example, hyperactivity in girls is more likely to manifest as hypertalkativeness or emotional reactivity than excessive motor activity. Furthermore, symptoms such as forgetfulness, disorganization, and daydreaming may easily go unnoticed by parents and teachers (Nadeau & Quinn, 2002). In general, girls with ADHD are less likely to exhibit behaviors consistent with DSM symptom criteria than boys (Barkley, 1990; DuPaul, 1991). This is perhaps a reflection of the fact that a majority of children in the DSM field trial were boys (Lahey et al., 1994). In addition, a large majority of the studies of ADHD have not included adequate numbers of girls to allow for statistically meaningful comparisons between girls and boys (Hartung & Widiger, 1998). This results in girls having to meet a higher threshold under DSM relative to other girls to be diagnosed with ADHD than do boys relative to other boys (Waschbusch & King, 2006).

Consequently, some researchers recommend that gender should be considered in the use of diagnostic criteria. This may entail (a) use of sex-specific diagnostic criteria, (b) addition of some remarks about the diagnosis of ADHD in girls, (c) decreasing the number of criteria needed to meet diagnostic thresholds for girls, or (d) a combination of these (Hudziak et al., 2007; Regier et al., 2007; Waschbusch & King, 2006).

9.3 The Diagnostic Criteria of ADHD in DSM-5

The conceptual development and planning of DSM-5 began in 1999 and the final manual was released at the 166th APA annual meeting in San Francisco on May 18, 2013. DSM-5 is the result of the collaborative effort between the DSM-5 Task Force, 13 work groups, and six study groups. ADHD was included in the responsibilities of the DSM-5 ADHD and Disruptive Behavior Disorders Workgroup. A striking change is that APA has decided to abandon the Roman numeral system and switch to Arabic numerals to more easily allow for multiple text revisions that can come along more frequently so that the manual can be more responsive to research.

In DSM-5, the section titled ***disorders usually first diagnosed in infancy, childhood or adolescence***, which previously included ADHD, has been removed. ADHD is now clustered within a new section, titled ***neurodevelopmental disorders.*** The same section also includes ID, communication disorders, ASD, SLD, and motor disorders. It is devoted to chronic conditions with a neurological substrate that affect functioning but manifest differently at various points of development.

The DSM-5 criteria for ADHD kept the bidimensional structure of ADHD and the same list of symptoms. They are presented below.[1]

A. A persistent pattern of inattention and/or hyperactivity-impulsivity that interferes with functioning or development, as characterized by (1) and/or (2):

   1. **Inattention**: Six (or more) of the following symptoms have persisted for at least 6 months to a degree that is inconsistent with developmental level and that negatively impacts directly on social and academic/occupational activities:

      Note: The symptoms are not solely a manifestation of oppositional behavior, defiance, hostility, or failure to understand tasks or instructions. For older adolescents and adults (age 17 and older), at least five symptoms are required.

      a. Often fails to give close attention to details or makes careless mistakes in schoolwork, at work, or during other activities (e.g., overlooks or misses details, work is inaccurate).
      b. Often has difficulty sustaining attention in tasks or play activities (e.g., has difficulty remaining focused during lectures, conversations, or lengthy reading).
      c. Often does not seem to listen when spoken to directly (e.g., mind seems elsewhere, even in the absence of any obvious distraction).
      d. Often does not follow through on instructions and fails to finish schoolwork, chores, or duties in the workplace (e.g., starts tasks but quickly loses focus and is easily sidetracked).

e. Often has difficulty organizing tasks and activities (e.g., difficulty managing sequential tasks; difficulty keeping materials and belongings in order; messy, disorganized work; has poor time management; fails to meet deadlines).
f. Often avoids, dislikes, or is reluctant to engage in tasks that require sustained mental effort (e.g., schoolwork or homework; for older adolescents and adults, preparing reports, completing forms, reviewing lengthy papers).
g. Often loses things necessary for tasks or activities (e.g., school materials, pencils, books, tools, wallets, keys, paperwork, eyeglasses, mobile telephones).
h. Is often easily distracted by extraneous stimuli (for older adolescents and adults, may include unrelated thoughts).
i. Is often forgetful in daily activities (e.g., doing chores, running errands; for older adolescents and adults, returning calls, paying bills, keeping appointments).

2. **Hyperactivity and impulsivity**: Six (or more) of the following symptoms have persisted for at least 6 months to a degree that is inconsistent with developmental level and that negatively impacts directly on social and academic/occupational activities:

Note: The symptoms are not solely a manifestation of oppositional behavior, defiance, hostility, or a failure to understand tasks or instructions. For older adolescents and adults (age 17 and older), at least five symptoms are required.

a. Often fidgets with or taps hands or feet or squirms in seat.
b. Often leaves seat in situations when remaining seated is expected (e.g., leaves his or her place in the classroom, in the office or other workplace, or in other situations that require remaining in place).
c. Often runs about or climbs in situations where it is inappropriate. (Note: In adolescents or adults, may be limited to feeling restless.)
d. Often unable to play or engage in leisure activities quietly.
e. Is often "on the go," acting as if "driven by a motor" (e.g., is unable to be or uncomfortable being still for extended time, as in restaurants, meetings; may be experienced by others as being restless or difficult to keep up with).
f. Often talks excessively.
g. Often blurts out an answer before a question has been completed (e.g., completes people's sentences; cannot wait for turn in conversation).
h. Often has difficulty waiting his or her turn (e.g., while waiting in line).
i. Often interrupts or intrudes on others (e.g., butts into conversations, games, or activities; may start using other people's things without asking or receiving permission; for adolescents and adults, may intrude into or take over what others are doing).

B. Several inattentive or hyperactive-impulsive symptoms were present prior to age 12 years.
C. Several inattentive or hyperactive-impulsive symptoms are present in two or more settings (e.g., at home, school, or work; with friends or relatives; in other activities).
D. There is clear evidence that the symptoms interfere with, or reduce the quality of, social, academic, or occupational functioning.
E. The symptoms do not occur exclusively during the course of schizophrenia or another psychotic disorder and are not better explained by another mental disorder (e.g., mood disorder, anxiety disorder, dissociative disorder, personality disorder, substance intoxication or withdrawal).

Specify whether:

314.01 (F90.2) Combined presentation: If both Criterion A1 (inattention) and Criterion A2 (hyperactivity-impulsivity) are met for the past 6 months.

314.00 (F90.0) Predominantly inattentive presentation: If Criterion A1 (inattention) is met but Criterion A2 (hyperactivity-impulsivity) is not met for the past 6 months.

314.01 (F90.1) Predominantly hyperactive/impulsive presentation: If Criterion A2 (hyperactivity-impulsivity) is met and Criterion A1 (inattention) is not met for the past 6 months.

Specify if:

in partial remission: When full criteria were previously met, fewer than the full criteria have been met for the past 6 months, and the symptoms still result in impairment in social, academic, or occupational functioning.

Specify current severity:

Mild: Few, if any, symptoms in excess of those required to make the diagnosis are present, and symptoms result in no more than minor impairments in social or occupational functioning.

Moderate: Symptoms or functional impairment between "mild" and "severe" are present.

Severe: Many symptoms in excess of those required to make the diagnosis, or several symptoms that are particularly severe, are present, or the symptoms result in marked impairment in social or occupational functioning.

It is noted that the manifestations of the disorder should be present in more than one setting (e.g., home and school or work), and confirmation of substantial symptoms across settings must be done by consulting informants who have seen the individuals in those settings. Finally, it is noted that symptoms may vary depending on context within a given setting. Signs of the disorder may be minimal or completely absent when the individual is receiving frequent rewards for appropriate behavior, is under close supervision, is in a novel setting, is engaged in especially interesting activities, has consistent external stimulation (e.g., via electronic screens), or is interacting in one on one situations (e.g., in a clinical setting).

9.4 Associated Features Supporting Diagnosis

Mild delays in language, motor, or social development are not specific to ADHD but often co-occur with this disorder. Associated features of ADHD may include low frustration tolerance, irritability, and emotional lability. Furthermore, even in the absence of an SLD, ADHD may negatively affect academic and professional performance. Inattentive behavior is associated with various underlying cognitive processes. Therefore, individuals with ADHD may exhibit cognitive problems on tests of attention, executive function, or memory, even though these tests are not sufficiently sensitive or specific to serve as diagnostic tools.

There are no biological markers for the diagnosis of ADHD. As a group, compared with peers, children with ADHD display increased slow wave EEGs, reduced total brain volume on magnetic resonance imaging, and a possible delay in prefrontal cortex maturation. However, these characteristics are not diagnostic. In the uncommon cases where there is a known genetic cause (e.g., Fragile X syndrome), the ADHD presentation should still be diagnosed. By early adulthood, ADHD is associated with an increased risk of suicide attempt, primarily when comorbid with DDs, CD, or SUD.

9.5 Summary of Modifications and Clinical Implications

The main modifications in the diagnostic criteria of ADHD in DSM-5 can be summarized as follows:

1. The section titled "disorders usually first diagnosed in infancy, childhood, or adolescence" has been removed and a new diagnostic category titled "neurodevelopmental disorders" has been created.

This is one of the most significant modifications for child and adolescent disorders, which reflects a general approach in DSM-5 to be representative over the life span (Doernberg & Hollander, 2016). The etiological basis of the disorders is now being emphasized instead of their age of onset. The predominant view about the neurobiological substrate of ADHD is clearly highlighted.

Furthermore, ADHD is separated conceptually from ODD and CD, which are clustered under a new section, titled "disruptive behavior, impulse control and conduct disorders." Classification of ADHD into the section of neurodevelopmental disorders may lead to earlier identification, more comprehensive assessment across multiple domains of functioning, and selection of more effective interventions that target the full array of impairments associated with this disorder (Tannock, 2013).

It is acknowledged that ADHD is a chronic neurodevelopmental disorder with childhood onset. However, some researchers suggest that ADHD shares significant behavioral overlap with disorders that are classified into the chapter titled "disruptive behavior, impulse control and conduct disorders" (Roberts & Milich, 2013). It has also been suggested that ADHD can be distinguished from other neurodevelopmental disorders with reference to early deviance in cognitive development, continuing course, and persistent failure in achieving maturational milestones, which are important facets of the neurodevelopmental cluster (Andrews, Pine, Hobbs, Anderson, & Sunderland, 2009). Maybe ADHD has yet to find its ideal place in the structure of DSM. However, its current place is certainly better than the previous one.

2. The three subtypes of ADHD have been eliminated and replaced with *specifiers for current presentation* to classify the current manifestation of the disorder at the time of assessment.

The underlying rationale is that the use of these specifiers over the life course might reveal different clinical courses, and help clarify the heterogeneity in symptom expression (Tannock, 2013). Diagnosis is now established on the basis of the clinical presentation that the individual has at the time of assessment and can be differentiated over the course of development. Although the etiological basis of the disorder does not change in each individual over the life span, the combination of prevalent symptoms in each developmental period usually does. It is now acknowledged that the different ADHD symptom clusters do not indicate clear and stable types. As children with ADHD can fluctuate in the degree and type of symptoms they experience over time, specifiers for current presentation reflect this vacillating characteristic. This modification also emphasizes the need to customize treatment according to individual areas of impairment.

However, the three suggested specifiers have the same name with the former subtypes of ADHD and, possibly, the change in philosophy that is hidden behind the distinction between subtypes and presentations may not be very clear to clinicians and, most importantly, to parents and teachers. Furthermore, a question that still remains is whether individuals with predominant symptoms of inattention without hyperactivity or impulsivity should receive the diagnosis of ADHD or constitute a distinct diagnostic category (Adams, Milich, & Fillmore, 2010; Roberts & Milich, 2013).

3. The age of onset criterion has been raised from 7 to 12 years, and requirement of impairment has been removed from this criterion.

This modification is expected to extend the ADHD diagnosis to older adolescents and adults who may not have demonstrated noticeable impairment until later in childhood due to the presence of various protective factors, including high intelligence or well-structured and supportive homes and classrooms (Sibley et al., 2013). A study by Polanczyk and colleagues (2010) concluded that using 12 years of age as an age at onset would not increase ADHD prevalence.

In addition although impairment is still required to make a diagnosis, the DSM-5 criteria require that impairment is documented only for current rather than past functioning. This subtle adjustment may increase ADHD prevalence rates.

4. Reduced requirement of current impairment has been noted in C and D criteria.

DSM-IV required that "some impairment from the symptoms is present in at least two settings," whereas DSM-5 requires that "the symptoms are apparent in two or more settings." Furthermore, DSM-IV stipulated that "there must be clear evidence of interference with developmentally appropriate social, academic, or occupational functioning," whereas DSM-5 states that "symptoms interfere with, or reduce the quality of functioning." Functioning of reduced quality does not necessitate impairment. Therefore, the diagnosis of ADHD is now possible in individuals who display symptoms of the disorder but function satisfactorily in their everyday life (Sibley et al., 2013). Reduced requirement of current impairment and the change in age of onset are expected to increase the prevalence of ADHD, especially in adults (Dalsgaard, 2013).

Several researchers, however, are skeptical about this modification because many of the ADHD criteria describe behaviors that are not necessarily impairing (Batstra & Frances, 2012). We appreciate that clinicians involved in the assessment of ADHD should be very experienced and knowledgeable of developmental psychopathology and the process of epigenesis in order to distinguish whether impairment results from the presence of ADHD, another disorder, or other factors.

5. The number of symptoms required for the diagnosis in older adolescents and adults has been reduced from six to five in both ADHD dimensions.

The aim of the lowered symptoms threshold for adults with ADHD is to take into account the consistent finding of an age-related decline in several symptoms but persistent impairment (Tannock, 2013). Therefore, the adjusted threshold for diagnosing ADHD in adults is more consistent with the symptom presentations of adults.

6. Specific parenthetical examples have been added under each criterion, including typical behaviors of older adolescents and adults with ADHD.

These examples of symptoms have been elaborated in order to enhance their developmental sensitivity. Furthermore, the new criteria incorporate developmentally ubiquitous descriptors to facilitate symptom identification in adolescents and adults.

The reduction of symptoms threshold as well as the adjustments to the wording of some symptoms to improve their adequacy to adults may lead to increased prevalence of adult ADHD and decrease of false negatives (Batstra & Frances, 2012). These modifications facilitate the diagnosis of ADHD in adults, making it clear that it is a persistent disorder that goes well beyond childhood.

7. The exclusionary criteria for pervasive developmental disorder have been removed, and comorbidity between ADHD and ASD (previously known as pervasive developmental disorder) has now been acknowledged.

Over the last years, there has been an increase in the reports about the presence of ASD symptoms in individuals with ADHD and vice versa (Hattori et al., 2006). From a neurobiological perspective, it is highly likely that ADHD and ASD coexist because adjoining brain regions are implicated (axon: frontal lobe-basal ganglia) (Holtmann, Bolte, & Poustica, 2007; Rommelse, Franke, Geurts, & Hartman, 2010). In DSM-5, comorbid diagnosis of ADHD and ASD is allowed, enhancing clinical management of these children.

8. Three severity specifiers have been added.

In DSM-5, it is required that a severity level is assigned to the disorder. This development is an attempt to incorporate dimensional aspects into the diagnostic criteria and has great clinical value, because it may facilitate goal setting in treatment. In the case of neurodevelopmental disorders, it is not a "disorder" that should be treated but a total of maladaptive behaviors that a certain individual may exhibit. These behaviors may belong to different diagnostic categories, and their prioritization should be an absolutely individualized process.

However, the definition of these specifiers is quite vague and is open to subjective interpretations. Severity is specified in terms of numbers of symptoms in excess of those required to make a diagnosis. However, we wonder how the following formulation can help clinicians: The severity of ADHD is assessed as moderate when "symptoms or functional impairment between 'mild' and 'severe' are present." The severity of a disorder should not be defined merely by the number of symptoms but by the degree and extent to which these symptoms cause impairment. For this reason, we believe that impairment should probably be incorporated into the criteria required for the diagnosis of the disorder instead of being an additional diagnostic criterion.

9. In addition to cross-domain impairment, it is now required that separate raters for each domain provide information about the individual.

The empirical evidence to support this requirement is strong because diagnosis based on data from a single informant may be of questionable validity. This modification may increase the burden of ADHD assessments but is expected to enhance diagnostic accuracy (Sibley et al., 2013).

10. Clinicians are required to document that ADHD symptoms do not extend exclusively from oppositional behavior.

This modification is also predicted to increase diagnostic accuracy (Dalsgaard, 2013). However, in clinical practice, it may be difficult to isolate the source of a behavior, given that half of children with ADHD also meet criteria for the diagnosis of ODD (Barkley, 2006a).

In conclusion, some of the weaknesses of DSM-IV were successfully addressed in DSM-5. It seems, however, that there were no profound or radical changes. Classification principally remains categorical, with the only dimensional aspect being the addition of severity specifiers, in spite of specific suggestions about other more substantial dimensional aspects (Hudziak, Achenbach, Althoff, & Pine, 2007; Krueger & Bezdjian, 2009).

Despite the fact that numerous research studies stress the necessity of taking gender into account for the diagnosis of ADHD, DSM-5 did not make any relevant modification. Furthermore, although an attempt has been made for the use of developmentally sensitive diagnostic criteria, relevant modifications referred only to adolescents and adults. There were no changes concerning preschoolers, despite the increased awareness of the importance of early intervention and the fact that the guidelines published in 2011 by the American Academy of Pediatrics clearly suggest that assessment and treatment of ADHD should start at the age of 4 years.

A recent evaluation of DSM-5 ADHD criteria in a large, representative, population-based sample of adults has shown that they would determine a 27% increase in the prevalence rate of ADHD in adults, compared with DSM-IV criteria (3.55% vs. 2.8%). However, the new criteria did not impact substantially on the factor structure of the disorder (Matte et al., 2015). Nevertheless, in order to fully assess the new diagnostic criteria, further research and use in clinical practice are needed.

9.6 The Diagnostic Criteria of ADHD in ICD-10[2]

ICD-10 classifies *hyperkinetic disorders* into the category *behavioral and emotional disorders with onset usually occurring in childhood and adolescence* (F90–F98). A detailed description of the behavioral characteristics of this type of disorders is provided. In addition, information is given both about their secondary characteristics and issues of differential diagnosis.

According to ICD-10, this group of disorders is characterized by (a) early onset; (b) a combination of overactive, poorly modulated behavior with marked inattention and lack of persistent task involvement; (c) pervasiveness over situations; and (d) persistence over time. The cardinal features are impaired attention and overactivity: both are necessary for the diagnosis and should be evident in more than one situation (e.g., home, classroom, clinic). Impaired attention is manifested by prematurely breaking off from tasks and leaving activities unfinished. The children change frequently from one activity to another, seemingly losing interest in one task because they become diverted to another (although laboratory studies do not generally show an unusual degree of sensory or perceptual distractibility). These deficits in persistence and attention should be diagnosed only if they are excessive for the child's age and IQ. Overactivity implies excessive restlessness, especially in situations requiring relative calm. It may, depending upon the situation, involve the child running and jumping around, getting up from a seat when he or she is supposed to remain seated, excessive talkativeness and noisiness, or fidgeting and wriggling. This behavioral feature is most evident in structured, organized situations that require a high degree of behavioral self-control. The standard for judgment should be that the activity is excessive in the context of what is expected in the situation and by comparison with other children of the same age and IQ.

The associated features are not sufficient for the diagnosis, or even necessary, but help to sustain it. Disinhibition in social relationships, recklessness in situations involving some danger, and impulsive flouting of social rules (as shown by intruding on or interrupting others' activities, prematurely answering questions before they have been completed, or difficulty in waiting turns) are all characteristic of children with this disorder. Secondary complications include dissocial behavior and low self-esteem.

Learning disorders and motor clumsiness occur with undue frequency, and should be noted separately (under F80–F89) when present; they should not, however, be part of the actual diagnosis of hyperkinetic disorder.

Symptoms of conduct disorder are neither exclusion nor inclusion criteria for the main diagnosis, but their presence or absence constitutes the basis for the main subdivision of the disorder. The characteristic behavior problems should be of early onset (before age 6 years) and long duration. However, before the age of school entry, hyperactivity is difficult to recognize because of the wide normal variation: only extreme levels should lead to a diagnosis in preschool children.

Diagnosis of hyperkinetic disorder can still be made in adult life. The grounds are the same, but attention and activity must be judged with reference to developmentally appropriate norms. When hyperkinesis was present in childhood, but has disappeared and been succeeded by another condition, such as dissocial personality disorder or substance abuse, the current condition rather than the earlier one is coded.

Diagnosis requires the exclusion of ADs, mood (affective) disorders, pervasive developmental disorders and schizophrenia.

Hyperkinetic disorders are encoded on the basis of four types:

F90.0 Disturbance of activity and attention

The main subdivision is made according to the presence or absence of associated aggression, delinquency, or dissocial behavior. The code used should be F90.0 when the overall criteria for hyperkinetic disorder (F90.–) are met but those for F91.– (conduct disorders) are not.

Includes: attention deficit disorder or syndrome with hyperactivity attention deficit hyperactivity disorder

Excludes: hyperkinetic disorder associated with conduct disorder (F90.1)

F90.1 Hyperkinetic conduct disorder

This coding should be used when both the overall criteria for hyperkinetic disorders (F90.–) *and* the overall criteria for conduct disorders (F91.–) are met.

F90.8 Other hyperkinetic disorders
F90.9 Hyperkinetic disorder, unspecified

This residual category is not recommended and should be used only when there is a lack of differentiation between F90.0 and F90.1 but the overall criteria for F90.– are fulfilled.

Includes: hyperkinetic reaction or syndrome of childhood or adolescence NOS.

9.7 Suggested Modifications in ICD-11[3]

It is the first time in the history of DSM and ICD that a revision of ICD has followed that of DSM and has not preceded it. ICD-11 is due for publication in May 2018, namely 5 years after the publication of DSM-5. Until the publication of ICD-11, 26 years will have passed by since its previous revision (ICD-10; WHO, 1992), and this is the longest time between ICD revisions. One of the work groups established for the production of the proposals for the classification of mental disorders within ICD-11 is the *Harmonization Coordination Group*. This group aims at reducing the differences between DSM and ICD, and ensuring that the structure of ICD-11 will be aligned with DSM-5 (Regier et al., 2009; Sartorius, 2010).

The second phase of the revision of ICD-10 started on May 14, 2012. ICD-11 is currently in the process of review by representatives from over 200 countries. As we are waiting for the final form of ICD-11, we will briefly present the suggested modifications for hyperkinetic disorders.

It seems that modifications approaching those in DSM-5 are recommended, bringing the two taxonomic systems closer. First, removal of the category ***Behavioral and emotional disorders with onset usually occurring in childhood and adolescence*** is suggested, as well as the creation of a new category with the title ***neurodevelopmental disorders***, into which ADHD will be also classified. Neurodevelopmental disorders are described as

> behavioural and cognitive disorders that arise during the developmental period that involve significant difficulties in the acquisition and execution of specific intellectual, motor, or social functions. Although behavioural and cognitive deficits are present in many mental and behavioural disorders that can arise during the developmental period (e.g., Schizophrenia, Bipolar disorder), only disorders whose core features are neurodevelopmental are included in this grouping. The presumptive etiology for neurodevelopmental disorders is complex, and in many individual cases is unknown.
>
> (ICD-11 Beta Draft)

It seems that the name also changes from ***hyperkinetic disorders*** to ADHD (6A42). The following definition is given:

> Attention deficit hyperactivity disorder is characterized by a persistent pattern (at least 6 months) of inattention and/or hyperactivity-impulsivity, with onset during the developmental period, typically early to mid-childhood. The degree of inattention and hyperactivity-impulsivity is outside the limits of normal variation expected for age and level of intellectual functioning and significantly interferes with academic, occupational, or social functioning. Inattention refers to significant difficulty in sustaining attention to tasks that do not provide a high level of stimulation or frequent rewards, distractibility and problems with organization. Hyperactivity refers to excessive motor activity and difficulties with remaining still, most evident in structured situations that require behavioural self-control. Impulsivity is a tendency to act in response to immediate stimuli, without deliberation or consideration of the risks and consequences. The relative balance and the specific manifestations of inattentive and hyperactive-impulsive characteristics vary across individuals, and may change over the course of development. In order for a diagnosis of disorder the behaviour pattern must be clearly observable in more than one setting.
>
> (ICD-11 Beta Draft)

The following presentations are proposed:

ADHD, predominantly inattentive presentation (6A42.1)

All definitional requirements for attention deficit hyperactivity disorder are met and inattentive symptoms are predominant in the clinical presentation. Inattention refers to significant difficulty in sustaining attention to tasks that do not provide a high level of stimulation or frequent rewards, distractibility and problems with organization. Some hyperactive-impulsive symptoms may also be present, but these are not clinically significant in relation to the inattentive symptoms.

ADHD, predominantly hyperactive-impulsive presentation (6A42.2)

All definitional requirements for attention deficit hyperactivity disorder are met and hyperactive-impulsive symptoms are predominant in the clinical presentation. Hyperactivity refers to excessive motor activity and difficulties with remaining still, most evident in structured situations that require behavioral self-control. Impulsivity is a tendency to act in response to immediate stimuli, without deliberation or consideration of the risks and consequences. Inattentive symptoms may or may not be clinically significant.

ADHD, combined presentation (6A42.3)

All definitional requirements for attention deficit hyperactivity disorder are met. Both inattentive and hyperactive-impulsive symptoms are clinically significant, with neither predominating in the clinical presentation. Inattention refers to significant difficulty in sustaining attention to tasks that do not provide a high level of stimulation or frequent rewards, distractibility and problems with organization. Hyperactivity refers to excessive motor activity and difficulties with remaining still, most evident in structured situations that require behavioral self-control. Impulsivity is a tendency to act in response to immediate stimuli, without deliberation or consideration of the risks and consequences.

ADHD, other specified presentation (6A42.Y)

This category is an 'other specified' residual category.

ADHD, presentation unspecified presentation (6A42.Z)

This category is an 'unspecified' residual category.

As it is highlighted, however, on the website of the World Health Organization, these suggestions are under discussion and are now being considered. Therefore, they may diverge from the final text and eventually not be definitive.

Notes

1 Reprinted with permission from the Diagnostic and Statistical Manual of Mental Disorders, Fifth Edition, (Copyright 2013). American Psychiatric Association.

2 Reprinted from The ICD-10 Classification of Mental and Behavioural Disorders, World Health Organization, Hyperkinetic disorders, Pages No. 262–266, Copyright (1992).

3 www.who.int/classifications/icd/revision/en/

10 Measures and Methods of Diagnosis

10.1 General Issues

Assessment of ADHD in children is initiated at the moment the parent or another adult becomes concerned with the child's behavior and decides to seek professional help. There is no specific diagnostic procedure for reliably diagnosing ADHD. An ADHD diagnosis is not reached as a result of a single objective test. Assessment of ADHD is a multidimensional and complex process that relies on several informants concerning the children's difficulties and strengths across multiple settings. It requires the use of multiple diagnostic methods that include (a) interviews with parents/caregivers, child, and teachers; (b) rating scales, psychometric tests, educational assessment, and behavioral observation; and (c) Functional Behavioral Analysis (FBA).

Several sets of guidelines for the evidence-based assessment of ADHD have been made available (American Academy of Child and Adolescent Psychiatry, 2007; Pelham, Fabiano, & Massetti, 2005). Consistent across specialty areas is the recommendation of a multi-informant and multisetting approach to assessment. In addition, the assessment of ADHD ought to consist of an evaluation of both symptoms and associated impairments. Brock and Clinton (2007) found that the four nearly universally recommended procedures are rating scales, interviews, laboratory/ psychological testing, and direct behavioral observations.

In planning and undertaking an assessment with a child referred for an evaluation of ADHD, clinicians should consider the essential information required to develop and monitor an appropriate personalized treatment plan. Mere recognition of the presence of the disorder is not enough to achieve this goal. In contrast, a thorough assessment of the individual and contextual factors is needed. A major goal of the assessment is also to determine whether ADHD is comorbid with other disorders in order to evaluate the effect that comorbidity may have on prognosis and treatment planning.

Initial findings regarding the child's difficulties usually guide the nature and depth of subsequent assessment. It should be noted that assessment continues throughout treatment, as clinicians evaluate its efficacy and review goal setting according to the specific needs that the individual and their family may have (see Section 8.4).

10.2 The Importance of the Impairment Criterion

In order to receive the diagnosis of any disorder, DSM-5 requires the presence of a minimum number of symptoms and stipulates that these symptoms must cause significant impairment in the individual's functioning. However, while the symptoms are clearly defined in the manual, there are no guidelines as to what constitutes impairment, making it difficult to assess uniformly.

Functioning is evidence of the way in which symptoms impact on the individual's capacity to perform in activities of daily living, learning, socialization, and work, and to maintain adequate and autonomous self-care. In assessment of ADHD, it is critically important to assess impairment specifically related to ADHD symptoms and not to other factors (Gibbins, & Weiss, 2007). Clinicians should adopt a developmental approach and be able to understand the epigenetic process in order to assess the effect of the symptoms on the individual's functioning. The thorough and accurate assessment of impairment is essential for diagnostic decision making but is also important in developing intervention plans and evaluating outcomes (Power et al., 2015).

However, many mental health professionals continue to base diagnostic decision predominantly on the number of symptoms and not on their functional outcomes. This practice might be a consequence of both the assumption that symptoms and impairment are one and the same and also a lack of clarity on how impairment is measured (Gathje, Lewandowski, & Gordon, 2008). However, it has been shown that the prevalence of psychiatric disorders can be decreased by 31% when diagnosis goes from using only symptoms to the inclusion of impairment (Simonoff et al., 1997). Especially for ADHD, this rate reaches 41% (Gathje et al., 2008).

According to Barkley, Cunningham, and colleagues (2006), the symptoms of ADHD basically constitute the "behavioral expressions associated with this disorder," whereas impairments are the "consequences that ensue for the individual as a result of these behaviors" (p. 2). In a study by Gordon and colleagues (2006), when an ADHD group was constituted based on current symptoms and then added an impairment criterion, the sample was reduced by 77%. Therefore, the majority of them would lose the diagnosis if the impairment criterion was used.

Contrariwise, Costello, Angold, & Keeler (1999) identified a group of children who had serious psychosocial impairment yet did not reach the threshold for any psychiatric diagnosis. Therefore, it appears that equating symptoms with impairment is invalid because ADHD symptoms and impairment are distinct constructs with little conceptual overlap (Gordon et al., 2006; Graetz, Sawyer, Hazell, Arney, & Baghurst, 2001; Romano, Tremblay, Vitaro, Zoccolillo, & Pagani, 2001).

According to Pelham and colleagues (2005), the primary symptoms of ADHD are not typically the reason for referral or the most meaningful intervention targets. Families seeking treatment for ADHD are often more concerned about impairment in academic, social, and family functioning than symptoms per se. Consequently, assessing symptoms alone does not provide sufficient information about the specific areas of impairment that seem to be the most appropriate targets for initial assessment, intervention, and monitoring (Gordon, Barkley, & Lovett, 2006). An important consideration is the development of specific impairment criteria that can be adhered to when making a diagnosis of ADHD (Healey, Miller, Castelli, Marks, & Halperin, 2008).

Furthermore, clinicians should be aware that all ADHD symptoms do not "perform" equivalently. Some ADHD symptoms may have a great impact on functioning; other symptoms may have a minor impact; still others may have no impact at all. According to our view, symptoms of hyperactivity usually have a minor impact on the functioning of children with ADHD, whereas symptoms of impulsivity and inattention may considerably impact functioning. Therefore, we appreciate that it is particularly important that future diagnostic manuals give different weight to each symptom for the diagnosis of the disorder, depending on the degree to which it affects the individual's functioning.

Power, Costigan, Leff, Eiraldi, & Landau (2001) have expressed a similar view, suggesting that not all items pertaining to ADHD are equal with regard to their predictive validity. It is a paradox that even though inattention and hyperactivity were differentially associated with ADHD diagnostic status in the DSM-IV field trials (Frick et al., 1994), all 18 symptoms are weighted equally in making diagnostic decisions, without regard to their different psychometric properties (Shemmassian & Lee, 2017).

Regarding clinical utility estimates for items on the inattention dimension, items such as "avoids tasks that require sustained mental effort" or "has difficulty sustaining attention in tasks or play activities" have greater predictive validity than "has difficulty organizing tasks and activities." Items on the hyperactivity-impulsivity dimension, such as "is on the go or acts as if driven by a motor" and "fidgets with hands or feet or squirms in seat" have greater predictive validity than "has difficulty awaiting turn." According to Power and colleagues (2001), the DSM polythetic practice of using any combination of items to make diagnostic decisions is challenged by current research. A better approach proposed is to combine the items that are the most highly predictive of diagnostic status.

In an effort to improve the validity of ADHD assessment, algorithms consisting of highly predictive symptoms have been created to predict ADHD caseness at different thresholds and functional impairment (Shemmassian & Lee, 2017). These algorithms incorporate multi-informant ratings and diverse measures of functional impairment. It is suggested that the implementation of such algorithms may improve treatment planning by allowing clinicians to target the most clinically significant symptoms.

Furthermore, the effect of ADHD symptoms on the individual's functioning may differ considerably by age. Therefore, while this effect is minimal during preschool years, it is major for adolescents and adults (Gordon et al., 2006). A study conducted by Mannuzza and colleagues (2011) found that there was a strong association between number of ADHD symptoms and degree of impairment in adults. All participants who met at least five of the criteria for the diagnosis of ADHD were clinically impaired by their symptoms. For this reason, the number of symptoms that are required in DSM-5 for the diagnosis of ADHD in older adolescents and adults was reduced from six to five.

In conclusion, an operational definition and valid measures of impairment, as well as diagnostic decision rules for incorporating impairment into the assessment of ADHD, are urgently needed.

Furthermore, clinicians should be aware that an individual's level of functioning is not only associated with the strengths and difficulties inherent in the individual but also, to a great extent, with social expectations and demands, which considerably depend on time and context. For example, it is possible that mild intellectual disability has a different impact on an individual's functioning depending on the extent to which academic knowledge and special skills are valued and required within their social environment. Similarly, impairment in individuals with ADHD may be minimal in case academic and social demands for conformity to rules are limited as well. However, contemporary societies place increased demands on individuals in all domains of life. Therefore, even mild forms of neurodevelopmental disabilities may cause functional impairment. This may be one of the main causes of the considerable increase in the prevalence of neurodevelopmental disorders, such as ADHD, over the last years.

Consequently, clinicians should perceive ADHD symptoms not merely as the individual's intrinsic weaknesses but as difficulties to respond adequately to certain demands of a particular environment. These difficulties would possibly not lead to impairment if the individual lived in a different environment or in an environment that placed different demands upon them.

10.3 The First Contact With the Clinician for the Assessment of ADHD in Children

Children rely on adult caretakers to identify and seek assistance for their behavior problems. Therefore, clinicians are usually contacted via a phone call made by an adult who is concerned with the child's behavior and asks for an appointment. The initial contact is usually with a social worker who gathers demographic information about the child and family, including the child's name, date of birth and school, parents' names and occupations, as well as family structure. In addition, the reason and source of referral are investigated. It is important that this person have the relevant knowledge and experience in order to collect efficiently the first significant information, which will be later incorporated into the main body of information that will be gathered during assessment.

This information initially concerns the request made by the individual who asks for the assessment and the major concerns regarding the child. Usually, the person who makes this call is one of the child's parents. In this case, the initiative for the child's referral is investigated. Parents, teachers, and pediatricians are the most frequent sources of referral. Furthermore, it is investigated whether the family has visited another mental health service in the past for the same or other reasons. Many times, a diagnosis has already been given to the child and parents are interested in a second evaluation. Other times, the child is already in treatment, and parents are interested in the evaluation of treatment efficacy.

This information may considerably facilitate assessment and help in saving valuable time, so that clinicians can seek additional information in time, before even see the child. For example, they may contact the child's school, study the information that was gathered in a previous assessment, or get in touch with professionals who had worked with the child before. However, clinicians should remain mindful that referral information may not match closely the child's clinical presentation (Sowerby & Tripp, 2009).

A packet of printed questionnaires and broadband rating scales is usually sent to parents and teachers following the first call. It is necessary that parental written permission is obtained for the contact with the school. This material is completed in advance of the scheduled appointment and is made available for review by the clinician on the day of the appointment, prior to meeting with the family.

10.4 Measures of Assessment of ADHD in Children

10.4.1 Rating Scales

Rating scales have been extensively validated for the assessment of ADHD and are efficient and practical for collecting data from multiple informants, concerning a child's functioning in multiple settings (Pelham et al., 2005). The use of rating scales requires that clinicians be well aware of the psychometric characteristics of these scales, the kind of information they offer, the purpose to which they are being applied, and their limitations and shortcomings as well.

Rating scales provide a structured format for documenting the presence and degree of ADHD symptoms using a normative frame of reference (Anastopoulos & Shelton, 2001). Most scales have parallel versions for parents and teachers. The rater is usually asked to rate each of the behaviors associated with ADHD on a 3-, 4-, or 5-point scale. Therefore, the rater might rate the scale's items at the level of "never," "sometimes," "often," or "not at all," "just a little," "pretty much," or "very much." Total scores are then calculated.

According to Barkley (1990), the advantages of these scales over other methods are multiple. First, they offer the opportunity to collect information from informants who have a wealth of information about children's functioning in multiple naturalistic contexts. Second, they allow identification of behaviors that occur very infrequently and are likely to be missed. Third, they are time efficient and cost-effective. Fourth, they provide developmental norms for establishing the statistical deviance of child behavior ratings. Fifth, they are available in various forms that allow assessment of several dimensions in child psychopathology. Sixth, they incorporate the views of different people who are involved with the child. Seventh, they provide an account for situational variation. Finally, they allow for quantitative distinctions in qualitatively different aspects of the child's behavior.

Despite the many benefits of using rating scales, there are a number of limitations to their use, including subjectivity and reporter bias. For example, parental depression may influence ratings, making children appear to have ADHD even though they do not (Chi & Hinshaw, 2002). Parental symptomatology may also impact ratings, which could compromise the validity of parent ratings (Sayal & Taylor, 2005).

Furthermore, teacher ratings may be influenced by variables that are irrelevant to child behavior, including teacher personality, management style, and expectations. Moreover, it has been shown that there is little correlation between teacher and parent ratings of ADHD symptoms, even between mothers and fathers (Collett, Ohan, & Myers, 2003a). Therefore, low interrater reliability is a significant drawback.

Several explanations for these discrepancies have been proposed. First, disagreement between raters may be due to genuine differences in children's behavior in different settings. Therefore, informants typically have access to nonoverlapping information. Second, informant ratings may also be influenced by the time period during which the child is observed or other environmental factors (Loughran, 2003). Finally, raters have different levels of tolerance and different interpretations of a child's behavior (Pelham et al., 2005).

Therefore, rating scales basically explore parent and teacher perceptions about child behavior and provide means of quantifying these perceptions. As a result, they are subject to prejudices and limitations on reliability and validity. Furthermore, these scales may be insensitive to low base rate or covert behaviors that may be of great significance but unknown to the rater (Pelham et al., 2005). It has also been shown that agreement between different informants, assessment instruments, and settings is usually only fair to moderate (Posserud et al., 2014). Finally, it seems that these scales share the weakness of the diagnostic systems in effectively detecting girls with ADHD. Consequently, despite their utility, rating scales should never be used in isolation to diagnose ADHD (Nahlik, 2004). In addition, the interpretation of these results should be made with particular caution, as it requires clinical experience and skillful clinical judgment.

A packet of these scales is often mailed out to parents and teachers prior to the visit to the clinical setting. This preliminary information permits the clinician to elucidate vague or significant answers and focus on the major child difficulties in the subsequent interview.

An initial step in the assessment of ADHD is the use of broadband scales that are designed to identify a wide range of childhood disorders and cover the major dimensions of childhood psychopathology. Moreover, these scales give information regarding the child's level of impairment and may be useful in differential diagnosis and identification of comorbid difficulties (Sowerby & Tripp, 2009). They can also assist in determining the developmental appropriateness of behavior. Commonly used broadband scales that evidence good reliability and validity include:[1]

1. Behaviour Assessment System for Children, Second Edition (BASC-2; Reynolds & Kamphaus, 2004)
2. Child Behavior Checklist (CBCL; Achenbach, 1991) and its different versions (Achenbach & Rescorla, 2001)
3. Strengths and Difficulties Questionnaire (SDQ; Goodman, 1997)
4. Conners' Parent and Teacher Rating Scales Revised (CRS-R; Conners, Sitarenios, Parker, & Epstein, 1998a,b).

Next, the use of narrowband scales, specific to ADHD, is recommended. These scales contribute to diagnostic decision making through identification of symptom presence or absence.

They focus more specifically on symptoms relevant to ADHD. Specifically, they are symptom lists that the respondent rates according to presence and severity. It should be noted that rating scales currently used to assess symptoms of ADHD will need to be revised according to DSM-5. Popular ADHD rating scales for children with good psychometric properties are the following:

1. ADHD Rating Scale-IV (ADHD RS-IV; DuPaul et al., 1998)
2. ADHD Symptom Checklist-4 (ADHD-SC4; Gadow & Sprafkin, 1997)
3. Attention-Deficit/Hyperactivity Disorder Test (ADHDT; Gilliam, 1995)
4. Attention Deficit Disorders Evaluation Scale, Third Edition (ADDES-3; McCarney & Arthaud, 2004)
5. The ADHD Rating Scale-5 (ARS-5; DuPaul et al., 2015).

In order to assess impairment related to ADHD, specific scales have been constructed.[2] The Vanderbilt AD/HD Diagnostic Teacher Rating Scale (VABS-2; Wolraich, 2003; Wolraich, Feurer, Hannah, Baumgaertel, & Pinnock, 1998) is a measure of ADHD symptoms that includes impairment items. The Impairment Rating Scale (IRS; Fabiano et al., 2006) is used in the assessment of impairment in school-aged children with ADHD. Parent and teacher versions assess children in various domains known to be often impaired in ADHD (e.g., academic progress, relationships, self-esteem, and influence on family functioning). The ADHD Rating Scale-5 (ARS-5; DuPaul et al., 2015) is a recently developed scale, allowing for simultaneous assessment of ADHD symptoms and symptom-related impairment. It was developed to incorporate symptom wording changes consistent with DSM-5 and to obtain current normative data for symptom ratings based on DSM-5 criteria. It provides a broad assessment of impairments associated with ADHD, integrates the assessment of symptoms and impairments in the same measure, and differentiates impairment related to each ADHD symptom dimension (Power et al., 2015). The Barkley Functional Impairment Scale-Children and Adolescents (BFIS-CA; Barkley, 2012b) provides parents a means to rate their child's degree of functional impairment in 15 domains of major life activities and school, social, and community adjustment.

Finally, clinicians may decide to explore additional features, including self-esteem, social skills, self-control, and so forth. More specialized rating scales can then be chosen, according to clinicians' judgment.

10.4.2 Parental Interview

Parental clinical interview is the cornerstone of the assessment in order to collect valuable information about the child and their family. Parents are typically able to provide the most detailed and ecologically relevant information to the assessment process.

However, parental interview can be subject to bias and therefore be of limited reliability and not provide a true picture of the child's functioning. The reliability of the interview depends to a great degree on the way it is conducted, and the specificity of the questions posed by the clinician. The diagnostic validity of parental interview is enhanced when questions are specific to symptoms of psychopathology that have been empirically demonstrated to have a high degree of association with particular disorders (Barkley, 2015b).

Parental interview serves multiple purposes. Initially, it contributes to establishing a trusting relationship with the parents, which may help in fostering parental cooperation during assessment and subsequent treatment. The clinician begins to establish rapport with parents by empathically listening to their concerns, accurately reflecting their thoughts and feelings, and offering an initial plan to address their worries (Weis, 2014).

The interview provides clinicians with the opportunity to explore the presence of child and family problems, including the context in which they occur, their onset, frequency, severity, chronicity, and impact on functioning (Sowerby & Tripp, 2009). In addition, interviews permit clinicians to form an impression of parent mental health and the nature of the parent–child interactions. It should be noted that parent and child behavior at the clinician's office may be very different from their usual behavior. Consequently, clinicians should always be cautious not to reach any conclusions on the basis of this behavior.

Finally, parental interview many times works as "sheer catharsis" because parents have the opportunity to share their worries about their child with a professional, express guilt for their own mistakes, and refresh their hopes of receiving help and support by someone who understands them and has the knowledge and expertise to manage such situations.

Clinicians often use structured or semistructured interviews that are based on the DSM diagnostic criteria. Structured interviews are conducted using an interview schedule designed to probe areas of specific concern. Interview questions are read in the order they are written, and responses are recorded categorically (Anastopoulos & Shelton, 2001). Semistructured interviews incorporate a specific set of questions while allowing the clinician to engage in open-ended inquiries to obtain further information about relevant points. These measures have superior psychometric properties including test-retest reliability and predictive validity. However, administration is often lengthy and impractical in clinical settings.

Several structured and semistructured interviews are now available for use with parents and children. They are designed to elicit the information required to make specific DSM-IV diagnoses.[3] The following is an indicative list of the most widely used and researched interviews for assessing psychopathology in children and adolescents:

1. NIMH Diagnostic Interview Schedule for Children, Version IV (NIMH DISC-IV; Shaffer, Fisher, Lucas, Dulcan, & Schwab-Stone, 2000)
2. Children's Interview for Psychiatric Syndromes (ChIPS; Weller, Weller, Fristad, Rooney, & Schecter, 2000)
3. Child and Adolescent Psychiatric Assessment (CAPA; Angold & Costello, 2000)
4. Interview Schedule for Children and Adolescents (ISCA; Sherrill & Kovacs, 2000)
5. Diagnostic Interview for Children and Adolescents—Revised (DICA; Reich, 2000).

It should be noted that although these structured or semistructured interviews aid in the identification of ADHD symptoms required for the diagnosis, they offer limited information about the nature and degree of impairment and associated difficulties, as well as child and family resources and potential barriers to intervention (Sowerby & Tripp, 2009). This information needs to be collected as part of a supplementary unstructured interview, which allows the clinician to follow an individualized process, customized to the needs of each family.

Initially, clinicians usually investigate the major parental concerns by asking parents to describe in detail the child's difficulties and impairment in various domains. Clinicians assist parents in organizing their descriptions by posing specific questions to elucidate the nature of the problems and providing a framework of operationally defined behaviors. In discussing parental concerns, clinicians explore the severity, frequency, and age of onset of the problematic behaviors. Particular emphasis is put on the situational and temporal variations in these behaviors, and their consequences both for child and family (Barkley, 2015d). Factors relating to the family's ability to cope and manage a child with ADHD are carefully examined. Clinicians explore whether there is disagreement between parents on parenting strategies and management approaches to difficult child behaviors. It is also important to investigate what prompted the referral at this particular time. Parental motivation for treatment as well as previous treatments received by the child should also be investigated.

A review of the child's developmental history in major developmental domains (motor, language, intellectual, academic, emotional, and social functioning) is essential for differential diagnosis and documentation of comorbidity (Barkley & Edwards, 2006). Prenatal and birth events with the potential to affect development also need to be established (Rappley, 2005). At each point, clinicians seek to identify information associated with the occurrence and progression of ADHD throughout development.

Review of the family history and significant life events is an indispensable part of the interview in order to identify mental or other medical problems in the extended family. It also provides information on the quality of family interactions, the nature of parenting skills, the burden that ADHD may pose on the family, and the possibility of acute stressors that may be shaping the context in which the child lives. It is suggested that clinicians determine whether siblings of the referred child are currently having or have experienced similar problems in the past (Goldstein & Goldstein, 1998).

It is always important to ask parents about their attributions regarding the causes of the child's difficulties. Modification of maladaptive beliefs often constitutes the first goal of treatment. It is also important to explore whether parents believe that the child has the potential to improve, as this belief may greatly influence their degree of motivation during treatment.

Finally, parents are often asked to report the strengths and positive attributes of their child. Some parents of children with ADHD often fail to find positive characteristics in their child, due to pervasive management problems. Guided by the clinician, parents are encouraged to identify such characteristics during the interview. This procedure is a first step toward the implementation of a behavior modification program, where parents are asked to focus on their child's desirable behaviors and reinforce them.

10.4.3 Teacher Interview

Problems in school are often the primary reason behind referrals for ADHD (Loe & Feldman, 2007), making teachers important informants of children's behavior. Teachers spend significantly more structured and unstructured time with children than nearly any other adult. Furthermore, teachers interact with many children of the same age, thus having a better reference point for making decisions regarding developmentally inappropriate behaviors. Therefore, they can more easily detect the difficulties that children with ADHD may encounter in learning, behavior, and interactions with peers, which may bring them to clinical attention (Loe & Feldman, 2007).

Practice guidelines recommend the use of multiple informants in the assessment of ADHD (American Academy of Child and Adolescent Psychiatry, 2007; American Academy of Pediatrics, 2011). Furthermore, DSM-5 criteria require the presence of impairment from symptoms in more than one setting. Therefore, teachers are a very important source of information because they interact with children over long time periods in a wide range of settings that vary in structure (Evans, Allen, Moore, & Strauss, 2005). Furthermore, teachers interact with many children of the same age, thus having a better reference point in order to make decisions regarding developmentally inappropriate behaviors. Parents and teachers provide two ecologically valid sources of indispensable information and have a unique contribution to the assessment process.

The initial contact with the teacher is usually made by telephone, after completion of the rating scales previously sent by the clinician. This process gives clinicians the opportunity to form a first impression about the child's behavior at school and focus on areas of dysfunction, in order to further discuss them during the subsequent telephone contact. In case time and resources permit, a visit to the child's school, and maybe later a teacher's visit to the clinical setting, can set the foundation for an effective collaboration between the teacher and the clinician and facilitate the planning of a behavioral intervention in classroom.

Teachers are usually asked to provide information on children's academic performance, classroom behavior, ability to follow rules, interactions with peers, position in the group, and behavior during team games. Teacher interviews can also serve as an additional opportunity to screen for the presence of an SLD.

The teacher interview should follow a behavioral analysis format. The settings, nature, frequency, consequences, and eliciting events of the major problematic behaviors, as well as teacher responses to them, should be explored (Barkley, 2015d). An analysis of antecedents and consequences in a variety of settings helps clinicians move from assessment to intervention. It is uncommon for children with ADHD to experience equal difficulty across *all* school activities and situational contexts. To the contrary, it is very likely that there are activities in which these difficulties do not appear at all. Detecting these activities is important for two reasons. The first reason is to reveal conditions in which the child is completely functional and on which emphasis should be placed. The second reason is that these activities can stimulate positive interaction between teacher and student, who is mainly used to frequent reprimands and comments about their shortcomings and failures.

Clinicians should take into consideration that teachers are usually susceptible to a halo effect. For example, it has been shown that teachers often rate children with ODD as having elevated levels of inattention and hyperactivity even when no behaviors directly indicative of these symptoms have been displayed (Abikoff et al., 1993). This bias is bidirectional, because teachers also rate children with ADHD as having elevated levels of oppositional behaviors (Hartung et al., 2010). It seems that factors other than observed child behavior may influence teacher ratings. Therefore, clinicians should be aware that teachers may engage in overreporting symptoms (Sims & Lonigan, 2012). The integrity of the information provided must always be weighed in judging its validity.

Clinicians should help the teacher distinguish behaviors that are symptoms of ADHD from behaviors that may be signs of the child's lack of motivation. A distinction should also be made between poor school performance related to SLD from poor school performance related to familial and psychosocial factors. Establishment of a positive relationship with the teacher may assist clinicians not only in detecting the child difficulties at school but also in determining the framework of their collaboration. Clinicians and teachers can work together on defining and prioritizing intervention targets, choosing effective techniques, and planning the implementation of school-based interventions.

10.4.4 Functional Behavioral Analysis (FBA)

FBA is a particularly useful tool that aims to operationalize behavioral problems and gather information on setting events and antecedents. FBA assesses whether an individual's characteristics or environmental contingencies influence the likelihood of development, maintenance, or exacerbation of problematic behaviors (Gresham, Watson, & Skinner, 2001). The desired outcome of FBA is to understand the function of specific behaviors and eventually manipulate behavior-environment relationships and promote more appropriate behaviors (Crone & Horner, 2003).

The process usually starts with the development of a precise definition of the problematic behavior in clear, observable terms, which can be used for the assessment of possible associations between a child's behavior and environmental variables. This information assists in determining the function a problematic behavior serves. This function could be to escape/avoid, obtain attention, or gain access to privileges (Olympia & Larsen, 2005). In FBA, observation is directed to (a) antecedents, namely the events that immediately precede the target behavior and act as a signal that a particular consequence is likely to follow; (b) the frequency of occurrence of a specific behavior; and (c) consequences, namely the events that follow behavior and serve to either maintain or weaken the behavior.

Moreover, an FBA is directed as establishing specific setting events, which are contextual factors that can affect a child's response to specific antecedents or consequences. Setting events that seem to influence children with ADHD include fatigue, medication, time of day, workload, negative peer interactions, presence or absence of specific individuals, class transitions, and so forth (Chandler & Dahlquist, 2002).

The use of this method is particularly helpful in providing information that can be directly targeted in treatment planning, as it can link assessment to intervention in very individualized contexts and be tailored to the needs of a specific child. If we consider, for example, the symptom "often does not seem to listen when spoken to directly," it does not give any information on the extent to which this behavior is a problem for the child and what causes, maintains, or exacerbates this behavior. For one child, the function of this behavior could be to avoid boring tasks and is limited to situations where a demand is placed on the child. For another child, this behavior may be caused by poor adult commands that fail to explain clearly the appropriate behavior to the child. A third child may have an attention deficit and may not be able to process the instructions effectively. An FBA would result in the development of three different treatment plans for the cases described. These plans would be based on three different hypothesized functions of the behavior in question (Gresham et al., 2001; Nelson-Gray, 2003). In other words, the symptom is not informative for treatment if we do not know the impaired function that it reflects and the context in which it is manifested.

An FBA can also considerably contribute to differential diagnosis, indicating, for example, that maladaptive behavior is manifested as a result of environmental contingencies and not as a result of the child's intrinsic psychopathology (Northup & Gulley, 2001). Finally, it may assist clinicians in detecting family factors that may perplex treatment and need to be addressed before the implementation of any intervention.

10.4.5 Clinical Assessment of the Child

10.4.5.1 Child Interview

Meeting with the child gives clinicians the opportunity to discuss with them, observe their behavior, and administer psychometric tests, if needed. During this interaction, clinicians can evaluate several areas of development, in which the child may encounter difficulties, according to the information that has been gathered so far. Above all, it is an opportunity to become acquainted and build rapport with the child.

The interview with the child is an indispensable part of the assessment, and its duration and content depend on the child's age, developmental level, and language abilities. This interview should be experienced by children as a pleasant interaction with an adult who is interested in knowing them. Encouragement and acknowledgement of positive aspects in the child are necessary features of this interaction. The assessment ambiance should be agreeable for the child in order to respond effectively to this process.

The interview with preschoolers is usually short and must be adjusted to their developmental and language level. It is often carried out while they are playing, drawing, doing a puzzle, or simply wandering about the office. It should be noted that the reliability of the child's answers at this age can be seriously called into question (Achenbach, McConaughy, & Howell, 1987).

With school-aged children and adolescents, the interview is longer and can be more focused on the way in which children perceive themselves and their difficulties in different settings (including home, school, neighborhood), with different people (including parents, teachers, friends), and in different activities (including homework, play, after-school activities, etc.). The clinician should also explore the child's causal attributions regarding these difficulties.

Clinicians informally observe the child's behavior and general demeanor during interview and testing procedures. The most important aspect of the interview is not usually its content but the quality of the child's responses, their ability to conform to the rules of conversation, and the kind of interaction that they develop with the clinician. Children with ADHD frequently respond impulsively, without thinking, even before the clinician finishes the question. Moreover, this interview gives clinicians the opportunity to observe the child's behavior and obtain valuable information about strengths and difficulties, functioning, and impairment.

The interview with the child can start with the question "Why do you think you came here today?," which gives clinicians the opportunity to clarify the reason for their visit and explain the procedure to be undertaken. It is particularly important that the child have a rough idea of the reasons that led to the assessment and the procedure to be followed. Clinicians should be honest with the child and prepared to answer any questions about the nature of the assessment. Our clinical experience has taught us that even preschoolers are usually aware of their difficulties, and, for this reason, they become very cooperative when they realize that they can get help to minimize them.

At the beginning, the interview may cover neutral topics, including child interests and hobbies, and then move to more specific areas, such as child views of peer relationships, school performance, family functioning, and other important aspects of their life. Clinicians may ask the child if they have friends, what they do together, or if they would like to have more friends, in order to explore social skills and the quality of peer relationships. Children with ADHD often complain that they are not popular, that they do not have as many friends as they would like, and that they often argue with their classmates.

The interview can progress to a review of school-related matters. Clinicians may ask the child about favorite and less-preferred subjects and investigate their attributions about the reasons that they may find certain subjects difficult. Clinicians may also ask if the teacher admonishes them frequently, if they prefer lesson or break time, if they believe that they can be better students, and so forth. By asking these questions, clinicians can obtain some information about the child's self-perception, self-esteem, and insight. Children with ADHD often attribute their learning difficulties to the fact that they are "less clever than other children" because they can not understand why they do not perform as well at school as their classmates do although they may try harder than them. Other children complain that the school subjects are very difficult, or that the teacher is very strict.

Finally, questions that refer to the kind and frequency of punishments imposed by parents, as well as activities that parents share with the child, may give information about the way in which the child perceives family relationships. These questions frequently reveal that the child may feel that parents are unfair, constantly reprimand them, usually criticize them, and often yell at them. Interviews may end by obtaining children's collaboration and ensuring treatment compliance (Nahlik, 2004).

It should be noted that clinicians have to be cautious about the diagnostic conclusions that they may draw based on the child's answers during the interview. Many children with ADHD try to behave in a socially pleasing direction and may hide or cover their actual difficulties. It has been acknowledged that children commonly report fewer symptoms than do parents and teachers, and try to give more socially acceptable answers, particularly in the realm of externalizing behaviors (Volpe, DuPaul, Loney, & Salisbury, 1999).

10.4.5.2 Behavioral Observation

The clinician's office provides an excellent observational opportunity during the child interview and the psychoeducational evaluation. Qualitative inferences made by experienced clinicians during direct contact with the child may be more valuable than standardized procedures. Direct behavioral observation lasts from the moment the clinician meets the child in the waiting room until the child leaves the office. Clinicians make informal observation of the child's appearance, behavior, and gross developmental skills. They also have the opportunity to observe interactions with parents and maybe with other children.

Behavioral observation provides the clinician with valuable information about differential diagnosis. The child's ability to separate from parents and accompany the clinician to the assessment room is one of the first behaviors the clinician observes. The majority of children with ADHD do not have difficulty separating from their parents and they willingly accompany the clinician (Goldstein & Goldstein, 1998).

The child's ability to make appropriate eye contact, the capacity to initiate and maintain conversation, and the quality of language abilities are carefully evaluated. Clinicians observe whether the child's speech is coherent or rapid and difficult to follow. Many children with ADHD have particular difficulty focusing and have the tendency to look around the room even when they answer to questions. Similar difficulties are noted in keeping a conversation, as they usually jump from one topic to another, giving the impression that they have not heard or understood the question. Moreover, they often have difficulty organizing their thoughts and expressing them with clarity. They may also have difficulty in articulation and auditory discrimination, particularly if they are younger. In this case, a complete speech-pathology evaluation is also needed. If motor clumsiness is observed, an occupational therapy evaluation should be added to the assessment plan.

Clinicians should also evaluate the child's affect. Affect refers to the child's short term emotional expression and is usually inferred by the child's facial expressions, posture, and body movements (Weis, 2014). Sometimes, it is difficult to distinguish if motor activity and restlessness are signs of ADHD or anxiety. However, if they are asked, anxious children usually acknowledge that they are feeling uncomfortable and nervous, whereas children with ADHD do not usually express such feelings unless anxiety coexists. Besides, the quality of increased motor activity differs between children with ADHD and children with ADs, and an experienced clinician can recognize this difference. Furthermore, it is important to note emotional lability, which is not typical of ADHD and may indicate the presence of DDs.

The ability to sustain attention, remain on task, and follow instructions should also be evaluated. If the child lacks task persistence and gives up quickly, it is important to distinguish whether this happens due to impulsive frustration or feelings of helplessness and low self-efficacy. In the case of preschoolers, clinicians should be able to differentiate developmentally appropriate responses from ADHD symptoms because younger children have shorter attention span, are overactive, and lose interest more easily. Developmentally appropriate distractibility and distractibility due to ADHD mainly differ quantitatively.

Finally, clinicians should be aware that the behavior observed in a clinical setting may not be representative of the child's usual behavior (Anastopoulos & Shelton, 2001; DuPaul & Stoner, 2003). It appears that the majority of children with ADHD do not show high levels of ADHD behaviors in clinical settings (Edwards et al., 2005). A relatively normal conduct in the clinician's office may be an unreliable indicator of the child's behavior in other settings. "ADHD reveals itself when tasks are routine rather than novel, when competing contingencies abound, when work gets difficult, and when self-regulation is at a premium" (Hinshaw & Scheffler, 2014, p. 36). Therefore, it is important for clinicians to dedicate plenty of time to the child and evaluate them in various situations. An evaluation of too short a duration is improbable to reveal their real difficulties. Significantly disruptive behavior during a lengthy clinical assessment may be a marker for similar behaviors in other settings as well (Barkley, 2015d).

In some cases, it may prove to be particularly useful if two clinicians participate simultaneously in the diagnostic session with the child. In this case, the first clinician can have the role of the observer and record the child's difficulties and behavior in general, and the second clinician can interact with the child. After the completion of this process, the two clinicians can discuss and compare their observations to reach the final conclusions.

10.4.5.3 Neuropsychological Assessment

Neuropsychological testing has been advocated by some researchers and clinicians to be an important part of the assessment of ADHD. Neuropsychological tests have been suggested to be sensitive to neuropsychological functioning including attention span, sustained attention, alertness, response inhibition, and working memory (Brock & Clinton, 2007). They have also been reported to effectively distinguish children with ADHD from typically developing children or from children with other disorders (for an overview, see Gordon et al., 2006). A comprehensive neuropsychological assessment offers a thorough consideration of the child's cognitive strengths and weaknesses, based on an understanding of brain structure and function (Pritchard, Nigro, Jacobson, & Mahone, 2012).

Neuropsychological tests that objectively assess ADHD behaviors are of interest to circumvent subjective bias, particularly when there is interrater disagreement found between informant ratings (Sims & Lonigan, 2012). They may increase diagnostic validity when used in combination with other measures and facilitate appropriate recommendations regarding treatment, given the heterogeneity in the neuropsychological phenotype of ADHD (Mahone & Slomine, 2008; Pritchard et al., 2012). Research suggests that select neuropsychological test batteries may be more sensitive and specific for the diagnosis of ADHD compared to any individual measure alone (Gupta, Kar, & Srinivasan, 2011; Hale et al., 2009).

Some individually administered assessment batteries designed specifically to measure executive functions related to ADHD have been developed. These include the *Delis Kaplan Executive Functioning System* (DKEFS; Delis, Kaplan, & Kramer, 2001) and the *Test of Everyday Attention for Children* (TEA-Ch; Manly, Robertson, Anderson, & Nimmo-Smith, 1999). In addition, computerized neuropsychological assessments designed to evaluate specific aspects of ADHD have been recommended. These include the *Continuous Performance Test* (CPT; Conners, 2000b), the *Test of Variables of Attention* (TOVA; Greenberg, Corman, & Kindschi, 2001), and the *Gordon Diagnostic System* (Gordon, McClure, & Aylward, 1996).

Among them, the CPT has been most widely researched. There are several well-validated CPTs (Hall et al., 2016). They typically involve the rapid presentation of visual or auditory stimuli. Participants are requested to respond to a target stimulus but not respond to nontargets. In doing so, the CPT measures the ability to sustain attention and inhibit responses.

A more recent measure is the QbTest (Qbtech Ltd.), which has been designed to measure the three core symptom domains of ADHD. Although it is not a stand-alone diagnostic tool, several UK NHS ADHD clinics have incorporated the implementation of the QbTest as an adjunct to standard clinical practice (Hall et al., 2016). It is suggested, however, that more rigorous clinical trials are needed to prove the utility of this test in facilitating standard ADHD assessment. Another relevant test is the Neuropsychiatric Electroencephalogram-Based ADHD Assessment Aid (NEBA; Snyder, Rugino, Hornig, & Stein, 2015), which is an EEG-based device designed to aid in the diagnostic process for ADHD by identifying individuals less likely to have ADHD by virtue of a lower theta/beta ratio. Both these tests have received Federal Drug Administration (FDA) marketing approval. However, as Arns and colleagues (2016) note, FDA marketing approval is not the same as a recommendation for best practices. Caution is warranted in any overreliance on such technologies for diagnostic assessments, given their current lack of empirical support for diagnostic validity and specificity (Arns & Gordon, 2014).

However, there is no convincing evidence with regard to the clinical utility of such tools in detecting ADHD. The administration of comprehensive neuropsychological test batteries is not recommended in the routine assessment of ADHD (AACAP, 2007). It has been suggested that there is no psychometric test that can be used with confidence for purposes of diagnostic decision (Nichols & Waschbusch, 2004; Rapport, Chung, Shore, Denney, & Isaacs, 2000). Even CPTs, which have adequate psychometric properties and almost ubiquitous findings of abnormal performance by children with ADHD, have questionable value as diagnostic tools (McGee, Clark, & Symons, 2000; Nigg, Hinshaw, & Halperin, 1996). Research has demonstrated low to moderate correlations between scores on these tests and other assessment measures for ADHD, including rating scales and direct behavioral observation (Egeland, Johansen, & Ueland, 2009; Sims & Lonigan, 2012).

Besides, performance of a child with ADHD on a test administered in the clinical setting may differ greatly from the performance of the same child at school or at home (Adams, Finn, Moes, Flannery, & Rizzo, 2009). Moreover, such measurements do not provide information about the environmental variables that may affect the child's attention, level of arousal, and consequently, their performance (Barkley, 1997b). Finally, they do not correlate significantly with parent and teacher ratings of executive functioning in the child's daily life activities (Toplak, West, & Stanovich, 2013).

Psychoeducational assessment can provide unique information to the diagnostic process as it provides information related to academic functioning, which is often impaired in children with ADHD. Detailed assessment of the major academic achievement skills (reading, reading comprehension, writing, spelling, and math) is essential, given the high likelihood of the coexistence of learning disabilities.

A significant amount of research has been conducted regarding the relevance of IQ testing to the ADHD diagnosis. Findings have been mixed, with some research indicating that children with ADHD are likely to perform several points lower than peers on IQ tests (Doyle, Biederman, Seidman, Weber, & Faraone, 2000; Fischer, Barkley, Fletcher, & Smallish, 1990), whereas others have found that ADHD and IQ function independent of one another (Shuck & Crinella, 2005). However, it has been suggested that IQ tests and achievement tests are important for understanding the individual's overall learning capacities and determining the possible effect of ADHD symptoms on academic achievement (Hechtman, 2000). They may also shed light on whether an individual's high IQ has allowed them to compensate for the effects of ADHD. For the interpretation of the results, clinicians should take into account that children's performance on such tests is in high correlation with measurements of attention and self-control (Aylward, Gordon, & Verhulst, 1997). Finally, the way in which these results are interpreted and used should be handled with high clinical sensitivity. Frequently, child behavior during the administration of a test may disclose more important information about overall functioning than performance scores.

10.4.5.4 Medical Evaluation

In some cases, a medical evaluation is rendered necessary, if a special reason arises from the child's developmental history or the clinical assessment. Depending on the features that dictate medical evaluation, an appointment with a pediatrician is usually enough. Rarely, more sophisticated laboratory examinations might be needed.

The need to include neurological examination in the assessment of ADHD is also justified due to increased prevalence rates of subtle neurological signs in children with ADHD (Ferrin & Vance, 2012). They are minor neurological abnormalities in motor, sensory, and integrative functions, including choreiform and athetoid movements, smoothness and accuracy of fine motor movements, conjugate eye gaze, and upper and lower limb cerebellar signs (Vance et al., 2006). Neurological subtle signs can be assessed with standardized measures, such as the Scored Developmental Neurological Examination (SDNE; Taylor, Sandberg, Thorley, & Giles, 1991). The utility of neurological subtle signs evaluation in the assessment of ADHD has been criticized, as these signs are nonspecific to ADHD but are often present in other neurodevelopmental disorders as well (Cardo, Casanovas, de la Banda, & Servera, 2008). However, recent studies have shown that it is possible to use these signs in clinical assessment for distinguishing between children with ADHD and typically developing children (Ferrin, & Vance, 2012).

A medical evaluation is important in order to rule out the contribution of any medical conditions to symptoms. Some medical conditions include ADHD symptomatology as part of their presentation (e.g., neurofibromatosis, fetal alcohol syndrome, and lead poisoning), whereas other conditions are commonly comorbid or may require differential diagnosis (Pearl, Weiss, & Stein, 2001). Clinicians should be particularly mindful of possible sleep disorders, epilepsy, and thyroid disorder.

Another purpose of the medical evaluation is to determine whether ADHD symptoms may constitute a side effect of medicines taken for other kinds of problems and whether physical conditions exist that contraindicate medication treatment for ADHD.

10.5 Synthesis of the Results and the Feedback Session

Once assessment has been completed, clinicians have at their disposal a plethora of information derived from multiple informants and measures. Clinicians must combine and integrate this data to reach a decision regarding whether the child meets current criteria for the diagnosis of ADHD. It should be noted that diagnostic manuals do not provide clear guidance on how the criteria for ADHD should be applied in practice, including how symptom counts should be obtained across informants (Barkley & Edwards, 2006). In addition, there is a lack of adequate models regarding how discrepant information across informants is best integrated into the diagnostic decision-making process (Sowerby & Tripp, 2009). It is obvious that reaching a diagnosis is a delicate and complex process that lies to a great degree on extensive clinical experience.

Synthesis of the results should lead to differential diagnosis. However, the most important issue for the clinician is not whether the child's symptoms reflect ADHD *or* another disorder but whether ADHD *coexists* with another disorder or whether secondary problems have developed on the basis of ADHD through the process of epigenesis. The interaction of ADHD with other disorders significantly affects symptom severity, outcomes, and treatment planning.

Announcing the diagnosis of ADHD to the child's parents is a very critical part of the assessment. Getting a diagnosis is usually a strong emotional experience for the parents (Klasen, 2000). Raising parents' awareness of their child's difficulties associated with ADHD and helping them understand the nature and etiology of this disorder provides the link between diagnosis and treatment. The feedback session may assist parents in modifying maladaptive causal attributions about their child's behavior, which may lead to positive changes in their own behavior toward the child.

Clinicians should explain that ADHD is a neurodevelopmental disorder and not a mental illness or the outcome of poor upbringing. Knowing that their child's difficulties are due to a neurodevelopmental disorder often helps parents to stop internalizing the problem as their own failure (Klasen, 2000). Clinicians should avoid using complex and extremely specialized scientific terminology and help parents understand why the child with ADHD is more energetic, impulsive, and inattentive than other children of the same age. At this point, tying ADHD symptoms to specific daily problems reported by parents might prove helpful.

Even though clinicians are not obliged to explain in detail how they reached diagnosis, it is recommended to walk parents through the data on which the diagnosis was based. In this way, clinicians can dispel possible doubts parents may have and convince them that the assessment was thorough and the diagnosis well-established. Clinicians should also provide reassurance that a diagnosis of ADHD is a positive step toward helping them manage their child's difficulties. Compassion and empathy are important elements of the clinician's attitude toward parents. This sense of security will counterbalance the disappointment they may experience as being told that their child has a neurodevelopmental disorder and will increase their confidence in the clinician in order to follow treatment recommendations. An adequate rationale for proposed interventions should also be provided.

When leaving the clinical setting, parents should have a rudimentary knowledge of the causes of their child's difficulties, have received answers to their basic questions, have understood that they are not responsible for their child's condition, and have developed realistic expectations with reference to treatment.

10.6 Assessment of ADHD in Adults

Assessment of ADHD in adults differs in many respects from the process that is followed for children and adolescents. Clinicians must be well aware of the differences in the clinical manifestations of the disorder in adults, as well as the developmental course of ADHD. Moreover, it is important that clinicians be familiar with the modifications in the diagnostic criteria of ADHD in adults in DSM-5 (see Section 9.3). It should be noted that a diagnosis of ADHD in adults can provide an explanation for, and means of dealing with, the difficulties that have transformed the life of the individual so far.

Adults with ADHD may be identified in three different ways. First, individuals who had received the diagnosis in childhood may require continued care and seek ongoing treatment in adulthood. Second, parents of children with ADHD may report that they had and continue to have the same difficulties as their offspring. Third, a number of adults may decide to seek professional help for the first time, either because they were informed about ADHD or because they need help for secondary problems and comorbid conditions (Gibbins, & Weiss, 2007).

An effective assessment of ADHD in adults requires the collection of a plethora of information through various methods and from various people (Canadian Attention Deficit Hyperactivity Disorder Resource Alliance; CADDRA, 2011; Nutt et al., 2007). Because individuals may distort their report of challenges, it is important to gather information from collateral informants (Surman, 2013). Another reason for the collection of information from third parties is the risk of false-positive diagnosis (e.g., in patients who are drug seeking) or false-negative diagnosis (patients who lack insight) (Gibbins & Weiss, 2007). It is fairly common that the person seeking assessment is accompanied by family members or significant others. With the person's permission, such guests are encouraged to participate in the assessment process (Ramsey, 2015).

A typical process for the assessment of ADHD in adults, as suggested by Gallagher & Blader (2001), includes the following steps.

10.6.1 Review of Current and Past Functioning Using Rating Scales

In these measures, individuals respond to questions on how well descriptions of problems with ADHD fit their experience. A number of scales have been proposed for the assessment of ADHD in adults with varied levels of psychometric development (Murphy & Adler, 2004). Some of them are the following:

1. The Brown Attention Deficit Disorders Scales (BADDS; Brown, 1996).
   They were created to obtain information regarding the frequency with which a person encounters difficulties with the cognitive and behavioral consequences of ADHD. They are available in a form that allows self-report and report from parents.
2. The Conners' Adult ADHD Rating Scale (CAARS; Conners, Erhardt, & Sparrow, 1999).
   It was developed to obtain information about the person's current difficulties. It includes inattention and hyperactivity/impulsivity items and provides self-report and observer rating scales. The long form of the CAARS also includes measures of impulsivity/emotional lability and problems with self-concept.
3. The Wender Utah Rating Scale (WURS; Ward, Wender, & Reimherr, 1993).
   It is a self-report measure, developed to obtain information about a person's developmental history and childhood experiences. It relies on retrospective self-report of adults.
4. The Adult Self Report Scale (ASRS; Adler, Kessler, & Spencer, 2004).
   It is based around the DSM-IV-TR items but incorporates more adult-appropriate item examples. It also provides a six-item Adult ADHD Self-Report Scale screener (ASRS-v1.1).
5. The Barkley Adult ADHD Rating Scales-IV (BAARS-IV; Barkley, 2011).
   It is a norm-based symptom checklist, including both self- and observer-report forms for both childhood and adult symptoms of ADHD.

10.6.2 Clinical Interview With the Person

Clinicians should address the reasons for seeking an evaluation as well as current concerns, presenting problems, functioning, and life circumstances. A review of the individual's typical everyday schedule, for weekdays and weekends, may help clinicians gain insight into issues relating to time management, organizational skills, and level of motivation. Present educational or occupational functioning should also be reviewed.

Clinical assessment also requires a detailed developmental and psychosocial history in order to determine that symptoms have precursors during the developmental years and had influenced functioning before the age of 12 years. Moreover, a full educational, occupational, and psychiatric history should be reviewed. Clinicians explore the possibility of frequent job changes and dismissals, difficulties with timely arrival to work, failure in meeting deadlines, and overall work productivity. In adults with ADHD, the cumulative effect of such difficulties often leads to lower productivity and more mistakes relative to coworkers, including safety issues in some jobs (Kessler et al., 2005). Furthermore, adults with ADHD typically have a long psychiatric history for other problems as well. Many may have received a variety of different interventions to assist them with maladaptive behaviors (Gibbins & Weiss, 2007).

Moreover, obtaining information about the person's relationships with family and friends is warranted. Adults with ADHD often report past or ongoing conflict with their family, childhood experiences of rejection and bullying by peers, low-level social anxiety, as well as unstable and short-lasting romantic relationships (Ramsey, 2015). The emotional reactions to the impact of ADHD symptoms on a person's life should also be scrutinized. The way the person copes with negative emotions, including anger, disappointment, and frustration should be explored.

10.6.3 Review of School Performance

School records in the form of report cards constitute a useful source of indication of a person's level and consistency of performance. Variability in performance is a hallmark of ADHD. Moreover, the teacher written comments often highlight problems with behavior, motivation, effort, and attentiveness. Reviewing school records may provide information regarding the age of onset of the problems and their persistence across the age span.

Particular emphasis should be given on the transition to middle school, as well as on organization of schoolwork during the teenage years. As Barkley notes, "Adequate grades can be maintained with inadequate study habits that may foretell later academic problems" (Barkley, 2015b, p. 483). Therefore, it is important to explore how academics and assignments were handled during this phase of schooling.

For example, adults with ADHD often report that they did not tend to complete assigned readings, but used to rely on information presented in class; they did not tend to complete homework properly, but used to do it in a rushed fashion in order to get rid of it; they used to rely on their parents to supervise them or even do their homework for them. All these practices, however, do not translate into adaptive study skills and influence negatively a person's educational history.

10.6.4 Neuropsychological Testing

In light of diagnostic difficulties in adults with ADHD, neuropsychological testing may play an important role (Gallagher & Blader, 2001). Neuropsychological evaluation is sometimes viewed as a way to objectively determine cognitive abilities. A novel neuropsychological tool developed for this purpose is Mindstreams (NeuroTrax Corp., NY), a computerized battery assessing multiple cognitive domains in adults with ADHD (Schweiger, Abramovitch, Doniger, & Simon, 2007). Robust construct and discriminant validity in the assessment of attention and executive functions have been provided. However, the use of neuropsychological testing is not required to establish the presence of ADHD symptomatology and associated impairment (Ramsey, 2015).

Numerous difficulties beset diagnosis of ADHD in adults. First, diagnosis requires evidence that the symptoms began before the age of 12 years. However, oftentimes self-report is flawed because, on the one hand, there are obvious difficulties in recalling symptoms that occurred many years ago, and on the other hand, adults sometimes deny symptoms that are verified by others.

Clinicians should be aware of the changes observed in ADHD presentation during a lifetime. In addition, the manifestations of ADHD may be quite clear, or in some adults, hidden by avoidance of challenges and compensatory efforts (Surman, 2013). Overt motoric hyperactivity usually declines with age due to ongoing brain development. Hyperactivity in adults usually manifests as an internal sense of physical and mental restlessness, leading to inability to slow down or relax. Adults with ADHD usually describe physical discomfort in situations in which they feel confined, which interferes with paying attention (Ramsey, 2015). Sometimes, this excessive energy is channeled into overwork or intense sports. Furthermore, hyperactivity in adulthood may be perceived as an umbrella term that also covers behaviors such as logorrhea, speeding when driving, and racing thoughts. In adults, there is less gross motor hyperactivity but continued fine motor expression of the internal push of driven-like behavior (Gibbins & Weiss, 2007).

Impulsivity is less obvious in adults but not necessarily more benign. It may be expressed in cognition, affect, sexual behavior, and life events. Impulsivity problems often appear to be poor judgment or not considering the long-term consequences of an action (Ramsey, 2015). Difficulties in emotional management are also associated with impulse control in adults. Anger and frustration management are common challenges for adults with ADHD. It seems that even a single impulsive action can have much more serious implications for a self-reliant adult than for a child who is under supervision (Gibbins & Weiss, 2007).

Inattention, distractibility, and poor sustained attention are the most persistent ADHD symptoms across development and a primary source of difficulty for adults with ADHD (Ramsey, 2015). Inattention is evident as a diminished capacity for forced effort, information processing, conceptualizing consequences, planning, prioritizing, and ability to turn out irrelevant distractions. Adults with ADHD often complain about procrastination and poor motivation. Procrastination refers to a maladaptive voluntary delay of an intended course of action despite the recognition of negative outcomes (Steel, 2007). Adults with ADHD also find it difficult to reengage in a task once their focus has been disrupted. These difficulties often prevent adults with ADHD from working efficiently, avoiding arguments, managing their finances, organizing a household, and doing many other activities that are taken for granted in adulthood (Gibbins & Weiss, 2007).

Unlike children, most adults with ADHD have the freedom to avoid overly structured situations. In addition, a strong base of support at home or at work can make it difficult to identify substantial impairment in multiple settings (Wigal & Wigal, 2007).

Differential diagnosis is also particularly important. A physical examination is often needed to check for medical homologues of ADHD, including head trauma, seizures, hyper- or hypothyroidism, migraines, and sleep disorders (Gibbins & Weiss, 2007). For the differential diagnosis, it is important to explore the presence of DDs, ADs, BDs, and SUD. In DDs, individuals describe their attention and memory difficulties as being related to their mood state. In other words, these problems do not seem to be present outside a depressive episode (Ramsey, 2015). In ADs, feelings of tension, irritability, difficulty concentrating, worry, and restlessness are experienced mainly in the presence or at the thought of specific triggers and are diminished when these triggers are not present (Ramsey, 2015). In BDs, irritability and difficulties in emotional self-regulation and self-control have longer duration during a manic episode, whereas ADHD outbursts are shorter and are usually recognized by the individual. In SUD, it is important to clarify whether the symptoms that resemble ADHD preceded the use of substances or followed them.

Differential diagnosis is particularly challenging in cases where personality disorders have been previously diagnosed. In this case, the developmental history and a family psychiatric history are particularly important. Strong evidence of ADHD in a first-degree relative would mean familial risk for ADHD in the person who is being assessed (Sowerby & Tripp, 2009).

Finally, the high rate of symptom overlap between comorbid psychiatric disorders in adults with ADHD may impede diagnosis. Any of the disorders mentioned earlier can coexist with ADHD, as over 80% of clinic-referred adults with ADHD exhibit at least one other comorbid disorder (Barkley, 2015b). In fact, such comorbidities may be the main complaint of the adult seeking evaluation. For this purpose, it is useful to obtain measures of other psychiatric symptoms, such as the Adult Symptom Inventory and Adult Self Report Inventory (Gadow et al., 2004). Recognizing the disorders that may co-occur with ADHD in adults is very important, particularly when medication is recommended because the presence of BDs or SUD may contraindicate medication for ADHD. It is anticipated that there will be revisions of relevant rating scales in order to be consistent with DSM-5.

The contrasting comorbid profiles of persons seeking help during adulthood with adults who are simply followed into adulthood suggests that clinical samples of adults with ADHD encountered in psychiatric settings have a referral bias. In the first case, adults with ADHD usually manifest internalized disorders, including DDs or ADs, whereas in the second case they usually have externalized disorders, including antisocial personality disorder and SUD. It seems that self-referred adults experience more emotional distress, which probably motivated them to seek help (Gallagher & Blader, 2001).

Notes

1 For further information regarding the scales typically used in the assessment of ADHD, the readers are referred to Pelham et al. (2005), and Collett, Ohan, & Myers (2003a,b).
2 Further information regarding the rating scales designed to assess functional impairment in children can be found in the review of Winters, Collett, & Myers (2005).
3 For a thorough description and comparison of these guides, the reader is referred to a series of articles in the first issue (volume 39) of the *Journal of the American Academy of Child and Adolescent Psychiatry* of 2000 as well as to the article by Anastopoulos & Shelton, 2001.

Part III

Treatment of ADHD

11 Interventions for ADHD

11.1 Introduction

ADHD is one of the most prevalent, impairing, costly, and refractory neurodevelopmental disorders (Page et al., 2016). Furthermore, it is associated with a great number of comorbid disorders. Individuals with ADHD are impaired across a range of domains in different settings, including numerous developmental, cognitive, emotional, social, and academic impairments, as well as various health risks that can significantly affect their quality of life. Children with the disorder are at greater risk for longer-term negative outcomes, such as lower educational and employment attainment. ADHD impacts not only on the child, but also on parents and siblings, causing disturbances to family and marital functioning. Finally, it affects the community, creating substantial burden for health, educational, and criminal justice systems.

The significant impairment experienced by individuals with ADHD results in enormous societal costs. Health economists estimate that the total annual societal cost for childhood and adolescent ADHD in the United States is $42.5 billion, which is allocated to treatment costs, special education services, and juvenile justice, plus low work productivity and employment lapses among adults (Hinshaw & Scheffler, 2014; Pelham, Foster, & Robb, 2007). Among these costs, the estimated annual costs of ADHD to the U.S. education system total $13.4 billion. Thus, the incremental lifetime cost of educating the population of children with ADHD is approximately $174 billion over 13 years of education (Robb et al., 2011).

For all these reasons, there is a critical need to develop efficacious interventions that affect the immediate impairments and adverse long-term outcomes associated with ADHD. One of the most central questions regarding ADHD has long been what constitutes effective treatment (Page et al., 2016).

According to evidence-based guidelines, the most common recommended treatment options for ADHD include pharmacological and psychosocial interventions (Seixas, Weiss, & Müller, 2012; Subcommittee on Attention-Deficit/Hyperactivity Disorder, 2011). These two modalities of treatment have been studied for decades, both separately and in combination. Medication has received considerable empirical support, and is often the first-line treatment due to its efficacy and rapid onset of action (Daughton & Kratochvil, 2009). Psychosocial interventions are also recommended and used in ADHD treatment. They include behavior modification, parent training, classroom management, cognitive-behavioral interventions, and social skills training. These interventions generally rely on parents and teachers to learn and implement contingency management procedures in order to address behavioral problems associated with ADHD and promote functional skill development. Systematic reviews of treatment trials have provided evidence to support their efficacy (Daley et al., 2014). Therefore, they are also offered as first-line interventions (Pelham & Fabiano, 2008). Dietary interventions, neurofeedback, and neurocognitive training are recommended as alternative or complementary treatments. Although these interventions have yet to be empirically verified, they appear to have beneficial effects on ADHD (Gevensleben et al., 2014; Sonuga-Barke et al., 2013).

The treatments currently available for ADHD address symptoms and function but are usually not curative (Subcommittee on Attention-Deficit/Hyperactivity Disorder, 2011). An effective intervention for school-aged individuals with ADHD or older should achieve *symptomatic remission* and optimization of functioning as well. Symptomatic remission indicates that the individual has symptom scores within the normal range with some remaining functional impairment. *Functional remission* means that the individual has achieved symptomatic remission and also shows no functional impairments due to any residual symptoms that may remain (Rostain, Jensen, Connor, Miesle, & Faraone, 2015). In the case of children younger than 4 years old, treatment goals may be more ambitious and include even *syndromal remission*, defined as loss of diagnostic criteria for meeting the ADHD diagnosis by means of normalization of deficient neurocognitive functioning via early intervention (see Section 11.7).

Understanding and accepting the benefits and limitations of treatment is very important in order to have realistic expectations and set attainable goals. ADHD treatment must be viewed as a lifelong enterprise that requires commitment, determination, stability, patience, and persistence in order to produce long-lasting and generalizable outcomes.

11.2 Pharmacological Interventions

Available research demonstrates the usefulness of two broad categories of psychotropic drugs in the treatment of ADHD: stimulants and nonstimulants. In both European and U.S. guidelines, stimulants are mentioned as the first-choice drugs in the pharmacological treatment of ADHD (Kutcher et al., 2004; Meijer, Faber, van den Ban, & Tobi, 2009).

Data demonstrating the short-term beneficial effects of stimulants on the symptoms of ADHD were well-established by the 1970s. Relevant studies constitute the largest body of treatment literature on any developmental disorder (Daughton & Kratochvil, 2009; Van der Oord, Prins, Oosterlaan, & Emmelkamp, 2008). The first stimulant for children with ADHD was *Ritalin*, initiated by Dr. Leon Eisenberg in the late 1950s, when he conducted the first randomized controlled study of the use of Ritalin for children with hyperactivity. In 1961, the U.S. FDA approved Ritalin for use with children (Grosswald, 2015). Since then, medication has advanced, and today stimulants include both methylphenidate (MPH) and amphetamine (AMP) compounds. For a complete list of MPH and AMP formulations FDA-approved for children with ADHD, the reader is referred to Connor (2015).

The main immediate-release MPH formulations used for the treatment of ADHD in children are *Ritalin* (MPH), *Methylin* (MPH), and *Focalin* (d-MPH). Ritalin is perhaps the most common MPH medication, which peaked in popularity throughout the 1990s but is still regarded as a very effective pharmaceutical option for managing symptoms of ADHD. Methylin is relatively similar to other forms of MPH. Focalin is a unique formulation that contains the "dextro" stereoisomer of MPH. It functions primarily as a norepinephrine-dopamine reuptake inhibitor and results in stimulation of the CNS.

The main immediate-release AMP formulations are *Dexedrine* (dextroamphetamine), *Dextrostat* (dextroamphetamine), and *Adderall* (mixed AMP salts). Dexedrine and Dextrostat are very potent stimulants used for the treatment of ADHD. Adderall is one of the most popular pharmaceutical medications for the treatment of ADHD. It contains 75% dextroamphetamine salts and 25% levoamphetamine salts.

Stimulants, as a class, enhance dopaminergic and noradrenergic neurotransmission in the CNS, but the mechanism involved differs between MPH and amphetamines. MPH is a dopamine reuptake inhibitor, which facilitates dopaminergic neurotransmission at the dopamine transporter and elicits little presynaptic dopamine release. Amphetamines block the reuptake of both norepinephrine and dopamine into the presynaptic neuron and facilitate neurotransmitter release through reverse transport (Faraone & Buitelaar, 2010). The immediate-release formulation of MPH is rapidly and almost completely absorbed and it reaches an initial maximum between one and three hours with significant intersubject variation. It provides relief from ADHD symptoms for approximately four hours. Thus, multiple daily dosing is necessary to maintain improvements throughout the day (Findling, 2008).

Over the last two decades, a new generation of stimulants has emerged in novel extended-release formulations that allow for one daily dosing, thus facilitating effective medicine use, avoiding stigma at school, and enhancing compliance to treatment. Long-acting compounds cover both the school day and the afterschool hours with a single-dose, given in the morning.

Concerta, an extended-release formulation of MPH, is one of the most commonly prescribed stimulants for ADHD nowadays. It reaches an initial maximum after one to two hours, and its action on behavior is stated to last about 10 to 12 hours (Swanson et al., 2003). Other long-acting MPH formulations are *Focalin XR* (d-MPH), *Quillivant XR* (MPH), and *Daytrana Patch* (MPH). Quillivant is a liquid formulation. Daytrana is a transdermal patch, which is usually utilized when oral formulations are poorly tolerated. Long-acting AMP formulations are *Adderall XR* (mixed AMP salts), *Dexedrine Spansule* (AMP), and *Vyvance* (lisdexamphetamine), a "prodrug" that is thought to have smoother absorption and eliminate some of the euphoric effects of other stimulants.

It is estimated that in 70% to 80% of the children with ADHD, treatment with stimulants leads to primary symptom improvement (DuPaul & Barkley, 1993; Findling, 2008). Similar effects have been found for adults (Faraone & Glatt, 2010). However, between 10% and 30% of children with ADHD do not respond to or do not tolerate stimulant medication (Pliszka, 2007; Spencer, Biederman, Wilens et al., 1996).

Stimulants improve a wide variety of abilities, including sustained attention, impulse inhibition, and reduction of purposeless activity, particularly in settings where behavioral control is required. In other words, medication reduces the core symptoms of the disorder and associated behaviors. In the classroom, stimulants have been found to reduce classroom disruption, and increase on-task behavior and compliance. Moreover, improvement is noted in social functioning, risk-taking behavior, and academic performance in the short term. However, this improvement does not seem to have long-term effects (Meijer et al., 2009; Van der Oord et al., 2008). Furthermore, it should be noted that stimulants do not improve core cognitive vulnerabilities due to learning disabilities, which require specific educational remediation (Connor, 2015).

While stimulants are generally well-tolerated, safety and adverse effects are the focus of significant clinical and public health concern. It has been found that side effects of stimulants increase with escalating dose and duration of exposure (Swanson et al., 2007). One of the most common side effects of stimulants is appetite reduction, which is reported for 13% to 60% of children with ADHD (Schachter, Pham, King, Langford, & Moher, 2001; Zachor, Roberts, Hodgens, Isaacs, & Merrick, 2006). This appetite reduction may be associated with a reduction in expected height and weight gain, at least in the first 1 to 3 years of treatment (Faraone, Biederman, Morley, & Spencer, 2008; Poulton, 2005). It has been argued that this growth suppression does not appear to raise clinical concerns for most children treated with stimulants, because it seems to be dose related and can be controlled by dose reduction. In addition, it is reversible after discontinuation of medication (Charach, Figueroa, Chen, Ickowicz, & Schachar, 2006; Spencer, Biederman, Harding et al., 1996).

However, a more recent longitudinal study showed that intensive consistent stimulant treatment over a 10-year period caused, on average, a nearly 1-inch growth lag the first year that was not caught up (Swanson et al., cited in Hinshaw, Arnold, & The MTA Cooperative Group, 2015).

Another longitudinal study of the long-term effects of stimulants on growth parameters reached similar results. Powell, Frydenberg, and Thomsen (2015) found a fall in weight and height growth for children with ADHD in stimulant treatment at 72 months after initial assessment. Attenuation in the decrease was observed after 12 to 47 months of treatment, but baseline values had not been reached at 72 months.

A rare but more severe adverse effect of both stimulants and ATX is their impact on cardiovascular function. These drugs can increase blood pressure, heart rate, and cardiac rhythm, although mostly on a clinically insignificant level (Rapport & Moffitt, 2002; Wernicke et al., 2003). For this reason, medication treatment for ADHD requires ongoing cardiovascular monitoring and should be cautiously used in individuals with pre-existing heart abnormalities (Hennissen et al., 2017).

Other side effects include dizziness, insomnia, and drowsiness (Barkley, 1997b). One in seven children who receive stimulants is reported to suffer from insomnia (Schachter et al., 2001). A small percentage of children may report stomachaches and headaches. Lastly, motor or vocal tics may occur in approximately 1% to 2% of children who have a personal or family history of tics and are treated with stimulants (Barkley, DuPaul, & Connor, 2013).

It should be noted that children with comorbid ASD or ID with an IQ less than 55 may experience elevated rates of side effects (Research Units on Pediatric Psychopharmacology, 2005). The use of stimulants is generally contraindicated in cases of children with known oversensitivity to these substances, structural cardiac defects, schizophrenia or other psychotic disorders, unstable hypertension, and severe TDs (Connor, 2015).

A secondary line of treatment involves the use of nonstimulant drugs when stimulants have been ineffective or poorly tolerated and when there is a history of substance abuse (Daughton & Kratochvil, 2009). Nonstimulant drugs approved by the U.S. FDA for the treatment of ADHD in children include ATX (*Strattera*), a long-acting formulation of clonidine (*Kapvay*), and a long-acting guanfacine preparation (*Intuniv*).

In 2002, Strattera was the first nonstimulant medication approved for use in the treatment of ADHD. Since its initial approval, it has been marketed in approximately 90 countries and is widely used, accounting for 6% of prescriptions for ADHD in the United States in 2010 (Garfield et al., 2012). ATX selectively blocks reuptake at noradrenergic neurons and increases catecholaminergic neurotransmission in the prefrontal cortex. The full treatment effect of ATX may take up to 12 weeks to emerge (Bushe & Savill, 2014). However, responders usually show some change by the 4-week point. Once full clinical effectiveness is established, it persists across the day at a fairly consistent level (Banaschewski et al., 2006).

A recent meta-analysis reviewed 25 randomized controlled trials with ATX and found that ATX was significantly better than placebo in relieving ADHD symptoms (Schwartz, S., & Correll, 2014). Another comprehensive meta-analysis reviewed 42 studies and found that ATX led to significant improvement in core ADHD symptomatology according to parent reports (Gayleard & Mychailyszyn, 2017). A meta-analysis comparing stimulants to nonstimulants found the effect sizes of long-acting stimulants to be significantly higher than the effect sizes of nonstimulants (Faraone & Glatt, 2010). However, gains noted during acute treatment are not necessarily further improved during long-term treatment (Childress, 2016).

Common adverse effects of ATX include headache, abdominal pain, decreased appetite, nausea, vomiting, and somnolence (Connor, 2015). Rare cases of severe liver toxicity have been reported (Bangs et al., 2008; Lim et al., 2006). Furthermore, suicidal ideation occurs with a frequency of 0.44%, although no deaths from suicide have been reported so far (Bangs et al., 2008; Wooltorton, 2005). However, a more recent meta-analysis found a low overall suicide risk and no significant difference between medication classes in suicide risk (Bushe & Savill, 2014). Finally, irritability, agitation, anger, or aggression may also occur in rare cases

(Banaschewski et al., 2006). Growth deficits have not been observed in studies of ATX (Donnelly et al., 2009; Spencer et al., 2007).

Alpha-agonists are also useful in the treatment of ADHD. The long-acting alpha-agonist, extended-release clonidine, and the long acting alpha-2A-agonist, extended-release guanfacine, have been approved by the U.S. FDA for the treatment of ADHD as monotherapy or adjunctive treatment in combination with a psychostimulant (Daughton, Corr, Liu, & West, 2012). Clonidine stimulates inhibitory presynaptic autoreceptors in the CNS and may facilitate the ability to focus attention by increasing norepinephrine in the prefrontal cortex (Rosenberg, 2002). Clonidine has also been found helpful for aggression, impulsivity, and sleep problems. Adverse reactions include somnolence, fatigue, and irritability (Daughton et al., 2012). Clonidine can produce intraventricular conduction delay and T wave abnormalities, so careful ECG-monitoring is recommended.

Antidepressants, including tricyclics and selective serotonin reuptake inhibitors, are also used as third- or fourth- line agents for ADHD treatment, although they are not clinically approved by the FDA for the treatment of ADHD. Their use has been limited by concerns raised about their potential increasing the risk of suicide in some individuals (Hammad, Laughren, & Racoosin, 2006; Schneeweiss et al., 2010). Other adverse effects include dry mouth, sedation, confusion, blurred vision, constipation, and urinary retention (Attia & Meseeha, 2016). However, they have distinct advantages that make them a relevant alternative or adjunct in the treatment of ADHD, including their potentially positive effects on mood, anxiety, sleep, and tics (Wood, Crager, Delap, & Heiskell, 2007).

A relatively recent trend in ADHD treatment is combined pharmacotherapy. This trend is based on the high comorbidity rates of ADHD with other disorders, and the belief that the synergy of combined medications may lead to better symptom control (Parritz & Troy, 2014). For example, antihypertensives are sometimes used in combination with stimulants for the treatment of sleep disturbances among children with ADHD or for the management of ADHD symptoms in the context of CD or BDs (Biederman, Hammerness et al., 2008).

However, medication seems to have differential effects on different domains of functioning, with evidence suggesting efficacy in reducing core ADHD symptoms, but less evidence to suggest improved academic performance and long-term benefit on adolescent or adult outcomes (Schachar et al., 2002). Medication can increase sustained attention and improve academic productivity, as indicated in the quality of note-taking, scores on worksheets, the amount of written-language output, and homework completion (Evans et al., 2001). However, medication does not remediate the underlying language mechanisms needed to perform optimally in academic subject matter (Hinshaw, 2009), nor can it provide the individual with social skills (Hoza et al., 2005). Furthermore, long term treatment with MPH may lead to loss of efficacy and upregulation of dopamine transporter availability, which could result in more severe inattention when the individual with ADHD is not medicated, and in need of higher doses of medication (Wang et al., 2013). Finally, parents may have concerns about the use of medication to manage their child's behavior (Berger, Dor, Nevo, & Goldzweig, 2008).

More recent findings suggest that medication may have some long-term beneficial effects on the functioning of individuals with ADHD, including higher educational level, better occupational status, fewer accidents, and less delinquency (Fredriksen, Halmoy, Faraone, & JanHaavik, 2013). However, these studies are still extremely limited and their results have not been corroborated. We appreciate that the possible long-term efficacy of medication in reducing the impairment associated with ADHD remains to be investigated.

A critical issue to be considered by clinicians is nonadherence and discontinuation of medication, which might undermine its effectiveness. Treatment nonadherence has an important short-term impact, affecting the initial efficacy and tolerability of treatment, and a longer-term impact, associated with poorer outcomes (Treuer, Méndez, Montgomery, & Wu, 2016). Reported levels of nonadherence in children and adults range between 15% and 87% (Adler & Nierenberg, 2010; Ahmed & Aslani, 2013). Particularly in adolescence, refusing and resisting stimulant medication is a documented problem (Charach & Gajaria, 2008; McCarthy et al., 2009). The main reasons for nonadherence include the adolescent's wish not to rely on psychiatric drugs indefinitely, lack of understanding the need for medication, a perceived lack of efficacy, and the belief that the disadvantages associated with medication outweigh the advantages (McCarthy, 2014). In general, nonadherence may result, in part, from a lack of understanding the importance of medication in achieving and maintaining the desired outcomes (Ahmed & Aslani, 2013).

Pharmacotherapy should always be preceded by a careful assessment of various factors. First, parent and child attitudes about medication should be evaluated. The attitudes toward the suggested treatment can affect compliance and be essential for the individual's maximal benefit and outcome (Berger et al., 2008). Some parents may overestimate the efficacy of medication and hold unrealistic expectations. Others may be inconsistent or not supportive. Parents with more reasonable beliefs about ADHD and its treatment were found to show greater acceptance and utilization of medication treatment, whereas those with false beliefs about ADHD were more likely to find alternative interventions as more acceptable (Johnston, Seipp, Hommersen, Hoza, & Fine, 2005).

A physical evaluation is required prior treatment in order to detect factors that may contraindicate medication. Comorbid disorders, any potential for drug misuse, and potential side effects should be taken into consideration. Furthermore, it is important to thoroughly assess for comorbid SLDs, because they require supplemental educational remediation. Specific issues related to compliance and ability to take the medication are also important. Finally, the prescribing doctor should systematically monitor the child in order to adjust dosage and evaluate effectiveness, safety, and tolerability of the medication over time (Connor, 2015).

11.3 Psychosocial Interventions

11.3.1 Behavioral Interventions

Psychosocial interventions for ADHD are supported by research as effective alternatives or complementary treatments to medication and are an important part of a multimodal treatment plan (Schoenfelder & Sasser, 2016). Multimodal treatment plans integrate a number of individual interventions to target symptoms across multiple functional domains (Hechtman et al., 2004). Psychosocial interventions are designed to address the behavioral, emotional, and interpersonal aspects of ADHD, using modalities such as behavior modification, skills training, and parent/teacher training.

Behavior modification has been identified as one of the main evidence-based psychosocial interventions for the treatment of ADHD (Daley et al., 2014; Evans, Owens, & Bunford, 2014; Fabiano, Pelham et al., 2009). Reviews and meta-analyses are based on more than 40 years of research on a total sample of 3,500 individuals (Pfiffner & Haack, 2014).

Behavioral interventions are grounded in learning theory and employ principles of classical conditioning, operant conditioning, cognitive-behavioral theory, and social learning theory to target ADHD-related behaviors directly with the child or indirectly via an adult. Although behavioral interventions are varied in scope, they all tend to focus on modifying undesirable behaviors, increasing desirable behaviors, and developing new functional behaviors that were previously absent from the child's behavioral repertoire.

Systematic reviews of treatment trials have provided evidence to support the efficacy of interventions using behavioral techniques in reducing behavioral problems exhibited by children with ADHD but not the core symptoms of the disorder (Charach, Carson, Fox, Ali, Beckett, & Lim, 2013; Fabiano, Pelham et al., 2009). This finding may be explicable by the fact that these interventions were initially developed and have been used extensively for children with oppositional and conduct problems. The rationale is that children's challenging behavior develops as a result of coercive interactional cycles that co-reinforce noncompliant behaviors in the child and inappropriate responses from significant adults. During intervention, adults are trained in the use of behavior modification techniques to reinforce appropriate and discourage inappropriate child behaviors, promote effective adult–child interactions, and turn negative interactional cycles to positive ones. It is therefore expected that such interventions are not as effective as treatments for core ADHD symptoms because these symptoms do not emerge along a similar environmentally mediated route as behavioral problems (Daley et al., 2014; Sonuga-Barke et al., 2006). Furthermore, effects appear to be short-term and limited to the period of treatment, and there is a lack of demonstrated effectiveness over the long term (Waschbusch & Hill, 2003).

However, the use of behavioral interventions in ADHD is justified in many respects because behavioral problems and poor social, academic, and organizational skills are often more impairing relative to core ADHD symptoms. Therefore, these difficulties constitute very important treatment targets because they are associated with substantial burden to the child, the child's family, and society through the criminal justice, special education, and health systems (Daley et al., 2014).

Additionally, the short-term effect of behavioral interventions may be attributed to parameters related to the delivery of treatment, including willingness of parents, knowledge and skills of therapist, or duration of delivery, and not to the potential effectiveness of treatment (Waschbusch & Hill, 2003). Long-term management plans for ADHD should include behavioral interventions over long periods. Therefore, behavioral interventions should be sustained, modified, and adapted over time to promote long-term usage by parents and schools (Pelham & Fabiano, 2008).

In conclusion, behavioral interventions constitute a standard component of the psychosocial interventions for ADHD. Fabiano and colleagues (2004) have shown an incremental benefit of adding additional behavior modification components to an ongoing behavioral program because it appears to improve functioning in a number of domains. However, according to Pfiffner & Haack (2014), it is important to acknowledge the following limitations of these interventions:

1. The outcomes of the intervention in one setting (e.g., at home) are not automatically generalized in other settings (e.g., at school), but it is required that the intervention be implemented in these settings as well.
2. In order to maintain the outcomes in the long term, it may be required that some components of the interventions be repeated periodically.
3. Even though the outcomes of these interventions are very satisfactory, they do not completely normalize behavior.

11.3.1.1 Parent Training

Parenting is a critical determinant of child outcomes. Parent–child interactions and the way in which parents structure the environment where children grow up are important elements in developmental outcomes for all children, but especially those at greatest risk (Davis & Williams, 2011).

Parenting is an important mechanism of change in psychosocial treatment. A key element of behavioral interventions is training parents of children with ADHD in the use of behavioral contingencies. It is suggested that changes in parent management strategies are essential in producing sustained changes in child behavior and subsequent improvements in parental well-being (DeGarmo, Patterson, & Forgatch, 2004). The main goal of this training is to enable parents to modify and enhance their parenting skills in order to cope with problem behaviors, improve parent–child relationships, and in some cases, target the underlying neuropsychological features of ADHD (Rimestad, Lambek, Christiansen, & Hougaard, 2016). Specifically, parents are taught to engage in positive attending and monitoring, set clear expectations, and provide consistent positive and negative consequences (Haack, Villodas, McBurnett, Hinshaw, & Pfiffner, 2016).

Parents of children with ADHD often experience stress, frustration, negative feelings, and low self-efficacy in their interactions with the child (Maniadaki, Sonuga-Barke, Kakouros et al., 2005). As a result, they often use inadequate and ineffective child-rearing practices, which usually reinforce rather than reduce child inappropriate behaviors. Parent training is therefore of utmost importance in order to effectively modify poor parenting practices to increase positive outcomes with children with ADHD. Poor parenting is one of the most robust predictors of negative long-term outcomes in children with behavior problems (Chronis et al., 2004).

Parents are taught to identify and manipulate the antecedents (e.g., setting structure) and consequences (e.g., adult attention) of child behavior, target and monitor problematic behaviors, reinforce desirable behavior through praise, positive attention, and tangible rewards, and decrease undesirable behavior through planned ignoring, time-out, and other disciplinary techniques (Chronis, Chacko, Fabiano, Wymbs, & Pelham, 2004) (see Section 12.2). Furthermore, from early beginnings in the 1960s, parent training has incorporated a range of factors that influence parenting, including interparental discord, low self-efficacy, and social isolation (Scott, 2002).

According to Chronis and colleagues (2004),[1] the typical sequence of sessions for parent training in a clinical behavioral intervention is the following:

(a) overview of the child's disorder, social learning theory, and behavior management principles
(b) establishing a home/school daily report card/establishing a home behavior checklist/rewarding home and school behavior
(c) attending to appropriate behavior (e.g., compliance) and ignoring minor, inappropriate behaviors (e.g., whining)
(d) giving effective commands and reprimands
(e) establishing and enforcing rules/When . . . then contingencies
(f) time-out procedures
(g) home point system-reward and response cost
(h) enforcing contingencies outside of the home; planning ahead for misbehavior outside the home
(i) problem-solving techniques
(j) maintenance of program after weekly therapist contact ends.

Parent training is particularly important during preschool years because prosocial and desirable behaviors as well as maladaptive and undesirable behaviors are established during this developmental period. Several structured parent training programs have demonstrated success in decreasing disruptive behavior in preschool children with ADHD, including the *Triple Programme* (Sanders, Markie-Dadds, Turner, & Ralph, 2004), the *Incredible Years Programme* (Jones, Daley, Hutchings, Bywater, & Eames, 2007), and the *New Forest Parenting Programme* (Sonuga-Barke, Thompson, Abikoff, Miller Brotman, & Klein, 2006). These programs encourage the development of parenting skills that promote positive parent–child interactions and strategies for setting boundaries and managing negative behavior.

Furthermore, adults may serve an important role in the development of attention and regulatory abilities in young children at risk for attention deficits and poor regulatory control (Davis & Williams, 2011). *Scaffolding* is a term that has been used to describe these supportive parenting behaviors (Robinson, Burns, & Davis, 2009). Parents provide only enough assistance, by offering suggestions, hints, and prompts, to allow the child to successfully complete the task at hand. Gradually, the parent withdraws support and the child takes over regulatory and attention functions.

Behavioral parent training has been evaluated as a well-established treatment for ADHD with substantial evidence of efficacy in improving child, parent, and family functioning (Fabiano, Pelham et al., 2009; Pelham & Fabiano, 2008). Specifically, this intervention results in improvements in several important areas, more notably parent ratings of oppositional and aggressive behavior and observed negative parent–child interaction. It may also increase positive parenting, reduce parent stress, and enhance parent self-efficacy (Pfiffner & Haack, 2014). It has been suggested that behavioral parent interventions may be beneficial even for children as young as 3 years old (Mulqueen, Bartley, & Bloch, 2015). However, according to several meta-analyses, there is no objective documentation of an effect on ADHD symptoms (Rimestad et al., 2016). Given the multifaceted nature of ADHD, this finding is quite understandable if parent training is delivered as a single component treatment.

The MTA study (see Section 11.4) revealed that for families showing the greatest reductions in power-assertive, harsh, and inconsistent/ineffective disciplinary practices, effects of combined medication plus behavioral treatment were pronounced so that teacher-reported disruptive behavior patterns and social behavior in the school setting were essentially normalized (Hinshaw et al., 2000). Other studies showed that parent training programs are more efficacious for parents who attend regularly training sessions but also apply newly acquired skills in real life (Clarke et al., 2015; Nix et al., 2009).

Although parent training is effective in treating a variety of child behavior problems associated with ADHD, not all families benefit from this form of treatment. It has been found that nearly half of families experience less positive outcomes (Nock & Ferriter, 2005). Barriers to optimal treatment response include maternal depression, single parenthood, and parental ADHD (Chronis et al., 2004). Furthermore, socioeconomic factors and family adversity have been found to negatively influence treatment outcome (Reyno & McGrath, 2006).

In case parents of children with ADHD experience psychopathology such as DDs, ADs, or SUD, they usually find it even more difficult to consistently manage child disruptive behavior (Johnston et al., 2012). Distressed individuals often lack the motivation or organization to complete effortful tasks that require ongoing work, such as the consistent implementation of behavioral management techniques (Chronis et al., 2006). Consequently, unless parental psychopathology is addressed prior to behavioral parent training, it is unlikely that parents will be able to make changes in their behavior management techniques (Chronis et al., 2004).

Parental ADHD may be a particular concern for understanding less optimal parent training outcomes, as at least 25% of children with ADHD have a parent with ADHD (Chronis et al., 2003). Parents who have difficulty with their own behavioral self-regulation are more likely to fail to manage child disruptive behavior. Parents with ADHD display higher levels of inconsistent discipline and less frequent monitoring. Furthermore, they provide a less organized and structured environment for their children. It has been found that maternal ADHD reduces the effectiveness of parent training for preschoolers with ADHD (Sonuga-Barke, Daley, & Thompson, 2002). Therefore, treatment of parental ADHD should be a first priority in order to improve outcomes of parent training (Hinshaw, 2009). However, other studies showed that these parents can also benefit considerably from parent behavioral training (Babinski, Waxmonsky, & Pelham, 2014).

11.3.1.2 School-Based Interventions

Treatments for ADHD should be implemented in each setting where the child exists in order to maximize positive outcomes. Given that school is a very important part of children's life, school-based interventions are an indispensable and empirically supported component of ADHD treatments (Chronis et al., 2006).

Students with ADHD typically exhibit a variety of difficulties with school functioning in both academic and behavioral domain. Problems in school are a key feature of ADHD, often bringing these children to clinical attention. Many of the core symptoms of ADHD interfere with a child's classroom behavior and ability to learn, resulting in lower academic achievement and impaired functioning (Chronis et al., 2006). Therefore, school is the ideal setting where behavioral interventions can be implemented and yield positive outcomes. Furthermore, teachers need to have a rudimentary knowledge of medication use among children with ADHD.

School-based interventions require adherence, cooperation, and co-ordination among family, professionals, and teachers to achieve optimal outcomes. These interventions integrate behavior modification and cognitive-behavioral techniques, adapted for application in the classroom setting to assist teachers and students to gain control of behavior at school (DuPaul, Helwig, & Slay, 2011; Miranda, Presentación, & Soriano, 2002; Miranda, Jarque, & Rosel, 2006).

A school-based behavioral intervention usually begins with psychoeducation about ADHD, so that teachers become able to recognize ADHD symptoms and modify maladaptive causal attributions about deliberate defiant behavior, indifference, or laziness on behalf of the child. Then, identification of specific target behaviors follows, based upon an FBA (see Section 10.4.4). The next stage refers to defining and prioritizing goals, depending on the child's developmental level and according to the principles of gradual shaping of behavior. Finally, teachers are instructed to use specific techniques adapted for classroom management (Chronis et al., 2006). Recent enhancements of behavioral classroom management strategies have also equipped teachers to foster peer relationships among children with ADHD (Mikami et al., 2013).

A meta-analysis of 63 studies from 1971 to 1995 showed that behavioral school-based interventions are particularly effective in treating inappropriate behaviors exhibited by children with ADHD in the school setting (DuPaul & Eckert, 1997). A more recent meta-analysis, which evaluated the effects of school-based interventions for students with ADHD by examining 60 outcome studies between 1996 and 2010, led to similar conclusions (DuPaul, Eckert, & Vilardo, 2012). This meta-analysis highlighted that school-based interventions should also address skill and performance deficits in students with ADHD.

Interventions directly addressing academic deficits are necessary because students with ADHD often experience difficulties with development of core reading and math skills. Academic interventions may also be considered preventative, as improvements in academic performance may be associated with enhancement of behavior control (DuPaul, 2007).

It should be noted, however, that beneficial treatment effects rely on the consistent use of behavior modification techniques by teachers. Level of intervention integrity is positively correlated with degree of effectiveness (Hirschstein, Van Schoiack Edstrom, Frey, Snell, & MacKenzie, 2007). Teachers vary widely in their investment and implementation of school-based interventions for children with ADHD, and sometimes they are resistant to implement such programs as intended (Biggs, Vernberg, Twemlow, Fonagy, & Dill, 2008; Chronis et al.,

2006). It has also been found that teacher implementation of these interventions is generally poor, and tends to decline after the initial phases of intervention (Noell et al., 2005). Consequently, assessing teacher engagement before intervention is necessary in that relatively low ratings of engagement may suggest the need for strategies to provide additional support for teachers to elicit greater investment (Power et al., 2009).

Evidence is accumulating to support the effectiveness of behavioral interventions that promote collaboration between family and school (Power & Mautone, 2008). The assumption underlying such collaborative partnerships is that appropriate behavior at school can be reinforced by rewards delivered at home, an environment that has a wider variety of highly salient reinforcers (DuPaul, 2007). Moreover, daily parent–school communication through a structured collaborative process enhances the relationship between parents and teachers, who work as partners aiming at mutually identifying, defining, analyzing, and addressing student concerns with the support of a professional (Sheridan et al., 2017). These combined interventions have been found to be effective for addressing academic performance deficits, behavioral problems, and social skills (Sheridan & Kratochwill, 2008; Power, Soffer, Clarke, & Mautone, 2006).

11.3.2 Cognitive-Behavioral Interventions

Cognitive-behavioral interventions are based on a scientific understanding of the complex interplay of thoughts, feelings, and behavior, emphasizing their modification in the mediation of new learning (Knouse, 2015). These approaches aim at identifying and modifying maladaptive ways of thinking, improving self-regulation and cognitive reappraisal, and helping individuals with ADHD learn and use specific compensatory skills in their daily life to ameliorate symptom-related deficits. They are based on the rationale that behavioral self-control can be increased by enhancing specific cognitive and metacognitive skills that are believed to underlie and promote impulse control and goal-oriented behavior (Hinshaw, 2006; Pelham, Wheeler, & Chronis, 1998).

In our view, cognitive restructuring, namely identifying and altering unhelpful belief systems, is an indispensable component of a multilevel approach to treatment. Cognitions including both attributions regarding child behavior and expectations regarding treatment are particularly important to address because the way in which parents and children interpret various behaviors determines how they respond to them.

In cognitive-behavioral interventions, individuals are taught problem solving, cognitive restructuring, and motivational strategies, such as self-talk, self-monitoring, and self-reinforcement, to develop self-control and rule-governed behavior (Purdie, Hattie, & Carroll, 2002). Furthermore, they include direct skills training of cognitive skills, including attention and working memory, and are directly related to the theoretical conceptualizations of ADHD (Toplak et al., 2008).

For example, a recent study showed that positive reinforcement improved sustained attention and vigilance in school-aged children with ADHD, and this effect was comparable to that obtained with a therapeutic dose of MPH (Bubnik, Hawk, Pelham, Waxmonsky, & Rosch, 2015). This finding is consistent with the Dynamic Developmental theory of ADHD (Sagvolden, Johansen et al., 2005), which associates difficulties in sustained attention with altered reinforcement sensitivity in individuals with ADHD (see Section 6.5).

Finally, cognitive-behavioral interventions often target several secondary symptoms of ADHD, including low self-esteem, demoralization related to repeated failures, and peer problems. Therefore, individual CBT may help the individual cope with the secondary emotional consequences of ADHD and manage everyday life situations more effectively (Hinshaw, 2009).

Evidence for the efficacy of cognitive-behavioral interventions for ADHD is equivocal. A controlled study suggested that it could be a promising intervention for the treatment of the core symptoms of ADHD in children (Froelich, Doepfner, & Lehmkuhl, 2002). However, negative findings have also been reported (Fehlings, Roberts, Humphries, & Dawe, 1991).

11.3.3 Social Skills Training

Impairment in peer relationships is one of the hallmark characteristics of children with ADHD. Common manifestations include children's high rejection and low acceptance in their peer group, and their tendency to have fewer reciprocated friendships. Children with ADHD are approximately four times more likely to be rejected by their peers relative to typical children, and they are about half as likely to have close friendships (Hoza et al., 2005). It is now widely accepted that a major contributing factor to the peer problems of children with ADHD is their largely unrestrained interaction style, characterized by several forms of controlling behavior that make them highly aversive to peers (Hoza et al., 2005). In peer-to-peer play interactions, children with ADHD have difficulty with sharing, supporting, responding to social cues, cooperative play, and perspective-taking. Additionally, they are usually more self-focused when negotiating compared to peers (Cordier, Bundy, Hocking, & Einfeld, 2010; Normand et al., 2011).

Peer problems of children with ADHD are of concern because they incrementally increase the likelihood that these children will experience a range of behavioral and mental health problems over time (Mikami & Normand, 2015). For example, it was found that childhood peer rejection was uniquely predictive of depression, delinquency, heavy smoking, substance abuse, school dropout, academic difficulties, and general impairment in middle adolescence (Mrug et al., 2012). Furthermore, peer rejection may actually exacerbate ADHD symptoms over the course of a year (Tseng, Kawabata, Gau, & Crick, 2014). It has been suggested that peer problems contribute to functional impairment by (a) increasing children's loneliness, which contributes to depression and anxiety; (b) leading children to dislike school, which hampers academic learning and encourages delinquency; and (c) depriving children of valuable opportunities to develop or practice social skills (Mikami & Normand, 2015).

The difficulty of children with ADHD in making and keeping friendships has been explained in terms of the social skills deficit model, which attributes peer rejection to social skills knowledge or performance deficits, and posits that teaching social skills will result in amelioration of peer problems (deBoo & Prins, 2007). Therefore, it has been suggested that socially incompetent children need a social skills training.

Social skills knowledge deficits refer to deficiencies in social cognition, namely the thought processes one uses in order to understand and relate to other people (Uekermann et al., 2010). For example, it has been found that children with ADHD often have difficulty interpreting accurately peers' intentions in ambiguous or conflict situations. As a result, they may exhibit ineffective responses (Thurber, Heller, & Hinshaw, 2002). Another social-cognitive deficit concerns the goals of children with ADHD in peer interactions, as they seem to prioritize attention seeking at the expense of rules and fairness (Melnick & Hinshaw, 1996). Other relevant deficits refer to the difficulty of children with ADHD in inferring cause-and-effect relationships between story events (Lorch, Milich, Astrin, & Berthiaume, 2006) and in understanding peers' emotions and perspectives (Marto et al., 2009). Finally, children with ADHD, inattentive type may have particular difficulty paying attention to social cues, for example, that peers are bored, so they fail to ask them if they want to play something else (Mikami, 2015).

Social skills training is typically therapist-led instruction to children about appropriate social behavior and is intended to target the deficits thought to be maintaining the peer problems of children with ADHD (Mikami & Normand, 2015). Specifically, children are trained to label peers' emotions accurately, interpret their intentions correctly, and find effective solutions to problematic social situations (de Boo & Prins, 2007). Common skills taught are sharing, keeping a conversation, joining groups of peers, following the rules of games, taking turns, calming down when upset, and identifying emotions (Pfiffner, 2008).

However, efficacy of traditional social skills training is limited because these skills do not seem to generalize out of the clinical setting, and long-term effects have not been established (de Boo & Prins, 2007). In addition, they seem more beneficial for children with ADHD, inattentive type, because they are less driven by oppositional defiant behavior and emotional regulation difficulties (Evans et al., 2014; Fabiano, Pelham et al., 2009).

A possible explanation is that the theoretical underpinnings of these interventions do not reflect current theoretical conceptualizations of ADHD. These interventions are based on the view that children with ADHD are characterized by social incompetence because they lack the appropriate skills to perform adequately on social tasks. However, it seems that the main difficulty of children with ADHD, combined type, is not an acquisition deficit, namely lack of particular social skills in their behavioral repertoire, but a performance deficit, namely failure to apply the social skills they possess in specific real-life situations. In other words, it is possible that children with ADHD possess social skills but fail to apply them in specific social situations due to difficulty in inhibiting various verbal, motoric, and affective competing impulses in the heat of the moment (Huang-Pollock, Mikami, Pfiffner, & McBurnett, 2009; Tseng & Gau, 2013).

Besides, deficits in self-regulation have been found to underlie disruptions in socializing because regulatory processes serve to modulate the reactivity of the individual (de Boo & Prins, 2007). Barkley (1997c) postulated that children with ADHD would demonstrate immediate emotional reactivity to emotionally charged events and fewer anticipatory emotions toward future events due to decreased capacity for forethought.

Therefore, social difficulties of children with ADHD cannot be overcome through training but through immediate reinforcement of desirable social behaviors by significant adults, including parents and teachers (Pfiffner, 2008). Parents may create social contexts for their children by networking with other families and by organizing playdates between their child and peers. They can also assist and encourage the child to practice the newly learned skills outside the clinical setting because they can provide direct and on-the-spot reinforcement for adaptive social behavior. Consequently, adaptive social behavior can mediate peer acceptance, leading to an improvement of social contact with peers (de Boo & Prins, 2007). It has also been empirically verified that active parental involvement in the training that the child is receiving has greater efficacy relative to interventions that focus exclusively on the child (Frankel, Myatt, Cantwell, & Feinberg, 1997; Pfiffner & McBurnett, 1997; Sheridan, Dee, Morgan, McCormick, & Walker, 1996). For example, the Parental Friendship Coaching (PFC) intervention instructs parents in order to become "friendship coaches" for their children with ADHD (Mikami, Lerner, Griggs, McGrath, & Calhoun, 2010). Unlike typical social skills training interventions, this approach has no child treatment component and instead focuses on training the parents to address peer group factors.

An additional explanation for the poor efficacy of the traditional social skills training approach is that it focuses exclusively on the characteristics of children with ADHD that contribute to social rejection by their peers and neglects the contribution of the peer group to these social problems. However, the social context in which peer interactions occur also influences rejection and is a factor impeding change (Mikami, Lerner, & Lun, 2010; Mikami & Normand, 2015). When typically developing children have cognitive biases against children whom they dislike, they are often resistant to changing their attitudes even in the face of improved behavior by the disliked children (Mrug, Hoza, Pelham, Gnagy, & Greiner, 2007). Thus, the negative reputation of children with ADHD within the peer group persists even after their behavior has changed. For instance, peers interpret the ambiguous behaviors of children whom they dislike as hostile in intent and interpret the ambiguous behaviors of children whom they like as benign (Peets, Hodges, Kikas, & Salmivalli, 2007).

Consequently, through the mechanism of self-fulfilling prophecy, peers' negative judgments about children with ADHD may actually lead peers to treat these children in a fashion that elicits poorer social skills from them (Mikami, 2015). The social psychology literature documents the occurrence of expectancy effects, by which individuals presume that outgroup members will be unfriendly and therefore unconsciously elicit evidence that confirms this expectation (Hilton & von Hippel, 1996).

It has been suggested that for social skills to be established and employed in the natural setting once they are learned, these skills must be reinforced by the peers in that setting (Hoza et al., 2005). Therefore, adjunctive procedures to help peers reduce social devaluation of ADHD symptoms, exclusionary behaviors, and reputational biases may be needed to maximize sociometric improvement (Mikami et al., 2013). A recent development in this area is the Play-Based Intervention, which used the context of play and a child treatment component with parent- and peer-mediated components. This intervention was demonstrated to be effective for improving the social play skills of children with ADHD aged 5 to 11 years in peer-to-peer interactions (Wilkes-Gillan, Bundy, Cordier, Lincoln, & Chen, 2016).

The role of the teacher is particularly important in enhancing relationships among children with ADHD and their typically developing peers. Interventions that focus on training teachers to increase peers' inclusiveness toward children with ADHD, by also addressing peers' negative social and affective judgments, show very positive outcomes (Mikami et al., 2013). Making Socially Accepting Inclusive Classrooms (MOSAIC) is a classroom-based intervention, designed by Mikami and colleagues (2013), administered by teachers in order to encourage peers to be more socially inclusive and welcoming of children with ADHD. Teachers are trained to provide warm versus frustrated responses to children with ADHD in order to provide peers with cues about whether ADHD behaviors should be socially devalued and whether children with ADHD symptoms should be rejected. Teachers are also trained to help the peer group to refrain from excluding children with ADHD. Finally, teachers are instructed to draw peer's attention to positive characteristics of children with ADHD, in order to address the negative cognitive biases that peers frequently possess toward these children.

In conclusion, it seems that traditional interventions for the development of social skills in children with ADHD have limited efficacy. Current recommendations point to the necessity of parent training, so that parents become their child's coaches for effective use of social skills in everyday real-life situations. The importance of training teachers is also highlighted, in order to support the child with ADHD, create a climate of acceptance and support, and enhance peer inclusion.

11.4 Comparison Between Pharmacological and Psychosocial Interventions

Worldwide use of stimulant medication for the treatment of ADHD has significantly increased over the last decades (Singh, 2008). In the United States, the prevalence of stimulant use among individuals with ADHD under 18 years of age increased threefold to sevenfold between 1987 and 1996 (Zito et al., 2003) and from 2.8% to 4.4% between 2000 and 2005 (Castle, Aubert, Verbrugge, Khalid, & Epstein, 2007). Another study documented an annual growth rate of stimulant use of 3.4% in children under 18 years from 1996 to 2008 (Zuvekas &

Vitiello, 2012). This overall increase raised global concerns and led to public and political debates regarding issues like the potential overdiagnosis and overtreatment of ADHD and the possibility that the use of stimulants by children is addictive (Buitelaar & Rothenberger, 2004; Safer, 2000; Rey & Sawyer, 2003).

However, data from the National Health and Nutrition Examination Survey suggest that half of the children with ADHD who participated in the study had not received any kind of treatment (Merikangas et al., 2010). Consequently, it is suggested that there is little scientific evidence to support concerns of ADHD overmedication in children (Connor, 2011). However, others argue that the debate as to whether ADHD medication is overprescribed still continues, as the number of prescriptions of these drugs is rising every year (Grosswald, 2015). It is noted that by 2004, the market for ADHD-related drugs in the United States had grown to over $3 billion annually and reached $13 billion in 2015 (Grosswald, 2015).

An important concern with respect to long-term stimulant treatment is the possibility that exposure to stimulant medications early in life could lead to the development of sensitization and cross-sensitization, which may facilitate the abuse of other similar substances (Barkley, Fischer, Smallish, & Fletcher, 2003; Biederman, Wilens, Mick, Spencer & Faraone, 1999). The majority of studies is reassuring and in favor of the view that treating ADHD with stimulants does not increase the risk of SUDs (Fredriksen et al., 2013; Humphreys et al., 2013). Some studies concluded that stimulant medication may even protect children with ADHD from developing a SUD (Groenman et al., 2013; Wilens, Faraone et al., 2003). However, this finding is not corroborated by other studies, which demonstrated no link between prior pharmacotherapy for ADHD and subsequent SUDs (Humphreys et al., 2013).

Prescription of medication to preschoolers with ADHD raises serious concerns because the effects of medication on the developing brain of very young children are not well understood (Parritz & Troy, 2014). Besides, the Preschool ADHD Treatment Study found that the efficacy of stimulants is decreased among preschoolers compared with school-aged children (Greenhill et al., 2006). Furthermore, the side-effect burden, including emotional outbursts, irritability, sleep difficulties, proneness to cry, repetitive behaviors/thoughts, and appetite loss, may be greater in preschoolers than that experienced by older children (Taylor et al., 2004; Wigal et al., 2006). As a result, neither MPH nor most medications that are commonly used for ADHD are approved by the U.S. FDA for children younger than 6 years (Davis & Williams, 2011).

Moreover, approximately 90% of teenagers discontinue ADHD medication before 18 years of age. As a result, this population is especially likely to forgo treatment and experience difficulties during a risky developmental period (McCarthy et al., 2009; Molina et al., 2009). Finally, many parents do not accept medication as a treatment option and seem to prefer psychosocial or alternative interventions (Berger et al., 2008).

A landmark, randomized clinical trial, known as the Multimodal Treatment Study of Children with ADHD (MTA), directly compared four distinct treatment strategies for 579 children aged 7 to 9.9 years with a diagnosis of ADHD, combined type: (a) systematic medication management; (b) multicomponent behavior therapy; (c) the combination of the first two interventions; and (d) usual community care (MTA Cooperative Group, 1999). At the end of the 14-month treatment phase, children in the combination and medication management groups showed significantly greater improvement in ADHD and ODD symptoms than those in behavior therapy and community care. Combination and medication management treatments did not differ significantly on any direct comparisons. Therefore, the first reports concluded that the medication management approach was superior to the behavior therapy and community care approaches for the reduction of ADHD core symptoms (MTA Cooperative Group, 1999).

This finding provided the scientific basis for the current clinical practice of stimulant monotherapy as the first-line intervention for school-aged children with ADHD in the United States

(Greenhill et al., 2002). On the basis of the MTA results, medication use for ADHD increased in Europe as well, even though European guidelines (National Institute for Health and Clinical Excellence, 2009) did not feature medication as a first-line treatment (Hinshaw et al., 2015).

However, additional analyses revealed that for composited outcomes of adult-rated symptoms, and particularly for functional impairment related to academic achievement, peer relationships, and parenting practices, the combined treatment was optimal (Conners, Epstein, & March, 2001; Swanson et al., 2001). Moreover, the addition of behavioral treatment to medication was necessary for complex cases with comorbid disorders (Foster et al., 2007). Finally, when accompanied by clinical significant improvements in parenting style, combined treatment yielded not just improvement but even normalization of behavioral problems at school (Hinshaw et al., 2000).

Besides, approximately half of the initial advantage of medication and combined intervention had dissipated by the first follow-up evaluation, 10 months after the termination of treatment. By the next follow-up, 3 years after enrollment, although the improvements over baseline for children in all four groups were maintained, the relative advantage associated with the intensive 14-month medication had dissipated. Follow-up assessments at 6 and 8 years after initial enrollment showed that the positive effects of the ADHD treatments had been minimized and the differential effects of treatments had attenuated (Molina et al., 2009; MTA Cooperative Group, 2004). This finding may reveal that medications targeting dopamine and norepinephrine neurotransmission may have an "expiration date" with respect to their efficacy over the course of continuous administration (Hinshaw, Arnold and the MTA Cooperative Group, 2015).

In conclusion, additional analyses of the MTA study revealed that the initial conclusion that medication alone was the best treatment of ADHD was erroneous and that eventually the combination of medication and behavioral intervention was superior to medication alone (Smith & Shapiro, 2015).

Furthermore, a recent study concluded that the sequence in which medication and behavioral interventions for ADHD are implemented is of great importance for the treatment's efficacy (Pelham et al., 2016). Treatment initiated with behavioral interventions was found to produce better outcomes than treatment initiated with medication. In the face of inadequate response to initial behavioral treatment, either more intensive behavioral intervention or the addition of a low dose of medication could produce improved outcomes. The simultaneous introduction of conditions in the combined treatment group in the MTA makes it impossible to evaluate whether a behavioral intervention employed before medication would have prevented the need for medication or reduced the dosage needed. Consequently, the failure to begin behavioral treatment before medication may have contributed to the relatively small advantage of combined treatment to medication alone in the MTA study. Additionally, ceiling effects may have occurred, in which the potential added benefit of psychosocial treatment could not be observed due to high rates of medication use in the control group (Haack et al., 2016). Pelham and colleagues (2016) conclude that reconsideration of the current practice of relying on medication as first-line and typically sole treatment for many children with ADHD is needed. It has been suggested that beginning treatment with a low dose of behavior modification is, by definition, the most cost-effective approach in treating children with ADHD (Page et al., 2016).

A meta-analysis of 26 studies published between 1985 and 2006 compared the effect of MPH, psychosocial interventions, and their combinations on ADHD (Van der Oord et al., 2008). Results suggested that although medication seems to be the most effective method in treating the core symptoms of ADHD, psychosocial interventions are very effective with regard to social behavior and parent rated ODD. Furthermore, a recent study aiming at evaluating the quality of 21 systematic reviews and meta-analyses conducted for psychosocial treatments of ADHD from 1998 to 2010 indicated that although psychosocial treatments contribute to improvements on behavioral and social outcomes, the interplay of ADHD and SLD in treatment outcomes in learning difficulties is largely unexplored (Watson, Richels, Michalek, & Raymer, 2015). Therefore, targeted interventions for learning disabilities in children with ADHD are largely needed.

Finally, children with comorbid difficulties are not likely to respond to a single treatment (Hinshaw, 2009). Besides, it is possible that the medication recommended for ADHD be contraindicated for the comorbid disorders.

In our opinion, which is consistent with a great number of professionals around the world, medication should not be the first-line treatment for ADHD, particularly for children. Medication cannot teach abilities and skills and should be offered only as a part of a comprehensive and multilevel treatment plan that includes a combination of psychosocial interventions (National Institute for Health and Clinical Excellence, 2009; Pliszka, 2007). The treatment goal for ADHD should be not only temporary symptom relief but also the establishment of a more favorable long-term developmental trajectory (Fredriksen et al., 2013; Pelham & Gnagy, 1999). Intervention does not equal reducing problem behavior but includes facilitating problem solving, planning, error correction, academic performance, and social skills to yield real impact on the quality of life of individuals with ADHD (Hinshaw et al., 2015). A treatment regimen that includes only medication cannot attain these goals and is not a viable treatment strategy for ADHD, as it confers no long-term benefit (Molina et al., 2009).

Psychosocial interventions address aspects of ADHD that medications cannot, such as skill and functional deficits, environmental stressors, or relational conflicts that exacerbate difficulties (Schoenfelder & Sasser, 2016). Consequently, psychosocial interventions are appropriate as a first and primary intervention for children with ADHD, and medication should be added as an adjunct when indicated (Pelham & Fabiano, 2008). In our view, a combination of psychosocial interventions provided within the framework of a multilevel approach is a clearly challenging path. However, this is currently best practice that can lead to generalized positive long-lasting change, given the lack of significant benefits of time-limited single interventions. Systematic multimodal and well-rounded treatments of ADHD, tailored to the individual's specific needs and implemented consistently over the long term in all settings in which impairments are present, have the potential to maximize the success of the intervention (Jensen et al., 2007; Young & Amarasinghe, 2010).

On the other hand, when more severe symptomatology or comorbidity are present, and when children and families do not respond adequately to psychosocial interventions, medication is an important means of enhancing the efficacy of these interventions. Medication can contribute to the reduction of the core ADHD symptoms, thus leading to better cooperation and adherence to psychosocial treatments.

According to Barkley (1998a), the factors that should be considered in the decision to employ medication for children with ADHD are the following: (a) the child's age; (b) duration and severity of symptoms; (c) the risk of injury to the child; (d) the success of previous interventions; (e) normal levels of anxiety; (f) the absence of stimulant abuse by the child or their parents; and (g) the likelihood that the parents will employ the medication responsibly, in compliance with physician recommendation.

In conclusion, we would like to stress that the empirical data concerning the efficacy of the predominant interventions for ADHD are particularly significant for the clinicians, who should take them into consideration when making treatment decisions. However, clinicians' experience and scientific perspective also play a decisive role in treatment planning. A move beyond data regarding the average efficacy of treatments is essential in order to identify the best treatment for each different and unique individual with ADHD. Besides, a recent development in psychiatry is ***personalized medicine***, which aims to provide the right treatment for the right person at the right time as opposed to the ***trial-and-error*** approach (Arns, Heinrich, & Strehl, 2014). In other words, the question "Which treatment is more effective for ADHD" is modified as follows: "Which treatment, delivered at which time intervals and at what levels of intensity is the most effective for the specific individual, in promoting maintained positive change across all areas of functioning?" Until evidence-based answers are given, this role is taken on by clinicians, reflecting their clinical experience and theoretical orientation. Beyond theories, empirical data, and statistical analyses that emerge in research laboratories, the degree of improvement that is eventually achieved in the clinical setting and the generalization of positive outcomes to the individual's everyday life are the most important factors in the evaluation of all interventions and therefore confirm or refute empirical data. Finally, it is up to each parent to entrust their child to the clinician who convinces them more and to evaluate the efficacy of intervention.

11.5 Alternative Interventions

11.5.1 The Need for Alternative Interventions

Current first-line interventions for childhood ADHD, including pharmacological and psychosocial interventions, aim at reducing the manifestation of primary symptoms, preventing secondary symptoms, and minimizing impairment. Despite their proven efficacy, it is now widely accepted that these interventions result in short-term benefits. Specifically, they are not associated with clinically significant gains in key areas of functioning, do not normalize behavior, are of negligible utility when not actively administered, seldom yield therapeutic benefits that are maintained over time, and do not generalize in all settings (Chacko et al., 2014).

The most important limitation of these interventions, however, is that they are not theoretically derived to address the underlying pathophysiology of recovery from ADHD (Antshel & Barkley, 2008; Rapport et al., 2015). For example, it has been found that children with ADHD exhibit a delay of approximately three years in attaining peak cortical thickness in prefrontal-frontal regions relative to typically developing children (Shaw et al., 2007). Therefore, activating these regions through stimulants or behavioral interventions may improve the core symptoms of ADHD but fails to improve processes related to more meaningful functional outcomes, such as academic performance and peer relationships. In addition, behavioral changes do not last over an extended time frame after treatment is withdrawn, due to the underdeveloped brain structures themselves and the cognitive functions these structures support (Rapport et al., 2015).

Consequently, the compelling need for therapeutic innovation is highlighted in order to develop effective nonpharmacologic interventions that will improve short- and long-term outcomes, and more directly address compensatory mechanisms associated with symptom recovery (Chacko, Kofler & Jarrett, 2014; Rapport, Orban, Kofler, Friedman, & Bolden, 2015; Sonuga-Barke, Brandeis, Holtmann, & Cortese, 2014).

11.5.2 Dietary Interventions

The idea that dietary interventions may modify the biochemistry of the brain and lead to symptom reduction spans for several decades, but research on the relationship between ADHD and diet has yielded inconsistent results.

A specific hypothesis that food additives, which include artificial food colorings, preservatives, and flavors, are etiologically associated with ADHD, via either allergenic or pharmacologic mechanisms, was introduced by Feingold (1975) in the 1970s and led to the promotion of an exclusion diet (see Sections 1.4.4 and 5.4.1). Feingold proposed a diet free of foods with a natural salicylate radical and all synthetic colors and flavors to treat hyperactivity. This diet, also referred to as the Kaiser Permanente diet, was welcome with great enthusiasm by the media and parental advocacy groups (Millichap & Yee, 2012; Nigg et al., 2012). Through the years, controlled studies failed to confirm the effectiveness of the diet to the extent claimed (Stevens, Kuczek, Burgess, Hurt, & Arnold, 2011). As a result, interest in food additives in relation to ADHD has waned in the United States. However, a meta-analysis of double-blind placebo-controlled trials concluded that there is evidence to support the theory that artificial food colors promote hyperactivity in already hyperactive children (Schab & Trinh, 2004). Since then, the Feingold diet shows an occasional, smoldering revival especially in the United Kingdom, Europe, and Australia (Millichap & Yee, 2012).

The relation of diet to ADHD has regained new interest in recent years. A provocative publication from Australia, the Raine study, supports that ADHD in adolescents may be associated with a "Western-style diet," which is high in fat, refined sugars, and sodium, and low in fibers, folic acid, and omega-3 fatty acids (Howard et al., 2011). Other researchers have tried to relate risk of ADHD with low-quality diets, even with lower adherence to specific traditional diets, such as the Korean (Woo et al., 2014) or the Mediterranean diet (Ríos-Hernández, Alda, Farran-Codina, Ferreira-García, & Izquierdo-Pulido, 2017).

The dietary changes that have been suggested as potential treatments of ADHD and have been tested in randomized clinical trials fall into two groups: (a) elimination interventions that remove elements from the diet (e.g., sugars, salicylic acid, gluten, corn, caffeine, artificial colorings, and preservatives); and (b) interventions that provide dietary supplements, including vitamins, minerals (zinc, iron, and magnesium), and omega-3 polyunsaturated fatty acids.

Food elimination diets vary in their specific content but take three main forms: (a) a single-food exclusion diet excludes one suspected food; (b) a multifood exclusion diet, such as the 6 Food Elimination diet, eliminates the most common food allergens; and (c) a few foods diet eliminates all but a few food items from the diet for a certain period (Nigg & Holton, 2014). This diet typically consists of two types of meat, two sources of carbohydrates, two vegetables, two fruits, oil and water (Carter et al., 1993). After a few weeks, food items are reintroduced in a controlled way to identify any specific food causing the child to react. The overall idea is to identify the food items to be avoided in each specific case and thus design an individual diet (Rytter et al., 2015).

The efficacy of diet treatments in ADHD was recently evaluated in three reviews that reached divergent conclusions (Nigg & Holton, 2014; Rytter et al., 2015; Stevenson et al., 2014). Elimination diets, either artificial food color exclusion or restricted food diets, seem to have positive but modest effects on ADHD symptoms, although they may be limited to children with ADHD with food sensitivities (Sonuga-Barke et al., 2013; Stevens et al., 2011). Therefore, restricted food diets could be helpful in managing ADHD in a clinically meaningful subset of cases and should continue to be investigated in high quality and bias-proof clinical trials (Nigg et al., 2012). A systematic review, conducted to synthesize meta-analytic results of diet interventions in children with ADHD in order to determine the effectiveness of diet treatments, showed that the effect sizes of the few foods diets are medium to large, possibly offering novel treatment opportunities (Pelsser, Frankena, Toorman, & Pereira, 2017).

However, it seems that these interventions have significant practical difficulties in their implementation. First, when eliminating some foods from the child's diet, it is important to add substitutions for nutritional balance. Furthermore, the implementation of such a dietary program requires a high degree of organization and structure, which is often difficult to achieve for the family of a child with ADHD. Finally, parents cannot always control their child's diet.

Consequently, the child may consume restricted foods at school or other settings. Oppositionality and limited self-control of children with ADHD could also pose barriers to the effective implementation of such interventions, especially in cases in which mealtimes are already challenging (Hurt & Arnold, 2015). It should be noted, however, that the removal of artificial food colors and other food additives from the diet of children seems to be beneficial not only for children with ADHD but for all children (Bateman et al., 2004; McCann et al., 2007).

The rationale for the dietary interventions that provide dietary supplements is that children with ADHD could have deficiencies in particular nutrients either because of a low intake or because of a higher requirement (Rytter et al., 2015). Among them, omega-3 fatty acid supplementation is one of the most studied alternative treatments for ADHD (Raz & Gabis, 2009).

Human infants require omega-6 and omega-3 fatty acids for neural development and to maintain neural integrity and function (Haag, 2003). Therefore, these fatty acids have been proclaimed as critical for intellectual growth and development in early childhood. Omega-3 fatty acids cannot be synthesized de novo by humans and must be sourced via the diet. The main dietary sources are fish, seals, and other kinds of seafood (Bloch & Qawasmi, 2011). Supplementation is usually achieved by administering a capsule containing oils or by introducing diets rich in fish products.

There is a concern that intake of omega-3 fatty acids has declined in the Western diet. It has been found that a high omega-6 to omega-3 ratio can alter cell membrane properties in the brain and cause inflammation (Simopoulos, 2002). By contrast, omega-3 fatty acids are anti-inflammatory. Therefore, it is speculated that increased omega-3 fatty acid concentration in the diet may alter the structure and function of the proteins that are embedded in CNS cell membrane fluidity and phospholipid composition, thus affecting serotonin and dopamine neurotransmission in the frontal cortex, which may impact directly on executive functioning (Bloch & Qawasmi, 2011; Gow & Hibbeln, 2014; Sinn & Bryan, 2007; Sinn, Bryan, & Wilson, 2008).

Some epidemiological studies have found associations between low seafood intake during pregnancy and the development of neurodevelopmental problems in children (Hibbeln et al., 2007). Furthermore, significantly lower plasma and blood concentrations of omega-3 fatty acids have been shown in children and adolescents with ADHD, suggesting that omega-3 fatty acid supplementation may reduce the attention and behavior problems associated with ADHD (Gillies, Sinn, Lad, Leach, & Ross, 2012).

Research results regarding the effectiveness of supplementation with polyunsaturated fatty acids on ADHD-related problems are inconclusive and often contradicting, with some studies making mention of "disappointing" and others of "hopeful" results. Recent meta-analyses show a small but statistically significant benefit of omega-3 fatty acid supplementation (Bloch & Qawasmi, 2011; Sonuga-Barke et al., 2013; Stevenson et al., 2014). Positive outcomes are reported with reference to core ADHD symptoms as well as to educational and behavioral problems (Richardson & Montgomery, 2005; Rytter et al., 2015). Recent findings provide initial evidence that omega-3 supplementation can also produce sustained reductions in internalizing and more general behavior problems (Raine, Portnoy, Liu, Mahhomed, & Hibbeln, 2015). However, given the small size of the beneficial effect reported, there is no suggestion at present that omega-3 supplementation should be considered a front-line treatment for ADHD but an adjunct to other more mainline treatments (Pelsser et al., 2017; Sonuga-Barke, 2015).

Recently, a combined intervention has been suggested with the administration of MPH and addition of omega-3/6 fatty acids into the diet. This intervention seems to allow for lower doses of MPH, contribute to the reduction of adverse effects, and improve treatment adherence compared with medication monotherapy (Barragán, Breuer & Döpfner, 2017). Finally, it has been found that children with ADHD whose parents reported no improvement after being treated with medication and behavioral therapy benefited from the supplementation of combined omega-3/6 fatty acids in both core ADHD symptoms and academic performance (Perera, Jeewandara, Senviratne, & Gurage, 2012).

In conclusion, research on the relationship between ADHD and nutrition has yielded inconsistent results and a dietary approach to ADHD treatment is still regarded as controversial without a comprehensive evidence base. Moreover, it is important to highlight that these interventions are supplementary, and under no circumstances can they substitute the mainline evidence-based treatments for ADHD.

11.5.3 Neurofeedback

In the search for complementary or alternative treatments for individuals with ADHD, neurofeedback emerged as a very promising option (Heinrich, Gevensleben, & Strehl, 2007). The most commonly used type of neurofeedback is based on EEG activity of the individual and is, therefore, also called EEG biofeedback. Neurofeedback is an operant conditioning procedure that aims at developing skills for self-regulation of brain activity and implementing these skills in daily life situations. In other words, it is a method of brain training based on real-time measurement and processing of electrical activity.

The first case study in which neurofeedback was used for the treatment of ADHD was conducted by Lubar and Shouse (1976), who applied neurofeedback in a child with hyperkinetic syndrome and found improvements in hyperactivity and distractibility. These findings were subsequently replicated several years later in a larger open label study (Shouse & Lubar, 1979). The first review of studies that had used neurofeedback was published in 2005 (Loo & Barkley, 2005). It reached the conclusion that although the reviewed studies claimed promising results, their methodological weaknesses did not permit to include neurofeedback in the evidence-based treatments of ADHD. Since then, a series of studies with significantly better and more reliable methodology has been carried out.

The growing acceptance of neurofeedback can be understood against the backdrop of an increased understanding of the neurodevelopmental basis of ADHD. The rationale for using neurofeedback as an intervention in ADHD derives from the conceptualization of ADHD as a disorder of neural regulation and underarousal. It is assumed that these neural deficiencies are amenable to change by repeated training of improved cortical (or subcortical) self-regulation, by making use of the brain's plasticity (Butnik, 2005; Holtmann, Sonuga-Barke, Cortese, & Brandeis, 2014).

ADHD is associated with two primary types of neurophysiologic abnormalities. Most individuals with ADHD demonstrate cortical hypoarousal, evidenced in excessive power recorded in theta frequencies and suppressed beta power over frontal and central midline regions. A minority of individuals with ADHD exhibit hyperarousal or no evidence of cortical slowing over these regions (Monastra, 2008). It has been argued that "signatures" of psychiatric conditions can be found based on these brain wave patterns (Butnik, 2005), with rates of sensitivity and specificity at 86% and 98%, respectively (Monastra et al., 1999).

In neurofeedback, the individual is trained to control particular brainwave patterns using electroencephalographic technology in order to achieve normal levels of brain waves. Therefore, it is a kind of functional brain activity modification, which enhances attention and concentration, providing a physiological means of self-control (Drechsler et al., 2007; Gevensleben et al., 2014).

Typically, three to five electrodes are attached to the scalp and are connected to an EEG that reads the brain waves. The procedure involves recording neural activity while the individual participates in a computer program that resembles a video game format. The EEG sends strong electrical signals to a computer, which in turn detects the EEG information and provides a visual or auditory display of activity in the targeted frequency band. Neurofeedback helps individuals with ADHD learn which brain waves are associated with sustained attention and teaches them to modify specific brainwaves associated with ADHD symptoms (Nooner, Leaberry, Keith, & Ogle, 2016).

Every time target neural activity is obtained, the individual is positively reinforced usually in the form of points earned and is then given a reward for earning a certain amount of points within each session (Gevensleben, Rothenberger, Moll, & Heinrich, 2012). After several sessions, it is hypothesized that a person will be able to produce the desired EEG brain waves through increased awareness of their own physiological processes (Loo & Barkley, 2005).

For obvious reasons, this treatment model seems to be particularly attractive to children (Gevensleben et al., 2014). Furthermore, given the fact that adolescents are monitored by adults less closely than younger children, and given the challenges associated with identifying salient rewards for adolescents, this treatment model may be particularly useful for youth in this age group (Evans et al., 2014).

Three basic types of training protocols are typically used in children with ADHD (Holtmann et al., 2014). The first one is a conventional protocol of theta/beta training that addresses tonic aspects of cortical arousal. It aims at increasing beta activity to target concentration and decreasing theta activity to target unfocused behavior (Egner & Gruzelier, 2004; Liechti et al., 2012). The second one is a protocol aimed at reducing hypermotoric symptoms and enhancing sensorimotor rhythm. Sometimes, it is used in addition to the theta-beta protocol (Russell-Chapin et al., 2013). The third one is aimed at modifying slow cortical potentials in order to regulate cortical excitation thresholds and is related to phasic regulation of cortical excitability (Christiansen, Reh, Schmidt, & Rief, 2014; Gevensleben et al., 2009). Recently, it has been suggested that a protocol modification aiming to increase beta and theta oscillatory power at the same time may have stronger therapeutic effects on executive functions in ADHD (Bluschke, Roessner, & Beste, 2016).

The efficacy of neurofeedback as treatment for ADHD is still debated. A series of studies provides evidence for positive effects of neurofeedback in children with ADHD, as decrease of behavioral problems and improved cognitive performance have been reported (Drechsler et al., 2007; Leins et al., 2007). A meta-analysis by Sonuga-Barke and colleagues (2013) demonstrated larger and significant effects by raters closest to the therapeutic setting, but diminishing and nonsignificant effects when blinded assessment was employed. A recent meta-analysis confirmed the beneficial effects of neurofeedback on core ADHD symptoms, when assessed by parents, and on inattention, when assessed by teachers (Micoulaud-Franchi et al., 2014). Other studies, however, found insufficient transfer of positive results to daily functioning and reported that training results were not related to behavioral changes (Janssen et al., 2016).

Several findings indicate normalization of neurophysiological EEG markers of ADHD (Bakhshayesh, Hansch, Wyschkon, Rezai, & Esser, 2011; Doehnert, Brandeis, Straub, Steinhausen, & Dreschler, 2008). According to a controlled fMRI study, neurofeedback appears to lead to normalization of neural activity within brain regions key to selective attention and response inhibition (Beauregard, & Lévesque, 2006). Another study employed high-density EEG recordings combined with source localization analyses using standardized low resolution brain electromagnetic tomography. According to the results, an 8-week theta/beta neurofeedback training was found to modulate medial frontal areas that are crucially involved in cognitive processes underlying impulsivity (Bluschke, Broschwitz, Kohl, Roessner, & Beste, 2016). However, it has been suggested that these beneficial effects might be explained by unspecific variables of the treatment setting, such as the reinforcement, which may in itself induce the production of cortical brain alterations in regions known to be involved in reinforcement processing (Holtmann et al., 2014).

An important advantage of neurofeedback over other interventions is the absence of severe or permanent side effects (Van Dongen-Boomsma, Vollebregt, Slaats-Willemse, & Buitelaar, 2013). Headaches and fatigue have been occasionally documented, which seem to be attributable to the intentional demands and associated muscular tension during training sessions (Nash, 2000). Another major advantage is the potential for sustained, long-term benefits after successful completion of treatment. Positive changes on the behavioral, neurophysiologic, and neuropsychological levels have been reported after as few as 20 and as many as 40 sessions of neurofeedback (Holtmann et al., 2014). It has been suggested that for sustained long-term change, neurofeedback may require up to 6 months of treatment (Fox, Tharp, & Fox, 2005). Positive outcomes have been reported to be stable 6 months after training. One study even reported stability 2 years after the end of treatment (Gani, Birbaumer, & Strehl, 2008). However, interpretation of these findings is complicated by the fact that most ratings of long-term effects were not blinded and thus subject to bias.

Some researchers suggest that neurofeedback reduces ADHD core symptoms and associated functional impairment to a similar extent as medication (Duric, Assmus, Gundersen, & Elgen, 2012; Meisel, Servera, Garcia-Banda, Cardo, & Moreno, 2014), whereas others have not found similar results (Geladé et al., 2016; Ogrim & Hestad, 2013). Other researchers suggest neurofeedback as a clinically effective module in combination with medication and psychosocial interventions within the framework of a multimodal treatment setting (Gevensleben et al., 2014; Loo & Makeig, 2012). It has been found that children receiving medication plus neurofeedback obtain higher benefits, namely higher values of cortical activation, better executive control, and a reduction of the observed symptomatology compared to children receiving medication alone (González-Castro, Cueli, Rodríguez, García, & Álvarez, 2016; Monastra, Monastra, & George, 2002). However, other studies showed similar behavioral improvements in children with ADHD receiving neurofeedback alone, stimulant medication, or combined stimulant medication and neurofeedback (Bink, van Nieuwenhuizen, Popma, Bongers, & van Boxtel, 2015; Van Dongen-Boomsma et al., 2013).

An interesting point of view regarding the effectiveness of neurofeedback has been expressed by Doehnert and colleagues (2008), who suggested that neurofeedback training should be regarded as a kind of behavioral psychotherapy, where positive expectations and the experience of self-efficacy are important nonspecific variables contributing to positive outcomes. Furthermore, parenting style may moderate the effectiveness of neurofeedback because children whose parents were systematically using reinforcement principles in their normal practice were more likely to demonstrate a reduction in the frequency of core ADHD symptoms following neurofeedback training than children of parents with a nonsystematic parenting style (Monastra et al., 2006).

Besides EEG-based neurofeedback, new neurofeedback techniques based on hemodynamic measures are emerging. On the one hand, functional near-infrared spectroscopy (NIRS) measures hemodynamic correlates of neural activity, with promising results (Marx et al., 2015; Mihara et al., 2012). In most NIRS studies, the comparison of children with ADHD to healthy controls in different executive functioning tasks showed altered prefrontal activity. Consequently, this method was supposed to lead to a more effective use of cognitive resources, similar to EEG-neurofeedback. In their pilot study, Marx and colleagues (2015) reported that NIRS-neurofeedback was effective in the reduction of the main symptoms of ADHD and possibly more time-effective in comparison to EEG-neurofeedback. However, this interpretation remains to be confirmed. On the other hand, real-time fMRI may also offer advantages in terms of targeting well-defined brain regions and opening the possibility for more rapid learning to regulate deep structures, such as the dopaminergic midbrain regions implicated in ADHD along with cortical regions (Holtmann et al., 2014).

In conclusion, in light of the most recent findings, better evidence from well-blinded, methodologically sound, and sensitive trials is required before neurofeedback can be supported as an evidence-based treatment for ADHD (Holtmann et al., 2014; Sonuga-Barke et al., 2013). Neurofeedback is a promising intervention because it provides a neurobiological means for the development of self-control, and the evidence is demonstrating some amelioration of performance on both cognitive and behavioral outcome measures.

11.5.4 Neurocognitive Training

ADHD is associated with a broad range of neuropsychological impairments, which involve several developmentally abnormal brain networks related to cognition, attention, emotion, and sensorimotor functions (Cortese et al., 2012). A growing evidence base suggests that many children with ADHD have significant deficits in aspects of executive functions (see Chapter 6). The executive functions that have been mostly investigated in neurocognitive training studies are working memory and sustained attention (Rapport et al., 2013). These developmentally deficient processes have been shown to contribute to core symptoms of ADHD as well as social problems and academic underachievement (Chacko et al., 2017; Kofler et al., 2011; Sarver et al., 2012).

Working memory is a limited capacity system for the temporary storage, rehearsal, processing, updating, and manipulating internally held information. This multicomponent system plays a significant role in guiding behavior and underlies the capacity to perform complex tasks, including learning, comprehension, reasoning, and planning (Rapport et al., 2015). The *working* (central executive) component of working memory, which involves mental processing, updating, and reordering internally held information for use in guiding behavior, as opposed to *memory* (storage-rehearsal), seems to be mostly related to ADHD. At least 81% of children with ADHD have deficits in this component (Rapport et al., 2015), which are functionally related to deficits in attention (Kofler, Rapport, Bolden, Sarver, & Raiker, 2010), impulsivity (Raiker, Rapport, Kofler, & Sarver, 2012), and hyperactivity (Rapport et al., 2009).

Sustained attention is a component of attention that refers to the ability to maintain a tonic state of alertness during prolonged mental activity. Approximately 33% to 55% of children with ADHD have deficits in sustained attention, which are closely associated with behavioral problems in class (Brocki, Tillman, & Bohlin, 2010; Epstein et al., 2003) and learning difficulties (Molina et al., 2009).

In current theories of ADHD, these deficits are conceptualized as pathophysiological mediating factors (endophenotypes) of pathways between the observed manifestations of the disorder on a behavioral level and its originating causes (Coghill, Nigg, Rothenberger, Sonuga-Barke, & Tannock, 2005). Therefore, these neuropsychological deficits constitute significant treatment targets because they sit between the etiopathogenesis and the development of ADHD. Neurocognitive training can strengthen the key brain networks implicated in ADHD and improve the cognitive processes they subserve, leading to improvement of related areas of functioning (Cortese et al., 2015). Therefore, neurocognitive training is defined as the process of improving cognitive functioning by means of intentional instruction, involving repetition, practice, and feedback (Jolles & Crone, 2012).

A central tenet of this intervention is that by improving the deficient neurocognitive functions that are related to ADHD, the benefits will generalize and transfer beyond the clinical setting. Resulting improvement is expected to transfer to untrained tasks that rely on nearly identical cognitive processes (near transfer), as well as to tasks that tap cognitive processes other than the trained ones (far transfer) (Rutledge, van den Bos, McClure, & Schweitzer, 2012). Generalizability of training benefits derives from the improvement of brain function at the neuronal level (Klingberg, 2010). Obviously, the ultimate objective of neurocognitive treatment is to demonstrate far transfer effects, given that the goal is not to improve the children's performance on laboratory-based tasks but to improve specific cognitive abilities and the functional outcomes that rely on these abilities (Shipstead, Redick, & Engle, 2012).

The idea of directly training cognitive deficits via a program designed to improve attention or working memory is rooted in cognitive rehabilitation for individuals suffering from a brain injury (Sohlberg & Mateer, 1987). In the first study to effectively use such a training program for children with ADHD, Kerns, Eso, and Thomson (1999) targeted attention and presumed that improvements would generalize to other domains beyond attention due to the broader function of the neural systems altered by the intervention.

The theoretical rationale for the use of neurocognitive training as a treatment for ADHD builds on contemporary developmental neuroscience. This approach is grounded on the notion of neuroplasticity and the reorganization of brain structure and neural functions in response to structured environmental experiences, which drive learning and promote the development of new cognitive skills (Sonuga-Barke et al., 2014). Neuroplasticity refers to the brain's ability to create new "pathways" (neurogenesis) and rearrange and expand existing ones (synaptogenesis) to improve neuronal communication. In other words, it is "the brain's solution to the challenge of integrating new information into its repertoire of neural networks" (Galvan, 2010, p. 887).

Age of training affects the utility of neurocognitive training, as neurological structures do not develop at the same rate from birth to adulthood (Galvan, 2010). It is also important to note that neuroplasticity of the brain differs among individuals, depending on genetic factors and prior environmental influences (Jolles & Crone, 2012). It seems that periods of increased brain sensitivity to the effects of training are not only influenced by age but also by brain maturation, which is associated with experience (Hensch, 2004; Munakata, Casey, & Diamond, 2004).

Neurocognitive training is usually based on structured activities that are provided through a computer. The duration of each training session, the number of sessions, and their frequency vary depending on the protocol employed, although they typically involve a large number of sessions spread over several weeks. The most widely used, commercially available computerized neurocognitive training programs for children with ADHD are the following: (a) *Cogmed Working Memory Training*; (b) *Captain's Log MindPower*; (c) *AIXTENT*; (d) *CogniPlus*; (e) *Locu Tour Acoustic*; (f) *Pay Attention!*; and (g) *RehaCom REMINDER* (partially computerized) (Sonuga-Barke et al., 2014). Computerized approaches are especially appropriate, given that the difficulty and intensity of the training is increased across the training regime to continually challenge the individual at the boundaries of their competence (Sonuga-Barke et al., 2014).

Neurocognitive training is a promising avenue for the improvement of underdeveloped neurocognitive functions. It has been demonstrated that neurocognitive training can change brain structures (Hoekzema et al., 2010; Klingberg, 2006) and density in dopamine receptors (McNab et al., 2009). Moreover, working memory training has shown effects on verbal and spatial working memory (Melby-Lervåg, & Hulme, 2013), and these effects generalized to improved sustained attention up to 6 months follow-up (Shinaver, Entwistle, & Söderqvist, 2014). Few studies have also shown improvements in academic abilities (Egeland, Aarlien, & Saunes, 2013; Gray et al., 2012), but there is no consensus yet as several newer studies had negative results (Chacko, Kofler & Jarrett, 2014; Redick et al., 2013). Attention training shows positive effects on vigilance and reading comprehension (Shalev, Tsal, & Mevorach, 2007).

However, three recent meta-analyses revealed minimal improvement on near-transfer measures of children's cognitive performance and on ADHD symptoms (Cortese et al., 2015;

Rapport et al., 2013; Sonuga-Barke et al., 2013). Although statistically significant effects on ADHD symptoms were found when raters were proximal to treatment delivery, these effects were reduced substantially when assessors were probably blind to treatment allocation. Furthermore, effects in terms of far transfer measures are also disputed.

An explanation provided is that currently available training programs do not target the neurocognitive mechanisms and processes most strongly associated with ADHD due to target misspecification (Chacko et al., 2014). For example, while most studies argue that they investigate the outcomes of neurocognitive training in working memory, they rely on tasks associated with short-term memory and not with central executive working memory. However, short-term memory deficits are minimally related to ADHD behavioral symptoms or functional impairments (Raiker et al., 2012).

Furthermore, these interventions focus on training a single domain of cognitive functioning in children with ADHD. However, most children with ADHD show deficits on multiple executive functions, related to different brain regions. Therefore, training of multiple executive functions might be a potentially more effective strategy to reduce executive functioning-related ADHD symptoms (Dovis, Van der Oord, Wiers, & Prins, 2015). For example, a recent randomized clinical trial reported positive effects of a cognitive computerized program that aimed to improve eight different cognitive functions (Bikic, Leckman, Lindschou, Christensen, & Dalsgaard, 2015).

Besides, given the clinical and pathophysiological heterogeneity of ADHD, inconsistencies in far transfer effects might be due to the fact that only certain subgroups of individuals with ADHD benefit from neurocognitive training (Van der Donk, Hiemstra-Beernink, Tjeenk-Kalff, van der Leij, & Lindauer, 2016; Sonuga-Barke et al., 2014). Specifically, neurocognitive interventions cannot be effective for those individuals with ADHD who do not have executive functions deficits (Willcutt et al., 2012). Consequently, consideration should be given to the role of baseline executive functions deficits in response to neurocognitive interventions (Chacko et al., 2017). Training regimens tailored to target the specific neuropsychological deficits experienced by individuals with ADHD as well as motivational and energetic deficits may be more effective (Sonuga-Barke et al., 2014).

Finally, it has been found that treatment outcome measures of neurocognitive interventions for children with ADHD can be influenced by initial cognitive abilities and clinical variables, including ADHD presentation and comorbidity. Consequently, neurocognitive training is not a "one size fits all" treatment (Van der Donk et al., 2016).

To date, evidence for corroborated core effects of neurocognitive training on ADHD remains inconsistent. Therefore, research moves toward the development of next-generation neurocognitive training protocols, which should intensely target core underdeveloped neurocognitive functions most closely related to ADHD. Future neurocognitive interventions should take into consideration developmental issues, including child age, their particular pattern of neurocognitive strengths and weaknesses, and the timing of developmentally sensitive periods for neural development. Furthermore, given the diverse developmental pathways to ADHD (Nigg, 2006), it may be beneficial to identify specific neurocognitive profiles at the individual level and tailor neurocognitive training approaches to these specific profiles. Finally, these interventions should lead to generalization of effects beyond the clinical setting (Rutledge et al., 2012).

In order to maximize potential outcomes, a combined targeted neurocognitive plus social skills treatment is suggested, requiring from parents and teachers to provide additional behavioral practice in real context. As Rapport, Chung, Shore, and Isaacs (2001) note, glasses allow children with farsightedness to see the printed letters and benefit from classroom instruction, but the glasses themselves do not teach children how to read. Similarly, strengthening neurocognitive functioning is expected to improve the child's potential due to the improved cortical foundation, but it may not sufficiently affect important areas of behavioral, peer, family, and academic functioning. Therefore, changing the trajectory of ADHD-related impairments requires targeted, individualized, skill-focused interventions (Chacko et al., 2014; Chacko et al., 2017; Neville et al., 2013).

11.6 Early Intervention and Secondary Prevention of ADHD

According to our clinical experience, a common view among parents is that delays in child language development, motor clumsiness, social ineptitude, or difficulties in concentrating constitute no reason to worry before the age of 5–6 years at the earliest. Parents, preschool educators, and often pediatricians usually attribute these difficulties to "immaturity" and believe that the child will overcome them on their own as they grow older. This view is even more widespread for boys, on account of the predominant view that "boys generally mature later than girls." Most parents usually seek professional help upon entry into formal schooling. Meanwhile, these difficulties may have become more complex, and time limits for their "automatic remission" have been dramatically reduced.

Many teachers and professionals also encourage parents to wait and not rush into considering treatment for their child's difficulties in order to avoid "stigmatization" or "traumatization" of the child. We would like to comment that if something can be "stigmatizing" or "traumatizing" for a child, is the disadvantageous position in which they may be placed among their peers due to the aforementioned difficulties and definitely not the attempt to treat these difficulties as early as possible.

All empirical data converge to the view that when the child's development is impaired in one or more domains and significantly deviates from what is developmentally expected, this deviation is due to a certain cause, possibly of neurological nature, and requires further investigation. As the child grows older, these difficulties are likely to increase and complicate, significantly impair the child's functioning, and compromise further development. The most important negative consequence, however, is the loss of valuable time during a critical developmental period in which brain plasticity gives the opportunity for the greatest possible alteration of neurological structures that may underpin the child's prominent behavioral and developmental problems. Therefore, the importance of early intervention cannot be overstated, because the earlier the intervention the better and more favorable the outcome (Kern et al., 2007; McGoey, DuPaul, Eckert, Volpe, & Van Brakle, 2005).

The benefits of early identification and treatment of health and developmental problems have long been recognized (Davis & Williams, 2010). Early intervention may function as secondary prevention for the emergence of ADHD. Primary prevention stops the development of a disorder before it occurs. Secondary prevention detects the emerging disorder at its earlier stages and attempts to inhibit its progress, slow its escalation in severity or persistence, modify its course, and reduce adverse outcomes through procedures that facilitate brain growth to alter its adverse long-term trajectory. Tertiary prevention reduces the impact of a disorder on the individual's functioning after the disorder has manifested (Halperin, Bedard, & Curchack-Lichtin, 2012).

The most recent scientific approach for the treatment of ADHD refers to the implementation of early intervention programs that aim at secondary prevention. On a clinical level, this means detecting infants with increased chances of developing ADHD before the full symptomatology of the disorder is manifested in order to implement psychosocial programs targeted at both children and their parents. Early intervention focuses on those processes that take place very early in development and have a causal relationship with ADHD, with the aim of modifying the underlying neurophysiology and producing generalized long-lasting change (Sonuga-Barke & Halperin, 2010). Within this developmental psychopathology framework, prodromal states and precursor processes are targets for intervention. Therefore, treatment targets shift from fixed core biological deficits to multiple developmental processes that mediate the disorder. For this reason, early intervention may be much more effective than waiting until problems are manifested and established and then trying to reverse the pathogenic process (Sonuga-Barke & Halperin, 2010).

The efficacy of early intervention mainly lies in the fact that it takes place during a period when brain plasticity is great. Plasticity is an intrinsic property of the brain that ensures dynamic modifications at multiple levels of neural organization, allowing the brain to process, encode, and implement new knowledge (Hoekzema et al., 2011). During the first 2 years of life, the human brain reaches 80% of its final size, while the processes of myelination and creation of neuronal synapses undergo a rapid development (Halperin & Healey, 2011). By age 6, neurons begin to form complex dendritic trees that constitute the neurological basis for learning. Therefore, early childhood is a critical period to implement interventions that facilitate development of highly malleable learning-dependent brain networks (Andersen & Navalta, 2011).

Although this neuronal development is to a great extent genetically programmed, it is widely acknowledged that environment also plays a major role through the process of epigenesis. Environment may moderate gene expression, for example 'switch on' or 'switch off' a susceptibility gene (Mill & Petronis, 2008), with subsequent alterations in brain structure and function (Dawson, 2008; Kieling, Goncalves, Tannock, & Castellanos, 2008) (see Section 5.5). As a consequence, the developing person is more susceptible to the influence of environmental factors during this period (Bischof, 2007; Vuksic, Rados, & Kostovic, 2008). For example, it has been found that developing attention circuitry is particularly amenable to experience between the ages of 3 and 7 (Rueda, Rothbart, McCandliss, Saccomanno, & Posner, 2005).

Another compelling argument for the efficacy of early intervention is that it is implemented before ADHD behaviors become compounded with secondary problems, such as academic failure, behavioral problems, poor social relationships, low self-esteem, hardening of adult attitudes, and negative parent–child relationships. Early intervention that is directed more toward prevention than treatment before the child is allowed to fail in several domains is of particular value. Finally, early intervention occurs before the child has developed strong behavioral habits that lead to functional impairment and before parents have established maladaptive attitudes that reduce their receptiveness and the efficacy of family-based interventions (Sonuga-Barke & Halperin, 2010).

Early intervention is also supported by most theories of ADHD. For example, the Dynamic Developmental theory argues that due to deficient extinction of undesired behaviors in children with ADHD, such behaviors are established during preschool age and are particularly difficult to become extinct later (see Section 6.5). For this reason, parents should be trained to manage reward and punishment in such a way that they can prevent and correct the undesired behavior in time, before it is established (Sagvolden, Russell, Aase, Johansen, & Farshbaf, 2005).

As we discussed in Section 3.3, infants predisposed to develop ADHD are often difficult infants who elicit negative parental responses, including anger, rigidity in setting boundaries, and punitiveness. This type of interaction increases disobedience and impulsivity and contributes to the establishment and aggravation of the initial difficult child behaviors. To the contrary, positive and creative upbringing may promote resilience factors and inhibit the progression of the disorder through permanent alterations in the neuroanatomy of the brain due to the "attenuation" of gene effects (Sonuga-Barke, 2005). Resilience refers to escaping adverse outcomes despite having a genetic susceptibility for risks. It has been found that the effect of low birthweight on the clinical emergence of the disorder in infants at risk for ADHD can be moderated by positive parenting practices in the first years of life (Tully, Arsenault, Caspi, Moffitt, & Morgan, 2004).

An additional argument in favor of early intervention emerges from findings about the use of medication for the treatment of ADHD in preschool children. It has been found that medication at this age has very limited results relative to the results usually observed in the cases of older children (Kollins & Greenhill, 2006). Furthermore, side effects of medication in younger children are more frequent in comparison to older children (Wigal et al., 2006). In general, clinical benefits from pharmacological interventions often dissipate over time, and long-term effects remain uncertain (Molina et al., 2009).

Research findings corroborate the efficacy of early intervention. It is known that both MPH and ATX act in the frontal region of the brain and facilitate activating and interconnecting dysfunctional brain areas (Chamberlain et al., 2009; Rubia et al., 2011) (see Section 11.2). A relatively recent pilot study with the use of fMRI has shown that cognitive training activates similar brain regions to those that are activated following MPH treatment. This finding suggests that the neural effects of psychosocial interventions on the brain may be comparable with those induced by medication (Hoekzema et al., 2010). Furthermore, it has been found that the characteristics of the psychosocial environment during critical periods early in development differentiate the expression of genes via epigenetic processes (Szyf, Weaver, & Meaney, 2007). The interaction of certain dopaminergic and serotoninergic genotypes with psychosocial factors affects the severity of ADHD symptoms in children (Nigg, Nikolas, & Burt, 2010).

Further evidence of the efficacy of early intervention is provided by the research carried out by Hoekzema and her colleagues (2011). With the use of neuroimaging techniques, they found focal volumetric gray matter increases in areas of the prefrontal cortex involved in the pathogenesis of ADHD in children who were placed in an intensive neurocognitive treatment program. These increases were associated with attentional performance. In other words, this study provides evidence for the efficacy of training in producing not only changes of neuronal functioning, but also dynamic structural alterations in the brain of children with ADHD. Thus, it has been found that some of the neuroanatomical deficits associated with ADHD may be reversible by adequate cognitive training.

The possibility of early intervention for the prevention of neurodevelopmental disorders has also been investigated in the case of ASD, with very encouraging results. For example, while previously only 50% of individuals with ASD developed spoken language, it has now been demonstrated that 75% to 95% of children who receive early intensive behavioral intervention until the age of 3 develop functional speech by age 5 (Dawson, 2008). Furthermore, three separate research groups have reported that a significant proportion of children receiving intensive intervention for ASD early in life make so exceptional progress that autistic symptoms diminish considerably and these children have no longer evidence of disability (Howard, Sparkman, Cohen, Green, & Stanislaw, 2005; McEachin, Smith, & Lovaas, 1993; Sallows & Graupner, 2005).

Applied early interventions for ADHD are still in their infancy and are less frequently used than similar programs for other disorders (Shaw, Dishion, Supplee, Gardner, & Arnds, 2006). However, the ones that have already been implemented are very hopeful. Sonuga-Barke, Thompson, Abikoff, Klein, and Brotman (2006) developed a specialized early intervention program (New Forest Parenting Programme; NFPP) in 3-year-old children who were at risk for ADHD. This program promoted cognitive enhancement within a general parent training approach. Mother and child are encouraged to practice together game-like activities at home that enhance attention, concentration, working memory, delay of gratification, and turn-taking. Furthermore, parents are trained to use real-world situations that require the use of self-regulatory skills as opportunities for generalization of the skills across settings. In this way, a naturalistic context is offered, which gives the opportunity of incorporating the child's training in everyday life. This program yielded very positive effects and reduced significantly primary ADHD symptoms in children (Thompson et al., 2009).

Halperin and colleagues (2013) have developed a program for children with ADHD, aged 4 to 5 years (Training Executive, Attention and Motor Skills; TEAMS). This program includes educational activities that target an array of cognitive and motor skills, such as inhibition, sustained attention, memory, planning, and visuospatial orientation. Parents are also trained in incorporating these activities into everyday life and in using techniques that promote positive interaction with their child. According to research findings, this program achieved significant and sustainable reduction of ADHD symptoms (Halperin et al., 2013).

Executive Training of Attention and Metacognition (ETAM) is a similar program for children aged 3 to 7 years, which targets executive function deficits through the use of behaviorally based skills training and practice, along with training in metacognitive strategies. It aims at helping the children to achieve well-regulated, goal-directed thought and behavior (Tamm, Nakonezny & Hughes, 2014).

Furthermore, Enhancing Neurocognitive Growth with the Aid of Games and Exercise (ENGAGE) is an early intervention for 3- and 4-year-old children that extends beyond cognitive skills, focusing on improving self-control on both emotional and behavioral levels (Healey & Halperin, 2015). Like all the previous problems, it involves parents as well.

Finally, a novel trial, investigating the potential efficacy of cognitive training applied to infants at increased risk of developing ADHD, is INTERSTAARS (Goodwin et al., 2016). This program aims to improve attention control in infants aged 10 to 14 months at familial risk of ADHD and is still in progress. If successful, INTERSTAARS could offer a promising new approach for developing early interventions for ADHD.

To sum up, programs that include the child's cognitive training, parent training, and incorporation of these activities into the child's daily routine have considerable results that seem to be generalizable and long-lasting (Halperin et al., 2012). In addition, the longitudinal findings that early responsive parenting predicts later ADHD symptoms offer further support for the clinical utility of parent training (Seipp and Johnston, 2005) and for including both fathers and mothers in early intervention programs. Furthermore, it has been highlighted that early intervention should not be confined to cognitive skills and behavior but should also aim at the acquisition of academic skills that promote school readiness in order to reduce the chance of developing learning difficulties (DuPaul, Kern, Gormley, & Volpe, 2011).

A reasonable question concerns the criteria for the selection of children who are eligible to participate in early intervention programs, as it is not feasible for every preschool child that has some ADHD symptoms to participate in such a program. These costly and time-consuming interventions should focus on children at an increased risk for developing this disorder. In addition, intervention should be based on sound evidence to ensure that the most effective treatments are implemented and that they do not impede optimal developmental progress unnecessarily (Davis & Williams, 2011). Therefore, a key task is to predict which preschool children with atypical patterns of inattentiveness and hyperactivity will go on to develop ADHD (Sonuga-Barke et al., 2005). Several early markers for the later emergence of ADHD have been discussed in Section 3.3.

Through our clinical experience, we have concluded that the chance of developing ADHD is particularly increased in cases in which hyperactivity, inability to focus attention, and difficulty in self-regulation during preschool years are accompanied by language problems (e.g., delayed language development, articulation problems, auditory discrimination problems), as well as difficulties with spatial orientation and motor coordination (see Sections 7.2.2 and 12.5.2).

Difficulties in language development, in particular, should not be seen as isolated difficulties, as they are usually manifested in the broader context of various developmental disorders, one of which is ADHD (Hagberg, Miniscalco, & Gillberg, 2010). Speech and language delays have been documented at 9 and 18 months in a retrospective chart review of children with ADHD relative to typically developing controls (Gurevitz et al., 2012). In addition, specific language features, including mispronouncing words, word-finding problems, trouble rhyming, and difficulty learning the alphabet are some of the most common early risks of learning disabilities (Shaywitz, 2003). Therefore, merely treating them with speech therapy, often without the establishment of a diagnosis, is not enough (see Section 12.5.2).

Furthermore, negative parenting, including provision of excessive amount of stimuli, lack of stability, excessive rigidity, punitive behavior, and constant interference are closely associated with the development of ADHD in preschool age, especially if they date back to infancy (Morrell & Murray, 2003).

A 5-year research program funded by the National Institute of Health Research is currently in progress in the University of Southampton (Programme for Early Detection and Intervention for ADHD; PEDIA). This program aims at developing a plan for the identification of preschool children with ADHD most at risk for a poor outcome and developing a risk index for poor outcome/high burden in order to be used as a criterion for their placement in an early intervention program (Sonuga-Barke et al., 2011).

ADHD could potentially be diagnosed early with better screening tools that would include behavioral and cognitive measures and would be more sensitive to developmental and early sex differences. Such early screeners for ADHD risk would measure externalizing and internalizing symptoms, sleep difficulties, social problems, cognitive performance, and physiological measures of behavioral and attention regulation (Arnett et al., 2013).

In conclusion, when specific child's characteristics are combined with a dysfunctional family environment, early intervention is imperative (Sonuga-Barke, Koerting, Smith, McCann, & Thompson, 2011). It has been shown that early emergence of ADHD symptoms, which impair functioning already from the preschool period, considerably increases the risk of developing the disorder during school-aged years. In these cases, up to 80% of children are likely to encounter difficulties upon entering elementary school (Lahey et al., 2004).

It is clear that preschool age is the most fertile period for the implementation of early intervention programs, not only for ADHD but also for other neurodevelopmental disorders. Parent training in the use of appropriate strategies to handle the difficult behaviors of a genetically vulnerable infant or preschooler gives the opportunity for creating resilience circumstances capable of inhibiting the process of the emergence of the disorder (Sonuga-Barke et al., 2005). Most importantly, preschool age is the only period in the course of development when secondary prevention of ADHD can be substantially achieved through alteration of the deficient brain structures and functions. Consequently, the chronically impaired course of the individual who was born with a predisposition to develop a neurodevelopmental disorder like ADHD can be radically altered.

Note

1 Reprinted by author's permission.

12 The Multilevel Approach of ADHD

12.1 Conceptual Framework

Professionals who work in the field of developmental psychopathology are usually confronted with a wide range of clinical decisions, including the choice of the best treatment or combination of treatments for children and their families. During this process, they need to consider a plethora of factors that may influence the child's behavior, set a wide range of treatment goals, use multiple strategies, and include all individuals involved in the child's upbringing and education. ADHD is not a disorder where we should be trying to identify specific ingredients leading to successful treatment, but create a multilevel approach addressing all the components that need to be addressed.

The multilevel approach is a theoretical clinical framework guiding individualized assessment and treatment plans for neurodevelopmental disorders. Treatment planning is tailored to the families' needs and is based on (a) a thorough assessment covering multiple domains of behavior, as well as parental cognitions and other crucial family and child factors; (b) official clinical guidelines for the treatment of neurodevelopmental disorders; (c) research evaluating the efficacy of evidence-based treatments; (d) professionals' theoretical background, orientation, and conceptualization of developmental psychopathology; and (e) professionals' clinical experience. For reasons of brevity, we will use the term "clinicians" from now on in order to refer to every specialty involved in the treatment of ADHD in the context of an interdisciplinary team.

The multilevel approach incorporates and combines several treatment modalities. These modalities are mainly psychosocial in nature and include a child, a parent, and a teacher component. It has been found that psychosocial interventions are of limited effectiveness when implemented only in one setting because outcomes do not lead to generalized gains, and improvements tend to be context specific (Valdez, Carlson, & Zanger, 2005; Webster-Stratton, Reid, & Beauchaine, 2011). Children experience their symptoms in multiple contexts, and therefore need treatment in each setting to obtain maximal benefit (Chronis et al., 2006). Improvements that result from parent training have limited effects at school, and similarly, gains from school-based interventions often fail to generalize to the home environment, unless active arrangements are made. For comorbid cases, in particular, several channels of intervention are mandated.

For these reasons, psychosocial impairments are best addressed with multilevel treatment programs, like the multilevel approach, which incorporate children, parents, and teachers, and equip all of the above with new skills. Such interventions are more likely to foster self-regulation and age-appropriate competencies and reduce impairment in individuals with ADHD (Hinshaw et al., 2015; Power et al., 2012; Sheridan et al., 2012; Villodas, McBurnett, Kaiser, Rooney, & Pfiffner, 2014). Randomized controlled trials investigating these multicomponent interventions for ADHD reveal broader effects across multiple contexts (Evans et al., 2011; Pfiffner et al., 2014; Power et al., 2012).

In the multilevel approach, clinicians, parents, teachers, and the child are considered active collaborators, form part of the same partnership, and reach agreement about treatment goals. The child component includes psychoeducation, cognitive restructuring, behavior modification, academic remediation, and specific skills training (e.g., neurocognitive, social skills, and organizational skills training). Where needed, speech therapy and/or occupational therapy are added. Finally, in collaboration with a physician, medication may be recommended in some cases under the conditions described in Section 11.2.

The parent component includes psychoeducation, cognitive restructuring, training in the use of behavioral techniques, counseling, and sometimes, individual psychotherapy in order to treat parental psychopathology, psychosocial adversity, or intrafamilial problems that may impede treatment adherence.

The school component includes teacher psychoeducation, teacher training in the use of behavioral techniques, and implementation of FBA and contingency management interventions at school. Therefore, parents and teachers are both recipients of treatment, via training, and providers of treatment, via implementation of behavioral interventions at home and school. Desirable behaviors displayed in one setting (e.g., at school) are reinforced in the other (e.g., home or clinical setting), as clinicians, parents, and teachers share responsibility for promoting positive, generalizable, and consistent behavioral and educational outcomes.

The multilevel approach sets a wide range of treatment goals beyond the reduction of ADHD symptomatology and associated impairments. Central goals of the multilevel approach for the parents include modification of dysfunctional causal attributions, enhancement of parenting practices, strengthening of parent self-efficacy, improvement of intrafamilial communication, and reduction of stress and negative feelings toward the child.

Central goals of the multilevel approach for the child include modification of maladaptive cognitions and behaviors, reduction of core symptomatology and associated impairment, improvement of social, academic, and organizational skills, and increase in motivation and self-esteem. The multilevel approach aims at addressing the cross-setting impairments of the disorder and fostering age-appropriate competencies across the life span. Target behaviors are prioritized in terms of severity and impact on functioning. For example, if ADHD co-occurs with ASD, the difficulties stemming from the latter will be treated first if they are mostly impairing child functioning. Moreover, if a child with ADHD displays learning difficulties and major behavioral problems, behavior modification may be implemented before addressing learning difficulties, because even the best educational interventions are doomed to failure unless the child learns to cooperate and follow rules.

Furthermore, the child is treated as a developing individual with skills, talents, and positive features, which should be further enhanced. A child with ADHD is not only a child with poor attention, increased motor activity, and impulsive behavior. This child usually has normal intelligence, typical developmental worries, exploratory tendencies, talents, and gifts, which are often obscured by the deficits associated with the disorder. Clinicians set these qualities as a starting point and aim at a balanced development of all child skills and personality aspects. Therefore, clinicians adopting the multilevel approach always bear in mind that treatment of a disorder should not take the lead over the development of a child's personality.

The multilevel approach is grounded on the idea that treatment of ADHD should be chronic, intensive, and pervasive. It is management of a complex condition that involves finding means to cope with, compensate for, and accommodate to developmental deficits and socioeducational demands. Short-term behavioral outcomes are beyond the scope of this approach. Engagement, patience, commitment, and adherence of children, parents, teachers, and clinicians for protracted periods of time are required. Implementing treatment for children with ADHD is a demanding task, often requiring major lifestyle changes. Brief and time-limited treatment regimens are not sufficient and effective interventions for ADHD (Pelham & Fabiano, 2008). Moreover, even in the case of successful interventions in childhood, it is likely that new interventions may be needed in adolescence and adulthood due to differential developmental needs of individuals with ADHD in response to new developmental challenges.

The multilevel approach is guided by cognitive-behavioral theory, and is conceptually a systemic approach. Maladaptive behaviors exhibited by child, parents, and teachers are treated as groups of systems that mutually affect each other as they are characterized by interdependence. The effect of each variable is evaluated from an ecological perspective. Therefore, emphasis is given on the dynamic nature of family and school systems and subsystems. It is acknowledged that treatment may result in reorganizing relationships and modifying family communication patterns.

An important aspect of any useful intervention is the theory that supports the specific intervention. Changes in the conceptualization of ADHD in line with current developments force clinicians to constantly evaluate the adequacy of their treatment approaches because their working theory of ADHD has an important impact on treatment and determines the goals to be set and the techniques to be used.

The multilevel approach adopts the basic principles of the developmental psychopathology framework. Developmental appropriateness of behavior is taken into consideration in setting treatment goals and appreciating environmental demands. Therefore, treatment goals are based on normative functioning for the child's age (Chronis et al., 2006). For example, some behaviors that are indicative of ADHD, including poor sustained attention and increased motor activity, are normative in preschool years but impairing in school-age years. Moreover, these behaviors may be perceived as maladaptive or not, depending on environmental demands.

The multilevel approach is developmentally sensitive in that the child's level of cognitive development and unique characteristics, such as individual developmental needs and challenges, are also taken into consideration and influence treatment decisions (Holmbeck, Greenley, & Franks, 2003). In this regard, treatment features differ across different age groups in order to adapt to the needs of preschoolers as well as to those of adolescents, although the basic principles that guide treatment are similar. Furthermore, particular emphasis is placed on the choice of targets and methods that are meaningful and motivating for the individual. Treatment is modified at developmental transitions, and developmentally sensitive strategies are used in order to target the behaviors that are most impairing at each developmental stage in accordance with the individual's cognitive development (Chronis et al., 2001).

The multilevel approach incorporates the difficulties encountered among children with ADHD throughout development into a cohesive developmental model. Several co-occurring difficulties are understood via epigenetic processes, and some of the most prevalent comorbid disorders are conceptualized as resulting from atypical brain development under the umbrella of ADHD and not as distinct clinical entities (see Chapter 7).

Let's consider, for example, the relationship among SLPs, SLD, and ADHD. In our view, deep understanding of this relationship could bridge an important gap in ADHD treatment literature. Medication mainly addresses the core ADHD symptoms. Behavioral interventions target maladaptive behaviors. Neurocognitive training aims at improving the deficient neurocognitive functions that are related to ADHD. Evidence-based educational interventions for the specific academic difficulties of children with ADHD are practically nonexistent, either as single treatments or as a component of combined treatments. It has been acknowledged that no reviews have looked exclusively at the nonmedical interventions used to improve the academic outcomes of these children (Trout, Lienemann, Reid, & Epstein, 2007).

This is surprising, given the significant overlap between ADHD and academic underachievement and the fact that learning difficulties are the rule rather than the exception among children with ADHD. Furthermore, the impact of academic underachievement on the child's self-esteem, motivation, behavior, and familial and social life is detrimental. If we further consider the consequences of the accumulation of failures, which can range from school dropout in adolescence to juvenile delinquency, it is worth wondering why this field is often neglected in the ADHD treatment literature.

In our view, this is possibly attributed to the fact that SLD and ADHD constitute two distinct diagnostic categories in DSM, and clinical scientists fail to perceive the nature of the association between them. Considerable advances have been made in developing effective interventions for each disorder separately, but surprisingly little research has directly evaluated interventions for children with ADHD and SLD (Miranda et al., 2011; Sexton et al., 2012). According to our clinical experience, SLD rarely occurs alone; in the majority of cases, it constitutes a part of the clinical presentation of children with ADHD (see Section 7.3). Unless conceptualized this way, interventions designed for ADHD, interventions designed for SLD, and the studies supporting them will continue to follow separate routes. It has been suggested that rather than treating each of these disorders in isolation, it is critical for clinicians and researchers to consider their overlap (Sexton et al., 2012).

In line with this view, SLPs of toddlers with ADHD usually constitute a precedent stage of SLD. Conceptualized this way, a wide range of SLPs could be understood as part of the broader symptomatology of ADHD at preschool. On the other hand, treatment of SLPs would be a priority of interventions for preschoolers with ADHD as it could serve a preventative role against the development of SLD at a later developmental stage. Consequently, several diagnoses within the range of SLPs and SLD, which are relatively meaningless and give limited information about the etiology of the child's problems, could be perceived under the umbrella of ADHD and be set as goals in a developmentally sensitive treatment plan. In conclusion, the multilevel approach views treatment of SLPs in preschoolers with ADHD as an integrative part of a multicomponent intervention, both because these problems impair the child's development and functioning, and because they are usually indices of forthcoming SLDs. Therefore, their treatment may function as therapy and prevention as well.

The multilevel approach suggests that the specialty of the professionals delivering treatment for ADHD should be a function of the child's age and predominant difficulties. Psychologists, occupational therapists, speech therapists, special educators, and child psychiatrists are some of the professionals who may be involved in the treatment of ADHD. However, speech therapy, occupational therapy, or psychotherapy should not be narrowly focused. In the case of ADHD, the speech therapist or the occupational therapist needs to be knowledgeable about the main principles of behavioral theory and must be trained in the use of behavior modification techniques in order to ensure the best possible cooperation of the child. On the other hand, a psychologist needs to have a vast knowledge of language and motor development but also of cognitive prerequisites for learning to write and read in order to holistically help the child with ADHD and associated learning difficulties. Finally, a special educator should understand the impact of the core ADHD symptoms and neurocognitive deficits on learning and target these deficits in parallel with academic remediation.

The multilevel approach suggests that professionals delivering treatment for ADHD need to work within a multidisciplinary team. This team should include psychologists, child psychiatrists, social workers, occupational therapists, speech therapists, special educators, developmental pediatricians, and child neurologists, so that every specialty can make a unique contribution toward diagnosis and treatment, on an individualized basis. Besides, the wide range of biological, behavioral, cognitive, social, and learning deficits associated with ADHD renders collaboration among professionals from different scientific backgrounds necessary.

The multilevel approach posits that professionals whose theoretical background encompasses multiple domains may be more efficient in coordinating ADHD treatments. For example, academic deficits among children with ADHD cannot be effectively treated merely via special education techniques. Treatment of these deficits should derive from the profound knowledge of current conceptualizations of ADHD and should be based on the use of methods that (a) increase self-control and self-management skills, (b) improve sustained attention, (c) enhance motivation, (d) increase frustration tolerance, and (e) use reinforcement effectively. Our long clinical experience has taught us that improvement in these domains leads to improvement in academic performance as well, because deficits in these domains are mainly responsible for impeding learning rather than difficulties in spelling or grammar. The important role of self-regulation as an efficient means of increasing academic productivity in ADHD has been widely acknowledged (Reid, Trout, & Schartz, 2005).

In our view, specialized child psychologists are well-equipped in order to coordinate psychosocial interventions for ADHD because they have comprehensive theoretical knowledge of developmental psychology, developmental psychopathology, cognitive psychology, counseling, and psychotherapy. This sound basis makes them suitable to coordinate multilevel interventions targeting multiple deficits and impairments across different areas of functioning.

However, the specialty alone does not render a therapist effective. The existence of a cohesive theoretical framework that guides the techniques chosen, the clinician's personal skills and experience after long supervised clinical work, several personality traits, including enthusiasm, self-control, stability, determination, persistence, and patience, are essential prerequisites for effectively working with children (see Section 12.5.1).

The multilevel approach is a dynamic process that constantly modifies its methods in order to incorporate the most recent developments regarding the etiology of ADHD and the evidence on the efficacy of several interventions. Clinicians adopting this approach should be entirely knowledgeable about the techniques that they use and know exactly why they use them. In other words, clinicians should know precisely what exactly they are trying to improve, what is the cause of what they are trying to improve, and why a specific technique is the most suitable for what they are trying to improve. Therefore, a well-organized and flexible theoretical framework is an essential guide to treatment.

Because of the heterogeneity of ADHD, there are no techniques that can be implemented in the *same* way in *all* children. Treatment is definitely a completely individualized process. For this reason, the multilevel approach does not provide therapeutic protocols with a fixed therapeutic plan, structure, and duration. This is probably the most important difference between the multilevel approach and existing multimodal approaches to the treatment of ADHD. We believe that prescriptive interventions implemented in the same manner for all children with ADHD cannot be effective for all children. One-size-fits-all treatment modalities cannot lead to optimal outcomes.

Therefore, the multilevel approach aims at providing clinicians with principles and techniques that should be tailored in a unique way for each individual with ADHD and their families according to "clinical wisdom." According to Jensen, Abikoff, & Brown (2009), "the essence of clinical skill is the clinician's ability to match the type, timing, and intensity of specific treatments and rehabilitative approaches to the particular clinical needs of the individual patient" (p. 415). Following this reasoning, treatment modalities to be presented in the subsequent sections are not ready-to-follow "recipes," implemented in a "cookbook" fashion, but means that should be used within the framework of a broader therapeutic philosophy. The main principles of this philosophy will be presented in this chapter, and six clinical illustrations will be presented in Chapter 14.

12.2 Behavioral Techniques

12.2.1 Introduction

Behavioral techniques constitute an indispensable part of parent training in managing issues related to ADHD. These techniques can be also used by teachers and therapists of all specialties implicated in treatment delivery. Therefore, parents, teachers, and therapists will be referred to as "adults" in this section. Especially for parents, it is highlighted that the use of behavioral contingency techniques needs to be integrated into the family's daily activities and routine in order to maximize outcomes. Furthermore, it has been suggested that there is an incremental benefit of adding several behavior modification components to an ongoing behavioral program (Fabiano et al., 2004).

Although behavior therapy shares a set of principles, individual programs introduce different techniques and strategies to achieve the same ends. At this point, we would like to emphasize that the efficacy of behavioral techniques lies in *the way* in which they are implemented and in *the person* who implements them. Techniques are only tools that can lead to different results depending on whether they are used by an inexperienced craftsman or a talented artist. In the previous chapter we presented research evaluating the effectiveness of several treatments. In our view, these quantitative data are simply indicative of effectiveness because the true effectiveness of an intervention is determined not only by the theoretical background that underpins it but, above all, by implementation integrity. Besides, it has been found that successful therapeutic outcomes may be more closely linked to therapeutic alliance between the receiver and the provider of intervention rather than the type of intervention (Wampold, 2001).

Particularly for behavioral techniques, their effectiveness lies in details. Personality characteristics of the individual who implements them (firmness, stability, consistency, determination, calmness, patience, and persistence) and precision in the time and way of implementation play a decisive role. Because several of these techniques are popularized in a simplistic way and may seem very easy to use, many parents and teachers are likely to claim that they have already tried them out without success. According to our experience, these attempts are usually isolated and inaccurate. They are not based on a deep understanding of the philosophy of behavioral theory and they do not guarantee implementation integrity. Furthermore, the effective use of these techniques requires great skill. Therefore, in order to ensure their success, it is important that they be used by people who have been fully trained and appropriately qualified.

For example, the technique of praise, which will be presented below, seems very simple. The power of praise, however, does not lie in the words that are spoken but behind these words. It is easy to say "well done," but it is magnificent to say it in a particular way and tone that can touch a child's heart, so that the child can believe in these positive words, incorporate their meaning in their self-image, be overwhelmed with pride, and feel that they have done something great, for which they are admirable. Children may often be praised, but only a few times will they be influenced in a decisive way. Words are soulless without the right emotional context. They come to life by the way they are expressed. In the same way, the techniques that will be presented below gain strength from their proper use, the emotional context in which they are implemented, and the appropriate style of the person using them. In case they do not function as expected, it is important that adults check carefully on implementation integrity before rejecting them as inefficient.

12.2.2 Rule Setting

Children with ADHD have difficulty in self-regulation of behavior through internalized rules. For this reason, adults need to use more explicit, concise, systematic, externalized, and compelling methods of setting rules and presenting instructions to these children.

Rule setting is more effective when it is not absolutely external, namely imposed by adults, but emerges through a Socratic dialogue with children. When children actively participate in this process, they develop a better understanding about rules, their importance, and the function each one serves. Consequently, they do not feel that rules are imposed on them against their will. When children are committed to a set of rules in the establishment of which they have participated and the value of which they have appreciated, they are more willing to follow them.

Adults can lead the conversation in a way that children formulate the rules they must follow by themselves. Subsequently, adults have the opportunity to verbally reward children for the correctness of their conclusions. This procedure has a double benefit. On the one hand, children are reinforced for their sound judgment; on the other hand, they come to realize that they are capable of setting rules on their own. Such an approach helps in enhancing self-esteem and reducing impulsive behavior, as children are convinced that they can find ways that lead to more frequent reinforcement.

Generally, the implementation of behavioral techniques should not only be based on enforcing rules and consequences but also on providing explanations for rules and expectations. Besides, it has been found that maintenance of behavior change might be enhanced if greater emphasis is placed on the internalization of rules and committed compliance (Lundahl, Risser, & Lovejoy, 2006).

12.2.3 Effective Commands

The way in which adults ask from a child to carry out a task or follow instructions is highly important and may increase or decrease the likelihood of child compliance and decrease the number and frequency of commands. Therefore, by providing appropriate commands, adults stand the best chance of minimizing noncompliant disruptive behaviors among children with ADHD.

Commands should be used conservatively, when it is absolutely necessary, within the framework of predetermined rules, and only when adults are able to follow through consequences for noncompliance. Otherwise, adults lose their credibility, and commands lose their power, thus reducing the chances of child compliance.

In case commands are necessary, they should be expressed clearly, in direct statement rather than question form. Giving commands means giving the child directions rather than making requests. Commands that are given in a straightforward, declarative manner leave no room for disputes and negotiations. For example, adults should state "It is time to do your homework" and not "Would you like to do your homework?" or "Don't you think it's time you did your homework?" Questions like these leave room for choice and negative answers. Similarly, adults should avoid pleading, which sends the message that the child has the power to choose not to follow the direction and to gain control of the situation.

In order to increase the likelihood of child compliance, commands should be given in a firm and assertive voice with accompanying nonverbal behavior of the same style. The child should be convinced that the adult is determined not to accept a negative answer and is ready to apply contingencies. In this way, the adult helps the child comply and has the opportunity to apply positive reinforcement. It is noted that firm and assertive tone should not be confused with a wild or angry tone, because the latter can produce the opposite outcomes.

Before a command is given, adults should have obtained the child's attention first. Otherwise, disobedience may be secondary to poor attention for children with ADHD. Adults should ensure physical proximity and direct eye contact with the child during commands. Sometimes, it is useful to ask the child to repeat the command verbally. This way, adults confirm that the child has paid attention to them and has understood what they expect. If the child has not either attended to the adult or understood the command, there is always an opportunity to correct any misunderstandings.

Commands should be simple, brief, firm, specific, and include a time frame for expected completion to elicit child compliance. Moreover, they should indicate one step at a time, because deficits in attention and executive functioning make it difficult for children with ADHD to retain and follow long and complex instructions.

It is also important that commands direct children toward behaviors that they are expected to exhibit and not toward behaviors they are expected to stop. Adults are used to responding when children exhibit aversive behaviors by using negative directions. However, this practice leaves a wide range of other possibilities open. For example, a child who is given the command "Don't put your feet on the couch" may take their feet off the couch and put them on the wall. The child will have followed the command, without doing what the adult really means. Commands that clearly direct children to what they should be doing, such as "Put your feet on the floor," are favored.

Children with ADHD may find it difficult to act upon a command immediately, for example when they are asked to switch off the television and get ready for a scheduled activity. Transitional warnings may be helpful, for example: "In five minutes you should switch off the TV and get ready for your basketball training."

In case of noncompliance, it is important to give the child a second chance, by repeating the command and accompanying it with a clear warning about the consequences that will follow. For example: "In five minutes you should switch off the TV and get ready for your basketball training. If you are not ready on time, you won't be allowed to play with your friend afterward." Alternatively: "If you are ready on time, we will go for an ice cream after training."

12.2.4 Planned Ignoring

Some of the child's problem behaviors may be maintained by social attention. For this reason, it is important that adults detect frequently occurring, mildly annoying behaviors (e.g., whining, complaining, or making disruptive noises) that serve the function of attention seeking and remove the reinforcing consequence, namely increased adult attention. Therefore, adults are instructed to ignore these behaviors, leading to their extinction, as they are not reinforced any longer via social attention (Chacko et al., 2015).

Parents in particular should anticipate that these behaviors are expected to increase initially, as children may increase the intensity and frequency of their negative behaviors in an effort to elicit parental attention (Chacko et al., 2015). If parents show consistency and do not get carried away by the child at this crucial point, problem behavior will be eventually reduced and new forms of gaining attention will be established.

It should also be highlighted that planned ignoring is one of the most difficult techniques for parents and teachers to practice effectively, because ignoring a defiant or persistent behavior may be exceptionally challenging. Children with ADHD are relentless attention seekers. Even an occasional verbal or nonverbal response (e.g., facial expressions, glances, gestures) can maintain the inappropriate behavior. Therefore, parents need to be equipped with coping strategies for the negative emotions that may overwhelm them in such a situation. First, it is particularly important to realize the provocative nature of these behaviors and not take seriously phrases like "I don't love you," "You are a bad mom," and "I will leave home." Furthermore, they can leave the immediate area of the child for a while, as provocation has no meaning without the presence of bystanders. Lastly, the use of relaxation techniques may be helpful.

Consistency is a concept of cardinal importance when implementing this technique. Consistency promotes trust. If rules are set and followed through, children understand that these rules are meaningful. If adults have been using planned ignoring for a period of time but sometimes provide attention to problematic child behavior out of frustration, the problematic behavior will have been unintentionally reinforced at an increased intensity, which will likely render future use of this technique more difficult (Chacko et al., 2015).

Finally, it is important to clarify that this technique is not appropriate for aggressive, harmful, or destructive behaviors, which should not be ignored under any circumstances.

12.2.5 Praise and Positive Attending

Praise and positive attending are positive reinforcement techniques that contribute to increasing the frequency of child desirable behavior and improve the quality of the adult–child interaction. The behaviors that will be the focus of praise have been usually identified prior to treatment. Positive reinforcement of desirable behavior is accompanied by specifying the behavior that is being praised (e.g., "Good job! You completed your exercises within the time limit we agreed upon" instead of "Good job! You did your homework!"), as a means of providing children with a clear understanding of what behaviors are being expected and praised. Praise should be given immediately after the manifestation of desirable behavior, be genuine and sincere, and include nonverbal behavior (e.g., positive affect, smile, hugs). Positive attending includes eye contact, attentive listening, reflecting upon the child's verbal and nonverbal behavior, and supportive conversation (Chacko et al., 2015).

Praise of the "positive opposites" of negative behaviors is also an effective technique. Parents and teachers are instructed to attend to and praise desirable behaviors (e.g., "Thanks for helping your little brother with his homework!") rather than provide negative attention for problem behaviors (e.g., "Stop talking to your brother while he is studying!"). Reinforcing a positive behavior at the expense of the negative one that is being extinct is called ***differential reinforcement***.

Adults usually attend to inappropriate behaviors and ignore appropriate ones. Parents and teachers usually seek for strategies aiming to reduce problematic behavior. They want to reduce child noncompliance, to stop fights among siblings or classmates, to make children study for school, and so forth. They rarely wonder how to react toward child compliance, cooperation among siblings or classmates, and willingness to study. Attending to problematic behavior usually reinforces this behavior and increases the likelihood of its reappearance. At the same time, it reduces the frequency of desirable behaviors, as the child learns that problematic behaviors attract adults' attention, whereas positive behaviors do not gain any kind of attention.

Clinicians should help parents and teachers understand that their attention is extremely important for children with ADHD and that they should use it effectively, by actively attending to ongoing prosocial and compliant child behaviors. Many parents and teachers complain that these children engage in very few behaviors that elicit positive attending. It has been found that parents of children with ADHD have difficulty identifying positive behaviors in their child (Chronis et al., 2004). However, there is no child that is constantly defiant, noncompliant, oppositional, and disobedient. Adults should learn to identify and comment on positive behaviors and on child's merits and talents, which are often overshadowed by the difficulties and problems of everyday life.

In case parents have great difficulty identifying behaviors that are worthy of praise and positive attending, clinicians can suggest the systematic use of some play activities in the family's everyday life, in order to provide the child with the opportunity to spend some quality time with their parents in a context free of judgment, corrections, or direction. During this child-centered quality time, there is increased likelihood that the child will behave appropriately and, therefore, trigger praise and positive attending. Parents are trained to observe themselves, reduce negative behaviors such as commands and criticisms, and increase positive behaviors, such as praising, describing, and touching. Systematic use of such activities within the day may considerably help in enhancing the parent–child relationship. Over time, it becomes easier for parents to use praise and positive attending in less structured and more challenging situations (Chacko et al., 2015).

In conclusion, there are two main rules for applying praise and positive attending. On the one hand, adults should attend to and praise positive behaviors that constitute the opposites of the negative behaviors that they wish to extinct, every time they are manifested. On the other hand, if adults cannot identify behaviors that justify praise and positive attending, they should create the context and the opportunities so that such behaviors can be exhibited on a daily basis.

12.2.6 Incentive Systems

Incentive systems are additional positive reinforcement procedures that are based on FBA (see Section 10.4.4) and are used whenever further motivation is needed beyond that of praise and positive attending. According to a recent meta-analysis of 82 studies, FBA-based interventions tend to be significantly more effective than non FBA-based interventions for students with ADHD (Miller & Lee, 2013). Therefore, including FBA in behavioral intervention planning has been considered an optimal practice (Gresham et al., 2001).

Incentive systems are created by establishing clear expectations of desirable behaviors and determining meaningful rewards for these behaviors. Several theories of ADHD emphasize dysregulation of reinforcement in the form of an elevated reinforcement threshold or reduced ability of delayed reinforcement to maintain control over behavior (see Section 6.5). Incentive systems are consistent with theories of ADHD that emphasize the role of reinforcement and view performance as an interaction of cognition and motivation. These systems provide a structured means of giving rewards in a way that is more effective for children with ADHD. Due to the increased sensitivity of children with ADHD to immediate consequences, rewards should be immediate, concrete, frequent, and intense. They should also be provided more systematically relative to the natural consequences that follow the behavior of typically developing children (Barkley, 1997c).

Incentive systems can take various forms and should match the child's cognitive maturity. The first stage of an incentive system is identifying and clearly defining behaviors that negatively affect the child's functioning. These behaviors should be first stated in specific and observable terms and then be prioritized. Afterward, a few of them are targeted for modification. Target behaviors should be defined as *positive opposites* of the behaviors to be substituted. For example, the target behavior for a child who is used to shouting when experiencing frustration may be defined as "I express my feelings by using words."

Targets should be of gradual difficulty, starting with those that can be achieved more easily and more quickly, in order to lead to an experience of success and motivate the child. These targets should correspond to the child's developmental level and abilities and be realistic and feasible. For example, targets like "I have to be a good child," "I have to obey my parents," and the like are general and unrealistic. Examples of feasible targets are: "I wash my hands before meals," "I start my homework at 5 p.m.," and "I prepare my schoolbag on my own."

Afterward, the tokens to be used as conditioned reinforcers and the backup reward are chosen, and the number of tokens awarded for each particular behavior is specified. Tokens are earned when children engage positively in target behaviors. The term "token" suggests physical objects, such as poker chips, printed cards with smiley faces, stickers, or even fake money. However, for older children, just a tick on a sheet of paper, a hole punched in a card, or a stamp put onto a card could be used as tokens. These "non-physical" tokens are sometimes called "points" (Miltenberger, 2008), and can be recorded on a token economy chart. These points or tokens are later exchanged for backup rewards, whenever the amount needed for a specific award has accumulated. Tokens are an immediate form of reinforcement and can be used to track progress toward the reward. Children should not have access to the reward unless they complete the target request.

The token economy is a form of "conditioned" or "secondary" reinforcement because tokens are not naturally occurring reinforcers (Malott & Trojan-Suarez, 2006). Food or candies are "unconditioned reinforcers" or "primary reinforcers" because they do not need to be paired with anything. The success of a token economy depends on the appeal of the backup rewards, which are meaningful objects, privileges, or activities that individuals receive in exchange for their tokens. Examples include food items, toys, extra free time, extra time on the computer, and outings. Children will only be motivated to earn tokens if they anticipate the future reward represented by the tokens. Therefore, backup rewards should be chosen in collaboration with the child. Moreover, reinforcers should often be rotated, because they lose their power over time as children get acquainted with them.

Another component of an incentive system based on a token economy is the schedule of reinforcement, which specifies whether every response or only some responses are followed by reinforcement A continuous schedule of reinforcement occurs when reinforcement is delivered after every single target behavior, whereas an intermittent schedule of reinforcement means reinforcement is delivered after *some* behaviors or responses but never after each one (Miltenberger, 2008). Generally, reinforcers should be provided only *after* the manifestation of expected behavior and never *prior* to it, on the basis of the child's promises. In the second case, the child might engage in desirable behaviors only when there is a promise of reward, whereas in the first case adults can gradually shift the child's interest from the extrinsic to the intrinsic reward, which is provided by the positive experience of achieving a goal.

Once target behaviors are fully achieved, the backup reward is provided and old targets are replaced by new ones, with greater degree of complexity and difficulty. The experience of success, adults' satisfaction, and the reward reinforce the child's willingness to continue being involved in this process. Initially, tokens should be awarded frequently and in higher amounts, but as children learn the desirable behavior, opportunities to earn tokens decrease. Moreover, verbal praise should accompany the awarding of tokens. As the time intervals between delivery of tokens and/or number of tokens required increase, token delivery should continue to be paired with lots of social praise, which teaches the child delayed gratification. In order to prevent the child from developing a dependence on the incentive system, a plan for fading the token economy is usually implemented. A token economy can be faded by dispensing tokens in an intermittent fashion and requiring more tokens to access the backup reinforcers. Additionally, the use of tangible reinforcers can be faded and replaced with reinforcers that are more readily available in the natural environment.

Sometimes, parents are reluctant and skeptical about the value of rewards because they may consider it as a form of "bribery" and claim that rewards may undermine intrinsic motivation. Clinicians should first address these erroneous beliefs and then move to the implementation of an incentive system because such erroneous beliefs can limit contingency management efficacy. Studies have shown that reward does not reduce the child's intrinsic motivation or task interest (Eisenberger & Cameron, 1996). To the contrary, a tangible reward that one perceives as being deserved for successful performance or desirable behavior is likely to maintain or enhance the perception of self-competence without undermining feelings of self-determination (Bandura, 1986).

After several weeks of positive reinforcement, a response cost component can be added wherein children lose tokens for inappropriate behavior (see Section 12.2.7). It is important, however, that this process not turn into a punitive process and a massive removal of points because this practice may undermine the system and reduce child engagement.

At this point, parents and teachers should acknowledge the intermediate stages between the extinction of a maladaptive behavior and its replacement by a functional one because many parents and teachers often expect drastic and complete change, which is both utopic and infeasible. Change is a gradual and time-consuming process. There is a need to consistently apply rewards and consequences as tasks are achieved, and then to gradually increase the expectations for each task as they are mastered to shape behaviors. Moreover, adults need to be consistent when working with a token economy in order to keep the child motivated and engaged in the process. Completing the token economy chart sporadically and occasionally, providing reinforcers inconsistently, using this strategy mainly as a punitive means, evaluating different target behaviors from those that have been agreed upon, and removing massive points, are factors that may doom a very powerful and effective technique to failure.

12.2.7 Response Cost and Time-Out

Response cost and time-out are punishment procedures, used to suppress maladaptive behaviors for which previous techniques have been proved unsuccessful, or dangerous behaviors that require an immediate and more dynamic response. These techniques should be implemented in very specific and limited cases. Besides, in our view, the more effectively adults use positive reinforcement and planned ignoring, the less necessary it is to resort to punishment.

Response cost involves loss of benefits contingent upon inappropriate behavior. The use of this technique requires consistency and commitment of adults, who should be prepared to impose the predetermined consequences contingent upon undesirable child behavior. Removing routine privileges is preferred to removing major life event–type rewards (e.g., attendance at a birthday party). Specifying for how long the privilege or reward is lost is also important. It is noted that losing something for a long period of time is rarely effective because the child habituates to its absence (Friedberg & McClure, 2002). Finally, the removal should be tied to the value of the misbehavior and not to high levels of parent emotion.

Under no circumstances should parental love for the child be at stake. Expressions like "I don't love you," "I don't want you," or "I wish you had never been born" may evoke insecurity and negativity in a child rather than positive behavior. Furthermore, response cost refers to specific behaviors and not to the child's overall behavior. Response cost is not imposed because the child "is aggressive" but because "they hit their younger sibling on the head."

Time-out from positive reinforcement is a behavior-modification procedure in which an individual is removed from a reinforcing situation to a situation that is not reinforcing following a target behavior (Fabiano et al., 2004). It should be used only for dangerous or aggressive behaviors and when the child is in a condition of extreme emotional tension that renders verbal communication difficult. Parents must implement time-out shortly after noncompliance and not wait until they are very upset. This technique gives the opportunity to the child to calm down and regulate emotions of anger, disappointment, deprivation, or frustration. Time-out should have a specific and short duration. The child is removed from the source of natural tension and is sent to a specific place designed for time-out. In case the child is placed in their bedroom, toys or other entertaining activities are previously removed. It has been found that, for approximately 50% of children with ADHD, a simple 5-minute time-out procedure will be an effective consequence for aggression, property destruction, or noncompliance, and such a time-out will be as effective as longer or more complicated time-out procedures (Fabiano et al., 2004).

Moreover, the use of this technique needs to be made in an emotional climate of absolute calmness on the part of the adult; otherwise, it may be perceived as a sign of rejection by the child. It is very difficult for a parent to remain calm in front of an emotionally dysregulated child, but the aim of behavioral techniques is to help children increase their capacity for self-control and not to provide them with a role model of an adult who has also lost self-control.

After using such techniques, it is important to create the conditions for the child to manifest desirable behaviors, which will give adults the opportunity to provide positive reinforcement.

12.3 Parent Participation in Treatment

12.3.1 The Framework of Collaboration Between Clinicians and Parents

Interventions applied to ADHD in childhood involve a reliance on parents for implementation and require that they be highly available. Parents usually recognize the need to receive training in child management and ask clinicians to help them change maladaptive parenting practices and equip them with new knowledge and skills (Maniadaki, Sonuga-Barke & Kakouros, 2006). However, according to our experience, there are many parents who perceive ADHD as a child-centered problem and do not recognize their own contribution in triggering several child behaviors. As a result, some parents expect the positive change to come exclusively from the child, expressing their covert or overt dissatisfaction about the need for their own active participation in treatment.

Parent involvement in treatment is critically important in order to promote generalization of the intervention benefits from the clinical setting to other contexts. In the initial phase, the framework of collaboration between the family and the coordinating clinician is established, and the structure and philosophy of the intervention are described. Parents are prepared to (a) be thoroughly informed about the nature and etiology of ADHD; (b) be helped to replace many of their own misconceptions about the causes of their child's behavior with new, scientifically driven ones; (c) be trained in more effective parenting strategies; (d) make family accommodations according to the child's needs; and (e) learn to implement simple but specialized and evidence-based behavioral contingency management techniques. More importantly, therapeutic alliance is established during this phase between clinician and parents, who make a joint effort for the maximum benefit of the child. Clinicians who are capable of active listening, absence of criticism, and empathy have better chances of developing a positive therapeutic relationship, which is based on trust, understanding, and respect.

The multilevel approach favors goal-directed and preference-based interventions, implemented through a process of shared decision-making, so that treatment can be fine-tuned and tailored to individual needs (Fiks, Mayne, DeBartolo, Power, & Guevara, 2013). A joint determination of the treatment plan helps both clinicians and parents to hold common expectancies about treatment outcomes. Expectancies about treatment refer to anticipatory beliefs that parents bring to treatment and can encompass beliefs about the procedures, outcomes, or any other facet of the intervention and its delivery. Parent expectancies play a significant role in participation in treatment. When these expectancies are consistent with characteristics of treatment delivery, parents are more likely to believe that treatment is worthwhile, remain in treatment, and achieve therapeutic change (Nock & Kazdin, 2001). Discrepancies between parent expectancies and the actual demands of treatment predict treatment dropout (Nock & Kazdin, 2001). Given the importance of parent engagement in treatment, clinicians are required to assess unrealistic parent expectancies, so that they modify them in order to strengthen not only parent attendance but parent adherence as well.

Prior to the initiation of treatment, clinicians assess possible barriers to optimal parent engagement and include them in the treatment plan in order to enhance parent engagement and treatment outcomes. Four main barriers to children's mental health treatment have been identified: (a) practical obstacles; (b) perceptions that treatment is too demanding; (c) perceptions that treatment is of little relevance to the child's problems; and (d) poor relationship or alliance with the therapist (Kazdin, Holland, Crowley, & Breton, 1997). Maladaptive causal attributions, low self-efficacy, lack of self-confidence, parental psychopathology, long working hours, and marital problems are also reported (Chronis et al., 2004). Overwhelmed and stressed parents are not in a position to consistently apply behavioral techniques in everyday life. Therefore, intervention is also targeted toward the parents' needs in addition to those of the child (Smith et al., 2015). For this reason, clinicians investigate whether parents need to consider treatment for their own difficulties prior to enrolling in the child's treatment (Chacko et al., 2015).

Within the framework of the multilevel approach, the clinician's collaboration with parents can take various forms. In some cases, it is required that some sessions with parents take place before the initiation of the child treatment component. In most cases, clinicians dedicate time on parent training and counseling at the end of every session with the child. During this meeting, clinicians are informed about significant events that took place between sessions, evaluate progress, and adapt counseling accordingly. At the same time, clinicians encourage and support parents in dealing with rising difficulties. School-related issues are systematically addressed in the context of collaboration with parents because they are a likely source of parent–child interaction difficulties. Moreover, separate sessions with parents take place whenever needed, either with both parents or on an individual basis, in order to discuss further issues.

Finally, emphasis is placed on helping parents to implement strategies at home through modeling and scaffolding. Parents are systematically asked to attend selected parts of the child session in order to be trained in vivo in techniques that they are asked to implement at home. In fact, a key mediator between treatment attendance and outcome may be the extent to which parents actually apply newly acquired skills in real life (Clarke et al., 2015). For this reason, clinicians may invite parents to perform certain activities with the child in their presence, so that they evaluate if techniques are implemented properly and observe the quality of parent–child interactions. It has been found that intervention efforts that assist parents in the effective implementation of behavioral strategies may promote the continued acceptance of and adherence to this form of treatment (Johnston, Hommersen, & Seipp, 2008). Furthermore, clinicians highlight improvements and progress explicitly throughout treatment.

Consequently, the role of parents extends to that of cotherapists because parents are also implementers of treatment, as they have the unique opportunity to apply the techniques taught in the clinical setting in real-life situations. Therefore, it is particularly important for parents to acknowledge the degree to which their personal participation in treatment is required and the influence of their collaboration with clinicians on the effectiveness and duration of the intervention. For example, if parents attend sessions consistently, follow guidelines systematically, and are willing to replace malpractices with effective techniques of child behavior management, the intervention is likely to progress at a faster rate and be completed sooner.

Fathers' participation in treatment is usually less frequent relative to mothers' (Chronis et al., 2004). This finding may reflect the traditional tendency of men not to engage in help-seeking behavior. Fathers usually claim that they have increased workload and often report that child-rearing is mostly mothers' responsibility. According to our experience, fathers may have greater difficulty than mothers accepting the diagnosis of a neurodevelopmental disorder and tend to attribute it to other causes, often blaming mothers. It is not rare to listen to fathers saying: "My wife needs help and not the child." For these reasons, many mothers seem to be relieved when the diagnosis of ADHD is established. In this way, clinicians confirm their worries about the presence of a problem in the child and dispel fathers' inappropriate beliefs about "immaturity" or "mother's responsibility."

Many times, fathers accept child treatment or accompany their child to the clinical setting in order to comply with the mother's wishes, without having been convinced about the necessity or usefulness of the intervention. Over the last years, there has been an increase in fathers who are more actively involved with their children and participate more systematically in clinical interventions, but those fathers are still fewer compared to mothers.

Increasing the involvement of fathers in treatment is a main goal of the multilevel approach. Fathers' engagement facilitates social support within the family unit and consistency in parenting and discipline. Sports activities may provide a father-friendly context, as it is an area where fathers may interact more easily with their child and implement various behavioral techniques (Fabiano, Chacko et al., 2009).

In conclusion, we would like to highlight that engagement of parents in treatment is not restricted to parent training in the use of behavioral techniques. In contrast, the collaboration between parents and clinicians is broader and multidimensional. It includes continuous parental counseling on any issue related to the child, emotional support, and promotion of the family's better functioning and well-being.

12.3.2 Psychoeducation and Cognitive Restructuring

Once the framework of collaboration between the coordinating clinician and the family is established, and initial issues have been clarified, parent psychoeducation is ready to begin. Psychoeducation is defined as a specific component of the therapeutic program, focusing on didactic communication of information and providing patients and families with coping skills (Montoya et al., 2014). Psychoeducation includes thorough information about the nature, developmental course, symptomatology, and etiology of ADHD. It also disentangles controversial issues that might have arisen from previous resources. Particularly, clinicians explain the way in which core symptoms of ADHD and underlying cognitive deficits may affect child learning and behavior.

The main aim of psychoeducation is to increase awareness of symptoms and underlying causes in order to assist parents in distinguishing symptoms from developmentally appropriate behaviors (Lopez, Toprac, Crismon, Boemer, & Baumgartner, 2005). Psychoeducation emphasizes the power parents have to influence developmental outcomes and makes them active agents in treatment. Increased understanding and active participation are also expected to increase the likelihood that parents will follow through with treatment recommendations (Lopez et al., 2005).

Psychoeducation is a mainly informative treatment modality that integrates both psychotherapeutic and educational interventions (Montoya, Colom, & Ferrin, 2011). Psychoeducation is a dynamic and active process that adapts to the level and needs of each family. Parents ask questions, express their worries about the child's present and future, and discuss issues that require prompt decisions (e.g., medication initiation, selection of school setting, etc.).

At this stage, many parents often ask questions about issues that refer to the distant future. It is important for the clinician to respond to parents' concerns but at the same time reassure them. Clinicians should explain that the difficulties related to ADHD are not generalized and do not prevent the child from performing optimally in a multitude of tasks and domains. Provided with the right help from a young age, children with ADHD can achieve anything their potential would allow them to if they did not have the disorder. Therefore, expectations and goals should not be fewer or qualitatively inferior because of the presence of ADHD. What differs is the route to the achievement of goals, which may be more effortful and strenuous. We cannot know for sure if a child with ADHD will study at university or find a good job, as we do not have answers to these questions about their siblings without ADHD. Therefore, clinicians should redirect parents to the present, as it is more effective to focus on what we can do for the child today rather than hypothesizing about the future.

Psychoeducation increases parental motivation to participate in treatment (Montoya et al., 2011). Parents' motivational readiness is explored with a view to incorporating techniques to help enhance motivation levels where necessary. Increase in parent motivation predicts the perception of fewer barriers to treatment participation and greater treatment attendance (Nock & Photos, 2006). Moreover, parents' enhanced understanding of the nature of ADHD facilitates medication acceptance, if required (Liu, Robin, Brenner, & Eastman, 1991).

Many times, parents look forward to seeing the positive outcomes of the intervention immediately. During psychoeducation, the factors that affect the progress and outcomes of the intervention are discussed, and the role of parental contribution is emphasized. It takes insistence, patience, and trust in the clinician and the treatment plan to see positive outcomes. Furthermore, time is required for new behaviors to emerge and even more time for them to be stabilized and established.

Through psychoeducation, parents are getting prepared for the difficulties they may face during the implementation of treatment as well as for the likelihood of setbacks. Parents should know that children often try to return to former behaviors, testing their parents' firmness. These fluctuations do not constitute signs of poor effectiveness of the intervention. Contrariwise they are pivotal points that will lead to the next stages of treatment once treated effectively.

Finally, additional introductory information is provided through printed handouts, which provide a brief explanation of the ADHD symptoms, etiology, and prognosis and include references to additional sources of information.

Psychoeducation is also intended to replace maladaptive beliefs because parents' way of thinking is highly likely to influence the success of the interventions for their children (Hoza et al., 2000). However, usually, the provision of new information is not enough to foster new cognitions in parents. Therefore, the use of cognitive techniques throughout treatment is required to directly modify dysfunctional parental cognitions. This is very important because parental responses toward children are not elicited directly by child behaviors but are mediated by parental cognitions. Therefore, parents' causal attributions for their children's misbehavior mediate the impact of these behaviors both on their immediate emotional and behavioral responses to the child and the long-term quality of family relationships (Sonuga-Barke & Balding, 1993).

Parents and teachers of children with ADHD often have false and maladaptive perceptions, mainly regarding the nature and etiology of the disorder (Akram, Thomson, Boyter, & McLarty, 2009; Bussing et al., 2012). For example, it was found that preschool teachers and parents of preschoolers tend to evaluate behaviors related to ADHD as symptoms of a disorder mainly when they are manifested by girls, whereas they tend to regard them as developmentally appropriate behaviors when manifested by boys (Maniadaki et al., 2003; Maniadaki, Sonuga-Barke & Kakouros, 2005). As a result, parents tend to attribute intentionality and respond punitively toward boys displaying ADHD symptoms more frequently relative to girls exhibiting similar behaviors.

Parents who attribute their child's behavior exclusively to enduring symptoms of ADHD are less willing to be involved in behavioral treatments that emphasize improving child behavior through altering contingencies in the environment (Johnston, Mah, & Regambal, 2010). To the contrary, parents who assume some responsibility for their child's behavior are more likely to participate actively and effectively in such programs (Peters, Calam, & Harrington, 2005).

However, assuming responsibility for child behavior is often unpleasant and painful. Parents may engage in attributions of self-blame followed by self-condemnation about inappropriate parenting practices used so far. Clinicians should provide emotional support and help parents realize which practices are beneficial and which are not in order to modify the nonbeneficial ones and enhance parent–child interaction. Guilt and remorse are unhelpful to this end because they upset parents and may undermine their ability to actively engage in treatment.

Parents of children with ADHD often have difficulty distinguishing intentional oppositionality from ADHD symptomatology. Research with typically developing children has revealed that, in general, parents attribute negative behaviors to external, situational factors, whereas parents of difficult children often attribute misbehavior to the child's negative dispositions and hold the child responsible for the misbehavior (Baden & Howe, 1992). Parental attributions for children's misbehavior are important because they are closely associated with functionality of parenting responses. When parents attribute child misbehavior to an intentional and controllable act, they are more likely to respond negatively to such behavior in ways that are often harsh and authoritative (Hoza et al., 2000). Cognitive restructuring helps parents realize that their child behavior has biological underpinnings and is not intentional. As a result, parent level of anger and frustration usually decreases, leading to more supportive responses toward the child.

Parents' cognitions about the nature of their child's problems may also affect their treatment preferences. For example, parents who consider learning difficulties as their child's predominant problem are usually more positive toward medication initiation in order to enhance child-sustained attention. To the contrary, when they consider behavioral problems as predominant difficulties, they may favor behavioral interventions (Fiks et al., 2013). Parent beliefs about ADHD have been found to predict treatment choices, with parents who have more accurate beliefs favoring evidence-based treatments, and those who have inaccurate beliefs being more likely to seek alternative, less empirically supported interventions (Johnston, Seipp, Hommersen, Hoza, & Fine, 2005).

Parents' cognitions about *themselves* are also important to address because they may influence their level of engagement in treatment (Hoza et al., 2000; Smith et al., 2015). Parents of children with ADHD usually report lack of parenting confidence and low self-efficacy (Maniadaki, Sonuga-Barke, Kakouros et al., 2005). These parents may find it hard to follow through behavioral recommendations and subsequently feel that any efforts at improving child behavior through parent training are futile (Johnston et al., 2010). Specifically, low self-esteem in mothers, low parenting efficacy in fathers, and fathers' attributions for child noncompliance are associated with poorer response to treatment (Hoza et al., 2000). To the contrary, parents with high efficacy in the parenting realm can deal better with the unique challenges associated with parenting a child with ADHD (Hoza et al., 2005).

Besides, optimistic parents focus on active treatment of problems, whereas pessimistic parents focus on feelings of disappointment that overwhelm them and tend to quit in face of difficulties during treatment (Carver & Scheier, 2001). Pessimistic thinking may lead to negative expectations that impede treatment progress. Therefore, cognitive restructuring of parent perceptions about their own parenting abilities and strengthening of their self-confidence are an important part of the clinician's work with parents.

More importantly, parents should be helped to truly accept their child with ADHD. Many parents find it difficult to accept that their own child is not an excellent student, does not perform well in sports, is not the most popular child among peers, and does not always have the prosocial behavior that would make them proud. Therefore, the primary goals of parent cognitive restructuring are acceptance of the child and modification of the negative feelings that child difficulties evoke in parents.

In conclusion, it is important to highlight that psychoeducation and cognitive restructuring do not take place only at the initial stage of the intervention but continue and evolve throughout treatment. Repetition and deeper processing of some issues are often required, as well as dealing with new questions regarding the disorder or new maladaptive attitudes that emerge in the process.

12.3.3 Basic Principles of Parent Training and Counseling

Once therapeutic alliance has been established and basic psychoeducation has been carried out, parents are ready to receive training and counseling on various issues detected by the clinician in the initial phase of intervention. Training refers to the instruction of optimal parenting strategies and specific contingency management techniques. It usually has short duration and is implemented at the beginning of treatment, although it can be repeated and extended at any time throughout treatment. Counseling refers to a type of continuous support offered to parents by providing the necessary knowledge, tools, and guidance in order to render them capable of understanding the needs of their child and cope with overall concerns regarding the child.

A part of the training/counseling provided to parents of children with ADHD may be also useful for children with other kinds of difficulties, or even children without difficulties. The factors that favor the development of all children also favor the development of children with ADHD. A stable family environment, positive familial relationships, use of proper discipline techniques, acknowledgment of the child's abilities, encouragement, praise, and absence of criticism form the basis for optimal development of children with or without difficulties.

The initial goal of treatment is to improve the quality of parent–child interactions, which are often characterized by conflict, anger, and frustration in families of children with ADHD. These children, like every child, need love, affection, support, and unconditional acceptance in order to be emotionally healthy and cope effectively with the difficulties related to ADHD. For example, let's consider a father who tells his noncompliant daughter: "I will love you only if you start complying." This father sets the ground for making the child believe that blind obedience is the prerequisite for being loved. Even if defiant behavior is reduced following this statement, the harmful effects on shaping this child's personality and beliefs about right and wrong are immeasurable.

The multilevel approach promotes a positive focus on the child. Raising independent, assertive children with high self-esteem, resilience, and emotional stability constitutes the principal axis around which all the rest revolves. Besides, if the emotional environment in which the child grows is characterized by negativity, even the most effective intervention will not yield the expected results. There is no effective technique for a rejecting parent. Finally, children are more likely to comply and follow rules when these are expressed within the framework of a warm and positive rather than authoritative and punitive relationship.

Parent training includes tenets of social learning theory. Parents are trained in the main behavioral techniques (see Section 12.2) in order to implement an individualized behavioral program at home as soon as children have been familiarized with the structure of such a program through their own training. However, parent training is not restricted to the mere implementation of behavioral techniques but helps parents understand the theoretical framework that guides development of behavioral intervention plans. Parents should be in a position to recognize the causes of specific child behaviors and make hypotheses about the function of these behaviors. For example, a behavior (e.g., aggressive behavior) that occurs every time homework (antecedent) is assigned and ends up in removal of the assignment (consequence) is likely to have an escape-motivated function. Further evaluation of this situation may reveal that the workload is too demanding for this child. Therefore, reducing the workload, allowing breaks, or dividing the material into smaller sections may constitute more effective strategies than assigning a time-out. Parents who learn to respond according to the function that each behavior has and not according to the behavior itself—in other words, parents who understand the conceptual framework of behavioral theory—are more likely to use these skills over time in novel contexts with novel behaviors (Chacko et al., 2015).

Janney and Snell (2000) suggest an interesting classification of several maladaptive behaviors, based on the severity of the problem and its potential effect on the child and others.

Distracting behaviors are simply annoying (e.g., interrupting people while speaking) but do not cause any harm to the child or others. *Disruptive behaviors* affect negatively successful learning in various settings (e.g., disobedience). Finally, *destructive behaviors* are potentially harmful to the child or others (e.g., aggression). The use of this classification may appear particularly useful in prioritizing treatment goals within the context of behavior modification.

Another approach is the one that classifies behaviors depending on the function that they serve: (a) behaviors that are due to a medical condition, such as a headache; (b) behaviors that allow escaping, namely the opportunity to avoid an unpleasant or aversive activity; (c) behaviors that serve attention seeking; (d) behaviors that serve obtaining a reward; and (e) behaviors that serve sensory stimulation (Chacko et al., 2015).

Parent counseling includes consideration of some central concepts that should determine their behavior toward children with ADHD. One of them is *predictability*. Children should be in a position to predict parental responses and associate them with their own behavior. To this end, clear and concise rules and consequences should be set regarding desirable and undesirable behaviors. Furthermore, the same behaviors should be always followed by the same consequences. In other words, parental responses should be dictated by the child's behavior on the basis of a predetermined set of rules and consequences, and not by parent emotional state. For example, if a rule violation sometimes leads to punishment and sometimes is ignored, then the child is thrown into confusion. As a consequence, operant learning does not occur because the child's behavior is not associated with a specific parental response. In this case, the child does not learn which behaviors are acceptable and which not, but which emotional state of the parent leads to punishment and which not.

Another main concept is *stability*. When parents set boundaries and rules, it is important that they follow through with them in spite of the child's nagging and grumbling. Stability does not mean that parents are always right or that the child's wishes should not be valued. In contrast, parents should always listen actively to the child's opinion. However, in case where the violation of rules and boundaries may harm the child, the long-term benefit of the child precedes the short-term benefit of stopping nagging. Stability means setting rules that have been already discussed with the child, requiring that they be followed, supervising their implementation, and reinforcing compliance immediately. As the intervention progresses, parents do not need to supervise rules constantly, because one of the main goals of treatment is to increase self-control and self-regulation of behavior and to decrease external control.

A third fundamental concept is *consistency*. As parents should be consistent in rule setting and compliance, similarly they should be consistent in keeping their promises and providing predetermined rewards. Besides, parents are strong role models in preschool and school-age years, and their own behavior shapes children's behavior within the context of social learning. Therefore, it is imperative that parents be the first to observe rules and keep promises before they expect children to do so.

A cardinal principle that should also be embraced by parents is the *common practice* between fathers and mothers. Under no circumstances should any possible disagreements between fathers and mothers be expressed in front of the child. Otherwise, parents' reliability is questioned, and the child is given the opportunity to escape rules, taking advantage of the dispute between parents.

Finally, adult demands and expectations should be guided by the *principle of success*. This means that adults should always lead children with ADHD to experience success by adapting the level of difficulty of tasks and demands to the level of children's abilities. When children manage to complete tasks effectively, achieve positive outcomes, and respond to parent expectations, they experience a strong feeling of satisfaction, which encourages them to repeat the activity in which they succeeded. To the contrary, if children constantly fail due to increased demands or specific difficulties, they are likely to experience frustration and quit.

Therefore, the process of reaching a goal and the way in which parents encourage their child during this process is often more important than the goal itself and the positive outcome. For example, the benefit of a child making a drawing does not lie in the perfection of the drawing but in the qualities of the process. When the drawing is being made in a pleasant and playful atmosphere, in which the child is allowed to get messy and decide for the materials, colors, and shapes, with parents encouraging and praising the child enthusiastically, there is a huge benefit for the child no matter what the artistic value of the drawing will be. To the contrary, a perfect drawing made under parent detailed guidance and accompanied by step-by-step instructions is of much less benefit for the child.

Encouragement, praise, and accumulation of successful experiences are the main means that lead to enhancement of self-confidence and self-esteem, which is a central goal of treatment. To this end, it is important that parents avoid any characterization that insults the child's intelligence and personality as well as any comparison of the child with ADHD to siblings and peers, which usually puts the child with ADHD in an inferior position.

Parents should be also advised not to go to the opposite extreme and have very low expectations of the child. Overprotecting children with ADHD and preventing them from participating in activities that may be difficult for them should be avoided. The fact that the principle of success is important for children with ADHD does not mean that they should not try, risk, and fight in the process of achieving a goal. Learning is achieved through effort expenditure and, therefore, ample opportunities for action, trial, and error should be given to the child.

It should be noted that cognitive therapy strategies are incorporated into parent counseling in order to replace several parent inaccurate perceptions that could interfere with the implementation of intervention. Parents often claim that they have already used some of the techniques recommended without positive outcomes. It is important for the clinician to contrast the details of previously used strategies to the ones recommended. Other times, the clinician needs to correct the overgeneralization in parent thinking, for example, when they claim that the child *never* complies or that praise *never* works. Some parents hesitate to implement techniques like response cost or time-out, claiming that the child will not like them. In order to decide to do so, parental control can be framed as a constructive responsibility that is in the best interests of the child (Barkley, 1998b). Cognitive restructuring techniques enhance parent motivation to implement recommended strategies at home.

Generally, warm and creative parent–child communication considerably contributes to the enhancement of cognitive functioning. More specifically, parental interactions characterized by positive affect, reduced criticism, supportiveness, and a less controlling or directive approach, are associated with higher cognitive competence and school achievement and give these children a developmental advantage (Connell & Prinz, 2002; Wacharasin, Barnard, & Spieker, 2003). Supportive parents, who are aware of their child's abilities and set appropriate and challenging goals, are those who contribute decisively to optimal child development and treatment (Sonuga-Barke et al., 2006).

12.3.4 Issues Regarding Homework and Other Daily Routines

ADHD contributes to functional impairments in homework, including low engagement, poor productivity, avoidance, non-compliance, off-task behavior, problematic time management, and poor organization (Power, Werba, Watkins, Angelucci, & Eiraldi, 2006). The homework process has a lot of steps that can be difficult for children with ADHD to complete because self-regulation of behavior and motivation are necessary for successful homework completion. However, both these factors are deficient in ADHD according to current theories of the disorder. As a result, children with ADHD are more likely than their peers to forget to bring materials from school to home and vice versa, to have homework assignments recorded inaccurately, to procrastinate when completing homework assignments, to have left work incomplete, and to forget to turn in assignments the next day (Evans et al., 2009). Approximately 75% of children with ADHD exhibit clinically significant homework problems in comparison to 30% of typically developing peers (Coghill et al., 2008).

By the time they sit down to do their homework, children with ADHD are already mentally exhausted from their day at school. As a result, homework usually represents a source of stressful interaction between children with ADHD and their parents (Rogers, Wiener, Marton, & Tannock, 2009b). Therefore, homework routine for many children with ADHD usually undergoes the following process: the parent sits next to the child, tries to redirect attention to homework when it is directed toward other activities, threatens with removal of privileges if homework is not completed, checks over the homework for accuracy, and demands that the child redo incorrect assignments. Over time, the child may develop learned helplessness, a sense of personal inefficiency, and even efforts to counter-control via increased defiance or spitefulness (Chacko et al., 2015).

Therefore, homework performance is an important treatment target because it constitutes a pathway to academic improvement. Longitudinal studies show that homework performance in elementary school is a key predictor of later academic success among individuals with ADHD (Langberg et al., 2011). Furthermore, homework completion problems are persistent across time and are unlikely to be ameliorated without intervention (Langberg et al., 2016). Behavioral treatments focused on child homework problems result in acute improvements in homework performance among children with ADHD (Merrill et al., 2017).

Within this context, it is important to take some measures to minimize distractions as well as avoidance behaviors during the homework period. A consistent homework routine should be established. First, children with ADHD are in need of a specific and dedicated homework location, which is simple, quiet, and free of common distractions, such as television or background noise. The kitchen or the living room do not fulfill the aforementioned requirements and are inappropriate places for homework. Moreover, it is obvious that the other family members should try to be quiet. A mother speaking on the phone in a loud voice and siblings watching TV in the living room do not constitute the ideal environment that will help a child with poor attention concentrate on homework. Besides, the child's desk should contain only the necessary books and pencils and no decorative objects, toys, or other irrelevant things, which are very likely to direct the child's attention away from studying.

Moreover, homework should begin ideally early in the afternoon. In this way, accumulation of exhaustion, which usually occurs later in the day, can be prevented. Furthermore, this schedule allows a child the opportunity to earn several rewards, including a game or a walk, following the completion of homework. Under no circumstances should homework start after a dispute during which parents beg or threaten the child to study. If after-school activities make a regular schedule difficult, the child's time management may be helped by posting a weekly calendar that lists homework start and end times each day. Short frequent breaks should be planned in order to help children with ADHD recharge.

In the case of school-aged children with ADHD and learning difficulties, it is important to discuss with their teacher the possibility of lightening the homework load or developing an upper limit on the amount of time the child should spend on homework completion. This arrangement is necessary so that homework will not turn into an aversive process, surrounded by negative feelings. In case homework is associated with this kind of attributes, neither the principle of success nor motivation for learning supports this process.

Finally, parents should try to be involved in homework completion as little as possible. They should monitor the process discreetly so that they can award praise when they catch their child studying appropriately and according to the rules.

Due to the long hours that homework usually takes for children with ADHD, parents do not usually have the time nor are they in the mood to engage in recreational activities with their children. Therefore, many times mothers are mainly associated with the unpleasant experience of homework. It is important for parents to find opportunities for creative and recreational activities with the child, because this quality time provides the possibility of using positive reinforcement and strengthens the bond between parents and child. Besides, there are many opportunities for learning without books. An outing may act as an opportunity for the development and application of social skills; a board game teaches children to wait their turn patiently, follow rules, and learn how to win or lose; a sports activity along with parents may form the basis for the development of numerous skills, including gross motor skills, cooperation, and self-control.

Overall, the daily routines of children with ADHD should be well-organized and relatively stable because consistent routines usually become habits. The use of visual prompts (e.g., notes of the basic rules placed in various parts of the house) and a watch or a timer are particularly helpful. A steady routine based on specific rules and time schedule creates predictability, which leaves limited room for disputes and conflicts. Incentive systems are recommended in order to monitor and reward adherence to a structured organizational skills system and meeting operationalized goals.

12.4 Teacher Participation in Treatment

12.4.1 Importance of Teacher Participation in Treatment

The success of education depends to a great extent on the ideals that animate both teachers and students. School traditionally constitutes the major source of knowledge. However, contemporary school should give equal attention to academic learning and personal development by promoting socialization, skills development, prosocial behavior development, and capacity for personal achievement. Emotional intelligence, impulse inhibition, problem-solving skills, resilience, frustration tolerance, persistence, emotion regulation, cooperative skills, and development of high self-esteem should also constitute major educational goals. Children spend a big part of their life at school during development. A successful school trajectory may help them build self-confidence, become self-reliant, and learn to love knowledge and the process of obtaining it.

Some children manage to develop these characteristics and respond relatively easily to school demands. Children with ADHD, however, have greater difficulty and need specialized help in order to succeed. Without it, school may be a detestable place with predominant experiences of failure, belittlement, rejection, and social isolation. Such experiences reinforce aggressive behavior, defiance, and quitting. A psychological climate like this may have negative effects not only on children with ADHD and their family but also on the rest of the children in class, on school functioning, and consequently on the broader society.

While, for the majority of children, school promotes skills development, in the case of children with ADHD it often reinforces risk factors and adds new difficulties to the already existing ones. For this reason, many children with ADHD develop secondary behavioral problems, partly as a result of their failure to conform to the rules and demands of the school setting. When these children face learning difficulties as well, repeated academic failures may intensify these behavioral problems and have detrimental effects on self-esteem.

Teacher training about ADHD is of primary importance because the degree of knowledge and preparedness to work effectively with students with ADHD is a major factor contributing to the success or failure of these children (Bekle, 2001). A properly qualified teacher should be in a position to recognize and understand the difficulties of children with ADHD and have the necessary skills to encourage desirable behaviors, discourage undesirable ones, and generally promote the child's psychosocial development. In this way, teachers can improve class functioning, promote mental health in a great number of children, and contribute to the prevention of school dropout and juvenile delinquency. Most importantly, this training is essential in order to help teachers implement one of the main democratic principles of education, that everyone is unique and learns in a different way. Therefore, school should provide equal opportunities for every student regardless of each one's starting point.

Unfortunately, teachers are not sufficiently well-versed in managing children with developmental difficulties in regular classrooms (Arcia, Frank, Sanchez-LaCay, & Fernandez, 2000). In our view, this lack of teacher expertise greatly impedes the school trajectory of children with ADHD. A lot of teachers ignore the main principles needed to design and implement an effective behavioral intervention for children with ADHD or adapt their teaching to the needs of these children.

Within the framework of the multilevel approach, every effort is made so that the teacher can learn at least some basic principles and techniques in order to contribute as much as possible to the management of ADHD and learning difficulties in class. Teacher participation in treatment contributes to the development of a conjoint intervention in the clinical, family, and school settings, so that generalizability across settings and maintenance of positive outcomes over time can be achieved.

12.4.2 The Framework of Collaboration Between Clinicians and Teachers

Collaboration between the coordinating clinician and teachers is based on the willingness of the latter to get involved in this process and their sincere desire to dedicate time and energy in order to help children with ADHD. Therefore, a good rapport between the two parts is particularly important because clinicians and teachers may constitute a therapeutic team whose members may have different knowledge but share common goals. The members of this team work together in order to identify problem behaviors, analyze associated antecedent and consequent events, develop a specific feasible treatment plan, implement it at home, school, and the clinical setting, and finally assess outcomes. Therefore, teachers are engaged in a full partnership, as opposed to traditional expert-driven methods of consultation.

According to our experience, there are many teachers who are willing to support these children and cooperate with clinicians and the family in a joint treatment plan. On the other hand, there are teachers who refuse to get involved and insist on common misconceptions about laziness or parental responsibility. Recently, a teacher of the first grade whom we contacted for one of his students denied the diagnosis of ADHD, claiming that ADHD cannot be recognized before the third grade. Therefore, he postponed our communication for two years.

The greatest difficulties regarding teacher participation in treatment are ignorance or misconceptions, mainly when they are surrounded by a certainty of possessing knowledge (Kakouros et al., 2004; Moore et al., 2015). Obtaining teacher collaboration for adolescents is usually even more challenging. The Pygmalion effect in the classroom very vividly describes how teachers' expectations about their students, even if they are completely erroneous relative to students' real abilities, will transform their behavior in ways that the student performance confirms the initial expectations (Rosenthal & Jacobson, 1968).

A pertinent difficulty in collaboration with teachers refers to the case in which teachers feel confident in their abilities to meet the demands of children with ADHD in the classroom regardless of whether they have had relevant training. In this case, they may implement weak and untailored behavioral interventions but not feel the need to improve them. In a study conducted on a sample of 149 teachers in the United States, most teachers reported practicing evidence-based classroom management procedures, although in fact these procedures were ineffective (Akin-Little, Little, & Laniti, 2007). For example, the most widespread techniques were verbal reprimands and moving the student closer to the teacher, which may act as positive reinforcers for misbehavior through the attention that they provide.

Therefore, before the initiation of school consultation, clinicians should explore teacher cognitions and willingness to participate in treatment in order to evaluate possible barriers and determine the extent to which teacher involvement is to the benefit of the child. There are few cases in which teacher involvement in treatment could prove to be detrimental to the child. For example, the teacher of a boy with ADHD, who was also a mother of a child with ADHD, characteristically told us that as nobody helped her with her own child, she would not help any other child as well. It is obvious that engagement of this teacher in treatment was out of question. In similar cases, transfer of the child to another classroom or school may be sometimes necessary.

A significant factor that may influence the effectiveness of school-based interventions is the extent to which teachers view strategies as acceptable, feasible, fair, and reasonable (Pfiffner & DuPaul, 2015). For example, it has been found that teachers consider medication as more acceptable for boys than girls with ADHD (Pisecco et al., 2001). Moreover, there are teachers who are opposed to the philosophy of behavioral interventions out of concern that they are too mechanistic. Others simply resist modifying their teaching methods or making classroom accommodations for children with ADHD. Finally, many teachers simply have little confidence in the effectiveness of commonly used interventions for ADHD (Graczyk et al., 2005).

Other important teacher factors appear to be tolerance of particular behaviors, teaching style, previous experience with students with ADHD, communication style, and time involvement for treatment delivery. The success of teacher involvement in treatment depends to a large extent upon the broad-mindedness of the teachers as well as their level of engagement and investment in the process. Teacher factors associated with student success include patience, knowledge of intervention techniques, ability to collaborate with an interdisciplinary team, use of gestures when communicating with students, and a positive attitude toward children with special needs.

Therefore, interventions are not effective or ineffective by definition, because variability in response to intervention depends on the people who implement them. Consequently, a behavioral intervention may work or not work within a classroom depending on the personality, the skills, and the degree of motivation demonstrated by the teacher. Assessing the level of teacher engagement and other teacher factors before implementing treatment at school is essential in order to define the need for additional support for teachers to elicit greater investment (Power et al., 2009). A critical responsibility for the clinician is to promote partnerships with parents and teachers, as well as between them, so that system dynamics are in place for positive collaboration (DuPaul & Power, 2008).

Clinicians can enhance teachers' engagement in treatment by highlighting the importance of their role in treatment and by showing understanding and empathy for the burden posed on teachers by children with ADHD. Moreover, it is important to lighten the workload involved for teachers because this might influence teacher engagement (Moore et al., 2015). Motivation can be also facilitated by helping teachers understand that intervention will be easily applicable and will be worth the effort in students' positive outcomes. Finally, clinicians should provide emotional support to teachers and help them handle disappointment and frustration.

In case the basic prerequisites for the collaboration between the clinician and teachers are fulfilled, the clinician may visit the school, and the teacher may visit the clinical setting. Contact by phone is arranged on a regular basis, depending on the needs of the intervention. It should be noted that a few consultation contacts are insufficient to yield significant teacher change in their approach to students with ADHD. Teachers usually require explicit instruction and guidance in the process of implementing a behavioral intervention at school. The emphasis of school consultation is on giving teachers specific strategies and skills to promote the child's use of newly acquired skills in the school environment (Braswell & Bloomquist, 1991). Based on the questionnaires filled in during the assessment, the clinician and the teacher set the goals of intervention at school. A daily report card is usually the means of communication among teachers, family, and clinicians. The exact use of this card will be presented in Section 12.4.5.

Teachers' attitudes influence classroom organization and management and teaching practices. It has been found that students with behavioral problems tend to be treated differently by even the most effective teachers, who typically call on them infrequently, praise them in a less positive way, and criticize them more often (Bekle, 2001). However, it is necessary for teachers not only to be knowledgeable about ADHD but to possess positive, non-discriminatory attitudes toward the disorder as well. Psychoeducation is pivotal so that teachers modify several misconceptions about ADHD and be better prepared to implement behavioral interventions in class. Besides, psychoeducation may build teachers' trust in the use of behavioral techniques (Houghton, Carroll, Taylor, & O'Donoghue, 2006).

Teachers should be helped to understand the neurobiological nature of ADHD; the fact that ADHD is a problem of sustaining attention, effort and motivation and does not represent a lack of skill or knowledge; the effect of comorbidities on functional impairment; and the need for more structure, frequent and salient positive consequences, consistent negative consequences, and classroom accommodations for students with ADHD (Pfiffner & DuPaul, 2015). They should also learn to define operationally problem behaviors in the classroom.

Another important issue is the quality of relationship between parents and teachers because conflicts between them may compromise student outcomes. Sometimes parents may hold the school responsible for their child's difficulties or consider that the school fails to address their child's needs adequately. On the other hand, teachers may think that child inappropriate behavior may stem from adverse family factors. However, positive and constructive relationships between teachers and parents are critical to children's academic achievement, prosocial behavior, and emotional development. Clinicians should help teachers and parents establish a good rapport and enhance family–school partnership. Family–school partnership emphasizes the bidirectional interactions between families and schools intended to create a context to resolve students' school problems through coordinated and consistent cross-system supports (Pfiffner & DuPaul, 2015; Sheridan & Kratochwill, 2008). The multilevel approach favors the theoretical framework of conjoint behavioral consultation, which is defined as

> a strength-based, cross-system problem-solving and decision-making model wherein parents, teachers, and other caregivers or service providers work as partners and share responsibility for promoting positive and consistent outcomes related to a child's academic, behavioral, and social-emotional development.
>
> (Sheridan & Kratochwill, 2008, p. 25)

Through this process, parents and teachers serve as joint consultees who mutually identify, define, analyze, and address student concerns with the support of the clinician who coordinates treatment and oversees implementation.

The treatment integrity, defined as the extent to which the treatment plan is implemented as designed, should be regularly monitored by the clinician, because teacher consistency in the implementation of behavioral interventions tends to decline after few weeks (Noell et al., 2005). Treatment integrity depends on several factors. In some cases, the teacher may feel burdened either due to the time needed for implementation or due to the complexity of some interventions. In other cases, the teacher's beliefs about the treatment's potential effectiveness, the degree of compatibility between teaching style and intervention, and the teacher's motivation to participate in treatment significantly affect treatment integrity (DuPaul, 2007).

However, accurate treatment implementation is closely associated with treatment effectiveness and child outcomes (Noell, Gresham, & Gansle, 2002). A means of sustaining treatment implementation is performance feedback, namely a frequent review of the effect of the intervention on student performance in the context of ongoing evaluation between the clinician and the teacher. Within this context, completed steps are discussed, problems are identified and solved, and next moves are designed (Noell et al., 2005). In addition, teacher self-efficacy is a critical element in treatment integrity. According to Bandura (2001), self-efficacy beliefs are learned, and much of this learning occurs through direct mastery experiences and vicarious learning experiences. Therefore, teachers should be supported in their efforts to work with students with ADHD and be provided with ongoing consultation in order to plan and troubleshoot behavioral interventions in class.

12.4.3 Behavior Management of ADHD in Class

The presence of a student with ADHD in class may easily disrupt regular class functioning and place a substantial demand on teacher skills and patience. Teachers need to follow some basic principles and use specific techniques for the management of ADHD in class in order to help students, enhance classroom functioning, and prevent class disorganization.

Classroom management is a set of procedures that can help teachers maintain order in the classroom and involve both proactive and reactive procedures. The main principles and techniques regarding parent participation in treatment apply for teachers as well. Moreover, many of the strategies that work for children with ADHD also help other children. A functional educational environment for children with ADHD is a good educational environment for all children (Reeve, 1994). The difference is that typically developing children have the ability to adapt to less favorable conditions, whereas children with ADHD need modification of these conditions in order to respond efficiently to school demands. Therefore, classwide strategies may be an option for teachers aiming to overall better classroom management.

A key contextual issue that may influence the effectiveness of a school-based intervention is the quality of relationship between children with ADHD and their teachers (Moore et al., 2015). Teachers frequently respond to the challenging behaviors of students with ADHD by becoming more commanding. Over time, teacher frustration may lead to less positive and more negative interactions with these students. However, children do not comply when they feel that they are not loved. Therefore, teachers should create a positive and supportive climate for the child with ADHD, being the first to exhibit acceptance and respect toward this child. Even in cases where correction for disruptive behavior is required, this correction should be brief, directed at the student's behavior, not the student, and provided in a calm manner and in proximity to the student (Pfiffner, 2011).

A significant consideration for teachers is to help children with ADHD integrate in the peer group and improve their ability to apply social skills in real-life situations. Teachers are often present during interactions of children with ADHD with their peers and can therefore provide not only reminders of appropriate behavior but also reinforcement in order to promote generalization out of the clinical setting. First, teachers should set explicit classroom rules for mutual respect and social inclusion, and systematically reinforce children who apply them and exhibit behaviors characterized by kindness and patience toward classmates. Second, teachers should provide a role model of positive interaction with children with ADHD and encourage the other students to follow their example. When teachers maintain an emotionally warm relationship with these children, respond in a calm and stable way to defiant behavior, and show personal interest, they convey the message that a child with ADHD is a person worthy of respect and affection and model the ways in which peers can approach this child (Mikami, 2015). Finally, teachers should emphasize the positive characteristics and genuine strengths of children with ADHD, acknowledging them publicly in order to shift peers' attention from maladaptive behaviors to positive characteristics of these children.

Teachers who take into account these issues considerably help students with ADHD conform to the rules of the classroom and increase socially competent behavior. Furthermore, they attenuate peer rejection by training the peer group to refrain from excluding and instead interact inclusively with children with ADHD (Mikami et al., 2013). Consequently, they give children with ADHD the opportunity to experience the positive aspects of school life, including improved peer relationships.

Children with ADHD function significantly better in consistent settings. Maintaining a well-organized, structured, and predictable class, in which the daily schedule is posted, the rules are explicit, and their consequences specific and applicable, definitely helps students with ADHD but also all the other students to comply with classroom rules. Rules should be phrased in a positive manner and posted in full view of all students. Rules delivered through visible and external modes of presentation, including posters, stop signs, charts, pictures, and color coding may contribute to reducing the need for frequent verbal repetitions. Rules should be clearly explained at the beginning and periodically throughout the year (DuPaul, Weyandt, & Janusis, 2011).

Classroom adaptations and arrangement of the learning environment in particular ways might be necessary, including reducing noise levels, structuring classrooms formally, and sitting children with ADHD in the front seats, in proximity to the teacher's desk and away from distractions, such as windows and the door. It is important that teachers maintain direct contact with students with ADHD and monitor their work. These children need more external signs for behavior regulation than typically developing peers. In case they get distracted, teachers can redirect their attention back to the lesson with the use of nonverbal and visual cues, including eye contact, hand gestures, or other signals that teach students to recognize the conditions that trigger specific behaviors. Verbal redirection should be done by using clear, concise, and inconspicuously delivered verbal cues rather than long explanations.

Providing children with ADHD with the opportunity to move during the lesson is of utmost importance. For this reason, teachers can give them the opportunity to release their energy by assigning some duties, including cleaning up the board, collecting notebooks, handing out notes, and supplying the classroom with markers. Providing frequent breaks between learning tasks is also important (Purdie et al., 2002).

In order to reduce undesirable behaviors, teachers can use the behavioral techniques introduced at the beginning of this chapter (see Section 12.2), adapted to the educational setting.

Differential reinforcement is a particularly effective technique. The common strategy of many teachers is to attend to off-task behaviors by reprimanding them and to ignore on-task and other positive behaviors. In this way, children with ADHD learn that they can attract attention by interrupting their work and being disruptive. Teachers should learn to purposely direct their attention to children when they work appropriately, by using verbal and nonverbal cues and positive gestures in order to help them remain on task and display desirable behaviors. Frequent feedback should be delivered for ongoing task performance.

Planned ignoring is the appropriate technique for nondisruptive minor motor and nonattending behaviors intended to gain teacher attention. This technique is contraindicated in case of destructive or aggressive behavior. Furthermore, the efficacy of this technique may increase when teachers ignore the undesirable behavior exhibited by the child with ADHD (e.g., talking without raising hand) while at the same time praise students who manifest the positive opposite of this behavior (e.g., raising hand in order to talk). The last step is praising children with ADHD as soon as they begin raising their hand when they wish to speak. In this case, vicarious learning occurs through modeling and the child's desire for positive teacher attention (Pfiffner & DuPaul, 2015).

The use of praise is essential following exhibition of positive target behaviors. Children with ADHD should be provided with more frequent and powerful praise when following rules than typical children (Purdie et al., 2002). However, the efficacy of praise depends on the *time* and the *way* it is provided. Praise should be delivered immediately following desirable behavior, specify the behavior being reinforced, and delivered with a warm tone of voice, appropriate facial expression, and varied content depending on the child's developmental level. Smiles, nods, and pats on the back are important social reinforcers for children.

Incentive systems (see Section 12.2.6) are very strong means for suppressing negative behaviors and developing positive ones in children with ADHD. The development, implementation, and evaluation of such systems should include clearly defined and realistic goals of graduated difficulty (DuPaul & Stoner, 2003). Teachers should be enthusiastic and make the visualization of the incentive system look funny and cheerful, by using beautiful colors and special words to describe the reward.

The use of powerful reinforcers is critical for the effectiveness of incentive systems. They can be detected either by discussing with children or by observing the kind of activities in which they engage more. Access to these activities can be used as a reinforcer. Common reinforcers for younger children are small gifts, stickers, or school supplies that are found in a grab bag. For older children, it could be computer game time, earning extra recess, being the teacher's assistant, or the leader in an activity or game. (Pfiffner & DuPaul, 2015). Moreover, reinforcers should be rotated or varied over time, so that children do not become bored. Many teachers tend to abandon incentive systems after a while because they do not consider them effective any more, whereas what is needed is reinforcer modification.

Incentive systems can be used on a team level, involving the entire class and not only the students with ADHD. There are many ways of implementing these programs (Pfiffner, 2011). For example, children can compete with teachers and win points by following rules, whereas teachers win points when children violate these rules. Whoever has the majority of points at the end of the day (students or teachers), chooses an activity for the whole class. In another version, students win points during the week and those who have the most points at the end of the week gain a benefit. Moreover, the class can be divided into competing teams and earn points for their respective team in order to win a group prize. In this way, students compete against each other in manifesting the best behavior. This practice has the advantage of not stigmatizing students with ADHD and preventing peer complaints about teacher special attention to children receiving treatment, although these concerns have not been substantiated in research studies (Pfiffner & DuPaul, 2015). Teachers implementing such a program should make sure to minimize peer pressure and subversion of the program by one or more children.

Response cost and time-out should be used judiciously and only for behaviors that are aggressive and dangerous or for those that resist modification through positive reinforcement. The loss of recess time is not recommended as a consequence, given that physical exercise benefits children with ADHD in coping with their symptoms during the lesson (Pontifex, Saliba, Raine, Picchietti, & Hillman, 2013). In addition, the efficacy of time-out is dependent on whether the classroom is viewed as a positive environment by the student; otherwise time-out can actually reinforce problematic behaviors (DuPaul et al., 2011).

Overall, it is important that teachers deliver consequences, positive or negative, immediately and consistently to children with ADHD. Smaller but immediate rewards are more effective than bigger but distant ones due to poor motivation and delay aversion of these children. The efficacy of penalties lies in their immediacy and consistency and not in their severity. Moreover, penalties should be administered privately and not in front of the entire class. Suspension from classroom or school is neither acceptable nor effective for children with ADHD (Pfiffner & DuPaul, 2015). It is not immediate, and many children may find staying in the playground or at home more enjoyable than being in class. For those children who are avoiding work, these approaches are equivalent to positive reinforcement. Furthermore, occasional praise and inconsistent reprimands do not seem to work on children with ADHD. Finally, when rewards and response costs are used together, the opportunity to earn tokens should be greater than the possibility of losing them. "Positives before negatives" is the order of the day for effective behavioral interventions (Barkley, 2008).

A widely used and effective means of communication among school, family, and the clinical setting is the *daily report card*. It is an operationalized list of a child's target behaviors and includes specific criteria for meeting each goal. A reasonable number of behavioral goals are targeted for change, stated in a positive manner, and set at an attainable level. Teachers track the child's progress on the card throughout the day by noting whether goals related to target behaviors were met (DuPaul, Eckert, & Vilardo, 2012; Fabiano et al., 2010; Vannest, Davis, Davis, Mason, & Burke, 2010). Target behaviors may include both behavior and academic performance.

A daily report card is an intervention tool that has been used to enhance functional outcomes, such as increasing work completion, reducing talk-outs during instruction, increasing on-task behavior, and remediating a range of behavioral problems (Vannest et al., 2010). This card may also contribute to improvements in academic achievement, given that it may target motivation and academic enablers that mediate the relationship between ADHD symptoms and academic achievement (Volpe et al., 2006). However, it should be noted that complementary academic intervention that directly targets peripheral learning outcomes is necessary to support educational achievement in children with ADHD (Fabiano et al., 2009).

This card returns home completed so that parents can monitor the child's progress, and provide contingencies on a consistent basis dependent on teacher ratings of goal attainment. The program requires a clear and consistent system for translating teacher reports into consequences at home. Statements on negative outcomes should be brief, neutral, and unemotional.

The number of target behaviors and frequency of feedback and reinforcement depend on the child's developmental level and severity of symptomatology. For example, younger or very impulsive children may require fewer goals and more frequent feedback and reinforcement than older or less impulsive children. In case there is a similar report card at home, these two cards can work in combination (Hinshaw, 2009). Goals are modified on an ongoing basis in accordance with student progress.

To maximize the effectiveness of this method, coordination among direct service providers should occur for students who are served by multiple teachers throughout the day. Furthermore, it is important to actively involve parents in planning and implementing this program (Vannest et al., 2010).

Home-based reward programs of school behavior have several beneficial effects. First, they give teachers the opportunity to monitor multiple behaviors and provide feedback to students with ADHD more frequently than is usually provided at school. There is flexibility in implementation and lack of interruption to instructional time. Parents are more directly informed about their child's behavior and performance at school. In addition, these programs take advantage of the variety of reinforcers available at home. Furthermore, communication between the child's teachers and parents is strengthened, and collaboration is fostered (Pfiffner & DuPaul, 2015). Finally, these programs may promote treatment integrity because calling attention to the child's goals and recording success related to goal attainment may serve to prevent teacher and parent drift (Fabiano et al., 2010).

12.4.4 Academic Intervention Strategies for ADHD

Students with ADHD have difficulty remaining on task when mental effort is required, particularly when their motivation is low, as is often the case with various school subjects. As a result, they do not often manage to follow the lesson all the way through, do not finish their projects, and benefit less from traditional teaching methods relative to their classmates. Boredom and avoidance of activities in which interest is lost usually leads to manifestation of disruptive behavior in class. This behavior is likely to prompt teachers to deliver reprimands or impose punishments, which further alienate students with ADHD from the educational process.

This vicious circle may break if teachers modify academic instruction and use specific academic intervention strategies, including computer-assisted instruction, peer tutoring, self-regulated strategy for written expression, directed note-taking, and task modification in order to enhance specific areas and overall academic performance (DuPaul, 2007). These strategies focus on increasing the structure of the child's environment and making tasks appear more manageable in order to reduce frustration, increase persistence, and help sustain attention (Raggi & Chronis, 2006).

Task modification involves reducing task length and complexity by creating smaller task units, paired with teacher praise contingent on task completion. As students succeed with shorter assignments, the length of assignments can be gradually increased, thereby matching classroom norms (DuPaul et al., 2011). It is important that time limits are externally and concretely represented by the use of timers, set to reflect the elapsed time available for task performance, as well as by frequent reminders before time is up (DuPaul & Stoner, 2003).

Task modification also includes variety and innovation in the stimulus properties of tasks assigned to children with ADHD. Children with ADHD have a greater need for stimulation and are less tolerant of situations involving minimal stimulation, which results in increased errors and excessive motor and verbal activity (Raggi & Chronis, 2006). Therefore, intra-task stimulation through the use of different colors, shapes, and textures, increased rate of material presentation, and frequent shifts in the nature of the task may enhance vigilance and learning in children with ADHD (DuPaul & Eckert, 1998). Presenting the same teaching material with small variations increases students' interest in the activity and helps them maintain motivation. Finally, low interest activities that require a passive response from students could be interspersed with interactive activities, which give students with ADHD the opportunity to better channel their need for action into learning activities and not into disruptive behavior. Given that fidgeting and out-of-seat behavior are common in children with ADHD, brief moments of recess and physical exercise are essential to reduce hyperactivity and diminish the monotony of long academic work periods (Pfiffner & DuPaul, 2015).

Instruction modification refers to simplifying instructions so that they are brief, explicit, and clear, and modifying the delivery or modality of instruction depending on the student's individual learning style. Extra time should be allowed for completing tasks. The use of positive feedback is important, as it serves to reinforce targeted behaviors and increase motivation and persistence at tasks. Furthermore, teacher proximity is highly effective for helping students with ADHD maintain attention. For example, the teacher may move closer to the student when giving directions and monitoring seatwork.

Multimedia use entails the presentation of specific instructional objectives at the beginning of each lesson, highlighting of essential material, division of content into smaller chunks of information, and use of repeated trials (DuPaul & Eckert, 1998). Computer-assisted instruction has intuitive appeal for children with ADHD because of its interactive format, use of multiple sensory modalities, and ability to provide immediate feedback about response accuracy (Loe & Feldman, 2007).

Strategy training involves teaching specific strategies to students that they can implement in academic situations to improve their performance (Evans, Pelham, & Grudberg, 1995). Some of these strategies are associated with homework demands, including note-taking and study skills. An assignment notebook and color-coded folders could be provided to help students organize assignments for different academic subjects. Other strategies are related to self-management, including self-verbalization, namely repeating out loud instructions before application (Pfiffner & DuPaul, 2015).

Peer tutoring is a strategy in which children with ADHD are paired with a peer tutor who aids them in learning academic material. This strategy facilitates the development of both academic and social skills and allows for instruction that is individually tailored to the child's academic ability (DuPaul & Stoner, 2003). It requires active responding on the part of the student and frequent, immediate feedback on the part of the tutor.

It is important that teachers evaluate the child's level of knowledge and skills and adapt their demands accordingly, by always adhering to the principle of success. According to this reasoning, it is important that teachers do not correct every mistake in written assignments, but rather focus on one kind of mistakes at a time. As students make progress, teachers can increase their demands and renew their educational goals. Finally, the level of difficulty of oral evaluation in class should give students with ADHD the opportunity to experience success and be reinforced. Changes could also be made to the examination environment to ensure that students' ADHD behaviors do not impact on exam performance. Students with ADHD could be assessed in smaller units, and the exam length could be reduced, so that attention remains focused on the examination (Raggi & Chronis, 2006).

12.5 Child Participation in Treatment

12.5.1 General Guidelines

In the multilevel approach, the focus of treatment is on the child, within a broad treatment context, which actively involves parents and teachers. Goals and methods vary according to the child's age, developmental level, severity of primary symptoms, comorbidity, and associated problems. The principles and techniques that have been described so far are also available in the clinicians' repertoire and are used in the child sessions as well. Prioritizing goals and developing an individualized treatment plan is achieved on the basis of the information that has been recorded and evaluated during assessment.

The main kinds of interventions that can be delivered to the child include speech therapy, occupational therapy, special education, psychotherapy, psychoeducational intervention for ADHD, and their combinations. Speech therapy is provided by a speech therapist, occupational therapy by an occupational therapist, psychoeducational intervention for ADHD by a child psychologist, special education by a special educator, and psychotherapy by a clinical child psychologist or a child psychiatrist, particularly in cases of comorbidity with certain disorders. However, within the multilevel approach, all these specialties adopt the general principles of the cognitive-behavioral theory, follow the main behavior modification techniques, and have received specialized training in implementing these methods on children with ADHD. In other words, we strongly believe that having the specialty of a speech therapist, an occupational therapist, a special educator, or a psychologist is not enough in order to be effective in the treatment of ADHD. In addition, extensive expertise in the *specific disorder* is needed. In case a combination of interventions is delivered to the child, one of the professionals is delegated to be the keyworker who coordinates treatment within the interdisciplinary team and with school, and oversees its implementation. The keyworker is usually the child psychologist or the child psychiatrist of the team.

Session frequency is usually determined at one to three times a week, with two times being the most common frequency. This frequency gradually decreases as intervention progresses until goals have been achieved and intervention is completed. In case medication is considered a necessary complementary option, the child's progress is also monitored by the physician who is prescribing medication.

We will now present some basic principles for the clinicians' collaboration with the child. Many of these principles may seem simplistic or self-evident. However, according to our experience, these minor details of *how* something is done are those that determine the efficacy of *what* is done. The difference in the efficiency of two therapists who have similar qualifications and theoretical background lies in the mastery with which they will implement the intervention and the minute details that will be taken into account.

The first and predominant goal of every therapeutic intervention is the development of a strong positive relationship between the clinician and the child. In the context of such a relationship, maximization of child collaboration and motivation for active participation in treatment can be achieved. For this reason, the clinicians who work with the child should not alternate often if there is no special reason. The degree of the participants' commitment in the intervention is a significant factor that affects treatment integrity. Even the most effective evidence-based interventions are of little value without *participant responsiveness*, defined as the degree to which intervention participants are engaged in treatment (Power et al., 2005). Particularly for children with ADHD, the quality of relationship with their therapists lays the foundation for positive outcomes. Given that these children usually exhibit limited self-control, low frustration tolerance, and noncompliance, it is obvious that establishment and maintenance of this relationship is not always an easy task.

Another key goal is limit setting. By knowing what is expected, children are facilitated to feel safe. The establishment of therapeutic boundaries communicates that the clinician cares about the child and the clinical setting becomes a safe place (Friedberg & McClure, 2002).

For the preceding reasons, neither the specialty nor the theoretical expertise in ADHD can guarantee the effectiveness of the clinicians who are implicated in the treatment of ADHD. The best theoretical expertise cannot lead to optimal outcomes if clinicians do not possess the basic skills to implement treatment correctly, in the same way that children with ADHD usually know what to do but do not always do what they know. The presence of certain personality traits is what allows clinicians to be successful in their collaboration with the child. To be more specific, clinicians need to be consistent, patient, persistent, and calm. They should have empathy, flexibility, and imagination. It is important that they be constantly vigilant and alert. They should have high self-esteem and high self-efficacy. Clinicians involved in the treatment of ADHD should truly love not only children in general but children with ADHD in particular. They should also find working with them pleasant. All the above cannot be taught, but constitute characteristics that can be developed. A recommended policy for clinicians is to have come into contact with children with ADHD, possibly within the framework of an internship or supervised work, before they decide to work with this population.

The workplace with the child should be simple and free from distracting visual and auditory stimuli. The material that will be used during the session should be kept in a place accessible only to the clinician and not to the child. It should be also out of the child's field of vision. Every toy, book, or other type of material should be presented successively, after previous material has been put away, because a plethora of objects in front of the child causes confusion and increases difficulty in focusing attention and remaining on task.

An important feature of the collaboration between the clinician and the child is eye contact, which should be constant. For this reason, the most suitable position for the clinician is to sit across from the child. The child should assume a proper sitting position, which will not allow bending, wiggling, or putting feet on the chair. The right position of the child and the clinician allows direct control of child behavior and maximization of attention span. Within such a context and with the clinician's appropriate manipulations, the child quickly starts to display appropriate behavior, experience success, and be reinforced. At the same time, the child learns how to self-regulate behavior in order to respond more effectively to the demands of the session.

Children with ADHD must be constantly alert and highly motivated to fully benefit from the intervention. A positive attitude toward the activities of the 45-minute session is also necessary. Therefore, the goals of the session and the activities underpinning these goals should be presented in a way that the child looks forward to being involved in the process and allocates the maximum effort. Child arousal can be achieved in many ways. Modulation of voice tone, as well as pace and pitch of speech, accompanied by expressive moves and gestures, may awaken children and intensify arousal. Innovation in the presentation of activities, frequent alteration of activities, and constant use of contingency techniques also contribute to this end. It is particularly important that the therapist be enthusiastic first. It is impossible for a child to maintain arousal and sustain effort and positive behavior in front of an adult who shows signs of boredom or underarousal.

Within the multilevel approach, the keyworker usually develops a token economy system in collaboration with the interdisciplinary team delivering treatment, the child, the parents, and the teachers. The keyworker coordinates goal setting, choice of tokens and backup rewards, reinforcement schedule, and the final design of the token economy chart or the daily report card, which constitutes the primary means of communication across participants and settings. The clinicians delivering treatment are persons of reference for the child, as they evaluate goal attainment in every session and provide the child with the appropriate feedback.

According to the multilevel approach, the broader goal of every intervention for children with ADHD, no matter whether it is delivered in the context of speech therapy, psychoeducational intervention, or occupational therapy, is the development of self-control skills, namely self-management and self-regulation of behavior on the basis of internalized rules due to the important role that deficits in these skills play in children's symptomatology and functioning, as both the Executive Dysfunction theory and the Dual Pathway model explain (see Sections 6.2 and 6.3, respectively). Applying these skills extends to all the key areas of functioning. Furthermore, every intervention is guided by recent scientific developments regarding etiopathogenesis and pathophysiology of ADHD and is influenced by the contemporary theories of the disorder (see Chapter 6).

12.5.2 Preschool Years

Treatment of ADHD at preschool years has the potential to lead to the most impressive outcomes. The optimal outcome refers to the secondary prevention of ADHD. During this period, interventions take maximum advantage of the brain's neuroplasticity and aim at restoring certain neuropsychological deficits that are directly or indirectly related to ADHD symptomatology and functional impairment.

During preschool years, rarely is a child with ADHD referred because of the core symptoms of the disorder. Even if a child is particularly hyperactive, impulsive, or inattentive, usually parents, teachers, and even pediatricians consider that these are normal developmental characteristics and often describe them with the general and scientifically meaningless term of "immaturity." There are two main reasons of referral of preschoolers with ADHD to child mental health services: speech and language problems and/or behavioral problems. In the first case, the most common difficulties are either speech delay or phonological difficulties. In the second case, defiant, noncompliant, and sometimes aggressive behavior is usually of concern, as it hinders daily cooperation with the child.

When a child is referred for assessment because of speech and language problems, speech therapy is usually recommended. However, according to our clinical experience, most of these children are placed into a narrowly focused speech language program after they have received a general diagnosis of SLPs, without a thorough developmental assessment that could associate these speech problems to ADHD or another neurodevelopmental disorder. However, delays in the attainment of early milestones may have negative consequences for development in other domains or may be a general risk indicator for a range of conditions, ADHD included (Johnson et al., 2015). Thus, attention difficulties may be responsible for language delays in children with ADHD (Kelly, Walker, & Norbury, 2013).

Infants during the first year of life are able to exercise little volitional control over their allocation of attention (Colombo & Cheatham, 2006). Toward the end of the first year, the capacity to exercise attentional control, namely to choose what is paid attention to and what is ignored, emerges as the neural circuitry substantiating this cognitive function matures (Deoni et al., 2011). The ability to exercise control over attention is thought to be a faculty required for the acquisition of skills in a range of other areas of cognitive and behavioral functioning and correlates longitudinally with later attentional development (Posner & Rothbart, 2007). Individual differences in aspects of attentional control have been shown to correlate with early language development (Rose, Feldman, & Jankowski, 2009), with early learning in academic settings (Rose, Feldman, & Jankowski, 2011; Steele, Karmiloff-Smith, Cornish, & Scerif, 2012), and with later hyperactive/impulsive behaviors (Lawson & Ruff, 2004).

Consequently, although speech therapy is indispensable when a child has a speech delay or when developmental milestones in language development have not been achieved, we strongly believe that omission of a thorough developmental assessment, which could reveal the presence of a neurodevelopmental disorder like ADHD, is never justified, for the following reasons. First, delayed language development may hinder the development of higher order cognitive functions, such as sustained attention and voluntary control (Gartstein et al., 2008; Ruf et al., 2008). Therefore, focusing exclusively on speech problems prevents from fully appreciating delays in the child's overall development, aspects of which may be attributed to completely erroneous causes by teachers or parents (e.g., laziness, immaturity, poor child-rearing), with the subsequent mistakes in parenting and teaching practices. Focusing on speech problems and ignoring the presence of ADHD behind a great number of them equals missing the forest for the trees. Second, the need for treatment in other areas is overlooked, for example motor coordination, learning difficulties, behavior problems, or peer problems. Third, speech therapy is not enriched with behavioral techniques that could simultaneously lead to improvements in other domains, such as self-regulation. Furthermore, available knowledge regarding the particular characteristics of children with ADHD is not taken into consideration. Finally, ignoring the presence of ADHD does not allow for prevention of secondary problems, including behavioral problems, low motivation, and low self-esteem.

For these reasons, within the multilevel approach, when a preschooler is referred for evaluation due to SLPs, a thorough developmental and psychological assessment is conducted and the underlying cause of these problems is investigated, as problems in language development usually constitute a symptom or an associated problem of some disorder (see Section 7.2). In case there is evidence that this disorder is ADHD, then the child's needs are evaluated and prioritized and treatment is suggested accordingly.

In cases of delay in the onset of speech and presence of early signs of ADHD (or in case of toddlers at high risk for ADHD), we recommend initiation of speech therapy between 2 and 3 years of age, dependent on the extent and severity of speech problems. According to our experience, speech therapists are often hesitant in placing a child of this age into speech therapy and rarely initiate treatment in children younger than 3 years old. However, contemporary research suggests that many of the difficulties of school-aged children not only in language but also in cognitive development may be detected in aspects of their language development at the age of 2 years (see Section 7.2). It seems that there is continuity between early and subsequent characteristics of language development, which also affect cognition.

Therefore, early difficulties in language development do not seem to recede merely with the passage of time. To the contrary, they foreshadow later difficulties and negatively affect cognitive functions, including attention and working memory, which play a central role in the process of learning. For example, early underdeveloped working memory abilities are associated with decreased learning and processing of new material in academic settings, which may result in accumulated delays in achievement over time that may eventually manifest as an SLD (Sarver et al., 2012).

Knowing that children with ADHD very often face difficulties in all domains of language development and academic achievement (see Section 7.2), and that deficits in working memory and attention constitute the main cognitive deficits in many cases of ADHD (see Sections 6.2 and 11.6), delay in placing children with slow language development into speech therapy is just loss of valuable time, which underpins the epigenesis of additional problems. Furthermore, we conceptualize speech therapy as one means of early intervention for ADHD, by constituting a broader therapeutic scheme within which a wide range of goals are set, far further from restoring language difficulties.

According to our experience, difficulties in auditory discrimination may be an early sign of dyslexia in children with ADHD. Auditory discrimination is the ability to notice, compare, and distinguish between distinct and separate sounds (see Section 7.2.2). Auditory discrimination difficulties, contrary to articulation difficulties (namely failure to properly pronounce certain phonemes) are not easily recognized by parents and teachers because children often avoid using those words that are difficult for them to pronounce. However, these difficulties are directly associated with emerging literacy skills and are those that will be later manifested as dyslexic symptoms in reading and writing. Phonemic decoding skills play a critical supporting role in reading ability. Weaknesses in the ability to process the phonological features of language are related to reading and writing difficulties (Torgesen, 2000). Furthermore, unless these difficulties are treated early, they may persist into adulthood.

Unfortunately, proper attention is rarely given to this kind of difficulties in conventional speech therapy. Within the multilevel approach, when phonological difficulties are restored, great emphasis is given to auditory discrimination difficulties. Restoring these difficulties has been proved a preventative measure against dyslexia (Young & Amarasinghe, 2010). Explicit instruction in phonemic awareness and phonetic decoding skills enhance reading abilities in these children. However, the exclusive treatment of phonological difficulties is not enough to this end (Torgesen, 2000). Therefore, it is required that the goals of speech therapy be broadened.

This idea is scientifically justified in multiple ways. Language abilities facilitate the development of cognitive processes (Marchman & Fernald, 2008). Restoring difficulties in all the domains of language development in preschool years, including articulation and auditory discrimination, vocabulary, and descriptive and pragmatic skills may have considerable beneficial secondary effects on academic achievement, particularly reading (Gremillion & Martel, 2014).

Within the multilevel approach, speech therapy in preschoolers with ADHD aims at enhancing the child's overall cognitive development through training of deficient neuropsychological functions in order to prevent learning and other difficulties. Treatment of language problems is also achieved through training of general cognitive functions (Gillam, Loeb, & Friel-Patti,

2001; Papaeliou et al., 2015). For example, it has been found that interventions designed to improve language skills may do so by training the neural mechanisms of selective auditory attention (Stevens et al., 2008).

However, all interventions during this period should have similar broadened goals and apply similar basic principles and behavioral techniques, no matter what their specialized focus would be. One of these goals is to exploit the brain's plasticity in order to improve the function of the brain networks thought to mediate the risk for ADHD and relate to functional impairment. In case speech and language difficulties are predominant, speech therapy is the recommended treatment. In case considerable difficulties exist in gross and fine motor skills and overall motor coordination, occupational therapy is suggested. In case children's predominant difficulties are behavioral, and parent/teacher training is not considered sufficient to address them, psychoeducational intervention is proposed. In many cases, preschoolers with ADHD may need a combined program (e.g., speech therapy *and* occupational therapy or occupational therapy *and* psychoeducational intervention). In these cases, interventions should be coordinated and clinicians should have a common treatment plan, constantly modified in an ongoing process.

Cognitive training has been considered as a candidate for early or preventative intervention in ADHD, and a series of research findings corroborates the efficacy of cognitive training among preschoolers with ADHD (Goodwin et al., 2016; Neville et al., 2009; Tamm et al., 2014). Cognitive training may be especially effective as core components of executive functions, such as attention, working memory, and inhibitory control, develop during the preschool period, are receptive to training, and set the stage for the development of higher cognitive processes. Particularly maturation of attentional capacity forms a foundation for the executive function abilities and may be the source of common variance underlying various executive function skills, allowing children to increasingly control what information they process (Garon, Bryson, & Smith, 2008). For example, differences in attention during infancy predict later ability to inhibit responses (Sethi, Mischel, Aber, Shoda, & Rodriguez, 2000), and attention control has been found to differentiate preschoolers with low and high working memory span (Espy & Bull, 2005). Evidence that atypicalities in attention may develop very early in individuals who later develop symptoms of ADHD indicates continuities in the developmental pathway from executive attention skills in infancy, to emerging symptoms of ADHD in preschool years (Goodwin et al., 2016).

The goal-directed activity that characterizes executive functioning is dependent not only on strictly effortful cognitive aspects of information processing but also on emotional systems within the brain. Preschoolers with ADHD are usually characterized by negative emotionality and, as a result, they experience difficulty in the application of higher order cognitive processes because their emotional responses do not call for reflective planning and problem solving. Therefore, one of the main features of the cognitive training of preschoolers with ADHD refers to the improvement of self-regulation, either defined as the regulation of emotion in appropriate social responding or the regulation of attention in the execution of cognitive tasks. High levels of self-regulation are associated with academic achievement and successful school adjustment (Blair, 2002; Nelson, 2000a). When affect can assist and support attention, memory, inhibitory control, and problem solving, it promotes optimal functioning (Carver & Scheier, 2000).

As the interaction of emotionality with rearing experience is central to the development of self-regulation, parent and teacher training is pivotal in this regard. A home environment and preschool education specifically designed to foster emotional competence promote the attention and cognitive self-regulation needed for both social and cognitive adaptation to the classroom (Blair, 2002).

Self-regulation training also aims at modifying response to reward, on the basis of the Dual Pathway model (see Section 6.3). The main reason why this age is the most appropriate for this training is the fact that the part of the brain that is responsible for response to reward, the corpus striatum, matures at this very period (Somerville & Casey, 2010). Schweitzer and Sulzer-Azaroff (1988) taught preschoolers to tolerate delayed reinforcement through a procedure designed to increase the proportion of children's choices of larger delayed over smaller immediate reinforcers by gradually introducing delays of increasing duration. Positive results were also brought by the intervention of Diamond, Barnett, Thomas, & Munro (2007) on children aged 4 to 5 years, aiming at promoting self-regulation of behavior.

In the case of preschoolers with ADHD aged 4 to 6 years, all interventions should also aim at promoting school readiness. It has been found that transition from preschool to a more structured environment may be particularly problematic for children who have not acquired basic skills of behavioral regulation, including paying attention, following instructions, and inhibiting inappropriate actions (McClelland et al., 2007). Research documents that behavioral regulation skills are particularly important for school success beyond the influence of other important child variables, such as a child's intelligence (Duckworth & Seligman, 2005; Von Suchodoletz, Trommsdorff, Heikamp, Wieber, & Gollwitzer, 2009).

Cognitive training of major executive functions described earlier contributes to school readiness. Attention allows children to focus on activities and complete them; working memory allows children to remember and follow instructions, as well as to plan and find solutions; inhibitory control allows children to escape false choices and choose more functional responses. These functions provide a foundation for the development of positive motivation and engagement in the school setting (McClelland et al., 2007; Schumacher, Greenberg, & Mezey, 2003). In addition, they are predictive of reading and math skills between kindergarten and sixth grade, regardless of child IQ (Blair & Razza, 2007; McClelland, Acock, & Morrison, 2006). In other words, there is remarkable consistency in the relation between kindergarten learning-related skills and math and reading achievement over the course of elementary school.

Furthermore, enhancement of language development, including developing phonological awareness, restoring difficulties in auditory discrimination, improving descriptive skills, enriching vocabulary, and increasing the complexity of speech, are important for the emergence of literacy skills and later reading proficiency. School readiness is also promoted via the development of learning-related skills, which are important for academic achievement. Although learning-related skills stem from children's executive function skills, they reflect the behavioral and social manifestation of these skills, such as listening and following directions, organizing materials, taking turns, and staying on task (McClelland, Morrison, & Holmes, 2000). Sáez and colleagues (2012) found that the effect of differentiated literacy instruction on kindergarten students' word reading achievement was stronger in children with attention problems only when the classroom teacher also provided frequent prompts that redirected children's focus to the task at hand. In general, learning-related skills tap the domains of self-regulation and social competence, including independence, responsibility, self-regulation, and cooperation.

To sum up, the multilevel approach integrates language, attention, working memory, self-regulation, and work-related skills in a coherent therapeutic framework in order to provide treatment in preschoolers with ADHD with both therapeutic and preventative goals concerning academic performance, behavior, and social relationships. In fact, a number of studies have linked language problems and attentional difficulties, while other research has revealed a relation between attentional difficulties and both lower work-related and social skills, and poorer academic achievement (McClelland, Morrison, & Holmes, 2000).

Sometimes parents and teachers dispute the necessity of such interventions, expressing the view that preschool years should be dedicated to play and that school-related skills should not be of concern prior to formal schooling. We strongly believe that the value of play is indisputable, but interventions that promote school readiness in children with ADHD offer the cognitive and behavioral background so that school adjustment and later academic performance will be successful. If we consider the implications of school failure for all aspects of a child's life, it is obvious that the benefit of such a preparation for entering a school career successfully is priceless for a child with high chances of school failure.

It has been empirically verified that early academic skills are important for later academic achievement (Mullis & Jenkins, 1990) and that early work-related skills are predictive of academic achievement at the end of the second grade (McClelland et al., 2000). In a survey conducted by the National Center for Early Development and Learning, 46% of a nationally representative sample of kindergarten teachers indicated that more than half of children in their class lacked basic regulatory skills that would enable them to do well in school (Rimm-Kaufman, Pianta, & Cox, 2000). This suggests that a great number of typically developing children go to school without having the necessary abilities to function productively in classroom. Moreover, it has been found that children at risk for reading failure benefit considerably from training in phonemic awareness and linking phonemes with letters before school entry (Hatcher, Hulme, & Snowling, 2004), as phonemic awareness supports children's ability to decode novel words and encode words into prints (Ehri et al., 2001).

Consequently, preschoolers with ADHD, who usually enter formal schooling with weaknesses in important basic regulatory and other work-related skills, are in paramount need of emergent literacy skills interventions and compensatory education programs aiming at promoting school readiness. These programs can affect the biological and physiological developmental processes underlying age-appropriate social and cognitive competence at school entry and prevent the onset of SLD in elementary school (Chacko et al., 2014).

Treatment of ADHD in preschool years takes advantage of the beneficial features of play. Materials and activities chosen have a playful character to a great extent. The intrinsic rewarding qualities of play make it an ideal delivery system for treatment of children with ADHD, who are known to be highly responsive to continuously rewarding contingencies (Halperin & Healey, 2011). Besides, play contributes to brain growth and has a direct relation to self-regulation of behavior (Bodrova, Germeroth, & Leong, 2013). As Vygotsky (1967) stated,

> The role the child plays, and her relationship to the object if the object has changed its meaning, will always stem from the rules, e.g., the imaginary situation will always contain rules. In play, the child is free. But this is an illusory freedom.
>
> (p. 10)

The creative use of directed play in child sessions, incorporating cognitive challenges and physical exercise, has the potential to increase child motivation to actively engage in the process. The use of play in treatment of ADHD in preschool years has been empirically substantiated (Halperin & Healey, 2011; Halperin et al., 2013).

To conclude, we would like to briefly refer to the case of Cathy, a 2-year-old girl with ADHD, being the youngest child treated in our clinic via an early intervention program. This program was completed at the age of 5. Cathy was referred to us due to language delay, as she did not use more than 4 to 5 words at this age. Moreover, there were a lot of early signs of ADHD, including highly hyperactive and impulsive behavior, low frustration tolerance, and defiant behavior. She participated in a speech therapy program, whose main goal was initially the development of expressive language, then the restoration of phonological difficulties, afterward the restoration of auditory discrimination difficulties, and finally the promotion of school readiness. At the same time, Cathy's parents attended an intensive parent training program. Moreover, collaboration with her preschool teachers was consistent and systematic. Predictive factors for the outcomes of this intervention were optimal. Early intervention was delivered at a very young age, the child had high intelligence, and her parents responded very well to parent training. Treatment integrity was systematically monitored. The clinician who worked with the child possessed the characteristics of an effective therapist and implemented an intervention that included all the features that were described in this section.

The outcomes of the intervention completely justified the commitment and effort of all the participants. Cathy is 11 years old today and is about to finish elementary school. She is still quite hyperactive and she likes talking a lot. She often needs more time for everyday activities, including getting dressed or having a shower, because she gets more easily distracted relative to other children and she tends to pay attention to several tasks simultaneously. She is a little stubborn and particularly assertive, therefore great patience, persistence, and flexibility are required within the family context. She hates to lose, she sometimes has difficulty managing her frustration, and she is a little anxious in tests and evaluations. These are the only still existent signs that this child was born with the pathophysiological substrate of ADHD.

With respect to functioning, however, after successful early intervention within the multilevel approach, Cathy did not encounter any kind of learning difficulty and she is by far the best student in her class. She is completely autonomous regarding homework completion, schedule organization, and time management. She is learning two foreign languages without any difficulty, and has a remarkable talent for music, as she started playing the violin at the age of 4 years and the piano at the age of 5 years. Today, she has won several international music competitions, and she is a member of a youth symphonic orchestra. She is also an athlete of rhythmic gymnastics. She is very sociable, popular, and beloved by her peers, and has a lot of friends. She has great leadership skills, high self-esteem, positive self-image, and a lot of goals for the future. She is happy and full of dreams. No one from her broader familial or social environment ever suspected that Cathy had any kind of developmental problem. In our view, early intervention within the multilevel approach led to secondary prevention of ADHD in the case of Cathy.

12.5.3 Middle Childhood

Interventions for children with ADHD in middle childhood are usually delivered due to the presence of learning difficulties, behavioral problems, or their combination. Intervention for this age within the multilevel approach usually takes the form of a psychoeducational program, which includes parent and teacher training.

In the previous section, we referred to the common practice of delivering speech therapy to preschoolers with ADHD without a thorough developmental assessment and without a meaningful diagnosis. Something similar usually happens with school-aged children with learning difficulties. They may receive a general and vague diagnosis of learning disabilities and be placed in educational remediation without a thorough developmental assessment and screening for ADHD. Even in case diagnosis of ADHD is given, restoring learning difficulties is usually considered an exclusively educational task.

However, profound knowledge of the nature of learning difficulties in children with ADHD makes it clear that these learning difficulties are closely associated with the core symptoms of ADHD; with concomitant language and speech problems that these children often experience at preschool age; with deficient executive functions (mainly attention, working memory, and self-regulation of behavior); and with psychological factors, including motivation, frustration tolerance, self-esteem, and self-efficacy. Therefore, we consider that restoring learning difficulties within the context of ADHD is more complicated than usually believed and that treatment efforts should be guided by understanding the nature of these difficulties. Consequently, more factors should be encompassed than remedial teaching. Interventions targeting learning difficulties of children with ADHD should be based on a holistic approach, taking into account all the aforementioned factors in order to lead to optimal outcomes.

Behavioral attention is a significant and unique predictor of word reading proficiency (Gray, Carter, Briggs-Gowan, Jones, & Wagmiller, 2014; Martinussen, Grimbos, & Ferrari, 2014), and inattentive behavior is associated with reduced ability to acquire emergent prereading skills and word reading efficiency (Dittman, 2016; Sims & Lonigan, 2013). Learning to read is a cognitively demanding task that requires sustained attention and on-task behavior over extended periods of time (Dittman, 2016). It has been found that the benefits of traditional academic interventions, such as tutoring, are substantially diminished in children with ADHD if deficits in these children's attention are not directly addressed simultaneously (Rabiner, Malone, & Conduct Problems Prevention Research Group, 2004). Moreover, reading programs modified to facilitate active engagement and to accommodate children's concurrent challenges with processing speed, working memory, and selective and sustained attention produced noteworthy treatment effects (Tannock et al., 2016). For all these reasons, we believe that psychoeducational interventions for ADHD in middle childhood are more effective when they are coordinated by qualified child psychologists.

In our view, psychosocial interventions for ADHD should always include a component aiming at restoring learning difficulties of these children. Therefore, treatment of ADHD in middle years in the context of the multilevel approach usually sets the following goals regarding the child:

1. Diminishing core ADHD symptoms
2. Managing behavioral problems
3. Enhancing motivation
4. Improving basic academic skills and academic performance
5. Improving skills that promote independence and self-reliance
6. Developing organizational skills
7. Improving social skills and peer relationships
8. Improving self-regulation and overall executive functioning
9. Increasing self-esteem and self-efficacy.

The development of a positive relationship between the child and the clinician is obviously of utmost importance. At school age, however, it is also important that children know exactly the reason of the intervention, its goals, and its methods. Children of this age are usually fully aware of their difficulties. With a little help, they can explicitly describe their weaknesses and express specific concerns they would like to be addressed. On the basis of the child's self-reports, the clinician explains to the child the kind of help that can be provided and sets the framework of their collaboration, by giving examples of activities, materials, and token economy, which usually highly motivates the child.

At this stage, it is very important to raise children's hope that they can be better students, make more friends, and respond effectively to parent and teacher demands. The clinician should foster a climate of optimism and convince the child that there are no dead ends, and that everyday situations such as homework, conflicts with friends, reprimands, and punishments can change. Children usually like to hear that they are going to learn "tricks" that will help them cope with challenging situations.

Older children are more likely to have experienced failure, reprimands, and punishments. Negative self-image and low self-esteem usually result from such experiences and make these children believe that they are less clever and capable than peers. It is very important that children understand the causes of their difficulties, through psychoeducation adapted to their developmental level and appropriate cognitive techniques, in order to modify common misconceptions. For example, instead of believing that they are less clever, they must realize their difficulty concentrating and the need to learn how to sustain attention. Instead of believing that they are not able to learn the school subject of history, they must realize that comprehension difficulties may be caused by reading mistakes, and that techniques that enhance reading accuracy and fluency may enhance history learning as well.

Therefore, in middle childhood, the initial stage of treatment is usually focused on elevating the child's mood, providing alternative interpretations on their difficulties, and enhancing motivation and engagement in the treatment process. Unless such a psychological climate is established, even the best techniques are bound to fail.

During treatment implementation, oftentimes school material is used. However, the use of this material does not imply that the session is a kind of private lesson for the child. For example, when the clinician works using a history text, the goal is not to teach the child history. The goals that can be achieved during this process, by the use of appropriate techniques, are the following:

1. Modifying the perception that history is a difficult subject
2. Enhancing self-efficacy in children who believe that they are not capable of learning history
3. Increasing the ability to sustain attention while studying a theoretical subject
4. Reducing impulsive behavior (e.g., the child's tendency to stop reading in order to say something irrelevant or jump from one answer to another when talking about the lesson)
5. Increasing frustration tolerance (e.g., the child's tendency to quit in front of a task perceived as difficult)
6. Improving reading skills with the aid of specific self-guidance techniques (e.g., with the use of two fingers, one finger pointing at the word and the other pointing at the line)
7. Improving the capacity for time orientation with the aid of a watch or timer
8. Learning strategies for studying texts
9. Gradually reinforcing self-reliance with the study of theoretical subjects
10. Enhancing self-esteem with the constant use of positive reinforcement.

Therefore, in the case of children with ADHD and learning difficulties, the use of techniques that restore their difficulties in the main academic domains of reading, writing, and mathematics is a fundamental aspect of psychoeducational intervention within the multilevel approach. Particular emphasis is given on improving reading skills, which form the basis for academic leaning.

It has been found that intensive comprehensive reading instruction among school-aged children leads to changes in brain function during performance of language tasks that resemble brain activation patterns characteristic of normal readers (Aylward et al., 2003; Meyler, Keller, Cherkassky, Gabrieli, & Just, 2008). Furthermore, Keller and Just (2009) demonstrated that the implementation of intensive remedial instruction in 8- to 10-year-old poor readers resulted in changes in the structural integrity of the white matter in the left hemisphere. This impressive result demonstrates the capability of a behavioral intervention to bring about a positive change in cortical white matter tracts, when provided within an age window in which maturation, experience, and development are still capable of influencing white matter microstructural organization. This is particularly important because the white matter supports communication between brain regions and structural connectivity supports higher order mental functions. Furthermore, reading difficulties have been associated with lower functional connectivity (the synchronization of neural activity) across areas of the reading cortical network (Hampson et al., 2006; Pugh et al., 2000). As it was mentioned in Section 5.3.1, white matter microstructural abnormalities have been documented in children with ADHD, leading to a disturbance in communication between brain regions, ultimately resulting in disrupted functioning (Nagel, 2011).

Therefore, reading difficulties and ADHD are likely to share some common neurological deficits, which are amenable to change through behavioral interventions, even in middle childhood. It seems that improvement of reading skills may lead to modification of the white matter, whose microstructural abnormalities are associated with ADHD. Therefore, systematically remediating reading difficulties within psychoeducational interventions for ADHD is absolutely justifiable and essential, and requires knowledge of neuropsychology beyond special education strategies.

As it has already been mentioned, improving self-regulation is a major goal of the multilevel approach to the treatment of ADHD. The neurological structures associated with high-order cognitive functions maintain their plasticity in response to experience until adulthood (Nelson, 2000b). In other words, reorganization of cortical pathways in the human brain is possible beyond early childhood. Therefore, cognitive training is still meaningful in middle childhood.

Furthermore, several cognitive-behavioral strategies are used in order to enhance self-regulation in school-aged children with ADHD. Self-talk is a powerful means of improving self-control (Reid et al., 2005). Self-talk may also be used in the learning process, as children practice in saying out loud every step toward completion of an activity, or saying out loud what they are writing (Reid & Lienemann, 2006). Moreover, reading comprehension is also facilitated when children with ADHD read out loud and not silently (Ghelani, Sidhu, Jain, & Tannock, 2004). Reading out loud adds auditory support to the information a child is studying, improving recall. By speaking study material aloud, children with ADHD help themselves to stay on task.

Self-control is also enhanced via training in problem-solving and self-instruction strategies. Children are trained how to recognize problems, generate alternative solutions, anticipate consequences and obstacles that may arise, and execute specific behaviors to solve problems. Self-instruction is a more specific form of problem solving that provides children with a verbal framework to guide their behavior when confronted with a problem (Meichenbaum & Goodman, 1971). Problem-solving techniques can be applied in interpersonal problems and academic tasks as well. They are also particularly useful in frustration management because they help children better modulate their emotional arousal.

Self-management, comprising self-monitoring, self-recording, self-evaluation, and self-reinforcement, is a particularly promising self-regulation strategy. Children initially implement these strategies in the clinical setting and later are encouraged to use them in classroom and other settings. Specifically, they are instructed to monitor, assess, and reward their own academic and social targeted behaviors. This self-evaluation may be recorded by the child and be compared with parent or teacher evaluation (Barry & Messer, 2003; Harris, Friedlander, Saddler, Frizzelle, & Graham, 2005). With the successful use of this technique, the need for systematically using incentive systems is reduced, particularly for older children.

Another major aspect of the psychoeducational intervention with a school-aged child is the development of organizational and planning skills. The multilevel approach borrows strategies from several evidence-based organizational skills interventions. Children are taught new tools and routines to record assignments and due dates, organize school materials, use checklists, manage projects, monitor the amount of time involved in completing assignments, and break larger tasks into smaller more manageable ones. They also learn to plan ahead for the completion of long-term projects and balance extracurricular activities and school responsibilities. Furthermore, they learn strategies for note-taking in class, which significantly improve lesson comprehension and reduce distractibility in the school setting (Langberg et al., 2006).

These strategies are routed in behavioral theory and utilize contingency management. Parents and teachers are trained to take over the monitoring of organization checklists and application of rewards. Results of randomized clinical trials demonstrate that youth receiving organizational skills training have significantly improved academic functioning and homework completion, less family conflict, and better ratings of organization (Abikoff et al., 2012; Pfiffner et al., 2007).

Finally, intervention for middle-aged children with ADHD is often enriched with elements of psychotherapy, due to comorbidity, low self-esteem, bullying at school, and other relevant experiences that require specialized treatment.

12.5.4 Adolescence

Adolescence is a challenging developmental period because youth are undergoing exponential changes in several domains. In the case of adolescents with ADHD, these challenges are magnified. In addition, during adolescence, individuals have to cope in a less structured but often more demanding environment. Therefore, it is necessary to take into account the increasing influence of the peer culture and the particular difficulties that adolescence may bring to teenagers with ADHD (Young & Amarasinghe, 2010).

Very little research has been conducted with adolescents with ADHD (Pelham & Fabiano, 2008). Particularly for adolescents with ADHD who receive treatment for the first time, treatment delivery can be extremely challenging. Many adolescents with ADHD have already experienced failures in their school careers and have been struggling to meet parent and teacher educational and behavioral demands. They may also have low self-esteem and a lot of learning gaps, which can further reduce their motivation for school achievement. It is likely that they have developed chronic feelings of demoralization, discouragement, disappointment, and frustration caused by persistent shortcomings (Murphy, 2005). Very often, interactions with parents are characterized by conflicts, which are magnified as adolescence moves forward. In the case of older adolescents, parents are usually concerned with behavioral problems, which may have taken the form of CD, even delinquent behavior, mostly among boys.

Furthermore, the psychological experience of puberty for boys and girls may entail a difference in course and comorbidity of ADHD. For example, boys may develop CD more frequently, whereas girls may develop ADs or DDs. Therefore, interventions need to address these gender differences in order to maximize the beneficial effects of treatment (Babinski, Sibley, Ross, & Pelham, 2013; Young & Amarasinghe, 2010). Boys may require treatments that have a greater focus on behavior control, whereas girls may require more social and mood-oriented treatments.

Therefore, clinicians often have to deal with a very complicated clinical presentation. Comorbidity and secondary problems developed through epigenetical processes may be more impairing for adolescents compared to core ADHD symptoms. According to our experience, adolescent poor self-regulation in combination with increasing peer influence and decreasing parent monitoring render adolescence the most risky period for individuals with ADHD.

In order to develop an appropriate intervention for adolescents with ADHD, it is important to take into consideration the particular developmental characteristics of adolescence. It is a period of intrapersonal change, during which the individual is gradually becoming independent, is taking on more responsibility, and is asked to make significant decisions about the future. According to Smith, Waschbusch, Willoughby, & Evans (2000), adolescence signals six significant developmental changes, which may considerably influence treatment. These include (a) a greater cognitive capacity that includes the ability to think more abstractly and solve problems in a more systematic manner; (b) increased self-awareness of behavior; (c) a focus on identity formation and increased independence; (d) greater reliance on peers for information and support; (e) a different daily routine at school involving increased educational demands; and (f) physiological changes such as growth and the development of secondary sex characteristics.

Therefore, ADHD treatment in adolescence should aim to increase the adolescent's involvement in the treatment planning, alter behavioral contingencies to include fewer tangible reinforcers and more privilege losses, increase the opportunities to interact with peers, take into account the adolescent's need for independence, and place emphasis on organizational skills, time management, homework issues, and use of self-monitoring strategies (Young & Amarasinghe, 2010).

Developing a collaborative relationship with adolescents with ADHD is more challenging relative to younger children. Defiance is usually greater, maladaptive cognitions are well-established, and persistence in goal attainment is weaker. Furthermore, oftentimes clinicians may be perceived as figures of authority, which adolescents tend to question and reject. Therefore, adolescents require a sympathetic informal approach in order to place confidence in the clinician and engage in treatment (Nahlik, 2004). It is important that clinicians approach adolescents by "speaking their language." In other words, clinicians should know the adolescent culture, including fashion trends, teenage jargon, music preferences, and sports idols, as well as particularities in the use of technology and social network systems. Clinicians who employ professional jargon and are acquainted with typical adolescent characteristics mainly through manuals may face serious difficulty establishing therapeutic alliance with adolescents with ADHD and motivating them to remain engaged in treatment.

Psychoeducation is an important component of the intervention in adolescence so that youth can understand the true nature of their lifelong difficulties and modify misconceptions about incompetence, laziness, immaturity, or low intelligence. The symptoms of ADHD can be portrayed to the adolescent as being merely more extreme forms of temperament traits that are quite normal, which may be put to advantage in life if brought under control (Nahlik, 2004). Clinicians should elicit adolescents' understanding of ADHD causes and course. Psychoeducation is also an opportunity to strengthen the therapeutic relationship because adolescents may experience relief at finally being understood regarding their everyday struggles. Moreover, better-informed adolescents are usually more cooperative. Finally, psychoeducation can help adolescents renew hope and set realistic and feasible goals for the future (Murphy, 2005).

Clear boundaries should be set with respect to communication between clinicians and parents in order to safeguard the therapeutic relationship. Adolescents are often very suspicious and should be convinced that session content will not be disclosed to their parents. Adolescents should feel that clinicians are primarily their own ally, who will defend them against school as well as against parents, if need be.

Within the multilevel approach, major treatment goals for adolescents with ADHD is the enhancement of academic performance, the development of organizational and study skills, the improvement of social skills, and the empowering of self-regulation skills. Enhancement of self-control and self-esteem are considered principal goals of ADHD treatment in adolescence because low self-control and low self-esteem are among the basic factors that make these adolescents vulnerable to engage in juvenile delinquency, substance abuse, and overall risky behavior. Autonomy, responsibility, and self-reliance are also strengthened. In case of comorbidity with CD, MDs, or ADs, specialized techniques for the treatment of these disorders are also implemented. However, the presentation of these techniques is beyond the scope of this book.

For adolescents, parent and teacher training is of limited efficacy because adolescents are monitored by adults less closely than younger children and encounter numerous teachers. However, incentive systems modified for adolescents with ADHD can be used. Adolescents are trained in self-management techniques in order to monitor, evaluate, and reinforce their own behavior. Moreover, a behavioral contract negotiation may be required to enlist the adolescent's willingness to participate in treatment and define goals, time schedules, and rewards (Wolraich & DuPaul, 2010). A great amount of adolescent input is essential for such a contract to be useful, given the challenges associated with identifying salient rewards for adolescents (Evans et al., 2014). Reinforcers are usually privileges related to the adolescents' outings, opportunities to use gadgets, bedtime, and watching TV. Loss of privileges, including talking on the phone, going to the mall with friends, and obtaining access to gadgets, are also used for adolescents (Chronis et al., 2001).

In conclusion, clinicians who work with adolescents with ADHD within the framework of the multilevel approach should be in a position to use all the techniques that were described in previous sections but adapt them to the particularities of this specific developmental period according to the teenage culture of each era.

13 Treatment of ADHD in Adults

13.1 Introduction

Adults with ADHD have usually suffered years of feeling demoralized and discouraged because of a multiplicity of negative life events, failures, and underachievement in school, work, family, and romantic relationships. Furthermore, many report having received consistent complaints and criticism about their behavior from parents, teachers, partners, and employers. As a result of their long-standing underachievement, they may not understand why they systematically fail to translate their assets into more positive outcomes. The accumulation of negative experiences affects the formation of their self-esteem and self-efficacy and often leads to a sense of anticipating failure as the predictable outcome of every effort (Murphy, 2015; Ramsay & Rostain, 2008). These negative expectations may lead them to give up and believe that nothing can change in their lives.

Consequently, most adults with ADHD need effective treatment in order to manage the challenges that ADHD presents over the life span, and maintain a positive long-term outcome. However, empirically based information about the efficacy of treatments for adults with ADHD is considerably limited relative to available information for children. Moreover, studies have almost exclusively investigated the efficacy of medication, as there are limited comparative studies between pharmacological and psychosocial interventions for adults with ADHD (Safren, Otto et al., 2005).

Many adults tend to underestimate the impact of the disorder on their life, mistakenly believe they just need to try a little harder, and adopt the view that they can handle their difficulties without using professional help (Murphy, 2015). Newly diagnosed adults usually need time to realize that, despite personal efforts to compensate for ADHD symptoms, the disorder disrupts functioning and produces impairment in multiple life domains.

Denial of the disorder seems stronger among young adults with ADHD, even if the diagnosis was given in childhood. In a 10-year follow-up of children with ADHD, when participants were between ages 16 and 22, it was found that they tended to deny the existence of ADHD symptoms and associated impairments and to attribute the blame for any difficulties they acknowledged on others (Barkley et al., 2008). In contrast, their parents reported the continuation of many ADHD symptoms and life impairments. At the next follow-up, when participants were between ages 27 and 32, the majority were no longer denying their symptoms and impairments. This delayed acceptance may have occurred only after having experienced a number of setbacks and failures and may have underscored the importance of treatment at a younger age.

The first goal of treatment is to foster acceptance and understanding of the disorder in adults with ADHD and to instill optimism, hope, and faith in the possibility of change. Acceptance and hope may activate individuals to get involved and engage in treatment. To this end, clinicians working with adults with ADHD need patience, tolerance, a good sense of humor, realistic expectations, and a genuine willingness to help them through crises, repeated mistakes, and failures they may experience during treatment (Murphy, 2015).

13.2 Pharmacological Interventions

Most guidelines suggest medication as first-line treatment for adults with ADHD. Currently, formulations of two types of extended-delivery stimulants (AMP and MPH), including Ritalin, Concerta, and Adderall, and one nonstimulant (ATX), namely Strattera, are the main approved drugs for the treatment of ADHD in adults (Prince, Wilens, Spencer, & Biederman, 2015).

Meta-analyses consistently show that stimulants significantly decrease core ADHD symptoms for many adults with the disorder, at least on a short-term basis (Faraone, Spencer, Aleardi, Pagano, & Biederman, 2004; Moriyama, Polanczyk, Terzi, Faria, & Rohde, 2013). Overall rates of efficacy of stimulants in adults are somewhat lower than they are among children, ranging between 25% and 78%, with the higher rates reported in studies employing higher doses (Spencer, Biederman, & Wilens, 2004). It has been found that 20% to 50% of adults with ADHD are considered nonresponders due to insufficient symptom reduction or inability to tolerate these medications (Wilens, Spencer et al., 2002). Furthermore, responders typically show a reduction in only 50% or less of the core ADHD symptoms (Wilens, Spencer et al., 2002). Hence, they do not achieve full remission and show significant residual symptoms, which may continue to cause significant impairments. Evidence shows that in adults, as in children, medications do not normalize neuropsychological outcomes, leaving room for improvement through other modalities (Advokat, 2010).

Similar side effects to those observed among children have been found in adults, including decreased appetite, nausea, headaches, dizziness, irritability, insomnia, dry mouth, and weight loss (Aagaard & Hansen, 2013). In addition, menstrual problems in women and decreased libido in both genders are also reported (Rösler, Fischer, Ammer, Ose, & Retz, 2009). Furthermore, complaints such as palpitations, tachycardia, and dyspnea occur in up to 20% of stimulant-treated adults. However, serious cardiovascular events are rarely seen in large-scale clinical trials (Habel et al., 2011; Hammerness, Perrin, Shelley-Abrahamson, & Wilens, 2011). The most annoying side effect is the rebound that occurs when the MPH wears off. Rebound refers to a temporary increase in the ADHD symptoms, irritability, and mood swings (Kooij, 2013).

Another issue that has been investigated regarding the use of stimulants among adults with ADHD is their interaction with other drugs or substances. It has been found that concurrent use of antihistamines reduces the efficacy of stimulants. Excessive intake of caffeine may also compromise their efficacy, and the combination of caffeine and/or nicotine with stimulants may exacerbate sleep difficulties (Prince et al., 2015). Furthermore, the use of stimulants may differentiate the body's response to alcohol.

ATX is prescribed in the case of nonresponse to MPH and dextroamphetamine, in the case of contraindications for stimulants or comorbidity with DDs, ADs, or TDs (Adler et al., 2009; Wilens et al., 2008). Its efficacy has been investigated in a limited number of studies up to date. However, the first outcomes are positive and show significant reduction in the core symptoms of ADHD (Adler et al., 2006; Marchant et al., 2011). The positive response to this medication has been investigated for a time period of up to two years of continuous administration. It has been found that ATX is far superior to placebo in treating adult ADHD and significantly more efficacious in treating inattention than impulsivity/hyperactivity (Ravishankar, Chowdappa, Benegal, & Muralidharan, 2016). A comparison of five head-to-head trials of ATX versus stimulants in treating ADHD showed ATX to have equal efficacy as stimulants, while both groups of medications were equally well tolerated (Gibson et al., 2006). However, stimulants were the preferred choice in the treatment of ADHD (Gibson, Bettinger, Patel, & Crismon, 2006).

In clinical practice, ATX is often prescribed in conjunction with stimulants. Reports suggest that this combination may be effective and well-tolerated (Hammerness et al., 2009). However, safety, tolerability, and efficacy of this combination have not been systematically studied yet. Common side effects of ATX among adults include dry mouth, insomnia, nausea, decreased appetite, constipation, decreased libido, dizziness, and sweating (Michelson et al., 2003). Therefore, clinicians should weigh the benefits against the risks for each patient before they prescribe this combination.

A significant number of adults with ADHD do not adhere to their prescribed regimen (Knouse & Safren, 2013), and many others discontinue medication after a few months (Fredriksen et al., 2013; Olfson, Marcus, Zhang, & Wan, 2007). More than 50% of patients quit stimulants after 90 days of treatment, and treatment maintenance for more than 180 days is unusual (Marcus, Wan, Kemner, & Olfson, 2005). Factors associated with non-adherence were found to be female gender and higher education level (Kooij et al., 2013).

In conclusion, pharmacotherapy provides an effective treatment for core symptoms of ADHD in most adults. Moreover, according to a recent review, stimulant therapy for ADHD in adulthood was associated with global functional improvement and improvement in interpersonal, occupational, academic, and leisure functioning (Surman, Hammerness, Pion, & Faraone, 2013). However, findings regarding the efficacy of medication in enhancing functioning are controversial. Pharmacotherapy can hardly provide adults with ADHD with compensatory strategies and skills for coping with associated functional impairment (Safren et al., 2004). Furthermore, in many clinical trials of ADHD medications, a 30% reduction in symptoms can qualify a patient as a treatment responder (Steele, Jensen, & Quinn, 2006). Therefore, for individuals who had high baseline levels of symptoms, there is substantial room for further improvement. For these reasons, individuals should be informed about the risks, benefits, and side effects of medication, as well as the availability of alternative treatments.

13.3 Cognitive-Behavioral Interventions

Despite the documented benefits of medication for most adults with ADHD, symptom reduction does not necessarily translate into functional improvement, and may not represent a sufficient level of treatment by itself (Gualtieri & Johnson, 2008). Consequently, there is a growing recognition that treatment options for adult ADHD should include additional cognitive and behavioral interventions that take into consideration the comprehensive implications of the disorder, its functional outcomes, and overall quality of life. Current clinical guidelines recommend adjunctive psychosocial treatments, either in combination with medication or as a next step approach to treating those who have been stabilized on medications but still show residual symptoms (Safren et al., 2010). It has been found that individuals diagnosed with ADHD de novo in adulthood are often highly motivated to receive psychosocial interventions (Young, Bramham, Gray, & Rose, 2008).

Among the most promising psychosocial treatments for adult ADHD is CBT (Ramsay & Rostain, 2008; Safren, 2006). CBT modified for ADHD is considered the second evidence-based treatment for adults (Ramsay, 2016). Whereas medications target core symptoms of ADHD, CBT targets functional impairments and involves the intentional teaching of strategies in order to enhance the individual's problem solving, promote emotion regulation, and motivate the gradual meeting on important behavioral goals (Hinshaw, 2009; Ramsay, 2010). These strategies include both behavioral and cognitive techniques to increase the likelihood of effective coping in the presence of negative thoughts and emotions (Knouse, 2015). Cognitive techniques usually include cognitive restructuring, reframing the past, organization and planning, and coping with distractibility. Anger management and communication skills training may also be used (Safren, Sprich, Chulvick, & Otto, 2004). Furthermore, CBT has a strong evidence base for many of the comorbid problems associated with ADHD, such as anxiety and depression. Treating these comorbid problems is important, as they may constitute the problems that led an individual to seek treatment.

CBT therapists initially provide psychoeducation about ADHD. Psychoeducation is an important mental framework because it reframes problems as stemming from neurological causes rather than from laziness, low intelligence, or lack of effort (Murphy, 2015). This process is more effective as an interactive dialogue with the individual rather than a lecture. Through psychoeducation, individuals come to understand and recognize the effects of ADHD in their life. Psychoeducation puts the patient's full history into context and is therapeutic in itself.

Afterward, CBT therapists usually engage individuals in a collaborative FBA in order to identify the factors that negatively affect goal achievement, so that they can develop the treatment plan and prioritize treatment goals. These goals should be meaningful to the individual and be framed in terms of how they will contribute to everyday functioning. For example, strategies to help the individual be more punctual may become more meaningful if they are framed as a means of improving the individual's relationships with friends and partners (Knouse & Safren, 2013).

Treatment usually proceeds with training adults with ADHD to change their behavior by developing new skills and habits. These skills require systematic practice for a long enough period of time so that use becomes less effortful and the new skills are incorporated into the individual's repertoire (Knouse & Safren, 2013). Problem solving and communication training are particularly important. Problem solving usually involves training in a five-step problem-solving approach, including problem definition, brain-storming solutions, negotiation, decision-making, and implementing the solution. Communication training helps individuals develop more effective communication and conflict management strategies. These skills do not correct the underlying neuropsychological deficits associated with ADHD but help individuals compensate for and cope with these deficits.

Clinicians also help individuals with *environmental engineering*. This concept refers to the process of setting up one's living, work, and study settings to make them more ADHD-friendly in terms of instituting systems designed to circumvent the effects of executive dysfunction (Ramsay, 2010). Reducing distractions in work or study areas, setting up automatic payment plans, making task lists, and using a calendar for appointments and a daily planner for scheduling and prioritizing, are coping strategies that support skill use and increase efficiency.

In order to cope with distractibility, clinicians help adults with ADHD become more aware of the environmental factors that contribute to distractibility and to develop techniques to reduce them. For example, they are encouraged to switch off the television, the radio, or the sound notification for e-mails when they have to focus on a task. Furthermore, they learn to break tasks into smaller units and schedule regular breaks after each unit completion. They are also taught cue-control procedures to cue awareness of whether they are on task. For example, they are encouraged to use a watch that beeps at certain intervals. Whenever the alarm sounds, they are instructed to assess whether they have been distracted from the main task at hand, and, if so, to return to that task. They are also instructed to make multiple sets of keys and set up specific locations where they will keep important objects to minimize the chance of misplacing them (Sprich, Knouse, Cooper-Vince, Burbridge, & Safren, 2010).

In order to cope with avoidance, the individual learns to use desired activities as incentives. For example, they may promise themselves a 5-minute phone call to a beloved person after having studied for half an hour.

It should be noted that CBT has to be adapted to the needs of adults with ADHD because the disorder involves symptoms that may impede the effectiveness of standard CBT (Ramsay, 2010). Individuals with ADHD usually have great difficulty turning their intentions into actions. The main challenge for the therapist is to help adults with ADHD consistently follow through on the use of these coping strategies (Ramsay, 2016). The benefit of CBT is not in the coping suggestions but in assisting their implementation. Effective implementation strategies hopefully result in *exposure* to previously avoided tasks that may counter negative thoughts and promote a sense of competence and resilience (Ramsey, 2010).

Implementation strategies include putting visual reminders in strategic locations. For example, many adults with ADHD find using a day planner ineffective with the excuse that they forget to look at it. The clinician may suggest a sticker note in the middle of the computer screen or another conspicuous spot, so that adults with ADHD can be reminded to use their day planner.

CBT clinicians should also attend to medication adherence in the cases of adults receiving combined treatment. To this end, the reasons of nonadherence should be explored so that clinicians can choose the right strategy. Adults with ADHD may simply forget to take their medicine and may need a reminder; they may experience side effects but be reluctant to discuss them with their physician; they may have negative attitude toward medication use that triggers avoidance (Knouse & Safren, 2013).

On a cognitive level, CBT therapists increase the individual's awareness of maladaptive thoughts that interfere with using appropriate skills effectively (Ramsay, 2010). As a result of chronic functional difficulties, recurring frustrations in most life settings can lead to the development of pessimistic outlooks, negative assumptions about one's abilities, and dysfunctional belief systems. Many adults with ADHD end up attributing their problems to characterological defects that are not amenable to change (Murphy, 2015). Typical maladaptive schemas in adults with ADHD are defectiveness, failure, and insufficient self-control (Ramsay & Rostain, 2003). Typical maladaptive thinking patterns are jumping to conclusions, overgeneralization, and all-or-nothing thinking (Ramsay & Rostain, 2008). Based on these cognitive distortions, adults with ADHD usually develop maladaptive compensatory strategies, such as avoidance and procrastination.

Therapists direct adults with ADHD toward change of these long existing dysfunctional beliefs. Individuals learn to identify automatic thoughts, challenge negative statements, evaluate judgments, and praise themselves for achievements. In addition, they are provided with strategies to develop confidence and to restart activities they have avoided. CBT has been found to be effective in raising self-esteem and self-efficacy in adults with ADHD, which are important factors in motivating treatment engagement (Young & Amarasinghe, 2010).

Behavior modification and cognition modification are synergistic because the cognitive changes generate adaptive behavioral changes. When these changes are reinforced, they in turn serve to generate more positive cognitions and self-attributions (Solanto, 2011).

In case it is considered feasible and beneficial, therapists can recruit significant others and family members of the individual with ADHD in order to increase support in daily routine. The individual's parents, partner, other family members, and close friends may considerably contribute to treatment if they are educated on the nature of ADHD symptoms, hold realistic expectations, and reduce conflicts, thus providing a secure and supportive environment.

More recently, mindfulness-based interventions and Dialectical Behavior Therapy (DBT)-based interventions have been developed for adults with ADHD, with effect sizes comparable to the ones found for CBT (Bueno et al., 2015; Fleming et al., 2015; Jansen et al., 2015). Mindfulness-based interventions are part of a "third generation" of behavior therapy (Hayes, Follette, & Linehan, 2004). Mindfulness meditation can be understood as a form of mental training (Bachmann, Lam, & Philipsen, 2016). At the intervention level, mindfulness meditation practices involve focusing attention on a particular object and returning to this object after becoming distracted in order to improve attentional control abilities (Keng, Smoski, & Robins, 2011). This can be thought of as a regulatory approach to attention that improves executive processes (Chiesa, Calati, & Serretti, 2011). Dialectical behavior therapy aims at balancing change-oriented skills (interpersonal effectiveness and emotion regulation) and acceptance-based skills (mindfulness and distress tolerance).

There is preliminary evidence that mindfulness meditation can improve the functioning of brain mechanisms underlying neuropsychological capacities impaired in ADHD, such as attention control and emotion regulation (Tang, Hölzel, & Posner, 2015). Neuroimaging studies suggest that mindfulness meditation engenders neuroplastic changes in brain areas associated with attentional functioning typically impaired in ADHD (Mitchell, Zylowska, & Kollins, 2015). Besides reducing core ADHD symptoms, these interventions are also effective in reducing the burden of the disease, which includes depression, anxiety, interpersonal difficulties, low self-esteem, and low quality of life and functioning (Cole et al., 2016; Philipsen et al., 2014).

It has been suggested that future research should investigate how to incorporate mindfulness with CBT in order to enhance treatment outcomes. Integrating mindfulness may be beneficial for nonresponders in CBT treatment, who are found to range from 33% to 58% (Safren, Perlman et al., 2005; Solanto, 2011). In addition, emotional functioning would be addressed as well, extending the focus of treatment to incorporate emotion dysregulation, which has been shown to improve following mindfulness meditation (Mitchell et al., 2013). Mindfulness may also enhance training in CBT strategies, by providing techniques that help individuals manage stress, focus in the session, cope with distractions, and manage overall negative affect (Mitchell et al., 2015).

The use of CBT interventions, including mindfulness meditation and dialectical behavior therapy in the treatment of adult ADHD, is a relatively new perspective that requires further empirical validation. However, to date there is significant evidence suggesting that these interventions have promise for ADHD treatment in adulthood (Canu & Wymbs, 2015; Jensen, Amdisen, Jørgensen, & Arnfred, 2016; Safren, Sprich, Mimiaga et al., 2010; Solanto et al., 2010). More than 20 peer-reviewed outcome studies have been published, including several recent randomized controlled trials, mostly reporting positive results when compared with active treatment control groups (Ramsay, 2016).

13.4 Coaching

Coaching is an increasingly popular intervention for adults with ADHD, deriving from cognitive-behavioral paradigms and the coaching model used in executive coaching and athletics (Prevatt, Lampropoulos, Bowles, & Garrett, 2011). ADHD coaching is a specialty area within the broader field of professional or personal coaching (Kubik, 2010). Despite limited scientific study on ADHD coaching as an intervention for adults with ADHD, this approach has grown significantly in recent years (Murphy, Ratey, Maynard, Sussman, & Wright, 2010). Within the framework of this approach, the person who participates in coaching is called a *client*.

Coaching has been defined as "collaboration between a coach and a client, through a creative process with cognitive challenges, thus inspiring the individual with ADHD to maximize their personal and professional potential" (Sleeper-Triplett, 2010, p. 2). It is a holistic, goal-driven, supportive, and cooperative process in which a coach and a client work together in order to identify goals, devise strategies to meet these goals, evaluate the effectiveness of the strategies, and make adjustments as necessary.

Coaches establish a nonjudgmental relationship with their clients and foster a climate of support and encouragement so that clients can discover how to replace defeating behaviors with positive patterns of success to cope with life challenges (Ratey & Sleeper-Triplett, 2011). The relationship is individualized to the client's needs and might include many areas that encompass daily life, such as work, exercise, nutrition, stress management, social relations, and recreational needs (Jaksa & Ratey, 1999). ADHD coaching draws on an individual's personal strengths and provides structure, support, and feedback. Furthermore, it helps adults with ADHD develop skills and strategies to cope with the core impairments associated with the disorder. Motivation is important to the success of coaching (Prevatt & Yelland, 2015). The process of delivery varies considerably, including face-to-face contact, brief regular telephone conversations, and email contact (Ratey, 2008; Young & Amarasinghe, 2010).

A review of the ADHD coaching literature states that a fundamental goal of coaching is to improve executive functioning skills (Goudreau & Knight, 2015). Therefore, coaching targets planning, time management, prioritization, goal setting, organization, problem solving, developing realistic plans, activating and sustaining effort over time, and regulating emotional reactions (Parker & Boutelle, 2009; Prevatt, 2016). Coaches use specific types of questioning with their clients to model effective executive functioning in order to increase their client's capacity to clarify, plan, and take action on goals (Field, Parker, Sawilowsky, & Rolands, 2013).

Coaching has a lot of similarities with traditional CBT counseling, and some researchers have questioned the extent to which coaching differs from CBT (Goldstein, 2005; Prevatt, 2016). Furthermore, coaching has evolved to encompass a wide range of CBT techniques (Kubik, 2010). However, several distinct differences can be identified.

First, CBT focuses on the overall functioning of the individual and attempts to train general coping skills that can be applied in a variety of contexts, whereas coaching provides the individual with support in achieving more concrete goals and handling specific problems. Second, coaching is a pragmatic, behavioral, results-oriented approach, as opposed to CBT, which is a more insight-oriented, intellectual approach (Murphy, 2005). CBT focuses on the mediational role of thoughts and beliefs in the implementation and maintenance of skills, whereas coaching focuses on the practical implementation of the client's goals (Ratey, 2002). However, it has been claimed that cognitive changes also occur in coaching as the result of behavioral interventions brought about by questioning, problem solving, modeling, and practicing (Prevatt et al., 2011). Third, the CBT therapist encourages the client to practice skills on their own through weekly homework, whereas the coach is generally more accessible to the client on an as-needed basis, without expecting behavioral changes to persist after the coaching relationship ends. Coaching may be more of an educational rather than a therapeutic process (Goldstein, 2005). Fourth, the CBT therapist has a specific and well-established theoretical orientation and uses evidence-based techniques. The theoretical orientation of coaching is usually vague and unspecified. Goldstein (2005) expressed his concern that "professionals from diverse mental health, business, and educational backgrounds" promote coaching as a service they offer without the support of scientific studies. Finally, coaching does not offer treatment but is suggested as an intervention that complements treatment (Ratey & Sleeper-Triplett, 2011).

The empirical corroboration for the efficacy of coaching for adults with ADHD is limited, and is basically examined as applied to the academic problems of students in a college setting (Kubik, 2010; Stevenson, Stevenson, & Whitmont, 2003; Swartz, Prevatt, & Proctor, 2005; Zwart & Kallemyn, 2001).

Evidence suggests that ADHD can impair academic achievement in college students. Only 9.1% of young adults with ADHD graduate from college, compared to 60.6% of typically developing individuals (Barkley, Murphy, & Fischer, 2008). College students with ADHD have demonstrated lower grades than their peers, have difficulty completing tests on time, require more time to complete assignments, have poorer study habits, withdraw from a greater number of courses, and take longer to complete their studies (Advokat, Lane, & Luo, 2011; Gormley et al., 2015). Furthermore, they are more likely to report depressive symptoms (Rabiner, Anastopoulos, Costello, Hoyle, & Swartzwelder, 2008).

Demands for self-regulation are very important upon entering college, not only with respect to educational tasks but also with respect to personal and social responsibilities (Anastopoulos & King, 2015). Prior to college, many supports may be in place to help manage the deficits in self-regulation. For example, parents provide structure, as they help their child get to school in the morning, oversee homework, keep a schedule of activities, and provide reminders of class assignments. Removal of external supports amplify developmental challenges for students with ADHD due to their deficits in self-regulation (Fleming & McMahon, 2012; Meaux, Green, & Broussard, 2009).

Although the research base on coaching is still emerging, the initial findings point toward the promise of this intervention to support students with ADHD to be more successful in postsecondary education (Canu & Wymbs, 2015; Field et al., 2013). A 5-year follow-up evaluated 148 coaching clients seen by 26 different coaches (Prevatt, & Yelland, 2015). Significant 8-week gains were found on ten different learning and study strategies, self-esteem, satisfaction with school and work, and a reduction in emotional distress. The largest effect sizes were found for time management and concentration. Additionally, several studies of ADHD coaching in college students found that participants engaged in more positive thoughts and behaviors, such as taking greater responsibility for one's actions, using goal-attainment skills, modulating emotions, and increasing positive expectations for performance (Parker, & Boutelle, 2009; Parker, Hoffman, Sawilowsky, & Rolands, 2011). Finally, it has been found that students who participated in coaching demonstrated statistically significant higher executive functioning compared to the comparison students and reported enhanced sense of well-being (Field et al., 2013).

A more recent approach is the combination of CBT and personal mentoring, as implemented in ACCESS (Accessing Campus Connections and Empowering Student Success), which is an intervention for students with ADHD on college campuses (Anastopoulos & King, 2015). ACCESS includes an 8-week active treatment protocol, followed by a maintenance phase, and provides group CBT accompanied by individual mentoring. It is designed to increase knowledge of ADHD and awareness of campus resources, improve organization, time management, and other behavioral skills, and teach cognitive therapy strategies for increasing adaptive thinking. Preliminary findings from this ongoing project are very encouraging.

14 Case Studies

14.1 Introduction

In the previous chapters of this book, we attempted to condense and present critically the current scientific knowledge about the most researched neurodevelopmental disorder of our era: ADHD. We relied on extensive, profound, and thorough study of the literature, as well as on our long clinical experience with children, adolescents, and adults with ADHD and their families. We also approached the disorder from the perspective of the researcher, the writer, and the academic teacher. However, the most significant part of our identity, which gives life to all the above, is that of a clinical child psychologist, who experiences on a daily basis the difficulties, the struggles, and the worries of children, adolescents, and young adults with ADHD, their parents, friends, and teachers. In this fascinating journey, we are not alone. We are accompanied by an outstanding interdisciplinary team, each member of which plays their own unique role in the provision of services of diagnosis and treatment for individuals with ADHD across the life span.

In the last chapter of this book, we chose to give the floor to some of the members of this team, in order to empirically present six cases of individuals with ADHD, for whom they served as keyworkers during treatment within the framework of the multilevel approach. These cases cover almost the whole spectrum of development up to adulthood, both genders, and several comorbidities. In some cases, treatment has been completed, whereas in other cases it is still in progress. Each of the following case studies is unique, as each person with ADHD is unique. Overall, they reflect the heterogeneity of the disorder and the wide range of treatment methods and techniques of the multilevel approach. In order to keep the text vivid, we chose not to report on test scores and procedures that were followed during assessment, but focus on case conceptualization and treatment. We aspire that the end of this book conveys a positive message. ADHD can be treated very effectively when some important requirements are fulfilled, one of which is that clinicians should know their job well!

14.2 Bryan, 4 Years[1]

Referral Question

Bryan visited our clinic accompanied by his parents, who were concerned about his noncompliant and aggressive behavior. Upon intake, he was 4 years old and was attending a private nursery school.

Brief Family History

Bryan was the only child born to his parents. Bryan's mother was a particularly active woman of high educational status. She was a diplomat required to travel a lot during the week. Bryan's father was a very busy entrepreneur, working long hours. During the parent interview, it was reported that there was no history of family members with learning or behavior difficulties.

Mother Profile

Bryan's mother had a successful professional career that had boosted substantially her self-esteem. However, she often felt inadequate and incompetent as a mother because she had considerable difficulty handling everyday issues with her son. Seeking an explanation for the child's defiant behavior, she had searched on the internet and had already suspected the presence of ADHD in her son. Despite the fact that she had read a lot about ADHD and was well-informed about optimal parenting practices, she failed to implement them appropriately. Bryan's mother was feeling ineffective and overwhelmed with guilt. Her husband, parents, and friends had reinforced these feelings, holding her responsible for her child's behavior. Bryan's mother often treated him as an older child. Her expectations were not developmentally realistic for a 4-year-old child, particularly a child with ADHD. As a result, disappointment and frustration intensified, wrong manipulations toward Bryan multiplied, and conflicts between Bryan and his mother increased.

Father Profile

Bryan's father was usually more lenient relative to his wife and quite permissive. He had realized that his own attitude negatively influenced the child's behavior, and he was willing to modify his maladaptive parenting practices. Due to the nature of his job, he was absent for most of the day and spent some time with Bryan mainly at weekends. Bryan's mother was the one who was systematically occupied with Bryan and dedicated a lot of time to various common activities with the child. The relationship between parents was fairly good.

Brief Developmental History

Bryan's mother indicated no complications with her pregnancy and reported that Bryan was born full-term with normal birth weight. He walked at the age of 10 months and had fast motor development. He had a late speech onset at 2 years, but a very rapid vocabulary development. At nights, he used to wake up and visit his parents' bed. Mild tics were present at the age of 3. Low frustration tolerance, delay aversion, difficulty following rules, and anger outbursts were also reported. His mother said: "When he wants something, he screams and thrashes about on the floor until he gets it."

Information From School

At the nursery school, Bryan avoided participating in most activities, did not complete tasks, and quitted easily. He was also oppositional, noncompliant, and easily lost temper. He constantly argued with his peers. His teacher said that he became overly excited or upset by different activities, transitions, or frustrations.

Initial Evaluation

The initial evaluation revealed that Bryan was a very intelligent child, with a wealth of knowledge. It was obvious that the child lived in a highly stimulating environment. His receptive language, including comprehension of spoken language and identification of vocabulary, was above average. However, he displayed a variety of phonological error patterns, including articulation and auditory discrimination difficulties. Bryan's phonological error patterns contributed to a level of speech intelligibility that was below average for his age group.

In the domain of motor development, Bryan exhibited decreased bilateral integration, motor planning, and eye-hand coordination during gross motor activities. He was also observed to use a cylindrical grip to hold a pencil during graphomotor tasks, exhibit a decreased speed when coloring, and difficulty with cutting with scissors. With respect to his behavior, Bryan was particularly impulsive, hyperactive, and very easily distracted. He was very talkative and had difficulty remaining seated. In addition, he had poor self-control skills and very low frustration tolerance, motivation, and self-efficacy.

Diagnosis

Bryan was diagnosed with ADHD, combined type, Speech-Sound Disorder, and ODD, according to the DSM-IV criteria. Today, Bryan is 6 years old and meets the DSM-5 criteria for the combined presentation of ADHD. Following treatment, he no longer fulfills the requirements for ODD or Speech-Sound Disorder.

Treatment Structure and Progress

The initial treatment plan for Bryan included speech therapy and psychoeducational intervention for ADHD. At the age of 5.5 years, speech therapy was extended to include a component for the promotion of school readiness. Occupational therapy was also recommended, but the family did not wish to engage in this kind of intervention. Parent training was inherent in every program the child attended, following some initial sessions of psychoeducation. It is highlighted that Bryan's parents were not particularly interested in speech therapy because they did not consider speech difficulties important, as they would like to focus on Bryan's behavior. However, they accepted this treatment plan. Their primary concern was Bryan's noncompliance and his limited ability to follow instructions, resulting in conflicts during everyday activities, play, and outings. However, the parents expected Bryan to get dressed without help, wash his hands without a reminder before lunch, make his bed every morning, and communicate effectively his thoughts and needs.

Initially, speech therapy focused on articulation problems and writing motor skills in order to partially compensate for the absence of occupational therapy from the treatment structure. Expressive language skills and auditory discrimination were also targeted. However, the major goals of the program were the improvement of sustained attention and impulse inhibition. Toward this end, Bryan's mother was regularly invited to attend parts of the speech therapy session in order to apply correctly the therapist's guidelines at home. Several oral exercises and assignments were provided for practice at home, following specific principles that mother and child were taught during speech therapy sessions.

The psychoeducational intervention primarily aimed at the reduction of the core ADHD symptoms and the modification of the child's maladaptive behaviors following an FBA, through behavior modification techniques. A behavioral chart was used at home, and the backup reward was provided by the clinician at the end of each week. Later on, the reward was provided once a month by parents. Parent training in behavioral techniques was provided at the end of each session with the child, and parent counseling was constant throughout treatment in order to support parents to handle concerns and worries about Bryan and other family matters. Techniques used with the child included stimulus control, gradual increase of attention span, and behavior modification techniques, such as positive reinforcement and response-cost. On the other hand, parents were trained in a wide range of behavioral, problem-solving, and anger management techniques. Monthly school consultation was also included.

Two months after initiation of treatment, Bryan was able to follow some basic rules and started to cooperate more effectively with his parents at home. Furthermore, anger outbursts were significantly reduced. His mother started to reinforce him systematically and developed more realistic expectations from him. In the domain of oral speech, Bryan had a very good progress rate and had already started to pronounce correctly some phonemes that were particularly difficult for him.

From time to time, Bryan's mother complained that Bryan was not always willing to complete tasks and exercises required by his speech therapist. He often tried to negotiate the quantity and the way in which these exercises should be done, thus often coming into conflict with his mother, who had been exhausted from managing Bryan. Each time these problems re-emerged, parent training and counseling intensified and, subsequently, the child's behavior normalized.

During our collaboration, Bryan's mother reported incidents that revealed that she was prone to lose her temper easily and that she did not always manage to be consistent and implement planned ignoring and differential reinforcement. For example, one day Bryan woke up in the morning and tried to get ready on his own in order to surprise his mother but he could not button his trousers. When his mother entered his room, Bryan was frustrated that he had not managed to get dressed, so he began shouting at his mother and burst into tears. His mother, instead of letting him calm down, as she had done in similar situations in the past, got angry and told him that they would not leave home unless he managed to put on his trousers. Eventually, the child put on his trousers, but his mother did not praise him. As a result, they were both in a bad mood for the rest of the day.

Treatment Outcome

Bryan is 6 years old today, he does not have any difficulty in articulation, and his speech is perfectly intelligible. Furthermore, the school readiness component of speech therapy has helped him improve significantly in various academic domains. Bryan has fewer auditory discrimination difficulties, recognizes all the alphabet letters without difficulty, and is able to read and write two-syllable words. With respect to his behavior, remarkable reduction of defiant and disobedient behavior is observed in both school and family settings. He has acquired better self-control, participates actively in class activities, and finishes tasks on time. Furthermore, he exhibits better emotional regulation and general self-regulation skills, has increased frustration tolerance, engages in activities that he previously avoided, and handles defeat in games more appropriately.

Bryan continues attending a psychoeducational program in our clinic. The current goals of treatment primarily include impulse control and sustained attention, because Bryan still manifests inattentive and off-task behavior when sustained mental effort is required. Furthermore, there is some evidence of SLD and, therefore, the school readiness component continues with the aim of preventing full manifestation of SLD upon entrance to formal schooling.

Conclusion

Bryan represents a typical case of a child with ADHD who received the diagnosis and appropriate treatment at preschool age. Although the child's parents were of high educational status, in many occasions they obstructed treatment progress, either due to their high expectations or due to their difficulty implementing recommended techniques. However, they showed trust in their child's therapists, engaged in treatment and, as a result, they can now enjoy Bryan's company, feel more effective in their parenting role, and have the knowledge and determination to implement appropriate techniques to manage Bryan's behavior. On the other hand, Bryan has now enhanced expressive language and communication skills, has acquired a wide range of self-regulatory skills, and has more friends, elevated self-esteem, and increased motivation for school achievement. His parents and teachers often express their satisfaction openly with respect to his behavior and performance, which are praised accordingly.

14.3 George, 5 Years[2]

Referral Question

George was referred for evaluation by his teacher to determine the nature of speech impairment. Upon intake, he was 5 years old and was attending kindergarten. Specific concerns included manifestation of hyperactive and inattentive behaviors both at home and school. His teacher was also concerned about the child's delayed response time, especially when multiple manipulations or sequencing was required.

Brief Family History

George lived with his parents and his older sister in a familial block of flats. His parents had graduated high school. His mother was a secretary and his father worked in a retail store. George's parents had a very good relationship and no conflicts between them were reported.

Mother Profile

George's mother was an anxious woman who wanted to have complete control over family life and had assumed the main responsibility of child-rearing. On the one hand, she was overprotective with her children and would not let anyone insult or underestimate them. On the other hand, she was extremely judgmental herself and did not believe in the use of praise. She particularly valued academic learning, and she expected her children to love school, read a lot of books, and have excellent school performance. Consequently, she was very worried about her son's difficulties. To the contrary, she was very proud of George's sister, Nancy, whom she described as the "perfect child." Nancy was a very good student, compliant, cooperative, agreeable, and popular among her peers. George's mother always compared George's behavior to that of Nancy's.

Father Profile

George's father was a low-profile person. He did not take much initiative within the family. He supported his wife's decisions about the children, but he believed that her worries were excessive. He often said that George took after him. He reported that he was also late to speak and experienced similar academic difficulties during schooling. He was reluctant to become involved in treatment.

Brief Developmental History

George's mother was put on bed rest during her second and third trimesters in order to avoid miscarriage due to placental abruption. George was born at 8 months gestation via C-section.

He was kept in the hospital for monitoring for 10 days. No other complications were noted. His mother stated that walking and toilet training were completed at a normal rate but language development was slower relative to her daughter.

Information From School

George's teacher reported that he constantly left the story circle time and wandered around the classroom. Furthermore, he was messy and careless, thus often losing his stuff and forgetting to take his jacket. George was rejected by his peers who never chose him to play with them. As a result, he often displayed inappropriate attention-seeking behaviors and played the class clown. George was fully aware of his difficulties and was motivated to engage in treatment since the first meeting. He was interested in learning how he could manage to display appropriate behaviors in order to get less reprimands, have better performance in school activities, and make friends.

Initial Evaluation

During the initial assessment, George moved ceaselessly, had great difficulty remaining seated, and was moving from one activity to the other as he was getting easily bored. He was noisy during play and had difficulty following complex instructions. He talked all the time and did not have turn-taking abilities. He was impulsive and displayed low frustration tolerance. He was able to complete all the tasks but had a delayed response time, especially when multiple manipulations or sequencing was required.

According to speech-language evaluation, George's receptive language was within average range. However, he displayed several expressive language difficulties, including the ability to participate in conversation appropriately, use of appropriate grammar, and the ability to provide information upon request. Furthermore, he revealed articulation skills to be below functional limits. Specifically, he demonstrated errors of articulation of /l/, /sh/, /j/, /v/, and /th/ sounds at the conversational level. Additionally, he demonstrated a substitution of fricatives (e.g., /s/, /f/). His cognitive ability was estimated to fall in the average range compared to same aged peers.

Diagnosis

George was diagnosed with ADHD, combined type, and Speech-Sound Disorder, according to the DSM-IV criteria. Today, George is 11 years old and meets the DSM-5 criteria for the combined presentation of ADHD. Following treatment, he does not fulfill the requirements for ODD or Speech-Sound Disorder anymore. However, he meets the criteria for SLD with impaired reading and writing.

Treatment Structure and Progress

The initial treatment plan for George included speech therapy and psychoeducational intervention for ADHD. Psychoeducation and cognitive restructuring helped the child distinguish behaviors and difficulties associated with ADHD from behaviors associated with other factors. George was trained in self-management skills in order to control the core ADHD symptoms. Toward this end, various techniques were used, including self-monitoring, self-evaluation, and self-reinforcement. The complete range of behavioral techniques was introduced as well. A daily report card was used jointly with his teacher and his mother. Furthermore, the child was trained in problem solving with the use of the technique Stop-Think-Act. Social skills training was also included with the use of anger management techniques, empathy, and role play, modeling, and relaxation techniques. His mother received training and counseling throughout treatment.

Upon entering elementary school, low academic performance was also added into the child's difficulties. George had difficulty learning how to read and write and began to reverse letters and words. As soon as he learned to read, it was obvious that his reading was slow and inaccurate. As soon as he learned to write, he faced difficulties with spelling and transferring ideas onto paper. In addition, his written work was without spacing and oblivious to the lines on the page. He soon met the diagnostic criteria for SLD with impaired reading and writing. His assignments were messy or incomplete and full of careless mistakes. He had a difficult time completing classroom assignments on time and needed frequent prompting and supervision to complete tasks.

As a result, George had low self-esteem and reduced motivation for school achievement. He believed that he could not succeed in school and began to avoid getting involved in activities requiring mental effort. Therefore, techniques for the treatment of learning difficulties, as well as CBT techniques for the enhancement of the child's self-esteem and self-efficacy, were introduced into the psychoeducational intervention.

George was exceptionally agreeable and cooperative during treatment. Within five months, the articulation and auditory discrimination difficulties had been eliminated. Within six months, his reading and writing scores had progressed one grade level. Remarkable improvement also was noted in his behavior. His father's attitude changed as well. He started to engage in treatment more actively and told the mother that "eventually she did not exaggerate when she insisted that the child should be referred for assessment." George's mother was particularly motivated to learn new parenting practices and strategies to cope with the child's difficulties effectively.

Within 18 months, George had completely changed attitude toward school and was motivated to participate actively in class. Furthermore, he was able to control his hyperactivity to such a degree that his teacher in the third grade could not identify any overt symptom of ADHD. Furthermore, George had made a very good friend and could hang out effectively with several peers. During the time period that followed, George had a steady improvement in all domains. From time to time, there were setbacks, which were dealt with lowering expectations and reintroducing fundamental goals that were achieved in the past.

Treatment Outcome

Treatment was completed in two years. George's grades and behavior in school had remarkably improved. Intermittently George would return to our clinic for booster sessions on the family's demand in order to reinforce or troubleshoot additional areas needed to be worked on. Currently, the child is receiving a short-term intervention aiming at enhancing organizational and social skills in order to prepare George for his transition to junior high school.

Conclusion

In conclusion, treatment in George's case was very successful. The key to George's progress was the excellent collaboration among the professionals, the child, and his family. However, we consider that the efficacy of treatment would be even greater and would become evident sooner if the head teacher of the elementary school that the child attended did not refuse collaboration, as he did not believe in the existence of ADHD as a disorder.

14.4 Anne, 7 Years[3]

Referral Question

Anne was referred for evaluation by her teacher in order to identify possible sources of school failure and conduct problems. Upon intake, she was a 7-year-old first-grade student. Specific concerns included attention difficulties, poor response inhibition, academic underachievement, poor homework completion, peer problems, and noncompliance. Parents reported that Anne frequently lost or misplaced homework, books, or other items, and seemed completely disorganized. In addition, she did not follow rules, refused to do her homework, and exhibited oppositionality on a daily basis.

Brief Family History

Anne was the second child of the family and she lived with her parents, her 9-year-old sister, and her 3-year-old brother. Her father was a physiotherapist, and her mother was a housewife. Anne's father came from France and her mother from Russia. It was reported that there was a history of severe learning disabilities within the family, concerning the mother's sister. Besides, Anne's mother met the diagnostic criteria for ADHD, although she had never been diagnosed.

Family Profile

Anne's mother exhibited particularly high levels of stress, whereas her father seemed more relaxed. Parents often argued on issues regarding child-rearing because they perceived their children's behavior in very different ways. Anne's father was responsible for financially supporting his family, whereas Anne's mother was almost exclusively responsible for the household and the child-rearing. Anne's father was physically absent from the house for most of the day. At home, arguments and conflicts among siblings often broke out, a fact that negatively influenced the family atmosphere. Parents appeared to implement inconsistent and lax parenting practices. For example, the mother often threatened Anne that she would throw all her dolls away if she did not finish homework, without having ever applied any consequences or having kept her word. Anne's mother felt overwhelmed by the task of raising her children without spousal help. Soon after Anne's assessment, both her siblings were also referred for assessment. All three children were given the diagnosis of ADHD and received treatment as well.

Brief Developmental History

Anne's mother indicated no complications with her pregnancy and that Anne was born at expected time with normal birth weight. Developmental milestones were reported as within normal range for gross motor development and toilet training. Nevertheless, Anne had received speech therapy for 3 months at the age of 3 years due to delay in language development. At the time, Anne was diagnosed with *Language Disorder*, and no other assessment had been recommended. It should be noted that the children were multilingual, as they spoke Russian, French, Greek, and English, and they attended a Greek-French school.

Anne was described as a difficult and restless baby. As soon as she walked, she started to run and engage in risky behaviors, which resulted in frequent minor injuries. At home, she could not remain seated during lunch but she moved up and down with her plate. Her mother likened her to a spinning top because she could neither concentrate and play with a toy for more than 10 minutes nor finish her drawings. Furthermore, she often displayed defiant and oppositional behavior, particularly toward her mother. On the whole, she tried to monopolize attention in every way. Similar behaviors were reported in nursery school and kindergarten. However, Anne's parents attributed her behavior to immaturity and did not realize that something was going wrong until they were prompted to seek evaluation by the child's teacher.

Information From School

According to her teacher's reports, Anne struggled with unstructured activities both in the classroom and at recess. She fidgeted constantly, called out, left her seat, and left assignments incomplete. She played with objects and manipulated any materials within her reach. She was described as disruptive and oppositional in class. She displayed refusal to follow directions, verbal aggression toward peers and teachers (threats, throwing objects, breaking items), and class disruptions (talking out and arguing). The teacher attributed these behaviors to poor child-rearing and parent difficulties in setting boundaries. She believed that Anne was a very clever girl who was not achieving her potential because she was lazy. As a result, she often reprimanded her, yelled at her, and punished her.

Initial Evaluation

Anne was a child of average intelligence, particularly sociable and cooperative. She was a very cute girl with a neat appearance. She enjoyed her beauty, and she made sure to show off her beautiful clothes and her impressive hair clips. She was particularly hyperactive, impulsive, and careless. Furthermore, she had auditory discrimination difficulties and difficulties in pronouncing multisyllable words. She also demonstrated little difficulty with thought organization and verbal expression. Anne exhibited difficulties in basic reading and writing skills, reading comprehension, and mathematics calculation. Although she had mastered the basic number facts in addition and subtraction, her inattention to the task demands created problems in their completion. The child seemed to be fully aware of her difficulties and she believed that she was not a good student compared to her classmates. She reported that she did not like school and that she often faked a stomachache in order to avoid going to school.

Diagnosis

From the available data, it was concluded that Anne met all the DSM-5 criteria for the diagnosis of ADHD, combined presentation, and SLD with impaired reading, writing, and mathematics.

Treatment Structure and Progress

A psychoeducational intervention for ADHD, which focused on behavior modification and improvement of academic performance, was implemented. The primary treatment goals included reducing the symptoms of impulsivity and hyperactivity, improving the ability to focus attention, and enhancing child compliance, self-esteem, and self-efficacy. Anger management and social skills training were also included, and participation in extracurricular activities was recommended. Anne's parents received intensive parent training apart from counseling provided within the psychoeducational intervention. Furthermore, the mother received personal help for anxiety management, enhancement of her self-efficacy, and management of her own ADHD symptomatology. Parent training included psychoeducation about ADHD, rule setting, and training in a wide range of behavioral techniques. Finally, joint school consultation was implemented, and a daily report card was introduced with targets concerning both school and home.

Anne developed a very close relationship with her therapist and engaged enthusiastically in treatment. Within 2 months, she could easily follow the rules of the clinical setting and control her impulsivity to a certain extent. Within 4 months, her academic performance, her relationship with her teacher, and her overall behavior showed great improvement. Anne joined the drama club and made good friends with whom she played happily during recess. Her motivation for school achievement increased, and she did not avoid school anymore. Within 6 months, great improvement was also noticed in parenting practices. The mother's anxiety level was reduced, she felt more competent in her parenting role, and she made progress in channeling Anne's energy productively and providing praise and negative consequences adequately, depending on Anne's behavior. In fact, she made the following statement about herself: "In the beginning, I constantly wondered why a child like this came to me. But now, I have realized what is happening with my child, and I feel relieved of a heavy burden. You helped me calm down and learn how to manage her."

Treatment Outcome

Anne's treatment is still in progress. Next targets include impulse inhibition, emotion regulation, and increase of attention span. Emphasis will be also given on organization and homework management skills, and further enhancing academic performance.

Conclusion

The success of treatment is closely associated with the quality of collaboration among the members of the therapeutic team, including parents and teachers. In Anne's case, her mother managed to overcome her initial difficulties because she was highly motivated to help her child. Both parents tried to systematically follow the instructions given to them, and the father became more supportive toward his wife. Finally, the good therapeutic relationship that was established with the child, her good mental ability, and the fact that treatment goals were mutually agreed upon and considered realistic and feasible were the main factors leading to positive outcomes.

14.5 Alex, 8 Years[4]

Referral Question

Alex was referred for evaluation due to mutual concern on the part of his mother and teacher to determine functional limitations related to communication, academic performance, and social behavior. Upon intake, Alex was an 8-year-old second-grade student. His mother described him as a hyperactive and inattentive child, with obsessions and serious difficulty in adapting to environmental changes. He was easily upset and often displayed anger outbursts. Furthermore, he interacted with his peers in an awkward way, which often resulted in peer rejection.

Brief Family History

Alex lived with his parents and his 3-year-old sister, who also caused her mother's concern due to delay in language development. Parent's relationship was reported to be problematic. No medical, behavioral, or psychiatric problems were reported in other family members.

Mother Profile

Alex's mother was an architect. She was a particularly nervous and overreacting woman, who lost her patience easily. She had high expectations from Alex and was very demanding. She spent a lot of time with Alex but did not end up enjoying her interaction with her son, as their relationship was conflictual. As a result, she felt inefficient in her parenting role and often got angry with herself. Her self-efficacy was low, and she often reported feelings of frustration and disappointment.

Father Profile

Alex's father did not seem to realize his child's difficulties. He mainly responded to noncompliance and other maladaptive behaviors with punishment, scolding, and beating. He underestimated the mother's worries about Alex, attributed the child's behavior to characterological defects, and was emotionally unavailable for his family.

Brief Developmental History

Information obtained from his mother, indicated that Alex was not an easy baby to tend. He was a colicky baby despite being breastfed. He was restless, grouchy, and had sleep disturbances. He was also very sensitive to light and noise. Early on, Alex exhibited delays and regressions in his speech development and social functioning. His mother reported that Alex knew how to say "mama" and "agua" at 11 months of age but stopped speaking soon afterward. Alex used mostly gestures and grunts to communicate his needs until he was almost 2 years old. For this reason, he went through a speech-language evaluation, but no diagnosis was reached. However, speech therapy was recommended. He also displayed several maladaptive behaviors, such as sensitivity to smells and tastes, excessive tantrums, and stereotypical movements, such as rocking and darting. Auditory tics were also reported. Furthermore, Alex developed phobias and obsessions with machinery and was easily upset when changes occurred in daily routines. He also displayed increased sensitivity to sensory input. When Alex was 4 years old, his mother realized that the child did not want people at home and that he was playing alone exclusively. Furthermore, he had difficulty following rules and his thought patterns appeared extremely rigid.

Information From School

In nursery school, Alex had great difficulty communicating with peers. He approached other children in an awkward and inappropriate way. At this time, he went through a developmental evaluation and was given the diagnosis of Asperger's syndrome. It was suggested that Alex was not ready for regular class placement; however, his parents did not welcome any other option. In the first grade, Alex had difficulty completing classroom assignments on time and needed frequent prompting and supervision to complete tasks. The quality of work he did manage to turn in was in the poor to satisfactory range. He had weakness in all areas of academic functioning. Alex had difficulty with other functional behaviors, including organization, planning, and sequencing of activities. When assigned a task, he often had difficulty knowing what to do to begin, how to break the task into smaller steps, and how to keep everything organized. He was often unprepared for class and had difficulty following multi-step directions. Socially, Alex had a difficult time integrating himself with the other children. During recess, he spent most of his time wandering in the playground.

Initial Evaluation

Alex's general intellectual functioning was measured to fall within the average range, with his overall thinking and reasoning abilities exceeding those of approximately 30% of his same-aged peers. Upon the initial meeting, Alex appeared a little shy and avoided the examiner's attempts to establish eye contact. However, he was cooperative and yearned intensely for praise. He was particularly hyperactive and impulsive, with severe distractibility. During testing, he had difficulty remaining seated and often sought out opportunities to stand up and move. He did not initiate conversation or make any comment as to how he was feeling. At times, Alex appeared anxious, especially when working on tasks he found difficult or tedious. Most of the time, Alex responded to questions posed by the examiner with one-word sentences, especially when asked questions pertaining to his hobbies, friendships, and family life. Toward the end, as Alex began to tire, he grew increasingly frustrated and worried.

In the domain of motor development, Alex had mild difficulties in gross motor skills and more serious difficulties in fine motor skills. He exhibited decreased bilateral integration, praxis/motor planning, and eye-hand coordination during gross motor activities. Furthermore, Alex was observed to use a cylindrical grip to hold an enlarged pencil during graphomotor tasks. He presented with decreased awareness of pressure by either not making marks on the paper when he intended to or pressing on the pencil so hard that the lead snapped off. He exhibited a decreased speed when writing. Alex demonstrated intact bilateral integration during graphomotor tasks as evidenced by manipulating writing utensils with his left hand and stabilizing the paper with his right hand. He occasionally attempted to write with both hands. Finally, Alex demonstrated difficulty donning shirt, pants, and socks, and frequently needed assistance for dressing.

In the domain of language development, it was observed that the child had a rich vocabulary but did not use verbal and nonverbal language for appropriate communication and social interaction. He was not capable of maintaining conversation in a socially appropriate way, did not demonstrate turn-taking abilities, and had difficulty understanding metaphors and humor. Moreover, he had mild auditory discrimination difficulties and often manifested echolalia. There were several phrases that he repeated even in irrelevant and inappropriate contexts. Finally, he had marked difficulties in reading fluency skills, reading comprehension, and written expression.

Diagnosis

According to DSM-5, Alex met the criteria for the diagnosis of ASD (Level 1), ADHD, combined presentation, DCD, and SLD with impaired reading and writing.

Treatment Structure and Progress

Alex was enrolled in a psychoeducational intervention for ASD, a psychoeducational intervention for ADHD, and occupational therapy for his motor difficulties. Due to the multimorbidity, the appropriate coordination of these interventions was given primary importance. The child's strengths and weaknesses in all developmental domains were carefully assessed, and treatment goals were prioritized through FBA.

The initial goals for Alex across interventions included reducing dysfunctional social behaviors, controlling ADHD primary symptoms, improving self-care skills, writing motor skills and visual-motor coordination, and enhancing self-regulation and self-efficacy. At the same time, Alex's mother was provided with psychoeducation, counseling, and training in behavioral and social skills techniques. It should be noted that she needed a lot of emotional support to accept the diagnosis. An illustrative example was her reaction after the announcement of the diagnosis. When she returned home, she started shaking Alex and saying: "Get out of my child and bring Alex back." Despite our repeated attempts to get the father involved in treatment too, he remained nonresponding because he did not believe that his child had any difficulties requiring treatment.

Techniques used included discrete-trial teaching, token economy, and prompting, which was sometimes provided in the form of verbal instruction or physical guidance and sometimes through modeling. Training in self-care was based on task analysis and backward chaining. Gradually, Alex's functioning significantly improved in all settings, and communication skills training intensified. Problem-solving skills training and stress management were also provided because Alex exhibited increased stress. In the first semester of treatment, steady improvement was observed in all domains. After the second semester, anger outbursts were limited, the child's social and motor skills were improved, tolerance to changes had increased, and ADHD symptoms were markedly reduced. However, when Alex attended the third grade, learning difficulties were more evident, and his mother started to express intense worries related to Alex's academic performance. She believed that "high academic performance would cover up Alex's deficits in other domains." These expectations, in conjunction with his attention and learning difficulties, caused Alex increased stress, as evidenced by school refusal and complaints about physical symptoms shortly before it was time to leave for school. For this reason, mother's counseling was intensified and academic remediation was added into the child's treatment plan.

Treatment Outcome

Today, Alex is 10 years old and impairments stem mainly from ASD and much less from ADHD. His attention span has increased and his academic performance is above average. He has one close friend, and he responds positively to initiatives of social interaction. However, he does not take such initiatives himself. Furthermore, his interests are still limited, and stereotypic behaviors occur under stress. The main treatment goals at present are the reduction of obsessive thoughts and stereotypic behaviors and the generalization of social and communication skills in real life situations.

Conclusion

In this case, comorbidity of ADHD with ASD, DCD, and SLD required very careful prioritization of the child's needs in order to address those symptoms that mostly caused functional impairment in each developmental stage. From our point of view, we did not have four different disorders to treat but a wide range of symptoms resulting from mild brain dysfunction. Therefore, following a systematic FBA, we targeted symptoms causing functional impairment and not disorders. Within this framework, symptoms in the spectrum of ADHD (learning difficulties included) were successfully treated and did not impair the child's functioning any longer. A well-coordinated multidisciplinary team of experts, capable of capturing the whole clinical picture of Alex and not isolated fragments, has helped this child overcome major difficulties and integrate satisfactorily in school and peer group. If his father had been able to understand Alex's difficulties and engage in treatment, the outcome would have been even better.

14.6 Tom, 15 Years[5]

Referral Question

Tom was a 15-year-old teenager referred for evaluation by his parents due to concerns about how his emotions and behaviors were impacting his ability to access and progress in the general curriculum. He was a student of the first grade of a professional high school. The parents' initial request was to screen for ADHD and then "find a way, so that this child will calm down and come to his senses." Tom himself was negative and did not want to get into this process. He agreed to the evaluation after a lot of pressure and numerous conflicts with his parents.

Brief Family History

Tom was the oldest son in the family and had a brother aged 12 years and twin sisters aged 8 years. Two of the three younger children of the family had been diagnosed with ADHD and were enrolled in treatment. Tom's mother had ADHD herself but had never received treatment.

Mother Profile

Tom's mother was a civil servant. She was a nervous, impulsive woman with frequent anger outbursts. On the other hand, she was deeply religious and had very rigid moral values. In her attempt to organize and set boundaries for her children, she often came into conflict with them. Her parenting style was harsh and authoritarian.

Father Profile

Tom's father was a carpenter. He had been diagnosed with depression but refused to take his medication. He did not spend any time with his children, nor did he assume any responsibility about them. He often became very judgmental toward them and underestimated them. Tom's relationship with his parents and his brother was conflictual, whereas he was protective and loving toward his sisters.

Brief Developmental History

According to his mother's reports, Tom had normal language and motor development. Developmental milestones were reported to have been acquired a little late but within the normal range. Hyperactivity was noticed from a very young age but had not been considered as an alarming behavior by his parents.

Information From School

In elementary school, Tom was very compliant and his teachers had not reported any problems. His mother helped him with his homework and had noticed that he was easily distracted. However, his increased motivation for school achievement counterbalanced this difficulty, and Tom was ranked among the top students.

Tom started to experience difficulties in his transition from elementary to junior high school with respect to his academic achievement. Homework was time-consuming for him and his performance started to drop. However, by the age of 15, no serious maladjustments were reported.

In the summer before entering high school, Tom started to spend a lot of time on the internet. In the first grade of high school, his performance dropped rapidly. Many times Tom went to school without his schoolbag and books. He would go to bed late at night and fail to get up for school in the morning. He was often out without parental consent, started going to football matches systematically, and got involved with organized sports fan clubs. His parents were extremely worried with his rebellious behavior.

Initial Evaluation

Tom's general intellectual functioning was measured to fall within the superior range. However, Tom was impulsive, with limited self-control. Although he had initially opposed to the evaluation, he was very compliant and soon confided to the examiner that he had begun ambushing fans of rival teams, getting into trouble with the police, and making use of alcohol and cannabis. He tried to give the impression of a "tough" child, who defied everything from the school system to family principles. Nonetheless, he was particularly vulnerable to negative criticism, and his self-esteem was seriously battered. He did not face any learning difficulties, apart from organizational problems that interfered with academic achievement. His academic skills were all within the average or above average level of ability, but he often failed to utilize his capacity to achieve up to his potential.

Diagnosis

According to the assessment's results, Tom met the DSM-5 criteria for the diagnosis of ADHD, combined presentation, comorbid with CD. An evaluation of his early development, cognitive capability, emotional status, and academic achievement resulted in a determination of a complex set of characteristics that were contributing to his difficulties.

Treatment Structure and Progress

Tom agreed to receive CBT psychotherapy on condition that he was not accompanied to sessions by his parents. He also gave his consent for a weekly contact by phone between his parents and his therapist. The initial goal of treatment was to gain Tom's trust and build therapeutic alliance. The next goals were set along with Tom and included increasing self-awareness, improving self-control, and enhancing self-esteem and motivation for academic achievement, through the development of appropriate cognitive and behavioral skills. Psychoeducation was initially provided so that Tom could understand how ADHD impacted his functioning.

He was trained in identifying and challenging negative automatic thoughts (e.g., "Whatever I do is wrong"), distorted cognitions (e.g., "The only way of letting off steam is to go to the football match and smash everything"), negative core beliefs (e.g., "I am probably stupid"), and demoralizing thoughts (e.g., "I will never succeed"). Moreover, he was trained in developing new cognitive mechanisms and problem-solving skills. Finally, he learned to associate his thoughts with his emotions and find new ways of coping with them. Later on, self-control techniques, anger management, and organizational skills training were added as treatment components.

In the first sessions, Tom was very suspicious and gave only one-word answers. He needed time to start trusting the therapist and expressing himself. It was very important for him to realize that the therapist accepted him just the way he was. The goals of intervention were prioritized from the easiest to the most difficult ones, so that Tom could start experiencing success. For example, he got into the process of trying to be more diligent in his school obligations and more cooperative with his teachers.

After several sessions, Tom felt the need to reveal some life events that he had been keeping secret until then. From early childhood until the age of 12 years, his parents often took him to monasteries with them, although he had repeatedly expressed his annoyance. He was feeling very angry with his parents having obliged him to follow religious routines against his will. The most significant revelation, however, referred to an incident with his godfather, who was a policeman. Tom's mother asked for his help in order to persuade Tom to spend fewer hours on the internet. He visited Tom and started to reprimand him for his excessive occupation with the computer. As Tom was not heedful of these reprimands, things got out of control, and his godfather started threatening and beating Tom. The parents did not intervene to help their child, who was finally taken to hospital with severe contusions all over his body. The family members never discussed this incident again neither with each other nor with anybody else.

From that moment on, Tom started avoiding staying at home and hanging out with people who belonged to organized sports fan clubs. Tom felt accepted and appreciated within these groups. In the face of all the policemen and every other figure of authority, he used to see his godfather and his parents. As a result, he was often being provocative and challenging toward them. "I don't fancy policemen and army officers because they are authoritarian," he characteristically stated.

These revelations considerably contributed to the progress of treatment. Since that session, Tom stopped feeling guilty and discussed everything. His mother's counseling intensified, as she had also reached the point of talking about these life-changing events. Tom started expending much greater effort to honor his agreements with his therapist, and the outcomes soon became evident.

Treatment Outcome

The intervention lasted almost two years and was completed with success. Tom is now at college, studying law. He has not made use of cannabis for 3 years and has left the sports fan clubs. He has become a happy, communicative, and responsive young man who can express his feelings instead of acting them out. Furthermore, his relationship with all the family members has improved, except for his godfather, with whom he still does not wish any contact. Tom tries to contribute financially to his family by doing a part-time job in parallel with his studies.

Conclusion

Tom is a typical case of an intelligent child with ADHD without learning difficulties, who manages to enter high school without particular problems. However, the combination of his impulsive behavior, low self-esteem, wrong manipulations on the part of the family, developmental characteristics of adolescence, some particular circumstances and incidents, and his susceptibility to negative influences from peers led this child to the development of CD and delinquent behavior. Thanks to his mother's insistence on his initiating treatment and Tom's constructive collaboration with his psychotherapist, the course of his life changed radically, and Tom is today a young adult who is ambitiously pursuing his dreams.

14.7 Susan, 30 Years[6]

Referral Question

Susan decided to seek help after having been prompted by her family in order to overcome chronic feelings of demoralization and failure in all domains of life, particularly in the professional and social domains. Susan was particularly upset by her inability to commit to her goals and reach achievement. As she stated, "I am easily bored and I am continually looking for something new to be occupied with. Therefore, I never achieve anything."

Brief Family History

Susan was brought up by her mother and her stepfather. Her parents got divorced when she was 5 years old after a long legal battle. Her father had remarried and had one more daughter. Susan had a very good relationship with her stepfather as well as with her father and his new family. She had a bachelor's in economics but she had been unemployed for a year and her parents had been supporting her financially. At the time of referral, she lived with her partner, Robert, aged 38 years.

Mother Profile

Her mother, aged 58 years, was an executive in a multinational company. Susan described her mother as a person with serious difficulties with organization, time management, and procrastination. Her parenting strategies were lax and permissive, and she failed to set boundaries and impose contingencies on Susan when she was a child. Moreover, her mother encouraged her to socialize with individuals of high socioeconomic status and was judgmental toward her when she chose friends of lower socioeconomic background.

Father Profile

Susan's father was a 65 year old civil engineer. Susan described him as a serious, responsible, and down-to-earth person. As a child, she kept in touch with him regularly, but later their contact diminished because of her procrastination and her difficulty with time management.

Brief Developmental History

Susan had Irritable Bowel Syndrome (IBS). Since she was a child, she had been experiencing intense abdominal pain and dysphoria, which exacerbated in stressful situations. Due to her delicate health, Susan received bullying at school until adolescence. In elementary school, her classmates called her derogatory names and avoided her. Therefore, she suffered peer rejection and had no friends. At the age of 19, Susan sought psychological help, but treatment lasted shortly because she moved abroad for studies.

Initial Evaluation

Susan reported that she had always had difficulty sustaining attention, a fact that seriously impaired her functioning. School had always been relatively hard for her. Although she presented no behavior problems, teachers consistently complained of her inattention and disorganization. Her difficulties with attention, concentration, and impulse control interfered with her ability to consistently access and progress in the general curriculum. Furthermore, she had poor time management skills and was many times late in her meetings. Susan always postponed her obligations until the last minute. As a result, she experienced heightened stress. Her procrastination had led to three job dismissals. Her family and friends believed she was lazy, an idea that she had also adopted about herself.

Susan always got bored easily and lost interest in the activities she was engaged in. She enjoyed risky activities, including riding fast motorcycles with high-capacity engines. She was also very impulsive and made even serious decisions on the spot. For example, she chose her subject of studies within an hour after the example of a friend who would enroll in the same studies. However, by the time of evaluation, she had regretted her choice and wished to change her professional career and become a teacher.

Susan had low self-esteem and was very insecure. She felt that she could not meet her parents' high expectancies for professional success, financial well-being, and high social status. She did not display assertive behavior and was always trying to fulfill other people's wishes. Furthermore, despite the fact that she had a large social circle, she did not have any close friends because she was afraid that if she let others get to know her better, she would be rejected.

Due to her attractive physical appearance, Susan received affirmation through her transient sexual relationships. She usually engaged in risky and even dangerous sexual behaviors because of her impulsivity and her need to be liked and accepted. Her relationship with Robert was her only long-term relationship. Even though he did not respond to her mother's expectations ("I can see it in her eyes that she thinks I could be with somebody much better!"), she stayed with him because he was the only partner who had fully accepted her with her virtues and weaknesses.

Diagnosis

According to the information that was collected during the psychological assessment and the DSM-5 diagnostic criteria, Susan received the diagnosis of ADHD, inattentive presentation. During the assessment, Susan described obsessive thoughts, mainly fear of getting seriously sick, and handwashing compulsions. However, soon after initiation of treatment, compulsions stopped, and only some occasional thoughts remained but did not cause any clinically significant impairment. Therefore, Susan did not meet the full criteria for the diagnosis of OCD.

Treatment Structure and Progress

Susan received CBT psychotherapy, adapted for ADHD. The main treatment goals for Susan included reducing the primary symptoms of ADHD and increasing self-control, enhancing self-esteem and assertiveness, improving organizational skills, stress management, and coping with obsessive thoughts.

Initially, psychoeducation was provided to Susan regarding the nature of ADHD and its etiology, so that Susan could gain self-awareness of what was thwarting her efforts. Later, organizational skills training was introduced, including techniques for organizing her daily routine and developing everyday habits, organizing a system for archiving documents with the use of file dividers or different folders, and keeping a day planner and task list system for appointments, schedule, and "to-do" items. Furthermore, Susan was taught to break down her task goals into manageable action steps. Implementation strategies were used to identify the potential barriers to follow through on these techniques, and plans were made for how to handle each of these potential barriers to introduce coping skills. Susan's partner had offered to act as her "assistant," by helping her in the implementation of the strategies taught.

For better management of her finances, Susan was encouraged to write down her expenses for a month, evaluate them, and develop ways to minimize unnecessary expenses and waste of money. Moreover, she adopted a system for archiving receipts, so that her expenses could be checked regularly. For better time management, Susan started wearing a watch, which was set 20 minutes ahead, so that she could offset any tardiness and increase her punctuality in appointments. In a subsequent phase of the intervention, the time she took to carry out her main obligations was recorded, so that the exact time that was needed for them would be determined and pointless wastes of time would be minimized. In order to reduce procrastination and impulsivity, problem solving and other appropriate techniques were implemented.

At the same time, Susan's cognitive distortions were identified, and her main maladaptive cognitions (e.g., "I am lazy") were challenged and reconstructed. Susan was encouraged to use positive self-talk to remain motivated and reinforce herself every time she was successful in task completion and goal attainment. A pivotal point was that she reconsidered the thought of changing her professional career, as she realized that this thought was undermined by her disappointment related to her difficulty in finding a job in her field.

Furthermore, Susan was trained in basic communication skills, including the following: "I listen without interrupting," "I stay on the topic of conversation," "I give feedback to my interlocutor to make sure that I have understood well what they have said," "I ask when I have not understood something," and "I control my body and avoid needless movements." Moreover, Susan was trained in assertiveness and stress management, which resulted in the reduction of the episodes of Irritable Bowel Syndrome.

Treatment Outcome

Susan was highly motivated and actively engaged in treatment. The diagnosis of ADHD helped her to reframe several core beliefs of inadequacy/incompetence and self-mistrust. She gained greater insight concerning her own subjective experience, which led to better management of her emotions and eliminated subjective distortion of events. Furthermore, Susan learned how to use effectively a great number of coping techniques in order to organize and follow daily routines, minimize distractions, stay on task, and become better at self-regulating and monitoring her own actions. She also regained trust in herself and her abilities and started to assert her desires and defend her interests. Her relationship with her partner and family improved, and she finally found a job that satisfied her.

Conclusion

Throughout the course of treatment, several barriers occurred, as Susan did not always follow the instructions given in a steady and systematic way. However, after a year of intervention, the treatment outcomes started to become generalized and established. Susan got control of her life and herself and reconstructed her self-image. She is now a young woman who leads a normal life and knows how to cope with the presence of ADHD so that it does not have a negative impact on her functioning any longer.

Notes

1 Bryan's case study is presented by Niki Kakourou, speech therapist.
2 George's case study is presented by Stylianna Christodoulea, psychologist.
3 Anne's case study is presented by Ifigeneia Kostopoulou, psychologist.
4 Alex's case study is presented by Anastasia Bouloubasi, psychologist.
5 Tom's case study is presented by Fanny Roidou, psychologist.
6 Susan's case study is presented by Vassiliki Tsatsou, psychologist.

References

Aagaard, L., & Hansen, E.H. (2013). Adverse drug reaction labeling for atomoxetine, methylphenidate and modafinil: Comparison of product information for oral formulations in Australia, Denmark and the United States. *Current Drug Safety, 8*, 162–168.

Aase, H., Meyer, A., & Sagvolden, T. (2006). Moment-to-moment dynamics of ADHD behaviour in South African children. *Behavioral and Brain Functions, 28*, 11.

Aase, H., & Sagvolden, T. (2005). Moment-to-moment dynamics of ADHD behaviour. *Behavioral and Brain Functions, 1*, 1–12.

Aase, H., & Sagvolden, T. (2006). Infrequent, but not frequent, reinforcers produce more variable responding and deficient sustained attention in young children with attention-deficit/hyperactivity disorder (ADHD). *Journal of Child Psychology and Psychiatry, 47*, 423–534.

Abidin, R.R. (1995). *The parenting stress index* (3rd ed.). Odessa, FL: Psychological Assessment Resources.

Abikoff, H., Courtney, M., Pelham, W.E., & Koplewicz, H.S. (1993). Teachers' ratings of disruptive behaviors: The influence of halo effects. *Journal of Abnormal Child Psychology, 21*, 519–533.

Abikoff, H., Gallagher, R., Wells, K.C., Murray, D.W., Huang, L., Lu, F., & Petkova, E. (2012). Remediating organizational functioning in children with ADHD: Immediate and long-term effects from a randomized controlled trial. *Journal of Consulting and Clinical Psychology, 81*, 113–28.

Abikoff, H., Gittelman-Klein, R., & Klein, D. (1977). Validation of a classroom intervention code for hyperactive children. *Journal of Consulting and Clinical Psychology, 45*, 772–783.

Abikoff, H., Jensen, P.S., Arnold, L.E., Hoza, B., Hechtman, L., Pollack, S., . . . Wigal, T. (2002). Observed classroom behavior of children with ADHD: Relationship to gender and comorbidity. *Journal of Abnormal Child Psychology, 30*, 349–359.

Accardo, P.J., Accardo, J.A., & Capute, A.J. (2008). A neurodevelopmental perspective on the continuum of developmental disabilities. In *Capute and Accardo's neurodevelopmental disabilities in infancy and childhood* (3rd ed., pp. 3–26). Baltimore: Paul H. Brookes.

Achenbach, T.M. (1985). *Assessment and taxonomy of child and adolescent psychopathology.* Beverly Hills, CA: Sage.

Achenbach, T. M. (1991). *Integrative guide for the 1991 CBCL/4–18 YSR and TRF profiles.* Burlington: University of Vermont, Department of Psychiatry.

Achenbach, T.M., Conners, C.K., Quay, H.C., Verhulst, F.C., & Howell, C.T. (1989). Replication of empirically derived syndromes as a basis for taxonomy of child/adolescent psychopathology. *Journal of Abnormal Child Psychology, 17*, 299–323.

Achenbach, T.M., & Edelbrock, C. (1991). *Normative data for the child behavior checklist* (rev. ed.). Burlington, VT: Department of Psychiatry.

Achenbach, T.M., Howell, C.T., McConaughy, S.H., & Stanger, C. (1995). Six-year predictors of problems in a national sample of children and youth: II. Signs of disturbance. *Journal of the American Academy of Child and Adolescent Psychiatry, 34*, 488–498.

Achenbach, T.M., McConaughy, S.H., & Howell, C.T. (1987). Child/adolescent behavioral and emotional problems: Implications of cross informant correlations for situational specificity. *Psychological Bulletin, 101*, 213–232.

Achenbach, T.M., & Rescorla, L. (2001). *Manual for the Achenbach system of empirically based assessment school-age forms profiles.* Burlington, VT: ASEBA.

Adams, R., Finn, P., Moes, E., Flannery, K., & Rizzo, A. (2009). Distractibility in Attention/Deficit/Hyperactivity Disorder (ADHD): The virtual reality classroom. *Child Neuropsychology, 15*, 120–135.

Adams, Z.W., Milich, R., & Fillmore, M. (2010). A case for the return of attention-deficit disorder in DSM-5. *The ADHD Report, 18*, 1–6.

Adler, L., Dietrich., A., Reimherr, F.W., Taylor, L.V., Sutton, V.K., Bakken, R., . . . Kelsey, D. (2006). Safety and tolerability of once versus twice daily atomoxetine in adults with ADHD. *Annals of Clinical Psychiatry, 18*, 107–113.

Adler, L., Kessler, R.C., & Spencer, T. (2004). *Adult ADHD Self-Report Scale- v1.1 (ASRSv1.1) symptom checklist.* New York. Retrieved from www.med.nyu.edu/psych/assets/adhdscreen18.pdf

Adler, L.A., Liebowitz, M., Kronenberger, W., Qiao, M., Rubin, R., Hollandbeck, M., . . . Durell, T. (2009). Atomoxetine treatment in adults with attention-deficit/hyperactivity disorder and comorbid social anxiety disorder. *Depression and Anxiety, 26*, 212–221.

Adler, L.D., & Nierenberg, A.A. (2010). Review of medication adherence in children and adults with ADHD. *Postgraduate Medicine, 122*, 184–191.

Advokat, C. (2010). What are the cognitive effects of stimulant medications? Emphasis on adults with attention-deficit/hyperactivity disorder (ADHD). *Neuroscience and Biobehavioral Reviews, 34*, 1256–1266.

Advokat, C., Lane, S.M., & Luo, C. (2011). College students with and without ADHD: Comparison of self-report of medication usage, study habits, and academic achievement. *Journal of Attention Disorders, 15*, 656–666.

Agapitou, P., & Andreou, G. (2008). Language deficits in ADHD preschoolers. *Australian Journal of Learning Difficulties, 13*, 39–49.

Agarwal, N., Port, J.D., Bazzocchi, M., & Renshaw, P.F. (2010). Update on the use of MR for assessment and diagnosis of psychiatric diseases. *Radiology, 255*, 23–41.

Agranat-Meged, A.N., Deitcher, C., Goldzweig, G., Leibenson, L., Stein, M., & Galili-Weisstub, E. (2005). Childhood obesity and attention deficit/hyperactivity disorder: a newly described comorbidity in obese hospitalized children. *International Journal of Eating Disorders, 37*, 357–359.

Ahmed, R., & Aslani, P. (2013). Attention-deficit/hyperactivity disorder: An update on medication adherence and persistence in children, adolescents and adults. *Expert Review of Pharmacoeconomics & Outcomes Research, 13*, 791–815.

Ahuja, A., Martin, J., Langley, K., & Thapar, A. (2013). Intellectual disability in children with Attention Deficit Hyperactivity Disorder. *Journal of Pediatrics, 163*, 890–895.

Akin-Little, K.A., Little, S.G., & Laniti, M. (2007). Teachers' use of classroom management procedures in the United States and Greece. A cross-cultural comparison. *School Psychology International, 28*, 53–62.

Akinci, G., Oztura, I., Hiz, S., Akdogan, O., Karaarslan, D., Ozek, H., & Akay, A. (2015). Sleep structure in children with attention-deficit/hyperactivity disorder. *Journal of Child Neurology, 30*, 1520–1525.

Akram, G., Thomson, A.H., Boyter, A.C., & McLarty, M. (2009). ADHD and the role of medication: Knowledge and perceptions of qualified and student teachers. *European Journal of Special Needs Education, 24*, 423–436.

Alban-Metcalfe, J., Cheng-Lai, A., & Ma, T. (2002). Teacher and student teacher ratings of attention-deficit/hyperactivity disorder in three cultural settings. *International Journal of Disability, Development and Education, 49*, 281–299.

Albayrak, Ö., Pütter, C., Volckmar, A.L., Cichon, S., Hoffmann, P., Nöthen, M.M., . . . Neale, B.M. (2013). Common obesity risk alleles in childhood attention-deficit/hyperactivity disorder. *American Journal of Medical Genetics Part B: Neuropsychiatric Genetics, 162*, 295–305.

Alfano, C.A., & Gamble, A.L. (2009). The role of sleep in childhood psychiatric disorders. *Child & Youth Care Forum, 38*, 327–340.

Alfonsson, S., Parling, T., & Ghaderi, A. (2012). Screening of adult ADHD among patients presenting for bariatric surgery. *Obesity Surgery, 22*, 918–926.

Aman, M.G., Armstrong, S., Buican, B., & Sillick, T. (2002). Four-year follow-up of children with low intelligence and ADHD: A replication. *Research in Developmental Disabilities*, *23*, 119–134.
American Academy of Child and Adolescent Psychiatry. (2007). Practice parameters for the assessment and treatment of children and adolescents with attention-deficit hyperactivity disorder. *Journal of the American Academy of Child and Adolescent Psychiatry*, *46*, 894–921.
American Academy of Pediatrics. (2011). ADHD: Clinical practice guideline for the diagnosis, evaluation, and treatment of attention-deficit/hyperactivity disorder in children and adolescents. *Pediatrics*, *128*, 1–8.
American Psychiatric Association. (1952). *Diagnostic and statistical manual of mental disorders.* Washington, DC: Author.
American Psychiatric Association. (1968). *Diagnostic and statistical manual of mental disorders* (2nd ed.). Washington, DC: Author.
American Psychiatric Association. (1980). *Diagnostic and statistical manual of mental disorders* (3rd ed.). Washington, DC: Author.
American Psychiatric Association. (1987). *Diagnostic and statistical manual of mental disorders* (3rd ed. rev.). Washington, DC: Author.
American Psychiatric Association. (1994). *Diagnostic and statistical manual of mental disorders* (4th ed.). Washington, DC: Author.
American Psychiatric Association. (2000). *Diagnostic and statistical manual of mental disorders* (4th ed., text rev.). Washington, DC: Author.
American Psychiatric Association. (2013). *Diagnostic and statistical manual of mental disorders* (5th ed.). Washington, DC: Author.
Anastopoulos, A.D., & King, K.A. (2015). A cognitive-behavior therapy and mentoring program for college students with ADHD. *Cognitive and Behavioral Practice*, *22*, 141–151.
Anastopoulos, A.D., & Shelton, T.L. (2001). *Assessing Attention-Deficit/Hyperactivity Disorder.* New York: Kluwer Academic/Plenum.
Andersen, S.L., & Navalta, C.P. (2011). Annual research review: New frontiers in developmental neuropharmacology: Can long-term therapeutic effects of drugs be optimized through carefully timed early intervention? *Journal of Child Psychology and Psychiatry*, *52*, 476–503.
Anderson, J.C. (1996). Is childhood hyperactivity the product of western culture? *Lancet*, *348*, 73–74.
Anderson, U. (2010). Skill development in different components of arithmetic and basic cognitive functions: Findings from a 3-year longitudinal study of children with different types of learning difficulties. *Journal of Educational Psychology*, *102*, 115–134.
Andreou, G., Agapitou, P., & Karapetsas, A. (2005). Verbal skills in children with ADHD. *European Journal of Special Needs Education*, *20*, 231–238.
Andreou, G., Karapetsas, A., Agapitou, P., & Gourgoulianis, K. (2003). Verbal intelligence and sleep disorders in children with ADHD. *Perceptual and Motor Skills*, *96*, 1283–1288.
Andreou, P., Neale, B.M., Chen, W., Christiansen, H., Gabriels, I., Heise, A., . . . Kuntsi, J. (2007). Reaction time performance in ADHD: Improvement under fast-incentive condition and familial effects. *Psychological Medicine*, *37*, 1703–1715.
Andrews, G., Pine, D.S., Hobbs, M.J., Anderson, T.M., & Sunderland, M. (2009). Neurodevelopmental disorders: Cluster 2 of the proposed meta-structure for DSM-V and ICD-11. *Psychological Medicine*, *39*, 2013–2023.
Angold, A. (1988). Childhood and adolescent depression I: Epidemiological and aetiological aspects. *British Journal of Psychiatry*, *152*, 601–617.
Angold, A., & Costello, E.J. (2000). The child and adolescent psychiatric assessment (CAPA). *American Academy of Child and Adolescent Psychiatry*, *39*, 39–48.
Angold, A., Costello, E.J., & Erkanli, A. (1999). Comorbidity. *Journal of Child Psychology and Psychiatry*, *40*, 57–87.
Angold, A., Costello, E.J., Farmer, E.M.Z., Burns, B.J., & Erkanli, A. (1999). Impaired but undiagnosed. *Journal of the American Academy of Child and Adolescent Psychiatry*, *38*, 129–137.
Antrop, I., Buysse, A., Roeyers, H., Van Oost, P. (2002). Stimulation seeking and hyperactive behavior in children with ADHD: A re-analysis. *Perceptual and Motor Skills*, *95*, 71–90.

Antshel, K.M., & Barkley, R.A (2008). Psychosocial interventions in attention-deficit/hyperactivity disorder. *Child and Adolescent Psychiatric Clinics of North America, 17*, 421–437.

Antshel, K.M., Hier, B.O., & Barkley, R.A. (2014). Executive functioning theory and ADHD. In S. Goldstein & J.A. Naglieri (Eds.), *Handbook of executive functioning* (pp. 107–120). New York: Springer.

Antshel, K.M., Phillips, M.H., Gordon, M., Barkley, R., & Faraone, S.V. (2006). Is ADHD a valid disorder in children with intellectual delays? *Clinical Psychology Review, 26*, 555–572.

Antshel, K.M., Polacek, C., McMahon, M., Dygert, K., Spenceley, L., Dygert, L., . . . Faisal, F. (2011). Comorbid ADHD and anxiety affect social skills group intervention treatment efficacy in children with autism spectrum disorders. *Journal of Developmental & Behavioral Pediatrics, 32*, 439–446.

Appelhans, B.M., Woolf, K., Pagoto, S.L., Schneider, K.L., Whited, M.C., & Liebman, R. (2011). Inhibiting food reward: Delay discounting, food reward sensitivity, and palatable food intake in overweight and obese women. *Obesity, 19*, 2175–2182.

Applegate, B., Lahey, B.B., Hart, E.L., Biederman, J., Hynd, G.W., Barkley, R.A., . . . Shaffer, D. (1997). Validity of the age-of-onset criterion for ADHD. A report from the DSM-IV field trials. *Journal of the American Academy of Child and Adolescent Psychiatry, 36*, 1211–1221.

Arble, D.M., Ramsey, K.M., Bass, J., & Turek, F.W. (2010). Circadian disruption and metabolic disease: findings from animal models. *Best Practice and Research Clinical Endocrinology & Metabolism, 24*, 785–800.

Arbuthnott, K., & Frank, J. (2000). Trail making test, part B as a measure of executive control: Validation using a set-switching paradigm. *Journal of Clinical and Experimental Neuropsychology, 22*, 518–528.

Archer, T., & Beninger, R.J. (2007). Movement disorders: Neurodevelopment and neurobehavioural expression. *Journal of Neural Transmission, 114*, xxxiii–xli.

Archer, T., Oscar-Berman, M., & Blum, K. (2011). Epigenetics in developmental disorder: ADHD and endophenotypes. *Journal of Genetic Syndrome & Gene Therapy, 2*(104): 100–104.

Arcia, E., & Conners, C.K. (1998). Gender differences in ADHD? *Journal of Developmental and Behavioural Pediatrics, 19*, 77–83.

Arcia, E., Frank, R., Sanchez-LaCay, A., & Fernandez, M.C. (2000). Teacher understanding of ADHD as reflected in attributions and classroom strategies. *Journal of Attention Disorders, 4*, 91–101.

Arcos-Burgos, M., & Acosta, M.T. (2007). Tuning major gene variants conditioning human behavior: The anachronism of ADHD. *Current Opinion in Genetics & Development, 17*, 234–238.

Arias, A., Gelernter, J., Chan, G., Weiss, R., Brady, K., Farrer, L., & Kranzler, H. (2008). Correlates of co-occurring ADHD in drug dependent subjects: Prevalence and features of substance dependence and psychiatric disorders. *Addictive Behaviors, 33*, 1199–1207.

Arnett, A.B., MacDonald, B., & Pennington, B.F. (2013). Cognitive and behavioral indicators of ADHD prior to school age. *Journal of Child Psychology and Psychiatry, 54*, 1284–1294.

Arnett, A.B., Pennington, B.F., Willcutt, E.G., DeFries, J.C., & Olson, R.K. (2015). Sex differences in ADHD symptom severity. *Journal of Child Psychology and Psychiatry, 56*, 632–639.

Arnold, L.E., Aman, M.G., Li, X., Butter, E., Humphries, K., Scahill, L., . . . Stigler, K.A. (2012). Research Units of Pediatric Psychopharmacology (RUPP) Autism Network randomized clinical trial of parent training and medication: One-year follow-up. *Journal of the American Academy of Child and Adolescent Psychiatry, 51*, 1173–1184.

Arnold, L.E., Demeter, C., Mount, K., Frazier, T.W., Youngstrom, E.A., Fristad, M., . . . Axelson, D.A. (2011). Pediatric bipolar spectrum disorder and ADHD: Comparison and comorbidity in the LAMS clinical sample. *Bipolar Disorders, 13*, 509–521.

Arnold, L.E., Vitello, B., McDougle, C., Scahill, L., Shah, B., Conazalez, N., . . . Tierney, E. (2003). Parent-defined target symptoms respond to risperidone in RUPP autism study: Customer approach to clinical trials. *Journal of the American Academy of Child and Adolescent Psychiatry, 42*, 1443–1450.

Arnold, P.D., Ickowicz, A., Chen, S., & Schachar, R. (2005). Attention-deficit hyperactivity disorder with and without obsessive-compulsive behaviours: Clinical characteristics, cognitive assessment, and risk factors. *Canadian Journal of Psychiatry, 50*, 59–66.

Arns, M., Heinrich, H., & Strehl, U. (2014). Evaluation of neurofeedback in ADHD: The long and winding road. *Biological Psychology*, *95*, 108–115.

Arns, M., Loo, S.K., Sterman, M.B., Heinrich, H., Kuntsi, J., Asherson, P., . . . Brandeis, D. (2016). Editorial Perspective: How should child psychologists and psychiatrists interpret FDA device approval? Caveat emptor. *Journal of Child Psychology and Psychiatry*, *57*, 656–658.

Arnsten, A.F., Berridge, C.W., & McCracken, J.T. (2009). The neurobiological basis of attention-deficit/hyperactivity disorder. *Primary Psychiatry*, *16*, 47–54.

Arnsten, A.F., & Li, B.M. (2005). Neurobiology of executive functions: Catecholamine influences on prefrontal cortical functions. *Biological Psychiatry*, *57*, 1377–1384.

Asherson, P. (2005). Clinical assessment and treatment of attention deficit hyperactivity disorder in adults. *Expert Review of Neurotherapeutics*, *5*, 525–539.

Asherson, P., Akehurst, R., Kooij, J.S., Huss, M., Beusterien, K., Sasané, R., . . . Hodgkins, P. (2012). Under diagnosis of adult ADHD: Cultural influences and societal burden. *Journal of Attention Disorders*, *16*(5 suppl), 20S–38S.

Attia, M., & Meseeha, M. (2016). Are tricyclic antidepressants effective at improving symptoms of ADHD in children and adolescents? *Evidence-based practice*, *19*(6), E-1-E-2.

Auerbach, J.G., Landau, R., Berger, A., Arbelle, S., Faroy, M., & Karplus, M. (2005). Neonatal behavior of infants at familial risk for ADHD. *Infant, Behavior and Development*, *28*, 220–224.

Aylward, E.H., Richards, T.L., Berninger, V.W., Nagy, W.E., Field, K.M., Grimme, A.C., . . . Cramer, S.C. (2003). Instructional treatment associated with changes in brain activation in children with dyslexia. *Neurology*, *61*, 212–219.

Aylward, G.P., Gordon, M., & Verhulst, S.J. (1997). Relationships between continuous performance task scores and other cognitive measures: causality or commonality? *Assessment*, *4*, 313–324.

Aymami, N., Jimenez-Murcia, S., Granero, R., Ramos-Quiroga, J.A., Fernandez-Aranda, F., Claes, L., . . . Menchon, J.M. (2015). Clinical, psychopathological, and personality characteristics associated with ADHD among individuals seeking treatment for Gambling Disorder. *BioMed Research International*. https://doi.org/10.1155/2015/965303.

Babinski, D.E., Pelham, W.E., Jr., Molina, B.S.G., Gnagy, E.M., Waschbusch, D.A., Yu, J., . . . Karch, K.M. (2010). Late adolescence and young adult outcomes of girls diagnosed with ADHD in childhood: An exploratory investigation. *Journal of Attention Disorders*, *15*, 204–214.

Babinski, D.E., Sibley, M.H., Ross, J.M., & Pelham, W.E. (2013). The effects of single versus mixed gender treatment for adolescent girls with ADHD. *Journal of Clinical Child & Adolescent Psychology*, *42*, 243–250.

Babinski, D.E., Waxmonsky, J.G., & Pelham, W.E., Jr. (2014). Treating parents with attention-deficit/hyperactivity disorder: The effects of behavioral parent training and acute stimulant medication treatment on parent—child interactions. *Journal of Abnormal Child Psychology*, *42*, 1129–1140.

Bachmann, K., Lam, A.P., & Philipsen, A. (2016). Mindfulness-based cognitive therapy and the adult ADHD brain: A neuropsychotherapeutic perspective. *Frontiers in Psychiatry*, *7*, 117.

Baden, A.D., & Howe, G.W. (1992). Mothers' attributions and expectancies regarding their conduct-disordered children. *Journal of Abnormal Child Psychology*, *20*, 467–486.

Baeyens, D., Roeyers, H., & Walle, J. (2006). Subtypes of attention-deficit/hyperactivity disorder (ADHD): Distinct or related disorders across measurement levels? *Clinical Psychiatry and Human Development*, *36*, 403–417.

Bagwell, C.L., Molina, B.S.G., Pelham, W.E., & Hoza, B. (2001). Attention-deficit hyperactivity disorder and problems in peer relations: Predictions from childhood to adolescence. *Journal of the American Academy of Child and Adolescence Psychiatry*, *40*, 1285–1292.

Baird, J., Stevenson, J.C., & Williams, D.C. (2000). The evolution of ADHD: A disorder of communication? *The Quarterly Review of Biology*, *75*, 17–35.

Bakare, M.O. (2012). Attention deficit hyperactivity symptoms and disorder (ADHD) among African children: A review of epidemiology and co-morbidities. *African Journal of Psychiatry*, *15*, 358–361.

Baker, B.L., Neece, C.L., Fenning, R.M., Crnic, K.A., & Blacher, J. (2010). Mental disorders in five-year-old children with or without developmental delay: Focus on ADHD. *Journal of Clinical Child and Adolescent Psychology*, *39*, 492–505.

Bakermans-Kranenburg, M.J., Van IJzendoorn, M.H., Pijlman, F.T., Mesman, J., & Juffer, F. (2008). Experimental evidence for differential susceptibility: Dopamine D4 receptor polymorphism (DRD4 VNTR) moderates intervention effects on toddlers' externalizing behavior in a randomized controlled trial. *Developmental Psychology, 44*, 293–300.

Bakhshayesh, A.R., Hansch, S., Wyschkon, A., Rezai, M.J., & Esser, G. (2011). Neurofeedback in ADHD: A single-blind randomized controlled trial. *European Child and Adolescent Psychiatry, 20*, 481–491.

Bakker, M.P., Ormel, J., Verhulst, F.C., & Oldehinkel, A.J. (2010). Peer stressors and gender differences in adolescents' mental health: the TRAILS study. *Journal of Adolescent Health, 46*, 444–450.

Ball, J.D., Tiernan, M., Janusz, J., & Furr, A. (1997). Sleep patterns among children with attention-deficit hyperactivity disorder: A reexamination of parent perceptions. *Journal of Pediatric Psychology, 22*, 389–398.

Ballard, W., Hall, M.N., & Kaufmann, L. (2010). Do dietary interventions improve ADHD symptoms in children? *Journal of Family Practice, 59*, 234–235.

Banaschewski, T., Coghill, D., Santosh, P., Zuddas, A., Asherson, P., Buitelaar, J., . . . Taylor, E. (2006). Long-acting medications for the hyperkinetic disorders: A systematic review and European treatment guideline. *European Child and Adolescent Psychiatry, 15*, 476–495.

Banaschewski, T., Neale, B., Rothenberger, A., & Roessner, V. (2007). Comorbidity of tic disorders & ADHD—conceptual and methodological considerations. *European Child and Adolescent Psychiatry [Suppl 1], 16*, I/5—I/14.

Bandura, A. (1986). *Social foundations of thought and action. A social cognitive theory.* Englewood Cliffs, NJ: Prentice Hall.

Bandura, A. (2001). Social cognitive theory: An agentic perspective. *Annual Review of Psychology, 52*, 1–26.

Bangs, M.E., Jin, L., Zhang, S., Desaiah, D., Allen, A.J., Read, H.A., . . . Wernicke, J.F. (2008). Hepatic events associated with atomoxetine treatment for attention-deficit hyperactivity disorder. *Drug Safety, 31*, 345–354.

Bangs, M.E., Tauscher-Wisniewski, S., Polzer, J., Zhang, S., Acharya, N., Desaiah, D. . . . Allen, A.J. (2008). Meta-analysis of suicide-related behavior events in patients treated with atomoxetine. *Journal of the American Academy of Child and Adolescent Psychiatry, 47*, 209–218.

Barbaresi, W.J., Colligan, R.C., Weaver, A.L., Voigt, R.G., Killian, J.M., & Katusic, S.K. (2013). Mortality, ADHD, and psychosocial adversity in adults with childhood ADHD: A prospective study. *Pediatrics, 131*, 637–644.

Barbarin, O.A., & Soler, R.E. (1993). Behavioral, emotional, and academic adjustment in a national probability sample of African American children: Effects of age, gender, and family structure. *Journal of Black Psychology, 19*, 423–446.

Barkley, R.A. (1981a). *Hyperactive children: A handbook for diagnosis and treatment.* New York: Guilford Press.

Barkley, R.A. (1981b). Hyperactivity. In E. Mash & L. Terdal (Eds.), *Behavioral assessment of childhood disorders.* NY: Guilford Press.

Barkley, R.A. (1990). *Attention-deficit hyperactivity disorder: A handbook for diagnosis and treatment.* New York: Guilford Press.

Barkley, R.A. (1995). A closer look at DSM-IV criteria for ADHD: Some unresolved issues. *The ADHD Report, 3*, 1–5.

Barkley, R.A. (1996). Attention-Deficit/ Hyperactivity Disorder. In E.J. Mash & R.A. Barkley (Eds.), *Child psychopathology* (pp. 63–112). New York: Guilford Press.

Barkley, R.A. (1997a). *ADHD and the nature of self-control.* New York: Guilford Press.

Barkley, R.A. (1997b). Attention-deficit/hyperactivity disorder. In E.J. Mash & L.G. Terdal (Eds.), *Assessment of childhood disorders* (3rd ed., pp. 71–129). New York: Guilford Press.

Barkley, R.A. (1997c). Behavioral inhibition, sustained attention, and executive functions: constructing a unifying theory of ADHD. *Psychological Bulletin, 121*, 65–94.

Barkley, R.A. (1998a). Attention-deficit/hyperactivity disorder. In E.J. Mash & R.A. Barkley (Eds.), *Treatment of childhood disorders* (2nd ed., pp. 55–110). New Yrok: Guilford Press.

Barkley, R.A. (1998b). *Attention-Deficit/Hyperactivity Disorder: A handbook for diagnosis and treatment.* (2nd ed.). New York: Guilford Press.

Barkley, R.A. (2002a). Major life activity and health outcomes associated with attention-deficit/hyperactivity disorder. *Journal of Clinical Psychiatry, 63(Suppl)*, 10–15.

Barkley, R.A. (2002b). ADHD and accident proneness. *The ADHD Report, 10*, 2–6.

Barkley, R.A. (2003). Issues in the diagnosis of attention-deficit/hyperactivity disorder in children. *Brain and Development, 25*, 77–83.

Barkley, R.A. (2006a). ADHD in adults: Developmental course and outcome of children with ADHD, and ADHD in clinic-referred adults. In R.A. Barkley (Ed.) *Attention-Deficit Hyperactivity Disorder: A handbook for diagnosis and treatment* (pp. 248–296). New York: Guilford Press.

Barkley, R.A. (2006b). *Attention-Deficit Hyperactivity Disorder: A handbook for diagnosis and treatment* (3rd ed.). New York: Guilford Press.

Barkley, R.A. (2008). Classroom accommodations for children with ADHD. *The ADHD Report, 16*, 7–10.

Barkley, R.A. (2011). *Barkley Adult ADHD Rating Scale-IV (BAARS-IV)*. New York: Guilford Press.

Barkley, R.A. (2012a). *Executive functions. What they are, how they work, and why they evolved.* New York: Guilford Press.

Barkley, R.A. (2012b). *Barkley Functional Impairment Scale-Children and Adolescents (BFIS-CA).* New York: Guilford Press.

Barkley, R.A. (2013). *Taking charge of ADHD: The complete, authoritative guide for parents* (3rd ed.). New York: Guilford Press.

Barkley, R.A. (2015a). History of ADHD. In R.A. Barkley (Ed.) *Attention-Deficit Hyperactivity Disorder* (4th ed., pp. 3–50). New York: Guilford Press.

Barkley, R.A. (2015b). Psychological assessment of children with ADHD. In R.A. Barkley (Ed.) *Attention-Deficit Hyperactivity Disorder* (4th ed., pp. 455–474). New York: Guilford Press.

Barkley, R.A. (2015c). Etiologies of ADHD. In R.A. Barkley (Ed.) *Attention-Deficit Hyperactivity Disorder* (4th ed., pp. 356–390). New York: Guilford Press.

Barkley, R.A. (2015d). Psychological assessment of children with ADHD. In R.A. Barkley (Ed.) *Attention-Deficit Hyperactivity Disorder* (4th ed., pp. 455–474). New York: Guilford Press.

Barkley, R.A., & Biederman, J. (1997). Toward a broader definition of the age-of-onset criterion for attention-deficit hyperactivity disorder. *Journal of the American Academy of Child and Adolescent Psychiatry, 36*, 1204–1210.

Barkley, R.A., & Cunningham, C.E. (1979). The effects of methylphenidate on the mother-child interactions of hyperactive children. *Archives of General Psychiatry, 36*, 201–208.

Barkley, R.A., Cunningham, C.E., Gordon, M., Faraone, S.V., Lewandowski, L., Murphy, K.R. (2006). ADHD symptoms vs. impairment: Revisited. *ADHD Report, 14*, 1–9.

Barkley, R. A., DuPaul, G. J., & Connor, D. F. (2013). Stimiulants. In J.Werry, & M. Aman (Eds.), *A practitioner's guide to psychoactive drugs for children and adolescnts* (2nd ed., pp. 213–248). New York: Springer Science & Business Media.

Barkley, R. A., DuPaul, G. J., & McMurray, M. B. (1990). Comprehensive evaluation of attention deficit disorder with and without hyperactivity as defined by research criteria. *Journal of Consulting and Clinical Psychology*, 58, 775–789.

Barkley, R.A., & Edwards, G. (2006). Diagnostic interview, behaviour rating scales and the medical examination. In R.A. Barkley (Ed.), *Attention-deficit hyperactivity disorder* (3rd ed., pp. 337–368). New York: Guilford Press.

Barkley, R.A., Fischer, M., Edelbrock, C.S., & Smallish, L. (1990). The adolescent outcome of hyperactive children diagnosed by research criteria: I. An 8-year prospective follow-up study. *Journal of the American Academy of Child & Adolescent Psychiatry, 29*, 546–557.

Barkley, R.A., Fischer, M., Smallish, L., & Fletcher, K. (2002). The persistence of attention-deficit/hyperactivity disorder into young adulthood as a function of reporting source and definition of disorder. *Journal of Abnormal Child Psychology, 111*, 279–289.

Barkley, R.A., Fischer, M., Smallish, L., & Fletcher, K. (2003). Does the treatment of attention-deficit/hyperactivity disorder with stimulants contribute to drug use/abuse? A 13-year prospective study. *Pediatrics, 111*, 97–109.

Barkley, R., Fischer, M., Smallish, L., & Fletcher, K. (2004). Young adult follow-up of hyperactive children: Antisocial activities and drug use. *Journal of Child Psychology and Psychiatry*, *45*, 195–211.

Barkley, R., Fischer, M., Smallish, L., & Fletcher, K. (2006). Young adult outcome of hyperactive children: adaptive functioning in major life activities. *Journal of the American Academy of Child and Adolescent Psychiatry*, *45*, 192–202.

Barkley, R.A., Grodzinsky, G., & DuPaul, G.J. (1992). Frontal lobe functions in attention deficit disorder with and without hyperactivity: A review and research report. *Journal of Abnormal Child Psychology*, *20*, 163–188.

Barkley, R.A., & Guevremont, D.C. (1992). A comparison of three family therapy programs for treating family conflicts in adolescents with Attention-Deficit/Hyperactivity Disorder. *Journal of Consulting and Clinical Psychology*, *60*, 450–462.

Barkley, R.A., Karlsson, J., Pollard, S., & Murphy, J.V. (1985). Developmental changes in the mother-child interactions of hyperactive boys: Effects of two dose levels of Ritalin. *Journal of Child Psychology and Psychiatry*, *26*, 705–715.

Barkley, R.A., & Murphy, K.R. (2006). Identifying new symptoms for diagnosing ADHD in adulthood. *The ADHD Report*, *14*, 7–11.

Barkley, R.A., & Murphy, K.R. (2010). Impairment in occupational functioning and adult ADHD: The predictive utility of executive function (EF) ratings versus EF tests. *Archives of Clinical Neuropsychology*, *25*, 157–173.

Barkley, R.A., Murphy, K.R., DuPaul, G.J., & Bush, T. (2002). Driving in young adults with attention deficit hyperactivity disorder: Knowledge, performance, adverse outcomes, and the role of executive functioning. *Journal of the International Neuropsychological Society*, *8*, 655–672.

Barkley, R.A., Murphy, K.R., & Fischer, M. (2008). *ADHD in adults: What the science says*. New York: Guilford Press.

Barkley, R.A., & Peters, H. (2012). The earliest reference to ADHD in the medical literature? Melchior Adam Weikard's description in 1775 of "Attention deficit" (Mangel der aufmerksamkeit, attention volubilis). *Journal of Attention Disorders*, *16*, 623–630.

Barkley, R.A., Terri, L., Shelton, T.L., Crosswait, C., Moorehouse, M., Fletcher, K., . . . Metevia, L. (2000). Multi-method psycho-educational Intervention for pre-school children with disruptive behaviour: Preliminary results at post treatment. *Journal of Child Psychology Psychiatry*, *41*, 319–332.

Barragán, E., Breuer, D., & Döpfner, M. (2017). Efficacy and safety of omega-3/6 fatty acids, methylphenidate, and a combined treatment in children with ADHD. *Journal of Attention Disorders*, *21*, 433–441.

Barrett, J.R., Tracy, D.K., & Giaroli, G. (2013). To sleep or not to sleep: A systematic review of the literature of pharmacological treatments of insomnia in children and adolescents with attention-deficit/hyperactivity disorder. *Journal of Child and Adolescent Psychopharmacology*, *23*, 640–647.

Barry, L.M., Johnstone, S.J., & Clarke, A.R. (2003). A review of electrophysiology in attention-deficit/hyperactivity disorder: II. Event-related potentials. *Clinical Neurophysiology*, *114*, 184–198.

Barry, L.M., & Kelly, M.A. (2006). Rule governed behavior and self-control in children with ADHD: A theoretical interpretation. *Journal of Early and Intensive Behavior Intervention*, *3*, 239–254.

Barry, L.M., & Messer, J.J. (2003). A practical application of self-management for students diagnosed with attention-deficit/hyperactivity disorder. *Journal of Positive Behavior Interventions*, *5*, 238–248.

Barry, R.J., Clarke, A.R., McCarthy, R., Selikowitz, M., Johnstone, S.J., & Rushby, J.A. (2004). Age and gender effects in EEG coherence: I. Developmental trends in normal children. *Clinical Neurophysiology*, *115*, 2252–2258.

Barry, R.J., Johnstone, S.J., & Clarke, A.R. (2003). A review of electrophysiology in attention-deficit/hyperactivity disorder: II. Event-related potentials. *Clinical Neurophysiology*, *114*, 184–198.

Barry, T.D., Lyman, R.D., & Klinger, L.G (2002). Academic underachievement and attention-deficit/hyperactivity disorder: The negative impact of symptom severity on school performance. *Journal of School Psychology*, *40*, 259–283.

Bateman, B., Warner, J.O., Hutchinson, E., Dean, T., Rowlandson, P., Gant, C., . . . Stevenson, J. (2004). The effects of a double blind, placebo controlled, artificial food colourings and benzoate preservative challenge on hyperactivity in a general population sample of preschool children. *Archives of Disease in Childhood*, *89*, 506–511.

Bates, E., Bretherton, I., & Snyder, L. (1988). *From first words to grammar: Individual differences and dissociable mechanisms.* New York: Cambridge University Press.

Batstra, L., Bosm, E.H., & Neeleman, J. (2002). Quantifying psychiatric comorbidity: Lessons from chronic disease epidemiology. *Social Psychiatry and Psychiatric Epidemiology, 37,* 105–111.

Batstra, L., & Frances, A. (2012). DSM-5 further inflates attention deficit hyperactivity disorder. *Journal of Nervous and Mental Disease, 200,* 486–488.

Battle, E.S., & Lacy, B. (1972). A context for hyperactivity in children over time. *Child Development, 43,* 757–773.

Bauermeister, J.J., Matos, M., Reina, G., Salas, C.C., Martínez, J.V., Cumba, E., & Barkley, R.A. (2005). Comparison of the DSM-IV combined and inattentive types of ADHD in a school-based sample of Latino/Hispanic children. *Journal of Child Psychology and Psychiatry, 46,* 166–179.

Baum, S.M., & Olenchak, F.R. (2002). The alphabet children: GT, ADHD, and more. *Exceptionality, 10,* 77–91.

Bax, M., & MacKeith, R. (1963). *Minimal cerebral dysfunction. Little Club Clinics in Developmental Medicine.* London: Heineman.

Beauchaine, T.P., Hinshaw, S.P., & Pang, K.L. (2010). Comorbidity of attention-deficit/hyperactivity disorder and early-onset conduct disorder: Biological, environmental, and developmental mechanisms. *Clinical Psychology: Science and Practice, 17,* 327–336.

Beauchaine, T.P., Klein, D.N., Erickson, N.L., & Norris, A.L. (2013). Developmental psychopathology and the Diagnostic and Statistical Manual of Mental Disorders. In T.H. Beauchaine & S.P. Hinshaw (Eds.), *Child and adolescent psychopathology* (pp. 29–110). Chichester, NJ: John Wiley & Sons.

Beauchaine, T.P., Neuhaus, E., Brenner, S.L., & Gatke-Kopp, L. (2008). Ten good reasons to consider biological processes in prevention and intervention research. *Development and Psychopathology, 20,* 745–774.

Beauregard, M., & Lévesque, J. (2006). Functional magnetic resonance imaging investigation of the effects of neurofeedback training on the neural bases of selective attention and response inhibition in children with attention-deficit/hyperactivity disorder. *Applied Psychophysiology and Biofeedback, 31,* 3–20.

Bechara, A. (2003). Risky business: Emotion, decision-making, and addiction. *Journal of Gambling Studies, 19,* 23–51.

Beck, A.T. (2008). The evolution of the cognitive model of depression and its neurobiological correlates. *American Journal of Psychiatry, 165,* 969–977.

Becker, K., El-Faddagh, M., Schmidt, M.H., Esser, G., & Laucht, M. (2008). Interaction of dopamine transporter genotype with prenatal smoke exposure on ADHD symptoms. *Journal of Pediatrics, 152,* 263–269.

Becker, S.P., Fite, P.J., Luebbe, A.M., Stoppelbein, L., & Greening, L. (2013). Friendship intimacy exchange buffers the relation between ADHD symptoms and later social problems among children attending an after-school care program. *Journal of Psychopathology and Behavioral Assessment, 35,* 142–152.

Becker, S.P., Luebbe, A.M., & Langberg, J.M. (2012). Co-occurring mental health problems and peer functioning among youth with attention-deficit/hyperactivity disorder: A review and recommendations for future research. *Clinical Child and Family Psychology Review, 15,* 279–302.

Beckett, C., Maughan, B., Rutter, M., Castle, J., Colvert, E., Groothues, C., . . . Sonuga-Barke, E.J.S. (2006). Do the effects of early severe deprivation on cognition persist into early adolescence? Findings from the English and Romanian adoptees study, *Child Development, 77,* 696–711.

Bédard, A., Schulz, K.P., Cook, E.H., Fan, J., Clerkin, S.M., Ivanov, I., . . . Newcorn, J.H. (2010). Dopamine transporter gene variation modulates activation of striatum in youth with ADHD. *Neuroimage, 53,* 935–942.

Befera, M.S., & Barkley, R.A. (1985). Hyperactive and normal girls and boys: mother-child interaction, parent psychiatric status and child psychopathology. *Journal of Child Psychology and Psychiatry, 26,* 439–452.

Beitchmann, J.H., Wilson, B., Brownlie, E.B., Walters, H., & Lancee, W. (1996). Long-term consistency in speech/language profiles: I. Developmental and academic outcomes. *Journal of the American Academy of Child and Adolescent Psychiatry, 35,* 804–811.

Bekle, B. (2001). Review of research on teachers' knowledge and attitudes about attention-deficit hyperactivity disorder (ADHD). *Australasian Journal of Special Education, 25*(1–2), 67–85.

Bell, A.S. (2011). A critical review of ADHD diagnostic criteria: What to address in the DSM-V. *Journal of Attention Disorders, 15*, 3–10.

Bender, L. (1942). Postencephalitic behavior disorders in children. In J.B. Neal (Ed.), *Encephalitis: A clinical study*. New York: Grune & Stratton.

Bendz, L.M., & Scates, A.C. (2010). Melatonin treatment for insomnia in pediatric patients with attention-deficit/hyperactivity disorder. *Annals of Pharmacotherapy, 44*, 185–191.

Benito, K.G., Conelea, C., Garcia, A.M., & Freeman, J.B. (2012). CBT specific process in exposure-based treatments: Initial examination in a pediatric OCD sample. *Journal of Obsessive-Compulsive and Related Disorders, 1*, 77–84.

Benninger, R.J. (1989). Dopamine and learning: Implications for attention deficit disorder and hyperkinetic syndrome. In T. Sagvolden & T. Archer (Eds.), *Attention deficit disorder: Clinical and basic research* (pp. 323–338). Hillsdale, NJ: Erlbaum.

Benton, A. (1991). Prefrontal injury and behavior in children. *Developmental Neuropsychology, 7*, 275–282.

Berger, I., Dor, T., Nevo, Y., & Goldzweig, G. (2008). Attitudes toward attention-deficit hyperactivity disorder (ADHD) treatment: Parents' and children's perspectives. *Journal of Child Neurology, 23*, 1036–1042.

Berridge, K.C., Ho, C.Y., Richard, J.M., & DiFeliceantonio, A.G. (2010). The tempted brain eats: Pleasure and desire circuits in obesity and eating disorders. *Brain Research, 1350*, 43–64.

Berry, A., Shaywitz, E., & Shaywitz, A. (1985). Girls with attention deficit disorder: A silent majority? A report on behavioral and cognitive characteristics. *Pediatrics, 75*, 801–809.

Berwid, O.G., Curko Kera, E.A., Marks, D.J., Santra, A., Bender, H.A., & Halperin, J.M. (2005). Sustained attention and response inhibition in young children at risk for attention deficit/hyperactivity disorder. *Journal of Child Psychology and Psychiatry, 46*, 1219–1229.

Best, J.R., Miller, P.H., & Naglieri, J.A. (2011). Relations between executive function and academic achievement from ages 5 to 17 in a large, representative national sample. *Learning and Individual Differences, 21*, 327–336.

Bettelheim, B. (1973). Bringing up children. *Ladies Home Journal*, p. 23.

Bezdjian, S., Baker, L.A., & Tuvblad, C. (2011). Genetic and environmental influences on impulsivity: A meta-analysis of twin, family and adoption studies. *Clinical Psychology Review, 31*, 1209–1223.

Bhatia, S., Nigam, R., Bohra, N., & Mallik, C. (1991). Attention deficit disorder with hyperactivity among paedritic outpatients. *Journal of Child Psychology and Psychiatry, 32*, 297–306.

Bhutta, A.T., Cleves, M.A., Casey, P.H., Cradock, M.M., & Anand, K.J. (2002). Cognitive and behavioral outcomes of school-aged children who were born preterm: A meta-analysis. *Journal of the American Medical Association, 288*, 728–737.

Bidwell, L.C., Henry, E.A., Willcutt, E.G., Kinnear, M.K., & Ito, T.A. (2014). Childhood and current ADHD symptom dimensions are associated with more severe cannabis outcomes in college students. *Drug and Alcohol Dependence, 135*, 88–94.

Biederman, J. (2011). The course and persistence of ADHD throughout the life-cycle. In J.K. Buitelaar, C.C. Kan, & P.J. Asherson (Eds.). *ADHD in adults: Characterization, diagnosis, and treatment* (pp. 1–8). Cambridge: Cambridge University Press.

Biederman, J., Ball, S.W., Monuteaux, M.C., Mick, E., Spencer, T., McCerary, B.A., . . . Faraone, S.V. (2008). New insights into the comorbidity between ADHD and major depression in adolescent and young adult females. *Journal of the American Academy of Child and Adolescent Psychiatry, 47*, 426–433.

Biederman, J., Ball, S.W., Monuteaux, M.C., Surman, C.B., Johnson, J.L., & Zeitlin, S. (2007). Are girls with ADHD at risk for eating disorders? Results from a controlled, five-year prospective study. *Journal of Developmental and Behavioral Pediatrics, 28*, 302–307.

Biederman, J., & Faraone, S.V. (2006). The effects of attention-deficit/hyperactivity disorder on employment and household income. *Medscape General Medicine, 8*(3), 12.

Biederman J., Faraone, S.V., Keenan, K., Knee, D., & Tsuang, M.T. (1990) Family-genetic and psychosocial risk factors in DSM-III attention deficit disorder. *Journal of the American Academy of Child and Adolescent Psychiatry, 29*, 526–533.

Biederman J., Faraone, S.V., Keenan, K., Steingard, R., & Tsuang, M.T. (1991) Family association between attention deficit disorder (ADD) and anxiety disorder. *American Journal of Psychiatry, 48*, 633–642.

Biederman, J., Faraone, S.V., & Lapey, K. (1992). Comorbidity of diagnosis in attention-deficit hyperactivity disorder. In G. Weiss (Ed.) *Child and adolescent psychiatric clinics of North America: Attention-deficit hyperactivity disorder* (pp. 335–360). Philadelphia: Saunders.

Biederman, J., Faraone, S.V., & Mick, E. (1996). Attention deficit hyperactivity disorder and juvenile mania: An overlooked comorbidity? *Journal of the American Academy of Child and Adolescent Psychiatry, 35*, 997–1008.

Biederman, J., Faraone, S.V., Mick, E., Spencer, T., Wilens, T., Kiley, K., . . . Warburton, R. (1995). High risk for attention deficit hyperactivity disorder among children of parents with childhood onset of the disorder: A pilot study. *American Journal of Psychiatry, 152*, 431–435.

Biederman, J., Faraone, S.V., Mick, E., Williamson, S., Wilens, T.E., Spencer, T.J., . . . Zallen, B. (1999). Clinical correlates of ADHD in females: Findings from a large group of girls ascertained from pediatric and psychiatric referral sources. *Journal of the American Academy of Child and Adolescent Psychiatry, 38*, 966–975.

Biederman, J., Faraone, S.V., Milberger, S., Jetton, J.G., Chen, L., Mick, E., . . . Russell, R.L. (1996). Is childhood oppositional defiant disorder a precursor to adolescent conduct disorder? Findings from a four-year follow-up study of children with ADHD. *Journal of the American Academy of Child and Adolescent Psychiatry, 35*, 1193–1204.

Biederman, J., Faraone, S.V., Monuteaux, M.C., & Feighner, J.A. (2000). Patterns of alcohol and drug use in adolescents can be predicted by parental substance use disorders. *Pediatrics, 106*, 792–797.

Biederman, J., Faraone, S.V., Spencer, T.J., Mick, E., Monuteaux, M.C., & Aleardi, M. (2006). Functional impairments in adults with self-reports of diagnosed ADHD: A controlled study of 1001 adults in the community. *Journal of Clinical Psychiatry, 67*, 524–540.

Biederman, J., Faraone, S.V., Spencer, T., Wilens, T., Norman, D., Lapey, K.A., . . . Doyle, A. (1993). Patterns of psychiatric comorbidity, cognition, and psychosocial functioning in adults with attention deficit hyperactivity disorder. *American Journal of Psychiatry, 150*, 1792–1798.

Biederman, J., Faraone, S.V., Taylor, A., Sienna, M., Williamson, S. & Fine, C. (1998). Diagnostic continuity between child and adolescent ADHD: Findings from a longitudinal clinical sample. *Journal of the American Academy of Child and Adolescent Psychiatry, 37*, 305–313.

Biederman, J., Hammerness, P., Doyle, R., Joshi, G., Aleardi, M., & Mick, E. (2008). Risperidone treatment for ADHD in children and adolescents with bipolar disorder. *Neuropsychiatric Disease and Treatment, 4*, 203–207.

Biederman, J., Kwon, A., Aleardi, M., Chouinard, V.A., Marino, T., Cole, H., . . . Faraone, S.V. (2005). Absence of gender effects on attention deficit hyperactivity disorder: findings in nonreferred subjects. *American Journal of Psychiatry, 162*, 1083–1089.

Biederman, J., Mick, E., & Faraone, S.V. (2000). Age-dependent decline of symptoms of attention deficit hyperactivity disorder: impact of remission definition and symptom type. *American Journal of Psychiatry, 157*, 816–818.

Biederman, J., Mick, E., Faraone, S.V., Braaten, E., Doyle, A., Spencer, T., . . . Johnson, M.A. (2002). Influence of gender on attention deficit hyperactivity disorder in children referred to a psychiatric clinic. *American Journal of Psychiatry, 159*, 36–42.

Biederman, J., Monuteaux, M.C., Mick, E., Spencer, T., Wilens, T., Klein, K.L., . . . Faraone, S.V. (2006). Psychopathology in females with attention deficit/hyperactivity disorder: A controlled, five-year prospective study. *Biological Psychiatry, 60*, 1098–1105.

Biederman, J., Monuteaux, M.C., Mick, E., Spencer, T., Wilens, T., Silva, J.M., . . . Faraone, S.V. (2006b). Young adult outcome of attention deficit hyperactivity disorder: A controlled 10-year follow-up study. *Psychological Medicine, 36*, 167–179.

Biederman, J., Petty, C., Clarke, A., Lomedico, A., & Faraone, S. (2011). Predictors of persistent ADHD: An 11-year follow-up study. *Journal of Psychiatric Research, 45*, 150–155.

Biederman, J., Petty, C. R., Evans, M., Small, J., & Faraone, S. V. (2010). How persistent is ADHD? A controlled 10-year follow-up study of boys with ADHD. *Psychiatry Research, 177*, 299–304.

Biederman, J., Spencer, T., Lomedico, A., Day, H., Petty, C. R., & Faraone, S. V. (2012). Deficient emotional self-regulation and pediatric attention deficit hyperactivity disorder: A family risk analysis. *Psychological Medicine, 42*, 639–646.

Biederman, J., Wilens, T., Mick, E., Faraone, S.V., Weber, W., Curtis, S., . . . Soriano, J. (1997). Is ADHD a risk factor for psychoactive substance use disorders? Findings from a four-year prospective follow-up study. *Journal of the American Academy of Child and Adolescent Psychiatry, 36*, 21–29.

Biederman, J., Wilens, T., Mick, E., Spencer, T., & Faraone, S. V. (1999) Pharmacotherapy of attention-deficit/hyperactivity disorder reduces risk for substance use disorder. *Pediatrics, 104*, e20.

Biggs, B. K., Vernberg, E. M., Twemlow, S. W., Fonagy, P., & Dill, E. J. (2008). Teacher adherence and its relation to teacher attitudes and student outcomes in an elementary school-based violence prevention program. *School Psychology Review, 37*, 533–549.

Bikic, A., Leckman, J. F., Lindschou, J., Christensen, T. Ø., & Dalsgaard, S. (2015). Cognitive computer training in children with attention deficit hyperactivity disorder (ADHD) versus no intervention: Study protocol for a randomized controlled trial. *Trials, 16*, 480.

Bink, M., van Nieuwenhuizen, C., Popma, A., Bongers, I. L., & van Boxtel, G. J. (2015). Behavioral effects of neurofeedback in adolescents with ADHD: A randomized controlled trial. *European Child & Adolescent Psychiatry, 24*, 1035–1048.

Birch, H. G. (1964). *Brain damage in children: The biological and social aspects.* Baltimore: Williams & Witkins.

Birmaher, B., Axelson, D., Goldstein, B., Monk, K., Kalas, C., Obreja, M., & Kupfer, D. (2010). Psychiatric disorders in preschool offspring of parents with bipolar disorder: the Pittsburgh Bipolar Offspring Study (BIOS). *American Journal of Psychiatry, 167*, 321–330.

Bischof, H. J. (2007). Behavioral and neuronal aspects of developmental sensitive periods. *Neuroreport, 18*, 461–465.

Bishop, D.V.M., & Baird, G. (2001). Parent and teacher report of pragmatic aspects of communication: Use of the children's communication checklist in a clinical setting. *Developmental Medicine and Child Neurology, 43*, 809–818.

Bishop, D. V., & Snowling, M. J. (2004). Developmental dyslexia and specific language impairment: Same or different? *Psychological Bulletin, 130*, 858–886.

Bitsakou, P., Psychogiou, L., Thompson, M., & Sonuga-Barke, E.J.S. (2008). Inhibitory deficits in attention-deficit/hyperactivity disorder are independent of basic processing efficiency and IQ. *Journal of Neural Transmission, 115*, 261–268.

Blachman, D. R., & Hinshaw, S. P. (2002). Patterns of friendship among girls with and without attention-deficit/hyperactivity disorder. *Journal of Abnormal Child Psychology, 30*, 635–640.

Black, D. W., Monahan, P. O., Temkit, M. H., & Shaw, M. (2006). A family study of pathological gambling. *Psychiatry Research, 141*, 295–303.

Black, D. W., Shaw, M., & Allen, J. (2008). Extended-release carbamazepine in the treatment of pathological gambling: An open-label study. *Progress in Neuro-Psychopharmacology and Biological Psychiatry, 32*, 1191–1194.

Black, D. W., Smith, M. M., Forbush, K. T., Shaw, M. C., McCormick, B. A., Moser, D. J., & Allen, J. M. (2013). Neuropsychological performance, impulsivity, symptoms of ADHD, and Cloninger's personality traits in pathological gambling. *Addiction Research and Theory, 21*, 216–226.

Blader, J. C., & Carlson, G. A. (2007). Increased rates of bipolar disorder diagnoses among U.S. child, adolescent, and adult inpatients, 1996–2004. *Biological Psychiatry, 62*, 107–114.

Blair, C. (2002). School readiness: Integrating cognition and emotion in a neurobiological conceptualization of children's functioning at school entry. *American Psychologist, 57*, 111–127.

Blair, C., & Razza, R. P. (2007). Relating effortful control, executive function, and false belief understanding to emerging math and literacy ability in kindergarten. *Child Development, 78*, 647–663.

Blasczynski, A. (1998) *Overcoming compulsive gambling.* London: Robinson.

Blase, S.L., Gilbert, A.N., Anastopoulos, A.D., Costello, E.J., Hoyle, R.H., Swartzwelder, H.S., & Rabiner, D.L. (2009). Self-reported ADHD and adjustment in college cross-sectional and longitudinal findings. *Journal of Attention Disorders, 13*, 297–309.

Blau, A. (1936). Mental changes following head trauma in children. *Archives of Neurology and Psychiatry, 35*, 722–769.

Bleck, J., DeBate, R., Levin, B.L., & Baldwin, J. (2016). Underlying mechanisms and trajectory of comorbid ADHD and eating disorders: Proposing an innovative systems framework for informing research. *International Journal of Mental Health and Addiction, 14*, 449–458.

Bloch, M.H., Peterson, B.S., Scahill, L., Otka, J., Katsovich, L., Zhang, H., & Leckman, J.F. (2006). Adulthood outcome of tic and obsessive-compulsive symptom severity in children with Tourette syndrome. *Archives of Pediatric and Adolescent Medicine, 160*, 65–69.

Bloch, M.H., & Qawasmi, A. (2011). Omega-3 fatty acid supplementation for the treatment of children with attention-deficit/hyperactivity disorder symptomatology: Systematic review and meta-analysis. *Journal of the American Academy of Child and Adolescent Psychiatry, 50*, 991–1000.

Block, G.H. (1977). Hyperactivity: A cultural perspective. *Journal of Learning Disabilities, 110*, 236–240.

Blum, K., Cull, J.G., Braverman, E.R., & Comings, D.E. (1996). Reward deficiency syndrome. *American Scientist, 84*, 132–145.

Bluschke, A., Broschwitz, F., Kohl, S., Roessner, V., & Beste, C. (2016). The neuronal mechanisms underlying improvement of impulsivity in ADHD by theta/beta neurofeedback. *Scientific Reports, 6*, 31178. https://doi.org/10.1038/srep31178

Bluschke, A., Roessner, V., & Beste, C. (2016). Editorial perspective: How to optimise frequency band neurofeedback for ADHD. *Journal of Child Psychology and Psychiatry, 57*, 457–461.

Boada, R., Willcutt, E.G., & Pennington, B.F. (2012). Understanding the comorbidity between dyslexia and attention-deficit/hyperactivity disorder. *Topics in Language Disorders, 32*, 264–84.

Bodrova, E., Germeroth, C., & Leong, D.J. (2013). Play and self-regulation. *American Journal of Play, 6*, 111–123.

Bohline, D.S. (1985). Intellectual and effective characteristics of attention deficit disordered children. *Journal of Learning Disabilities, 18*, 604–608.

Bolton, P.F., Golding, J., Emond, A., & Steer, C.D. (2012). Autism spectrum disorder and autistic traits in the Avon longitudinal study of parents and children: Precursors and early signs. *Journal of the American Academy of Child and Adolescent Psychiatry, 51*, 249–260.

Bonath, B., Tegelbeckers, J., Wilke, M., Flechtner, H.H., & Krauel, K. (2016). Regional gray matter volume differences between adolescents with ADHD and typically developing controls further evidence for anterior cingulate involvement. *Journal of Attention Disorders*. https://doi.org/1087054715619682

Bond, E.D., & Appel, K.E. (1931). *The treatment of behavior disorders following encephalitis*. New York: Commonwealth Fund.

Boonstra, A.M., Oosterlaan, J., Sergeant, J.A., & Buitelaar, J.K. (2005). Executive functioning in adult ADHD: A meta-analytic review. *Psychological Medicine, 35*, 1097–1108.

Borger, N., & van der Meere, J. (2000). Motor control and state regulation in children with ADHD: a cardiac response study. *Biological Psychiatry, 51*, 247–267.

Bouchard, M.F., Bellinger, D.C., Wright, R.O., & Weisskopf, M.G. (2010). Attention-deficit/hyperactivity disorder and urinary metabolites of organophosphate pesticides. *Pediatrics, 125*, e1270–1277.

Bourneville, D.-M. (1895). *Assistance, traitement et education den enfants idiots et dégénérés* (F. Alcan, Ed.). Paris: Progrès Médical.

Bowen, R., Chavira, D.A., Bailey, K., Stein, M.T., & Stein, M.B. (2008). Nature of anxiety comorbid with attention deficit hyperactivity disorder in children from a pediatric primary care setting. *Psychiatry Research, 157*, 201–209.

Bradley, W. (1937). The behavior of children receiving benzedrine. *American Journal of Psychiatry, 94*, 577–585.

Bradley, W., & Bowen, C. (1940). School performance of children receiving amphetamine (benzedrine) sulfate. *American Journal of Orthopsychiatry, 10*, 782–788.

Bradshaw, J. L. (2001) *Developmental disorders of the frontostriatal system: Neuropsychological, neuropsychiatric, and evolutionary perspectives.* Philadelphia, PA: Psychology Press.

Bradshaw, J. L., & Sheppard, D. M. (2000). The neurodevelopmental fronto-striatal disorders: Evolutionary adaptiveness and anomalous lateralization. *Brain and Language, 73,* 297–320.

Brand, N., Geenen, R., Oudenhoven, M., Lindenborn, B., van der Ree, A., Cohen-Kettenis, P., & Buitelaar, J. K. (2002). Brief report: Cognitive functioning in children with Tourette's syndrome with and without comorbid ADHD. *Journal of Pediatric Psychology, 27,* 203–208.

Brandon, C. L., Marinelli, M., Baker, L. K., & White, F. J. (2001). Enhanced reactivity and vulnerability to cocaine following methylphenidate treatment in adolescent rats. *Neuropsychopharmacology, 25,* 651–658.

Braswell, L., & Bloomquist, M. L. (1991). *Cognitive-behavioral therapy with ADHD children.* New York: Guilford Press.

Brault, M. C., & Lacourse, É. (2012). Prevalence of prescribed attention-deficit hyperactivity disorder medications and diagnosis among Canadian preschoolers and school-age children: 1994–2007. *Canadian Journal of Psychiatry, 57,* 93–101.

Braun, J. M., Kahn, R. S., Froehlich, T., Auinger, P., & Lanphear, B. P. (2006). Exposures to environmental toxicants and attention-deficit/hyperactivity disorder in U.S. children. *Environmental Health Perspectives, 114,* 1904–1909.

Breen, M. J., & Altepeter, T. S. (1990). Situational variability in boys and girls identified as ADHD. *Journal of Clinical Psychology, 46,* 486–490.

Breen, M. J., & Barkley, R. A. (1988). Child psychopathology and parenting stress in girls and boys having attention deficit disorder with hyperactivity. *Journal of Pediatric Psychology, 13,* 265–280.

Breggin, P. (2007). *Talking back to Ritalin: What doctors aren't telling you about stimulants and ADHD.* Da Capo Press.

Brem, S., Grünblatt, E., Drechsler, R., Riederer, P., & Walitza, S. (2014). The neurobiological link between OCD and ADHD. *Attention Deficit and Hyperactivity Disorders, 6,* 175–202.

Breyer, J. L., Botzet, A. M., Winters, K. C., Stinchfield, R. D., August, G., & Realmuto, G. (2009). Young adult gambling behaviors and their relationship with the persistence of ADHD. *Journal of Gambling Studies, 25,* 227–238.

Briscoe-Smith, A. M., & Hinshaw, S. P. (2006). Linkages between child abuse and attention-deficit/hyperactivity disorder in girls: Behavioral and social correlates. *Child Abuse & Neglect, 30,* 1239–1255.

Brock, S. E., & Clinton, A. (2007). Diagnosis of Attention Deficit/Hyperactivity Disorder (AD/HD) in childhood: A review of the literature. *California School Psychologist, 12,* 73–91.

Brocki, K. C., Tillman, C. M., & Bohlin, G. (2010). CPT performance, motor activity, and continuous relations to ADHD symptom domains: A developmental study. *European Journal of Developmental Psychology, 7,* 178–197.

Brod, M., Johnston, J., Able, S., & Swindle, R. (2006). Validation of the adult attention-deficit/hyperactivity disorder quality-of-life scale (AAQoL): A disease-specific quality-of-life measure. *Quality of Life Questionnaire, 15,* 117–129.

Brody, L. R., & Hall, J. A. (2000). Gender, emotion, and expression. In M. Lewis & J. M. Haviland (Eds.), *Handbook of emotions* (2nd ed., pp. 338–349). New York: Guilford Press.

Brook, D. W., Brook, J. S., Zhang, C., & Koppel, J. (2010). Association between attention-deficit/hyperactivity disorder in adolescence and substance use disorders in adulthood. *Archives of Pediatrics and Adolescent Medicine, 164,* 930–934.

Brook, J. S., Brook, D. W., Zhang, C., Seltzer, N., & Finch, S. J. (2013). Adolescent ADHD and adult physical and mental health, work performance and financial stress. *Pediatrics, 131,* 5–13.

Brook, U., & Boaz, M. (2005). Attention deficit and hyperactivity disorder (ADHD) and learning disabilities (LD): Adolescents perspective. *Patient Education and Counseling, 58,* 187–191.

Brookes, K. J., Mill, J., Guindalini, C., Curran, S., Xu, X., Knight, J., . . . Asherson, P. (2006). A common haplotype of the dopamine transporter gene associated with attention-deficit/hyperactivity disorder and interacting with maternal use of alcohol during pregnancy. *Archives of General Psychiatry, 63,*74–81.

Brotman, M.A., Schmajuk, M., Rich, B., Dickstein, D., Guyer, A.E., Costello, E.J., . . . Leibenluft, E. (2006). Prevalence, clinical correlates and longitudinal course of severe mood dysregulation in children. *Biological Psychiatry*, *60*, 991–997.

Brown, R.T., & Borden, K.A. (1986). Hyperactivity in adolescence: Some misconceptions and new directions. *Journal of Clinical Child Psychology*, *15*, 194–209.

Brown, R.T., Madan-Swain, A., & Baldwin, K. (1991). Gender differences in a clinic-referred sample of attention-deficit-disordered children. *Child Psychiatry and Human Development*, *22*, 111–128.

Brown, T.A., & Barlow, D.H. (2005). Dimensional versus categorical classification of mental disorders in the fifth edition of the Diagnostic and Statistical Manual of Mental Disorders and beyond: Comment on the special section. *Journal of Abnormal Psychology*, *114*, 551–556.

Brown, T.E. (1996). *Brown Attention-Deficit Disorder Scales*. San Antonio, TX: Psychological Corporation.

Brown, T.E. (2009). ADD/ADHD and impaired executive function in clinical practice. *Current Attention Disorders Reports*, *1*, 37–41.

Bruce, B., Thernlund, G. & Nettelbladt, U. (2006). ADHD and language impairment: A study of the parent questionnaire FTF (Five to Fifteen). *European Child & Adolescent Psychiatry*, *15*, 52–60.

Bubnik, M.G., Hawk, L.W., Jr., Pelham, W.E., Jr., Waxmonsky, J.G., & Rosch, K.S. (2015). Reinforcement enhances vigilance among children with ADHD: Comparisons to typically developing children and to the effects of methylphenidate. *Journal of Abnormal Child Psychology*, *43*, 149–161.

Buckner, R.L., Andrews-Hanna, J.R., & Schachter, D.L. (2008). The brain's default network. *Annals of the New York Academy of Sciences*, *1124*, 1–38.

Bueno, V.F., Kozasa, E.H., da Silva, M.A., Alves, T.M., Louzã, M.R., & Pompéia, S. (2015). Mindfulness meditation improves mood, quality of life, and attention in adults with attention deficit hyperactivity disorder. *BioMed Research International*, *2015*. http://doi.org/10.1155/2015/962857.

Bugental, D.B., & Johnston, C. (2000). Parental and child cognitions in the context of the family. *Annual Review of Psychology*, *51*, 315–344.

Buitelaar, J.K., & Rothenberger, A. (2004). Foreword-ADHD in the scientific and political context. *European Child and Adolescent Psychiatry*, *13* (Suppl. 1), i1–i6.

Bunte, T.L., Schoemaker, K., Hessen, D.J., van der Heijden, P.G., & Matthys, W. (2014). Stability and change of ODD, CD and ADHD diagnosis in referred preschool children. *Journal of Abnormal Child Psychology*, *42*, 1213–1224.

Burke, J.D., Loeber, R., & Birmaher, B. (2002). Oppositional defiant disorder and conduct disorder: A review of the past 10 years, part II. *Journal of the American Academy of Child and Adolescent Psychiatry*, *41*, 1275–1293.

Burke, J.D., Loeber, R., & Lahey, B.B. (2001). Which aspects of ADHD are associated with tobacco use in early adolescence? *Journal of Child Psychology and Psychiatry*, *42*, 493–502.

Burke, J.D., Loeber, R., Lahey, B.B., & Rathouz, P.J. (2005). Developmental transitions among affective and behavioral disorders in adolescent boys. *Journal of Child Psychology and Psychiatry*, *46*, 1200–1210.

Bush, G. (2008). Neuroimaging of attention deficit hyperactivity disorder: Can new imaging findings be integrated in clinical practice? *Child and Adolescent Psychiatric Clinics of North America*, *17*, 385–404.

Bush, G. (2010). Attention-deficit/hyperactivity disorder and attention networks. *Neuropsychopharmacology*, *35*, 278–300.

Bush, G. (2011). Cingulate, frontal, and parietal cortical dysfunction in attention-deficit/hyperactivity disorder. *Biological Psychiatry*, *69*, 1160–1167.

Bush, G., Valera, E.M., & Seidman, L.J. (2005). Functional neuroimaging of attention-deficit/hyperactivity disorder: a review and suggested future directions. *Biological Psychiatry*, *57*, 1273–1284.

Bushe, C.J., & Savill, N.C. (2014). Systematic review of atomoxetine data in childhood and adolescent attention-deficit hyperactivity disorder 2009–2011: Focus on clinical efficacy and safety. *Journal of Psychopharmacology*, *28*, 204–211.

Bussing, R., Gary, F.A., Leon, C.E., Garvan, C.W., & Reid, R. (2002). General classroom teachers' information and perceptions of attention deficit hyperactivity disorder. *Behavioral Disorders*, *27*, 327–339.

Bussing, R., Gary, F., Mills, T., & Garvan, C. (2007). Cultural variations in parental health beliefs, knowledge, and information sources related to attentiondeficit/hyperactivity disorder. *Journal of Family Issues*, *28*, 291–318.

Bussing, R., Schoenberg, N.E., Rogers, K.M., Zima, B.T., & Angus, S. (1998). Explanatory models of ADHD: Do they differ by ethnicity, child gender, or treatment status? *Journal of Emotional and Behavioral Disorders*, *6*, 233–243.

Bussing, R., Zima, B.T., Mason, D.M., Meyer, J.M., White, K., & Garvan, C.W. (2012). ADHD knowledge, perceptions, and information sources: Perspectives from a community sample of adolescents and their parents. *Journal of Adolescent Health*, *51*, 593–600.

Butnik, S.M. (2005). Neurofeedback in adolescents and adults with attention deficit hyperactivity disorder. *Journal of Clinical Psychology*, *61*, 621–625.

Byers, R.K. & Lord, E.E. (1943). Late effects of lead poisoning on mental development. *American Journal of Diseases of Children*, *66*, 471–494.

Byrd, H.M., Curtin, C., & Anderson, S.E. (2013). Attention-deficit/hyperactivity disorder and obesity in US males and females, age 8–15 years: National Health and Nutrition Examination Survey 2001–2004. *Pediatric Obesity*, *8*, 445–453.

Byrne, J., Bawden, H., Beattie, T., & DeWolfe, N. (2000). Preschoolers classified as having ADHD: DSM-IV symptom endorsement pattern. *Journal of Child Neurology*, *15*, 533–538.

Cairney, J., Hay, J.A., Faught, B.E., & Hawes, R. (2005). Developmental coordination disorder and overweight and obesity in children aged 9–14 y. *International Journal of Obesity*, *29*, 369–372.

Camarata, S., & Gibson, T. (1999). Pragmatic language deficits in attention-deficit hyperactivity disorder (ADHD). *Mental Retardation and Developmental Disabilities Research Reviews*, *5*, 207–214.

Campbell, S.B. (1973). Mother-child interaction in reflective, impulsive and hyperactive children. *Developmental Psychology*, *8*, 341–349.

Campbell, S.B. (1985). Hyperactivity in preschoolers: Correlates and prognostic implications. *Clinical Psychology Review*, *5*, 405–428.

Campbell, S.B. (1987). Parent-referred problem three-year olds: Developmental changes in symptoms. *Journal of Child Psychology and Psychiatry*, *28*, 835–846.

Campbell, S.B. (2002). *Behavior problems in preschool children: clinical and developmental issues* (2nd ed.). New York: Guilford Press.

Campbell, S.B., & Ewing, L.J. (1990). Follow-up of hard-to-manage preschoolers: Adjustment at age nine years and predictors of continuing symptoms. *Journal of Child Psychology and Psychiatry*, *31*, 891–910.

Campbell, S.B., Halperin, J.M., & Sonuga-Barke, E.J.S. (2014). A developmental perspective on attention-deficit/hyperactivity disorder (ADHD). In M. Lewis & K. Rudolph (Eds.), *Handbook of developmental psychopathology* (pp. 427–448). Boston: Springer.

Canadian Attention Deficit Hyperactivity Disorder Resource Alliance (CADDRA) (2011). *Canadian ADHD practice guidelines* (3rd ed.). Toronto: CADDRA.

Canino, G., Shrout, P.E., Rubio-Stipec, M., Bird, H.R., Bravo, M., Ramírez, R., . . . Ribera, J. (2004). The DSM-IV rates of child and adolescent disorders in Puerto Rico: Prevalence, correlates, service use, and the effects of impairment. *Archives of General Psychiatry*, *61*, 85–93.

Cantell, M.H., Smyth, M.M., & Ahonen, T.P. (2003). Two distinct pathways for developmental coordination disorder: persistence and resolution. *Human Movement Science*, *22*, 413–431.

Cantwell, D. (1981). Foreword. In R.A. Barkley, *Hyperactive children: A handbook for diagnosis and treatment*. New York: Guilford Press.

Cantwell, D. (1987). *The clinical description of AD-HD individuals.* Workshop presented at the Conference of Attention-Deficit Hyperactivity Disorders in Children and Adolescents: Assessment and Intervention Techniques, Minneapolis, MN.

Canu, W.H., & Wymbs, B.T. (2015). Novel approaches to cognitive-behavioral therapy for adult ADHD. *Cognitive and Behavioral Practice, 22*, 111–115.

Capaldi, D.M. (1991). Co-occurrence of conduct problems and depressive symptoms in early adolescent boys: I. Familial factors and general adjustment at grade 6. *Development and Psychopathology, 3*, 277–300.

Capaldi, D.M. (1992). Co-occurrence of conduct problems and depressive symptoms in early adolescent boys: II. A 2-year follow-up at grade 8. *Development and Psychopathology, 4*, 125–144.

Capano, L., Minden, D., Chen, S.X., Schachar, R.J., & Ickowicz, A. (2008). Mathematical learning disorder in school-age children with attention-deficit/hyperactivity disorder. *Canadian Journal of Psychiatry, 53*, 392–399.

Capusan, A.J., Bendtsen, P., Marteinsdottir, I., Kuja-Halkola, R., & Larsson, H. (2015). Genetic and environmental contributions to the association between attention deficit hyperactivity disorder and alcohol dependence in adulthood: A large population-based twin study. *American Journal of Medical Genetic, Part B.* https://doi.org/10.1002/ajmg.b.32300

Cardinal, R.N., Pennicott, D.R., Lakmali, C., Robbins, T.W., & Everitt, B.J. (2001). Impulsive choice induced in rats by lesions of the nucleus accumbens core. *Science, 292*(5526), 2499–2501.

Cardo, E., Casanovas, S., de la Banda, G., & Servera, M. (2008). Soft neurological signs: Are they of any value in the assessment and diagnosis of attention deficit hyperactivity disorder? *Revista de Neurologia, 46*(Suppl. 1), S51–S54.

Cardy, J.E.O., Tannock, R., Johnson, A.M., & Johnson, C.J. (2010). The contribution of processing impairments to SLI: Insights from attention-deficit/hyperactivity disorder. *Journal of Communication Disorders, 43*, 77–91.

Carlson, C.L., & Mann, M. (2002). Sluggish cognitive tempo predicts a different pattern of impairment in the attention deficit hyperactivity disorder, predominantly inattentive type. *Journal of Clinical Child and Adolescent Psychology, 31*, 123–129.

Carlson, C.L., Tamm, L., & Gaub, M. (1997). Gender differences in children with ADHD, ODD, and co-occurring ADHD/ODD identified in a school population. *American Academy of Child and Adolescent Psychiatry, 36*, 1706–1714.

Carlson, G.A. (2009). Treating the childhood bipolar controversy: A tale of two children. *American Journal of Psychiatry, 166*, 18–24.

Carlson, S.M. (2005). Developmentally sensitive measures of executive function in preschool children. *Developmental Neuropsychology, 28*, 595–616.

Carmona, S., Vilarroya, O., Bielsa, a., Tremols, V., Soliva, J.C., Rovira, M., . . . Bulbena, A. (2005). Global and regional grey matter reduction in ADHD: a voxel-based morphometric study. *Neuroscience Letters, 389*, 88–93.

Caron, C., & Rutter, M. (1991). Comorbidity in child psychopathology: Concepts, issues and research strategies. *Journal of Child Psychology & Psychiatry, 32*, 1063–1080.

Carr, K.A., Daniel, T.O., Lin, H., & Epstein, L.H (2011). Reinforcement pathology and obesity. *Current Drug Abuse Reviews, 4*, 190–196.

Carrasco, X., Lopez, V., & Aboitiz, F. (2005). Frontal and executive dysfunction is a central aspect of ADHD. *Behavioral and Brain Sciences, 28*, 427–428.

Carrellas, N., Wilens, T.E., & Anselmo, R. (2016). Treatment of comorbid substance use disorders and ADHD in youth. *Current Treatment Options in Psychiatry, 3*, 15–27.

Carrey, N., & Gregson, J. (2008). A context for classification in child psychiatry. *Journal of the Canadian Academy of Child and Adolescent Psychiatry, 17*, 50–57.

Carroll, J.M., Maughan, B., Goodman, R., & Meltzer, H. (2005). Literacy difficulties and psychiatric disorders: Evidence for comorbidity. *Journal of Child Psychology and Psychiatry, 46*, 524–532.

Carte, E.T., Nigg, J.T., & Hinshaw, S.P. (1996). Neuropsychological functioning, motor speed, and language processing in boys with and without ADHD. *Journal of Abnormal Child Psychology, 24*, 481–498.

Carter, C. M., Urbanowicz, M., Hemsley, R., Mantilla, L., Strobel, S., Graham, P. J., & Taylor, E. (1993). Effects of a few food diet in attention deficit disorder. *Archives of Disease in Childhood, 69*, 564–568.
Carter, A. S., O'Donnell, D. A., Schultz, R. T., Scahill, L., Leckman, J. F., & Pauls, D. L. (2000). Social and emotional adjustment in children affected with Gilles de la Tourette's syndrome: Associations with ADHD and family functioning. *Journal of Child Psychology and Psychiatry, 41*, 215–223.
Carver, C. S., & Scheier, M. F. (2000). On the structure of behavioral self-regulation. In M. Boekaerts, P. Pintrich, & M. Zeidner (Eds.), *Handbook of self-regulation*, (pp. 42–85). San Diego, CA: Academic Press.
Carver, C. S., & Scheier, M. F. (2001). Optimism, pessimism, and self-regulation. In *Optimism and pessimism: Implications for theory, research, and practice* (pp. 31–51).
Caspi, A., Hariri, A. R., Holmes, A., Uher, R., & Moffitt, T. E. (2010). Genetic sensitivity to the environment: The case of the serotonin transporter gene and its implications for studying complex diseases and traits. *American Journal of Psychiatry, 167*, 509–527.
Caspi, A., Langley, K., Milne, B., Moffitt, T. E., O'Donovan, M. C., Owen, M. J., & Thapar, A. (2008). A replicated molecular genetic basis for subtyping antisocial behavior in children with attention-deficit/hyperactivity disorder. *Archives of General Psychiatry, 65*, 203–210.
Cassoff, J., Wiebe, S. T., & Gruber, R. (2012). Sleep patterns and the risk for ADHD: A review. *Nature and Science of Sleep, 4*, 73–80.
Castellani, B., & Rugle, L. (1995). A comparison of pathological gamblers to alcoholics and cocaine misusers on impulsivity, sensation seeking, and craving. *International Journal of the Addictions, 30*, 275–289.
Castellanos, F. X. (2015). Is adult-onset ADHD a distinct entity? *American Journal of Psychiatry, 172*, 929–931.
Castellanos, F. X., Giedd, J. N., Marsh, W. L., Hamburger, S. D., Vaituzis, A. C., Dickstein, D. P., . . . Rapoport, J. L. (1996). Quantitative brain magnetic resonance imaging in attention-deficit hyperactivity disorder. *Archives of General Psychiatry, 53*, 607–616.
Castellanos, F. X., Lee, P. P., Sharp, W., Jeffries, N. O., Greenstein, D. K., Clasen, L. S., . . . Rapoport, J. L. (2002). Developmental trajectories of brain volume abnormalities in children and adolescents with attention-deficit/hyperactivity disorder. *JAMA: The Journal of the American Medical Association, 288*, 1740–1748.
Castellanos, F. X., Margulies, D. S., Kelly, C., Uddin, L. Q., Ghaffari, M., Kirsch, A., . . . Milham, M. P. (2008). Cingulate-precuneus interactions: A new locus of dysfunction in adult attention-deficit/hyperactivity disorder. *Biological Psychiatry, 63*, 332–337.
Castellanos, F. X., Marvasti, F. F., Durcharme, J. L., Walter, J. M., Israel, M. E., Krain, A., . . . Hommer, D. W. (2000). Executive function oculomotor tasks in girls with ADHD. *Journal of the American Academy of Child and Adolescent Psychiatry, 39*, 644–650.
Castellanos, F. X., & Proal, E. (2012). Large-scale brain systems in ADHD: Beyond the prefrontal-striatal model. *Trends in Cognitive Sciences, 16*, 17–26.
Castellanos, F. X., Sonuga-Barke, E. J., Milham, M. P., & Tannock, R. (2006). Characterizing cognition in ADHD: Beyond executive dysfunction. *Trends in Cognitive Sciences, 10*, 117–123.
Castellanos, F. X., & Tannock, R. (2002). Neuroscience of attention-deficit/hyperactivity disorder: the search for endophenotypes. *Nature Reviews Neuroscience, 3*, 617–628.
Castle, L., Aubert, R. E., Verbrugge, R. R., Khalid, M., & Epstein, R. S. (2007). Trends in medication treatment for ADHD. *Journal of Attention Disorders, 10*, 335–342.
Catalá-López, F., Peiró, S., Ridao, M., Sanfélix-Gimeno, G., Gènova-Maleras, R., & Catalá, M. A. (2012). Prevalence of attention deficit hyperactivity disorder among children and adolescents in Spain: A systematic review and meta-analysis of epidemiological studies. *BMC Psychiatry, 12*, 1.
Caye, A., Spadini, A. V., Karam, R. G., Grevet, E. H., Rovaris, D. L., Bau, C. H., . . . Kieling, C. (2016). Predictors of persistence of ADHD into adulthood: A systematic review of the literature and meta-analysis. *European Child & Adolescent Psychiatry, 25*, 1151–1159.

Chacko, A., Allan, C.C., Uderman, J., Cornwell, M., Anderson, L., & Chimiklis, A. (2015). Training parents of youth with ADHD. In R.A. Barkley (Ed.) *Attention-Deficit Hyperactivity Disorder* (4th ed., pp. 513–536). New York: Guilford Press.

Chacko, A., Bedard, A.C., Marks, D., Gopalan, G., Feirsen, N., Uderman, J., . . . Zwilling, A. (2017). Sequenced neurocognitive and behavioral parent training for the treatment of ADHD in school-age children. *Child Neuropsychology*. https://doi.org/10.1080/09297049.2017.1282450

Chacko, A., Kofler, M., & Jarrett, M. (2014). Improving outcomes for youth with ADHD: A conceptual framework for combined neurocognitive and skill-based treatment approaches. *Clinical Child and Family Psychology Review, 17*, 368–384.

Chacko, A., Wakschlag, L., Hill, C., Danis, B., & Espy, K.A. (2009). Viewing preschool disruptive behavior disorders and attention-deficit/hyperactivity disorder through a developmental lens: What we know and what we need to know. *Child and Adolescent Psychiatric Clinics of North America, 18*, 627–643.

Chacko, A., Wymbs, B.T., Flammer-Rivera, L.M., Pelham, W.E., Walker, K.S., Arnold, F.W., . . . Herbst, L. (2008). A pilot study of the feasibility and efficacy of the Strategies to Enhance Positive Parenting (STEPP) Program for single mothers of children with ADHD. *Journal of Attention Disorders, 12*, 270–280.

Chamberlain, S.R., Derbyshire, K., Leppink, E., & Grant, J.E. (2015). Impact of ADHD symptoms on clinical and cognitive aspects of problem gambling. *Comprehensive Psychiatry, 57*, 51–57.

Chamberlain, S.R., Hampshire, A., Muller, U., Rubia, K., Del, C.N., Craig, K., . . . Sahakian, B.J. (2009). Atomoxetine modulates right inferior frontal activation during inhibitory control: A pharmacological functional magnetic resonance imaging study. *Biological Psychiatry, 65*, 550–555.

Chandler, L., & Dahlquist, C. (2002). *Functional assessment: Strategies to prevent and remediate challenging behaviors in school settings*. Upper Saddle River, NJ: Merrill Prentice Hall.

Chaplin, T. M., Cole, P. M., & Zahn-Waxler, C. (2005). Parental socialization of emotion expression: Gender differences and relations to child adjustment. *Emotion, 5*, 80–88.

Charach, A., Carson, P., Fox, S., Ali, M.U., Beckett, J., & Lim, C.G. (2013). Interventions for preschool children at high risk for ADHD: A comparative effectiveness review. *Pediatrics, 131*, E1584–E1604.

Charach, A., Figueroa, M., Chen, S., Ickowicz, A., & Schachar, R. (2006). Stimulant treatment over 5 years: Effects on growth. *Journal of the American Academy of Child and Adolescent Psychiatry, 45*, 415–421.

Charach, A., & Gajaria, A. (2008). Improving psychostimulant adherence in children with ADHD. *Expert Review of Neurotherapeutics, 8*, 1–14.

Charach, A., Yeung, E., Climans, T., & Lillie, E. (2011). Childhood attention-deficit/hyperactivity disorder and future substance use disorders: Comparative meta-analyses. *Journal of the American Academy of Child and Adolescent Psychiatry, 50*, 9–21.

Chelune, G.J., Ferguson, W., Koon, R., & Dickey, T.O. (1986). Frontal lobe disinhibition in attention deficit disorder. *Child Psychiatry and Human Development, 16*, 221–234.

Chen, C.S., Burton, M., Greenberger, E., & Dmitrieva, J. (1999). Population migration and the variation of dopamine D4 receptor (DRD4) allele frequencies around the globe. *Evolution and Human Behavior, 20*, 309–324.

Chen, H.F., & Cohn, E.S. (2003). Social participation for children with developmental coordination disorder: Conceptual, evaluation and intervention considerations. *Physical and Occupational Therapy in Pediatrics, 23*, 61–78.

Chen, M.H., Chen, Y.S., Hsu, J.W., Huang, K.L., Li, C.T., Lin, W.C., . . . Bai, Y.M. (2015). Comorbidity of ADHD and subsequent bipolar disorder among adolescents and young adults with major depression: A nationwide longitudinal study. *Bipolar Disorders, 17*, 315–322.

Chess, S. (1960). Diagnosis and treatment of the hyperactive child. *New York State Journal of Medicine, 60*, 2379–2385.

Cheung, C.H., Rijsdijk, F., McLoughlin, G., Brandeis, D., Banaschewski, T., Asherson, P., & Kuntsi, J. (2016). Cognitive and neurophysiological markers of ADHD persistence and remission. *British Journal of Psychiatry, 208*, 548–555.

Cheung, C.H., Rijsdijk, F., McLoughlin, G., Faraone, S.V., Asherson, P., & Kuntsi, J. (2015). Childhood predictors of adolescent and young adult outcome in ADHD. *Journal of Psychiatric Research*, *62*, 92–100.

Chhabildas, N., Pennington, B.F., & Willcutt, E.G. (2001). A comparison of the neuropsychological profiles of the DSM-IV subtypes of ADHD. *Journal of Abnormal Child Psychology*, *29*, 529–540.

Chi, T.C., & Hinshaw, S.P. (2002). Mother-child relationships of children with ADHD: The role of maternal depressive symptoms and depression-related distortions. *Journal of Abnormal Child Psychology*, *30*, 387–400.

Chiesa, A., Calati, R., & Serretti, A. (2011). Does mindfulness training improve cognitive abilities? A systematic review of neuropsychological findings. *Clinical Psychology Review*, *31*, 449–464.

Childress, A.C. (2016). A critical appraisal of atomoxetine in the management of ADHD. *Therapeutics and Clinical Risk Management*, *12*, 27–39.

Choudhry, Z., Sengupta, S.M., Grizenko, N., Harvey, W.J., Fortier, M.E., Schmitz, N., & Joober, R. (2013). Body weight and ADHD: Examining the role of self-regulation. *PloS One*, *8*, e55351.

Christiansen, H., Chen, W., Oades, R.D., Asherson, P., Taylor, E.A., Lasky-Su, J., . . . Faraone, S.V. (2008). Co-transmission of conduct problems with attention-deficit/hyperactivity disorder: Familial evidence for a distinct disorder. *Journal of Neural Transmission*, *115*, 163–175.

Christiansen, H., Reh, V., Schmidt, M.H., & Rief, W. (2014). Slow cortical potential neurofeedback and self-management training in outpatient care for children with ADHD: Study protocol and first preliminary results of a randomized controlled trial. *Frontiers in Human Neuroscience*, *8*, 943.

Chronis, A.M., Chacko, A., Fabiano, G.A., Wymbs, B.T., & Pelham, W.E., Jr. (2004). Enhancements to the behavioral parent training paradigm for families of children with ADHD: Review and future directions. *Clinical Child and Family Psychology Review*, *7*, 1–27.

Chronis, A.M., Fabiano, G.A., Gnagy, E.M., Wymbs, B., Burrows-MacLean, L., & Pelham, W.E. (2001). Comprehensive, sustained behavioral and pharmacological treatment for ADHD: A case study. *Cognitive and Behavioral Practice*, *8*, 346–359.

Chronis, A.M., Jones, H.A., & Raggi, V.L. (2006). Evidence-based psychosocial treatments for children and adolescents with attention-deficit/hyperactivity disorder. *Clinical Psychology Review*, *26*, 486–502.

Chronis, A.M., Lahey, B.B., Pelham, W.E., Jr., Kipp, H.L., Baumann, B.L., & Lee, S.S. (2003). Psychopathology and substance abuse in parents of young children with attention deficit/hyperactivity disorder. *Journal of the American Academy of Child and Adolescent Psychiatry*, *42*, 1424–1432.

Chronis, A.M., Lahey, B.B., Pelham, W.E., Jr., Williams, S.H., Baumann, B.L., Kipp, H., . . . Rathouz, P.J. (2007). Maternal depression and early positive parenting predict future conduct problems in young children with attention-deficit/hyperactivity disorder. *Developmental Psychology*, *43*, 70 82.

Chronis-Tuscano, A., Molina, B.S., Pelham, W.E., Applegate, B., Dahlke, A., Overmyer, M.A., Lahey, B.B. (2010). Very early predictors of adolescent depression and suicide attempts in children with Attention-Deficit/Hyperactivity Disorder. *Archives of General Psychiatry*, *67*, 1044–1051.

Cicchetti, D., & Cohen, D.J. (2006). *Developmental psychopathology: Vol. 3. Risk, disorder, and adaptation* (2nd ed.). Hoboken, NJ: Wiley.

Cicchetti, D., & Manly, J.T. (2001). Editorial: Operationalizing child maltreatment: Developmental processes and outcomes. *Development and Psychopathology*, *13*, 755–757.

Clark, C., Nower, L., & Walker, D.M. (2013). The relationship of ADHD symptoms to gambling behaviour in the USA: Results from the National Longitudinal Study of Adolescent Health. *International Gambling Studies*, *13*, 37–51.

Clarke, A. T., Marshall, S.A., Mautone, J.A., Soffer, S.L., Jones, H.A., Costigan, T.E., . . . Power, T.J. (2015). Parent attendance and homework adherence predict response to a family-school intervention for children with ADHD. *Journal of Clinical Child and Adolescent Psychology*, *44*, 58–67.

Clarke, D. (2004). Impulsiveness, locus of control, motivation and problem gambling. *Journal of Gambling Studies*, *20*, 319–345.

Clavenna, A., & Bonati, M. (2014). Safety of medicines used for ADHD in children: A review of published prospective clinical trials. *Archives of Disease in Childhood*, *99*, 866–872.

Clements, S.D. (1966a). *Task force one: Minimal brain dysfunction in children.* U.S. Public Health Service. U.S. Department of Health, Education, and Welfare.

Clements, S.D. (1966b). *Minimal brain dysfunction in children; terminology and identification. Phase I of a three-phase project.* NINDB Monograph No. 3. U.S. Department of Health, Education, and Welfare. www.ncjrs.gov/pdffiles1/Digitization/54558NCJRS.pdf

Clouston, T.S. (1899). Stages of over-excitability, hypersensitiveness and mental explosiveness in children and their treatment by their bromides. *Scottish Medical and Surgical Journal*, *4*, 481–490.

Coghill, D., & Banaschewski, T. (2009). The genetics of attention-deficit/hyperactivity disorder. *Expert Review of Neurotherapeutics*, *9*, 1547–1565.

Coghill, D., Nigg, J., Rothenberger, A., Sonuga-Barke, E., & Tannock, R. (2005) Whither causal models in the neuroscience of ADHD? *European Society for Developmental Science*, *8*, 105–114.

Coghill, D., Soutullo, C., d'Aubuisson, C., Preuss, U., Lindback, T., Silverberg, M., & Buitelaar, J. (2008). Impact of attention-deficit/hyperactivity disorder on the patient and family: Results from a European survey. *Child and Adolescent Psychiatry and Mental Health*, *2*, 31.

Cohen, N.J., Barwick, M.A., Horodezky, N.B., Vallance, D.D., & Im. N. (1998). Language, achievement, and cognitive processing in psychiatrically disturbed children with previously identified and unsuspected language impairments. *Journal of Child Psychology and Psychiatry*, *39*, 865–877.

Cohen, N.J., Vallance, D.D., Barwick, M., Im, N., Menna, R., Horodezky, N.B., & Isaacson, L. (2000). The interface between ADHD and language impairment: An examination of language, achievement, and cognitive processing. *Journal of Child Psychology and Psychiatry*, *41*, 353–362.

Cohen, P. (1998). Issues in the disruptive behavior disorders: Attention deficit disorder without hyperactivity and the differential validity of oppositional defiant and conduct disorders. In: T. Widiger & M. Flory (Eds.), *DSM-IV sourcebook* (Vol. 4, pp. 455–463). Washington, DC: American Psychiatric Press.

Cohen, P., Cohen, J., Kasen, S., Velez, C.N., Hartmark, C., Johnson, J., . . . Streuning, E.L. (1993). An epidemiological study of disorders in late childhood and adolescence. I. Age- and gender-specific prevalence. *Journal of Child Psychology and Psychiatry*, *34*, 851–867.

Cohen-Zion, M., & Ancoli-Israel, S. (2004). Sleep in children with attention-deficit hyperactivity disorder (ADHD): A review of naturalistic and stimulant intervention studies. *Sleep Medicine Reviews*, *8*, 379–402.

Cole, P., Weibel, S., Nicastro, R., Hasler, R., Dayer, A., Aubry, J.M., . . . Perroud, N. (2016). CBT/DBT skills training for adults with attention deficit hyperactivity disorder (ADHD). *Psychiatria Danubina*, *28*(Suppl. 1), 103–107.

Collett, B.R., Ohan, J.L., & Myers, K.M. (2003a). Ten-year review of rating scales, V: Scales assessing attention-deficit/hyperactivity disorder. *Journal of the American Academy of Child and Adolescent Psychiatry*, *42*, 1015–1037.

Collett, B.R., Ohan, J.L., & Myers, K.M. (2003b). Ten-year review of rating scales. VI: scales assessing externalizing behaviours. *Journal of the American Academy of Child and Adolescent Psychiatry*, *42*, 1143–1170.

Colombo, J. (2004). Visual attention in infancy: process and product in early cognitive development. In: M. Posner, (Ed.), *Cognitive neuroscience of attention* (pp. 329–341). New York: Guilford Press.

Colombo, J., & Cheatham, C.L. (2006). The emergence and basis of endogenous attention in infancy and early childhood. *Advances in Child Development and Behavior*, *34*, 283–322.

Comings, D.E., & Comings, B.G. (1990). A controlled family history study of Tourette's syndrome, I: Attention deficit hyperactivity disorder and learning disorders. *Journal of Clinical Psychiatry*, *51*, 275–280.

Comings, D.E., Comings, B.G., Muhleman, D., Dietz, G., Shahbahrami, B., Tast, D., . . . Flanagan, S.D. (1991). The dopamine D2 receptor locus as a modifying gene in neuropsychiatric disorders. *Journal of the American Medical Association*, *266*, 1793–1800.

Conlon, K. E., Strassle, C. G., Vinh, D., & Trout, G. (2008). Family management styles and ADHD: Utility and treatment implications. *Journal of Family Nursing*, *14*, 181–200.

Connell, C. M., & Prinz, R. J. (2002). The impact of childcare and parent—child interactions on school readiness and social skills development for low-income African American children. *Journal of School Psychology*, *40*, 177–193.

Conners, C. K. (2000a). Attention-deficit/hyperactivity disorder: Historical development and overview. *Journal of Attention Disorders*, *3*, 173–191.

Conners, C. K. (2000b). *Conners' continuous performance test II*. North Tonawanda, NY: Multi Health Systems.

Conners, C. K. (2015). History of Attention-deficit hyperactivity disorder. In L. A. Adler, T. J. Spencer, & T. E. Wilens (Eds.), *Attention-Deficit Hyperactivity Disorder in adults and children* (pp. 1–15). Cambridge: Cambridge University Press.

Conners, C. K., Epstein, J. N., March, J. S. (2001). Multimodal treatment of ADHD in the MTA: An alternative outcome analysis. *Journal of the American Academy of Child and Adolescent Psychiatry*, *40*, 159–167.

Conners, C. K., Erhardt, D., & Sparrow, M. A. (1999). *Conners Adult ADHD Rating Scales (CAARS)*. New York: Multi Health Systems.

Conners, C. K., Sitarenios, G., Parker, J. D., & Epstein, J. N. (1998a). Revision and restandardization of the Conners' Teacher Rating Scale (CTRS-R): Factor structure reliability, and criterion validity. *Journal of Abnormal Child Psychology*, *26*, 279–291.

Conners, C. K., Sitarenios, G., Parker, J. D., & Epstein, J. N. (1998b). The revised Conners' Parent Rating Scale (CPRS-R): Factor structure, reliability, and criterion validity. *Journal of Abnormal Child Psychology*, *26*, 257–268.

Connor, D. F. (2011). Problems of overdiagnosis and overprescribing in ADHD: Are they legitimate? *Psychiatric Times*, *28*, 14–18.

Connor, D. F. (2015). Stimulant and nonstimulant medication for childhood ADHD. In R. A. Barkley (Ed.) *Attention-Deficit Hyperactivity Disorder* (4th ed., pp. 666–685). New York: Guilford Press.

Conrad, P. (1975). The discovery of hyperkinesis: Notes on the medicalization of deviant behavior. *Social Problems*, *23*, 12–21.

Conrad, P. (2007). *The medicalization of society: On the transformation of human conditions into treatable disorders*. Baltimore: Johns Hopkins University Press.

Copeland, W. E., Angold, A., MRCPsych, Costello, E. J., & Egger, H. (2013). Prevalence, comorbidity and correlates of DSM-5 proposed Disruptive Mood Dysregulation Disorder. *American Journal of Psychiatry*, *170*, 173–179.

Cordier, R., Bundy, A., Hocking, C., & Einfeld, S. (2010). Empathy in the play of children with attention deficit hyperactivity disorder. *OTJR: Occupation, Participation and Health*, *30*, 122–132.

Corkum, P., Moldofsky, H., Hogg-Johnson, S., Humphries, T., & Tannock, R. (1999). Sleep problems in children with attention-deficit/hyperactivity disorder: Impact of subtype, comorbidity, and stimulant medication. *Journal of the American Academy of Child and Adolescent Psychiatry*, *38*, 1285–1293.

Corkum, P., Tannock, R., Moldofsky, H., Hogg-Johnson, S., & Humphries, T. (2001). Actigraphy and parental ratings of sleep in children with attention deficit hyperactivity disorder. *Sleep*, *24*, 303–312.

Cornoldi, C., Del Prete, F., Gallani, A., Sella, F., & Re, A. M. (2010). Components affecting expressive writing in typical and disabled writers. *Advances in Learning and Behavioral Disabilities*, *23*, 269–286.

Cortese, S. (2012). The neurobiology and genetics of attention-deficit/hyperactivity disorder (ADHD): What every clinician should know. *European Journal of Pediatric Neurology*, *16*, 422–433.

Cortese, S. (2015). Sleep and ADHD: What we know and what we do not know. *Sleep Medicine*, *16*, 5–6.

Cortese, S., Angriman, M., Maffeis, C., Isnard, P., Konofal, E., Lecendreux, M., . . . Mouren, M. C. (2008). Attention-deficit/hyperactivity disorder (ADHD) and obesity: A systematic review of the literature. *Critical Reviews in Food Science and Nutrition*, *48*, 524–537.

Cortese, S., Azoulay, R., Castellanos, F.X., Chalard, F., Lecendreux, M., Chechin, D., . . . Bernardina, B.D. (2012). Brain iron levels in attention-deficit/hyperactivity disorder: A pilot MRI study. *World Journal of Biological Psychiatry, 13*, 223–231.

Cortese, S., Brown, T.E., Corkum, P., Gruber, R., O'Brien, L.M., Stein, M., . . . Owens, J. (2013). Assessment and management of sleep problems in youths with attention-deficit/hyperactivity disorder. *Journal of the American Academy of Child and Adolescent Psychiatry, 52*, 784–796.

Cortese, S., & Castellanos, F.X. (2014). The relationship between ADHD and obesity: Implications for therapy. *Expert Review of Neurotherapeutics, 14*, 473–479.

Cortese, S., Dalla Bernardina, B., & Mouren, M.C. (2007). Attention-deficit/hyperactivity disorder (ADHD) and binge eating. *Nutrition Reviews, 65*, 404–411.

Cortese, S., Faraone, S.V., Bernardi, S., Wang, S., & Blanco, C. (2013). Adult attention-deficit hyperactivity disorder and obesity: Epidemiological study. *British Journal of Psychiatry, 203*, 24–34.

Cortese, S., Faraone, S.V., Konofal, E., & Lecendreux, M. (2009). Sleep in children with attention-deficit/hyperactivity disorder: meta-analysis of subjective and objective studies. *Journal of the American Academy of Child and Adolescent Psychiatry, 48*, 894–908.

Cortese, S., Ferrin, M., Brandeis, D., Buitelaar, J., Daley, D., Dittmann, R.W., . . . Zuddas, A. (2015). Cognitive training for attention-deficit/hyperactivity disorder: meta-analysis of clinical and neuropsychological outcomes from randomized controlled trials. *Journal of the American Academy of Child and Adolescent Psychiatry, 54*, 164–174.

Cortese, S., Kelly, C., Chabernaud, C., Di Martino, A., Milham, M.P., Castellanos, F.X. (2012). Toward systems neuroscience of ADHD: A meta- analysis of 55 fMRI studies. *American Journal of Psychiatry, 169*, 1038–55.

Cortese, S., Konofal, E., Dalla Bernardina, B., Mouren, M.C., & Lecendreux, M. (2009). Sleep disturbances and serum ferritin levels in children with attention-deficit/hyperactivity disorder. *European Child and Adolescent Psychiatry, 18*, 393–399.

Cortese, S., Konofal, E., Yateman, N., Mouren, M., & Lecendreux, M. (2006). Sleep and alertness in children with attention-deficit/hyperactivity disorder: A systematic review of the literature. *Sleep, 29*, 504–501.

Cortese, S., Maffeis, C., Konofal, E., Lecendreux, M., Comencini, E., Angriman, M., . . . Dalla Bernardina, B. (2007). Parent reports of sleep/alertness problems and ADHD symptoms in a sample of obese adolescents. *Journal of Psychosomatic Research, 63*, 587–590.

Cortese, S., Moreira-Maia, C.R., St. Fleur, D., Morcillo-Peñalver, C., Rohde, L.A., & Faraone, S.V. (2016). Association between ADHD and obesity: A systematic review and meta-analysis. *American Journal of Psychiatry, 173*, 34–43.

Cortese, S., Olazagasti, M.A.R., Klein, R.G., Castellanos, F.X., Proal, E., & Mannuzza, S. (2013). Obesity in men with childhood ADHD: A 33-year controlled, prospective, follow-up study. *Pediatrics, 131*, e1731–e1738.

Cortese, S., & Vincenzi, B. (2012). Obesity and ADHD: Clinical and neurobiological implications. In C. Stanford & R. Tannock (Eds.) *Behavioral neuroscience of Attention Deficit Hyperactivity Disorder and its treatment* (pp. 199–218). Verlag Berlin Heidelberg: Springer.

Cosgrove, L., & Krimsky, S. (2012). A comparison of DSM-IV and DSM-5 panel members' financial associations with industry: A pernicious problem persists. *PLoS Med, 9*, e1001190.

Costa, N.M., Weems, C.F., Pellerin, K., & Dalton, R. (2006). Parenting stress and childhood psychopathology: An examination of specificity to internalizing and externalizing symptoms. *Journal of Psychopathology and Behavioral Assessment, 28*, 113–122.

Costello, E.J., Angold, A., & Keeler, G. (1999). Adolescent outcomes of childhood disorders: the consequences of severity and impairment. *Journal of the American Academy of Child and Adolescent Psychiatry, 38*, 121–128.

Cousins, M., & Smyth, M.M. (2003). Developmental coordination impairments in adulthood. *Human Movement Science, 22*, 433–459.

Coutin-Churchman, P., Anez, Y., Uzcategui, M., Alvarez, L., Vergara, F., Mendez, L., . . . Fleitas, R. (2003). Quantitative spectral analysis of EEG in psychiatry revisited: drawing signs out of numbers in a clinical setting. *Clinical Neurophysiology, 114*, 294–306.

Cramer, A. O., Waldorp, L. J., van der Maas, H. L., & Borsboom, D. (2010). Comorbidity: A network perspective. *Behavioral and Brain Sciences*, *33*, 137–193.

Crichton, A. (1798). *An inquiry into the nature and origin of mental derangement: Comprehending a concise system of the physiology and pathology of the human mind and a history of the passions and their effects.* London, England: T. Cadell Hr. & W. Davies (Reprinted by AMS Press, New York, 1976).

Crone, D. & Horner, R. (2003). *Building positive behavior support systems in schools: Functional behavior assessment.* New York: Guilford Press.

Cross-Disorder Group of the Psychiatric Genomics Consortium. (2013). Genetic relationship between five psychiatric disorders estimated from genome-wide SNPs. *Nature Genetics*, *45*, 984–994.

Cumyn, L., French, L., & Hechtman, L. (2009). Comorbidity in adults with attention-deficit hyperactivity disorder. *Canadian Journal of Psychiatry*, *54*, 673–683.

Cunningham, C. E., & Boyle, H. M. (2002). Preschoolers at risk for Attention-Deficit Hyperactivity Disorder and Oppositional Defiant Disorder: Family, parenting, and behavioral correlates. *Journal of Abnormal Child Psychology*, *30*, 555–569.

Curchack-Lichtin, J. T., Chacko, A., & Halperin, J. M. (2014). Changes in ADHD symptom endorsement: Preschool to school age. *Journal of Abnormal Child Psychology*, *42*, 993–1004.

D'Onofrio, B. M., Van Hulle, C. A., Waldman, I. D., Rodgers, J. L., Harden, K. P., Rathouz, P. J., & Lahey, B. B. (2008). Smoking during pregnancy and offspring externalizing problems: An exploration of genetic and environmental confounds. *Development and Psychopathology*, *20*, 139–164.

Dai, Z., Harrow, S. E., Song, X., Rucklidge, J., & Grace, R. (2016). Gambling, delay, and probability discounting in adults with and without ADHD. *Journal of Attention Disorders*, *20*, 968–978.

Daley, D., Sonuga-Barke, E., Thompson, M., & Chen, W. (2008). Gene-social environment interplay in relation to attention deficit hyperactivity disorder. *Psychiatry*, *7*, 520–524.

Daley, D., van der Oord, S., Ferrin, M., Danckaerts, M., Doepfner, M, Cortese, S., . . . Sonuga-Barke, E.J.S. (2014). Behavioral interventions in attention-deficit/hyperactivity disorder: a meta-analysis of randomized controlled trials across multiple outcome domains. *Journal of the American Academy of Child and Adolescent Psychiatry*, *53*, 835–847.

Dalsgaard, S. (2013). Attention-deficit/hyperactivity disorder. *European Child and Adolescent Psychiatry*, *22*(Suppl. 1), S43–S48.

Dalsgaard, S., Mortensen, P. B., Frydenberg, M., & Thomsen, P. H. (2002). Conduct problems, gender, and adult psychiatric outcome of children with attention-deficit hyperactivity disorder. *British Journal of Psychiatry*, *181*, 416–421.

Dalsgaard, S., Mortensen, P. B., Frydenberg, M., & Thomsen, P. H. (2013). Long-term criminal outcome of children with attention deficit hyperactivity disorder. *Criminal Behaviour and Mental Health*, *23*, 86–98.

Danforth, J. S., Barkley, R. A., & Stokes, T. F. (1991). Observations of parent-child interactions with hyperactive children: Research and clinical implications. *Clinical Psychology Review*, *11*, 703–727.

Danforth, J. S., Connor, D. F., & Doerfler, L. A. (2016). The development of comorbid conduct problems in children with ADHD: An example of an integrative developmental psychopathology perspective *Journal of Attention Disorders*, *20*, 214–229.

Daughton, J., Corr, L., Liu, H., & West, M. (2012). Clonidine extended-release tablets for the treatment of ADHD. *Neuropsychiatry*, *2*, 117–123.

Daughton, J. M., & Kratochvil, C. J. (2009). Review of ADHD pharmacotherapies: Advantages, disadvantages, and clinical pearls. *Journal of the American Academy of Child and Adolescent Psychiatry*, *48*, 240–248.

Davies, W. (2014). Sex differences in attention Deficit Hyperactivity Disorder: Candidate genetic and endocrine mechanisms. *Frontiers in Neuroendocrinology*, *35*, 331–346.

Davis, C. (2013). From passive overeating to "food addiction": A spectrum of compulsion and severity. *ISRN Obesity*, 435027. https://doi.org/10.1155/2013/435027.

Davis, C., Levitan, R. D., Smith, M., Tweed, S., & Curtis, C. (2006). Associations among overeating, overweight, and attention deficit/hyperactivity disorder: A structural equation modelling approach. *Eating Behaviors*, *7*, 266–274.

Davis, C., Strachan, S., & Berkson, M. (2004). Sensitivity to reward: Implications for overeating and overweight. *Appetite*, *42*, 131–138.

Davis, D.W., & Williams, P.G. (2011). Attention deficit/hyperactivity disorder in preschool-age children: Issues and concerns. *Clinical Pediatrics*, *50*, 144–152.

Davis, N.O., & Kollins, S.H. (2012). Treatment for co-occurring attention deficit/hyperactivity disorder and autism spectrum disorder. *Neurotherapeutics*, *9*, 518–530.

Daviss, W.B. (2008). A review of co-morbid depression in pediatric ADHD: Etiologies, phenomenology, and treatment. *Journal of Child and Adolescent Psychopharmacology*, *18*, 565–571.

Dawson, G. (2008). Early behavioral intervention, brain plasticity, and the prevention of autism spectrum disorder. *Development and Psychopathology*, *20*, 775–803.

Deater-Deckard, K. (1998). Parenting stress and child adjustment: Some old hypotheses and new questions. *Clinical Psychology: Science and Practice*, *5*, 314–332.

Deault, L.C. (2010). A systematic review of parenting in relation to the development of comorbidities and functional impairments in children with attention-deficit/hyperactivity disorder (ADHD). *Child Psychiatry and Human Development*, *41*, 168–192.

de Boo, G.M., & Prins, P.J.M. (2007). Social incompetence in children with ADHD: Possible moderators and mediators in social-skills training. *Clinical Psychology Review*, *27*, 78–97.

De Crescenzo, F., Licchelli, S., Ciabattini, M., Menghini, D., Armando, M., Alfieri, P., . . . Quested, D. (2016). The use of actigraphy in the monitoring of sleep and activity in ADHD: A meta-analysis. *Sleep Medicine Reviews*, *26*, 9–20.

Defoe, I.N., Farrington, D.P., & Loeber, R. (2013). Disentangling the relationship between delinquency and hyperactivity, low achievement, depression, and low socioeconomic status: Analysis of repeated longitudinal data. *Journal of Criminal Justice*, *41*, 100–107.

DeGarmo, D.S., Patterson, G.R., & Forgatch, M.S. (2004). How do outcomes in a specified parent training intervention maintain or wane over time? *Prevention Science*, *5*, 73–89.

Dehaene, S., Molko, N., Cohen, L., & Wilson, A.J. (2004). Arithmetic and the brain. *Current Opinion in Neurobiology*, *14*, 218–218.

Dehaene, S., Piazza, M., Pinel, P., & Cohen, L. (2005). Three parietal circuits for number processing. In J.I.D. Campbell (Ed.), *Handbook of mathematical cognition* (pp. 433–453). New York: Psychology Press.

Dekker, M.C., & Koot, H.M. (2003). DSM-IV disorders in children with borderline to moderate intellectual disability, I:prevalence and impact. *Journal of the American Academy of Child and Adolescent Psychiatry*, *42*, 915–922.

De La Fuente, A., Xia, S., Branvh, C., & Li, X. (2013). A review of attention-deficit hyperactivity disorder from the perspective of brain networks. *Frontiers in Human Neuroscience*, *7*, 192.

del Campo, N., Chamberlain, S.R., Sahakian, B.J., & Robbins, T.W. (2011). The roles of dopamine and noradrenaline in the pathophysiology and treatment of attention-deficit/hyperactivity disorder. *Biological Psychiatry*, *69*, e145–e157.

Delis, D., Kaplan, E., & Kramer, J. (2001). *The Delis-Kaplan executive function system.* San Antonio, TX: The Psychological Corporation.

Denckla, M., & Rudel, R. (1978). Anomalies of motor development in hyperactive boys. *Annual Neurology*, *3*, 231–233.

Dennis, M., Spiegler, B.J., Juranek, J.J., Bigler, E.D., Snead, O.C., & Fletcher, J.M. (2013). Age, plasticity, and homeostasis in childhood brain disorders. *Neuroscience and Biobehavioral Reviews*, *37*, 2760–2773.

Deoni, S.C.L., Mercure, E., Blasi, A., Gasston, D., Thomson, A., Johnson, M., . . . Murphy, D.G. (2011). Mapping infant brain myelination with magnetic resonance imaging. *Journal of Neuroscience*, *31*, 784–791.

de Ramírez, R.D., & Shapiro, E.S. (2005). Effects of student ethnicity on judgments of ADHD symptoms among Hispanic and White teachers. *School Psychology Quarterly*, *20*, 268–287.

De Sanctis, V.A., Nomura, Y., Newcorn, J.H., & Halperin, J.M. (2012). Childhood maltreatment and conduct disorder: Independent predictors of criminal outcomes in ADHD youth. *Child Abuse and Neglect*, *36*, 782–789.

Dewey, D., Kaplan, B.J., Crawford, S.G., & Wilson, B.N. (2002). Developmental coordination disorder: Associated problems in attention, learning, and psychosocial adjustment. *Human Movement Science, 21*, 905–918.

De Zeeuw, P., Zwart, F., Schrama, R., Van Engeland, H., & Durston, S. (2012). Prenatal exposure to cigarette smoke or alcohol and cerebellum volume in attention-deficit/hyperactivity disorder and typical development. *Translational Psychiatry, 2*, e84.

Diamantopoulou, S., Henricsson, L., & Rydell, A.M. (2005). ADHD symptoms and peer relations of children in a community sample: Examining associated problems, self-perceptions, and gender differences. *International Journal of Behavioral Development, 29*, 388–398.

Diamantopoulou, S., Verhulst, F.C., & van der Ende, J. (2011). The parallel development of ODD and CD symptoms from early childhood to adolescence. *European Child & Adolescent Psychiatry, 20*, 301–309.

Diamond, A., Barnett, W.S., Thomas, J., & Munro, S. (2007). Preschool program improves cognitive control. *Science, 318*, 1387–1388.

Dickstein, S.G., Bannon, K., Castellanos, F.X., & Milham, M.P. (2006). The neural correlates of attention deficit hyperactivity disorder: An ALE meta-analysis. *Journal of Child Psychology and Psychiatry, 47*, 1051–1062.

Diekelmann, S., & Born, J. (2010). The memory function of sleep. *Nature Reviews Neuroscience, 11*, 114–126.

DiPerna, J.C., Volpe, R.J., & Elliott, S.N. (2005). An examination of academic enablers and achievement in mathematics. *Journal of School Psychology, 43*, 379–392.

Dirks, E., Spyer, G., van Lieshout, E.C., & de Sonneville, L. (2008). Prevalence of combined reading and arithmetic disabilities. *Journal of Learning Disabilities, 41*, 460–473.

Dirlikov, B., Rosch, K.S., Crocetti, D., Denckla, M.B., Mahone, E.M., & Mostofsky, S.H. (2015). Distinct frontal lobe morphology in girls and boys with ADHD. *NeuroImage: Clinical, 7*, 222–229.

Dittman, C.K. (2016). The impact of early classroom inattention on phonological processing and word-reading development. *Journal of Attention Disorders, 20*, 653–664.

Docherty, S.J., Kovas, Y., Petrill, S.A., & Plomin, R. (2010). Generalist genes analysis of DNA markers associated with mathematical ability and disability reveals shared influence across ages and abilities. *BMC Genetics, 11*, 61.

Doehnert, M., Brandeis, D., Straub, M., Steinhausen, H.C., & Dreschler, R. (2008). Slow cortical potential neurofeedback in attention deficit hyperactivity disorder: Is there neurophysiological evidence for specific effects? *Journal of Neural Transmission, 115*, 1445–1456.

Doernberg, E., & Hollander, E. (2016). Neurodevelopmental disorders (ASD and ADHD): DSM-5, ICD-10, and ICD-11. *CNS Spectrums, 21*, 295–299.

Dolphin, J.E., & Cruickshank, W.M. (1951). Pathology of concept formation in children with cerebral palsy. *American Journal of Mental Deficiency, 56*, 386–392.

Dols, A., Sienaert, P., van Gerven, H., Schouws, S., Stevens, A., Kupka, R., & Stek, M.L. (2013). The prevalence and management of side effects of lithium and anticonvulsants as mood stabilizers in bipolar disorder from a clinical perspective: A review. *International Clinical Psychopharmacology, 28*, 287–296.

Donfrancesco, R., Miano, S., Martines, F., Ferrante, L., Melegari, M.G., & Masi, G. (2011). Bipolar disorder co-morbidity in children with attention deficit hyperactivity disorder. *Psychiatry Research, 186*, 333–337.

Donnelly, C., Bangs, M., Trzepacz, P., Jin, L., Zhang, S., Witte, M.M., . . . Spencer, T.J. (2009). Safety and tolerability of atomoxetine over 3 to 4 years in children and adolescents with ADHD. *Journal of the American Academy of Child and Adolescent Psychiatry, 48*, 176–185.

Döpfner, M., Rothenberger, A., & Sonuga-Barke, E. (2004). Areas for future investment in the field of ADHD: preschoolers and clinical networks. *European Child & Adolescent Psychiatry, 13*, i130–i135.

Douglas, V.I. (1972). Stop, look and listen: The problem of sustained attention and impulse control in hyperactive and normal children. *Canadian Journal of Behavioural Science, 4*, 259–282.

Douglas, V.I. (1980a). Higher mental processes in hyperactive children: Implications for training. In R. Knights & D. Bakker (Eds.), *Treatment of hyperactive and learning disordered children* (pp. 65–92). Baltimore: University Park Press.

Douglas, V.I. (1980b). Treatment and training approaches to hyperactivity: Establishing internal or external control. In C. Whalen & B. Henker (Eds.), *Hyperactive children: The social ecology of identification and treatment* (pp. 283–318). New York: Academic Press.

Douglas, V.I. (1983). Attention and cognitive problems. In M. Rutter (Ed.), *Developmental neuropsychiatry* (pp. 280–329). New York: Guilford Press.

Dovis, S., Van der Oord, S., Wiers, R.W., & Prins, P.J. (2015). Improving executive functioning in children with ADHD: Training multiple executive functions within the context of a computer game. A randomized double-blind placebo controlled trial. *PloS one*, *10*(4), e0121651.

Doyle, A.E., Biederman, J., Seidman, L.J., Weber, W., & Faraone, S.V. (2000). Diagnostic efficiency of neuropsychological test scores for discriminating boys with and without ADHD. *Journal of Consulting Clinical Psychology*, *68*, 477–488.

Drabick, D.A., & Kendall, P.C. (2010). Developmental psychopathology and the diagnosis of mental health problems among youth. *Clinical Psychology: Science and Practice*, *17*, 272–280.

Drechsler, R., Straub, M., Doehnert, M., Heinrich, H., Steinhausen, H.C., & Brandeis, D. (2007). Controlled evaluation of a neurofeedback training of slow cortical potentials in children with attention deficit/hyperactivity disorder (ADHD). *Behavioral and Brain Functions*, *3*, 1–13.

Duckworth, A.L., & Seligman, M.E.P. (2005). Self-discipline outdoes IQ in predicting academic performance of adolescents. *Psychological Science*, *16*, 939–944.

Duffy, A. (2012). The nature of the association between childhood ADHD and the development of Bipolar Disorder: A review of prospective high-risk studies. *American Journal of Psychiatry*, *169*, 1247–1255.

DuPaul, G.J. (1991). Parent and teacher ratings of ADHD symptoms: Psychometric properties in a community-based sample. *Journal of Clinical Child Psychology*, *20*, 242–253.

DuPaul, G.J. (2007). School-based interventions for students with attention deficit hyperactivity disorder: Current status and future directions. *School Psychology Review*, *36*, 183–194.

DuPaul, G.J. & Barkley, R. (1993). Behavioral contributions to pharmacology: The utility of behavioral methodology in medication treatment of children with attention deficit hyperactivity disorder. *Behavior Therapy*, *24*, 47–65.

DuPaul, G.J., & Eckert, T.L. (1997). The effect of school-based interventions for ADHD: A meta-analysis. *School Psychology Review*, *26*, 5–27.

DuPaul, G.J., & Eckert, T. (1998). Academic interventions for students with attention-deficit/hyperactivity disorder: A review of the literature. *Reading and Writing Quarterly*, *14*, 59–82.

DuPaul, G.J., Eckert, T.L., & Vilardo, B. (2012) The effects of school-based interventions for attention deficit hyperactivity disorder: A meta-analysis 1996–2010. *School Psychology Review*, *41*, 387–412.

DuPaul, G.J., Gormley, M.J., & Laracy, S.D. (2013). Comorbidity of LD and ADHD: Implications of DSM-5 for assessment and treatment. *Journal of Learning Disabilities*, *46*, 43–51.

DuPaul, G.J., Helwig, J.R., & Slay, P.M. (2011). Classroom interventions for attention and hyperactivity. In M.A. Bray & T.J. Kehle (Eds.), *The Oxford handbook of school psychology* (pp. 428–441). New York: Oxford University Press.

DuPaul, G.J., Kern, L., Gormley, M.J., & Volpe, R.J. (2011). Early intervention for young children with ADHD: Academic outcomes for responders to behavioral treatment. *School Mental Health*, *3*, 117–126.

DuPaul, G.J., & Langberg, J.M. (2015). Educational impairments in children with ADHD. In R.A. Barkley (Ed.) *Attention-Deficit Hyperactivity Disorder* (4th ed., pp. 169–190). New York: Guilford Press.

DuPaul, G.J., McGoey, K.E., Eckert, T.L., & VanBrakle, J. (2001). Preschool children with attention-deficit/hyperactivity disorder: Impairment in behavioral, social, and school functioning. *Journal of the American Academy of Child and Adolescent Psychiatry*, *40*, 508–515.

DuPaul, G., & Power, T.J. (2008). Improving school outcomes for students with ADHD: Using the right strategies in the context of the right relationships. *Journal of Attention Disorders*, *11*, 519–521.

DuPaul, G.J., Power, T.J., Anastopoulos, A.D., & Reid, R. (1998). *ADHD Rating Scale-IV. Checklists, norms and clinical implications.* New York: Guilford Press.

DuPaul, G.J., Reid, R., Anastopoulos, A.D., Lambert, M.C., Watkins, M.W., & Power, T.J. (2016). Parent and teacher ratings of attention-deficit/hyperactivity disorder symptoms: Factor structure and normative data. *Psychological Assessment, 28*, 214–225.

DuPaul, G.J. & Stoner, G. (2003). *ADHD in the schools: Assessment and intervention strategies* (2nd ed.). New York: Guilford Press.

DuPaul, G.J., & Volpe, R.J. (2009). ADHD and learning disabilities: research findings and clinical implications. *Current Attention Disorders Reports, 1*, 152–155.

DuPaul, G.J., & Weyandt., L.L. (2009). Behavioral interventions with externalizing disorders. In A. Akin-Little, M. Bray, & T. Kehle (Eds.), *Behavioral intervention in schools: Evidence-based positive strategies* (pp. 265–280). Washington, DC: American Psychological Association.

DuPaul, G.J., Weyandt, L.L., & Janusis, G.M. (2011). ADHD in the classroom: Effective intervention strategies. *Theory into Practice, 50*, 35–42.

Duric, N.S., Assmus, J., Gundersen, D., & Elgen, I.B. (2012). Neurofeedback for the treatment of children and adolescents with ADHD: A randomized and controlled clinical trial using parental reports. *BMC Psychiatry, 12*, 107.

Durston, S., Fossella, J.A., Casey, B.J., Hulshoff Pol, H.E., Galvan, A., Schnack, H.G., . . . (2005). Differential effects of DRD4 and DAT1 genotype on fronto-striatal gray matter volumes in a sample of subjects with attention deficit hyperactivity disorder, their unaffected siblings and controls. *Molecular Psychiatry, 10*, 678–685.

Durston, S., Hulshoff Pol, H.E., Schnack, H.G., Buitelaar, J.K., Steenhuis, M.P., Minderaa, R.B., . . . van Engeland, H. (2004). Magnetic resonance imaging of boys with attention-deficit/hyperactivity disorder and their unaffected siblings. *Journal of the American Academy of Child and Adolescent Psychiatry, 43*, 332–340.

Dwivedi, K.N., & Banhatti, R.G. (2005). Attention deficit/hyperactivity disorder and ethnicity. *Archives of Disease in Childhood, 90*, i10–i12.

Dyck, M.J., Ferguson, K., & Shochet, I.M. (2001). Do autism spectrum disorders differ from each other and from nonspectrum disorders on emotion recognition tests? *European Child and Adolescent Psychiatry, 10*, 105–116.

Dykman, R.A., Ackerman, P.T., Clements, S.D., & Peters, J.E. (1971). Specific learning disabilities: An attentional deficit syndrome. *Progress in Learning Disabilities, 2*, 56–93.

Ebaugh, F.G. (1923). Neuropsychiatric sequelae of acute epidemic encephalitis in children. *American Journal of Diseases of Children, 25*, 89–97.

Edelbrock, C., Costello, A.J., & Kessler, M.D. (1984). Empirical corroboration of attention deficit disorder. *Journal of the American Academy of Child Psychiatry, 23*, 285–290.

Eden, G., & Vaidy, C. (2008). ADHD and Developmental Dyslexia: Two pathways leading to impaired learning. *Annals of the New York Academy of Sciences, 1145*, 316–327.

Edwards, G., Barkley, R., Laneri, M., Fletcher, K., & Metevia, L. (2001). Parent-adolescent conflict in teenagers with ADHD and ODD. *Journal of Abnormal Child Psychology, 29*, 557–572.

Edwards, M.C., Schulz, E.G., Chelonis, J., Gardner, E., Philyaw, A., & Young, J. (2005). Estimates of the validity and utility of unstructured clinical observations of children in the assessment of ADHD. *Clinical Pediatrics, 44*, 49–56.

Egeland, J., Aarlien, A.K., & Saunes, B.K. (2013). Few effects of far transfer of working memory training in ADHD: A randomized controlled trial. *PLoS One, 8*(10):e75660.

Egeland, J., Johansen, S.N., & Ueland, T. (2009). Differentiating between ADHD sub-types on CCPT measures of sustained attention and vigilance. *Scandinavian Journal of Psychology, 50*, 347–354.

Egger, H.L., & Angold, A. (2006). Common emotional and behavioral disorders in preschool children: presentation, nosology, and epidemiology. *Journal of Child Psychology and Psychiatry, 47*, 313–337.

Egger, H.L., Kondo, D., & Angold, A. (2006). The epidemiology and diagnostic issues in preschool attention-deficit/hyperactivity disorder: A review. *Infants and Young Children, 19*, 109–122.

Egner, T., & Gruzelier, J.H. (2004). EEG biofeedback of low beta band components: Frequency-specific effects on variables of attention and event-related brain potentials. *Clinical Neurophysiology, 115*, 131–139.

Ehri, L.C. (2005). Learning to read words: Theory, findings, and issues. *Scientific Studies of Reading, 9*, 167–188.

Ehri, L.C., Nunes, S.R., Willows, D.M., Schuster, B.V., Yaghoub-Zadeh, Z., & Shanahan,T. (2001). Phonemic awareness instruction helps children learn to read: Evidence from the National Reading Panel's meta-analysis. *Reading Research Quarterly, 36*, 250–287.

Eichele, T., Debener, S., Calhoun, V.D., Specht, K., Engel, A.K., Hugdahl, K., . . . Ullsperger, M. (2008). Prediction of human errors by maladaptive changes in event-related brain networks. *Proceedings of the National Academy of Sciences of the United States of America, 105*, 6173–6178.

Eisenberg, D.T., Campbell, B., Gray, P.B., & Sorenson, M.D. (2008). Dopamine receptor genetic polymorphisms and body composition in undernourished pastoralists: An exploration of nutrition indices among nomadic and recently settled Ariaal men of northern Kenya. *BMC Evolutionary Biology, 8*, 173.

Eisenberg, N. (2002). Emotion-related regulation and its relation to quality of social functioning. *Minnesota Symposia on Child Psychology, 32*, 133–171.

Eisenberger, R., & Cameron, J. (1996). Detrimental effects of reward: Reality or myth? *Journal of the American Psychological Association, 51*, 1153–1166.

Ek, U., Westerlund, J., Holmberg, K., & Fernell, E. (2008). Self-esteem in children with attention and/or learning deficits: The importance of gender. *Acta Paediatrica, 97*, 1125–1130.

Elia, J., Ambrosini, P., & Berrettini, W. (2008). ADHD characteristics: I. Concurrent co-morbidity patterns in children & adolescents. *Child and Adolescent Psychiatry and Mental Health, 2*, 15–23.

Elkins, I.J., McGue, M., & Iacono, W.G. (2007). Prospective effects of attention-deficit/hyperactivity disorder, conduct disorder, and sex on adolescent substance use and abuse. *Archives of General Psychiatry, 64*, 1145–1152.

Ellison-Wright, I., Ellison-Wright, Z., & Bullmore, E. (2008). Structural brain change in attention deficit hyperactivity disorder identified by meta-analysis. *BMC Psychiatry, 8*, 51–58.

Elsabbagh, M., Fernandes, J., Webb, S.J., Dawson, G., Charman, T., Johnson, M.H., & British Autism Study of Infant Siblings Team. (2013). Disengagement of visual attention in infancy is associated with emerging autism in toddlerhood. *Biological Psychiatry, 74*, 189–194.

Elsabbagh, M., Gliga, T., Pickles, A., Hudry, K., Charman, T., Johnson, M.H., & BASIS Team. (2013). The development of face orienting mechanisms in infants at-risk for autism. *Behavioural Brain Research, 251*, 147–154.

Eme, R.F. (1992). Selective female affliction in development of disorders of childhood: A literature review. *Journal of Clinical Child Psychology, 21*, 354–364.

Emerson, E. (2003). Prevalence of psychiatric disorders in children and adolescents with and without intellectual disability. *Journal of Intellectual Disability Research, 47*, 51–58.

Engel, S.M., Wetmur, J., Chen, J., Zhu, C., Barr, D.B., Canfield, R.L., & Wolff, M.S. (2011). Prenatal exposure to organophosphates, paraoxonase 1, and cognitive development in childhood. *Environmental Health Perspectives, 119*, 1182–1188.

Engelhardt, C.R., Mazurek, M.O., & Sohl, K. (2013). Media use and sleep among boys with autism spectrum disorder, ADHD, or typical development. *Pediatrics, 132*, 1081–1089.

Epstein, J.N., Erkanli, A., Conners, C.K., Klaric, J., Costello, J.E., & Angold, A. (2003). Relations between continuous performance test performance measures and ADHD behaviors. *Journal of Abnormal Child Psychology, 31*, 543–554.

Epstein, J.N., Willoughby, M., Valencia, E.Y., Tonev, S.T., Abikoff, H.B., Arnold, L.E., & Hinshaw, S.P. (2005). The role of children's ethnicity in the relationship between teacher ratings of attention-deficit/hyperactivity disorder and observed classroom behavior. *Journal of Consulting and Clinical Psychology, 73*, 424–434.

Ercan, E.S., Coskunol, H., Varan, A., & Toksoz, K. (2003). Childhood attention deficit/hyperactivity disorder and alcohol dependence: A 1-year follow-up. *Medical Council on Alcohol, 38*, 352–356.

Eskenazi, B., Marks, A.R., Bradman, A., Harley, K., Barr, D.B., Johnson, C., . . . Jewell, N.P. (2007). Organophosphate pesticide exposure and neurodevelopment in young Mexican-American children. *Environmental Health Perspectives, 118*, 792–798.

Espy, K.A., & Bull, R. (2005). Inhibitory processes in young children and individual variation in short-term memory. *Developmental Neuropsychology, 28*, 669–688.

Esquirol, E. (1845). *Mental maladies: Treatise on insanity.* Philadelphia: Lee & Blanchard.

Eubig, P.A., Aguiar, A., & Schantz, S.L. (2010). Lead and PCBs as risk factors for attention-deficit/hyperactivity disorder. *Environmental Health Perspectives, 118*, 1654–1667.

Evans, S.W., Allen, J.A., Moore, S., & Strauss, V. (2005). Measuring symptoms and functioning of youth with ADHD in middle school. *Journal of Abnormal Child Psychology, 33*, 695–706.

Evans, S.W., Langberg, J.M., Raggi, V., Allen, J., & Buvinger, E. (2005). Evaluation of a school-based treatment program for middle school youth with ADHD. *Journal of Attention Disorders, 9*, 343–353.

Evans, S.W., Owens, J., & Bunford, N. (2014). Evidence-based psychosocial treatments for children and adolescents with attention-deficit/hyperactivity disorder. *Journal of Clinical Child and Adolescent Psychology, 43*, 527–551.

Evans, S.W., Pelham, W., & Grudberg, M.V. (1995). The efficacy of notetaking to improve behavior and comprehension of adolescents with attention deficit hyperactivity disorder. *Exceptionality, 5*, 1–17.

Evans, S.W., Pelham, W.E., Smith, B.H., Bukstein, O., Gnagy, E.M., Greiner, A.R., . . . Baron-Myak, C. (2001). Dose—response effects of methylphenidate on ecologically valid measures of academic performance and classroom behavior in adolescents with ADHD. *Experimental and Clinical Psychopharmacology, 9*, 163–175.

Evans, S.W., Schultz, B.K., DeMars, C.E., & Davis, H. (2011). Effectiveness of the Challenging Horizons after-school program for young adolescents with ADHD. *Behavior Therapy, 42*, 462–474.

Evans, S.W., Schultz, B.K., White, L.C., Brady, C., Sibley, M.H., & Van Eck, K. (2009). A school-based organization intervention for young adolescents with attention-deficit/hyperactivity disorder. *School Mental Health, 1*, 78–88.

Fabiano, G.A., Chacko, A., Pelham, W.E., Jr., Robb, J., Walker, K.S., Wymbs, F., . . . Pirvics, L. (2009). A comparison of behavioral parent training programs for fathers of children with attention-deficit/hyperactivity disorder. *Behavior Therapy, 40*, 190–204.

Fabiano, G.A., Pelham, W.B., Waschbusch, D.A., Gnagy, E.M., Lahey, B.B., Chronis, A.M., . . . Burrows-Maclean, L. (2006). A practical measure of impairment: Psychometric properties of the impairment rating scale in samples of children with attention deficit hyperactivity disorder and two school-based samples. *Journal of Clinical Child and Adolescent Psychology, 35*, 369–385.

Fabiano, G.A., Pelham, W.E., Coles, E.K., Gnagy, E.M., Chronis-Tuscano, A., & O'Connor, B.C. (2009). A meta-analysis of behavioral treatments for attention-deficit/hyperactivity disorder. *Clinical Psychology Review, 29*, 129–140.

Fabiano, G.A., Pelham, W.E., Jr., Manos, M.J., Gnagy, E.M., Chronis, A.M., Onyago, A.N., . . . Caserta, D.A. (2004). An evaluation of three time-out procedures for children with Attention-Deficit/Hyperactivity Disorder. *Behavior Therapy, 34*, 449–469.

Fabiano, G.A., Vujnovic, R.K., Pelham, W.E., Waschbusch, D.A., Massetti, G.M., Pariseau, M.E., . . . Volker, M. (2010). Enhancing the effectiveness of special education programming for children with attention deficit hyperactivity disorder using a daily report card. *School Psychology Review, 39*, 219–239.

Fallone, G., Owens, J.A., & Deane, J. (2002). Sleepiness in children and adolescents: Clinical implications. *Sleep Medicine Reviews, 6*, 287–306.

Fantuzzo, J., Bulotsky, R., McDermott, P., Mosca, S., & Lutz, M.N. (2003). A multivariate analysis of emotional and behavioral adjustment and preschool educational outcomes. *School Psychology Review, 32*, 185–203.

Faraone, S.V., & Biederman, J. (1997). Do attention deficit hyperactivity disorder and major depression share familial risk factors: *Journal of Nervous and Mental Disease, 185*, 533–541.

Faraone, S.V., & Biederman, J. (2004). *A controlled study of functional impairments in 500 ADHD adults*. Paper presented at the 157th Annual APA Meeting; May 6, 2004, New York.

Faraone, S.V., Biederman, J., Chen, W.J., Milberger. S., Warburton, R., & Tsuang, M.T. (1995). Genetic heterogeneity in attention-deficit hyperactivity disorder (ADHD): Gender, psychiatric comorbidity and maternal ADHD. *Journal of Abnormal Psychology, 104*, 334–345.

Faraone, S.V., Biederman, J., Doyle, A., Murray, K., Petty, C., Adamson, J.J., & Seidman, L. (2006). Neuropsychological studies of late onset and subthreshold diagnoses of adult attention-deficit/hyperactivity disorder. *Biological Psychiatry, 60*, 1081–1087.

Faraone, S.V., Biederman, J., Jetton, J.G., & Tsuang, M.T. (1997). Attention deficit disorder and conduct disorder. Longitudinal evidence for a familial subtype. *Psychological Medicine, 27*, 291–300.

Faraone, S.V., Biederman, J., Lehman, B., Keenan, K., Norman, D., Seidman, L.J., . . . Chen, W. (1993). Evidence for the independent familial transmission of attention deficit hyperactivity disorder and learning disabilities: Results from a family genetic study. *American Journal of Psychiatry, 150*, 891–895.

Faraone, S.V., Biederman, J., Mennin, D., Gershon, J., & Tsuang, M.T. (1996). A prospective four-year follow-up study of children at risk for ADHD: Psychiatric, neuropsychological, and psychosocial outcome. *Journal of the American Academy of Child and Adolescent Psychiatry, 35*, 1449–1459.

Faraone, S.V., Biederman, J., Mennin, D., Wozniak, J., & Spencer, T. (1997). Attention-deficit hyperactivity disorder with bipolar disorder: A familial subtype? *Journal of the American Academy of Child and Adolescent Psychiatry, 36*, 1378–1387.

Faraone, S.V., Biederman, J., & Monuteaux, M.C. (2000). Toward guidelines for pedigree selection in genetic studies of attention deficit hyperactivity disorder. *Genetic Epidemiology, 18*, 1–16.

Faraone, S.V., Biederman, J., & Monuteaux, M.C. (2001). Attention deficit hyperactivity disorder with bipolar disorder in girls: Further evidence for a familial subtype? *Journal of Affective Disorders, 64*, 19–26.

Faraone, S.V., Biederman, J., Morley, C.P., & Spencer, T.J. (2008). Effect of stimulants on height and weight: A review of the literature. *Journal of the American Academy of Child and Adolescent Psychiatry, 47*, 994–1009.

Faraone, S.V., & Buitelaar, J. (2010). Comparing the efficacy of stimulants for ADHD in children and adolescents using meta-analysis. *European Child & Adolescent Psychiatry, 19*, 353–364.

Faraone, S.V., & Glatt, S.J. (2010). A comparison of the efficacy of medications for adult attention-deficit/hyperactivity disorder using meta-analysis of effect sizes. *Journal of Clinical Psychiatry, 71*, 754–763.

Faraone, S.V., Perlis, R.H., Doyle, A.E., Smoller, J.W., Goralnick, J.J., Holmgren, M.A., & Sklar, P. (2005). Molecular genetics of attention-deficit/hyperactivity disorder. *Biological Psychiatry, 57*, 1313–1323.

Faraone, S.V., Spencer, T., Aleardi, M., Pagano, C., & Biederman, J. (2004). Meta-analysis of the efficacy of methylphenidate for treating adult attention-deficit/hyperactivity disorder. *Journal of Clinical Psychopharmacology, 24*, 24–29.

Faraone, S., Wilens, T., Petty, C., Antshel, K., Spencer, T., & Biederman, J. (2007). Substance use among ADHD adults: Implications of late onset and subthreshold diagnoses. *American Journal on Addictions, 16*(Suppl. 1), 24–32.

Farrell, L., & Barrett, P. (2006). Obsessive-compulsive disorder across developmental trajectory: Cognitive processing of threat in children, adolescents and adults. *British Journal of Psychology, 97 (Pt 1)*, 95–114.

Favuluri, M.N., Yang, S., Kamineni, K., Passarotti, A.M., Srinivasan, G., Harral, E.M., . . . Zhou, X.J. (2009). Diffusion tensor imaging study of white matter fiber tracts in pediatric bipolar disorder and attention-deficit/hyperactivity disorder. *Biological Psychiatry, 65*, 586–593.

Fayyad, J., De Graaf, R., Kessler, R., Alonso, J., Angermeyer, M., Demyttenaere, K., . . . Lépine, J.P. (2007). Cross—national prevalence and correlates of adult attention—deficit hyperactivity disorder. *British Journal of Psychiatry, 190*, 402–409.

Fedele, D.A., Lefler, E.K., Hartung, C.M., & Canu, W.H. (2012). Sex differences in the manifestation of ADHD in emerging adults. *Journal of Attention Disorders, 16*, 109–117.

Fehlings, D.L., Roberts, W., Humphries, T., & Dawe, G. (1991). Attention deficit hyperactivity Ddisorder: Does cognitive behavioral therapy improve home behavior? *Journal of Developmental & Behavioral Pediatrics, 12*, 223–228.

Feingold, B. (1975). *Why your child is hyperactive*. New York: Random House.

Feldman, H.M., Dale, P.S., Campbell, T.F., Colborn, D.K., Jurs-Lasky. M., Rockette, H.E., & Paradise, J.L. (2005). Concurrent and predictive validity of parent reports of child language at ages 2 and 3 years. *Child Development, 76*, 856–868.

Fergusson, D.M., Horwood, J., & Lynskey, T. (1993). Prevalence and comorbidity of DSM-III-R diagnoses in a birth cohort of 15 year olds. *Journal of the American Academy of Child and Adolescent Psychiatry, 32*, 1127–1134.

Fergusson, D.M., & Horwood, L.J. (1992). Attention deficit and reading achievement. *Journal of Child Psychology and Psychiatry, 33*, 375–385.

Fergusson, D.M., Horwood, L.J., & Ridder, E.M. (2007). Conduct and attentional problems in children and adolescence and later substance use. *Drug and Alcohol Dependence, 88*, S14—S26.

Fernández-Aranda, F., Agüera, Z., Castro, R., Jiménez-Murcia, S., Ramos-Quiroga, J.A., Bosch, R., . . . Sánchez, I. (2013). ADHD symptomatology in eating disorders: a secondary psychopathological measure of severity? *BMC Psychiatryy, 13*, 166.

Ferrin, M., & Vance, A. (2012). Examination of neurological subtle signs in ADHD as a clinical tool for the diagnosis and their relationship to spatial working memory. *Journal of Child Psychology and Psychiatry 53*, 390–400.

Field, S., Parker, D.R., Sawilowsky, S., & Rolands, L. (2013). Assessing the impact of ADHD coaching services on university students' learning skills, self-regulation, and well-being. *Journal of Postsecondary Education and Disability, 26*, 67–81.

Fiks, A.G., Mayne, S., DeBartolo, E., Power T.J., & Guevara, J.P. (2013). Parental preferences and goals regarding ADHD treatment. *Pediatrics, 132*, 692–703.

Filipek, P. (1999). Neuroimaging in the developmental disorders: The state of science. *Journal of Child Psychology and Psychiatry, 40*, 113–128.

Findling, R.L. (2008). Evolution of the treatment of Attention-Deficit/Hyperactivity Disorder in children: A review. *Clinical Therapeutics, 30*, 942–957.

First, M.B., Pincus, H.A., Levine, J.B., Williams, J.B., Ustun, B., & Peele, R. (2004). Clinical utility as a criterion for revising psychiatric diagnoses. *American Journal of Psychiatry, 16*, 946–954.

First, M.B., & Westen, D. (2007). Classification for clinical practice: How to make ICD and DSM better able to serve clinicians. *International Review of Psychiatry, 19*, 473–481.

Fischer, A.G., Bau, C.H.D., Grevet, E.H., Salgado, C.A., Victor, M.M., Kalil, K.L., . . . Belmonte-de-Abreu, P. (2007). The role of comorbid major depressive disorder in the clinical presentation of adult ADHD. *Journal of Psychiatric Research, 41*, 991–996.

Fischer, M. (1990). Parenting stress and the child with attention deficit hyperactivity disorder. *Journal of Clinical Child Psychology. Special Issue: The Stresses of Parenting, 19*, 337–346.

Fischer, M., Barkley, R.A., Edelbrock, C.S., & Smallish, L. (1990). The adolescent outcome of hyperactive children diagnosed by research criteria, II: Academic, attentional and neuropsychological status. *Journal of Consulting and Clinical Psychology, 58*, 550–588.

Fischer, M., Barkley, R.A., Edelbrock, C.S., & Smallish, L. (1993). The adolescent outcome of hyperactive children diagnosed by research criteria, V: Predictors of outcome. *Journal of the American Academy of Child and Adolescent Psychiatry, 32*, 324–332.

Fischer, M., Barkley, R.A., Fletcher, K.E., & Smallish, L. (1993). The stability of dimensions of behavior in ADHD and normal children over an 8-year followup. *Journal of Abnormal Child Psychology, 21*, 315–337.

Fleming, A.P., & McMahon, R.J. (2012). Developmental context and treatment principles for ADHD among college students. *Clinical Child and Family Psychology Review, 15*, 303–329.

Fleming, A.P., McMahon, R.J., Moran, L.R., Peterson, A.P., & Dreessen, A. (2015). Pilot randomized controlled trial of dialectical behavior therapy group skills training for ADHD among college students. *Journal of Attention Disorders, 19*, 260–271.

Fletcher, K.E., Fischer, M., Barkley, R.A., & Smallish, L. (1996). A sequential analysis of the mother-adolescent interactions of ADHD, ADHD/ODD, and normal teenagers during neutral and conflict discussions. *Journal of Abnormal Child Psychology, 24*, 271–297.

Flicek, M. (1992). Social status of boys with both academic problems and attention-deficit hyperactivity disorder. *Journal of Abnormal Child Psychology, 20*, 353–366.

Fliers, E.A., Buitelaar, J.K., Maras, A., Bul, K., Höhle, E., Faraone, S.V., . . . Rommelse, N.N. (2013). ADHD is a risk factor for overweight and obesity in children. *Journal of Developmental and Behavioral Pediatrics, 34*, 566–574.

Fliers, E.A., Rommelse, N., Vermeulen, S.H., Altink, M., Buschgens, C.J., Faraone, S.V., . . . Buitelaar, J.K. (2008). Motor coordination problems in children and adolescents with ADHD rated by parents and teachers: effects of age and gender. *Journal of Neural Transmission, 115*, 211–220.

Fliers, E.A., Vasquez, A.A., Poelmans, G., Rommelse, N., Altink, M., Buschgens, C., . . . Miranda, A. (2012). Genome-wide association study of motor coordination problems in ADHD identifies genes for brain and muscle function. *World Journal of Biological Psychiatry, 13*, 211–222.

Fliers, E., Vermeulen, S., Rijsdijk, F., Altink, M., Buschgens, C., Rommelse, N., . . . Franke, B. (2009). ADHD and poor motor performance from a family genetic perspective. *Journal of the American Academy of Child & Adolescent Psychiatry, 48*, 25–34.

Flory, K., & Lynam, D.R. (2003). The relation between attention deficit hyperactivity disorder and substance abuse: What role does conduct disorder play? *Clinical Child and Family Psychology Review, 6*, 1–16.

Flory, K., Molina, B.S.G., Pelham, W.E., Gnagy, E., & Smith, B. (2006). Childhood ADHD predicts risky sexual behavior in young adulthood. *Journal of Clinical Child and Adolescent Psychology, 35*, 571–577.

Forbush, K.T., Shaw, M., Graeber, M.A., Hovick, L., Meyer, V.J., Moser, D., . . . Black, D.W. (2008). Neuropsychological characteristics and personality traits in pathological gambling. *CNS Spectrums, 13*, 306–315.

Foster, E.M., Jensen, P.S., Schlander, M., Pelham, W.E., Hechtman, L., Arnold, L.E., . . . Wigal, T. (2007). Treatment for ADHD: Is more complex treatment cost effective for more complex cases? *Health Services Research, 42*, 165–182.

Fox, D.J., Tharp, D.F., & Fox, L.C. (2005). Neurofeedback: an alternative and efficacious treatment for attention deficit hyperactivity disorder. *Applied Psychophysiology and Biofeedback, 30*, 365–373.

Fraga, M.F., Ballestar, E., Paz, M.F., Ropero, S., Setien, F., Ballestar, M.L., . . . Esteller, M. (2005). Epigenetic differences arise during the lifetime of monozygotic twins. *Proceedings of the National Academy of Sciences, 102*, 10604–10609.

Franc, N., & Purper-Ouakil, D. (2009). ADHD medications and ethnicity. *Current Attention Disorders Reports, 1*, 159–164.

Frances, A., Pincus, A., Widiger, T., & Davis, H.A. (1989). The development of DSM-IV. *Archives of General Psychiatry, 46*, 373–375.

Frank, H., Stewart, E., Walther, M., Benito, K., Freeman, J., Conelea, C., & Garcia, A. (2014). Hoarding behavior among young children with obsessive-compulsive disorder. *Journal of Obsessive-Compulsive and Related Disorders, 3*, 6–11.

Frank, M.J. (2005). Dynamic dopamine modulation in the basal ganglia: A neurocomputational account of cognitive deficits in medicated and nonmedicated Parkinsonism. *Journal of Cognitive Neuroscience, 17*, 51–72.

Franke, B., Faraone, S.V., Asherson, P. Buitelaar, J., Bau, C.H., Ramos-Quirogra, J.A., . . . Reif, A. (2012). The genetics of attention-deficit/hyperactivity disorder in adults, a review. *Molecular Psychiatry, 18*, 1–28.

Franke, B., Neale, B.M., & Faraone, S.V. (2009). Genome-wide association studies in ADHD. *Human Genetics, 126*, 13–50.

Frankel, F., Myatt, R., Cantwell, D.P., & Feinberg, D.T. (1997). Parent-assisted transfer of children's social skills training: Effects on children with and without attention-deficit hyperactivity disorder. *Journal of the American Academy of Child and Adolescent Psychiatry, 36*, 1056–1064.

Frazier, T.W., Demaree, H.A., & Youngstrom, E.A. (2004). Meta-analysis of intellectual and neuropsychological test performance in attention-deficit/hyperactivity disorder. *Neuropsychology, 18*, 543–555.

Frazier, T.W., Youngstrom, E.A., Glutting, J.J., & Watkins, M.W. (2007). ADHD and achievement meta-analysis of the child, adolescent, and adult literatures and a concomitant study with college students. *Journal of Learning Disabilities, 40*, 49–65.

Fredriksen, M., Halmoy, A. Faraone, S.V., & Haavik, J. (2013). Long-term efficacy and safety of treatment with stimulants and atomoxetine in adult ADHD: A review of controlled and naturalistic studies. *European Neuropsychopharmacology, 23*, 508–527.

Freeman, R.D., Fast, D.K., Burd, L., Kerbeshian, J., Robertson, M.M., & Sandor, P. (2000). An international perspective on Tourette syndrome: Selected findings from 3500 individuals in 22 countries. *Developmental Medicine and Child Neurology, 42*, 436–447.

Freibergs, V., & Douglas, V. (1969) Concept learning in hyperactive and normal children. *Journal of Abnormal Psychology, 74*, 388–395.

Friars, P.M., & Mellor, D.J. (2007). Drop out from behavioral management training programs for ADHD: A prospective study. *Journal of Child and Family Studies, 16*, 427–441.

Frick, P.J., Lahey, B.B., Applegate, B., Kerdyck, L., Ollendick, T., Hynd, G.W., . . . Waldman, I. (1994). DSM-IV field trials for the disruptive behavior disorders: Symptom utility estimates. *Journal of the American Academy of Child and Adolescent Psychiatry, 33*, 529–539.

Friedberg, R.D., & McClure, J.M. (2015). *Clinical practice of cognitive therapy with children and adolescents: The nuts and bolts*. New York: Guilford Press.

Frith, U. (1995). Dyslexia: Can we have a shared theoretical framework? *Educational and Child Psychology, 12*, 6–17.

Frodl, T. (2010). Comorbidity of ADHD and substance use disorder (SUD): A neuroimaging perspective. *Journal of Attention Disorders, 14*, 109–120.

Frodl, T., & Skokauskas, N. (2012). Meta-analysis of structural MRI studies in children and adults with attention deficit hyperactivity disorder indicates treatment effects. *Acta Psychiatrica Scandinavica, 125*, 114–126.

Froelich, J., Doepfner, M., & Lehmkuhl, G. (2002). Effects of combined cognitive behavioural treatment with parent management training in ADHD. *Behavioural and Cognitive Psychotherapy, 30*, 111–115.

Fuchs, L.S., Compton, D.L., Fuchs, D., Paulsen, K., Bryant, J.D., & Hamlett, C.L. (2005). The prevention, identification, and cognitive determinants of math difficulty. *Journal of Educational Psychology, 97*, 493–513.

Fullana, M.A., Vilagut, G., Mataix-Cols, D., Adroher, N.D., Bruffaerts, R., Bunting, B., . . . Graaf, R. (2013). Is ADHD in childhood associated with lifetime hoarding symptoms? An epidemiological study. *Depression and Anxiety, 30*, 741e748.

Fuller, C.G., & Sabatino, D.A. (1998). Diagnosis and treatment considerations with comorbid developmentally disabled populations. *Journal of Clinical Psychology, 54*, 1–10.

Fuller, P.M., Gooley, J.J., & Saper, C.B. (2006). Neurobiology of the sleep-wake cycle: sleep architecture, circadian regulation, and regulatory feedback. *Journal of Biological Rhythms, 21*, 482–493.

Furman, L.M. (2008). Attention-deficit hyperactivity disorder (ADHD): Does new research support old concepts? *Journal of Child Neurology, 23*, 775–84.

Gadde, K.M., Yonish, G.M., Wagner, H.R., Foust, M.S., & Allison, D.B. (2006). Atomoxetine for weight reduction in obese women: a preliminary randomised controlled trial. *International Journal of Obesity, 30*, 1138–1142.

Gadow, K.D., DeVincent, C.J., & Pomeroy, J. (2006). ADHD symptom subtypes in children with pervasive developmental disorder. *Journal of Autism and Developmental Disorders, 36*, 271–283.

Gadow, K.D., & Sprafkin, J. (1997). *Child Symptom Inventory 4: Norms manual*. Stony Brook, NY: Checkmate Plus.

Gadow, K.D., Sprafkin, J., & Weiss, M. (2004). *Manual for the Adult Self Report Inventory and Adult Symptom Inventory*. Stony Brook, NY: Checkmate Plus.

Gagne, J.R., Saudino, K.J., & Asherson, P. (2011). The genetic etiology of inhibitory control and behavior problems at 24 months of age. *Journal of Child Psychology and Psychiatry, 52*, 1155–1163.

Galéra, C., Cote, S.M., Bouvard, M.P., Pingault, J.B., Melchior, M., Michel, G., . . . Tremblay, R.E. (2011). Early risk factors for hyperactivity-impulsivity and inattention trajectories from age 17 months to 8 years. *Archives of General Psychiatry, 68*, 1267–1275.

Galéra, C., Melchior, M., Chastang, J.F., Bouvard, M.P., & Fombonne, E. (2009). Childhood and adolescent hyperactivity-inattention symptoms and academic achievement 8 years later: The GAZEL Youth study. *Psychological Medicine, 39*, 1895–1906.

Gallagher, R., & Blader, J. (2001). The diagnosis and neuropsychological assessment of adult Attention Deficit/Hyperactivity Disorder. *Annals of the New York Academy of Sciences, 931*, 148–171.

Galland, B.C., Tripp, E., & Taylor, B.J. (2010). The sleep of children with attention deficit hyperactivity disorder on and off methylphenidate: a matched case—control study. *Journal of Sleep Research, 19*, 366–373.

Galvan, A. (2010). Neural plasticity of development and learning. *Human Brain Mapping, 31*, 879–890.

Gani, C., Birbaumer, N., & Strehl, U. (2008). Long term effects after feedback of slow cortical potentials and of theta-beta amplitudes in children with attention-deficit/hyperactivity disorder (ADHD). *International Journal of Bioelectromagnetism, 10*, 209–232.

Garfield, C.F., Dorsey, E.R., Zhu, S., Huskamp, H.A., Conti, R., Dusetzina, S.B., . . . Alexander, G.C. (2012). Trends in attention deficit hyperactivity disorder ambulatory diagnosis and medical treatment in the United States, 2000–2010. *Academic Pediatrics, 12*, 110–116.

Gargaro, B.A., Rinehart, N.J., Bradshaw, J.L., Tonge, B.J., & Sheppard, D.M. (2011). Autism and ADHD: How far have we come in the comorbidity debate? *Neuroscience and Biobehavioral Reviews, 35*, 1081–1098.

Garland, A.F., Lau, A.S., Yeh, M., McCabe, K.M., Hough, R.L., & Landsverk, J.A. (2005). Racial and ethnic differences in utilization of mental health services among high-risk youths. *American Journal of Psychiatry, 162*, 1336–1343.

Garon, N., Bryson, S.E., & Smith, I.M. (2008). Executive function in preschoolers: A review using an integrative framework. *Psychological Bulletin, 134*, 31–60.

Gartstein, M.A., Crawford, J., & Robertson, C.D. (2008). Early markers of language and attention: Mutual contributions and the impact of parent-infant interactions. *Child Psychiatry and Human Development, 39*, 9–26.

Gathje, A.R., Lewandowski, J.L., & Gordon, M. (2008). The role of impairment in the diagnosis of ADHD. *Journal of Attention Disorders, 11*, 529–537.

Gatzke-Kopp, L.M., & Beauchaine, T.P. (2007). Direct and passive prenatal nicotine exposure and the development of externalizing psychopathology. *Child Psychiatry and Human Development, 38*, 255–269.

Gau, S.S., Kessler, R.C., Tseng, W., Wu, Y., Chiu, Y., Yeh, C., & Hwu, H. (2007). Association between sleep problems and symptoms of attention-deficit/hyperactivity disorder in young adults. *Sleep, 30*, 195–201.

Gaub, M., & Carlson, C.L. (1997). Gender differences in ADHD: A meta-analysis and critical review. *Journal of American Academy of Child and Adolescent Psychiatry, 36*, 1036–1045.

Gautier, T., & Droit-Volet, S. (2002). Attentional distraction and time perception in children. *International Journal of Psychology, 37*, 27–34.

Gayan, J., Willcutt, E.G., Fisher, S.E., Francks, C., Cardon, L.R., Olson, R.K., . . . DeFries, J.C. (2005). Bivariate linkage scan for reading disability and attention deficit/ hyperactivity disorder localizes pleiotropic loci. *Journal of Child Psychology and Psychiatry, 46*, 1045–1056.

Gayleard, J.L., & Mychailyszyn, M.P. (2017). Atomoxetine treatment for children and adolescents with Attention-Deficit/Hyperactivity Disorder (ADHD): A comprehensive meta-analysis of outcomes on parent-rated core symptomatology. *ADHD Attention Deficit and Hyperactivity Disorders*. https://doi.org/10.1007/s12402-017-0216-y

Geary, D.C. (2004). Mathematics and learning disabilities. *Journal of Learning Disabilities, 37*, 4–15.

Geladé, K., Bink, M., Janssen, T.W., van Mourik, R., Maras, A., & Oosterlaan, J. (2016). An RCT into the effects of neurofeedback on neurocognitive functioning compared to stimulant medication and physical activity in children with ADHD. *European Child & Adolescent Psychiatry.* https://doi.org/10.1007/s00787-016-0902-x

Geller, D.A., Petty, C., Vivas, F., Johnson, J., Pauls, D., & Biederman, J. (2007). Further evidence for co-segregation between pediatric obsessive compulsive disorder and attention deficit hyperactivity disorder: A familial risk analysis. *Biological Psychiatry, 61*, 1388–1394.

Gerdes, A. C., Haack, L.M., & Schneider, B.W. (2012). Parental functioning in families of children with ADHD: Evidence for behavioral parent training and importance of clinically meaningful change. *Journal of Attention Disorders, 16*, 147–156.

Gerdes, A.C., Hoza, B., Arnold, L.E., Pelham, W.E., Swanson, J.M., Wigal, T., & Jensen, P.S. (2007). Maternal depressive symptomatology and parenting behavior: Exploration of possible mediators. *Journal of Abnormal Child Psychology, 35*, 705–714.

Gershon, J. (2002). A meta-analytic review of gender differences in ADHD. *Journal of Attention Disorders, 5*, 143–154.

Geurts, H.M., & Embrechts, M. (2008). Language profiles in ASD, SLI, and ADHD. *Journal of Autism and Developmental Disorders, 38*, 1931–1943.

Geurts, H.M., Verte, S., Oosterlaan, J., Roeyers, H., & Sergeant, J.A. (2004). How specific are executive functioning deficits in attention deficit hyperactivity disorder and autism? *Journal of Child Psychology and Psychiatry, 45*, 836–54.

Geuze, R.H. (2005). Postural control in children with developmental coordination disorder. *Neural Plasticity, 12*, 183–196.

Gevensleben, H., Holl, B., Albrecht, B., Vogel, C., Schlamp, D., Kratz, O., . . . Heinrich, H. (2009). Is neurofeedback an efficacious treatment for ADHD? A randomized controlled clinical trial. *Journal of Child Psychology and Psychiatry, 50*, 780–789.

Gevensleben, H., Kleemeyer, M., Rothenberger, L., Studer, P., Flaig-Rohr, A., Moll, G., Rothenberger, A., & Heinrich, H. (2014). Neurofeedback in ADHD: Further pieces of the puzzle. *Brain Topography, 27*, 20–32.

Gevensleben, H., Rothenberger, A., Moll, G.H., & Heinrich, H. (2012). Neurofeedback in children with ADHD: validation and challenges. *Expert Review of Neurotherapeutics, 12*, 447–460.

Ghelani, K., Sidhu, R., Jain, U., & Tannock, R. (2004). Reading comprehension and reading related abilities in adolescents with reading disabilities and attention-deficit/hyperactivity disorder. *Dyslexia, 10*, 364–384.

Gibbins, C., & Weiss, M (2007). Clinical recommendations in current practice guidelines for diagnosis and treatment of ADHD in adults. *Current Psychiatry Reports, 9*, 420–426.

Giblin, J.M., & Strobel, A.L. (2011). Effect of lisdexamfetamine dimesylate on sleep in children with ADHD. *Journal of Attention Disorders,15*, 491–498.

Gibson, A.P., Bettinger, T.L., Patel, N.C., & Crismon, M.L. (2006). Atomoxetine versus stimulants for treatment of attention deficit/hyperactivity disorder. *Annals of Pharmacotherapy, 40*, 1134–1142.

Gilger, J.W., & Kaplan, B.J. (2001). Atypical brain development: A conceptual framework for understanding developmental learning disabilities. *Developmental Neuropsychology, 20*, 465–481.

Gillam, R., Loeb, D., & Friel-Patti, S. (2001). Looking back: A summary of five exploratory studies of Fast ForWord. *American Journal of Speech-Language Pathology, 10*, 269–273.

Gillberg, C. (2003). Deficits in attention, motor control, and perception: a brief review. *Archives of Disease in Childhood, 88*, 904–910.

Gillberg, C. (2010). The ESSENCE in child psychiatry: Early symptomatic syndromes eliciting neurodevelopmental clinical examinations. *Research in Developmental Disabilities, 31*, 1543–1551.

Gillberg, C., Gillberg, I.C., Rasmussen, P., Kadesjo, B., Soderstrom, H., Rastam, M. . . . Niklasson, L. (2004). Co-existing disorders in ADHD—implications for diagnosis and intervention. *European Child and Adolescent Psychiatry, 13*(Suppl 1), I80–I92.

Gillberg, C., & Kadesjö, B. (2003). Why bother about clumsiness? The implications of having developmental coordination disorder (DCD). *Neural Plasticity, 10*, 59–68.

Gillberg, C., & Kadesjö, B. (2009). ADHD with Developmental Coordination Disorder. In. T. Brown (Ed.) *ADHD Comorbidities. Handbook for ADHD complications in children and adults* (pp. 305–314). Washington, DC: American Psychiatric.
Gilliam, J. E. (1995). *Attention-Deficit/Hyperactivity Disorder Test.* USA: PRO-ED.
Gilliam, W. S., & Demesquita, P. B. (2000). The relationship between language and cognitive development and emotional-behavior problems in financially-disadvantaged preschoolers: A longitudinal investigation. *Early Child Development and Care, 162*, 9–24.
Gillies, D., Sinn, J. K., Lad, S. S., Leach, M. J., & Ross, M. J. (2012). Polyunsaturated fatty acids (PUFA) for attention deficit hyperactivity disorder (ADHD) in children and adolescents. *Cochrane Database of Systematic Reviews, 7*, CD007986. https://doi.org/10.1002/14651858.CD007986.pub2
Gingerich, K. J., Turnock, P., Litfin, J. K., & Rosen, L. A. (1998). Diversity and attention deficit hyperactivity disorder. *Journal of Clinical Psychology, 54*, 415–426.
Ginsberg, Y., Hirvikoski, T., & Lindefors, N. (2010). Attention deficit hyperactivity disorder (ADHD) among longer-term prison inmates is a prevalent, persistent and disabling disorder. *BMC Psychiatry, 10*, 112.
Gizer, I. R., Ficks, C., Waldman, I. D. (2009). Candidate gene studies of ADHD: A meta-analytic review. *Human Genetics, 126*, 51–90.
Glover, V. (2011). Annual Research Review: Prenatal stress and the origins of psychopathology: An evolutionary perspective. *Journal of Child Psychology and Psychiatry, 52*, 356–367.
Glow, P. H., & Glow, R. A. (1979). Hyperkinetic impulse disorder: A developmental defect of motivation. *Genetic Psychological Monographs, 100*, 159–231.
Golan, N., Shahar, E., Ravid, S., & Pillar, G. (2004). Sleep disorders and daytime sleepiness in children with attention-deficit/hyperactive disorder. *Sleep, 27*, 261–266.
Goldsmith, M., Singh, M., & Chang, K. (2011). Antidepressants and psychostimulants in pediatric populations. *Pediatric Drugs, 13*, 225–243.
Goldstein, K. (1942). *After-effects of brain injuries in war.* New York: Grune and Stratton.
Goldstein, L. H., Harvey, E. A., & Friedman-Weieneth, J. L. (2007). Examining subtypes of behavior problems among 3-year-old children, part III: Investigating differences in parenting practices and parenting stress. *Journal of Abnormal Child Psychology, 35*, 125–136.
Goldstein, S. (2005). Editorial: Coaching as a treatment for ADHD. *Journal of Attention Disorders, 9*, 379–81.
Goldstein, S., & Goldstein, M. (1998). *Managing Attention Deficit Hyperactivity Disorder in Children* (2nd ed.). Chichester, NJ: John Wiley & Sons, Inc
González-Castro, P., Cueli, M., Rodríguez, C., García, T., & Álvarez, L. (2016). Efficacy of neurofeedback versus pharmacological support in subjects with ADHD. *Applied Psychophysiology and Biofeedback, 41*, 17–25.
Goodman, D. W. (2009). ADHD in adults: Update for clinicians on diagnosis and assessment. *Primary Psychiatry, 16*, 38–47.
Goodman, L. S., & Gilman, A. (Eds.). (1975). *The pharmacological basis of therapeutics* (5th ed.). New York: Macmillan.
Goodman, R. (1997). The Strengths and Difficulties Questionnaire: a research note. *Journal of Child Psychology and Psychiatry, 38*, 581–586.
Goodman, R., Ford, T., Richards, H., Gatward, R., & Meltzer, H. (2000). The development and well-being assessment: description and initial validation of an integrated assessment of child and adolescent psychopathology. *Journal of Child Psychology and Psychiatry, 41*, 645–655.
Goodwin, A., Salomone, S., Bolton, P., Charman, T., Jones, E. J., Pickles, A., . . . Johnson, M. H. (2016). Attention training for infants at familial risk of ADHD (INTERSTAARS): study protocol for a randomised controlled trial. *Trials, 17*(1), 608.
Gordon, M., Antshel, K., Faraone, S., Barkley, R., Lewandowski, L., Hudziak, J. J., . . . Cunningham, C. (2006). Symptoms versus impairment: The case for respecting DSV-IV's Criterion D. *Journal of Attention Disorders, 9*, 465–475.
Gordon, M., Barkley, R. A., & Lovett, B. J. (2006). Tests and observational measures. In R. A. Barkley (Ed.), *Attention-deficit hyperactivity disorder: A handbook for diagnosis and treatment* (3rd ed., pp. 369–388). New York: Guilford Press.

Gordon, M., McClure, F. D., & Aylward, G. P. (1996). *The Gordon diagnostic system*. DeWitt, NY: GSI.

Gordon, M., & Mettelman, B. B. (1994). Gender differences in ADHD referrals: IQ, laboratory measures and behaviour ratings. *ADHD/Hyperactivity Newsletter*, *21*, 7–9.

Gormley, M. J., Pinho, T., Pollack, B., Puzino, K., Franklin, M. K., Busch, C., . . . Anastopoulos, A. D. (2015). Impact of study skills and parent education on first-year GPA among college students with and without ADHD: A moderated mediation model. *Journal of Attention Disorders*. https://doi.org/1087054715594422

Gottesman, I. I., & Gould, T. D. (2003). The endophenotype concept in psychiatry: Etymology and strategic intentions. *American Journal of Psychiatry*, *160*, 636–645.

Goudreau, S. B., & Knight, M. (2015). Executive function coaching assisting with transitioning from secondary to postsecondary education. *Journal of Attention Disorders*. https://doi.org/1087054715583355

Gow, R. V., & Hibbeln, J. R. (2014). Omega-3 and treatment implications in Attention Deficit Hyperactivity Disorder (ADHD) and associated behavioral symptoms. *Lipid Technology*, *26*, 7–10.

Gowey, M. A., Stromberg, S. E., Lim, C. S., & Janicke, D. M. (2017). The moderating role of body dissatisfaction in the relationship between ADHD symptoms and disordered eating in pediatric overweight and obesity. *Children's Health Care*, *46*, 15–33.

Graczyk, P. A., Atkins, M. S., Jackson, M. M., Letendre, J. A., Kim-Cohen, J., Baumann, B. L., & McCoy, J. (2005). Urban educators' perceptions of interventions for students with attention deficit hyperactivity disorder: A preliminary investigation. *Behavioral Disorders*, *30*, 95–105.

Grados, M. A., Mathews, C. A., & Tourette Syndrome Association International Consortium for Genetics. (2008). Latent class analysis of Gilles de la Tourette syndrome using comorbidities: Clinical and genetic implications. *Biological Psychiatry*, *64*, 219–225.

Graetz, B. W., Sawyer, M. G., Hazell, P. L., Arney, F., & Baghurst, P. (2001). Validity of DSM-IV ADHD subtypes in a nationally representative sample of Australian children and adolescents. *Journal of the American Academy of Child and Adolescent Psychiatry*, *40*, 1410–1417.

Grall-Bronnec, M., Wainstein, L., Augy, J., Bouju, G., Feuillet, F., Venisse, J. L., & Sebille-Rivain, V. (2011). Attention deficit hyperactivity disorder among pathological and at-risk gamblers seeking treatment: A hidden disorder. *European Addiction Research*, *17*, 231–240.

Granero, R., Penelo, E., Stinchfield, R., Fernandez-Aranda, F., Savvidou, L. G., Fröberg, F., . . . Jiménez-Murcia, S. (2014). Is pathological gambling moderated by age? *Journal of Gambling Studies*, *30*, 475–492.

Granic, I., & Patterson, G. R. (2006). Toward a comprehensive model of antisocial development: A dynamic systems approach. *Psychological Review*, *113*, 101–131.

Grattan, M., & Eslinger, J. (1991). Frontal lobe damage in children and adults: A comparative review. *Developmental Neuropsychology*, *7*, 283–326.

Gray, S. A., Carter, A. S., Briggs-Gowan, M. J., Jones, S. M., & Wagmiller, R. L. (2014). Growth trajectories of early aggression, overactivity, and inattention: Relations to second-grade reading. *Developmental Psychology*, *50*, 2255–2263.

Gray, S. A., Chaban, P., Martinussen, R., Golberg, R., Gotlieb, H., Kronitz, R., . . . Tannock, R. (2012). Effects of a computerized working memory training program on working memory, attention, and academics in adolescents with severe LD and comorbid ADHD: a randomized controlled trial. *Journal of Child Psychology and Psychiatry*, *53*, 1277–1284.

Green, D., Chambers, M. E., & Sugden, D. A. (2008). Does subtype of developmental coordination disorder count: Is there a differential effect on outcome following intervention? *Human Movement Science*, *27*, 363–382.

Green, J., & Goldwyn, R. (2002). Annotation: Attachment disorganisation and psychopathology: new findings in attachment research and their potential implications for developmental psychopathology in childhood. *Journal of Child Psychology and Psychiatry*, *43*, 835–846.

Green, L., & Myerson, J. (2004). A discounting framework for choice with delayed and probabilistic rewards. *Psychological Bulletin*, *130*, 769–792.

Green, L., Myerson, J., & Ostaszewski, P. (1999). Amount of reward has opposite effects on the discounting of delayed and probabilistic outcomes. *Journal of Experimental Psychology: Learning, Memory, and Cognition*, *25*, 418–427.

Greenberg, L. M., Corman, C. L., & Kindschi, C. L. (2001). *Test of variables of attention*. Los Alamitos, CA: Universal Attention Disorders.

Greenhill, L. L., Findling, R. L., & Swanson, J. M. (2002). A double-blind, placebo-controlled study of modified-release methylphenidate in children with attention-deficit/hyperactivity disorder. *Pediatrics*, *109*, e39–e39.

Greenhill, L., Kollins, S., Abikoff, H., McCracken, J., Riddle, M., Swanson, J., . . . Cooper, T. (2006). Efficacy and safety of immediate-release methylphenidate treatment for preschoolers with ADHD. *Journal of the American Academy of Child and Adolescent Psychiatry*, *45*, 1284–1293.

Gregory, A. M., Agnew-Blais, J. C., Matthews, T., Moffitt, T. E., & Arseneault, L. (2016). ADHD and sleep quality: Longitudinal analyses from childhood to early adulthood in a twin cohort. *Journal of Clinical Child and Adolescent Psychology*, 1–11.

Gremillion, M. L., & Martel, M. M. (2012). Semantic language as a mechanism explaining the association between ADHD symptoms and reading and mathematics underachievement. *Abnormal Child Psychology*, *40*, 1339–1349.

Gremillion, M. L., & Martel, M. M. (2014). Merely misunderstood?: Receptive, expressive and pragmatic language in young children with disruptive behavior disorders. *Journal of Clinical Child and Adolescent Psychology*, *43*, 765–776.

Gresham, F. M., Watson, T. S., & Skinner, C. H. (2001). Functional behavioral assessment: Principles, procedures, and future directions. *School Psychology Review*, *30*, 156–172.

Greven, C. U., Kovas, Y., Willcutt, E. G., Petrill, S. A., & Plomin, R. (2014). Evidence for shared genetic risk between ADHD symptoms and reduced mathematics ability: a twin study. *Journal of Child Psychology and Psychiatry*, *55*, 39–48.

Grodzinsky, G. M., & Diamond, R. (1992). Frontal lobe functioning in boys with attention-deficit hyperactivity disorder. *Developmental Neuropsychology*, *8*, 427–445.

Groenman, A. P., Oosterlaan, J., Rommelse, N. N., Franke, B., Greven, C. U., Hoekstra, P. J., . . . Faraone, S. V. (2013). Stimulant treatment for attention-deficit hyperactivity disorder and risk of developing substance use disorder. *British Journal of Psychiatry*, *203*, 112–119.

Gross, M. D. (1995). Origin of stimulant use for treatment of attention deficit disorder. *American Journal of Psychiatry*, *152*, 298–299.

Grosswald, S. J. (2015). Evolution of a disorder and insights into prevention of ADHD. In J. M. Norvilitis (Ed.), *ADHD—New directions in diagnosis and treatment* (pp. 279–292). InTech. https://doi.org/10.5772/61069

Gruber, R. (2009). Sleep characteristics of children and adolescents with attention deficit-hyperactivity disorder. *Child and Adolescent Psychiatric Clinics of North America*, *18*, 863–876.

Gruber, R., Fontil, L., Bergmame, L., Wiebe, S. T., Amsel, R., Frenette, S., & Carrier, J. (2012). Contributions of circadian tendencies and behavioral problems to sleep onset problems of children with ADHD. *BMC Psychiatry*, *12*, 212.

Gruber, R., Grizenko, N., Schwartz, G., Bellingham, J., Guzman, R., & Joober, R. (2007). Performance on the continuous performance test in children with ADHD is associated with sleep efficiency. *Sleep*, *30*, 1003–1009.

Gruber, R., & Sadeh, A. (2004). Sleep and neurobehavioral functioning in boys with attention-deficit/hyperactivity disorder and no reported breathing problems. *Sleep*, *27*, 267–273.

Gruber, R., Sadeh, A., & Raviv, A. (2000). Instability of sleep patterns in children with attention-deficit/hyperactivity disorder. *Journal of the American Academy of Child and Adolescent Psychiatry*, *39*, 495–501.

Gualtieri, C. T., & Johnson, L. G. (2008). Medications do not necessarily normalize cognition in ADHD patients. *Journal of Attention Disorders*, *11*, 459–469.

Gudjonsson, G., Sigurddsson, J., Young, S., Newton, A. & Peersen, M. (2009). Attention deficit hyperactivity disorder (ADHD). How do ADHD symptoms relate to personality among prisoners? *Personality and Individual Differences*, *47*, 64–68.

Gupta, R., Kar, B. R., & Srinivasan, N. (2011). Cognitive—motivational deficits in ADHD: Development of a classification system. *Child Neuropsychology*, *17*, 67–81.

Gureasko-Moore, S., DuPaul, G., & White, G. (2007). Self-management of classroom preparedness and homework: Effects on school function of adolescents with attention deficit hyperactivity disorder. *School Psychology Review*, *36*, 647–664.

Gurevitz, M., Geva, R., Varon, M., & Leitner, Y. (2012). Early markers in infants and toddlers for development of ADHD. *Journal of Attention Disorders*, *18*, 14–22.

Haack, L.M., Villodas, M., McBurnett, K., Hinshaw, S., & Pfiffner, L.J. (2016). Parenting as a mechanism of change in psychosocial treatment for youth with ADHD, predominantly inattentive presentation. *Journal of Abnormal Child Psychology*. https://doi.org/10.1007/s10802-016-0199-8

Haag, M. (2003). Essential fatty acids and the brain. *Canadian Journal of Psychiatry*, *48*, 3195–203.

Haapasalo, J., & Hämäläinen, T. (1996). Childhood family problems and current psychiatric problems among young violent and property offenders. *Journal of the American Academy of Child and Adolescent Psychiatry*, *35*, 1394–1401.

Habel, L.A., Cooper, W.O., Sox, C.M., Chan, K.A., Fireman, B.H., Arbogast, P.G., . . . Selby, J.V. (2011). ADHD medications and risk of serious cardiovascular events in young and middle-aged adults. *Journal of the American Medical Association*, *306*, 2673–2683.

Haber, S.N. (2004). The primate basal ganglia: parallel and integrative networks. *Journal of Chemical Neuroanatomy*, *26*, 317–330.

Hacker, L.E., Park, J.M., Timpano, K.R., Cavitt, M.A., Alvaro, J.L., Lewin, A.B., . . . & Storch, E.A. (2016). Hoarding in children with ADHD. *Journal of Attention Disorders*, *20*, 617–626.

Hackman, D.A., Farah, M.J., & Meaney, M.J. (2010) Socioeconomic status and the brain: Mechanistic insights from human and animal research. *Nature Reviews Neuroscience*, *11*, 651–659.

Hagberg, B.S., Miniscalco, C., & Gillberg, C. (2010). Clinic attenders with autism or attention-deficit/hyperactivity disorder: Cognitive profile at school age and its relationship to preschool indicators of language delay. *Research in Developmental Disabilities*, *31*, 1–8.

Hale, J.B., Reddy, L.A., Decker, S.L., Thompson, R., Henzel, J., Teodori, A., & Denckla, M.B. (2009). Development and validation of an attention-deficit/hyperactivity disorder (ADHD) executive function and behavior rating screening battery. *Journal of Clinical and Experimental Neuropsychology*, *31*, 897–912.

Hale, T.S., Bookheimer, S., McGough, J.J., Phillips, J.M., & MacCracken, J.T. (2007). Atypical brain activation during simple & complex levels of processing in adult ADHD. An fMRI Study. *Journal of Attention Disorders*, *11*, 125–139.

Halfon, N., Larson, K., & Slusser, W. (2013). Associations between obesity and comorbid mental health, developmental, and physical health conditions in a nationally representative sample of US children aged 10 to 17. *Academic Pediatrics*, *13*, 6–13.

Hall, C.L., Selby, K., Guo, B., Valentine, A.Z., Walker, G.M., & Hollis, C. (2016). Innovations in practice: An objective measure of attention, impulsivity and activity reduces time to confirm attention deficit/hyperactivity disorder diagnosis in children a completed audit cycle. *Child and Adolescent Mental Health*. https://doi.org/10.1111/camh.12140

Hallahan, D.P., & Kauffman, J.M. (2005). *Exceptional learners: An introduction to special education*. Boston, MA: Pearson Education.

Halldorsdottir, T., & Ollendick, T.H. (2014). Comorbid ADHD: Implications for the treatment of anxiety disorders in children and adolescents. *Cognitive and Behavioral Practice*, *21*, 310–322.

Halperin, J.M., Bedard, A-C., & Curchack-Lichtin, J.T. (2012). Preventive interventions for ADHD: A neurodevelopmental perspective. *Neurotherapeutics*, *9*, 531–541.

Halperin, J.M., & Healey, D.M. (2011). The influences of environmental enrichment, cognitive enhancement, and physical exercise on brain development: Can we alter the developmental trajectory of ADHD? *Neuroscience and Biobehavioral Reviews*, *36*, 621–634.

Halperin, J.M., Marks, D.J., Bedard, A.C., Chacko, A., Curchack, J.T., Yoon, C.A., & Healey, D. (2013). Training executive, attention, and motor skills: A proof-of-concept study in preschool children with ADHD. *Journal of Attention Disorders*, *17*, 711–721.

Halperin, J.M., Newcorn, J.H., Matier, K., Bedi, G., Hall, S. & Sharma, V. (1995). Impulsivity and the initiation of fights in children with disruptive behaviors disorders. *Journal of Child Psychology and Psychiatry, 36*, 1199–1211.

Halperin, J.M., Trampush, J.W., Miller, C.J., Marks, D.J., & Newcorn, J.H. (2008). Neuropsychological outcome in adolescents/young adults with childhood ADHD: profiles of persisters, remitters and controls. *Journal of Child Psychology and Psychiatry, 49*, 958–966.

Hamblin, R.J., Lewin, A.B., Salloum, A., Crawford, E.A., McBride, N.M., & Storch, E.A. (2015). Clinical characteristics and predictors of hoarding in children with anxiety disorders. *Journal of Anxiety Disorders, 36*, 9–14.

Hamilton, L.S., Levitt, J.G., O' Neill, J., Alger, J.R., Luders, E., Phillips, O.R., & . . . (2008). Reduced white matter integrity in attention-deficit/hyperactivity disorder. *Neuroreport, 19*, 1705–1708.

Hammad, T.A., Laughren, T., & Racoosin, J. (2006). Suicidality in pediatric patients treated with antidepressant drugs. *Archives of General Psychiatry, 63*, 332–339.

Hammerness, P., Georgiopoulos, A., Doyle, R.L., Utzinger, L., Schillinger, M., Martelon, M., . . . Wilens, T.E. (2009). An open study of adjunct OROS-methylphenidate in children who are atomoxetine partial responders: II. Tolerability and pharmacokinetics. *Journal of Child and Adolescent Psychopharmacology, 19*, 493–499.

Hammerness, P.G., Perrin, J.M., Shelley-Abrahamson, R., & Wilens, T.E. (2011). Cardiovascular risk of stimulant treatment in pediatric attention-deficit/hyperactivity disorder: Update and clinical recommendations. *Journal of the American Academy of Child and Adolescent Psychiatry, 50*, 978–990.

Hampson, M., Tokoglu, F., Sun, Z., Schafer, R.J., Skudlarski, P., Gore, J.C., & Constable, R.T. (2006). Connectivity-behavior analysis reveals that functional connectivity between left BA39 and Broca's area varies with reading ability. *Neuroimage 31*, 513–519.

Handen, B.L., & Valdes, L. (2007). Preschoolers with developmental disabilities: A comparison of an ADHD and a NonADHD group. *Journal of Developmental and Physical Disabilities, 19*, 579–592.

Hannesdottir, H., Tyrfingsson, T., & Piha, J. (2001). Psychosocial functioning and psychiatric comorbidity among substance-abusing Icelandic adolescents. *Nordic Journal Psychiatry, 55*, 43–48.

Happe, F., Booth, R., Charlton, R., & Hughes, C. (2006). Executive function deficits in autism spectrum disorders and attention-deficit/hyperactivity disorder: Examining profiles across domains and ages. *Brain and Cognition, 61*, 25–39.

Harlaar, N., Kovas, Y., Dale, P.S., Petrill, S.A., & Plomin, R. (2012). Mathematics is differentially related to reading comprehension and word decoding: Evidence from a genetically-sensitive design. *Journal of Educational Psychology, 104*, 622–635.

Harpold, T., Biederman, J., Gignac, M., Hammerness, P., Surman, C., Potter, A., & Mick, E. (2007). Is oppositional defiant disorder a meaningful diagnosis in adults? Results from a large sample of adults with ADHD. *Journal of Nervous and Mental Disease, 195*, 601–605.

Harris, K.R., Friedlander, B.D., Saddler, B., Frizzelle, R. & Graham, S. (2005). Self-monitoring of attention versus self-monitoring of academic performance: Effects among students with ADHD in the general education classroom. *Journal of Special Education, 39*, 145–156.

Harrison, B.J., Soriano-Mas, C., Pujol, J., Ortiz, H., Lopez-Sola, M., Hernandez-Ribas, R., & Cardoner, N. (2009). Altered corticostriatal functional connectivity in obsessive—compulsive disorder. *Archives of General Psychiatry, 66*, 1189–1200.

Harrison, C., & Sofronoff, K. (2002). ADHD and parental psychological distress: Role of demographics, child behavioral characteristics, and parental cognitions. *Journal of the American Academy of Child and Adolescent Psychiatry, 41*, 703–711.

Hart, E.L., Lahey, B.B., Loeber, R., Applegate, B., & Frick, P. (1995). Developmental change in attention-deficit hyperactivity disorder in boys: A four-year longitudinal study. *Journal of Abnormal Child Psychology, 23*, 729–749.

Hart, S.A., Petrill, S.A., & Thompson, L.A. (2010). A factorial analysis of timed and untimed measures of mathematics and reading abilities in school aged twins. *Learning and Individual Differences, 20*, 63–69.

Hartmann, T. (1995). *ADD success stories: a guide to fulfillment for families with attention deficit disorder: maps, guidebooks, and travelogues for hunters in this farmer's world*. Grass Valley, California: Underwood Books.

Hartnett, N.D., Nelson, J.M., & Rinn, A.N. (2004). Gifted or ADHD? The possibilities of misdiagnosis. *Roeper Review, 26*, 73–76.

Hartocollis, P. (1968). The syndrome of minimal brain dysfunction in young adult patients. *Bulletin of the Menninger Clinic, 32*, 102–114.

Hartsough, C.S., & Lambert, N.M. (1985). Medical factors in hyperactive and normal children. *American Journal of Orthopsychiatry, 55*, 190–201.

Hartung, C.M., Lefler, E.K., Tempel, A.B., Armendariz, M.L., Sigel, B.A., & Little, C.S. (2010). Halo effects in ratings of ADHD and ODD: Identification of susceptible symptoms. *Journal of Psychopathology and Behavioral Assessment, 32*, 128–137.

Hartung, C.M., Van Pelt, J.C., Armendariz, M.L., & Knight, L.A. (2006). Biases in ratings of disruptive behavior in children effects of sex and negative halos. *Journal of Attention Disorders, 9*, 620–630.

Hartung, C.M., & Widiger, T.A. (1998). Gender differences in the diagnosis of mental disorders: Conclusions and controversies of the DSM-IV. *Psychological Bulletin, 123*, 260–278.

Harvard Mental Health Letter. (2011). Options for conduct disorder: Treatment works best when it involves and empowers parents. *Harvard Mental Health Letter, 27*, 1–3.

Harvey, E.A., Breaux, R.P., & Lugo-Candelas, C.I. (2016). Early development of comorbidity between symptoms of attention-deficit/hyperactivity disorder (ADHD) and oppositional defiant disorder (ODD). *Journal of Abnormal Psychology, 125*, 154–167.

Harvey, E.A., Danforth, J.S., McKee, T.E., Ulaszek, W.R., & Friedman, J.L. (2003). Parenting of children with attention-deficit/hyperactivity disorder (ADHD): The role of parental ADHD symptomatology. *Journal of Attention Disorders, 7*, 31–42.

Harvey, E.A., Friedman-Weieneth, J.L., Goldstein, L.H., & Sherman, A.H. (2007). Examining subtypes of behavior problems among 3-year-old children, Part I: Investigating validity of subtypes and biological risk-factors. *Journal of Abnormal Child Psychology, 35*, 97–110.

Harwood, V. (2015). Leaving melancholia: Disruptive mood dysregulation disorder. In M. O'Reilly & J.N. Lester (Eds.), *The Palgrave handbook of child mental health: discourse and conversation studies* (pp. 175–193). London: Palgrave Macmillan.

Haslam, J. (1809). *Observations of madness and melancholy including practical remarks on these diseases together with cases*. London: J. Callow.

Hasson, R., & Fine, J.G. (2012). Gender differences among children with ADHD on continuous performance tests a meta-analytic review. *Journal of Attention Disorders, 16*, 190–198.

Hastings, E., & Felt, B.T. (2012). ADHD and sleep problems in children. In J.M. Norvilitis (Ed.), *Current directions in ADHD and its treatment* (pp. 61–88). InTech. https://doi.org/10.5772/30964

Hastings, R.P., Beck, A., Daley, D., & Hill, C. (2005). Symptoms of ADHD and their correlates in children with intellectual disabilities. *Research in Developmental Disabilities, 26*, 456–468.

Hatcher, P.J., Hulme, C., & Snowling, M.J. (2004). Explicit phonological training combined with reading instruction helps young children at risk of reading failure. *Journal of Child Psychology and Psychiatry, 45*, 338–358.

Hattori, J., Ogino, T., Abiru, K., Nakano, K., Oka, M., & Ohtsuka, Y. (2006). Are pervasive developmental disorder and attention deficit/hyperactivity disorder distinct disorders? *Brain and Development, 28*, 371–374.

Hayes, S.C., Follette, V.M., & Linehan, M. (Eds.). (2004). *Mindfulness and acceptance: Expanding the cognitive-behavioral tradition*. New York: Guilford Press.

Healey, D., & Halperin, J.M. (2015). Enhancing neurocognitive growth with the aid of games and exercise (ENGAGE): A novel early-intervention fostering the development of preschoolers' self-control. *Child Neuropsychology, 21*, 465–480.

Healey, D.M., Miller, C.J., Castelli, K.L., Marks, D.J., & Halperin, J.M. (2008). The impact of impairment criteria on rates of ADHD diagnoses in preschoolers. *Journal of Abnormal Child Psychology, 36*, 771–778.

Hecht, S.A., Torgesen, J.K., Wagner, R.K., & Rashotte, C.A. (2001). The relations between phonological processing abilities and emerging individual differences in mathematical computation skills: A longitudinal study from second to fifth grades. *Journal of Experimental Child Psychology, 79*, 192–227.

Hechtman, L. (1999). Predictors of long term outcome in children with ADHD. *Pediatric Clinics of North America, 46*, 1039–1052.

Hechtman L. (2000). Assessment and diagnosis of attention-deficit/hyperactivity disorder. *Child and Adolescent Psychiatric Clinics of North America, 9*, 481–498.

Hechtman, L., Abikoff, H., Klein, R.G., Weiss, G., Respitz, C., Kouri, J., . . . Pollack, S. (2004). Academic achievement and emotional status of children with ADHD treated with long-term methylphenidate and multimodal psychosocial treatment. *Journal of the American Academy of Child and Adolescent Psychiatry, 43*, 812–819.

Hedtke, K.A., Kendall, P.C., & Tiwari, S. (2009). Safety-seeking and coping behavior during exposure tasks with anxious youth. *Journal of Clinical Child and Adolescent Psychology*, 38, 1–15.

Heilman, M., Voeller, S., & Nadeau, E. (1991). A possible pathophysiological substrate of attention deficit hyperactivity disorder. *Journal of Child Neurology, 6*, 74–79.

Heinrich, H., Gevensleben, H., & Strehl, U. (2007). Annotation: Neurofeedback-train your brain to train your behavior. *Journal of Child Psychology and Psychiatry, 48*, 3–16.

Hennissen, L., Bakker, M.J., Banaschewski, T., Carucci, S., Coghill, D., Danckaerts, M., . . . Nagy, P. (2017). Cardiovascular effects of stimulant and non-stimulant medication for children and adolescents with ADHD: A systematic review and meta-analysis of trials of methylphenidate, amphetamines and atomoxetine. *CNS Drugs, 31*, 119–215.

Hensch, T.K. (2004). Critical period regulation. *Annual Review of Neuroscience, 27*, 549–579.

Herman, K.C., Lambert, S.F., Ialongo, N.S., & Ostrander, R. (2007). Academic pathways between attention problems and depressive symptoms among urban African American children. *Journal of Abnormal Child Psychology, 35*, 265–274.

Hermens, D.F., Kohn, M.R., Clarke, S.D., Gordon, E., & Williams, L.M. (2005). Sex differences in adolescent ADHD: Findings from concurrent EEG and EDA. *Clinical Neurophysiology, 116*, 1455–1463.

Hibbeln, J.R., Davis, J.M., Steer, C., Emmett, P., Rogers, I., Williams, C., & Golding, J. (2007). Maternal seafood consumption in pregnancy and neurodevelopmental outcomes in childhood (ALSPAC study): An observational cohort study. *Lancet*, 369, 578–585.

Hill, E.L. (2001). Non-specific nature of specific language impairment: A review of the literature with regard to concomitant motor impairments. *International Journal of Language & Communication Disorders, 36*, 149–171.

Hilton, J.L., & von Hippel, W. (1996). Stereotypes. *Annual Review of Psychology, 46*, 237–271.

Hingson, R.W., & Zha, W. (2009). Age of drinking onset, alcohol use disorders, frequent heavy drinking, and unintentionally injuring oneself and others after drinking. *Pediatrics, 123*, 1477–1484.

Hinshaw, S.P. (2001). Is the inattentive type of ADHD a separate disorder? *Clinical Psychology-Science and Practice, 8*, 498–501.

Hinshaw, S.P. (2002). Preadolescent girls with attention-deficit/hyperactivity disorder: I. Background characteristics, comorbidity, cognitive and social functioning, and parenting practices. *Journal of Consulting and Clinical Psychology, 70*, 1086–1098.

Hinshaw, S.P. (2006). Treatment for children and adolescents with Attention-Deficit/Hyperactivity Disorder. In P.C. Kendall (Ed.), *Child and adolescent therapy: Cognitive-behavioral procedures* (3rd ed). New York: Guilford Press.

Hinshaw, S.P. (2009). Psychosocial interventions for ADHD and comorbidities. In. Brown, T.E. (Ed.), *ADHD Comorbidities. Handbook for ADHD complications in children and adults* (pp. 385–398). Washington, DC: American Psychiatric.

Hinshaw, S.P., Arnold, L.E., & The MTA Cooperative Group (2015). Attention-deficit hyperactivity disorder, multimodal treatment, and longitudinal outcome: evidence, paradox, and challenge. *WIREs Cognitive Science, 6*, 39–52.

Hinshaw, S.P., & Blachman, D.R. (Eds.). (2005). *Attention-deficit/hyperactivity disorder.* New York: Kluwer Academic/Plenum.

Hinshaw, S.P., Lahey, B.B., & Hart, E.L. (1993). Issues of taxonomy and comorbidity in the development of conduct disorder. *Development and Psychopathology, 5,* 31–49.

Hinshaw, S.P., Owens, E.B., Sami, N., & Fargeon, S. (2006). Prospective follow-up of girls with attention-deficit/hyperactivity disorder into adolescence: Evidence for continuing cross-domain impairment. *Journal of Consulting and Clinical Psychology, 74,* 489–499.

Hinshaw, S.P., Owens, E.B., Wells, K.C., Kraemer, H.C., Abikoff, H.B., Arnold, L.E., . . . Wigal, T. (2000). Family processes and treatment outcome in the MTA: negative/ineffective parenting practices in relation to multimodal treatment. *Journal of Abnormal Child Psychology, 28,* 555–568.

Hinshaw, S.P., & Scheffler, R.M. (2014). *The ADHD explosion. Myths, medication, money, and today's push for performance.* London: Oxford University Press.

Hinshaw, S.P., Scheffler, R.M., Fulton, B.D., Aase, H., Banaschewski, T., Cheng, W., ... Weiss, M.D. (2011). International variation in treatment procedures for ADHD: Social context and recent trends. *Psychiatric Services, 62,* 459–464.

Hirschstein, M.K., Edstrom, L.V.S., Frey, K.S., Snell, J.L., & MacKenzie, E.P. (2007). Walking the talk in bullying prevention: Teacher implementation variables related to initial impact of the Steps to Respect program. *School Psychology Review, 36,* 3–21.

Hiscock, H., Canterford, L., Ukoumunne, O.C., & Wake, M. (2007). Adverse associations of sleep problems in Australian preschoolers: National Population Study. *Pediatrics, 119,* 86–93.

Hiscock, H., Sciberras, E., Mensah, F., Gerner, B., Efron, D., Khano, S., & Oberklaid, F. (2015). Impact of a behavioural sleep intervention on symptoms and sleep in children with attention deficit hyperactivity disorder, and parental mental health: randomised controlled trial. *BMJ, 350,* h68.

Hoekzema, E., Carmona, S., Ramos-Quiroga, J.A., Barba, E., Bielsa, A., Tremols, V., . . . Vilarroya, O. (2011). Training-induced neuroanatomical plasticity in ADHD: A tensor-based morphometric study. *Human Brain Mapping, 32,* 1741–1749.

Hoekzema, E., Carmona, S., Tremols, V., Gispert, J.D., Guitart, M., Fauquet, J., . . . Rovira, M. (2010). Enhanced neural activity in frontal and cerebellar circuits after cognitive training in children with attention-deficit/hyperactivity disorder. *Human Brain Mapping, 31,* 1942–1950.

Hoffman, H. (1865). Die Geschichte vom Zappel-Philipp [Fidgetty Phil]. In H. Hoffman, *Der Struwwelpeter [Shock-headed Peter].* Erlangen, Germany: Pestalozzi-Verlag.

Holbrook, J.R., Cuffe, S.P., Cai, B., Visser, S.N., Forthofer, M.S., Bottai, M., . . . McKeown, R.E. (2016). Persistence of parent-reported ADHD symptoms from childhood through adolescence in a community sample. *Journal of Attention Disorders, 20,* 11–20.

Holmbeck, G.N., Greenley, R.N., & Franks, E.A. (2003). Developmental issues and considerations in research and practice. In A. Kazdin, & J. Weisz (Eds.), *Evidence-based psychotherapies for children and adolescents* (pp. 21–40). New York: Guilford Press.

Holtmann, M., Bolte, S., & Poustica, F. (2007). Attention deficit/hyperactivity disorder symptoms in pervasive developmental disorders: Association with autistic behaviour domains and coexisting psychopathology. *Psychopathology, 40,* 172–177.

Holtmann, M., Sonuga-Barke, E., Cortese, S., & Brandeis, D. (2014). Neurofeedback for ADHD: A review of current evidence. *Child and Adolescent Psychiatric Clinics of North America, 23,* 789–806.

Hooper, S.R., Swartz, C.W., Montgomery, J.W., & Reed, M.S. (1993). Prevalence of writing problems across three middle school samples. *School Psychology Review, 22,* 610–622.

Hooper, S.R., Swartz, C.W., Wakely, M.B., deKruif, R.E.L., & Montgomery, J.W. (2002). Executive functions in elementary school children with and without problems in written expression. *Journal of Learning Disabilities, 35,* 57–68.

Houghton, S., Carroll, A., Taylor, M., & O'Donoghue, T. (2006). *From traditional to ecological: Understanding attention deficit disorders through quantitative and qualitative research.* New York: Nova Science.

Howard, A.L., Robinson, M., Smith, G.J., Ambrosini, G.L., Piek, J.P., & Oddy, W.H. (2011). ADHD is associated with a "Western" dietary pattern in adolescents. *Journal of Attention Disorders, 15,* 403–411.

Howard, J.S., Sparkman, C.R., Cohen, H.G., Green, G., & Stanislaw, H. (2005). A comparison of intensive behavior analytic and eclectic treatments for young children with autism. *Research in Developmental Disabilities, 26*, 359–383.

Hoza, B., Gerdes, A.C., Mrug, S., Hinshaw, S.P., Bukowski, W.M., Gold, J.A., . . . Wigal, T. (2005). Peer-assessed outcomes in the multimodal treatment study of children with attention deficit hyperactivity disorder. *Journal of Clinical Child and Adolescent Psychology, 34*, 74–86.

Hoza, B., Mrug, S., Gerdes, A.C., Hinshaw, S.P., Bukowski, W.M., Gold, J.A., . . . Arnold, L.E. (2005). What aspects of peer relationships are impaired in children with ADHD? *Journal of Consulting and Clinical Psychology, 73*, 411–423.

Hoza, B., Owens, J.S., Pelham, W.E., Swanson, J.M., Conners, C.K., Hinshaw, S.P., . . . Kraemer, H.C. (2000). Parent cognitions as predictors of child treatment response in attention-deficit hyperactivity disorder. *Journal of Abnormal Child Psychology, 28*, 569–584.

Huang, Y.S., Guilleminault, C., Li, H.Y., Yang, C.M., Wu, Y.Y., & Chen, N.H. (2007). Attention-deficit/hyperactivity disorder with obstructive sleep apnea: A treatment outcome study. *Sleep Medicine, 8*, 18–30.

Huang-Pollock, C., Mikami, A., Pfiffner, L., & McBurnett, K. (2009). Can executive functions explain the relationship between attention deficit hyperactivity disorder and social adjustment? *Journal of Abnormal Child Psychology, 37*, 679–691.

Hudson, J.I., Hiripi, E., Pope, H.G., & Kessler, R.C. (2007). The prevalence and correlates of eating disorders in the National Comorbidity Survey Replication. *Biological Psychiatry, 61*, 348–358.

Hudziak, J.J., Achenbach, T.A., Althoff, R.R., & Pine, D.S. (2007). A dimensional approach to developmental psychopathology. *International Journal of Methods in Psychiatric Research, 16 (SI)*, S16–S23.

Huggins, S.P., Rooney, M.E., & Chronis-Tuscano, A. (2015). Risky sexual behavior among college students with ADHD. Is the mother—child relationship protective? *Journal of Attention Disorders, 19*, 240–250.

Hulme, C., & Snowling, M.J. (2009). *Developmental disorders of language, learning and cognition.* Chichester, UK: Wiley-Blackwell.

Humphreys, K., Eng, H., & Lee, S. (2013). Stimulant medication and substance use outcomes: A meta-analysis. *JAMA Psychiatry, 70*, 740–749.

Hunsley, J., & Mash, E.J. (2007). Evidence-based assessment. *Annual Review of Clinical Psychology, 3*, 29–51.

Huntley, Z., Maltezos, S., Williams, C., Morinan, A., Hammon, A., Ball, D., . . . Asherson, P.J. (2012). Rates of undiagnosed attention deficit hyperactivity disorder in London drug and alcohol detoxification units. *MC Psychiatry, 12*, 223.

Hurt, E., & Arnold, L.E. (2015). Dietary management of ADHD. In R.A. Barkley (Ed.) *Attention-Deficit Hyperactivity Disorder* (4th ed., pp. 630–640). New York: Guilford Press.

Hurt, E.A., Hoza, B., & Pelham, W.E. (2007). Parenting, family loneliness, and peer functioning in boys with attention-deficit/ hyperactivity disorder. *Journal of Abnormal Child Psychology, 35*, 543–555.

Hvolby, A., Jørgensen, J., & Bilenberg, N. (2008). Actigraphic and parental reports of sleep difficulties in children with attention-deficit/hyperactivity disorder. *Archives of Pediatrics and Adolescent Medicine, 162*, 323–329.

Hynd, G.W., Semrud-Clikeman, M., Lorys, A.R., Novey, E.S., Eliopoulos, D., & Lyytinen, H. (1990). Brain morphology in developmental dyslexia and attention deficit disorder/hyperactivity. *Archives of Neurology, 47*, 919–926.

Hysing, M. (2014). Review: recommendations for the assessment and management of sleep disorders in ADHD. *Evidence Based Mental Health, 17*, 22–22.

Iacono, W.G., Malone, S.M., & McGue, M. (2008). Behavioral disinhibition and the development of early-onset addiction: Common and specific influences. *Annual Review of Clinical Psychology, 4*, 325–348.

Individuals with Disabilities Education Improvement Act, Pub. L. No. 108–446, 118 Stat. 2647 (2004).

Insel, T. (2013). *Transforming diagnosis.* Bethesda, MD: National Institute of Mental Health.

Ishii, T., Takahashi, O., Kawamura, Y., & Ohta, T. (2003). Comorbidity in attention deficit-hyperactivity disorder. *Psychiatry & Clinical Neuroscience, 57,* 457–463.

Ivanov, I., Bansal, R., Hao, X., Zhu, H., Kellendonk, C., Miller, L., . . . Peterson, B.S. (2010). Morphological abnormalities of the thalamus in youths with attention deficit hyperactivity disorder. *American Journal of Psychiatry, 167,* 397–408.

Ivarsson, T., & Melin, K. (2008). Autism spectrum traits in children and adolescents with obsessive-compulsive disorder (OCD). *Journal of Anxiety Disorders, 22,* 969–978.

Ivarsson, T., Melin, K., & Wallin, L. (2008). Categorical and dimensional aspects of co-morbidity in obsessive—compulsive disorder (OCD). *European Child and Adolescent Psychiatry, 17,* 20–31.

Jacobson, L.A., Ryan, M., Martin, R.B., Ewen, J., Mostofsky, S.H., Denckla, M.B., & Mahone, E.M. (2011). Working memory influences processing speed and reading fluency in ADHD. *Child Neuropsychology, 17,* 209–224.

Jaksa, P., & Ratey, N. (1999). Therapy and ADD coaching: Similarities, differences, and collaboration. *FOCUS, 6,* 3–11.

James, A., & Taylor, E. (1990). Sex differences in the hyperkinetic syndrome of childhood. *Journal of Child Psychology and Psychiatry, 31,* 437–446.

James, W. (1890/1950). *The principles of psychology.* London: Dover.

Janney, R., & Snell, M.E. (2000). *Teacher's guide to inclusive practices: Behavioral support.* Baltimore: Brookes.

Janssen, L., Kan, C.C., Carpentier, P.J., Sizoo, B., Hepark, S., Grutters, J., . . . Speckens, A.E. (2015). Mindfulness based cognitive therapy versus treatment as usual in adults with attention deficit hyperactivity disorder (ADHD). *BMC Psychiatry, 15*(1), 216.

Janssen, T.W., Bink, M., Weeda, W.D., Geladé, K., van Mourik, R., Maras, A., & Oosterlaan, J. (2016). Learning curves of theta/beta neurofeedback in children with ADHD. *European Child & Adolescent Psychiatry.* https://doi.org/10.1007/s00787-016-0920-8

Jarrett, M.A., Wolff, J.C., Davis, T.E., 3rd, Cowart, M.J., & Ollendick, T.H. (2016). Characteristics of children with ADHD and comorbid anxiety. *Journal of Attention Disorders,* 20, 636–644.

Jensen, C.M., Amdisen, B.L., Jørgensen, K.J., & Arnfred, S.M. (2016). Cognitive behavioural therapy for ADHD in adults: Systematic review and meta-analyses. *ADHD Attention Deficit and Hyperactivity Disorders, 8,* 3–11.

Jensen, P.S., Abikoff, H., & Brow, T.E. (2009). Tailoring treatments for individuals with ADHD and their families. In. T.E. Brown (Ed.), *ADHD Comorbidities. Handbook for ADHD complications in children and adults* (pp. 415–428). Washington, DC: American Psychiatric.

Jensen, P.S., Arnold, L.E., Swanson, J.M., Vitiello, B., Abikoff, H., Greenhill, L.L., . . . Hur, K. (2007). 3-year follow-up of the NIMH MTA study. *Journal of the American Academy of Child and Adolescent Psychiatry, 46,* 989–1002.

Jensen, P.S., Hinshaw, S.P., Kraemer, H.C., Lenora, N., Newcorn, J.H., Abikoff, H.B., . . . Vitiello, B. (2001). ADHD comorbidity findings from the MTA study: Comparing comorbid subgroups. *Journal of the American Academy of Child and Adolescent Psychiatry, 40,* 147–158.

Jensen, P.S., Mrazek, D., Knapp, P.K., Steinberg, L., Pfeffer, C., Schowalter, J., & Shapiro, T. (1997). Evolution and revolution in child psychiatry: ADHD as a disorder of adaptation. *Journal of American Academy of Child and Adolescent Psychiatry, 36,* 1672–1679; discussion 1679–1681.

Jensen, P.S., Shervette, R., Xenakis, S.N., & Richters, J. (1993). Anxiety and depressive disorders in attention deficit disorder with hyperactivity: New findings. *American Journal of Psychiatry, 150,* 1203–1209.

Jerome, L., Habinski, L., & Segal, A. (2006). Attention-deficit/hyperactivity disorder (ADHD) and driving risk: A review of the literature and a methodological critique. *Current Psychiatry Reports, 8,* 416–426.

Jiménez-Murcia, S., Alvarez-Moya, E.M., Stinchfield, R., Fernández-Aranda, F., Granero, R., Aymamí, N., . . . Menchón, J.M. (2010). Age of onset in pathological gambling: clinical, therapeutic and personality correlates. *Journal of Gambling Studies, 26,* 235–248.

Johansen, E. B., Aase, H., Meyer, A., & Sagvolden, T. (2002). Attention-deficit/hyperactivity disorder (ADHD) behaviour explained by dysfunctioning reinforcement and extinction processes. *Behavioural Brain Research, 130*, 37–45.

Johansen, E. B., Killeen, P. R., Russell, V. A., Tripp, G., Wickens, J. R., Tannock, R., . . . Sagvolden, T. (2009). Origins of altered reinforcement effects in ADHD. *Behavioral and Brain Functions, 5*, 7.

Johansen, E. B., Killeen, P. R., & Sagvolden, T. (2007). Behavioral variability, elimination of responses, and delay-of-reinforcement gradients in SHR and WKY rats. *Behavioral and Brain Functions, 3*, 60.

Johansen, E. B., Sagvolden, T., Aase, H., & Russell, V. A. (2005). The dynamic developmental theory of attention-deficit/hyperactivity disorder (ADHD): Present status and future perspectives. *Behavioral and Brain Sciences, 28*, 451–454.

Johansen, E. B., Sagvolden, T., & Kvande, G. (2005). Effects of delayed reinforcers on the behaviour of an animal model of attention-deficit/hyperactivity disorder (ADHD). *Behavioural Brain Research, 162*, 47–61.

Johnson, J., & Reid, R. (2011). Overcoming executive function deficits with students with ADHD. *Theory into Practice, 50*, 61–67.

Johnson, K. A., Kelly, S. P., Bellgrove, M. A., Barry, E., Cox, M., Gill, M., & Robertson, I. H. (2007). Response variability in attention deficit hyperactivity disorder: Evidence for neuropsychological heterogeneity. *Neuropsychologia, 45*, 630–638.

Johnson, K. A., Wiersema, J. R., & Kuntsi, J. (2009). What would Karl Popper say? Are current psychological theories of ADHD falsifiable? *Behavioral and Brain Functions, 5*, 15.

Johnson, M. H. (2012). Executive function and developmental disorders: The flip side of the coin. *Trends in Cognitive Sciences, 16*, 454–457.

Johnson, M. H., Gliga, T., Jones, E., & Charman, T. (2015). Annual Research Review: Infant development, autism, and ADHD—early pathways to emerging disorders. *Journal of Child Psychology and Psychiatry, 56*, 228–247.

Johnson, M. H., Jones, E., & Gliga, T. (2015). Brain adaptation and alternative developmental trajectories. *Development & Psychopathology, 27*, 425–442.

Johnston, C. (1996). Parent characteristics and parent—child interactions in families of nonproblem children and ADHD children with higher and lower levels of oppositional-defiant behavior. *Journal of Abnormal Child Psychology, 24*, 85–104.

Johnston, C., Chen, M., & Ohan, J. (2006). Mothers' attributions for behavior in nonproblem boys, boys with attention deficit hyperactivity disorder, and boys with attention deficit hyperactivity disorder and oppositional defiant disorder. *Journal of Clinical Child & Adolescent Psychology, 35*, 60–71.

Johnston, C., Hommersen, P., & Seipp, C. (2008). Acceptability of behavioral and pharmacological treatments for attention-deficit/hyperactivity disorder: Relations to child and parent characteristics. *Behavior Therapy, 39*, 22–32.

Johnston, C., & Jassy, J. S. (2007). Attention-deficit/hyperactivity disorder and oppositional/conduct problems: Links to parent-child interactions. *Journal of the Canadian Academy of Child and Adolescent Psychiatry, 16*, 74–79.

Johnston, C., Lui, J. H., & Williamson, D. (2014). Adult ADHD and positive parenting. Is there a relationship? *The ADHD Report, 22*, 1–5.

Johnston, C., Mah, J.W.T., & Regambal, M. (2010). Parenting cognitions and treatment beliefs as predictors of experience using behavioral parenting strategies in families of children with attention-deficit/hyperactivity disorder. *Behavior Therapy, 41*, 491–504.

Johnston, C., & Mash, E. J. (2001). Families of children with attention-deficit/hyperactivity disorder: Review and recommendations for future research. *Clinical Child and Family Psychology Review, 4*, 183–207.

Johnston, C., Mash, E. J., Miller, N., & Ninowski, J. E. (2012). Parenting in adults with attention-deficit/hyperactivity disorder. *Clinical Psychology Review, 32*, 2154–2228.

Johnston, C., & Ohan, J. L. (2005). The importance of parental attributions in families of children with attention-deficit/hyperactivity and disruptive behavior disorders. *Clinical Child and Family Psychology Review, 8*, 167–182.

Johnston, C., Seipp, C., Hommersen, P., Hoza, B., & Fine, S. (2005). Treatment choices and experiences in attention deficit and hyperactivity disorder: Relations to parents' beliefs and attributions. *Child: Care, Health and Development, 31*, 669–677.

Johnstone, S.J., Barry, R.J., & Clarke, A.R. (2012). Ten years on: A follow-up review of ERP research in attention-deficit/hyperactivity disorder. *Clinical Neurophysiology, 124*, 644–657.

Jolles, D.D., & Crone, E.A. (2012). Training the developing brain: A neurocognitive perspective. *Frontiers in Human Neuroscience, 6*, 76.

Jones, D.E., & Foster, E.M. (2009). Service use patterns for adolescents with ADHD and comorbid conduct disorder. *Journal of Behavioral Health Services & Research, 36*, 436–449.

Jones, K., Daley, D., Hutchings, J., Bywater, T., & Eames, C. (2007). Efficacy of the Incredible Years Basic Parent Training Programme as an early intervention for children with conduct problems and ADHD. *Child Care, Health and Development, 33*, 740–756.

Jones, L.B., Rothbart, M.K., & Posner, M. (2003). Development of executive attention in preschool children. *Developmental Science, 6*, 498–504.

Jones, S., & Lynam, D.R. (2009). In the eye of the impulsive beholder: The interaction between impulsivity and perceived informal social control on offending. *Criminal Justice and Behavior, 36*, 307–321.

Jopp, D.A., & Keys, C.B. (2001). Diagnostic overshadowing reviewed and reconsidered. *American Journal of Mental Retardation, 106*, 416–433.

Justice, L.M. (2006). Evidence-based practice, response to intervention, and the prevention of reading difficulties. *Language, Speech, and Hearing Services in Schools, 37*, 284–297.

Kadesjö, B. (2000). *Neuropsychiatric and neurodevelopmental disorders in a young school-age population. Epidemiology and comorbidity in a school health perspective*, Doctoral Dissertation. Department of Child and Adolescent Psychiatry, University of Gothenburg.

Kahn, R.S., Khoury, J., Nichols, W.C., & Lanphear, B.P. (2003). Role of dopamine transporter genotype and maternal prenatal smoking in childhood hyperactive-impulsive, inattentive, and oppositional behaviors. *Journal of Pediatrics, 143*, 104–110.

Kaiser, N.M., McBurnett, K., & Pfiffner, L.J. (2011). Child ADHD severity and positive and negative parenting as predictors of child social functioning: Evaluation of three theoretical models. *Journal of Attention Disorders, 15*, 193–203.

Kakouros, E., Maniadaki, K., & Karaba, R. (2005). The relationship between Attention Deficit/Hyperactivity Disorder and aggressive behaviour in preschool boys and girls. *Early Child Development and Care, 175*, 203–214.

Kakouros, E., Maniadaki, K., & Papaeliou, Ch. (2004). How Greek teachers perceive school functioning of pupils with ADHD. *Emotional and Behavioural Difficulties, 9*, 41–53.

Kalff, A.C., De Sonneville, L.M., Hurks, P.P., Hendriksen, J.G., Kroes, M., Feron, F.J., . . . Jolles, J. (2003). Low-and high-level controlled processing in executive motor control tasks in 5–6-year-old children at risk of ADHD. *Journal of Child Psychology and Psychiatry, 44*, 1049–1057.

Kaminski, P.L., Jones, H., & Harshaw, A.A. (2004). *Low parental warmth and conduct problems in ADHD boys*. Poster presented at the 112th annual convention of the American Psychological Association, Honolulu, HI.

Kamphaus, R.W., & Frick, P.J. (2002). *Clinical assessment of child and adolescent personality and behavior*. Boston: Allyn & Bacon.

Kaplan, B., Crawford, S., Cantell, M., Kooistra, L., & Dewey, D. (2006). Comorbidity, co-occurrence, continuum: what's in a name? *Child: Care, Health and Development, 32*, 6, 723–731.

Kaplan, B.J., Dewey, D.M., Crawford, S.G. & Wilson, B.N. (2001) The term 'comorbidity' is of questionable value in reference to developmental disorders: data and theory. *Journal of Learning Disabilities, 34*, 555–565.

Kaplan, B.J., Wilson, B.N., Dewey, D.M., & Crawford, S.G. (1998). DCD may not be a discrete disorder. *Human Movement Science, 17*, 471–490.

Kaplan, R.F., & Stevens, M.C. (2002). A review of adult ADHD: A neuropsychological and neuroimaging perspective. *CNS Spectrums, 7*, 355–362.

Karalunas, S.L., Fair, D., Musser, E.D., Aykes, K., Iyer, S.P., & Nigg, J.T. (2014). Subtyping attention-deficit/hyperactivity disorder using temperament dimensions: Toward biologically based nosologic criteria. *JAMA Psychiatry, 79*, 1015–1024.

Karalunas, S. L., & Huang-Pollock, C. L. (2011). Examining relationships between executive functioning and delay aversion in attention deficit hyperactivity disorder. *Journal of Clinical Child & Adolescent Psychology*, *40*, 837–847.

Karam, R. G., Breda, V., Picon, F. A., Rovaris, D. L., Victor, M. M., Salgado, C.A.I., . . . Caye, A. (2015). Persistence and remission of ADHD during adulthood: A 7-year clinical follow-up study. *Psychological Medicine*, *45*, 2045–2056.

Karatekin, C. (2005). A comprehensive and developmental theory of ADHD is tantalizing but premature. *Behavioral and Brain Sciences*, *28*, 430–431.

Kaya, A., Taner, Y., Guclu, B., Taner, E., Kaya, Y., Bahcivan, H. G., & Benli, I. T. (2008) Trauma and adult attention deficit hyperactivity disorder. *Journal of International Medical Research*, *3*, 9–16.

Kazdin, A. E. (1995). Child, parent and family dysfunction as predictors of outcome in cognitive-behavioral treatment of antisocial children. *Behaviour Research and Therapy*, *33*, 271–281.

Kazdin, A. E. (2001). *Behavior modification in applied settings.* USA: Wadsworth Thomson Learning.

Kazdin, A. E., Holland, L., Crowley, M., & Breton, S. (1997). Barriers to treatment participation scale: Evaluation and validation in the context of child outpatient treatment. *Journal of Child Psychology and Psychiatry*, *38*, 1051–1062.

Keenan, K., & Shaw, D. (1997). Developmental and social influences on young girls' early problem behaviour. *Psychological Bulletin*, *121*, 95–113.

Keenan, K., & Wakschlag L. (2002). Can a valid diagnosis of disruptive disorder be made in preschool children? *American Journal of Psychiatry*, *159*, 351–358.

Keller, T. A., & Just, M. A. (2009). Altering cortical connectivity: Remediation-induced changes in the white matter of poor readers. *Neuron*, *64*, 624–631.

Kelly, D. J., Walker, R., & Norbury, C. F. (2013). Deficits in volitional oculomotor control align with language status in autism spectrum disorders. *Developmental Science*, *16*, 56–66.

Kendall, J. (1998). Outlasting disruption: The process of reinvestment in families with ADHD children. *Qualitative Health Research*, *8*, 839–857.

Kendall, J. (1999). Sibling accounts of attention deficit hyperactivity disorder (ADHD). *Family Processes*, *38*, 117–136.

Kendall, J., Leo, M. C., Perrin, N., & Hatton, D. (2005). Modeling ADHD child and family relationships. *Western Journal of Nursing Research*, *27*, 500–518.

Kendall, J., & Shelton, K. (2003). A typology of management styles in families with children with ADHD. *Journal of Family Nursing*, *9*, 257–280.

Keng, S. L., Smoski, M. J., & Robins, C. J. (2011). Effects of mindfulness on psychological health: A review of empirical studies. *Clinical Psychology Review*, *31*, 1041–1056.

Kent, K., Pelham, W. E., Jr., Molina, B.S.G., Waschbush, D. A., Yu, J., Sibley, M. H., . . . Karch, K. M. (2011). The academic experience of male high school students with ADHD. *Journal of Abnormal Child Psychology*, *39*, 451–462.

Kent, L., & Craddock, N., (2003). Is there a relationship between attention deficit hyperactivity disorder and bipolar disorder? *Journal of Affective Disorders*, *73*, 211–221.

Keown, L. J. (2012). Predictors of boys' ADHD symptoms from early to middle childhood: The role of father—child and mother—child interactions. *Journal of Abnormal Child Psychology*, *40*, 569–581.

Kern, L., DuPaul, G. J., Volpe, R. J., Sokol, N. G., Lutz, G., Arbolino, L. A., . . . VanBrakle, J. D. (2007). Multisetting assessment-based intervention for young children at risk for attention deficit hyperactivity disorder: Initial effects on academic and behavioral functioning. *School Psychology Review*, *36*, 237–255.

Kerns, K. A., Eso, K., & Thomson, J. (1999). Investigation of a direct intervention for improving attention in young children with ADHD. *Developmental Neuropsychology*, *16*, 273–295.

Kerr, M., Lambert, W. W., Stattin, H., & Klackenberg-Larsson, I. (1994). Stability of inhibitioh in a Swedish longitudinal sample. *Child Development*, *65*, 138–146.

Kerr, M., Stattin, H., & Burk, W. J. (2010). A reinterpretation of parental monitoring in longitudinal perspective. *Journal of Research on Adolescence*, *20*, 39–64.

Kessler, J.W. (1980). History of minimal brain dysfunction. In H. Rie & E. Rie (Eds.), *Handbook of minimal brain dysfunctions: A critical view* (pp. 18–52). New York: Wiley.

Kessler, R.C., Adler, L., Ames, M., Barkley, R.A., Birnbaum, H., Greenberg, P., . . . Ustün, T.B. (2005). The prevalence and effects of adult attention deficit/hyperactivity disorder on work performance in a nationally representative sample of workers. *Journal of Occupational and Environmental Medicine, 47*, 565–572.

Kessler, R.C., Adler, L.A., Barkley, R., Biederman, J., Conners, C.K., Faraone, S.V., . . . Zaslavsky, A.M. (2005). Patterns and predictors of attention-deficit/hyperactivity disorder persistence into adulthood: Results from the national comorbidity survey replication. *Biological Psychiatry, 57*, 1442–1451.

Kessler, R C., Adler, L., Barkley, R., Biederman, J., Conners, C.K., Demler, O., . . . Zaslavsky, A.M. (2006). The prevalence and correlates of adult ADHD in the United States: results from the National Comorbidity Survey Replication. *American Journal of Psychiatry, 163*, 716–723.

Khalifa, N., & von Knorring, A.L. (2005). Tourette syndrome and other tic disorders in a total population of children: Clinical assessment and background. *Acta Paediatrica, 94*, 1608–1614.

Khalife, N., Kantomaa, M., Glover, V., Tammelin, T., Laitinen, J., Ebeling, H., . . . Rodriguez, A. (2014). Childhood attention-deficit/hyperactivity disorder symptoms are risk factors for obesity and physical inactivity in adolescence. *Journal of the American Academy of Child and Adolescent Psychiatry, 534*, 425–436.

Kieling, C., Goncalves, R.R., Tannock, R., & Castellanos, F.X. (2008). Neurobiology of attention deficit hyperactivity disorder. *Child and Adolescent Psychiatric Clinics of North America, 17*, 285–307.

Kieling, C., Kieling, R.R., Rohde, L.A., Frick, P.J., Moffitt, T., Nigg, J.T., & Castellanos, F.X. (2010). The age at onset of attention deficit hyperactivity disorder. *American Journal of Psychiatry, 167*, 14–16.

Killeen, P.R., Russell, V.A., & Sergeant, J.A. (2013). A behavioral neuroenergetics theory of ADHD. *Neuroscience and Biobehavioral Reviews, 37*, 625–657.

Kim, B.N., Lee, J.S., Shin, M.S., Cho, S.C., & Lee, D.S. (2002). Regional cerebral perfusion abnormalities in attention deficit/hyperactivity disorder. *European Archives of Psychiatry and Clinical Neuroscience, 252*, 219–225.

Kim, H.W., Yoon, I.Y., Cho, S.C., Kim, B.N., Chung, S., Lee, H., . . . Yoo, H.J. (2010). The effect of OROS methylphenidate on the sleep of children with attention-deficit/hyperactivity disorder. *International Clinical Psychopharmacology, 25*, 107–115.

Kim, J., Mutyala, B., Agiovlasitis, S., & Fernhall, B. (2011). Health behaviors and obesity among US children with attention deficit hyperactivity disorder by gender and medication use. *Preventive Medicine, 52*, 218–222.

Kim, O.H., & Kaiser, A.P. (2000). Language characteristics of children with ADHD. *Journal of Attention Disorders, 21*, 154–165.

Kinsbourne, M. (1977). The mechanism of hyperactivity. In M. Blau, I. Rapin, & M. Kinsbourne (Eds.), *Topics in child neurology* (pp. 289–306). New York: Spectrum.

Kirk, S.A. (1963). Behavioral diagnoses and remediation of learning disabilities. In *Proceedings of the annual meeting: Conference on exploration into the problems of the perceptually handicapped child* (Vol. 1, pp. 1–7). Evanston, IL.

Kirk, S.A., & Kutchins, H. (1992). *The selling of DSM: The rhetoric science in psychiatry.* New York: Aldine de Gruyter.

Kirov, R. (2013). REM sleep and dreaming functions beyond reductionism. *Behavioral and Brain Sciences, 36*, 621–622.

Kirov, R., & Brand, S. (2014). Sleep problems and their effect in ADHD. *Expert Review of Neurotherapeutics, 14*, 287–299.

Klasen, H. (2000). A name, what's in a name? The medicalization of hyperactivity, revisited. *Harvard Review of Psychology, 7*, 334–344.

Klassen, L.J., Katzman, M.A., & Chokka, P. (2010). Adult ADHD and its comorbidities, with a focus on bipolar disorder. *Journal of Affective Disorders, 124*, 1–8.

Klein, C., Wendling, K., Huettner, P., Ruder, H., & Peper, M. (2006). Intra-subject variability in attention-deficit hyperactivity disorder. *Biological Psychiatry, 60,* 1088–1097.
Klein, D. N., & Riso, L. P. (1993). Psychiatric disorders: Problems of boundaries and comorbidity. In C. G. Costello (Ed.), *Basic issues in psychopathology* (pp. 19–66). New York: Guilford Press.
Klein, R. G., Mannuzza, S., Olazagasti, M.A.R., Roizen, E., Hutchison, J. A., Lashua, E., & Castellanos, X. (2012). Clinical and functional outcome of childhood attention-deficit/hyperactivity disorder 33 years later. *Archives of General Psychiatry, 69,* 1295–1303.
Klingberg, T. (2006). Development of a superior frontal-intraparietal network for visuospatial working memory. *Neuropsychologia, 44,* 2171–2177.
Klingberg, T. (2010). Training and plasticity of working memory. *Trends in Cognitive Science, 14,* 317–324.
Knell, E. R., & Comings, D. E. (1993). Tourette's syndrome and attention-deficit hyperactivity disorder: Evidence for a genetic relationship. *Journal of Clinical Psychiatry, 54,* 331–337.
Knopik, V. S., Heath, A. C., Jacob, T., Slutske, W. S., Bucholz, K. K., Madden, P. A., . . . Martin, N. G. (2006). Maternal alcohol use disorder and offspring ADHD: disentangling genetic and environmental effects using a children-of-twins design. *Psychological Medicine, 36,* 1461–1472.
Knouse, L. E. (2015). Cognitive-behavioral therapies for ADHD. In R. A. Barkley (Ed.) *Attention-Deficit Hyperactivity Disorder* (4th ed., pp. 757–773). New York: Guilford Press.
Knouse, L. E., & Safren, S. A. (2013). Psychosocial treatment for adult ADHD. In S.B.A. Surman (Ed.), *ADHD in adults* (pp. 119–136). New York: Humana Press.
Knouse, L., Zvorsky, I., & Safren, S. (2013). Depression in adults with Attention-Deficit/Hyperactivity Disorder (ADHD): The mediating role of cognitive-behavioral factors. *Cognitive Therapy and Research, 37,* 1220–1232.
Knutson, B., Adams, C. M., Fong, G. W., & Hommer, D. (2002). Anticipation of increasing monetary reward selectively recruits nucleus accumbens. *Journal of Neuroscience, 22,* 3303–3305.
Kofler, M. J., Rapport, M. D., Bolden, J., Sarver, D. E., & Raiker, J. S. (2010). ADHD and working memory: The impact of central executive deficits and exceeding storage/rehearsal capacity on observed inattentive behavior. *Journal of Abnormal Child Psychology, 38,* 149–161.
Kofler, M. J., Rapport, M. D., Bolden, J., Sarver, D. E., Raiker, J. S., & Alderson, R. M. (2011). Working memory deficits and social problems in children with ADHD. *Journal of Abnormal Child Psychology, 39,* 805–817.
Koller, H., Richardson, S. A., Katz, M., & McLaren, J. (1983). Behavior disturbance since childhood among a 5-year birth cohort of all mentally retarded young adults in a city. *American Journal of Mental Deficiency, 87,* 386–395.
Kollins, S. H., & Greenhill, L. (2006). Evidence base for the use of stimulant medication in preschool children with ADHD. *Infants & Young Children, 19,* 132–141.
Kolpe, M., & Carlson, G. (2007). Influence of attention-deficit/hyperactivity disorder symptoms on methadone treatment outcome. *American Journal on Addictions, 16,* 46–48.
Komro, K. A., Maldonado-Molina, M. M., Tobler, A. L., Bonds, J. R., Muller, K. E. (2007). Effects of home access and availability of alcohol on young adolescents' alcohol use. *Addiction, 102,* 1597–1608.
Konofal, E., Lecendreux, M., & Cortese, S. (2010). Sleep and ADHD. *Sleep Medicine, 11,* 652–658.
Konrad, K., & Eickhoff, S. B. (2010). Is the ADHD brain wired differently? A review on structural and functional connectivity in attention deficit hyperactivity disorder. *Human Brain Mapping, 31,* 904–916.
Kooij, J. J. (2013). *Adult ADHD: Diagnostic assessment and treatment.* London: Springer-Verlag.
Kooij, J. J., Rösler, M., Philipsen, A., Wächter, S., Dejonckheere, J., van der Kolk, A., . . . Schäuble, B. (2013). Predictors and impact of non-adherence in adults with attention-deficit/hyperactivity disorder receiving OROS methylphenidate: Results from a randomized, placebo-controlled trial. *BMC Psychiatry, 13,* 36.
Koten, J. W., Jr., Wood, G., Hagoort, P., Goebel, R., Propping, P., Willmes, K., & Boomsma, D. I. (2009). Genetic contribution to variation in cognitive function: An FMRI study in twins. *Science, 323,* 1737–1740.

Kraemer, H.C., Stice, E., Kazdin, A., Offord, D., & Kupfer, D. (2001). How do risk factors work together? Mediators, moderators, and independent, overlapping, and proxy risk factors. *American Journal of Psychiatry, 158*, 848–856.

Kramer, F., & Pollnow, H. (1932) Über eine hyperkinetische Erkrankung im Kindesalter. Aus der Psychiatrischen und Nerven-Klinik der Charité in Berlin (Direktor: Geh. Med.-Rat Prof. Dr. Bonhoeffer). *Monatsschrift für Psychiatrie und Neurologie, 82*, 21–40 [Reprint in Rothenberger, A., & Neumärker, K.J. (2005) Wissenschaftsgeschichte der ADHS. Kramer-Pollnow im Spiegel der Zeit. Steinkopff, Darmstadt].

Kroes, M., Kessels, A.G., Kalff, A.C., Feron, F.J., Vissers, Y.L., Jolles, J., & Vles, J.S. (2002). Quality of movement as predictor of ADHD: Results from a prospective population study in 5-and 6-year-old children. *Developmental Medicine & Child Neurology, 44*, 753–760.

Krone, B., & Newcorn, J.H. (2015). Comorbidity of ADHD and Anxiety Disorders. In L.A. Adler, T.J. Spencer, & T.E. Wilens (Eds.), *Attention-Deficit Hyperactivity Disorder in adults and children* (pp. 98–110). Cambridge: Cambridge University Press.

Krueger, R.F., & Bezdjian, S. (2009). Enhancing research and treatment of mental disorders with dimensional concepts: toward DSM-V and ICD-11 *World Psychiatry, 8*, 3–6.

Krueger, R.F., Hicks, B.M., Patrick, C.J., Carlson, S.R., Iacono, W.G., & McGue, M. (2002). Etiologic connections among substance dependence, antisocial behavior, and personality: Modeling the externalizing spectrum. *Journal of Abnormal Psychology, 111*, 411–424.

Krueger, R.F., & Markon, K.E. (2006). Reinterpreting comorbidity: A model-based approach to understanding and classifying psychopathology. *Annual Review of Clinical Psychology, 2*, 111–133.

Kruger, M., & Kendell, J. (2001). Description of self: An exploratory study of adolescents with ADHD. *Journal of Child and Adolescent Psychiatric Nursing, 14*, 61–72.

Kubik, J.A. (2010). Efficacy of ADHD coaching for adults with ADHD. *Journal of Attention Disorders, 13*, 442–453.

Kuhl, P.K., Conboy, B.T., Padden, D., Nelson, T., & Pruitt, J. (2005). Early speech perception and later language development: implications for the 'critical period'. *Language, Learning and Development, 1*, 237–264.

Kuhne, M., Schachar, R., & Tannock, R. (1997). Impact of comorbid oppositional or conduct problems on attention-deficit hyperactivity disorder. *Journal of the American Academy of Child and Adolescent Psychiatry, 36*, 1715–1725.

Kuntsi, J., Andreou, P., Ma, J., Borger, N.A., van der Meere, J.J. (2005). Testing assumptions for endophenotype studies in ADHD: Reliability and validity of tasks in a general population sample. *BMC Psychiatry, 5*, 40.

Kuperman, S., Johnson, B., Arndt, S., Lindgren, S., & Wolraich, M. (1996). Quantitative EEG differences in a non clinical sample of children with ADHD and undifferentiated ADD. *Journal of the American Academy of Child and Adolescent Psychiatry, 1*, 121–124.

Kuriyan, A.B., Pelham, W.E., Jr., Molina, B.S.G., Waschbusch, D.A., Gnagy, E.M., Sibley, M.H., . . . Kent, K.M. (2013). Young adult educational and vocational outcomes of children diagnosed with ADHD. *Journal of Abnormal Child Psychology, 41*, 27–41.

Kurlan, R., Como, P.G., Miller, B., Palumbo, D., Deeley, C., Andresen, EM., . . . McDermott, M.P. (2002). The behavioral spectrum of tic disorders: A community-based study. *Neurology, 59*, 414–420.

Kutcher, S., Aman, M., Brooks, S.J., Buitelaar, J., van Daalen, E., Fegert, J., . . . Tyano, S. (2004). International consensus statement on attention-deficit/hyperactivity disorder (ADHD) and disruptive behaviour disorders (DBDs): Clinical implications and treatment practice suggestions. *European Neuropsychopharmacology, 14*, 11–28.

LaBrie, R.A., Shaffer, H.J., LaPlante, D.A., & Wechsler, H. (2003). Correlates of college student gambling in the United States. *Journal of American College Health, 52*, 53–62.

Lahey, B.B., Applegate, B., McBurnett, K., Biederman, J., Greenhill, L., Hynd, G.W., et al. (1994). DSM-IV field trials for attention-deficit/hyperactivity disorder in children and adolescents. *American Journal of Psychiatry, 151*, 1673–1685.

Lahey, B.B., Hartung, C.M., Loney, J., Pelham, W.E., Chronis, A.M., & Lee, S.S. (2007). Are there sex differences in the predictive validity of DSM-IV ADHD among younger children? *Journal of Clinical Child and Adolescent Psychology, 36*, 113–126.

Lahey, B.B., Pelham, W.E., Loney, J., Kipp, H., Erhardt, A., Lee, S.S., . . . Massetti, G. (2004). Three-year predictive validity of DSM-IV attention deficit hyperactivity disorder in children diagnosed at 4–6 years of age. *American Journal of Psychiatry*, *61*, 2014–2020.

Lahey, B.B., Pelham, W.E., Loney, J., Lee, S.S., & Willcutt, E. (2005). Instability for the DSM-IV subtypes of ADHD from preschool through elementary school. *Archives of General Psychiatry*, *62*, 896–902.

Lahey, B.B., Rathouz, P.J., Lee, S.S., Chronis-Tuscano, A., Pelham, W.E., Waldman, I.D., & Cook, E.H. (2011). Interactions between early parenting and a polymorphism of the child's dopamine transporter gene in predicting future child conduct disorder symptoms. *Journal of Abnormal Psychology*, *120*, 33–45.

Lahey, B.B., Schaughency, E.A., Hynd, G.W., Carlson, C.L., & Nieves, N. (1987). Attention deficit disorder with and without hyperactivity: Comparison of behavioral characteristics of clinic-referred children. *Journal of the American Academy of Child and Adolescent* Psychiatry, 26, 718–723.

Lambert, N. (2005). The contribution of childhood ADHD, conduct problems, and stimulant treatment to adolescent and adult tobacco and psychoactive substance abuse. *Ethical Human Psychology and Psychiatry*, *7*, 197–221.

Landerl, K., Bevan, A., & Butterworth, B. (2004). Developmental dyscalculia and basic numerical capacities: A study of 8–9 year old students. *Cognition*, *93*, 99–125.

Langberg, J.M., Dvorsky, M.R., Marshall, S., & Evans, S.W. (2013). Clinical implications of daytime sleepiness for the academic performance of middle school-aged adolescents with attention deficit hyperactivity disorder. *Journal of Sleep Research*, *22*, 542–548.

Langberg, J.M., Dvorsky, M.R., Molitor, S.J., Bourchtein, E., Eddy, L.D., Smith, Z., . . . Evans, S.W. (2016). Longitudinal evaluation of the importance of homework assignment completion for the academic performance of middle school students with ADHD. *Journal of School Psychology*, *55*, 27–38.

Langberg, J.M., Molina, B.S., Arnold, L.E., Epstein, J.N., Altaye, M., Hinshaw, S.P., . . . Hechtman, L. (2011). Patterns and predictors of adolescent academic achievement and performance in a sample of children with attention-deficit/hyperactivity disorder. *Journal of Clinical Child & Adolescent Psychology*, *40*, 519–531.

Langberg, J.M., Smith, B.H., Bogle, K.E., Schmidt, J.D., Cole, W.R., & Pender, C. (2006). A pilot evaluation of Small Group Challenging Horizons Program: A randomized trial. *Journal of Applied School Psychology*, *23*, 31–58.

Lange, K.W., Reichl, S., Lange, K.M., Tucha, L., & Tucha, O. (2010). The history of attention deficit hyperactivity disorder. *ADHD Attention Deficit and Hyperactivity Disorders*, *2*, 241–255.

Langley, K., Heron, J., O'Donovan, M.C., Owen, M.J., & Thapar, A. (2010). Genotype link with extreme antisocial behavior: The contribution of cognitive pathways. *Archives of General Psychiatry*, *67*, 1317–1323.

Langley, K., Heron, J., Smith, G.D., & Thapar, A. (2012). Maternal and paternal smoking during pregnancy and risk of ADHD symptoms in offspring: Testing for intrauterine effects. *American Journal of Epidemiology*, *176*, 261–268.

Langley, K., Rice, F., Van der Bree, M., & Thapar, A. (2005). Maternal smoking during pregnancy as an environmental risk factor for attention-deficit/hyperactivity disorder behaviour. A review. *Minerva Pediatrica*, *57*, 359–371.

Langner, H. (2002). Role expectations. In P.O. Quinn, & K.C. Nadeau (Eds.), *Gender issues and ADHD* (pp. 70–80). USA: Advantage Books.

Lara, C., Fayyad, J., de Graaf, R., Kessler, R.C., Aguilar-Gaxiola, S., Angermeyer, M., . . . Sampson, N. (2009). Childhood predictors of adult attention-deficit/hyperactivity disorder: Results from the World Health Organization World Mental Health Survey Initiative. *Biological Psychiatry*, *65*, 46–54.

Larson, K., Russ, S.A., Kahn, R.S., & Halfon, N. (2011). Patterns of comorbidity, functioning, and service use for US children with ADHD. *Pediatrics*, *127*, 462–470.

Laucht, M., Skowronek, M.H., Becker, K.B., Schmidt, M.H., Esser, G., Schulze, T.G., & Rietschel, M. (2007). Interacting effects of the dopamine transporter gene and psychosocial adversity on attention-deficit/hyperactivity disorder symptoms among 15-year-olds from a high-risk community sample. *Archives of General Psychiatry*, *64*, 585–590.

Laufer, M.W., & Denhoff, E. (1957). Hyperkinetic behavior syndrome in children. *Journal of Pediatrics*, *50*, 463–474.

Laufer, M.W., Denhoff, E., & Solomons, G. (1957). Hyperkinetic impulse disorder in children's behavior problems. *Psychosomatic Medicine*, *19*, 38–49.

Lavigne, J.V., Arend, R., Rosenbaum, D., Binns, H.J., Christoffel, K.K., & Gibbons, R.D. (1998). Psychiatric disorders with onset in the preschool years: I stability of diagnoses. *Journal of the American Academy of Child and Adolescent Psychiatry*, *37*, 1246–1254.

Lawson, K.R., & Ruff, H.A. (2004). Early attention and negative emotionality predict later cognitive and behavioural function. *International Journal of Behavioral Development*, *28*, 157–165.

LeBourgeois, M.K., Avis, K., Mixon, M., Olmi, J., & Harsh, J. (2004). Snoring, sleep quality, and sleepiness across attention-deficit/hyperactivity disorder subtypes. *Sleep*, *27*, 520–526.

Lee, D.H., Jacobs, D.R., & Porta, M. (2007). Association of serum concentrations of persistent organic pollutants with the prevalence of learning disability and attention deficit disorder. *Journal of Epidemiology and Community Health*, *61*, 591–96.

Lee, S.L., Falk, A.E., & Aguirre, V.P. (2012). Association of comorbid anxiety with social functioning in school-age children with and without attention-deficit/hyperactivity disorder (ADHD). *Psychiatry Research*, *197*, 90–96.

Lee, S.S., Humphreys, K.L., Flory, K., Liu, R., & Glass, K. (2011). Prospective association of childhood attention-deficit/hyperactivity disorder (ADHD) and substance use and abuse/dependence: A meta-analytic review. *Clinical Psychology Review*, *31*, 328–341.

Lee, S.S., Lahey, B.B., Owens, E.B., & Hinshaw, S. (2008). Few preschool boys and girls are well-adjusted during adolescence. *Journal of Abnormal Child Psychology*, *36*, *373–383*.

LeFevre, J., Fast, L., Skwarchuk, S., Smith-Chant, B.L., Bisanz, J., Kamawar, D., & Penner-Wilger, M. (2010). Pathways to mathematics: Longitudinal predictors of performance. *Child Development*, *81*, 1753–1767.

Le Foll, B., Gallo, A., Le Strat, Y., Lu, L., & Gorwood, P. (2009). Genetics of dopamine receptors and drug addiction: A comprehensive review. *Behavioural Pharmacology*, *20*, 1–17.

Lehn, H., Derks, E.M., Hudziak, J.J., Heutink, P., van Beijsterveldt, T.C., & Boomsma, D.I. (2007). Attention problems and attention-deficit/hyperactivity disorder in discordant and concordant monozygotic twins: Evidence of environmental moderators. *Journal of the American Academy of Child and Adolescent Psychiatry*, *46*, 83–91.

Lehtonen, L., Korhonen, T., & Korvenranta, H. (1994). Temperament and sleeping patterns on colicky infants during the first year of life. *Developmental and Behavioral Pediatrics*, *15*, 416–420.

Leibenluft, E., Charney, D.S., Towbin, K.E., Bhangoo, R.K., & Pine, D.S. (2003). Defining clinical phenotypes of juvenile mania. *American Journal of Psychiatry*, *160*, 430–437.

Leins, U., Goth, G., Hinterberger, T., Klinger, C., Rumpf, N., & Strehl, U. (2007). Neurofeedback for children with ADHD: A comparison of SCP and Theta/Beta protocols. *Applied Psychophysiology and Biofeedback*, *32*, 73–88.

Leitner, Y. (2014). The co-occurrence of autism and attention deficit hyperactivity disorder in children—what do we know? *Frontiers in Human Neuroscience*, *8*, 268.

Lenroot, R.K., Schmitt, J.E., Ordaz, S.J., Wallace, G.L., Neale, M.C., Lerch, J.P., . . . Giedd, J.N. (2009). Differences in genetic and environmental influences on the human cerebral cortex associated with development during childhood and adolescence. *Human Brain Mapping*, *30*, 163–174.

Levin, P.M. (1938). Restlessness in children. *Archives of Neurology and Psychiatry*, *39*, 764–770.

Levy, F. (2005). ADHD, comorbidity, synaptic gates and re-entrant circuits. *Behavioral and Brain Sciences*, *28*, 434–435.

Levy, F., Hay, A., McStephen, M., Wood, C., & Waldman, I. (1997). Attention deficit hyperactivity disorder: A category or a continuum? Genetic analysis of a large-scale twin study. *Journal of the American Academy of Child and Adolescent Psychiatry*, *36*, 737–744.

Levy, L.D., Fleming, J.P., & Klar, D. (2009). Treatment of refractory obesity in severely obese adults following management of newly diagnosed attention deficit hyperactivity disorder. *International Journal of Obesity*, *33*, 326–334.

Lewis, B.A., Short, E.J., Iyengar, S.K., Taylor, H.G., Freebairn, M.L., Tag, M.J., . . . Stein, C.M. (2012). Speech-sound disorders and attention-deficit/hyperactivity disorder symptoms. *Topics in Language Disorders, 32*, 247–263.

Leyfer, O.T., Folstein, S.E., Bacalman, S., Davis, N.O., Dinh, E., Morgan, J., . . . Lainhart, J.E. (2006). Comorbid psychiatric disorders in children with autism: Interview development and rates of disorders. *Journal of Autism and Developmental Disorders, 36*, 849–861.

Li, C.S., Yan, P., Bergquist, K.L., & Sinha, R. (2007). Greater activity of the "default" brain regions predicts stop signal errors. *Neuroimage, 38*, 640–648.

Li, D., Sham, P.C., Owen, M.J., & He, L. (2006). Meta-analysis shows significant association between dopamine system genes and attention deficit hyperactivity disorder (ADHD). *Human Molecular Genetics, 15*, 2276–2284.

Li, J.J., & Lee, S.S. (2012). Interaction of dopamine transporter (DAT1) genotype and maltreatment for ADHD: A latent class analysis. *Journal of Child Psychology and Psychiatry, 53*, 997–1005.

Li, X., Sroubek, A., Kelly, M.S., Lesser, I., Sussman, E., He, Y., . . . Foxe, J.J. (2012). Atypical pulvinar-cortical pathways during sustained attention performance in children with attention-deficit/hyperactivity disorder. *Journal of the American Academy of Child and Adolescent Psychiatry, 51*, 1197–1207.

Lie, N. (1992). Follow-ups of children with attention deficit hyperactivity disorder (ADHD): Review of literature. *Acta Psychiatrica Scandinavica, 85*(Suppl. 368), 40.

Liechti, M.D., Maurizio, S., Heinrich, H., Jancke, L., Meier, L., Steinhausen, H.C., . . . Brendeis, D. (2012). First clinical trial of tomographic neurofeedback in attention-deficit/hyperactivity disorder: Evaluation of voluntary cortical control. *Clinical Neurophysiology, 123*, 1989–2005.

Lilienfeld, S.O. (2003). Comorbidity between and within childhood externalizing and internalizing disorders: Reflections and directions. *Journal of Abnormal Child Psychology, 31*, 285–291.

Lim, J.R., Faught, P.R., Chalasani, N.P., & Molleston, J.P. (2006). Severe liver injury after initiating therapy with atomoxetine in two children. *Journal of Pediatrics, 148*, 831–834.

Lin, Y.J., Lai, M.C., & Gau, S.S.F. (2012). Youths with ADHD with and without tic disorders: Comorbid psychopathology, executive function and social adjustment. *Research in Developmental Disabilities, 33*, 951–963.

Lindsay, R.L., Tomazic, T., Levine, M.D., & Accardo, P.J. (2001). Attentional function as measured by a Continuous Performance Task in children with dyscalculia. *Journal of Developmental & Behavioral Pediatrics, 22*, 287–292.

Lindsey, M. (2002). Comprehensive health care services for people with learning disabilities. *Journal of Advances in Psychiatric Treatment, 8*, 138–147.

Lingam, R., Hunt, L., Golding, J., Jongmans, M., & Emond, A. (2009). Prevalence of developmental coordination disorder using the DSM-IV at 7 years of age: A UK population-based study. *Pediatrics, 123*, e693–e700.

Linnet, K.M., Dalsgaard, S., Obel, C., Wisborg, K., Henriksen, T.B., Rodriguez, A., . . . Jarvelin, M.R. (2003). Maternal lifestyle factors in pregnancy risk of attention deficit hyperactivity disorder and associated behaviors: Review of the current evidence. *American Journal of Psychiatry, 160*, 1028–1040.

Liston, C., Cohen, M.M., Teslovich, T., Levenson, D., & Casey, B.J. (2011). Atypical prefrontal connectivity in attention-deficit/hyperactivity disorder: Pathway to disease or pathological end point?. *Biological Psychiatry, 69*, 1168–1177.

Listug-Lunde, L., Zevenbergen, A.A., & Petros, T.V. (2008). Psychological symptomatology in siblings of children with ADHD. *Journal of Attention Disorders, 12*, 239–247.

Liu, C., Robin, A.L., Brenner, S., & Eastman, J. (1991). Social acceptability of methylphenidate and behavior modification for treating attention deficit hyperactivity disorder. *Pediatrics, 88*, 560–565.

Liu, W., Lee, G.P., Goldweber, A., Petras, H., Storr, C.L., Ialongo, N.S., & Martins, S.S. (2013). Impulsivity trajectories and gambling in adolescence among urban male youth. *Addiction, 108*, 780–788.

Livingston, R. (1999). Cultural issues in diagnosis and treatment of ADHD. *Journal of the American Academy of Child and Adolescent Psychiatry, 38*, 1591–1594.

Locascio, G., Mahone, E.M., Eason, S.H., & Cutting, L.E. (2010). Executive dysfunction among reading comprehension deficits. *Journal of Learning Disabilities*, *43*, 441–451.

Lochman, J.E., & Wayland, K.K. (1994). Aggression, social acceptance, and race as predictors of negative adolescent outcomes. *Journal of the American Academy of Child and Adolescent Psychiatry*, *33*, 1026–1035.

Loe, I.M., & Feldman, H.M. (2007). Academic and educational outcomes of children with ADHD. *Journal of Pediatric Psychology*, *32*, 643–654.

Loeber, R., Green, S.M., Lahey, B.B., Christ, M.A.G., & Frick, P.J. (1992). Developmental sequences in the age of onset of disruptive child behaviors. *Journal of Child and Family Studies*, *1*, 21–41.

Logan, G. (1997). Automaticity and reading: Perspectives from the instance theory of automatization. *Reading and Writing Quarterly: Overcoming Learning Disabilities*, *13*, 123–146.

Loo, S.K., & Barkley, R.A. (2005). Clinical utility of EEG in attention deficit hyperactivity disorder. *Applied Neuropsychology*, *12*, 64–76.

Loo, S.K., & Makeig, S. (2012). Clinical utility of EEG in attention-deficit/hyperactivity disorder: A research update. *Neurotherapeutics*, *9*, 569–587.

Lopes-Silva, J.B., Moura, R., Júlio-Costa, A., Haase, V.G., & Wood, G. (2014). Phonemic awareness as a pathway to number transcoding. *Frontiers in Psychology*, *28*, 13.

Lopez, M.A., Toprac, M.G., Crismon, M.L., Boemer, C., & Baumgartner, J. (2005). A psychoeducational program for children with ADHD or depression and their families: results from the CMAP feasibility study. *Community Mental Health Journal*, *41*, 51–66.

Lorch, E.P., Milich, R., Astrin, C.C., & Berthiaume, K.S. (2006). Cognitive engagement and story comprehension in typically developing children and children with ADHD from preschool through elementary school. *Developmental Psychology*, *42*, 1206–1219.

Lorch, E.P., Milich, R., Flake, R.A., Ohlendorf, J., & Little, S. (2010). A developmental examination of story recall and coherence among children with ADHD. *Journal of Abnormal Child Psychology*, *38*, 291–301.

Lou, H.C., Henriksen, L., & Bruhn, P. (1984). Focal cerebral hypoperfusion in children with dysphasia and/or attention deficit disorder. *Archives of Neurology*, *41*, 825–829.

Lou, H.C., Henriksen, L., & Bruhn, P., Borner, H., & Nielsen, J.B. (1989). Striatal dysfunction in attention deficit and hyperkinetic disorder. *Archives of Neurology*, *46*, 48–52.

Loughran, S.B. (2003). Agreement and stability of teacher rating scales for assessing ADHD in preschoolers. *Early Childhood Education Journal*, *30*, 247–253.

Lougy, R.A., & Rosenthal, D.K. (2002). *ADHD. A survival guide for parents and teachers.* Duarte: Hope Press.

Lourenço, B.H., Arthur, T., Rodrigues, M.D., Guazzelli, I., Frazzatto, E., Deram, S., . . . Villares, S.M. (2008). Binge eating symptoms, diet composition and metabolic characteristics of obese children and adolescents. *Appetite*, *50*, 223–230.

Lovejoy, M.C., Graczyk, P.A., O'Hare, E., & Neuman, G. (2000). Maternal depression and parenting behavior: A meta-analytic review. *Clinical Psychology Review*, *20*, 561–592.

Lubar, J.F., & Shouse, M.N. (1976). EEG and behavioral changes in a hyperkinetic child concurrent with training of the sensorimotor rhythm (SMR): A preliminary report. *Biofeedback and Self Regulation*, *1*, 293–306.

Lubke, G.H., Hudziak, J.J., Derks, E.M., van Bijsterveldt, T.C.E.M., & Boomsma, D.I. (2009). Maternal ratings of attention problems in ADHD: Evidence for the existence of a continuum. *Journal of the American Academy of Child and Adolescent Psychiatry*, *48*, 1085–1093.

Lubke, G.H., Muthen, B., Moilanen, I.K., McGough, J.J., Loo, S.K., Swanson, J.M., . . . Smalley, S.L. (2007). Subtypes versus severity differences in attention-deficit/hyperactivity disorder in the northern Finnish birth cohort. *Journal of the American Academy of Child and Adolescent Psychiatry*, *46*, 1584–1593.

Luman, M., Oosterlaan, J., & Sergeant, J. (2005). The impact of reinforcement contingencies on AD/HD: A review and theoretical appraisal. *Clinical Psychology Review*, *25*, 183–213.

Luman, M., Tripp, G., & Scheres, A. (2010). Identifying the neurobiology of altered reinforcement sensitivity in ADHD: A review and research agenda. *Neuroscience and Biobehavioral Reviews, 34*, 744–754.

Luman, M., van Noesel, S. J., Papanikolau, A., van Oostenbruggen-Scheffer, J., Veugelers, D., Sergeant, J. A., & Oosterlaan, J. (2009). Inhibition, reinforcement sensitivity and temporal information processing in ADHD and ADHD + ODD: Evidence of a separate entity? *Journal of Abnormal Child Psychology, 37*, 1123–1135.

Lundahl, B., Risser, H. J., Lovejoy, M. C. (2006). A meta-analysis of parent training: Moderators and follow-up effects. *Clinical Psychology Review, 26*, 86–104.

Lyon, G. R., Shaywitz, S. E., & Shaywitz, B. A. (2003). A definition of dyslexia. *Annals of Dyslexia, 53*, 1–14.

Maddox, C., & Wilson, K. B. (2004, July). *Race matters: Disparities in African American children with attention deficit hyperactivity disorder*. Paper presented at the McNair Scholars Conference at Penn State University, State College, PA.

Mahajan, M., Hong, N., Wigal, T., & Gehricke, J. (2010). Hyperactive-impulsive symptoms associated with self-reported sleep quality in nonmedicated adults with ADHD. *Journal of Attention Disorders, 14*, 132–137.

Mahone, E. M., & Slomine, B. S. (2008). Neurodevelopmental disorders. In J. Morgan & J. Ricker (Eds.), *Textbook of clinical neuropsychology* (pp. 105–127). New York: Taylor & Francis.

Maj, M. (2005). 'Psychiatric comorbidity': An artefact of current diagnostic systems? *British Journal of Psychiatry, 186*, 182–184.

Mallett, C. A., Natarajan, A., & Hoy, J. (2014). Attention Deficit/Hyperactivity Disorder: A DSM Timeline Review. *International Journal of Mental Health, 43*, 36–60.

Malott, R. W., & Trojan-Suarez, E. A. (2006). *Principles of behaviour*. Upper Saddle River, NJ: Pearson Prentice Hall.

Manassis, K., Tannock, R., & Barbosa, J. (2000). Dichotic listening and response inhibition in children with comorbid anxiety disorders and ADHD. *Journal of the American Academy of Child and Adolescent Psychiatry, 39*, 1152–1159.

Maniadaki, K. (2003). *Social perceptions about attention deficit/hyperactivity disorder and other disruptive behaviour disorders: the effect of the child's sex*. Doctoral Dissertation. University of Southampton. [Available at: www.didaktorika.gr/eadd/handle/10442/15022].

Maniadaki, K., & Kakouros, E. (2007). A new approach to the etiology and treatment of stuttering. *Signal. The newsletter of SIG disorders of fluency, 28*, 2–3.

Maniadaki, K., & Kakouros, E. (2008). Social profiles and mental health problems of young offenders in detention in Greece. *Criminal Behaviour and Mental Health, 18*, 207–215.

Maniadaki, K., & Kakouros, E. (2011). Attention problems and learning disabilities in young offenders in detention in Greece. *Psychology, 2*, 53–59.

Maniadaki, K., Kakouros, E., & Karaba, R. (2009). Juvenile delinquency and mental health. In. A. Kakanowski & M. Narusevich (Eds.), *Handbook of social justice* (pp. 1–44). New York: Nova.

Maniadaki, K., Kakouros, E., & Karaba, R. (2010). *Psychopathology in juvenile delinquents*. New York: Nova.

Maniadaki, K., Sonuga-Barke, E., & Kakouros, E. (2003). Trainee nursery teachers' perceptions of disruptive behaviour disorders; the effect of sex of child on judgments of typicality and severity. *Child: Care, Health and Development, 29*, 433–440.

Maniadaki, K., Sonuga-Barke, E., & Kakouros, E. (2005). Parents' causal attributions about Attention Deficit/Hyperactivity Disorder: the effect of child and parent sex. *Child: Care, Health and Development, 31*, 331–340.

Maniadaki, K., Sonuga-Barke, E., & Kakouros, E. (2006). Adults' self-efficacy beliefs and referral attitudes for boys and girls with AD/HD. *European Child and Adolescent Psychiatry, 15*, 132–140

Maniadaki, K., Sonuga-Barke, E., Kakouros, E., & Karaba, R. (2005). Maternal emotions and self-efficacy beliefs in relation to boys and girls with AD/HD. *Child Psychiatry and Human Development, 35*, 245–263.

Maniadaki, K., Sonuga-Barke, E., Kakouros, E., & Karaba, R. (2006a). Parental beliefs about the nature of AD/HD behaviours and their relationship to referral intentions in preschool children. *Child: Care, Health and Development*, *33*, 188–195.

Maniadaki, K., Sonuga-Barke, E., Kakouros, E., & Karaba, R. (2006b). AD/HD symptoms and conduct problems: Similarities and differences in maternal perceptions. *Journal of Child and Family Studies*, *15*, 460–474.

Manly, T., Robertson, I. H., Anderson, V., & Nimmo-Smith, I. (1999). *The test of everyday attention for children*. Bury St. Edmunds, UK: Thames Valley Test Company.

Mann, E. M., Ikeda, Y., Mueller, C. W., Takahashi, A., Tao, K. T., Humris, E., . . . Chin, D. (1992). Cross-cultural differences in rating hyperactive-disruptive behaviors in children. *American Journal of Psychiatry*, *149*, 1539–1542.

Mannuzza, S., Castellanos, F., Roizen, E., Hutchison, J., Lashua, E., & Klein, R. (2011). Impact of the impairment criterion in the diagnosis of adult ADHD: 33-Year Follow-up study of boys with ADHD. *Journal of Attention Disorders*, *15*, 122–129.

Mannuzza, S., Gittelman-Klein, R., Bessler, A., Malloy, P., & LaPadula, M. (1993). Adult outcome of hyperactive boys: Educational achievement, occupational rank, and psychiatric status. *Archives of General Psychiatry*, *50*, 565–576.

Mannuzza, S., & Klein, R. (1992). Predictors of outcome of children with attention-deficit hyperactivity disorder. In G. Weiss (Ed.), *Child and adolescent psychiatric clinics of North America: Attention-Deficit Hyperactivity Disorder* (pp. 567–578). Philadelphia: Saunders.

Mannuzza, S., & Klein, R. G. (2000). Long-term prognosis in attention deficit/ hyperactivity disorder. *Child and Adolescent Psychiatric Clinics of North America*, *9*, 711–726.

Mannuzza, S., Klein, R. G., Konig, P. H., & Giampino, T. L. (1989). Hyperactive boys almost grown up. IV: Criminality and its relationship to psychiatric status. *Archives of General Psychiatry*, *46*, 1073–1079.

Mannuzza, S., Klein, R. G., & Moulton, J. L. (2008). Lifetime criminality among boys with ADHD: A prospective follow-up study into adulthood using official arrest records. *Psychiatry Research*, *160*, 237–246.

Mannuzza, S., Klein, R. G., & Moulton, J. L., 3rd. (2003). Persistence of Attention-Deficit/Hyperactivity Disorder into adulthood: what have we learned from the prospective follow-up studies? *Journal of Attention Disorders*, *7*, 93–100.

March, J. S., Swanson, J. M., Arnold, L. E., Hoza, B., Conners, C. K., Hinshaw, S. P., . . . Pelham, W. E. (2000). Anxiety as a predictor and outcome variable in the Multimodal Treatment Study of children with ADHD (MTA). *Journal of Abnormal Child Psychology*, *28*, 527–541.

Marchant, B. K., Reimherr, F. W., Halls, C., Williams, E. D., Strong, R. E., Kondo, D., . . . Robison, R. J. (2011). Long-term open-label response to atomoxetine in adult ADHD: Influence of sex, emotional dysregulation, and double-blind response to atomoxetine. *Attention Deficit and Hyperactivity Disorders*, *3*, 237–244.

Marchman, V. A., & Bates, E. (1994). Continuity in lexical and morphological development: a test of the critical mass hypothesis. *Journal of Child Language*, *21*, 339–366.

Marchman, V. A., & Fernald, A. (2008). Speed of word recognition and vocabulary knowledge in infancy predict cognitive and language outcomes in later childhood. *Developmental Science*, *11*, F9—F16.

Marco, R., Miranda, A., Schlotz, W., Melia, A., Mulligan, A., Muller, U. . . . Medad, S. (2009). Delay and choice in ADHD: a test of the delay aversion hypothesis. *Neuropsychology*, *23*, 367–380.

Marcus, S. C., Wan, G. J., Kemner, J. E., & Olfson, M. (2005). Continuity of methylphenidate treatment for attention-deficit/hyperactivity disorder. *Archives of Pediatrics & Adolescent Medicine*, *159*, 572–578.

Margulies, D., Weintraub, S., Basile, J., Grover, P., & Carlson, G. (2012). Will Disruptive Mood Dysregulation Disorder reduce false diagnosis of Bipolar Disorder in children? *Bipolar Disorders*, *14*, 488–496.

Marino, C., Mascheretti, S., Riva, V., Cattaneo, D., Rigoletto, M., Rusconi, M., . . . Molteni, M. (2011). Pleiotropic effects of DCDC2 and DYX1C1 genes on language and mathematics traits in nuclear families of developmental dyslexia. *Behavior Genetics*, *41*, 67–76.

Marks, D.J., Mlodnicka, A., Bernstein, M., Chacko, A., Rose, S., & Halperin, J.M. (2009). Profiles of service utilization and the resultant economic impact in preschoolers with attention deficit/hyperactivity disorder. *Journal of Pediatric Psychology*, *34*, 681–689.

Marsh, R., Maia, T.V., & Peterson, B.S. (2009). Functional disturbances within frontostriatal circuits across multiple childhood psychopathologies. *American Journal of Psychiatry*, *166*, 664–674.

Marshal, M.P., Molina, B.S.G., & Pelham, W.E. (2003). Childhood ADHD and adolescent substance use: An examination of deviant peer group affiliation as a risk factor. *Psychology of Addictive Behaviors*, *17*, 293–302.

Martel, M.M., Lucia, V.C., & Nigg, J.T. (2007). Sex differences in the pathway from low birth weight to inattention/hyperactivity. *Journal of Abnormal Child Psychology*, *35*, 87–96.

Martell, C.R., Addis, M.E., & Jacobson, N.S. (2001). *Depression in context: Strategies for guided action*. New York: W.W. Norton.

Martin, N.C., Piek, J.P., & Hay, D. (2006). DCD and ADHD: A genetic study of their shared aetiology. *Human Movement Science*, *25*, 110–124.

Martin, R. (2009). Temperament and the zone of diagnostic ambiguity. *Newlett Temperament Consortium*, *1*, 6–7.

Martinez-Badía, J., & Martinez-Raga, J. (2015). Who says this is a modern disorder? The early history of attention deficit hyperactivity disorder. *World Journal of Psychiatry*, *5*, 379–386.

Martinussen, R., Grimbos, T., & Ferrari, J.L. (2014). Word-level reading achievement and behavioral inattention: Exploring their overlap and relations with naming speed and phonemic awareness in a community sample of children. *Archives of Clinical Neuropsychology*, *29*, 680–690.

Martinussen, R., & Tannock, R. (2006). Working memory impairments in children with attention-deficit hyperactivity disorder with and without comorbid language learning disorders. *Journal of Clinical and Experimental Neuropsychology*, *28*, 1073–1094.

Marton, I., Wiener, J., Rogers, M., Moore, C., & Tannock, R. (2009). Empathy and social perspective taking in children with attention-deficit/hyperactivity disorder. *Journal of Abnormal Child Psychology*, *37*, 107–118.

Marx, A.M., Ehlis, A.C., Furdea, A., Holtmann, M., Banaschewski, T., Brandeis, D., . . . Fallgatter, A.J. (2015). Near-infrared spectroscopy (NIRS) neurofeedback as a treatment for children with attention deficit hyperactivity disorder (ADHD)-a pilot study. *Frontiers in Human Neuroscience*, *8*, 1038.

Mash, E.J., & Johnston, C. (1983a). Sibling interactions of hyperactive and normal children and their relationship to reports of maternal stress and self-esteem. *Journal of Child Clinical Psychology*, *12*, 91–99.

Mash, E.J., & Johnston, C. (1983b). Parental perceptions of child behavior problems, parenting self-esteem, and mothers' reported stress in younger and older hyperactive and normal children. *Journal of Consulting and Clinical Psychology*, *51*, 68–99.

Mash, E.J., & Johnston, C. (1990). Determinants of parenting stress: Illustrations from families of hyperactive children and families of physically abused children. *Journal of Clinical Child Psychology*, *19*, 313–328.

Mash, E.J., & Terdal, L.G. (1988). Behavioral assessment of childhood disturbance. In E.J. Mash & L.G. Terdal (Eds.), *Behavioral assessment of childhood disorders* (2nd ed., pp. 3–65). New York: Guilford Press.

Masi, G., Millepiedi, S., Mucci, M., Bertini, N., Pfanner, C., & Arcangeli, F. (2006). Comorbidity of obsessive-compulsive disorder and attention-deficit/hyperactivity disorder in referred children and adolescents. *Comprehensive Psychiatry*, *47*, 42–47.

Mason, M.J., & Scior, K. (2004). 'Diagnostic overshadowing' amongst clinicians working with people with intellectual disabilities in the UK. *Journal of Applied Research in Intellectual Disabilities*, *17*, 85–91.

Mason, M.J., Walker, L.R., Wine, L.A., Knoper, T.S., & Tercyak, K.P. (2007). Child and adolescent tobacco and substance use within the context of ADHD: Implications for prevention and treatment. *Journal of Clinical Psychology in Medical Settings*, *14*, 227–237.

Massetti, G.M., Lahey, B.B., Pelham, W.E., Loney, J., Ehrhardt, A., Lee, S.S., & Kipp, H. (2008). Academic achievement over 8 years among children who met modified criteria for attention-deficit/hyperactivity disorder at 4–6 years of age. *Journal of Abnormal Child Psychology*, *36*, 399–410.

Mathers, M.E. (2006). Aspects of language in children with ADHD. *Journal of Attention Disorders, 9*, 523–533.
Mathews, C.A., & Grados, M.A. (2011). Familiality of Tourette Syndrome, Obsessive-Compulsive Disorder, and Attention-Deficit\Hyperactivity Disorder: Heritability analysis in a large sib-pair sample. *Journal of the American Academy of Child and Adolescent Psychiatry, 50*, 46–54.
Mathews, H.L., & Janusek, L.W. (2011). Epigenetics and psychoneuroimmunology: Mechanisms and models. *Brain, Behavior, and Immunity, 25*, 25–39.
Mathiesen, K.S., & Sanson, A. (2000). Dimensions of early childhood behavior problems: stability and predictors of change from 18 to 30 months. *Journal of Abnormal Child Psychology, 28*, 15–31.
Matsumoto, T., Kamijo, A., Yamaguchi, A., Iseki, E., & Hirayasu, Y. (2005). Childhood histories of attention-deficit hyperactivity disorders in Japanese methamphetamine and inhalant abusers: preliminary report. *Psychiatry and Clinical Neurosciences, 59*, 102–105.
Matte, B., Anselmi, L., Salum, G.A., Kieling, C., Gonçalves, H., Menezes, A., . . . Rohde, L.A. (2015). ADHD in DSM-5: A field trial in a large, representative sample of 18-to 19-year-old adults. *Psychological Medicine, 45*, 361–373.
Matte, B., Rohde, L.A., & Grevet, E.H. (2012). ADHD in adults: A concept in evolution. *Attention Deficit and Hyperactivity Disorders 4*, 53–62.
Mattes, A. (1980). The role of frontal lobe dysfunction in childhood hyperkinesis. *Comprehensive Psychiatry*, 21, 358–369.
Mattos, P., Saboya, E., Ayrão, V., Segenreich, D., Duchesne, M., & Coutinho, G. (2004). Comorbid eating disorders in a Brazilian attention-deficit/hyperactivity disorder adult clinical sample. *Revista Brasileira de Psiquiatria, 26*, 248–250.
Maudsley, H. (1867). *The physiology and pathology of the mind*. New York: D. Appleton.
Mayes, R., Bagwell, C., & Erkulwater, J. (2008). Medicating children: The enduring controversy over ADHD and pediatric stimulant pharmacotherapy. *Child and Adolescent Psychopharmacology News, 13*, 1–5.
Mayes, S.D., & Calhoun, S.L. (2006). Frequency of reading, math and writing disabilities in children with clinical disorders. *Learning and Individual Differences, 16*, 145–157.
Mayes, S.D., & Calhoun, S.L. (2007). Learning attention, writing, and processing speed in typical children and children with ADHD, autism, anxiety, depression, and oppositional- defiant disorder. *Child Neuropsychology, 13*, 469–493.
Mayes, S.D., Calhoun, S.L., Bixler, E.O., Vgontzas, A.N., Mahr, F., Hillwig-Garcia, J., . . . Parvin, M. (2009). ADHD subtypes and comorbid anxiety, depression, and oppositional-defiant disorder: differences in sleep problems. *Journal of Pediatric Psychology, 34*, 328–337.
Mayes, S.D., Calhoun, S.L., & Crowell, E.W. (2000). Learning disabilities and ADHD: Overlapping spectrum disorders. *Journal of Learning Disabilities, 33*, 417–424.
Mayes, S.D., Calhoun, S.L., Mayes, R.D., & Molitoris, S. (2012). Autism and ADHD: Overlapping and discriminating symptoms. *Research in Autism Spectrum Disorders, 6*, 277–285.
Mayes, S.D., Waxmonsky, J., Calhoun, S.L., Kokotovich, C., Mathiowetz, C., & Baweja, R. (2015). Disruptive mood dysregulation disorder (DMDD) symptoms in children with autism, ADHD, and neurotypical development and impact of co-occurring ODD, depression, and anxiety. Research in Autism Spectrum Disorders, *18*, 64–72.
McAweeney, M., Rogers, N.L., Huddleston, C., Moore, D., & Gentile, J.P. (2010). Symptom prevalence of ADHD in a community residential substance abuse treatment program. *Journal of Attention Disorders, 13*, 601–608.
McBurnett, K., Pfiffner, L.J., & Frick, P.J. (2001). Symptom properties as a function of ADHD type: An argument for continued study of sluggish cognitive tempo. *Journal of Abnormal Child Psychology, 29*, 207–213.
McBurnett, K., Pfiffner, L.J., Willcutt, E., Tamm, L., Lerner, M., Ottolini, Y.L., . . . Furman, M.B. (1999). Experimental cross-validation of DSM-IV types of attention-deficit/hyperactivity disorder. *Journal of the American Academy of Child and Adolescent Psychiatry, 38*, 17–24.
McCann, D., Barrett, A., Cooper, A., Crumpler, D., Dalen, L., Grimshaw, K., . . . Stevenson, J. (2007). Food additives and hyperactive behaviour in 3-year-old and 8/9-year-old children in the community: A randomised, double-blinded, placebo-controlled trial. *The Lancet, 370*, 1560–1567.

McCarney, S.B., & Arthaud, T.J. (2004). *Attention Deficit Disorders Evaluation Scale—Third Edition (ADDES-3) Home Version Technical Manual.* Columbia, MO: Hawthorne Educational Services.

McCarthy, S. (2014). Pharmacological interventions for ADHD: how do adolescent and adult patient beliefs and attitudes impact treatment adherence? *Patient Preference and Adherence, 8*, 1317–1327.

McCarthy, S., Asherson, P., Coghill, D., Hollis, C., Murray, M., Potts, L., . . . Wong, I.C. (2009). Attention-deficit hyperactivity disorder: Treatment discontinuation in adolescents and young adults. *British Journal of Psychiatry, 194*, 273–277.

McCleary, L. (2002). Parenting adolescents with attention deficit hyperactivity disorder: Analysis of the literature for social work practice. *Health & Social Work, 27*, 285–292.

McClelland, M.M., Acock, A.C., & Morrison, F.J. (2006). The impact of kindergarten learning-related skills on academic trajectories at the end of elementary school. *Early Childhood Research Quarterly, 21*, 471–490.

McClelland, M.M., Cameron, C.E., Connor, C.M., Farris, C.L., Jewkes, A.M., & Morrison, F.J. (2007). Links between behavioural regulation and preschoolers' literacy, vocabulary, and math skills. *Developmental Psychology, 43*, 947–959.

McClelland, M.M., Morrison, F.J., & Holmes, D.L. (2000). Children at risk for early academic problems: the role of learning-related social skills. *Early Childhood Research Quarterly*, 15, 307–329.

McCown, W.G., & Chamberlain, L.L. (2000). *Best possible odds: Contemporary treatment strategies for gambling disorders.* New York: Wiley.

McEachin, J.J., Smith, T., & Ivar Lovaas, O. (1993). Long-term outcome for children with autism who received early intensive behavioral treatment. *American Journal of Mental Retardation, 97*, 359–359.

McGee, R., Clark, S.E., & Symons, D.K. (2000). Does the Conners' Continuous Performance Test aid in ADHD diagnosis? *Journal of Abnormal Child Psychology, 28*, 415–424.

McGee, R., & Feehan, M. (1991). Are girls with problems of attention underrecognized? *Journal of Psychopathology and Behavioral Assessment,13*, 187–198.

McGee, R., & Share, D.L. (1988). Attention deficit disorder-hyperactivity and academic failure: Which comes first and what should be treated? *Journal of the American Academy of Child and Adolescent Psychiatry, 27*, 318–327.

McGee, R., Williams, S., & Feehan, M. (1992). Attention deficit disorder and age of onset of problem behaviors. *Journal of Abnormal Child Psychology, 20*, 487–502.

McGoey, K.E., DuPaul, G.J., Eckert, T.L., Volpe, R.J., & Van Brakle, J. (2005). Outcomes of a multi-component intervention for preschool children at-risk for attention-deficit/hyperactivity disorder. *Child & Family Behavior Therapy, 27*, 33–56.

McGough, J.J., & Barkley, R.A. (2004). Diagnostic controversies in adult attention deficit hyperactivity disorder. *American Journal of Psychiatry, 161*, 1948–1956.

McGrath, L.M., Pennington, B.F., Shanahan, M.A., Santerre-Lemmon, L.E., Barnard, H.D., Willcutt, E.G., . . . Olson, R K. (2011). A multiple deficit model of reading disability and attention-deficit/hyperactivity disorder: Searching for shared cognitive deficits. *Journal of Child Psychology and Psychiatry, 52*, 547–557.

McIntyre, R.S., Kennedy, S.H., Soczynska, J.K., Nguyen, H.T., Bilkey, T.S., Woldeyohannes, H.O., . . . Muzina, D.J. (2010). Attention-deficit/hyperactivity disorder in adults with bipolar disorder or major depressive disorder: results from the international mood disorders collaborative project. *Primary Care Companion to the Journal of Clinical Psychiatry, 12*, PCC.09m00861.

McKee, T.E., Harvey, E., Danforth, J.S., Ulaszek, W.R., & Friedman, J.L. (2004). The relation between parental coping styles and parent—child interactions before and after treatment for children with ADHD and oppositional disorder. *Journal of Clinical Child and Adolescent Psychology, 33*, 158–168.

McMahon, W.M., Carter, A.S., Fredine, N., & Pauls, D.L. (2003). Children at familial risk for Tourette's disorder: Child and parent diagnoses. *American Journal of Medical Genetics, 121B* (1), 105–111.

McNab, F., Varrone, A., Farde, L., Jucaite, A., Bystritsky, P., Forssberg, H., & Klingberg, T. (2009). Changes in cortical dopamine D1 receptor binding associated with cognitive training. *Science, 323*, 800–802.

McPartland, J. C., & Dawson, G. (2014). DSM-5 criteria for ASD: Research review and commentary. In T. E. Davis III, S.W. White, & T.H. Ollendick (Eds.), *Handbook of autism and anxiety* (pp. 231–245). New York: Springer.

Meaney, M.J. (2010). Epigenetics and the biological definition of gene×environment interactions. *Child Development, 81*, 41–79.

Meaux, J.B., Green, A., & Broussard, L. (2009). ADHD in the college student: A block in the road. *Journal of Psychiatric and Mental Health Nursing, 16*, 248–256.

Meichenbaum, D.H., & Goodman, J. (1971). Training impulsive children to talk to themselves: A means of developing self-control. *Journal of Abnormal Psychology, 77*, 115–126.

Meijer, W. M., Faber, A., van den Ban, E., & Tobi, H. (2009). Current issues around the pharmacotherapy of ADHD in children and adults. *Pharmacy World and Science, 31*, 509–516.

Meisel, V., Servera, M., Garcia-Banda, G., Cardo, E., & Moreno, I. (2014). Reprint of "Neurofeedback and standard pharmacological intervention in ADHD: A randomized controlled trial with six-month follow-up". *Biological Psychology, 95*, 116–125.

Melby-Lervåg, M., & Hulme, C. (2013). Is working memory training effective? A meta-analytic review. *Developmental Psychology, 49*, 270–291.

Melnick, S. M., & Hinshaw, S. P. (1996). What they want and what they get: The social goals of boys with ADHD and comparison boys. *Journal of Abnormal Child Psychology, 24*, 169–185.

Merikangas, K.R., He, J.P., Brody, D., Fischer, P.W., Bourdon, K., & Koretz, D.S. (2010). Prevalence and treatment of mental disorders among US children in the 2001–2004 NHANES. *Pediatrics, 125*, 75–81.

Merrell, C., & Tymms, P.B. (2001). Inattention, hyperactivity and impulsiveness: their impact on academic achievement and progress. *British Journal of Educational Psychology, 71*, 43–56.

Merrill, B.M., Morrow, A.S., Altszuler, A.R., Macphee, F.L., Gnagy, E.M., Greiner, A.R., . . . Pelham, W.E. (2017). Improving homework performance among children with ADHD: A randomized clinical trial. *Journal of Consulting and Clinical Psychology, 85*, 111–122.

Metin, B., Roeyers, H., Wiersema, J.R., van der Meere, J., & Sonuga-Barke, E. (2012). A meta-analytic study of event rate effects on Go/No-Go performance in attention-deficit/hyperactivity disorder. *Biological Psychiatry, 72*, 990–996.

Metin, B., Wiersema, J.R., Verguts, T., Gasthuys, R., van Der Meere, J.J., Roeyers, H., & Sonuga-Barke, E. (2016). Event rate and reaction time performance in ADHD: testing predictions from the state regulation deficit hypothesis using an ex-Gaussian model. *Child Neuropsychology, 22*, 99–109.

Meyler, A., Keller, T.A., Cherkassky, V.L., Gabrieli, J.D.D., & Just, M.A. (2008). Modifying the brain activation of poor readers during sentence comprehension with extended remedial instruction: A longitudinal study of neuroplasticity. *Neuropsychologia, 46*, 2580–2592.

Miano, S., Donfrancesco, R., Bruni, O., Ferri, R., Galiffa, S., Pagani, J., . . . Pia, V.M. (2006). NREM sleep instability is reduced in children with attention-deficit/hyperactivity disorder. *Sleep, 29*, 797–803.

Michelson, D., Adler, L., Spencer, T., Reimherr, F.W., West, S.A., Allen, A.J., . . . Milton, D. (2003). Atomoxetine in adults with ADHD: Two randomized, placebo controlled studies. *Biological Psychiatry, 53*, 112–120.

Mick, E., Biederman, J., Faraone, S.V., Sayer, J., & Kleinman, S. (2002). Case-control study of attention-deficit/hyperactivity disorder and maternal smoking, alcohol use and drug use during pregnancy. *Journal of the American Academy of Child and Adolescent Psychiatry, 41*, 378–385.

Mick, E., Biederman, J., Jetton, J., & Faraone, S.V. (2000). Sleep disturbances associated with attention deficit hyperactivity disorder: The impact of psychiatric comorbidity and pharmacotherapy. *Journal of Child and Adolescent Psychopharmacology, 10*, 223–231.

Mick, E., Byrne, D., Fried, R., Monuteaux, M., Faraone, S.V., & Biederman, J. (2011). Predictors of ADHD persistence in girls at 5-year follow-up. *Journal of Attention Disorders, 15*, 183–192.

Mick, E., Faraone, S.V., Spencer, T., Zhang, H.F., & Biederman, J. (2008). Assessing the validity of the Quality of Life Enjoyment and Satisfaction Questionnaire-short form in adults with ADHD. *Journal of Attention Disorders, 11*, 508–509.

Micoulaud-Franchi, J., Geoffroy, P., Fond, G., Lopez, R., Bioulac, S., & Philip, P. (2014). EEG Neurofeedback treatments in 44 children with ADHD: An updated meta-analysis of randomized controlled trials. *Frontiers in Human Neuroscience, 8*, 906.

Mihara, M., Miyai, I., Hattori, N., Hatakenaka, M., Yagura, H., Kawano, T., . . . Kubota, K. (2012). Neurofeedback using real-time near-infrared spectroscopy enhances motor imagery related cortical activation. *PloS One, 7*(3), e32234.

Mikami, A.Y. (2015). Social skills training for youth with ADHD. In R.A. Barkley (Ed.) *Attention-Deficit Hyperactivity Disorder* (4th ed., pp. 569–595). New York: Guilford Press.

Mikami, A.Y., Griggs, M.S., Lerner, M.D., Emeh, C.C., Reyland, M.M., Jack, A., & Anthony, M.R. (2013). A randomized trial of a classroom intervention to increase peers' social inclusion of children with attention-deficit/hyperactivity disorder. *Journal of Consulting and Clinical Psychology, 81*, 100–112.

Mikami, A.Y., Hinshaw, S.P., Patterson, K.A., & Lee, J.C. (2008). Eating pathology among adolescent girls with attention-deficit/hyperactivity disorder. *Journal of Abnormal Psychology, 117*, 225–235.

Mikami, A.Y., Lerner, M.D., Griggs, M.S., McGrath, A. & Calhoun, C.D. (2010). Parental influence on children with attention-deficit/hyperactivity disorder: II. Results of a pilot intervention training parents as friendship coaches for children. *Journal of Abnormal Child Psycho*logy, *38*, 737–749.

Mikami, A.Y., Lerner, M.D., & Lun, J. (2010). Social context influences on children's rejection by their peers. *Child Development Perspectives, 4*, 123–130.

Mikami, A.Y., & Lorenzi, J. (2011). Gender and conduct problems predict peer functioning among children with attention-deficit/hyperactivity disorder. *Journal of Clinical Child & Adolescent Psychology, 40*, 777–786.

Mikami, A.Y., & Normand, S. (2015). The importance of social contextual factors in peer relationships of children with ADHD. *Current Developmental Disorders Reports, 2*, 30–37.

Mikami, A.Y., & Pfiffner, L.J. (2008). Sibling relationships among children with ADHD. *Journal of Attention Disorders, 11*, 482–492.

Mikami, A.Y., Ransone, M.L., & Calhoun, C.D. (2011). Influence of anxiety on the social functioning of children with and without ADHD. *Journal of Attention Disorders, 15*, 473–484.

Milich, R., Balentine, A.C., & Lynam, D.R. (2001). ADHD Combined Type and ADHD Predominantly Inattentive Type are distinct and unrelated disorders. *Clinical Psychology—Science and Practice, 8*, 463–488.

Milich, R., & Okazaki, M. (1991). An examination of learned helplessness among attention deficit hyperactivity disordered boys. *Journal of Abnormal Child Psychology, 19*, 607–623.

Mill, J., & Petronis, A. (2008). Pre- and peri- natal environmental risks for attention-deficit/hyperactivity disorder (ADHD): The potential role of epigenetic processes in mediating susceptibility. *Journal of Child Psychology and Psychiatry, 49*, 1020–1030.

Miller, C.J., Miller, S.R., Newcorn, J.H., & Halperin, J.M. (2008). Personality characteristics associated with persistent ADHD in late adolescence. *Journal of Abnormal Child Psychology, 36*, 165–173.

Miller, F.G., & Lee, D.L. (2013). Do functional behavioral assessments improve intervention effectiveness for students diagnosed with ADHD?: *A single-subject meta-analysis. Journal of Behavioral Education, 22*, 253–282.

Miller, G.E., & Prinz, R.J. (1990). Enhancement of social learning family interventions for childhood conduct disorder. *Psychological Bulletin, 108*, 291–307.

Miller, T.W., Nigg, J.T., & Faraone, S.V. (2007). Axis I and II comorbidity in adults with ADHD. *Journal of Abnormal Psychology, 116*, 519–528.

Miller, T.W., Nigg, J.T., & Miller, R.L. (2009). Attention deficit hyperactivity disorder in African American children: What can be concluded from the past ten years? *Clinical Psychology Review, 29*, 77–86.

Miller-Johnson, S., Coie, J.D., Maumary-Gremaud, A., & Bierman, K. (2002). Peer rejection and aggression and early starter models of conduct disorder. *Journal of Abnormal Child Psychology*, *30*, 217–230.

Millichap, J.G., Millichap, J.J., & Stack, C.V. (2011). Utility of the electroencephalogram in attention deficit hyperactivity disorder. *Clinical EEG and Neuroscience*, *42*, 180–184.

Millichap, J.G., & Yee, M.M. (2012). The diet factor in attention-deficit/hyperactivity disorder. *Pediatrics*, *129*, 330–337.

Miltenberger, R. (2008). *Behaviour modification*. Belmont, CA: Wadsworth.

Mindell, J.A., & Owens, J.A. (2010). *A clinical guide to pediatric sleep: Diagnosis and management of sleep problems* (2nd ed.). Philadelphia: Lippincott Williams & Wilkins.

Mindell, J.A., & Owens, J.A. (2015). *A clinical guide to pediatric sleep: Diagnosis and management of sleep problems*. China: Wolters Kluwer.

Miniscalco, C., Nygren, G., Hagberg, B., Kadesjo, B., & Gillberg, C. (2006). Neuropsychiatric and neurodevelopmental outcome at school age 6 and 7 years of children who screened positive for language problems at 2.5 years. A community-based study. *Developmental Medicine and Child Neurology*, *48*, 361–366.

Miranda, A., Colomer, C., Berenguer, C., Roselló, R., & Roselló, B. (2016). Substance use in young adults with ADHD: Comorbidity and symptoms of inattention and hyperactivity/impulsivity. *International Journal of Clinical and Health Psychology*, *16*, 157–165.

Miranda, A., Jarque, S., & Rosel, J. (2006). Treatment of children with ADHD: Psychopedagogical program at school versus psychostimulant medication. *Psicothema*, *18*, 335–341.

Miranda, A., Marco, R., & Grau, D. (2007). Parenting stress in families of children with attention-deficit/hyperactivity disorder: The impact of adhd subtype and oppositional defiant disorder comorbidity. *Advances in Learning and Behavioral Disabilities*, *20*, 139–162.

Miranda, A., Mercader, J., Fernández, M.I., & Colomer, C. (2017). Reading performance of young adults with ADHD diagnosed in childhood: Relations with executive functioning. *Journal of Attention Disorders*, *21*, 294–304.

Miranda, A., Presentación, J., & Soriano, M. (2002). Effectiveness of a school-based multicomponent program for the treatment of children with ADHD. *Journal of Learning Disabilities*, *35*, 546–562.

Miranda, A., Presentación, M.J., Siegenthaler, R., Colomer, C., & Pinto, V. (2011). Comorbidity between attention deficit hyperactivity disorder and reading disabilities: Implications for assessment and treatment. *Advances in Learning and Behavioral Disabilities*, *24*, 171–211.

Missiuna, C., Gaines, R., McLean, J., Delaat, D., Egan, M., & Soucie, H. (2008). Description of children identified by physicians as having developmental coordination disorder. *Developmental Medicine and Child Neurology*, *50*, 839–844.

Missiuna, C., Gaines, R., Soucie, H., & McLean, J. (2006). Parental questions about developmental coordination disorder: a synopsis of current evidence. *Paediatrics and Child Health*, *11*, 507–512.

Mitchell, J.T., Benson, J., Knouse, L.E., Kimbrel, N.A., & Anastopoulos, A.D. (2013). Are negative automatic thoughts associated with ADHD in adulthood? *Cognitive Therapy and Research*, *37*, 851–859.

Mitchell, J.T., McIntyre, E.M., English, J.S., Dennis, M.F., Beckham, J.C., & Kollins, S.H. (2013). A pilot trial of mindfulness meditation training for attention-deficit/hyperactivity disorder in adulthood: Impact on core symptoms, executive functioning, and emotion dysregulation. *Journal of Attention Disorders*. https://doi.org/10.1177/1087054713513328

Mitchell, J.T., Zylowska, L., & Kollins, S.H. (2015). Mindfulness meditation training for attention-deficit/hyperactivity disorder in adulthood: Current empirical support, treatment overview, and future directions. *Cognitive and Behavioral Practice*, *22*, 172–191.

Miyahara, M., & Piek, J. (2006). Self-esteem of children and adolescents with physical disabilities: Quantitative evidence from meta-analysis. *Journal of Developmental and Physical Disabilities*, *18*, 219–234.

Miyahara, M., Piek, J., & Barrett, N. (2006). Accuracy of drawing in a dual-task and resistance-to-distraction study: motor or attention deficit? *Human Movement Science*, *25*, 100–109.

Moderato, P., & Presti, G. (2005). What is the purpose of a new behaviorally based dynamic developmental theory of ADHD? The perspective of the educational psychologist. *Behavioral and Brain Sciences*, *28*, 435–436.

Moffitt, T.E. (1990). Juvenile delinquency and attention deficit disorder: Developmental trajectories from age 3 to 15. *Child Development*, *61*, 893–910.

Moffitt, T.E., Houts, R., Asherson, P., Belsky, D.W., Corcoran, D.L., Hammerle, M., . . . Poulton, R. (2015). Is adult ADHD a childhood-onset neurodevelopmental disorder? Evidence from a four-decade longitudinal cohort study. *American Journal of Psychiatry*, *172*, 967–977.

Moffitt, T.E., & Melchior, M. (2007). Why does the worldwide prevalence of childhood attention deficit hyperactivity disorder matter? *American Journal of Psychiatry*, *164*, 856–858.

Molina, B.S.G., Bukstein, G., & Lynch, G. (2002). Attention-deficit/hyperactivity disorder and conduct disorder symptomatology in adolescents with alcohol use disorder. *Psychology of Addictive Behaviors*, *16*, 161–164.

Molina, B.S.G., Flory, K., Hinshaw, S.P., Greiner, A.R., Arnold, L.E., Swanson, J.M. . . . Wigal. T. (2007). Delinquent behavior and emerging substance abuse in the MTA at 36 months: Prevalence, course and treatment effects. *Journal of the American Academy of Child and Adolescent Psychiatry*, *46*, 1028–1040.

Molina, B.S., Hinshaw, S.P., Arnold, L.E., Swanson, J.M., Pelham, W.E., Hechtman, L., . . . Greenhill, L.L. (2013). Adolescent substance use in the multimodal treatment study of attention-deficit/hyperactivity disorder (ADHD)(MTA) as a function of childhood ADHD, random assignment to childhood treatments, and subsequent medication. *Journal of the American Academy of Child and Adolescent Psychiatry*, *52*, 250–263.

Molina, B.S.G., Hinshaw, S., Swanson, J., Arnold, L., Vitiello, B., Jensen, P., . . . MTA Cooperative Group. (2009). The MTA at 8 years: prospective follow-up of children treated for combined-type ADHD in a multisite study. *Journal of the American Academy of Child and Adolescent Psychiatry*, *48*, 484–500.

Molina, B.S., & Pelham, W.E., Jr. (2003). Childhood predictors of adolescent substance use in a longitudinal study of children with ADHD. *Journal of Abnormal Psychology*, *112*, 497–507.

Molina, B.S.G., Pelham, W.E., Cheong, J., Marshal, M.P., Gnagy, E.M., & Curran, P.J. (2012). Childhood ADHD and growth in adolescent alcohol use: The roles of functional impairments, ADHD symptom persistence, and parental knowledge. *Journal of Abnormal Psychology*, *121*, 922–935.

Molina, B.S.G., Walther, C.A., Cheong, J., Pedersen, S.L., Gnagy, E.M., & Pelham, W.E., Jr. (2014). Heavy alcohol use in early adulthood as a function of childhood ADHD: Developmentally specific mediation by social impairment and delinquency. *Experimental and Clinical Psychopharmacology*, *22*, 110–121.

Moll, K., Göbel, S.M., Gooch, D., Landerl, K., & Snowling, M.J. (2016). Cognitive risk factors for specific learning disorder processing speed, temporal processing, and working memory. *Journal of Learning Disabilities*, *49*, 272–281.

Möller, H.J. (2009). Development of DSM-V and ICD-11: Tendencies and potential of new classifications in psychiatry at the current state of knowledge. *Psychiatry and Clinical Neurosciences*, *63*, 595–612.

Monastra, V.J. (2008). Quantitative electroencephalography and attention-deficit/hyperactivity disorder: Implications for clinical practice. *Current Psychiatry Reports*, *10*, 432–438.

Monastra, V.J., Lubar, J.F., Linden, M., VanDeusen, P., Green, G., Wing, W., . . . Fenger, T.N. (1999). Assessing attention deficit hyperactivity disorder via quantitative electroencephalography: An initial validation study. *Neuropsychology*, *13*, 424–433.

Monastra, V.J., Lynn, S., Linden, M., Lubar, J.F., Gruzelier, J., & La Vaque, T.J. (2006). Electroencephalographic biofeedback in the treatment of attention-deficit/hyperactivity disorder. *Journal of Neurotherapy*, *9*, 5–34.

Monastra, V.J., Monastra, D.M., & George, S. (2002). The effects of stimulant therapy, EEG biofeedback, and parenting style on the primary symptoms of attention-deficit/hyperactivity disorder. *Applied Psychophysiology and Biofeedback*, *27*, 231–249.

Monti, J.M., & Monti, D. (2007). The involvement of dopamine in the modulation of sleep and waking. *Sleep Medicine Reviews*, *11*, 113–133.

Montoya, A., Colom, F., & Ferrin, M. (2011). Is psychoeducation for parents and teachers of children and adolescents with ADHD efficacious? A systematic literature review. *European Psychiatry, 26*, 166–175.

Montoya, A., Hervás, A., Fuentes, J., Cardo, E., Polavieja, P., Quintero, J., & Tannock, R. (2014). Cluster-randomized, controlled 12-month trial to evaluate the effect of a parental psychoeducation program on medication persistence in children with attention-deficit/hyperactivity disorder. *Neuropsychiatric Disease and Treatment, 10*, 1081–1092.

Monuteaux, M. C., Biederman, J., Doyle, A.E., Mick, E., & Faraone, S.V. (2010). Genetic risk for conduct disorder symptom subtypes in an ADHD sample: Specificity to aggressive symptoms. *Journal of the American Academy of Child and Adolescent Psychiatry, 48*, 757–764.

Monuteaux, M. C., Mick, E., Faraone, S.V., & Biederman, J. (2010). The influence of sex on the course and psychiatric correlates of ADHD from childhood to adolescence: A longitudinal study. *Journal of Child Psychology and Psychiatry, 51*, 233–241.

Moore, D.A., Richardson, M., Gwernan-Jones, R., Thompson-Coon, J., Stein, K., Rogers, M., . . . Ford, T.J. (2015). Non-pharmacological interventions for ADHD in school settings: An overarching synthesis of systematic reviews. *Journal of Attention Disorders*. https://doi.org/10.1177/1087054715573994

Moreau, V., Rouleau, N., & Morin, C.M. (2014). Sleep of children with attention deficit hyperactivity disorder: actigraphic and parental reports. *Behavioral Sleep Medicine, 12*, 69–83.

Moreno, C., Laje, G., Blanco, C., Jiang, H., Schmidt, A.B., & Olfson, M. (2007). National trends in the outpatient diagnosis and treatment of bipolar disorder in youth. *Archives of General Psychiatry, 64*, 1032–1039.

Morgan, A.B., & Lilienfeld, S.O. (2000). A meta-analytic review of the relation between antisocial behavior and neuropsychological measures of executive function. *Clinical Psychology Review, 20*, 113–136.

Morgan, J., Robinson, D., & Aldridge, J. (2002). Parenting stress and externalizing child behaviour. *Child and Family Social Work, 7*, 219–225.

Morgan, W.P. (1896). A case of congenital word blindness. *British Medical Journal, 2*, 1378.

Moriyama, T. S., Polanczyk, G.V., Terzi, F.S., Faria, K.M., & Rohde, L.A. (2013). Psychopharmacology and psychotherapy for the treatment of adults with ADHD—a systematic review of available meta-analyses. *CNS Spectrums, 6*, 296–306.

Morrell, J., & Murray, L. (2003). Parenting and the development of conduct disorder and hyperactive symptoms in childhood: a prospective longitudinal study from 2 months to 8 years. *Journal of Child Psychology and Psychiatry, 44*, 489–508.

Mowinckel, A.M., Pedersen, M.L., Eilertsen, E., & Biele, G. (2015). A meta-analysis of decision-making and attention in adults with ADHD. *Journal of Attention Disorders, 19*, 355–387.

Mrug, S., Hoza, B., Pelham, W.E., Gnagy, E.M., & Greiner, A.R. (2007). Behavior and peer status in children with ADHD: Continuity and change. *Journal of Attention Disorders, 10*, 359–371.

Mrug, S., Molina, B.S.G., Hoza, B., Gerdes, A.C., Hinshaw, S.P., Hechtman, L., & Arnold, L.E. (2012). Peer rejection and friendship in children with attention-deficit/hyperactivity disorder: Contributions to long-term outcomes. *Journal of Abnormal Child Psychology, 40*, 1013–1026.

MTA Cooperative Group. (1999). A 14-month randomized clinical trial of treatment strategies for attention-deficit/hyperactivity disorder. *Archives of General Psychiatry, 56*, 1073–1086.

MTA Cooperative Group. (2004). National Institute of Mental Health Multimodal Treatment Study of ADHD follow-up: 24-month outcomes of treatment strategies for attention-deficit hyperactivity disorder. *Pediatrics, 113*, 754–761.

Mueller, K.L., & Tomblin, J.B. (2012). Examining the comorbidity of language disorders and ADHD. *Topics in Language Disorders, 32*, 228–246.

Mukolo, A., & Hefilnger, C.A. (2011). Factors associated with attributes about child health conditions and social distance preferences. *Community Mental Health Journal, 47*, 286–299.

Mulligan, A., Anney, R.J., O'Regan, M., Chen, W., Butler, L., Fitzgerald, M., . . . Gill, M. (2009). Autism symptoms in attention deficit/hyperactivity disorder: a familial trait which correlates with

conduct, oppositional defiant, language and motor disorders. *Journal of Autism and Developmental Disorders, 39*, 197–209.
Mullis, I.V.S., & Jenkins, L.B. (1990). *The reading report card, 1971–1988: Trends from the nation's report card.* Princeton, NJ: Educational Testing Service.
Mulqueen, J.M., Bartley, C.A., & Bloch, M.H. (2015). Meta-analysis: Parental interventions for preschool ADHD. *Journal of Attention Disorders, 19*, 118–124.
Mulraney, M., Giallo, R., Lycett, K., Mensah, F., & Sciberras, E. (2016). The bidirectional relationship between sleep problems and internalizing and externalizing problems in children with ADHD: A prospective cohort study. *Sleep Medicine, 17*, 45–51.
Munakata, Y., Casey, B.J., & Diamond, A. (2004). Developmental cognitive neuroscience: progress and potential. *Trends in Cognitive Sciences, 8*, 122–128.
Muraven, M., & Baumeister, R.F., (2000). Self-regulation and depletion of limited resources: Does self-control resemble a muscle? *Psychological Bulletin, 126*, 247–259.
Murphy, K.R. (2005). Psychosocial treatments for ADHD in teens and adults: A practice-friendly review. *Journal of Clinical Psychology, 61*, 607–619.
Murphy, K.R. (2006). Psychological counseling of adults with ADHD. In R.A. Barkley (Ed.), *Attention-deficit hyperactivity disorder: A handbook for diagnosis and treatment* (pp. 692–703). New York: Guilford Press.
Murphy, K.R. (2015). Psychological counseling of adults with ADHD. In R.A. Barkley (Ed.) *Attention-Deficit Hyperactivity Disorder* (4th ed., pp. 741–756). New York: Guilford Press.
Murphy, K.R., & Adler, L.A. (2004). Assessing attention-deficit/hyperactivity disorder in adults: Focus on rating scales. *Journal of Clinical Psychiatry, 65*(Suppl3), 8–11.
Murphy, K.R., Ratey, N., Maynard, S., Sussman, S., & Wright, S.D. (2010). Coaching for ADHD. *Journal of Attention Disorders, 13*, 546–552.
Murray-Close, D., Hoza, B., Hinshaw, S.P., Arnold, E., Swanson, J., Jensen, P.S., Hechtman, L., & Wells, K. (2010). Developmental processes in peer problems of children with attention-deficit/hyperactivity disorder in The Multimodal Treatment Study of Children with ADHD: Developmental cascades and vicious cycles. *Development and Psychopathology, 22*, 785–802.
Muzur, A., Pace-Schott, E.F., & Hobson, J.A. (2002). The prefrontal cortex in sleep. *Trends in Cognitive Sciences, 6*, 475–481.
Nadeau, K.C., & Quinn, P.O. (2002). The history of ADHD—An unexamined gender bias. In P.O. Quinn & K.C. Nadeau (Eds.), *Gender issues and ADHD* (pp. 2–22). USA: Advantage Books.
Nagel, B.J. (2011). Altered white matter microstructure in children with attention-deficit/hyperactivity disorder. *Journal of the American Academy of Child and Adolescent Psychiatry, 50*, 283–292.
Nahlik, J. (2004). Issues in the diagnosis of attention-deficit/hyperactivity disorder in adolescents. *Clinical Pediatrics,43*, 1–10.
Nakao, T., Radua, J., Rubia, K., Mataix-Cols, D. (2011). Gray matter volume abnormalities in ADHD: voxel-based meta-analysis exploring the effects of age and stimulant medication. *American Journal of Psychiatry, 168*, 1154–1163.
Narr, K.L., Woods, R.P., Lin, J., Kim, J., Phillips, O.R., Del' Homme, M., . . . Levitt, J.G. (2009). Widespread cortical thinning is a robust anatomical marker for attention-deficit/hyperactivity disorder. *Journal of the American Academy of Child and Adolescent Psychiatry, 48*, 1014–1022.
Narrow, W.E., First, M.B., Sirovatka, M.S., & Regier, M.D. (2007). Disruptive behavior disorders & ADHD in preschool children: characterizing heterotypic continuities for a developmentally-informed nosology for DSM-V. In D. Regier, M. First, & W. Narrow (Eds.), *Age and gender considerations in psychiatric diagnosis: A research agenda for DSM-V.* Washington: DC: American Psychiatric.
Nash, J.K. (2000). Treatment of attention deficit hyperactivity disorder with neurotherapy. *Clinical Electroencephalography, 31*, 30–37.
Nasrallah, H.A. (2013). Pleiotropy of psychiatric disorders will reinvent DSM. *Current Psychiatry, 12*(04), 6.
National Advisory Committee on Hyperkinesis and Food Additives. (1980). [*Report*]. New York: Nutrition Foundation.

National Institute for Health and Clinical Excellence. (2008). *Attention Deficit Hyperactivity Disorder: Pharmacological and Psychological Interventions in Children, Young People and Adults. (Clinical Guideline 72)*. London, UK: British Psychological Society and the Royal College of Psychiatrists.

National Institute for Health and Clinical Excellence. (2009). *Attention deficit hyperactivity disorder: Diagnosis and management of ADHD in children, young people and adults.* NICE Clinical Guideline 72. London: Author.

Nazar, B. P., de Sousa Pinna, C. M., Suwwan, R., Duchesne, M., Freitas, S. R., Sergeant, J., & Mattos, P. (2016). ADHD rate in obese women with binge eating and bulimic behaviors from a weight-loss clinic. *Journal of Attention Disorders, 20*, 610–616.

Neale, M. C., & Kendler, K. S. (1995). Models of comorbidity for multifactorial disorders. *American Journal of Human Genetics, 57*, 935–953.

Nederkoorn, C., Houben, K., Hofmann, W., Roefs, A., & Jansen, A. (2010). Control yourself or just eat what you like? Weight gain over a year is predicted by an interactive effect of response inhibition and implicit preference for snack foods. *Health Psychology, 29*, 389–393.

Neece, C., Baker, B., Crnic, K., & Blacher, J. (2013). Examining the validity of ADHD as a diagnosis for adolescents with intellectual disabilities: Clinical presentation. *Journal of Abnormal Child Psychology, 41*, 597–612.

Nelson, C. A. (2000a). The neurobiological bases of early intervention. In J. Shonkoff & S. Meisels (Eds.), *Handbook of early childhood intervention* (2nd ed., pp. 204–230.) New York: Cambridge University Press.

Nelson, C. A. (2000b). Neural plasticity and human development: The role of early experience sculpting memory systems. *Developmental Science, 3*, 115–130.

Nelson-Gray, R. O. (2003). Treatment utility of psychological assessment. *Psychological Assessment, 15*, 521–531.

Nemoda, Z., Szekely, A., & Sasvari-Szekely, M. (2011). Psychopathological aspects of dopaminergic gene polymorphisms in adolescence and young adulthood. *Neuroscience & Biobehavioral Reviews, 35*, 1665–1686.

Neuman, R., Sitdhiraksa, N., Reich, W., Ji, T.H.C., Joyner, C., Sun, L-W., & Todd, R. D. (2005). Estimation of prevalence of DSM-IV and latent class-defined ADHD subtypes in a population-based sample of child and adolescent twins. *Twin Research and Human Genetics, 8*, 392–401.

Neville, H., Andersson, A., Bagdade, O., Bell, T., Currin, J., Fanning, J., . . . Yamada, Y. (2009). How can musical training improve cognition. In S. Dehaene & C. Petit (Eds.), *The origins of human dialog: Speech and music* (pp. 277–290). Paris, France: Odile Jacob.

Neville, H. J., Steven, C., Pakulak, E., Bell, T. A., Fanning, J., Klein, S., & Isbell, E. (2013). Family-based training program improves brain function, cognition, and behavior in lower socioeconomic status preschoolers. *Proceedings of the National Academy of Sciences, 110*, 12138–12143.

Newcorn, J. H., Miller, S. R., Ivanova, I., Schulz, K. P., Kalmar, J., Marks, D. J., & Halperin, J. M. (2004). Adolescent outcome of ADHD: Impact of childhood conduct and anxiety disorders. *CNS Spectrums, 9*, 668–678.

Newman, R., Ratner, N. B., Jusczyk, A. M., Jusczyk, P. W., & Dow, K. A. (2006) Infants' early ability to segment the conversational speech signal predicts later language development: A retrospective analysis. *Developmental Psychology, 42*, 643–655.

Nichamin, S. J. (1972). Recognizing minimum cerebral dysfunction in the infant and toddler. *Clinical Pediatrics, 11*, 255–257.

Nichols, S. L., & Waschbusch, D. A. (2004). A review of the validity of laboratory cognitive tasks used to assess symptoms of ADHD. *Child Psychiatry and Human Development, 34*, 297–315.

Nieoullon, A., & Coquerel, A. (2003). Dopamine: A key regulator to adapt action, emotion, motivation and cognition. *Current Opinion in Neurology, 16*, S3–S9.

Nigg, J. T. (2005a). Neuropsychologic theory and findings in attention-deficit/hyperactivity disorder: The state of the field and salient challenges for the coming decade. *Biological Psychiatry, 57*, 1424–1435.

Nigg, J.T. (2005b). Reinforcement gradient, response inhibition, genetic versus experiential effects, and multiple pathways to ADHD. *Behavioral and Brain Sciences, 28*, 437–438.
Nigg, J.T. (2006). *What causes ADHD? Understanding what goes wrong and why.* New York: Guilford Press.
Nigg, J.T. (2013a). Attention-deficit/hyperactivity disorder and adverse health outcomes. *Clinical Psychology Review, 33*, 215–228.
Nigg, J.T. (2013b). Attention deficits and hyperactivity—impulsivity: What have we learned, what next? *Development and Psychopathology, 25*, 1489–1503.
Nigg, J.T., Blaskey, L., Stawicki, J., & Sachek, J. (2004). Evaluating the endophenotype model of ADHD neuropsychological deficit: Results for parents and siblings of children with DSM-IV ADHD combined and inattentive subtypes. *Journal of Abnormal Psychology, 113*, 614–625.
Nigg, J.T., & Casey, B.J. (2005). An integrative theory of attention-deficit/hyperactivity disorder based on the cognitive and affective neurosciences. *Development and Psychopathology, 17*, 785–806.
Nigg, J.T., & Hinshaw, S.P. (1998). Parent personality traits and psychopathology associated with antisocial behaviors in childhood attention-deficit hyperactivity disorder. *Journal of Child Psychology and Psychiatry, 39*, 145–159.
Nigg, J.T., Hinshaw, S.P., & Halperin, J.M. (1996). Continuous performance test in boys with attention deficit hyperactivity disorder: Methylphenidate dose response and relations with observed behaviors. *Journal of Clinical Child & Adolescent Psychology, 25*, 330–340.
Nigg, J.T., & Holton, K. (2014). Restriction and elimination diets in ADHD treatment. *Child and Adolescent Psychiatric Clinics of North America, 23*, 937–953.
Nigg, J.T., Johnstone, J.M., Musser, E.D., Long, H.G., Willoughby, M., & Shannon, J. (2016). Attention-deficit/hyperactivity disorder (ADHD) and being overweight/obesity: New data and meta-analysis. *Clinical Psychology Review, 43*, 67–79.
Nigg, J.T., Lewis, K., Edinger, T., & Falk, M. (2012). Meta-analysis of attention deficit hyperactivity disorder or attention deficit hyperactivity disorder symptoms, restriction diet and synthetic food color additives. *Journal of the American Academy of Child and Adolescent Psychiatry, 51*, 86–97.
Nigg, J.T., Nikolas, M., & Burt, S.A. (2010). Measured gene-by-environment interaction in relation to attention-deficit/hyperactivity disorder. *Journal of the American Academy of Child and Adolescent Psychiatry, 49*, 863–873.
Nigg, J.T., Willcutt, E.G., Doyle, A., & Sonuga-Barke, E.J.S. (2005). Causal heterogeneity in attention-deficit/hyperactivity disorder: Do we need neuropsychologically impaired subtypes. *Biological Psychiatry, 57*, 1224–1230.
Nijmeijer, J.S., Hoekstra, P.J., Minderaa, R.B., Buitelaar, J.K., Altink, M.E., Buschgens, C.J., . . . Hartman, C.A. (2009). PDD symptoms in ADHD, an independent familial trait? *Journal of Abnormal Child Psychology, 37*, 443–53.
Nijmeijer, J.S., Minderaa, R.B., Buitelaar, J.K., Mulligan, A., Hartman, C.A., & Hoekstra, P.J. (2008). Attention-deficit/hyperactivity disorder and social dysfunctioning. *Clinical Psychology Review, 28*, 692–708.
Ninowski, J.E. (2010). *Early temperament and emotion regulation in infants at familial risk for ADHD: the role of maternal parenting.* Unpublished Doctoral Dissertation, University of Calgary.
Niv, S., & Baker, L.A. (2013). Genetic markers for antisocial behavior. In C.R. Thomas & K. Pope (Eds.), *The origins of antisocial behavior: A developmental perspective* (pp. 3–38). New York: Oxford University Press.
Nix, R.L., Bierman, K.L., McMahon, R.J., & The Conduct Problems Prevention Research Group (2009). How attendance and quality of participation affect treatment response to parent management training. *Journal of Consulting and Clinical Psychology, 77*, 429–438.
Nock, M.K., & Ferriter, C. (2005). Parent management of attendance and adherence in child and adolescent therapy: A conceptual and empirical review. *Clinical Child and Family Psychology Review, 8*, 149–166.
Nock, M.K., & Kazdin, A.E. (2001). Parent expectancies for child therapy: Assessment and relation to participation in treatment. *Journal of Child and Family Studies, 10*, 155–180.

Nock, M.K., & Photos, V. (2006). Parent motivation to participate in treatment: Assessment and prediction of subsequent participation. *Journal of Child and Family Studies*, *15*, 333–346.

Noel, M.P., Seron, X., & Trovarelli, F. (2004). Working memory as a predictor of addition skills and addition strategies in children. *Current Psychology of Cognition*, *22*, 3–25.

Noell, G.H., Gresham, F.M., & Gansle, K.A. (2002). Does treatment integrity matter? A preliminary investigation of instructional implementation and mathematics performance. *Journal of Behavioral Education*, *11*, 51–67.

Noell, G.H., Witt, J.C., Slider, N.J., Connell, J.E., Gatti, S.L., & Wi, K.L. (2005). Treatment implementation following behavioral consultation in schools: A comparison of three follow-up strategies. *School Psychology Review*, *34*, 87–106.

Nooner, K.B., Leaberry, K.D., Keith, J.R., & Ogle, R.L. (2016). Clinic outcome assessment of a brief course neurofeedback for childhood ADHD symptoms. *Journal of Behavioral Health Services & Research*. https://doi.org/10.1007/s11414-016-9511-1

Normand, S., Schneider, B.H., Lee, M D., Maisonneuve, M.F., Kuehn, S.M., & Robaey, P. (2011). How do children with ADHD (mis) manage their real-life dyadic friendships? A multi-method investigation. *Journal of Abnormal Child Psychology*, *39*, 293–305.

Northup, J., & Gulley, V. (2001). Some contributions of functional analysis to the assessment of behaviours associated with attention deficit hyperactivity disorder and the effects of stimulant medication. *School Psychology Review*, *30*, 227–238.

Nováková, M., Paclt, I., Ptáček, R., Kuželová, H., Hájek, I., & Sumová, A. (2011). Salivary melatonin rhythm as a marker of the circadian system in healthy children and those with attention-deficit/hyperactivity disorder. *Chronobiology International*, *28*, 630–637.

Novik, T.S., Hervas, A., Ralston, S.J., Dalsgaard, S., Rodrigues Pereira, R., & Lorenzo, M.J. (2006). Influence of gender on attention-deficit/hyperactivity disorder in Europe—ADORE. *European Child and Adolescent Psychiatry, 15 (Suppl. 1)*, 115–124.

Nussbaum, N.L. (2012). ADHD and female specific concerns: A review of the literature and clinical implications. *Journal of Attention Disorders*, *16*, 87–100.

Nutt, D.J., Fone, K., Asherson, P., Bramble, D., Hill, P., Mathews, K., . . . Young, S. (2007). Evidence-based guidelines for management of attention-deficit/hyperactivity disorder in adolescents in transition to adult services and in adults: Recommendations from the British Association for Psychopharmacology. *Journal of Psychopharmacology*, *21*, 10–41.

O'Brien, L.M., Ivanenko, A., Crabtree, V.M., Holbrook, C.R., Bruner, J.L., Klaus, C.J., & Gozal, D. (2003). Sleep disturbances in children with attention deficit hyperactivity disorder. *Pediatric Research*, *54*, 237–243.

O'Callaghan, F.V., Al Mamun, A., O'Callaghan, M., Clavarino, A., Williams, G.M., Bor, W., . . . Najman, J.M. (2010). The link between sleep problems in infancy and early childhood and attention problems at 5 and 14years: Evidence from a birth cohort study. *Early Human Development*, *86*, 419–424.

Ogrim, G., & Hestad, K.A. (2013). Effects of neurofeedback versus stimulant medication in attention-deficit/hyperactivity disorder: A randomized pilot study. *Journal of Child and Adolescent Psychopharmacology*, *23*, 448–457.

Ohan, J.L., & Visser, T.A. (2009). Why is there a gender gap in children presenting for attention deficit/hyperactivity disorder services?. *Journal of Clinical Child & Adolescent Psychology*, *38*, 650–660.

Ohlmeier, M.D., Peters, K., Kordon, A., Seifert, J., Wildt, B.T., Wiese, B., . . . Schneider, U. (2007). Nicotine and alcohol dependence in patients with comorbid attention-deficit/hyperactivity disorder (ADHD). *Alcohol and Alcoholism*, *42*, 539–543.

Ohlmeier, M.D., Peters, K., Wildt, B.T., Zedler, M., Ziegenbein, M., Wiese, B., . . . Schneider, U. (2008). Comorbidity of alcohol and substance dependence with attention-deficit/hyperactivity disorder (ADHD). *Alcohol & Alcoholism*, *43*, 300–304.

Olfson, M., Blanco, C., Liu, L., Moreno, C., & Laje, G. (2006). National trends in the outpatient treatment of children and adolescents with antipsychotic drugs. *Archives of General Psychiatry*, *63*, 679–685.

Olfson, M., Gameroff, M.J., Marcus, S.C., & Jensen, P.S. (2003). National trends in the treatment of attention deficit hyperactivity disorder. *American Journal of Psychiatry, 160*, 1071–1077.

Olfson, M., Marcus, S.C., Zhang, H.F., & Wan, G.J. (2007). Continuity in methylphenidate treatment of adults with Attention-Deficit/Hyperactivity Disorder. *Journal of Managed Care Pharmacy, 13*, 570–577.

Oliveira, K.L.D.C., & Costa, R.C.C. (2012). Phonemic discrimination and its relation to phonological disorder. *Revista CEFAC, 14*, 1209–1214.

Oliver, M.L., Nigg, J.T., Cassavaugh, N.D., & Backs, R.W. (2012). Behavioral and cardiovascular responses to frustration during simulated driving tasks in young adults with and without attention disorder symptoms. *Journal of Attention Disorders, 16*, 478–490.

Olympia, D., & Larsen, J. (2005). Functional Behavioral Assessment: An emerging component of best school practices for ADHD. *The ADHD Report, 13*, 1–5.

Oner, P., Dirik, E.B., Taner, Y., Caykoylu, A., & Anlar, O. (2007). Association between low serum ferritin and restless legs syndrome in patients with attention deficit hyperactivity disorder. *The Tokoku Journal of Experimental Medicine, 213*, 269–276.

Oram, J., Fine, J., Okamoto, C., & Tannock, R. (1999). Assessing the language of children with attention deficit hyperactivity disorder: Role of executive function. *American Journal of Speech-Language Pathology, 8*, 72–80.

Ornoy, A., Uriel, L., & Tennenbaum, A. (1993). Inattention, hyperactivity and speech delay at two-four years of age as a predictor for ADD-ADHD syndrome. *Israel Journal of Psychiatry and Related Sciences, 30*, 155–163.

O'Rourke, J.A., Scharf, J.M., Platko, J., Stewart, S.E., Illmann, C., Geller, D.A., . . . Pauls, D.L. (2011). The familial association of Tourette's disorder and ADHD: The impact of OCD symptoms. *American Journal of Medical Genetics Part B: Neuropsychiatric Genetics, 156*, 553–560.

O'Rourke, J.A., Scharf, J., Platko, J., Stewart, S.E., Illmann, C., Geller, D.A. . . . Pauls, D.L. (2011). The familial association of Tourette's Disorder and ADHD: the impact of OCD symptoms. *American Journal of Medical Genetics, 156B*, 553–560.

Ostrander, R., Crystal, D.S., & August, G. (2006). Attention deficit-hyperactivity disorder, depression, and self- and other-assessments of social competence: A developmental study. *Journal of Abnormal Child Psychology, 34*, 773–787.

Ottenbreit, N.D., & Dobson, K.S. (2004). Avoidance and depression: The construction of the Cognitive-Behavioral Avoidance Scale. *Behaviour Research and Therapy, 42*, 293–313.

Ouellette, G.P. (2006). What's meaning got to do with it: The role of vocabulary in word reading and reading comprehension. *Journal of Education Psychology, 98*, 554–566.

Ouyang, L., Fang, X., Mercy, J., Perou, R., & Grosse, S.D. (2008). Attention-deficit/hyperactivity disorder symptoms and child maltreatment: A population-based study. *Journal of Pediatrics, 153*, 851–856.

Owens, E.B., Hinshaw, S.P., Kraemer, H.C., Arnold, L.E., Abikoff, H.B., Cantwell, D.P., . . . Hoza, B. (2003). Which treatment for whom for ADHD? Moderators of treatment response in the MTA. *Journal of Consulting and Clinical Psychology, 71*, 540–552.

Owens, J.A. (2005). The ADHD and sleep conundrum: A review. *Journal of Developmental and Behavioral Pediatrics, 26*, 312–322.

Owens, J.A. (2008). Classification and epidemiology of childhood sleep disorders. *Primary Care: Clinics in Office Practice 35*, 533–546.

Owens, J., Cardoos, S.L., & Hinshaw, S.P. (2015). Developmental progression and gender differences among individuals with ADHD. In R.A. Barkley (Ed.) *Attention-Deficit Hyperactivity Disorder* (4th ed., pp. 223–255). New York: Guilford Press.

Owens, J., Gruber, R., Brown, T., Corkum, P., Cortese, S., O'Brien, L., . . . Weiss, M. (2013). Future research directions in sleep and ADHD report of a consensus working group. *Journal of Attention Disorders, 17*, 550–564.

Pace-Schott, E.F., & Hobson, J.A. (2002). The neurobiology of sleep: Genetics, cellular physiology and subcortical networks. *Nature Reviews Neuroscience, 3*, 591–605.

Pagani, L.S., Derevensky, L., & Japel, C. (2009). Predicting gambling behavior in sixth grade from kindergarten impulsivity: A tale of developmental continuity. *Archives of Pediatric and Adolescent Medicine, 163*, 238–243.

Page, T.F., Pelham, W.E., III, Fabiano, G.A., Greiner, A.R., Gnagy, E.M., Hart, K.C., . . . Pelham, W.E., Jr. (2016). Comparative cost analysis of sequential, adaptive, behavioral, pharmacological, and combined treatments for childhood ADHD. *Journal of Clinical Child & Adolescent Psychology, 45*, 416–427.

Pagoto, S.L., Curtin, C., Lemon, S.C., Bandini, L.G., Schneider, K.L., Bodenlos, J.S., & Ma, Y. (2009). Association between adult attention deficit/hyperactivity disorder and obesity in the US population. *Obesity, 17*, 539–544.

Palili, A., Kolaitis, G., Vassi, I., Veltsista, A., Bakoula, C., & Gika, A. (2010). Inattention, hyperactivity, impulsivity—epidemiology and correlations: A nationwide Greek study from birth to 18 years. *Journal of Child Neurology, 26*, 199–204.

Palmer, E. D., & Finger, S. (2001). An early description of ADHD (inattentive subtype): Dr. Alexander Crichton and "Mental Restlessness" (1798). *Child Psychology and Psychiatry Review, 6*, 66–73.

Palmer, R.C., Young, S.E., Hopfer, C.J., Corley, R.P., Stallings, M.C., Crowley, T.J., & Hewitt, J.K. (2009). Developmental epidemiology of drug use and abuse in adolescence and young adulthood: Evidence of generalized risk. *Drug and Alcohol Dependence, 102*, 78–87.

Palumbo, D., Maughan, A., & Kurlan, R. (1997). Hypothesis III. Tourette syndrome is only one of several causes to a development basal ganglia syndromes. *Archives of Neurology, 54*, 475–481.

Papaeliou, C.F., Maniadaki, K. & Kakouros, E. (2015). Association between story recall and other language abilities in schoolchildren with ADHD. *Journal of Attention Disorders, 19*, 53–62.

Papavasiliou, A.S., Nikaina, I., Rizou, I., & Alexandrou, S. (2007). Effects of psycho-educational training and stimulant medication on visual perceptual skills in children with attention deficit hyperactivity disorder. *Neuropsychiatric Disease and Treatment, 3*, 949–954.

Papavasiliou, A., Nikaina, I., Spyridonidou, A., & Nianiou, E. (2013). Difficulties in recognizing ADHD in an urban population and treatment satisfaction with a short and a long acting stimulant. In: S. Banerjee (Ed.), *Attention Deficit Hyperactivity Disorder in children and adolescents.* https://doi.org/10.5772/53791

Park, J., Samuels, J.F., Grados, M.A., Riddle, M.A., Bienvenu, O.J., Goes, F.S., . . . Rasmussen, S.A. (2016). ADHD and executive functioning deficits in OCD youths who hoard. *Journal of Psychiatric Research, 82*, 141–148.

Parker, D.R., & Boutelle, K. (2009). Executive function coaching for college students with learning disabilities and ADHD: A new approach for fostering self-determination. *Learning Disabilities Research & Practice, 24*, 204–215.

Parker, D.R., Hoffman, S.F., Sawilowsky, S., & Rolands, L. (2011). An examination of the effects of ADHD coaching on university students' executive functioning. *Journal of Postsecondary Education and Disability, 24*, 115–132.

Parrino, L., Ferrillo, F., Smerieri, A., Spaggiari, M.C., Palomba, V., Rossi, M., & Terzano, M.G. (2004). Is insomnia a neurophysiological disorder? The role of sleep EEG microstructure. *Brain Research Bulletin, 63*, 377–383.

Parritz, R.H., & Troy, M.F. (2014). Disorders of childhood. *Development and psychopathology* (2nd ed). USA: Wadsworth.

Parry, P.A., & Douglas, V. (1976). Effects of reinforcement on concept identification in hyperactive children. *Journal of Abnormal Child Psychology, 11*, 327–340.

Parush, S., Sohmer, H., Steinberg, A., & Kaitz, M. (1997). Somatosensory functioning in children with ADHD. *Developmental Medicine and Child Neurology, 39*, 464–468.

Pasamanick, B., Rogers, M., & Lilienfeld, A.M. (1956). Pregnancy experience and the development of behavior disorder in children. *American Journal of Psychiatry, 112*, 613–617.

Passolunghi, M.C., & Siegel, L.S. (2004). Working memory and access to numerical information in children with disability in mathematics. *Journal of Experimental Child Psychology, 88*, 348–367.

Pastor, P.N., & Reuben, C.A. (2005). Racial and ethnic differences in ADHD and LD in young school-age children: parental reports in the National Health Interview Study. *Public Health Reports, 120*, 383–392.

Pastor, P.N., & Reuben, C.A. (2008). Diagnosed attention deficit hyperactivity disorder and learning disability: United States, 2004–2006. *Vital and Health Statistics, 10*, 1–14.

Patel, N.C., Delbello, M.P., Bryan, H.S., Adler, C.M., Kowatch, R.A., Stanford, K., & Strakowski, S.M. (2006). Open-label lithium for the treatment of adolescents with bipolar depression. *Journal of the American Academy of Child and Adolescent Psychiatry, 45*, 289–297.

Patte, K.A., Davis, C.A., Levitan, R.D., Kaplan, A S., Carter-Major, J., & Kennedy, J.L. (2016). A behavioral genetic model of the mechanisms underlying the link between obesity and symptoms of ADHD. *Journal of Attention Disorders*. https://doi.org/1087054715618793

Patterson, G.R. (1982). *Coercive family process*. Eugene, OR: Castalia.

Patterson, G.R., & Capaldi, D.M. (1990). A mediational model for boys' depressed mood. In J. Rolf, A.S. Masten, D. Cicchetti, K.H. Nuechterlein, & S. Weintraub (Eds.), *Risk and protective factors in the development of psychopathology* (pp. 141–163). New York: Cambridge University Press.

Patterson, G.R., DeGarmo, D.S., & Knutson, N. (2000). Hyperactive and antisocial behavior: Comorbid or two points in the same process? *Development and Psychopathology, 12*, 91–106.

Patterson, G.R., Reid, J., & Dishion, T. (1992). *Antisocial boys*. Eugene, OR: Castalia Press.

Pauli-Pott, U., & Becker, K. (2011). Neuropsychological basic deficits in preschoolers at risk for ADHD: A meta-analysis. *Clinical Psychology Review, 31*, 626–637.

Pauls, D.L., Alsobrook, J.P., Goodman, W., Rasmussen, S., & Leckman, J. (1995). A family study of obsessive-compulsive disorder. *American Journal of Psychiatry, 152*, 76–84.

Pauls, D.L., Hurst, C.R., Kruger, S.D., Leckman, J.F., Kidd, K.K., & Cohen, D.J. (1986). Gilles de la Tourette's syndrome and attention deficit disorder with hyperactivity: Evidence against a genetic relationship. *Archives of General Psychiatry, 43*, 1177–1179.

Pauls, D.L., Leckman, J.F., & Cohen, D.J. (1993). Familial relationship between Gilles de la Tourette's syndrome, attention deficit disorder, learning disabilities, speech disorders, and stuttering. *Journal of the American Academy of Child and Adolescent Psychiatry, 32*, 1044–1050.

Pearl, P.L., Weiss, R.E., & Stein, M.A. (2001). Medical mimics: Medical and neurological conditions simulating ADHD. *Annals of the New York Academy of Sciences, 931*, 97–112.

Pearsall-Jones, J.G., Piek, J.P., Rigoli, D., Martin, N.C., & Levy, F. (2009). An investigation into etiological pathways of DCD and ADHD using a monozygotic twin design. *Twin Research and Human Genetics, 12*, 381–391.

Pearson, D.A., & Aman, M.G. (1994). Ratings of hyperactivity and developmental indices: Should clinicians correct for developmental level? *Journal of Autism and Developmental Disorders, 24*, 395–411.

Peets, K., Hodges, E.V., Kikas, E., & Salmivalli, C. (2007). Hostile attributions and behavioral strategies in children: Does relationship type matter? *Developmental Psychology, 43*, 889–900.

Pelham, W.E., Jr., & Fabiano, G.A. (2008) Evidence-based psychosocial treatments for attention-deficit/hyperactivity disorder. *Journal of Clinical Child and Adolescent Psychology, 37*, 184–214.

Pelham, W.E., Jr., Fabiano, G.A., & Massetti, G.M. (2005). Evidence-based assessment of attention deficit hyperactivity disorder in children and adolescents. *Journal of Clinical Child and Adolescent Psychology, 34*, 449–476.

Pelham, W. E., Jr., Fabiano, G.A., Waxmonsky, J.G., Greiner, A.R., Gnagy, E.M., Pelham, W.E., III, . . . Karch, K. (2016). Treatment sequencing for childhood ADHD: A multiple-randomization study of adaptive medication and behavioral interventions. *Journal of Clinical Child & Adolescent Psychology, 45*, 396–415.

Pelham, W.E., Foster, E.M., & Robb, J.A. (2007). The economic impact of attention-deficit/hyperactivity disorder in children and adolescents. *Journal of Pediatric Psychology, 32*, 711–727.

Pelham, W.E., & Gnagy, E.M. (1999). Psychosocial and combined treatments for ADHD. *Mental Retardation and Developmental Disabilities, 5*, 225–236.

Pelham, W.E., Lang, A.R., Atkeson, B., Murphy, D.A., Gnagy, E.M., Greiner, A.R., . . . Greenslade, K.E. (1998). Effects of deviant child behavior on parental alcohol consumption: Stress-induced drinking in parents of ADHD children. *American Journal on Addictions, 7*, 103–114.

Pelham, W. E., & Milich, R. (1984). Peer relations of children with hyperactivity/attention deficit disorder. *Journal of Learning Disabilities*, *17*, 560–568.

Pelham, W. E., Walker, J. L., Sturges, J., & Hoza, J. (1989). Comparative effects of methylphenidate on ADD girls and ADD boys. *Journal of the American Academy of Child and Adolescent Psychiatry*, *28*, 773–776.

Pelham, W. E., Wheeler, T., & Chronis, A. (1998). Empirically supported psychosocial treatments for attention deficit hyperactivity disorder. *Journal of Clinical Child Psychology*, *27*, 190–205.

Pelkonen, M., Marttunen, M., Laippala, P., Lonngvist, J., & Aro, H. (1997). Psychosocial functioning in adolescent psychiatric patients: A prospective study of changes in psychosocial functioning among severely and moderately impaired adolescent outpatients. *Acta Psychiatrica Schandinavica*, *96*, 217–224.

Pelsser, L. M., Frankena, K., Toorman, J., & Pereira, R. R. (2017). Diet and ADHD, reviewing the evidence: A systematic review of meta-analyses of double-blind placebo-controlled trials evaluating the efficacy of diet interventions on the behavior of children with ADHD. *PLoS One*, *12*, e0169277.

Pennington, B.F. (1991). *Diagnosing learning disorders. A neuropsychological framework.* New York: Guilford Press.

Pennington, B. F. (2005). Commentary. Toward a new neuropsychological model of attention-deficit hyperactivity disorder: Subtypes and multiple deficits. *Biological Psychiatry*, *57*, 1221–1223.

Pennington, B. F. (2006). From single to multiple deficit models of developmental disorders. *Cognition*, *101*, 385–413.

Pennington, B. F., & Bishop, D. V. (2009). Relations among speech, language, and reading disorders. *Annual Review of Psychology*, *60*, 283–306.

Pennington, B. F., & Lefly, D. L. (2001). Early reading development in children at family risk for dyslexia. *Child Development*, *72*, 816–833.

Pennington, B. F., McGrath, L. M., Rosenberg, J., Barnard, H., Smith, S. D., Willcutt, E. G., . . . Olson, R. K. (2009). Gene×environment interactions in reading disability and attention-deficit/hyperactivity disorder. *Developmental Psychology*, *45*, 77–89.

Pennington, B. F., & Ozonoff, S. (1996). Executive functions and developmental psychopathology. *Journal of Child Psychology and Psychiatry*, *37*, 51–87.

Perera, H., Jeewandara, K. C., Seneviratne, S., & Guruge, C. (2012). Combined ω3 and ω6 supplementation in children with attention-deficit hyperactivity disorder (ADHD) refractory to methylphenidate treatment: A double-blind, placebo-controlled study. Journal *of Child Neurology*, *27*, 747–753.

Peters, S., Calam, R., & Harrington, R. (2005). Maternal attributions and expressed emotion as predictors of attendance at parent management training. *Journal of Child Psychology and Psychiatry*, *46*, 436–448.

Pfiffner, L. J. (2008). Social skills training. In K.McBurnett & L. J. Pfiffner (Eds.), *Attention-deficit/hyperactivity disorder: Concepts, controversies, new directions* (pp. 179–190). New York: Informa Healthcare.

Pfiffner, L. J. (2011). All about ADHD: *The complete practical guide for classroom teachers* (2nd ed.). New York: Scholastic.

Pfiffner, L. J., & Barkley, R. A. (1990). Educational placement and classroom management. In R. A. Barkley (Ed.), *Attention-deficit hyperactivity disorder: A handbook for diagnosis and treatment.* New York: Guilford Press.

Pfiffner, L. J., & DuPaul, G. J. (2015). Treatment of ADHD in school settings. In R. A. Barkley (Ed.) *Attention-Deficit Hyperactivity Disorder* (4th ed., pp. 596–629). New York: Guilford Press.

Pfiffner, L. J., & Haack, L. M. (2014). Nonpharmacological treatments for childhood ADHD and their combination with medication. In. P. E. Nathan, J. M. Gordon (Eds). *A guide to treatments that work* (4th ed). New York: Oxford University Press.

Pfiffner, L. J., Hinshaw, S. P., Owens, E., Zalecki, C., Kaiser, N. M., Villodas, M., & McBurnett, K. (2014). A two-site randomized clinical trial of integrated psychosocial treatment for ADHD-inattentive type. *Journal of Consulting and Clinical Psychology*, *82*, 1115–1127.

Pfiffner, L. J., & McBurnett, K. (1997). Social skills training with parent generalization: Treatment effects for children with attention deficit disorder. *Journal of Consulting and Clinical Psychology, 65*, 749–757.

Pfiffner, L. J., McBurnett, K., Rathouz, P. J., & Judice, S. (2005). Family correlates of oppositional and conduct disorders in children with attention-deficit/hyperactivity disorder. *Journal of Abnormal Child Psychology, 33*, 551–563.

Pfiffner, L. J., Mikami, A. Y., Huang-Pollock, C., Easterlin, B., Zalecki, C., & McBurrnet, K. (2007). A randomized, comparison led trial of integrated home-school behavioral treatment for ADHD, predominately inattentive type. *Journal of the American Academy of Child and Adolescent Psychiatry, 46*, 1041–1050.

Pham, A. V., & Hasson, R. M. (2014). Verbal and visuospatial working memory as predictors of children's reading ability. *Archives of Clinical Neuropsychology, 29*, 467–477.

Pham, A. V., & Riviere, A. (2015). Specific Learning Disorders and ADHD: Current issues in diagnosis across clinical and educational settings. *Current Psychiatry Reports, 17*, 1–7.

Pheula, G. F., Rohde, L. A., & Schmitz, M. (2011). Are family variables associated with ADHD, inattentive type? A case control study in schools. *European Child and Adolescent Psychiatry, 20*, 137–145.

Philipsen, A., Graf, E., Jans, T., Matthies, S., Borel, P., Colla, M., . . . Sobanski, E. (2014). A randomized controlled multicenter trial on the multimodal treatment of adult attention-deficit hyperactivity disorder: Enrollment and characteristics of the study sample. *ADHD Attention Deficit and Hyperactivity Disorders, 6*, 35–47.

Picchietti, D., Allen, R. P., Walters, A. S., Davidson, J. E., Myers, A., & Ferini-Strambi, L. (2007). Restless legs syndrome: Prevalence and impact in children and adolescents-the Peds REST study. *Pediatrics, 120*, 253–266.

Piek, J. P., Baynam, G. B., & Barrett, N. C. (2006). The relationship between fine and gross motor ability, self-perceptions and self-worth in children and adolescents. *Human Movement Science, 25*, 65–75.

Piek, J. P., Dawson, L., Smith, L. M., & Gasson, N. (2008). The role of early fine and gross motor development on later motor and cognitive ability. *Human Movement Science, 27*, 668–681.

Piek, J. P., Pitcher, T., & Hay, D. (1999). Motor coordination and kinaesthesis in boys with attention deficit hyperactivity disorder. *Developmental Medicine and Child Neurology, 41*, 159–165.

Pimperton, H., & Nation, K. (2010). Understanding words, understanding numbers: An exploration of the mathematical profiles of poor comprehenders. *British Journal of Educational Psychology, 14*, 225–268.

Pinto, C., Turton, P., Hughues, P., White, S., & Gillberg, C. (2006). ADHD and infant disorganized attachment. A prospective study of children next-born after stillbirth. *Journal of Attention Disorders, 10*, 83–91.

Pisecco, S., Huzinee, C., & Curtis, D. (2001). The effects of child characteristics on teachers' acceptability of classroom-based behavioral strategies and psychostimulant medication for the treatment of ADHD. *Journal of Clinical Child Psychology, 30*, 413–421.

Pitcher, T. M., Piek, J. P., & Hay, D. A. (2003). Fine and gross motor ability in males with ADHD. *Developmental Medicine and Child Neurology, 45*, 525–535.

Piven, J., Arndt, S., Bailey, J., & Andreasen, N. (1996). Regional brain enlargement in autism: A magnetic resonance imaging study. *Journal of the American Academy of Child & Adolescent Psychiatry, 35*, 530–536.

Plessen, K. J., Bansal, R., Zhu, H., Whiteman, R., Amat, J., Quackenbush, G. A., . . . Peterson, B. S. (2006). Hippocampus and amygdale morphology in attention-deficit/hyperactivity disorder. *Archives of General Psychiatry, 63*, 795–807.

Plichta, M., Vasic, N., Wolf, R. C., Lesch, K. P., Brummer, D., Jacob, C., Fallgatter, A. J., & Gron G. (2009). Neural hyporesponsiveness and hyperresponsiveness during immediate and delayed reward processing in adult attention-deficit/hyperactivity disorder. *Biological Psychiatry, 65*, 7–14.

Pliszka, S. R. (1992). Comorbidity of attention-deficit hyperactivity disorder and overanxious disorder. *Journal of the American Academy of Child and Adolescent Psychiatry, 31*, 197–203.

Pliszka, S. R. (2007). Practice parameter for the assessment and treatment of children and adolescents with attention-deficit/hyperactivity disorder. *Journal of the American Academy of Child and Adolescent Psychiatry*, *46*, 894–921.

Pliszka, S. R. (2015). Comorbid Psychiatric Disorders in children with ADHD. In R. A. Barkley (Ed.) *Attention-Deficit Hyperactivity Disorder* (4th ed., pp. 140–168). New York: Guilford Press.

Pliszka, S. R., Crismon, M. L., Hughes, C. W., Corners, C. K., Emslie, G. J., Jensen, P. S. . . . Texas Consensus Conference Panel on Pharmacotherapy of Childhood Attention Deficit Hyperactivity Disorder. (2006). The Texas Children's Medication Algorithm Project: Revision of the algorithm for pharmacotherapy of attention-deficit/hyperactivity disorder. *Journal of the American Academy of Child and Adolescent Psychiatry*, *45*, 642–657.

Plomin, R. (1995). Genetics and children's experiences in the family. *Journal of Child Psychology and Psychiatry*, *36*, 33–68.

Podolski, C., & Nigg, J. T. (2001). Parent stress and coping in relation to child ADHD severity and associated child disruptive behavior problems. *Journal of Clinical Child Psychology*, *4*, 503–513.

Poelmans, G., Pauls, D. L., Buitelaar, J. K., & Franke, B. (2011). Integrated genome-wide association study findings: Identification of a neurodevelopmental network for attention deficit hyperactivity disorder. *American Journal of Psychiatry*, *168*, 365–377.

Polanczyk, G., Caspi, A., Houts, R., Kollins, S. H., Rohde, L. A., & Moffitt, T. E. (2010). Implications of extending the ADHD age-of-onset criterion to age 12: Results from a prospectively studied birth cohort. *Journal of the American Academy of Child and Adolescent Psychiatry*, *49*, 210–216.

Polanczyk, G., De Lima, M. S., Horta, L., Biederman, J., & Rohde L. A. (2007). The worldwide prevalence of ADHD: A systematic review and metaregression analysis. *American Journal of Psychiatry*, *164*, 942–948.

Polanczyk, G. V., Willcutt, E. G., Salum, G. A., Kieling, C., & Rohde, L. A. (2014). ADHD prevalence estimates across three decades: an updated systematic review and meta-regression analysis. *International Journal of Epidemiology*, *43*, 434–442.

Polanska, K., Jurewicz, J., & Hanke, W. (2013). Review of current evidence on the impact of pesticides, polychlorinated biphenyls and selected metals on attention-deficit/hyperactivity disorder in children. *International Journal of Occupational Medicine and Environmental Health*, *26*, 16–38.

Polatajko, H. J., & Cantin, N. (2005). Developmental coordination disorder (dyspraxia): An overview of the state of the art. *Seminars in Pediatric Neurology*, *12*, 250–258.

Pomerleau, O. F., Downey, K. K., Stelson, F. W., & Pomerleau, C. S. (1995). Cigarette smoking in adult patients diagnosed with attention deficit hyperactivity disorder. *Journal of Substance Abuse*, *7*, 373–378.

Pontifex, M. B., Saliba, B. J., Raine, L. B., Picchietti, D. L., & Hillman, C. H. (2013). Exercise improves behavioral, neurocognitive, and scholastic performance in children with attention-deficit/hyperactivity disorder. *Journal of Pediatrics*, *162*, 543–551.

Posner, K., Melvin, G. A., Murray, D. W., Gugga, S. S., Fisher, P., Skrobala, A., . . . Greenhill, L. L. (2007). Clinical presentation of attention-deficit/hyperactivity disorder in preschool children: The Preschoolers with Attention-Deficit/Hyperactivity Disorder Treatment Study (PATS). *Journal of Child and Adolescent Psychopharmacology*, *17*, 547–562.

Posner, M. I., & Peterson, S. E. (1990). The attention system of the human brain. *Annual Review of Neuroscience*, *13*, 25–42.

Posner, M. I., & Rothbart, M. K. (2007). Research on attention networks as a model for the integration of psychological science. *Annual Review of Psychology*, *58*, 1–23.

Posner, M. I., Rothbart, M. K., & Rueda, M. R. (2014). Developing attention and self-regulation in childhood. In A. C. Nobre, & S. Kastner (Eds.), *The Oxford handbook of attention*. Oxford: Oxford University Press.

Posserud, M-B., Ullebø, A. K., Plessen, K. J., Stormark, K. M., Gillberg, C., Lundervold, A. J. (2014). Influence of assessment instrument on ADHD diagnosis. *European Child and Adolescent Psychiatry*, *23*, 197–205.

Poulton, A. (2005). Growth on stimulant medication; clarifying the confusion: A review. *Archives of Disease in Childhood, 90*, 801–806.

Powell, R.P., & Bishop, D.V.M. (1992). Clumsiness and perceptual problems in children with specific language impairment. *Developmental Medicine and Child Neurology, 34*, 755–765.

Powell, S.G., Frydenberg, M., & Thomsen, P.H. (2015). The effects of long-term medication on growth in children and adolescents with ADHD: An observational study of a large cohort of real-life patients. *Child and Adolescent Psychiatry and Mental Health, 9*, 50.

Power, J.T., Blom-Hoffman, J., Clarke, A.T., Riley-Tilman, T.C., Kelleher, C., & Manz, P.H. (2005). Reconceptualizing intervention integrity: A partnership-based framework for linking research with practice. *Psychology in the Schools, 42*, 495–507.

Power, T.J., Costigan, T.E., Leff, S.S., Eiraldi, R.B., & Landau, S. (2001). Assessing ADHD across settings: Contributions of behavioral assessment to categorical decision making. *Journal of Clinical Child Psychology, 30*, 399–412.

Power, T.J., & Mautone, J.A. (2008). Best practices in linking families and schools to educate children with attention problems. In A. Thomas, & J. Grimes (Eds.), *Best practices in school psychology V*. Bethesda, MD: National Association of School Psychologists.

Power, T.J., Mautone, J.A., Soffer, S.L., Clarke, A.T., Marshall, S.A., Sharman, J., . . . Jawad, A.F. (2012). Family-school intervention for children with ADHD: Results of a randomized clinical trial. *Journal of Consulting and Clinical Psychology, 80*, 611–623.

Power, T.J., Soffer, S.L., Clarke, A.T., & Mautone, J.A. (2006). Multisystemic intervention for children with ADHD. *Report on Emotional and Behavioral Disorders in Youth, 6*, 51–52.

Power, T.J., Soffer, S.L., Mautone, J.A., Costigan, T.E., Jones, H.A., Clarke, A.T., & Marshall, S.A. (2009). An analysis of teacher investment in the context of a family—school intervention for children with ADHD. *School Mental Health, 1*, 107–117.

Power, T.J., Watkins, M.W., Anastopoulos, A.D., Reid, R., Lambert, M.C., & DuPaul, G.J. (2015). Multi-informant assessment of ADHD symptom-related impairments among children and adolescents. *Journal of Clinical Child & Adolescent Psychology*, 1–14. https://doi.org/10.1080/15374416.2015.1079781

Power, T.J., Werba, B.E., Watkins, M.W., Angelucci, J.G., & Eiraldi, R.B. (2006). Patterns of parent-reported homework problems among ADHD-referred and non-referred children. *School Psychology Quarterly, 21*, 13–33.

Pressman, L.J., Loo, S.K., Carpenter, E.M., Asarnow, J.R., Lynn, D., McCracken, J.T., . . . Smalley, S.L. (2006). Relationship of family environment and parental psychiatric diagnosis to impairment in ADHD. *Journal of the American Academy of Child and Adolescent Psychiatry, 45*, 346–354.

Prevatt, F. (2016). Coaching for college students with ADHD. *Current Psychiatry Reports, 18*, 110.

Prevatt, F., Lampropoulos, G.K., Bowles, V., & Garrett, L. (2011). The use of between session assignments in ADHD coaching with college students. *Journal of Attention Disorders, 15*, 18–27.

Prevatt, F., & Yelland, S. (2015). An empirical evaluation of ADHD coaching in college students. *Journal of Attention Disorders, 19*, 666–677.

Pribram, K.H., & McGuinness, D. (1975). Arousal, activation, and effort in the control of attention. *Psychological Review, 82*, 116–149.

Prince, J.B. (2008). Catecholamine dysfunction in attention-deficit/hyperactivity disorder: An update. *Journal of Clinical Psychopharmacology, 28*, S39–S45.

Prince, J.B., Wilens, T.E., Spencer, T.J., & Biederman, J. (2015). Pharmacotherapy of ADHD in adults. In R.A. Barkley (Ed.) *Attention-Deficit Hyperactivity Disorder* (4th ed., pp. 826–860). New York: Guilford Press.

Prior, M., & Sanson, A. (1986). Attention deficit disorder with hyperactivity: A critique. *Journal of Child Psychology and Psychiatry, 27*, 307–319.

Pritchard, A. E., Nigro, C.A., Jacobson, L.A., & Mahone, E.M. (2012). The role of neuropsychological assessment in the functional outcomes of children with ADHD. *Neuropsychology Review, 22*, 54–68.

Ptacek, R., Kuzelova, H., Stefano, G. B., Raboch, J., Sadkova, T., Goetz, M., & Kream, R. M. (2014). Disruptive patterns of eating behaviors and associated lifestyles in males with ADHD. *Medical Science Monitor*, *20*, 608–613.

Pugh, K. R., Mencl, W. E., Shaywitz, B. A., Shaywitz, S. E., Fulbright, R. K., Constable, R. T., . . . Gore, J. C. (2000). The angular gyrus in developmental dyslexia: Task-specific differences in functional connectivity within posterior cortex. *Psychological Science*, *11*, 51–56.

Purdie, N., Hattie, J., & Carroll, A. (2002). A review of the research on interventions for Attention Deficit Hyperactivity Disorder: What works best? *Review of Educational Research*, *72*, 61–99.

Qiu, A., Crocetti, D., Adler, M., Mahone, E. M., Denckla, M. B., Miller, M. I., & Mostofsky, S. H. (2009). Basal ganglia volume and shape in children with attention deficit hyperactivity disorder. *American Journal of Psychiatry*, *166*, 74–82.

Quay, H. C. (1988). Attention deficit disorder and the behavioral inhibition system: The relevance of the neuropsychological theory of Jeffrey A. Gray. In L. M. Bloomingdale & J. Sergeant (Eds.), *Attention deficit disorder: Criteria, cognition, intervention* (pp. 117–126). New York: Pergamon Press.

Quay, H. C. (1999). Classification of the disruptive behavior disorders. In H. C. Quay, & A. E. Hogan (Eds.), *Handbook of disruptive behavior disorders* (pp. 3–21). New York: Kluwer Academic/ Plenum.

Quinn, P. O. (2005). Treating adolescent girls and women with ADHD: Gender specific issues. *Journal of Clinical Psychology*, *61*, 579–587.

Quinn, P. O., & Madhoo, M. (2014). A review of attention-deficit/hyperactivity disorder in women and girls: uncovering this hidden diagnosis. *The Primary Care Companion for CNS Disorders*, *16*, pii: PCC.13r01596.

Qureshi, I. A., & Mehler, M. F. (2013). Towards a 'systems'-level understanding of the nervous system and its disorders. *Trends in Neurosciences*, *36*, 674–684.

Rabiner, D. L., Anastopoulos, A. D., Costello, J., Hoyle, R. H., & Swartzwelder, H. S. (2008). Adjustment to college in students with ADHD. *Journal of Attention Disorders*, *11*, 689–699.

Rabiner, D., & Coie, J. D. (2000). Early attention problems and children's' reading achievement: a longitudinal investigation. *Journal of the American Academy of Child and Adolescent Psychiatry*, *39*, 859–867.

Rabiner, D. L., Malone, P. S., and Conduct Problems Prevention Research Group (2004). The impact of tutoring on early reading achievement for children with and without attention problems. *Journal of Abnormal Child Psychology*, *32*, 273–284.

Racicka, E., Hanć, T., Giertuga, K., Bryńska, A., & Wolańczyk, T. (2015). Prevalence of overweight and obesity in children and adolescents with ADHD: The significance of comorbidities and pharmacotherapy. *Journal of Attention Disorders*. https://doi.org/1087054715578272

Radek, K. (2013). Are actiwatch recordings useful in the diagnosis and treatment of attention deficit disorder and hyperactivity. *Sleep Disorders and Therapy*, *2*, 2167–2277.

Raggi, V. L. & Chronis, A. M. (2006) Interventions to address the academic impairment of children and adolescents with ADHD. *Clinical Child and Family Psychology Review*, *9*, 85–111.

Raiker, J. S., Rapport, M. D., Kofler, M. J., & Sarver, D. E. (2012). Objectively-measured impulsivity and attention-deficit/hyperactivity disorder (ADHD): Testing competing predictions from the working memory and behavioral inhibition models of ADHD. *Journal of Abnormal Child Psychology*, *40*, 699–713.

Raine, A., Portnoy, J., Liu, J., Mahoomed, T., & Hibbeln, J. R. (2015). Reduction in behavior problems with omega-3 supplementation in children aged 8–16 years: A randomized, double-blind, placebo-controlled, stratified, parallel-group trial. *Journal of Child Psychology and Psychiatry*, *56*, 509–520.

Ramsay, J. R. (2010). *Nonmedication treatments for adult ADHD: Evaluating impact on daily functioning and well-being*. Washington, DC: American Psychological Association.

Ramsay, J. R. (2015). Psychosocial assessment of adults with ADHD. In R. A. Barkley (Ed.) *Attention-Deficit Hyperactivity Disorder* (4th ed., pp. 475–500). New York: Guilford Press.

Ramsay, J.R. (2016). "Turning intentions into actions" CBT for adult ADHD focused on implementation. *Clinical Case Studies, 15*, 179–197.

Ramsay, J.R., & Rostain, A.L. (2003). A cognitive therapy approach for adult Attention Deficit/Hyperactivity Disorder. *Journal of Cognitive Psychotherapy, 17*, 319–334.

Ramsay, J.R., & Rostain, A.L. (2008). *Cognitive-behavioral therapy of adult ADHD: An integrative psychosocial and medical approach.* New York: Routledge.

Rao, P.A., & Landa, R.J. (2013). Association between severity of behavioral phenotype and comorbid attention deficit hyperactivity disorder symptoms in children with autism spectrum disorders. *Autism, 18*, 272–280.

Rapin, I. (1964). Brain damage in children. In J. Brennemann (Ed.), *Practice of pediatrics* (Vol. 4). Hagerstown, MD: Prior.

Rappley, M.D. (2005). Attention-deficit/hyperactivity disorder. *New England Journal of Medicine*, 352, 165–175.

Rapport, M.D., Bolden, J., Kofler, M.J., Sarver, D.E., Raiker, J.S., & Alderson, R.M. (2009). Hyperactivity in boys with attention deficit/hyperactivity disorder (ADHD): A ubiquitous core symptom or manifestation of working memory deficits? *Journal of Abnormal Child Psychology, 37*, 521–534.

Rapport, M.D., Chung, K.M., Shore, G., Denney, C.B., & Isaacs, P. (2000). Upgrading the science and technology of assessment and diagnosis: Laboratory and clinic-based assessment of children with ADHD. *Journal of Clinical Child Psychology, 29*, 555–568.

Rapport, M.D., Chung, K., Shore, G., & Isaacs, P. (2001). A conceptual model of child psychopathology: Implications for understanding attention deficit hyperactivity disorder and treatment efficacy. *Journal of Clinical Child Psychology, 30*, 48–58.

Rapport, M.D., & Moffitt, C. (2002). Attention deficit/hyperactivity disorder and methylphenidate. A review of height/weight, cardiovascular, and somatic complaint side effects. *Clinical Psychology Review, 22*, 1107–1131.

Rapport, M.D., Orban, S.A., Kofler, M.J., & Friedman, L.M. (2013). Do programs designed to train working memory, other executive functions, and attention benefit children with ADHD: A meta-analytic review of cognitive, academic, and behavioral outcomes. *Clinical Psychology Review, 33*, 1237–1252.

Rapport, M.D., Orban, S.A., Kofler, M.J., & Friedman, L.M., & Bolden, J. (2015). Executive function training for children with ADHD. In R.A. Barkley (Ed.) *Attention-Deficit Hyperactivity Disorder* (4th ed., pp. 641–665). New York: Guilford Press.

Rapport, M.D., Scanlan, S.W., & Denney, C.B. (1999). Attention-deficit/hyperactivity disorder and scholastic achievement: A model of dual developmental pathways. *Journal of Child Psychology and Psychiatry, 40*, 1169–1183.

Rasmussen, C., & Bisanz, J. (2005). Representation and working memory in early arithmetic. *Journal of Experimental Child Psychology, 91*, 137–157.

Rasmussen, K., & Levander, S. (2009). Untreated ADHD in adults: Are there sex differences in symptoms, comorbidity, and impairment? *Journal of Attention Disorders, 12*, 353–360.

Rasmussen, P., & Gillberg, C. (2000). Natural outcome of ADHD with developmental coordination disorder at age 22 years: A controlled, longitudinal, community-based study. *Journal of the American Academy of Child and Adolescent Psychiatry, 39*, 1424–1431.

Ratey, N.A. (2002). Life coaching for adult ADHD. In. S. Goldstein & A.T. Ellison (Eds.), *Clinician's guide to adult ADHD. Assessment and intervention* (pp. 261–277). San Diego, CA: Academic Press.

Ratey, N. A. (2008). *The disorganized mind: Coaching your ADHD brain to take control of your time, tasks, and talents.* New York: St. Martin's Press.

Ratey, N., & Sleeper-Triplett, J. (2011). Strategic coaching for LD and ADHD. In. S. Goldstein, J.A. Naglieri, & M. DeVries (Eds.), *Learning and attention disorders in adolescence and adulthood: Assessment and treatment*, (2nd ed., pp. 433–455). Chichester, NJ: John Wiley & Sons.

Ravishankar, V., Chowdappa, S.V., Benegal, V., & Muralidharan, K. (2016). The efficacy of atomoxetine in treating adult attention deficit hyperactivity disorder (ADHD): A meta-analysis of controlled trials. *Asian Journal of Psychiatry, 24*, 53–58.

Raz, R., & Gabis, L. (2009). Essential fatty acids and attention-deficit-hyperactivity disorder: A systematic review. *Developmental Medicine and Child Neurology, 51*, 580–92.

Re, A. M., Pedron, M., & Cornoldi, C. (2007). Expressive writing difficulties in children described as exhibiting ADHD symptoms. *Journal of Learning Disabilities, 40*, 244–255.

Reader, S. K., Stewart, L. M., & Johnson, J. H. (2009). Assessing ADHD-related family stressors with the Disruptive Behavior Stress Inventory (DBSI): A replication and extension. *Journal of Clinical Psychology in Medical Settings, 16*, 148–160.

Realmuto, G. M., Winters, K. C., August, G. J., Lee, S., Fahnhorst, T., & Botzet, A. (2009). Drug use and psychosocial functioning of a community-derived sample of adolescents with childhood ADHD. *Journal of Child & Adolescent Substance Abuse, 18*, 172–192.

Redick, T. S., Shipstead, Z., Harrison, T. L., Hicks, K. L., Fried, D. E., Hambrick, D. Z., . . . Engle, R. W. (2013). No evidence of intelligence improvement after working memory training: A randomized, placebo-controlled study. *Journal of Experimental Psychology: General, 142*, 359–379.

Redmond, S. (2004). Conversational profiles of children with ADHD, SLI and typical development. *Clinical Linguistics & Phonetics, 18*, 107–125.

Reeve, R. E. (1994). The academic impact of ADD. *Attention, 1*, 8–12.

Regier, D. A., First, M., & Narrow, W. (Eds.). (2007). *Age and gender considerations in psychiatric diagnosis: A research agenda for DSM-V.* Washington: DC: American Psychiatric.

Regier, D. A., Narrow, W. E., Kuhl, E. A., & Kupfer, D. J. (2009). The conceptual development of DSM-V. *American Journal of Psychology, 166*, 645–650.

Reich, W. (2000). Diagnostic Interview for Children and Adolescents (DICA). *Journal of the American Academy of Child and Adolescent Psychiatry, 39*, 59–66.

Reid, A. M., Graziano, P., McNamara, J., Paneto, A., & Geffken, G. (2015). Functional impairment differences among youth with ADHD: The role of comorbid anxiety and Mood Disorders. *Journal of Nature and Science, 1*, e31.

Reid, R., Casat, C. D., Norton, H. J., Anastopoulos, A. D., & Temple, E. P. (2001). Using behavior rating scales for ADHD across ethnic groups: The IOWA Conners. *Journal of Emotional and Behavioral Disorders, 8*, 38–48.

Reid, R., & Lienemann, T. O. (2006). *Strategy instruction for students with learning disabilities: What works for special needs learners.* New York: Guilford Press.

Reid, R., Riccio, C. A., Kessler, R. H., DuPaul, G. J., Power, T. J., Anastopoulos, A. D., . . . Noll, N. B. (2000). Gender and ethnic differences in ADHD as assessed by behavior ratings. *Journal of Emotional and Behavioral Disorders, 8*, 38–48.

Reid, R., Trout, A., & Schartz, M. (2005). Self-regulation interventions for children with attention deficit/hyperactivity disorder. *Exceptional Children, 71*, 361–378.

Reiersen, A. M., Constantino, J. N., & Todd, R. D. (2008). Co-occurrence of motor problems and autistic symptoms in attention deficit/hyperactivity disorder. *Journal of the American Academy of Child and Adolescent Psychiatry, 47*, 662–672.

Reiersen, A. M., Constantino, J. N., Volk, H. E., & Todd, R. D. (2007). Autistic traits in a population-based ADHD twin sample. *Journal of Child Psychology and Psychiatry, 48*, 464–472.

Reiersen, A. M., & Todd, R. D. (2008). Co-occurrence of ADHD and autism spectrum disorders: Phenomenology and treatment. *Expert Review of Neurotherapeutics, 8*, 657–669

Reinblatt, S. P., Leoutsakos, J.M.S., Mahone, E. M., Forrester, S., Wilcox, H. C., & Riddle, M. A. (2015). Association between binge eating and attention-deficit/hyperactivity disorder in two pediatric community mental health clinics. *International Journal of Eating Disorders, 48*, 505–511.

Research Units on Pediatric Psychopharmacology. (2005). Randomized, controlled, crossover trial of methylphenidate in pervasive developmental disorders with hyperactivity. *Archives of General Psychiatry, 62*, 1266–1274.

Rey, J. M., & Sawyer, M. G. (2003). Are psychostimulant drugs being used appropriately to treat child and adolescent disorders? *British Journal of Psychiatry, 182*, 284–286.

Reyno, S. M., & McGrath, P. J. (2006). *Journal of Child Psychology and Psychiatry, 47*, 99–111.

Reynolds, B. (2006). A review of delay-discounting research with humans: Relations to drug use and gambling. *Behavioural Pharmacology, 17*, 651–667.

Reynolds, C.R., & Kamphaus, R.W. (2004). *Behavior Assessment System for Children, Second Edition (BASC-2)*. Bloomington, MN: Pearson Assessments.

Reynolds, M., & Besner, D. (2006). Reading aloud is not automatic: Processing capacity is required to generate a phonological code from print. *Journal of Experimental Psychology: Human Perception and Performance, 32*, 1303–1323.

Reynolds, S., & Lane, S.J. (2009). Sensory overresponsivity and anxiety in children with ADHD. *American Journal of Occupational Therapy, 63*, 433–440.

Rhee, S.H., Waldman, I.D., Hay, D.A., & Levy, F. (1999). Sex differences in genetic and environmental influences on DSM-III-R attention-deficit/hyperactivity disorder. *Journal of Abnormal Psychology, 108*, 24–41.

Rhee, S.H., Waldman, I.D., Hay, D.A., & Levy, F. (2001). Aetiology of the sex difference in the prevalence of DSM-III-R ADHD: A comparison of two models. In F. Levy & D. Hay (Eds.), *Attention, Genes, and ADHD* (pp. 139–156). Philadelphia: Brunner-Routledge.

Rhee, S.H., Willcutt, E.G., Hartman, C.A., Pennington, B.F., & DeFries, J.C. (2008). Test of alternative hypotheses explaining the comorbidity between attention-deficit/hyperactivity disorder and conduct disorder. *Journal of Abnormal Child Psychology, 36*, 29–40.

Richardson, A.J., & Montgomery, P. (2005). The Oxford-Durham Study: A randomized, controlled trial of dietary supplementation with fatty acids in children with Developmental Coordination Disorder. *Pediatrics, 115*, 1360–1366.

Riddle, M.A., Yershova, K., Lazzaretto, D., Paykina, N., Yenokyan, G., Greenhill, L., . . . Posner, K. (2013). The Preschool Attention-Deficit/Hyperactivity Disorder Treatment Study (PATS) 6-year follow-up. *Journal of the American Academy of Child and Adolescent Psychiatry, 52*, 264–278.

Rie, H.E., & Rie, E.D. (Eds.). (1980). *Handbook of minimal brain dysfunction: A critical review*. New York: Wiley.

Rimestad, M.L., Lambek, R., Christiansen, H.Z., & Hougaard, E. (2016). Short-and long-term effects of parent training for preschool children with or at risk of ADHD: A systematic review and meta-analysis. *Journal of Attention Disorders*. https://doi.org/1087054716648775

Rimm-Kaufman, S., Pianta, R.C., & Cox, M. (2000). Teachers' judgments of problems in the transition to school. *Early Childhood Research Quarterly, 15*, 147–166.

Ríos-Hernández, A., Alda, J.A., Farran-Codina, A., Ferreira-García, E., & Izquierdo-Pulido, M. (2017). The Mediterranean diet and ADHD in children and adolescents. *Pediatrics, 139(2)*, e20162027.

Robb, J.A., Sibley, M.H., Pelham, W.E., Foster, M.E., Molina, B.S.G., Gnagy, E.M., . . . Kuriyan, A.B. (2011). The estimated annual cost of ADHD to the US education system. *School Mental Health, 3*, 169–177.

Roberts, W., & Milich, R. (2013). Examining the changes to ADHD in the DSM-5: One step forward and two steps back. *The ADHD Report, 21*, 1–6.

Roberts, W., Peters, J.R., Adams, Z.W., Lynam, D.R., & Milich, R. (2014). Identifying the facets of impulsivity that explain the relation between ADHD symptoms and substance use in a nonclinical sample. *Addictive Behaviors, 39*, 1272–1277.

Robins, P.M. (1992). A comparison of behavioural and attentional functioning in children diagnosed as hyperactive or learning disabled. *Journal of Abnormal Child Psychology, 20*, 65–82.

Robinson, J.B., Burns, B.M., & Davis, D.W. (2009). Maternal scaffolding and attention regulation in children living in poverty. *Journal of Applied Developmental Psychology, 30*, 82–91.

Robinson, L.M., Sclar, D.A., Skaer, T.L., & Galin, R.S. (2004). Treatment modalities among US children diagnosed with attention-deficit hyperactivity disorder: 1995–99. *International Clinical Psychopharmacology, 19*, 17–22.

Robison, S.D., Frick, P.J., & Sheffield Morris, A. (2005). Temperament and parenting: implications for understanding developmental pathways to conduct disorder. *Minerva Pediatrica, 57*, 373–388.

Robson, A.L. & Pederson, D.R. (1997). Predictors of individual differences in attention among low birth weight children. *Developmental and Behavioral Pediatrics, 18*, 13–21.

Rodgers, A.Y. (1998). Multiple sources of stress and parenting behavior. *Children and Youth Services Review, 20*, 525–546.

Rodriguez-Jimenez, R., Avila, C., Jimenez-Arriero, M.A., Ponce, G., Monasor, R., Jimenez, M.E.E.A., . . . Palomo, T. (2006). Impulsivity and sustained attention in pathological gamblers: Influence of childhood ADHD history. *Journal of Gambling Studies, 22*, 451–461.

Rodriguez-Lafora, G. (1917). *Los ninos mentalmente anormales.* [The mentally abnormal children]. Madrid: Ediciones de la Lectura.

Roessner, V., Banaschewski, T., Uebel, H., Becker, A., & Rothenberger, A. (2004). Neuronal network models of ADHD—lateralization with respect to interhemispheric connectivity reconsidered. *European Child and Adolescent Psychiatry, 13*(Suppl 1), I71-I79.

Roessner, V., Becker, A., Banaschewski, T., & Rothenberger, A. (2007). Psychopathological profile in children with chronic tic disorder and co-existing ADHD: Additive effects. *Journal of Abnormal Child Psychology, 35*, 79–85.

Rogers, M.A., Wiener, J., Marton, I., & Tannock, R. (2009a). Supportive and controlling parental involvement as predictors of children's academic achievement: Relations to children's ADHD symptoms and parenting stress. *School Mental Health, 2*, 89–102.

Rogers, M.A., Wiener, J., Marton, I., & Tannock, R. (2009b). Parental involvement in children's learning: Comparing parents of children with and without Attention-Deficit/Hyperactivity Disorder. *Journal of School Psychology, 47*, 167 185.

Rohde, L.A., Barbosa, G., Polanczyk, G. Eizrik, M., Rasmussen, E.R., Neuman, R.J., & Todd, R.D. (2001). Factor and latent class analysis of DSM-IV ADHD symptoms in a school sample of Brazilian adolescents. *Journal of the American Academy of Child and Adolescent Psychiatry, 40*, 711–718.

Rohde, L.A., Biederman, J., Zimmermann, H., Schmitz, M., Martins, S., & Tramontina, S. (2000). Exploring ADHD age-of-onset criterion in Brazilian adolescents. *European Child and Adolescent Psychiatry, 9*, 212–218.

Rohde, P., Clarke, G.N., Lewinsohn, P.M., Seeley, J.R., & Kaufman, N.K. (2001). Impact of comorbidity on a cognitive-behavioral group treatment for adolescent depression. *Journal of the American Academy of Child and Adolescent Psychiatry, 40*, 795–802.

Rohde, L.A., Szobot, C., Polanczyk, G., Schmitz, M., Martins, S., & Tramontina, S. (2005). Attention-deficit/hyperactivity disorder in a diverse culture: Do research and clinical findings support the notion of a cultural construct for the disorder? *Biological Psychiatry, 57*, 1436–1441.

Romano, E., Tremblay, R.E., Vitaro, F., Zoccolillo, M., & Pagani, L. (2001). Prevalence of psychiatric diagnoses and the role of perceived impairment: Findings from an adolescent community sample. *Journal of the American Academy of Child and Adolescent Psychiatry, 42*, 451–462.

Romirowsky, A. M., & Chronis-Tuscano, A. (2014). Paternal ADHD symptoms and child conduct problems: is father involvement always beneficial? Child Care Health and Development, 40, 706–714.

Rommelse, N.N.J., Franke, B., Geurts, H.M., & Hartman, J.B. (2010). Shared heritability of attention-deficit/hyperactivity disorder and autism spectrum disorder. *European Child and Adolescent Psychiatry, 19*, 281–295.

Rommelse, N.N.J., Peters, C.T.R., Oosterling, I.J., Visser, J.C., Bons, D., van Steijn, D.J., . . . Buitelaar, J.K. (2011). A pilot study of abnormal growth in autism spectrum disorders and other childhood psychiatric disorders. *Journal of Autism and Developmental Disorders, 41*, 44–54.

Ronald, A., Edelson, L., Asherson, P. & Saudino, K. (2010) Exploring the relationship between autistic-like traits and ADHD behaviors in early childhood: Findings from a community twin study of 2-year-olds. *Journal of Abnormal Child Psychology, 38*, 185–196.

Ronald, A., Larsson, H., Anckarsäter, H., & Lichtenstein, P. (2014). Symptoms of autism and ADHD: A Swedish twin study examining their overlap. *Journal of Abnormal Psychology, 123*, 440–451.

Ronald, A., Pennell, C.E., & Whitehouse, A.J.O. (2011). Prenatal maternal stress associated with ADHD and autistic traits in early childhood. *Frontiers in Psychology, 1*, 223.

Rooney, M., Chronis-Tuscano, A.M., & Huggins, S. (2015). Disinhibition mediates the relationship between ADHD and problematic alcohol use in college students. *Journal of Attention Disorders, 19*, 313–327.

Rooney, M., Chronis-Tuscano, A., & Yoon, Y. (2012). Substance use in college students with ADHD. *Journal of Attention Disorders, 16*, 221–234.

Rose, E., Bramham, J., Young, S., Paliokostas, E., & Xenitidis, K. (2009). Neuropsychological characteristics of adults with comorbid ADHD and borderline/mild intellectual disability. *Research in Developmental Disabilities, 30*, 496–502.

Rose, S.A., Feldman, J.F., & Jankowski, J.J. (2009). A cognitive approach to the development of early language. *Child Development, 80*, 134–150.

Rose, S.A., Feldman, J.F., & Jankowski, J.J. (2011). Modeling a cascade of effects: The role of speed and executive functioning in preterm/full-term differences in academic achievement. *Developmental Science, 14*, 1161–1175.

Rosenberg, D. (2002). Adrenergic agents in child and adolescent psychiatry. In D. Rosenberg, P. Davanzo, & S. Gershon (Eds.), *Pharmacotherapy for child and adolescent psychiatric disorders* (2nd ed., pp 543–555). New York: Marcel Dekker.

Rosenberg, J., Pennington, B.F., Willcutt, E.G., Olson, R.K. (2012). Gene by environment interactions influencing reading disability and the inattentive symptom dimension of attention deficit/hyperactivity disorder. *Journal of Child Psychology and Psychiatry, 53*, 243–251.

Rosenthal, R.H. & Allen, T.W. (1978). An examination of attention, arousal and learning dysfunctions of hyperkinetic children. *Psychological Bulletin, 85*, 689–715.

Rosenthal, R., & Jacobson, L. (1968). *Pygmalion in the classroom: Teacher expectation and pupils' intellectual development.* New York: Rinehart & Winston.

Rösler, M., Fischer, R., Ammer, R., Ose, C., & Retz, W.A (2009). Randomised, placebo-controlled, 24-week, study of low-dose extended-release methylphenidate in adults with attention-deficit/hyperactivity disorder. *European Archives of Psychiatry and Clinical Neuroscience, 259*,120–129.

Rösler, M., Retz, W., Retz-Junginger, P., Hengesch, G., Schneider, M., Supprian, T., . . . Thome, J. (2004). Prevalence of attention deficit-/hyperactivity disorder (ADHD) and comorbid disorders in young male prison inmates. *European Archives of Psychiatry and Clinical Neuroscience, 254*, 365–371.

Rösler, M., Retz, W., Yaqoobi, K., Burg, E., & Retz-Yunginger, P. (2008). Attention deficit/hyperactivity disorder in female offenders: Prevalence, psychiatric comorbidity and psychosocial implications. *European Archives of Psychiatry and Clinical Neurosciences, 259*, 98–105.

Ross, D.M., & Ross, S.A. (1976). *Hyperactivity: Research, theory and action.* New York: Wiley.

Ross, D.M., & Ross, S.A. (1982). *Hyperactivity: Current issues, research and theory.* New York: Wiley.

Rosselli, M., Matute, E., Pinto, N., & Ardila, A. (2006). Memory abilities in children with subtypes of dyscalculia. *Developmental Neuropsychology, 30*, 801–818.

Rostain, A., Jensen, P.S., Connor, D.F., Miesle, L.M., & Faraone, S.V. (2015). Toward quality care in ADHD: Defining the goals of treatment. *Journal of Attention Disorders, 19*, 99–117.

Rothbart, M.K., Sheese, B.E., Rueda, M.R., & Posner, M.I. (2011). Developing mechanisms of self-regulation in early life. *Emotion Review, 3*, 207–213.

Rothenberger, A., & Kirov, R. (2005). Changes in sleep-wake behavior may be more than just an epiphenomenon of ADHD. *Behavioral and Brain Sciences, 28*, 439.

Rothenberger, A., Roessner, V., Banaschewski, T., & Leckman, J.F. (2007). Co-existence of tic disorders and attention-deficit/hyperactivity disorder: Recent advances in understanding and treatment. *European Child and Adolescent Psychiatry, 16*(Suppl. 1), 1–4.

Rousselle, L., & Noel, M.P. (2007). Basic numerical skills in children with mathematical learning disabilities: A comparison of symbolic vs non-symbolic number magnitude processing. *Cognition, 102*, 361–395.

Rowe, R., Costello, E.J., Angold, A., Copeland, W.E., & Maughan, B. (2010). Developmental pathways in Oppositional Defiant Disorder and Conduct Disorder. *Journal of Abnormal Psychology, 119*, 726–738.

Rowland, A.S., Skipper, B.J., Umbach, D.M., Rabiner, D.L., Campbell, R.A., Naftel, A.J., & Sandler, D.P. (2015). The prevalence of ADHD in a population-based sample. *Journal of Attention Disorders, 19*,741–754.

Roy, A., Hartman, C.A., Veenstra, R., & Oldehinkel, A.J. (2015). Peer dislike and victimisation in pathways from ADHD symptoms to depression. *European Child and Adolescent Psychiatry, 24*, 887–895.

Rubia, K. (2005). RED: ADHD under the "micro-scope" of the rat model. *Behavioral and Brain Sciences, 28*, 439–440.

Rubia, K., Halari, R., Cubillo, A., Smith, A.B., Mohammad, A.M., Brammer, M., & Taylor, E. (2011). Methylphenidate normalizes fronto-striatal underactivation during interference inhibition in medication-naïve boys with attention-deficit/hyperactivity disorder. *Neuropsychopharmacology, 36*, 1575–1586.

Rubia, K., Overmery, S., Taylor, E., Brammer. M., Williams, S.C., Simmons, A., . . . Bullmore, E.T. (2000). Functional frontalisation with age: Mapping neurodevelopmental trajectories with fMRI. *Neuroscience and Biobehavioral Reviews, 24*, 13–19.

Rubinsten, O., Bedard, A.C., & Tannock, R. (2008). Methylphenidate improves general but not core numerical abilities in ADHD children with co-morbid dyscalculia or mathematical difficulties. *Journal of Open Psychology, 1*, 11–17.

Rubinsten, O., & Henik, A. (2006). Double dissociation of functions in developmental dyslexia and dyscalculia. *Educational Psychology, 98*, 854–867.

Rucklidge, J.J. (2010). Gender differences in attention-deficit/hyperactivity disorder. *Psychiatric Clinics of North America, 33*, 357–373.

Rucklidge, J.J., & Tannock, R. (2001). Psychiatric, psychosocial and cognitive functioning of female adolescents with ADHD. *Journal of the American Academy of Child and Adolescent Psychiatry, 40*, 530–540.

Rucklidge, J.J., & Tannock, R. (2002). Neuropsychological profiles of adolescents with ADHD: Effects of reading difficulties and gender. *Journal of Child Psychology and Psychiatry, 43*, 988–1003.

Rueda, M.R., Posner, M.I., & Rothbart, M.K. (2005). The development of executive attention: Contributions to the emergence of self-regulation. *Developmental Neuropsychology, 28*, 573–594.

Rueda, M.R., Rothbart, M.K., McCandliss, B.D., Saccomanno, L., & Posner, M.I. (2005). Training, maturation, and genetic influences on the development of executive attention. *Proceedings of the National Academy of Sciences of the United States of America, 102*, 14931–14936.

Ruf, H., Schmidt, N., Lemery-Chalfant, K., Goldsmith, H.H. (2008). Components of childhood impulsivity and inattention: Child, family, and genetic correlates. *European Journal of Developmental Science, 2*, 52–76.

Ruff, H.A., & Lawson, K.R. (1990). Development of sustained focused attention in young children during free play. *Developmental Psychology, 26*, 85–93.

Rush, A.J., Kilner, J., Fava, M., Wisniewski, S.R., Warden, D., Nierenberg, A.A., . . . Trivedi, M.H. (2008). Clinically relevant findings from STAR* D. *Psychiatric Annals, 38*, 188–193.

Rush, B. (1962). *Medical inquiries and observations upon the diseases of the mind.* New York: Macmillan-Hafner Press. (Original work published 1812).

Russell-Chapin, L., Kemmerly, T., Liu, W.C., Zagardo, M.T., Chapin, T., Dailey, D., & Dinh, D. (2013). The effects of neurofeedback in the default mode network: Pilot study results of medicated children with ADHD. *Journal of Neurotherapy, 17*, 35–42.

Russo, M.F., & Biedel, D.C. (1994). Comorbidity of childhood anxiety and externalizing disorders: Prevalence, associated characteristics, and validation issues. *Clinical Psychology Review, 14*, 199–221.

Rutledge, K.J., van den Bos, W., McClure, S.M., & Schweitzer, J.B. (2012). Training cognition in ADHD: Current findings, borrowed concepts, and future directions. *Neurotherapeutics, 9*, 542–558.

Rutter, M. (1977). Brain damage syndromes in childhood: Concepts and findings. *Journal of Child Psychology and Psychiatry, 18*, 1–21.

Rutter, M. (1982). Syndromes attributable to "minimal brain dysfunction" in childhood. *American Journal of Psychiatry, 139*, 21–33.

Rutter, M. (1989). Attention deficit disorder/hyperkinetic syndrome: Conceptual and research issues regarding diagnosis and classification, In T. Sagvolden & T. Archer (Eds.), *Attention deficit disorder: Clinical and basic research* (pp. 1–24). Hillsdale, NJ: Erlbaum.

Rutter, M. (1997). Comorbidity: concepts, claims and choices. *Criminal Behaviour and Mental Health, 7*, 265–285.

Rutter, M. (2006a). *Genes and behavior: Nature-nurture interplay explained.* London: Blackwell.
Rutter, M. (2006b). Gene—environment interplay and psychopathology: multiple varieties but real effects. *Journal of Child Psychology and Psychiatry, 47*, 226–261.
Rutter, M. (2007). Gene—environment interdependence. *Developmental Science, 10*, 12–18.
Rutter, M. (Ed.). (2008). *Genetic effects on environmental vulnerability to disease.* Chichester, UK: Wiley.
Rutter, M. (2010). Gene—environment interplay. *Depression and Anxiety, 27*, 1–4.
Rutter, M. (2011). Research review: Child psychiatric diagnosis and classification: Concepts, findings, challenges and potential. *Journal of Child Psychology and Psychiatry, 52*, 647–660.
Rutter, M., Beckett, C., Castle, J., Colvert, E., Kreppner, J., Mehta, M., . . . Sonuga-Barke, E. (2007). Effects of profound early institutional deprivation: An overview of findings from a UK longitudinal study of Romanian adoptees. *European Journal of Developmental Psychology, 4*, 332–350.
Rutter, M., Bishop, D., Pine, D., Scott, S., Stevenson, J., Taylor, E., . . . Thapar, A. (2008). *Rutter's child and adolescent psychiatry* (5th ed). Oxford, UK: Blackwell Scientific.
Rutter, M., & Sroufe, L.A. (2000). Developmental psychopathology: Concepts and challenges. *Development and psychopathology, 12*, 265–296.
Rutter, M., Tizard, J., Yule, W., Graham, P., & Whitmore, K. (1976). Research report: Isle of Wight studies. 1964–1974. *Psychological Medicine, 6*, 313–332.
Rybak, Y.E., McNeely, H.E., Mackenzie, B.E., Jain, U.R., & Levitan, R.D. (2006). An open trial of light therapy in adult attention-deficit/hyperactivity disorder. *Journal of Clinical Psychiatry, 67*, 1527–1535.
Rytter, M.J., Andersen, L.B., Houmann, T., Bilenberg, N., Hvolby, A., Molgaard, C., . . . Lauritzen, L. (2015). Diet in the treatment of ADHD in children—A systematic review of the literature. *Nordic Journal of Psychiatry, 69*, 1–18.
Sadeh, A., Pergamin, L., & Bar-Haim, Y. (2006). Sleep in children with attention-deficit hyperactivity disorder: A meta-analysis of polysomnographic studies. *Sleep Medicine Reviews, 10*, 381–398.
Sáez, L., Folsom, J.S., Al Otaiba, S., & Schatschneider, C. (2012). Relations among student attention behaviors, teacher practices, and beginning word reading skill. *Journal of Learning Disabilities, 45*, 418–432.
Safer, D.J. (2000). Are stimulants overprescribed for youths with ADHD? *Annals of Clinical Psychiatry, 12*, 55–62.
Safren, S.A. (2006). Cognitive-behavioral approaches to ADHD treatment in adulthood. *Journal of Clinical Psychiatry, 67*, 46–50.
Safren, S.A., Otto, M.W., Sprich, S., Winett, C.L., Wilens, T.E., & Biederman, J. (2005). Cognitive-behavioral therapy for ADHD in medication-treated adults with continued symptoms. *Behaviour Research and Therapy, 43*, 831–842.
Safren, S.A., Perlman, C.A., Sprich, S., & Otto, M.W. (2005). *Mastering your adult ADHD: a cognitive- behavioral therapy approach.* New York: Oxford University Press.
Safren, S.A., Sprich, S., Chulvick, S., & Otto, M.W. (2004). Psychosocial treatments for adults with attention-deficit/hyperactivity disorder. *Psychiatric Clinics of North America, 27*, 349–360.
Safren, S.A., Sprich, S.E., Cooper-Vince, C., Knouse, L.E., & Lerner, J.A. (2010). Life impairments in adults with medication-treated ADHD. *Journal of Attention Disorders, 13*, 524–531.
Safren, S.A., Sprich, S., Mimiaga, M.J., Surman, C., Knouse, L., Groves, M., & Otto, M.W. (2010). Cognitive behavioral therapy vs. relaxation with educational support for medication-treated adults with ADHD and persistent symptoms. *Journal of the American Medical Association, 304*, 857–880.
Sagvolden, T., Aase, H., Zeiner, P., & Berger, D. (1998). Altered reinforcement mechanisms in attention-deficit/hyperactivity disorder. *Behavioural Brain Research, 94*, 61–71.
Sagvolden, T., Johansen, E.B., Aase, H., & Russell, V.A. (2005). A dynamic developmental theory of attention-deficit/hyperactivity disorder (ADHD) predominantly hyperactive/impulsive and combined subtypes. *Behavioral and Brain Sciences, 28*, 397–468.
Sagvolden, T., Russell, V.A., Aase, H., Johansen, E.B., & Farshbaf, M. (2005). Rodent models of attention-deficit/hyperactivity disorder. *Biological Psychiatry, 57*, 1231–1238.

Sallows, G.O., & Graupner, T.D. (2005). Intensive behavioral treatment for children with autism: Four-year outcome and predictors. *American Journal on Mental Retardation, 110*, 417–438.
Sameroff, A.J. (2000). Dialectical processes in developmental psychopathology. In A.J. Sameroff, M. Lewis, & S.M. Miller (Eds.), *Handbook of developmental psychopathology* (2nd ed.). New York: Wiley.
Sanders, A.F. (1983). Towards a model of stress and performance. *Acta Psychologica, 53*, 61–97.
Sanders, A.F. (1998). *Elements of human performance: Reaction processes and attention in human skill.* Mahwah: Erlbaum.
Sanders, M.R., Markie-Dadds, C., Turner, K.M.T., & Ralph, A. (2004). Using the Triple P system of intervention to prevent behavioural problems in children and adolescents. In P. Barrett, & T. Ollendick (Eds.), *Handbook of interventions that work with children and adolescents: Prevention and treatment* (pp. 489–516). Chichester, NJ: John Wiley & Sons.
Santosh, P.J., Baird, G., Pityaratstian, N., Tavare, E., & Gringras, P. (2006). Impact of comorbid autism spectrum disorders on stimulant response in children with attention deficit hyperactivity disorder: A retrospective and prospective effectiveness study. *Child Care Health and Development, 32*, 575–583.
Sartorius, N. (2010). Revision of the classification of mental disorders in ICD—11 and DSM—V: work in progress. *Advances in Psychiatric Treatment, 16*, 2–9.
Sarver, D.E., Rapport, M.D., Kofler, M.J., Scanlan, S.W., Raiker, J.S., Altro, T.A., & Bolden, J. (2012). Attention problems, phonological short-term memory, and visuospatial short-term memory: Differential effects on near- and long-term scholastic achievement. *Learning and Individual Differences, 22*, 8–19.
Satterfield, J.H., Cantwell, D.P., & Satterfield, B.T. (1974). Pathophysiology of the hyperactive child syndrome. *Archives of General Psychiatry, 31*, 839–844.
Satterfield, J.H., Faller, K.J., Crinella, F.M., Schell, A.M., Swanson, J.M., & Homer, L.D. (2007). A 30-year prospective follow-up study of hyperactive boys with conduct problems: adult criminality. *Journal of the American Academy of Child and Adolescent Psychiatry, 46*, 601–610.
Satterfield, J.H., & Schell, A. (1997). A perspective study of hyperactive boys with conduct problems and normal boys: Adolescent and adult criminality. *Journal of the American Academy of Child and Adolescent Psychiatry, 36*, 1726–1735.
Sax, L., & Kautz, K.J. (2003). Who first suggests the diagnosis of attention-deficit/hyperactivity disorder? *Annals of Family Medicine, 1*, 171–174.
Sayal, K., & Taylor, E. (2005). Parent-ratings of school behaviour in children at risk of attention deficit/hyperactivity disorder. *Acta Psychiatrica Scandinavica, 111*, 460–465.
Scarborough, H.S., & Dobrich, W. (1990). Development of children with early language delay. *Journal of Speech and Hearing Research, 33*, 70–83.
Scassellati, C., Bonvicini, C., Faraone, S.V., & Gennarelli, M. (2012). Biomarkers and attention-deficit/hyperactivity disorder: A systematic review and meta-analyses. *Journal of the American Academy of Child and Adolescent Psychiatry, 51*, 1003–1019.
Schab, D.W., & Trinh, N.T. (2004). Do artificial food colours promote hyperactivity in children with hyperactive syndromes? A meta-analysis of double-blind placebo-controlled trials. *Journal of Developmental and Behavioral Pediatrics, 25*, 423–434.
Schachar, R., Jadad, A.R., Gauld, M., Boyle, M., Booker, L., Snider, A., . . . Cunningham, C. (2002). Attention-deficit hyperactivity disorder: Critical appraisal of extended treatment studies. *Canadian Journal of Psychiatry, 47*, 337–348.
Schachter, H.M., Pham, B., King, J., Langford, S., & Moher, D. (2001). How efficacious and safe is short-acting methylphenidate for the treatment of attention-deficit hyperactivity disorder in children and adolescents? A meta-analysis. *Canadian Medical Association Journal, 165*, 1475–1488.
Schatz, D.B., & Rostain, A.L. (2006). ADHD with comorbid anxiety: A review of the current literature. *Journal of Attention Disorders, 10*, 141–149.
Scheres, A., Lee, A., & Sumiya, M. (2008). Temporal reward discounting and ADHD: Task and symptom specific effects. *Journal of Neural Transmission, 115*, 221–226.
Schneeweiss, S., Patrick, A.R., Solomon, D.H., Dormuth, C.R., Miller, M., Mehta, J., . . . Wang, P.S. (2010). Comparative safety of antidepressant agents for children and adolescents regarding suicidal acts. *Pediatrics, 125*, 876–888.

Schneider, H., & Eisenberg, D. (2006). Who receives a diagnosis of attention-deficit/hyperactivity disorder in the United States elementary school population?. *Pediatrics, 117*, e601-e609.

Schneider, J.W., & Hans, S.L. (1996). Effects of pre-natal exposure to opiodis on focused attention in toddlers during free play. *Journal of Developmental Behavioral Pediatrics, 17*, 240–247.

Schneider, M.F., Krick, C.M., Retz, W., Hengesch, G., Retz-Junginger, P., Reith, W., & Rösler, M. (2010). Impairment of fronto-striatal and parietal cerebral networks correlates with attention deficit hyperactivity disorder (ADHD psychopathology in adults—A functional magnetic resonance imaging (fMRI) study). *Psychiatry Research: Neuroimaging, 183*, 75–84.

Schoenfelder, E.N., & Sasser, T. (2016). Skills versus pills: Psychosocial treatments for ADHD in childhood and adolescence. *Pediatric Annals, 45*, e367–e372.

Schrag, P., & Divoky, D. (1976). *The myth of the hyperactive child and other means of child control.* New York: Pantheon Books.

Schredl, M., Alm, B., & Sobanski, E. (2007). Sleep quality in adult patients with attention deficit hyperactivity disorder (ADHD). *European Archives of Psychiatry and Clinical Neuroscience, 257*, 164–168.

Schuch, V., Utsumi, D.A., Costa, T.V.M.M., Kulikowski, L.D., & Muszkat, M. (2015). Attention deficit hyperactivity disorder in the light of the epigenetic paradigm. *Frontiers in Psychiatry, 6, 126.*

Schulenberg, J.E., Sameroff, A.J., & Cicchetti, D. (2004). The transition to adulthood as a critical juncture in the course of psychopathology and mental health. *Development and Psychopathology, 16*, 799–806.

Schumacher, R.M., Greenberg, M., & Mezey, J. (2003). *Head Start reauthorization: A preliminary analysis of H.R. 2210, the "School Readiness Act of 2003."* Washington, DC: Center for Law and Social Policy.

Schwartz, S., & Correll, C.U. (2014). Efficacy and safety of atomoxetine in children and adolescents with attention-deficit/hyperactivity disorder: Results from a comprehensive meta-analysis and metaregression. *Journal of the American Academy of Child and Adolescent Psychiatry, 53*, 174–187.

Schweiger, A., Abramovitch, A., Doniger, G.M., & Simon, E.S. (2007). A clinical construct validity study of a novel computerized battery for the diagnosis of ADHD in young adults. *Journal of Clinical and Experimental Neuropsychology, 29*, 100–111.

Schweitzer, J.B., & Sulzer-Azaroff, B. (1988). Self-control: Teaching tolerance for delay in impulsive children. *Journal of the Experimental Analysis of Behavior, 50*, 173–186.

Sciberras, E., Fulton, M., Efron, D., Oberklaid, F., & Hiscock, H. (2011). Managing sleep problems in school aged children with ADHD: A pilot randomised controlled trial. *Sleep Medicine, 12*, 932–935.

Sciberras, E., Mueller, K., Efron, D., Bisset, M., Anderson, V., Schilpzand, E., . . . Nicholson, J. (2014). Language problems in children With ADHD: A community-based study. *Pediatrics, 133*, 793–800.

Scime, M., & Norvilitis, J.M. (2006). Task performance and response to frustration in children with attention deficit hyperactivity disorder. *Psychology in the Schools, 43*, 377–386.

Sciutto, M.J., Nolfi, C.J., & Bluhm, M. (2004). Effects of child gender and symptom type on referrals for ADHD by elementary school teachers. *Journal of Emotional and Behavioral Disorders, 12*, 247–253.

Scott, N., Blair, P.S., Emond, A.M., Fleming, P.J., Humphreys, J.S., Henderson, J., & Gringras, P. (2013). Sleep patterns in children with ADHD: a population-based cohort study from birth to 11 years. *Journal of Sleep Research, 22*, 121–128.

Scott, S. (2002). Parent training programmes. In M. Rutter, & E. Taylor (Eds.), *Child and adolescent psychiatry* (4th ed., pp. 949–967). Oxford: Blackwell.

Sedky, K., Bennett, D.S., & Carvalho, K.S. (2014). Attention deficit hyperactivity disorder and sleep disordered breathing in pediatric populations: A meta-analysis. *Sleep Medicine Reviews, 18*, 349–356.

Seidman, L.J., Biederman, J., Faraone, S.V., Weber, W., & Ouellette, C. (1997). Toward defining a neuropsychology of attention-deficit hyperactivity disorder: Performance of children and adolescence from a large clinically referred sample. *Journal of Consulting and Clinical Psychology, 65*, 150–160.

Seidman, L.J., Biederman, J., Monuteaux, M.C., Doyle, A.E., & Faraone, S.V. (2001). Learning disabilities and executive dysfunction in boys with attention-deficit/hyperactivity disorder. *Neuropsychology, 15*, 544–556.

Seidman, L.J., Biederman, J., Monuteaux, M.C., Valera, E., Doyle, A.E., & Faraone, S.V. (2005). Impact of gender and age on executive functioning: Do girls and boys with and without attention deficit hyperactivity disorder differ neuropsychologically in preteen and teenage years? *Development Neuropsychology, 27*, 79–105.

Seidman, L.J., Biederman, J., Valera, E.M., Monuteaux, M.C., Doyle, A.E., & Faraone, S.V. (2006). Neuropsychological functioning in girls with attention-deficit/hyperactivity disorder with and without learning disabilities. *Neuropsychology, 20*, 166–177.

Seipp, C.M., & Johnston, C. (2005). Mother-son interactions in families of boys with attention-deficit/hyperactivity disorder with and without oppositional behavior. *Journal of Abnormal Child Psychology, 33*, 87–98.

Seixas, M., Weiss, M., & Müller, U. (2012). Systematic review of national and international guidelines on attention-deficit hyperactivity disorder. *Journal of Psychopharmacology, 26*,753–765.

Semrud-Clikeman, M., Guy, K., Griffin, J.D., & Hynd, G.W. (2000). Rapid naming deficits in children and adolescent with reading disabilities and attention deficit hyperactivity disorder. *Brain and Language, 74*, 70–83.

Sergeant, J. (2000). The cognitive-energetic model: An empirical approach to attention-deficit/hyperactivity disorder. *Neuroscience and Biobehavioral Reviews, 24*, 7–12.

Sergeant, J. (2005). Modelling attention-deficit/hyperactivity disorder: A critical appraisal of the cognitive-energetic model. *Biological Psychiatry, 57*, 1248–1255.

Sergeant, J., Geurts, H., Huijbregts, S., Scheres, A., & Oosterlaan, J. (2003). The top and bottom of ADHD: A neuropsychological perspective. *Neuroscience and Biobehavioral Reviews, 27*, 583–592.

Sergeant, J., Oosterlaan, J., & van der Meere, J. (1999). Information processing and energetic factors in attention-deficit/hyperactivity disorder. In H.C. Quay & A.E. Hogan (Eds.), *Handbook of disruptive behavior disorders* (pp. 75–104). New York: Kluwer Academic.

Sergeant, J.A., Piek, J.P., & Oosterlaan, J. (2006). ADHD and DCD: A relationship in need of research. *Human Movement Science, 25*, 76–89.

Sesma, H.W., Mahone, E.M., Levine, T., Eason, S.H., & Cutting, L.E. (2009). The contribution of executive skills to reading comprehension. *Child Neuropsychology, 15*, 232–246.

Sethi, A., Mischel, W., Aber, J.L., Shoda, Y., & Rodriguez, M.L. (2000). The role of strategic attention deployment in development of self-regulation: Predicting preschoolers' delay of gratification from mother–toddler interactions. *Developmental Psychology, 36*, 767–777.

Sexton, C.C., Gelhron, H.L., Bell, J.A., & Classi, P.M. (2012). The co-occurrence of reading disorder and ADHD: Epidemiology, treatment, psychosocial impact, and economic burden. *Journal of Learning Disabilities, 45*, 538–564.

Seymour, K.E., Reinblatt, S.P., Benson, L., & Carnell, S. (2015). Overlapping neurobehavioral circuits in ADHD, obesity, and binge eating: Evidence from neuroimaging research. *CNS Spectrums, 20*, 401–411.

Shaffer, D., Fisher, P., Lucas, C.P., Dulcan, M.K., & Schwab-Stone, M.E. (2000). NIMH Diagnostic Interview Schedule for Children Version IV (NIMH DISC—IV): Description, differences from previous versions, and reliability of some common diagnoses. *Journal of the American Academy of Child and Adolescent Psychiatry, 39*, 28–38.

Shalev, L., Tsal, Yy, & Mevorach, C. (2007). Computerized Progressive Attentional (CPAT) Program: effective direct intervention for children with ADHD. *Child Neuropsychology, 13*, 382–388.

Shalev, R.S. (2004). Developmental dyscalculia. *Journal of Child Neurology, 19*, 765–771.

Shanahan, M.J., & Hofer, S.M. (2005). Social context in gene—environment interactions: Retrospect and prospect. *Journals of Gerontology Series B: Psychological Sciences and Social Sciences, 60*(Special Issue 1), 65–76.

Sharp, W.S., Walter, J.M., Marsh, W.L., Ritchie, G.F., Hamburger, S.D., & Castellanos, F.X. (1999). ADHD in girls: clinical comparability of a research sample. *Journal of the American Academy of Child and Adolescent Psychiatry, 38*, 40–47.

Sharp, S., Walter, M., Hamburger, D., Marsh, L., Rapoport, L., & Castellanos, X. (1997 Dec.). *Comparison between girls and boys with ADHD: A controlled study.* Paper presented at the annual meeting of the American Academy of Child and Adolescent Psychiatry, Toronto, Canada.
Shaw, D.S., Dishion, T.J., Supplee, L., Gardner, F., & Arnds, K. (2006). Randomized trial of a family centered approach to the prevention of early conduct problems: 2-year effects of the family check-up in early childhood. *Journal of Consulting and Clinical Psychology, 74*, 1–9.
Shaw, P., Eckstrand, K., Sharp, W., Blumenthal, J., Lerch, J.P., Greenstein, D., . . . Rapoport, J.L. (2007). Attention-deficit/hyperactivity disorder is characterized by a delay in cortical maturation. *Proceedings of the National Academy of Sciences of the United States of America, 104*, 19649–19654.
Shaw, P., Gilliam, M., Liverpool, M., Weddle, C., Malek, M., Sharp, W., . . . Giedd, J. (2011). Cortical development in typically developing children with symptoms of hyperactivity and impulsivity: Support for a dimensional view of Attention Deficit Hyperactivity Disorder. *American Journal of Psychiatry, 168*, 143–151.
Shaw, P., Lerch, J., Greenstein, D., Sharp, W., Clasen, L., Evans, A., . . . Rapoport, J. (2006). Longitudinal mapping of cortical thickness and clinical outcome in children and adolescents with attention-deficit hyperactivity disorder. *Archives of General Psychiatry, 63*, 540–549.
Shaw, P., & Robin, C. (2009). New insights into attention-deficit/hyperactivity disorder using structural neuroimaging. *Current Psychiatry Reports, 11*, 393–398.
Shaw, P., Stringaris, A., Nigg, J., & Leibenluft, E. (2014). Emotion dysregulation in attention deficit hyperactivity disorder. *American Journal of Psychiatry, 171*, 276–293.
Shaywitz, B.A., & Shaywitz, S.E. (1991). Comorbidity: A critical issue in attention deficit disorder. *Journal of Child Neurology, 6*(Suppl.), S13–122.
Shaywitz, B., Shaywitz, S., Blachman, B., Pugh, K., Fulbright, R., Skudlarski, P., . . . Gore, J.C. (2004). Development of left occipitotemporal systems for skilled reading in children after a phonologically-based intervention. *Biological Psychiatry, 55*, 926–933.
Shaywitz, S. (2003). *Overcoming dyslexia: A new and complete science-based program for reading problems at any level.* New York: Vintage.
Shaywitz, S., Fletcher, J., & Shaywitz, B. (1994). Issues in the definition and classification of attention deficit disorder. *Topics in Language Disorders, 14*, 1–25.
Shaywitz, S.E., & Shaywitz, B.A. (1988). Attention deficit disorder: Current perspectives. In J.F. Kavanaugh & T.J. Truss (Eds.), *Learning disabilities: Proceeding of the national conference* (pp. 330–347). New York: Guilford Press.
Shaywitz, S.E., & Shaywitz, B.A. (2008). Paying attention to reading: The neurobiology of reading and dyslexia. *Development and Psychopathology, 20*, 1329–1349.
Shaywitz, S.E., Shaywitz, B.A., Fletcher, J.M., & Escobar, M.D. (1990). Prevalence of reading disability in boys and girls. *JAMA, 264*, 998–1002.
Shemmassian, S.K., & Lee, S.S. (2017). Comparative validity of *DSM-IV* and alternative empirically derived for the assessment of ADHD. *Journal of Attention Disorders, 21*, 405–415.
Sher, K.J., Grekin, E.R., & Williams, N.A. (2005). The development of alcohol use disorders. *Annual Review of Clinical Psychology, 1*, 493–523.
Sheridan, S.M., Bovaird, J.A., Glover, T.A., Garbacz, S.A., Witte, A., & Kwon, K. (2012). A randomized trial examining the effects of conjoint behavioral consultation and the mediating role of the parent-teacher relationship. *School Psychology Review, 41*, 23–46.
Sheridan, S.M., Dee, C.C., Morgan, J.C., McCormick, M.E., & Walker, D. (1996). A multimethod intervention for social skills deficits in children with ADHD and their parents. *School Psychology Review, 25*, 57–76.
Sheridan, S.M., & Kratochwill, T.R. (2008). Conjoint behavioral consultation: Promoting family-school connections and interventions (2nd ed.). New York: Springer-Verlag.
Sheridan, S.M., Witte, A.L., Holmes, S.R., Coutts, M.J., Dent, A.L., Kunz, G.M., & Wu, C. (2017). A randomized trial examining the effects of Conjoint Behavioral Consultation in rural schools: Student outcomes and the mediating role of the teacher—parent relationship. *Journal of School Psychology, 61*, 33–53.

Sherman, J., Rasmussen, C., & Baydala, L. (2008). The impact of teacher factors on achievement and behavioural outcomes of children with Attention Deficit/Hyperactivity Disorder (ADHD): A review of the literature. *Educational Research*, *50*, 347–360.

Sherman, K., Iacono, G., & McGue, K. (1997). Attention deficit hyperactivity disorder dimensions: A twin study of inattention and impulsivity-hyperactivity. *Journal of the American Academy of Child and Adolescent Psychiatry*, *36*, 745–753.

Sherrill, J.T., & Kovacs, M. (2000). Interview schedule for children and adolescents (ISCA). *Journal of the American Academy of Child and Adolescent Psychiatry*, *39*, 67–75.

Shields, S.A. (2002). *Speaking from the heart: Gender and the social meaning of emotion*. Cambridge: Cambridge University Press.

Shinaver, C.S., 3rd, Entwistle, P.C., & Söderqvist, S. (2014). Cogmed WM training: Reviewing the reviews. *Applied Neuropsychology: Child*, *3*, 163–172.

Shipstead, Z., Redick, T.S., & Engle, R.W. (2012). Is working memory training effective? *Psychological Bulletin*, *138*, 628–654.

Shirley, M. (1939). A behavior syndrome characterizing prematurely born children. *Child Development*, *10*, 115–128.

Shouse, M.N., & Lubar, J.F. (1979). Operant conditioning of EEG rhythms and ritalin in the treatment of hyperkinesis. *Biofeedback and Self Regulation*, *4*, 299–312.

Shriberg, L.D. (2003). Diagnostic markers for child speech-sound disorders: Introductory comments. *Clinical Linguistics & Phonetics*, *17*, 501–505.

Shuck, S., & Crinella, F. (2005). Why children with ADHD do not have low IQs. *Journal of Learning Disabilities*, *38*, 262–280.

Sibley, M.H., Pelham, W.E., Jr., Molina, B.S., Coxe, S., Kipp, H., Gnagy, E.M., . . . Lahey, B.B. (2014). The role of early childhood ADHD and subsequent CD in the initiation and escalation of adolescent cigarette, alcohol, and marijuana use. *Journal of Abnormal Psychology*, *123*, 362–374.

Sibley, M.H., Pelham, W.E., Molina, B.S.G., Gnagy, E.M., Waschbusch, D.A., Biswas, A., . . . Karch, K.M. (2011). The delinquency outcomes of boys with ADHD and without comorbidity. *Journal of Abnormal Child Psychology*, *39*, 21–32.

Sibley, M.H., Waxmonsky, J.G., Robb, J.A., & Pelham, W.E., (2013). DSM-5: Implications of changes for the field of ADHD. *Journal of Learning Disabilities*, *46*, 34–42.

Silverman, W., & Ragusa, M. (1992). A short-term longitudinal study of the early development of self regulation. *Journal of Abnormal Child Psychology*, *20*, 415–435.

Silverthorn, P., Frick, P.J., Kuper, K., & Ott, J. (1996). Attention deficit hyperactivity disorder and sex: A test of two etiological models to explain the male predominance. *Journal of Clinical Child Psychology*, *25*, 52–59.

Silvestri, R., & Aricò, I. (2012). Sleep disorders diagnosis and management in children with attention deficit/hyperactivity disorder (ADHD). In C. Idzikowski (Ed.), *Sleep disorders*. InTech. https://doi.org/10.5772/27560

Silvestri, R., Gagliano, A., Aricò, I., Calarese, T., Cedro, C., Bruni, O., . . . Bramanti, P. (2009). Sleep disorders in children with Attention-Deficit/Hyperactivity Disorder (ADHD) recorded overnight by video-polysomnography. *Sleep Medicine*, *10*, 1132–1138.

Simmons, F.R., & Singleton, C. (2008). Do weak phonological representations impact on arithmetic development? A review of research into arithmetic and dyslexia. *Dyslexia*, *14*, 77–94.

Simmons, F.R., Singleton, C., & Horne, J. (2008). Phonological awareness and visual-spatial sketchpad functioning predict early arithmetic attainment: Evidence from a longitudinal study. *European Journal of Cognitive Psychology*, *20*, 711–722.

Simon, V., Czobor, P., Bálint, S., Mészáros, Á., & Bitter, I. (2009). Prevalence and correlates of adult attention-deficit hyperactivity disorder: meta-analysis. *British Journal of Psychiatry*, *194*, 204–211.

Simonoff, E., Pickles, A., Charman, T., Chandler, S., Loucas, T., & Baird, G. (2008). Psychiatric disorders in children with autism spectrum disorders: Prevalence, comorbidity, and associated factors in a population-derived sample *Journal of the American Academy of Child and Adolescent Psychiatry*, *47*, 921–929.

Simonoff, E., Pickles, A., Meyer, J.M., Silberg, J.L., Maes, H.H., Loeber, R., . . . Eaves, L.J. (1997). The Virginia twin study of adolescent behavioral development: Influence of age, sex, and impairment on rates of disorder. *Archives of General Psychiatry, 54*, 801–808.

Simopoulos, A.P. (2002). Omega-3 fatty acids in inflammation and autoimmune diseases. *Journal of the American College of Nutrition, 21*, 495–505.

Sims, D.M., & Lonigan, C.J. (2012). Multi-method assessment of ADHD characteristics in preschool children: Relations between measures. *Early Childhood Research Quarterly, 27*, 329–337.

Sims, D.M., & Lonigan, C.J. (2013). Inattention, hyperactivity, and emergent literacy: Different facets of inattention relate uniquely to preschoolers' reading-related skills. *Journal of Clinical Child & Adolescent Psychology, 42*, 208–219.

Singer, B. (1997). The psychological experience of siblings of children with ADHD. Doctoral dissertation. Massachusetts School of Professional Psychology. *Dissertation Abstracts International, 58*, 2700.

Singh, I. (2008). Beyond polemics: Science and ethics of ADHD. *Nature Reviews, 9*, 957–964.

Singh, K.D., & Fawcett, I.P. (2008). Transient and linearly graded deactivation of the human default-mode network by a visual detection task. *Neuroimage, 41*, 100–112.

Sinn, N., & Bryan, J. (2007). Effect of supplementation with polyunsaturated fatty acids and micronutrients on learning and behavior problems associated with child ADHD. *Journal of Developmental & Behavioral Pediatrics, 28*, 82–91.

Sinn, N., Bryan, J., & Wilson, C. (2008). Cognitive effects of polyunsaturated fatty acids in children with attention deficit hyperactivity disorder symptoms: A randomised controlled trial. *Prostaglandins, Leukotrienes, & Essential Fatty Acids, 78*, 311–326.

Sireteanu, R., Goertz, R., Bachert, I., & Wandert, T. (2005). Children with developmental dyslexia show a left visual "minineglect." *Vision Research, 45*, 3075–3082.

Sjöwall, D., Bohlin, G., Rydell, A.M., & Thorell, L.B. (2017). Neuropsychological deficits in preschool as predictors of ADHD symptoms and academic achievement in late adolescence. *Child Neuropsychology, 23*, 111–128.

Skirbekk, B., Hansen, B.H., Oerbeck, B., & Kristensen, H. (2011). The relationship between sluggish cognitive tempo, subtypes of attention-deficit/hyperactivity disorder, and anxiety disorders. *Journal of Abnormal Child Psychology, 39*, 513–525.

Skirrow, C., Hosang, G.M., Farmer, A.E., & Asherson, P. (2012). An update on the debated association between ADHD and bipolar disorder across the lifespan. *Journal of Affective Disorders 141*, 143–159.

Skounti, M., Philalithis, A., & Galanakis, E. (2007). Variations in prevalence of attention deficit hyperactivity disorder worldwide. *European Journal of Pediatrics, 166*, 117–123.

Skutle, A., Hellandsjø Bu, E.T., Konow Jellestad, F., van Emmerik-van Oortmerssen, K., Dome, G., Verspreet, S., . . . Geurt van de Glind, G. (2015). Early developmental, temperamental and educational problems in 'substance use disorder' patients with and without ADHD. Does ADHD make a difference? *Addictive Behaviors Reports, 2*, 13–18.

Sleeper-Triplett, J. (2010). *Empowering youth with ADHD: Your guide to coaching adolescents and young adults.* Plantation, FL: Specialty Press.

Slutske, W.S., Caspi, A., Moffitt, T.E., & Poulton, R. (2005). Personality and problem gambling: A prospective study of a birth cohort of young adults. *Archives of General Psychiatry, 62*, 769–775.

Smalley, S.L., McGough, J.J., Del'Homme, M., NewDelman, J., Gordon, E., Kim, T., & McKracken, J.T. (2000). Familial clustering of symptoms and disruptive behaviors in multiplex families with attention-deficit/hyperactivity disorder. *Journal of the American Academy of Child and Adolescent Psychiatry, 39*, 1135–1143.

Smith, A.J., Brown, R.T., Bunke, V., Blount, R.L., & Christophersen, E. (2002). Psychosocial adjustment and peer competence of siblings of children with attention-deficit/hyperactivity disorder. *Journal of Attention Disorders, 5*, 165–177.

Smith, B.H., & Shapiro, C.J. (2015). Combined treatments for ADHD. In R.A. Barkley (Ed.) *Attention-Deficit Hyperactivity Disorder* (4th ed., pp. 686–704). New York: Guilford Press.

Smith, B.H., Waschbusch, D.A., Willoughby, M.T., & Evans, S. (2000). The efficacy, safety, and practicality of treatments for adolescents with attention-deficit/hyperactivity disorder. *Clinical Child and Family Psychology Review*, *3*, 243–267.

Smith, E., Koerting, J., Latter, S., Knowles, M.M., McCann, D.C., Thompson, M., & Sonuga-Barke, E.J. (2015). Overcoming barriers to effective early parenting interventions for attention-deficit hyperactivity disorder (ADHD): Parent and practitioner views. Child Care Health and Development, *41*, 93–102.

Smith, L. (1975). *Your child's behavior chemistry*. New York: Random House.

Smits-Engelsman, B.C., Westenberg, Y., & Duysens, J. (2008). Children with developmental coordination disorder are equally able to generate force but show more variability than typically developing children. *Human Movement Science*, *27*, 296–309.

Snowling, M.J., Gallagher, A., & Frith, U. (2003). Family risk of dyslexia is continuous: Individual differences in the precursors of reading skill. *Child Development*, *74*, 358–373.

Snyder, S.M., & Hall, J.R. (2006). A meta-analysis of quantitative EEG power associated with attention-deficit/hyperactivity disorder. *Journal of Clinical Neurophysiology*, *23*, 440–455.

Snyder, S.M., Rugino, T.A., Hornig, M., & Stein, M.A. (2015). Integration of an EEG biomarker with a clinician's ADHD evaluation. *Brain and Behavior*, *5*, e00330.

Sobanski, E., Banaschewski, T., Asherson, P., Buitelaar, J., Chen, W., Franke, B. . . . Faraone, S.V. (2010). Emotional lability in children and adolescents with attention deficit/hyperactivity disorder (ADHD): Clinical correlates and familial prevalence. *Journal of Child Psychology and Psychiatry*, *51*, 915–923.

Sobanski, E., Bruggemann, D., Alm, B., Kern, S., Philipsen, A., Schmalzried, H., . . . Rietschel, M. (2007). Psychiatric comorbidity and functional impairment in a clinically referred sample of adults with attention-deficit/hyperactivity disorder (ADHD). *European Archives of Psychiatry and Clinical Neuroscience*, *257*, 371–377.

Sobanski, E., Schredl, M., Kettler, N., & Alm, B. (2008). Sleep in adults with attention deficit hyperactivity disorder (ADHD) before and during treatment with methylphenidate: a controlled polysomnographic study. *Sleep*, *31*, 375–381.

Sohlberg, M.M., & Mateer, C.A. (1987). Effectiveness of an attention-training program. *Journal of Clinical and Experimental Neuropsychology*, *9*, 117–130.

Sokol, M.S., Gray, N.S., Goldstein, A., & Kaye, W.H. (1999). Methylphenidate treatment for bulimia nervosa associated with a cluster B personality disorder. *International Journal of Eating Disorders*, *25*, 233–237.

Solanto, M.V. (2011). *Cognitive-behavioral therapy for adult ADHD: Targeting executive dysfunction*. New York: Guilford Press.

Solanto, M.V., Abikoff, H., Sonuga-Barke, E., Schachar, R., Logan, G.D., Wigal, T., . . . Turkel, E. (2001). The ecological validity of delay aversion and response inhibition as measures of impulsivity in AD/HD: A supplement to the NIMH multimodal treatment study of AD/HD. *Journal of Abnormal Child Psychology*, *29*, 215–228.

Solanto, M.V., Marks, D.J., Wasserstein, J., Mitchell, K., Abikoff, H., Alvir, J.M., & Kofman, M.D. (2010). Efficacy of metacognitive therapy for adult ADHD. *American Journal of Psychiatry*, *167*, 958–968.

Solomons, G. (1965). The hyperactive child. *Journal of the Iowa Medical Society*, *55*, 464–469.

Somerville, L.H., Casey, B.J. (2010). Developmental neurobiology of cognitive control and motivational systems. *Current Opinion in Neurobiology*, *20*, 236–241.

Sonuga-Barke, E.J.S. (1998). Categorical models of childhood disorder: a conceptual and empirical analysis. *Journal of Child Psychology and Psychiatry*, *39*, 115–133.

Sonuga-Barke, E.J.S. (2010). Editorial: 'It's the environment stupid!' On epigenetics, programming and plasticity in child mental health. *Journal of Child Psychology and Psychiatry*, *51*, 113–115.

Sonuga-Barke, E.J.S. (2002). Psychological heterogeneity in AD/HD-a dual pathway model of behaviour and cognition. *Behavioural Brain Research*, *130*, 29–36.

Sonuga-Barke, E.J.S. (2003). The dual pathway model of AD/HD: an elaboration of neuro-developmental characteristics. *Neuroscience and Biobehavioral Reviews*, *27*, 593–604.

Sonuga-Barke, E.J.S. (2004). On the reorganization of incentive structure to promote delay tolerance: A therapeutic possibility for AD/HD?. *Neural Plasticity*, *11*, 23–28.

Sonuga-Barke, E.J.S. (2005). Causal models of attention-deficit/hyperactivity disorder: from common simple deficits to multiple developmental pathways. *Biological Psychiatry*, *57*, 1231–1238.

Sonuga-Barke, E.J.S. (2011). Editorial: ADHD as a reinforcement disorder-moving from general effects to identifying (six) specific models to test. *Journal of Child Psychology and Psychiatry*, *52*, 917–918.

Sonuga-Barke, E.J.S. (2015). Editorial: Diet and children's behaviour problems—disentangling urban myth from clinical reality. *Journal of Child Psychology and Psychiatry*, *56*, 497–499.

Sonuga-Barke, E.J.S., Auerbach, J., Campbell, S.B., Daley, D., & Thompson, M. (2005). Varieties of preschool hyperactivity: Multiple pathways from risk to disorder. *Developmental Science*, *8*, 141–150.

Sonuga-Barke, E.J.S., & Balding, J. (1993) British parents' beliefs about the causes of three forms of psychological disturbance. *Journal of Abnormal Child Psychology*, *21*, 367–376.

Sonuga-Barke, E.J.S., Bitsakou, P., & Thompson, M. (2010). Beyond the dual pathway model: evidence for the dissociation of timing, inhibitory, and delay-related impairments in attention-deficit/hyperactivity disorder. *Journal of the American Academy of Child and Adolescent Psychiatry*, *49*, 345–355.

Sonuga-Barke, E.J.S., Brandeis, D., Cortese, S., Daley, D., Ferrin, M., Holtmann, M., . . . Sergeant, J. (2013). Nonpharmacological interventions for ADHD: Systematic review and meta-analyses of randomized controlled trials of dietary and psychological treatments. *American Journal of Psychiatry*, *170*, 275–289.

Sonuga-Barke, E., Brandeis, D., Holtmann, M., & Cortese, S. (2014). Computer-based cognitive training for Attention-Deficit/Hyperactivity Disorder. *Child and Adolescent Psychiatric Clinics of North America*, *23*, 807–824.

Sonuga-Barke, E.J.S., & Castellanos, F.X. (2007). Spontaneous attentional fluctuations in impaired states and pathological conditions: A neurobiological hypothesis. *Neuroscience and Biobehavioral Reviews*, *31*, 977–986.

Sonuga-Barke, E.J.S., & Coghill, D. (2014). Editorial Perspective: Laying the foundations for next generation models of ADHD neuropsychology. *Journal of Child Psychology and Psychiatry*, *55*, 1215–1217.

Sonuga-Barke, E.J.S., Dalen, L., & Remington, B. (2003). Do executive deficits and delay aversion make independent contributions to preschool attention-deficit/hyperactivity disorder symptoms? *Journal of the American Academy of Child and Adolescent Psychiatry*, *42*, 1335–1342.

Sonuga-Barke, E.J.S., Daley, D., & Thompson, M. (2002). Does maternal ADHD reduce the effectiveness of parent training for preschool children's ADHD? *Journal of the American Academy of Child and Adolescent Psychiatry*, *41*, 696–702.

Sonuga-Barke, E.J.S., Daley, D., Thompson, M., & Swanson, J. (2003). Preschool ADHD: Exploring uncertainties in diagnostic validity and utility, and treatment efficacy and safety. *Expert Review of Neurotherapeutics*, *3*, 465–476.

Sonuga-Barke, E.J.S., De Houwer, J., De Ruiter, K., Azensten, M., & Holland, S. (2004). ADHD and the capture of attention by briefly exposed delay-related cues. Evidence from a conditioning paradigm. *Journal of Child Psychology and Psychiatry*, *45*, 274–283.

Sonuga-Barke, E.J.S., & Halperin, J. (2010). Developmental phenotypes and causal pathways in attention deficit/hyperactivity disorder: Potential targets for early intervention? *Journal of Child Psychology and Psychiatry*, *51*, 368–389.

Sonuga-Barke, E.J.S., Houlberg, K., & Hall, M. (1994). When is "impulsiveness" not impulsive? The case of hyperactive children's cognitive style. *Journal of Child Psychology and Psychiatry*, *35*, 1247–1253.

Sonuga-Barke, E.J.S., Koerting, J., Smith, E., McCann, D.C., & Thompson, M. (2011). Early detection and intervention for attention-deficit/hyperactivity disorder. *Expert Review of Neurotherapeutics*, *11*, 557–563.

Sonuga-Barke, E.J.S., Kumsta, R., Schlotz, W., Lasky-Su, J., Marco, R., Miranda, A., & Faraone, S.V. (2011). A functional variant of the serotonin transporter gene (SLC6A4) moderates impulsive choice in attention-deficit/hyperactivity disorder boys and siblings. *Biological Psychiatry*, *70*, 230–236.

Sonuga-Barke, E.J.S., Minocha, K., Taylor, E.A., & Sandberg, S. (1993). Inter-ethnic bias in teachers' ratings of childhood hyperactivity. *British Journal of Developmental Psychology, 11*, 187–200.

Sonuga-Barke, E.J.S., Sergeant, J.A., Nigg, J., & Willcutt, E. (2008). Executive dysfunction and delay aversion in attention deficit hyperactivity disorder: Nosologic and diagnostic implications. *Child and Adolescent Psychiatric Clinics of North America, 17*, 367–384.

Sonuga-Barke, E.J.S., Taylor, E., Sembi, S., & Smith, J. (1992). Hyperactivity and delay aversion: I. The effective delay on choice. *Journal of Child Psychology and Psychiatry, 33*, 387–398.

Sonuga-Barke, E.J.S., Thompson, M., Abikoff, H., Klein, R., & Brotman, L.M. (2006). Nonpharmacological interventions for preschoolers with ADHD: The case for Specialized Parent Training. *Infants & Young Children, 19*, 142–153.

Sonuga-Barke, E.J.S., Wiersema, J.R., van der Meere, J.J., & Roeyers, H. (2010). Context-dependent dynamic processes in attention deficit/hyperactivity disorder: Differentiating common and unique effects of state regulation deficits and delay aversion. *Neuropsychology Review, 20*, 86–102.

Sorensen, L., Plessen, K.J., Nicholas, J., & Lundervold, A.J. (2011). Is behavioral regulation in children with ADHD aggravated by comorbid anxiety disorders? *Journal of Attention Disorders, 15*, 56–66.

Sowell, E.R., Thompson, P.M., Welcome, S.E., Henkenius, A.L., Toga, A.W., & Peterson, B.S. (2003). Cortical abnormalities in children and adolescents with attention-deficit/hyperactivity disorder. *Lancet, 362*, 1699–1717.

Sowerby, P. & Tripp, G. (2009). Evidence-based assessment of Attention-Deficit/Hyperactivity Disorder. In. J.L. Matson, F. Andrasik, & M.L. Matson (Eds.), *Assessing childhood psychopathology and developmental disabilities* (pp. 209–239). New York: Springer.

Spencer, T.J. (2006). ADHD and comorbidity in childhood. *Journal of Clinical Psychiatry, 67*, 27–31.

Spencer, T.J., Biederman, J., Faraone, S., Mick, E., Coffey, B., Geller, D., . . . Wilens, T. (2001). Impact of tic disorders on ADHD outcome across the life cycle: Findings from a large group of adults with and without ADHD. *American Journal of Psychiatry, 158*, 611–617.

Spencer, T.J., Biederman, J., Harding, M., O'Donnell, D., Faraone, S.V., & Wilens, T.E. (1996). Growth deficits in ADHD children revisited: Evidence of disorder-associated growth delays? *Journal of the American Academy of Child and Adolescent Psychiatry, 35*, 1460–1469.

Spencer, T.J., Biederman, J., Harding, M., O'Donnell, D., Wilens, T., Faraone, S., . . . Geller, D. (1998). Disentangling the overlap between Tourette's disorder and ADHD. *Journal of Child Psychology & Psychiatry, 39*, 1037–1044.

Spencer, T., Biederman, J., & Wilens, T. (2004). Stimulant treatment of adult attention-deficit/hyperactivity disorder. *Psychiatric Clinics, 27*, 361–372.

Spencer, T.J., Biederman, J., Wilens, T., Harding, M., O'Donnell, D., & Griffin, S. (1996). Pharmacotherapy of attention/deficit hyperactivity disorder across the life cycle. *Journal of Child Psychology & Psychiatry, 35*, 409–432.

Spencer, T.J., Kratochvil, C.J., Sangal, R.B., Saylor, K.E., Bailey, C.E., Dunn, D.W., . . . Allen, A.J. (2007). Effects of atomoxetine on growth in children with attention- deficit/hyperactivity disorder following up to five years of treatment. *Journal of Child and Adolescent Psychopharmacology, 17*, 689–700.

Spessot, A.L., & Peterson, B.S. (2006). Tourette syndrome: A multifactorial, developmental pychopathology. In: D. Cicchetti, & D.J. Cohen (Eds.) *Manual of Developmental psychopathology* (2nd ed., Vol. 3, pp 436–469). New York: John Wiley.

Spira, E.G., & Fischel, J.E. (2005). The impact of preschool inattention, hyperactivity, and impulsivity on social and academic development: A review. *Journal of Child Psychology and Psychiatry, 46*, 755–773.

Sprich, S.E., Knouse, L.E., Cooper-Vince, C., Burbridge, J., & Safren, S.A. (2010). Description and demonstration of CBT for ADHD in adults. *Cognitive and Behavioral Practice, 17*, 9–15.

Staikova, E., Gomes, H., Tartter, V., McCabe, A., & Halperin, J.M. (2013). Pragmatic deficits and social impairment in children with ADHD. *Journal of Child Psychology and Psychiatry, 54*, 1275–1283.

Stanovich, K.E. (1986). Matthew effects in reading. Some consequences of individual in the acquisition of literacy. *Reading Research Quarterly*, *21*, 360–406.

Stark, R., Bauer, E., Merz, C.J., Zimmermann, M., Reuter, M., Plichta, M.M., . . . Herrmann, M.J. (2011). ADHD related behaviors are associated with brain activation in the reward system. *Neuropsychologia*, *49*, 426–434.

Steel, P. (2007). The nature of procrastination: A meta-analytic and theoretical review of quintessential self-regulatory failure. *Psychological Bulletin*, *133*, 65–94.

Steele, A., Karmiloff-Smith, A., Cornish, K.M., & Scerif, G. (2012). The multiple sub-functions of attention: Differential developmental gateways to literacy and numeracy. *Child Development*, *83*, 2028–2041.

Steele, M., Jensen, P.S., & Quinn, D.M.P. (2006). Remission versus response as the goal of therapy in ADHD: A new standard for the field? *Clinical Therapeutics*, *28*, 1892.

Stefanatos, G.A., & Baron, I.S. (2007). Attention-Deficit/Hyperactivity Disorder: A neuropsychological perspective towards DSM-V. *Neuropsychology Review*, *17*, 5–38.

Steinberg, L. (2005). Cognitive and affective development in adolescence. *Trends in Cognitive Sciences*, *9*, 69–74.

Stephen, V.F., & Kevin, M.A. (2008). Diagnosing and treating attention-deficit hyperactivity/disorder in adults. *World Psychiatry*, *7*, 131–136.

Stergiakouli, E., Hamshere, M., Holmans, P., Langley, K., Zaharieva, I., Hawi, Z., & Thapar, A. (2012). Investigating the contribution of common genetic variants to the risk and pathogenesis of ADHD. *American Journal of Psychiatry*, *169*, 186–194.

Stergiakouli, E., & Thapar, A. (2010). Fitting the pieces together: Current research on the genetic basis of attention-deficit/hyperactivity disorder (ADHD). *Neuropsychiatric Disease and Treatment*, *6*, 551–560.

Stevens, C., Fanning, J., Coch, D., Sanders, L., & Neville, H. (2008). Neural mechanisms of selective auditory attention are enhanced by computerized training: Electrophysiological evidence from language-impaired and typically developing children. *Brain Research*, *1205*, 55–69.

Stevens, L.J., Kuczek, T., Burgess, J.R., Hurt, E., & Arnold, L.E. (2011). Dietary sensitivities and ADHD symptoms: Thirty-five years of research. *Clinical Pediatrics*, *50*, 279–293.

Stevens, S.E., Kumsta, R., Kreppner, J.M., Brookes, K., Rutter, M., & Sonuga-Barke, E. (2009). Dopamine transporter gene polymorphism moderates the effects of severe deprivation on ADHD symptoms: Developmental continuities in gene-environment interplay. *American Journal of Medical Genetics Part B*, *150B*, 753–761.

Stevens, T., Peng, L., & Barnard-Brak, L. (2016). The comorbidity of ADHD in children diagnosed with autism spectrum disorder. *Research in Autism Spectrum Disorders*, *31*, 11–18.

Stevenson, C.S., Stevenson, R.J., & Whitmont, S. (2003). A self directed psychosocial intervention with minimal therapist contact for adults with attention deficit hyperactivity disorder. *Clinical Psychology and Psychotherapy*, *10*, 93–101.

Stevenson, J., Buitelaar, J., Cortese, S., Ferrin, M., Konofal, E., Lecendreux, M., . . . Sonuga-Barke, E.J. (2014). Research Review: The role of diet in the treatment of attention-deficit/hyperactivity disorder—an appraisal of the evidence on efficacy and recommendations on the design of future studies. *Journal of Child Psychology and Psychiatry*, *55*, 416–427.

Stevenson, J., Sonuga-Barke, E., McCann, D., Grimshaw, K., Parker, K.M., Rose-Zerilli, M.J., . . . Warner, J.O. (2010). The role of histamine degradation gene polymorphisms in moderating the effects of food additives on children's ADHD symptoms. *American Journal of Psychiatry*, *167*, 1108–1115.

Stewart, M.A. (1970). Hyperactive children. *Scientific American*, *222*, 94–98.

Still, G.F. (1902). Some abnormal psychical conditions in children. *Lancet, i*, 1008–1012, 1077–1082, 1163–1168.

Storch, E.A., Nadeau, J.M., Johnco, C., Timpano, K., McBride, N., Mutch, P.J., . . . Murphy, T.K. (2016). Hoarding in youth with autism spectrum disorders and anxiety: Incidence, clinical correlates, and behavioral treatment Response. *Journal of Autism and Developmental Disorders*, *46*, 1602–1612.

Strauss, A.A., & Lehtinen, L.E. (1947). *Psychopathology and education of the brain-injured child.* New York: Grune & Stratton.

Stringaris, A., & Goodman, R. (2009). Longitudinal outcome of youth oppositionality: Irritable, headstrong, and hurtful behaviors have distinctive predictions. *Journal of the American Academy of Child and Adolescent Psychiatry, 48*, 404–412.

Strømme, P., & Diseth, T.H. (2000). Prevalence of psychiatric diagnoses in children with mental retardation: Data from a population-based study. *Journal of Developmental Medicine and Child Neurology, 42*, 266–70.

Stryker, S. (1925). Encephalitis lethargica-The behavior residuals. *Training School Bulletin, 22*, 152–157.

Stulz, N., Hepp, U., Gächter, C., Martin-Soelch, C., Spindler, A., & Milos, G. (2013). The severity of ADHD and eating disorder symptoms: a correlational study. *BMC Psychiatry, 13*, 44.

Stuss, D.T., & Alexander, M.P. (2000). Executive functions and the frontal lobes: A conceptual view. *Psychological Research, 63*, 289–298.

Stuss, T., & Benson, F. (1986). *The frontal lobes.* New York: Raven.

Subcommittee on Attention-Deficit/Hyperactivity Disorder & Steering Committee on Quality Improvement and Management. (2011). ADHD: clinical practice guideline for the diagnosis, evaluation, and treatment of attention-deficit/hyperactivity disorder in children and adolescents. *Pediatrics, 128*, 1007–1022.

Sukhodolsky, D.G., do Rosario-Campos, M.C., Scahill, L., Katsovich, L., Pauls, D.L., Peterson, B.S., . . . Leckman, J.F. (2005). Adaptive, emotional, and family functioning of children with obsessive-compulsive disorder and comorbid attention deficit hyperactivity disorder. *American Journal of Psychiatry, 162*, 1125–1132.

Sullivan, E.L., Holton, K.F., Nousen, E.K., Barling, A.N., Sullivan, C.A., Propper, C.B., & Nigg, J.T. (2015). Early identification of ADHD risk via infant temperament and emotion regulation: a pilot study. *Journal of Child Psychology and Psychiatry, 56*, 949–957.

Sullivan, M., & Rudnik-Levin, F. (2001). *Attention deficit/hyperactivity disorder and substance abuse: Diagnostic and therapeutic considerations. Adult attention deficit disorder: Brain mechanisms and life outcomes* (pp. 251–270). New York: New York Academy of Sciences.

Sung, V., Hiscock, H., Sciberras, E., & Efron, D. (2008). Sleep problems in children with attention-deficit/hyperactivity disorder—Prevalence and the effect on the child and family. *Archives of Pediatrics and Adolescent Medicine, 162*, 336–342.

Surman, B. H., Hammerness, P.G., Pion, K., & Faraone, S.V. (2013). Do stimulants improve functioning in adults with ADHD? A review of the literature. *European Neuropsychopharmacology, 23*, 528–533.

Surman, C.B. (2006). Adults with ADHD and sleep complaints: A pilot study identifying sleep-disordered breathing using polysomnography and sleep quality assessment. *Journal of Attention Disorders, 9*, 550–555.

Surman, C.B. (2013). Clinical assessment of ADHD in adults. In C.B.H. Surman (Ed.), *ADHD in adults. A practical guide to evaluation and management* (pp. 19–44). New York: Humana Press.

Surman, C.B., Randall, E.T., & Biederman, J. (2006). Association between attention-deficit/hyperactivity disorder and bulimia nervosa: analysis of 4 case-control studies. *Journal of Clinical Psychiatry, 67*, 351–354.

Swain, J.E., Scahill, L., Lombroso, P.J., King, R.A., & Leckman, J.F. (2007). Tourette syndrome and tic disorder: A decade of progress. *Journal of the American Academy of Child and Adolescent Psychiatry, 46*, 947–968.

Swanson, J.M., Gupta, S., Lam, A., Shoulson, I., Lerner, M., Modi, N., . . . Wigal, S. (2003). Development of a new once-a-day formulation of methylphenidate for the treatment of attention-deficit/hyperactivity disorder: Proof-of-concept and proof-of-product studies. *Archives of General Psychiatry, 60*, 204–211.

Swanson, J.M., Hinshaw, S.P., Arnold, L.E., Gibbons, R.D., Marcus, S.U.E., Hur, K., . . . Hechtman, L. (2007). Secondary evaluations of MTA 36-month outcomes: propensity score and growth mixture model analyses. *Journal of the American Academy of Child and Adolescent Psychiatry, 46*, 1003–1014.

Swanson, J.M., Kraemer, H.C., Hinshaw, S.P., Arnold, L.E., Conners, C.K., Abikoff, H.B., . . . Wu, M. (2001). Clinical relevance of the primary findings of the MTA: Success rates based on severity of symptoms at the end of treatment. *Journal of the American Academy of Child and Adolescent Psychiatry, 40*, 168–179.

Swanson, J.M., Lakes, K., Wigal, T., & Volkow, N.D. (2013). Multiple origins of sex differences in attention deficit hyperactivity disorder. In D.W. Pfaff & Y. Christen (Eds.), *Multiple origins of sex differences in brain* (pp. 103–122). New York: Springer.

Swanson, J.M., Oosterlaan, J., Murias, M., Schuck, S., Flodman, P., Spence, M.A., . . . Mann, M. (2000). Attention deficit/hyperactivity disorder children with a 7-repeat allele of the dopamine receptor D4 gene have extreme behavior but normal performance on critical neuropsychological tests of attention. *Proceedings of the National Academy of Sciences, 97*, 4754–4759.

Swanson, J.M., Wigal, T., Lakes, K., & Volkow, N.D. (2011). Attention deficit hyperactivity disorder: defining a spectrum disorder and considering neuroethical implications. In J. Illes, B.J. & Sahakian (Eds.), *Oxford handbook of neuroethics*. Oxford: Oxford University Press.

Swartz, S.L., Prevatt, F., & Proctor, B.E. (2005). A coaching intervention for college students with Attention-Deficit/Hyperactivity Disorder. *Psychology in the Schools, 42*, 647–56.

Szasz, T.S. (2001). *Pharmacracy: Medicine and politics in America*. Westport, Connecticut: Praeger.

Szyf, M., Weaver, I., & Meaney, M. (2007). Maternal care, the epigenome and phenotypic differences in behavior. *Reproductive Toxicology, 24*, 9–19.

Tait, G. (2005). The ADHD debate and the philosophy of truth. *International Journal of Inclusive Education, 9*, 17–38.

Takeda, T., Ambrosini, P., deBerardinis, R., & Elia, J. (2012). What can ADHD without comorbidity teach us about comorbidity? *Research in Developmental Disabilities, 33*, 419–425.

Tamam, L., Karakus, G., & Ozpoyraz, N. (2008). Comorbidity of adult attention-deficit hyperactivity disorder and bipolar disorder: prevalence and clinical correlates. *European Archives of Psychiatry and Clinical Neuroscience, 258*, 385–393.

Tamm, L., Nakonezny, P.A., & Hughes, C.W. (2014). An open trial of a metacognitive executive function training for young children with ADHD. *Journal of Attention Disorders, 18*, 551–559.

Tandon, M., Si, X., & Luby, J. (2011). Preschool onset attention-deficit/hyperactivity disorder: Course and predictors of stability over 24 months. *Journal of Child and Adolescent Psychopharmacology, 21*, 321–330.

Tang, Y.Y., Hölzel, B.K., & Posner, M.I. (2015). The neuroscience of mindfulness meditation. *Nature Reviews Neuroscience, 16*, 213–225.

Tannock, R. (2000). Attention-deficit/hyperactivity disorder with anxiety disorders. In T.E. Brown (Ed.), *Attention-deficit disorders and comorbidities in children, adolescents, and adults* (pp. 125–170). Washington, DC: American Psychiatric Press.

Tannock, R. (2002) Language, reading, and motor control problems in ADHD. A potential behavioral phenotype. In: L.L. Greenhill (Ed.), *Learning disabilities, Implications for psychiatric treatment*. Washington, DC: American Psychiatric Press.

Tannock, R. (2009). ADHD with anxiety disorders. In. T. Brown (Ed.) *ADHD Comorbidities. Handbook for ADHD complications in children and adults* (pp. 131–155). Washington, DC: American Psychiatric.

Tannock, R. (2013). Rethinking ADHD and LD in DSM-5: Proposed changes in diagnostic criteria. *Journal of Learning Disabilities, 46*, 5–25.

Tannock, R., Frijters, J.C., Martinussen, R., White, E.J., Ickowicz, A., Benson, N.J., & Lovett, M.W. (2016). Combined modality intervention for ADHD with comorbid reading disorders: A proof of concept study. *Journal of Learning Disabilities*. https://doi.org/0022219416678409

Tannock, R., Ickowicz, A., & Schachar, R. (1995). Differential effects of methylphenidate on working memory in ADHD children with and without comorbid anxiety. *Journal of the American Academy of Child and Adolescent Psychiatry, 34*, 886–896.

Tannock, R., & Schachar, R. (1996). Executive dysfunction as an underlying mechanism of behavior and language problems in attention deficit hyperactivity disorder. In M.M. Konstantareas, R. Tannock, J.H. Beitchman & N.J. Cohen (Eds.). *Language, learning, and behavior disorders: Developmental, biological, and clinical perspectives.* New York: Cambridge University Press.

Tanofsky-Kraff, M., & Yanovski, S.Z. (2004). Eating disorder or disordered eating? Non-normative eating patterns in obese individuals. *Obesity Research, 12,* 1361–1366.

Taurines, R., Schwenck, C., Westerwald, E., Sachse, M., Siniatchkin, M., & Freitag, C. (2012). ADHD and autism: Differential diagnosis or overlapping traits? A selective review. *Attention Deficit Hyperactivity Disorders, 4,* 115–139.

Taylor, D.C., & Ounsted, C. (1972). The nature of gender differences explored through ontogenic analysis of sex ratios in disease. In C. Ounsted & D.S. Taylor (Eds.), *Gender differences: Their ontogeny and significance* (pp. 215–240). London: Churchill-Livingstone.

Taylor, E.A. (1983). Drug response and diagnostic validation. In M. Rutter (Ed.), *Developmental neuropsychiatry* (pp. 348–368). New York: Guilford Press.

Taylor, E.A. (1988). Diagnosis of hyperactivity—A British perspective. In L. Bloomingdale & J. Sergeant (Eds.), *Attention deficit disorder: Criteria, cognition and intervention* (pp. 141–160). New York: Pergamon Press.

Taylor, E.A. (2011). Antecedents of ADHD: A historical account of diagnostic concepts. *Attention Deficit Hyperactivity Disorder, 3,* 69–75.

Taylor, E.A., Döpfner, M., Sergeant, J., Asherson, P., Banaschewski, T., Buitelaar, J., . . . Steinhausen, H.C. (2004). European clinical guidelines for hyperkinetic disorder—first upgrade. *European Child & Adolescent Psychiatry, 13,* i7–i30.

Taylor, E.A., Sandberg, S., Thorley, G., & Giles, S. (1991). *The epidemiology of childhood hyperactivity.* New York: Oxford University Press.

Taylor, E.A., & Sonuga-Barke, E.J.S. (2008). Disorders of attention and activity. In M. Rutter, D. Bishop, D. Pine, S. Scott, J.S. Stevenson, E.A. Taylor, & A. Thapar, (Eds.*), Rutter's child and adolescent psychiatry* (pp. 521–542). Oxford: Wiley-Blackwell.

Tercyak, K.P., Lerman, C., & Audrain, J. (2002). Association of attention deficit/ hyperactivity disorder symptoms with levels of cigarette smoking in a community sample of adolescents. *Journal of American Academy of Child and Adolescent Psychiatry, 41,* 799–805.

Thamotharan, S., Lange, K., Zale, E.L., Huffhines, L., & Fields, S. (2013). The role of impulsivity in pediatric obesity and weight status: A meta-analytic review. *Clinical Psychology Review, 33,* 253–262.

Thapar, A., Bree, M., Fowler, T., Langley, K., & Whittinger, N. (2006). Predictors of antisocial behaviour in children with attention deficit hyperactivity disorder. *European Child and Adolescent Psychiatry, 15,* 118–125.

Thapar, A., Cooper, M., Eyre, O., & Langley, K. (2013). Practitioner review: What have we learnt about the causes of ADHD? *Journal of Child Psychology and Psychiatry, 54,* 3–16.

Thapar, A., Harold, G., Rice, F., Langley, K., & O'Donovan, M. (2007) The contribution of gene-environment interaction to psychopathology. *Development and Psychopathology, 19,* 989–1004.

Thapar, A., Harrington, R., & McGuffin, P. (2001). Examining the comorbidity of ADHD-related behaviours and conduct problems using a twin study design. *British Journal of Psychiatry, 179,* 224–229.

Thapar, A., Langley, K., Fowler, T., Rice, F., Turic, D., Whittinger, N., & . . . O'Donovan, M. (2005). Catechol O-methyltransferase gene variant and birth weight predict early-onset antisocial behavior in children with attention-deficit/hyperactivity disorder. *Archives of General Psychiatry, 62,* 1275–1278.

Thapar, A., Langley, K., & Muñoz-Solomando, A. (2013). The ADHD debate: Being mindful of complexity and wary of reductionist explanations and polarization. *Journal of Family Therapy, 35,* 219–223.

Thapar, A., O'Donovan, M., & Owen, M.J. (2005). The genetics of attention deficit hyperactivity disorder. *Human Molecular Genetics, 14,* R275–282.

Thapar, A., Rice, F., Hay, D., Bolvin, J., Langley, K., van den Bree, M., . . . Harold, G. (2009). Prenatal smoking might not cause attention-deficit/hyperactivity disorder: Evidence from a novel design. *Biological Psychiatry, 66*, 722–727.

Thapar, A., & Rutter, M. (2009). Do prenatal risk factors cause psychiatric disorder? Be wary of causal claims. *British Journal of Psychiatry, 195*, 100–101.

Thapar, A., van den Bree, M., Fowler, T., Langley, K., & Whittinger, N. (2006). Predictors of antisocial behaviour in children with attention deficit hyperactivity disorder. *European Child & Adolescent Psychiatry, 15*, 118–125.

Theule, J., Hurl, K.E., Cheung, K., Ward, M., & Henrikson, B. (2016). Exploring the relationships between problem gambling and ADHD A Meta-Analysis. *Journal of Attention Disorders.* https://doi.org/1087054715626512

Theule, J., Wiener, J., Tannock, R., & Jenkins, J.M. (2013). Parenting stress in families of children with ADHD: A meta-analysis. *Journal of Emotional and Behavioral Disorders, 21*, 3–17.

Thomas, A., & Chess, S. (1977). *Temperament and development.* New York: Brunner/Mazel.

Thompson, M., Laver-Bradbury, C., Ayres, M., Le Poidevin, E., Mead, S., Dodds, C., . . . Sonuga-Barke, E.J.S. (2009). A small-scale randomized controlled trial of the revised new forest parenting programme for preschoolers with attention deficit hyperactivity disorder. *European Child and Adolescent Psychiatry, 18*, 605–616.

Thomsen, P.H. (2013). Obsessive-compulsive disorders. *European Child and Adolescent Psychiatry, 22*(Suppl 1), S23–S28.

Thorell, L.B. (2007). Do delay aversion and executive function deficits make distinct contributions to the functional impact of ADHD symptoms? A study of early academic skill deficits. *Journal of Child Psychology and Psychiatry, 48*, 1061–1070.

Thorell, L.B., & Rydell, A.M. (2008). Behaviour problems and social competence deficits associated with symptoms of attention-deficit/hyperactivity disorder: effects of age and gender. *Child: Care, Health and Development, 34*, 584–595.

Thurber, J.R., Heller, T.L., & Hinshaw, S.P. (2002). The social behaviors and peer expectation of girls with attention-deficit/hyperactivity disorder and comparison girls. *Journal of Clinical Child and Adolescent Psychology, 31*, 443–452.

Timimi, S. (2002). *Pathological child psychiatry and the medicalization of childhood.* Hove: Brunner-Routledge.

Timimi, S., & Taylor, E. (2004). ADHD is best understood as a cultural construct. Debate. *British Journal of Psychiatry, 184*, 8–9.

Timmers, M., Fischer, A.H., & Manstead, A.S.R. (1998). Gender differences in motives for regulating emotions. *Personality and Social Psychology Bulletin, 24*, 974–985.

Tirosh, E., & Cohen, A. (1998). Language deficit with attention-deficit disorder: A prevalent comorbidity. *Journal of Child Neurology, 13*, 493–497.

Todd, R.D., Huang, H., & Henderson, C.A. (2008). Poor utility of the age of onset criterion for DSM-IV attention deficit/hyperactivity disorder: Recommendations for DSM-IV and ICD-11. *Journal of Child Psychology and Psychiatry, 49*, 942–949.

Todd, R.D., Huang, H., Todorov, A.A., Neuman. R.J., Reiersen, A.M., Henderson, C.A., & Reich, W. (2008). Predictors of stability of attention deficit/hyperactivity disorder subtypes from childhood to young adulthood. *Journal of the American Academy of Child and Adolescent Psychiatry, 47*, 76–85.

Tomasi, D., Wang, G.J., Wang, R., Caparelli, E.C., Logan, J., & Volkow, N.D. (2015). Overlapping patterns of brain activation to food and cocaine cues in cocaine abusers. *Human Brain Mapping, 36*, 120–136.

Tomblin, J.B., & Mueller, K.L. (2012). How can the comorbidity with ADHD aid understanding of language and speech disorders? *Topics in Language Disorders, 32*, 198–206.

Toplak, M.E., Connors, L., Shuster, J., Knezevic, B., & Parks, S. (2008). Review of cognitive, cognitive behavioral, and neural-based interventions for attention- deficit/hyperactivity disorder (ADHD). *Clinical Psychology Review, 28*, 801–823.

Toplak, M.E., West, R.F., & Stanovich, K.E. (2013). Practitioner review: Do performance-based measures and ratings of executive function assess the same construct? *Journal of Child Psychology and Psychiatry, 54*, 131–143.

Torgersen, T., Gjervan, B., & Rasmussen, K. (2006). ADHD in adults: A study of clinical characteristics, impairment and comorbidity. *Nordic Journal of Psychiatry*, *60*, 38–43.

Torgesen, J.K. (2000). Individual differences in response to early interventions in reading: The lingering problem of treatment resisters. *Learning Disabilities Research and Practice*, *15*, 55–64.

Townsend, L., Flisher, A.J., & King, G. (2007). A systematic review of the relationship between high school dropout and substance use. *Clinical Child and Family Psychology Review*, *10*, 295–317.

Treacy, L., Tripp, G., & Baird, A. (2005). Parent stress management training for Attention-Deficit/Hyperactivity Disorder. *Behavior Therapy*, *36*, 223–233.

Tredgold, A.F. (1908). *Mental deficiency (amentia)*. New York: W. Wood.

Treuer, T., Méndez, L., Montgomery, W., & Wu, S. (2016). Factors affecting treatment adherence to atomoxetine in ADHD: A systematic review. *Neuropsychiatric Disease and Treatment*, *12*, 1061–1083.

Treuting, J.J., & Hinshaw, S.P. (2001). Depression and self-esteem in boys with ADHD: Associations with comorbid aggression and explanatory attributional mechanisms. *Journal of Abnormal Child Psychology*, *29*, 23–39.

Tripp, G., & Alsop, B. (2001). Sensitivity to reward delay in children with attention deficit hyperactivity disorder (ADHD). *Journal of Child Psychology and Psychiatry*, *42*, 691–698.

Tripp, G., & Wickens, J.R. (2008). Research review: Dopamine transfer deficit: a neurobiological theory of altered reinforcement mechanisms in ADHD. *Journal of Child Psychology and Psychiatry*, *49*, 691–704.

Trout, A. L., Lienemann, T.O., Reid, R., & Epstein, M.H. (2007). A review of non-medication interventions to improve the academic performance of children and youth with ADHD. *Remedial and Special Education*, *28*, 207–226.

Tsang, T., Kohn, M., Efron, D., Clarke, S., Clark, R., Lamb, C., & Williams, L. (2015). Anxiety in young people with ADHD: Clinical and self-report outcomes. *Journal of Attention Disorders*, *19*, 18–26.

Tseng, W.L., & Gau, S.S.F. (2013). Executive function as a mediator in the link between attention-deficit/hyperactivity disorder and social problems. *Journal of Child Psychology and Psychiatry*, *54*, 996–1004.

Tseng, W.L., Kawabata, Y., Gau, S.S.F., & Crick, N.R. (2014). Symptoms of attention-deficit/hyperactivity disorder and peer functioning: A transactional model of development. *Journal of Abnormal Child Psychology*, *42*, 1353–1365.

Tully, L.A., Arsenault, L., Caspi, A., Moffitt, T.E., & Morgan, J. (2004). Does maternal warmth moderate the effects of birthweight on twins' attention-deficit/hyperactivity disorder (ADHD) symptoms and low IQ? *Journal of Consulting and Clinical Psychology*, *72*, 219–226.

Tupper, D. (1987). *The issues with "Soft Signs"*. Orlando, FL: Grune & Stratton.

Turecki, S. (1989). The difficult child center. In W.B. Carey & S.C. McDevitt (Eds.), *Clinical and educational applications of temperament research* (pp. 141–153). Berwin, Pa: Swets North American.

Tuvblad, C., Raine, A., Zheng, M., & Baker, L.A. (2009). Genetic and environmental stability differs in reactive and proactive aggression. *Aggressive Behavior*, *35*, 437–452.

Uebel, H., Albrecht, B., Asherson, P., Börger, N.A., Butler, L., Chen, W., . . . Andreou, P. (2010). Performance variability, impulsivity errors and the impact of incentives as gender-independent endophenotypes for ADHD. *Journal of Child Psychology and Psychiatry*, *51*, 210–218.

Uekermann, J., Kraemer, M., Abdel-Hamid, M., Schimmelmann, B.G., Hebebrand, J., & Daum, I. (2010). Social cognition in attention-deficit/hyperactivity disorder (ADHD). *Neuroscience and Biobehavioral Reviews*, *34*, 734–743.

Ullebø, A.K., Posserud, M.B., Heiervang, E., Obel, C., & Gillberg, C. (2012). Prevalence of the ADHD phenotype in 7-to 9-year-old children: Effects of informant, gender and non-participation. *Social Psychiatry and Psychiatric Epidemiology*, *45*, 763–769.

Vaa, T. (2014). ADHD and relative risk of accidents in road traffic: A meta-analysis. *Accident Analysis & Prevention*, *62*, 415–425.

Vaidya, C.J. (2011). Neurodevelopmental abnormalities in ADHD. In C. Stanford and R. Tannock (Eds.), *Behavioral neuroscience of Attention Deficit Hyperactivity Disorder and its treatment* (pp. 49–66). Berlin: Springer.

Väisänen, R., Loukusa, S., Moilanen, I., & Yliherva, A. (2014). Language and pragmatic profile in children with ADHD measured by Children's Communication Checklist 2nd edition. *Logopedics Phoniatrics Vocology*, *39*, 179–187.

Valdez, C.R., Carlson, C., & Zanger, D. (2005). Evidence-based parent training and family interventions for school behavior change. *School Psychology Quarterly*, *20*, 403–433.

Valera, E.M., Brown, A., Biederman, J., Faraone, S.V., Makris, N., Monuteaux, M.C., . . . Seidman, L.J. (2009). Sex differences in the functional neuroanatomy of working memory in adults with ADHD. *American Journal of Psychiatry*, *167*, 86–94.

Valera, E.M., Faraone, S.V., Murray, K.E., & Seidman, L.J. (2007). Meta-analysis of structural imaging findings in attention-deficit/hyperactivity disorder. *Biological Psychiatry*, *61*, 1361–1369.

Vance, A., Arduca, Y., Sanders, M., Karamitsios, M., Hall, N., & Hetrick, S. (2006). DHD, combined type, dysthymic disorder and anxiety disorders: Differential patterns of neurodevelopmental deficits. *Psychiatry Research*, *143*, 213–222.

Van de Glind, G., Van Emmerik-van Oortmerssen, K., Carpentier, P.-J., Levin, F.R., Koeter, M., Kaye, S., & van den Brink, W. (2013). The International ADHD in Substance use disorders Prevalence (IASP) study: Background, methods and study population. *International Journal of Methods in Psychiatric Research*, *2*, 32–244.

Van der Donk, M.L., Hiemstra-Beernink, A.C., Tjeenk-Kalff, A.C., van der Leij, A., & Lindauer, R.J. (2016). Predictors and moderators of treatment outcome in cognitive training for children with ADHD. *Journal of Attention Disorders*. https://doi.org/1087054716632876

Van der Heijden, K.B., Smits, M.G., Someren, E.J.V., & Boudewijn Gunning, W. (2005). Idiopathic chronic sleep onset insomnia in attention-deficit/hyperactivity disorder: A circadian rhythm sleep disorder. *Chronobiology International*, *22*, 559–570.

Van der Meer, J.M., Oerlemans, A.M., van Steijn, D.J., Lappenschaar, M.G., de Sonneville, L.M., Buitelaar, J.K., & Rommelse, N.N. (2012). Are autism spectrum disorder and attention-deficit/hyperactivity disorder different manifestations of one overarching disorder? Cognitive and symptom evidence from a clinical and population-based sample. *Journal of the American Academy of Child and Adolescent Psychiatry*, *51*, 1160–1172.

Van der Meere, J.J., Gunning, B., & Stemerdink, N. (1995). The effect of presentation rate on task performance in ADHD children with and without tics. *Journal of Perceptual and Motor Skills*, *81*, 259–262.

Van der Meere, J., & Sergeant J. (1988). Focused attention in pervasively hyperactive children. *Journal of Abnormal Child Psychology*, *16*, 627–640.

Van der Oord, S., Prins, P.J., Oosterlaan, J., & Emmelkamp, P.M. (2008). Efficacy of methylphenidate, psychosocial treatments and their combination in school-aged children with ADHD: A meta-analysis. *Clinical Psychology Review*, *28*, 783–800.

Van Dongen-Boomsma, M., Vollebregt, M.A., Slaats-Willemse, D., & Buitelaar, J.K. (2013). A randomized placebo-controlled trial of electroencephalographic (EEG) neurofeedback in children with attention-deficit/hyperactivity disorder. *Journal of Clinical Psychiatry*, *74*, 821–827.

Van Egmond-Fröhlich, A.W., Weghuber, D., & de Zwaan, M. (2012). Association of symptoms of attention-deficit/hyperactivity disorder with physical activity, media time, and food intake in children and adolescents. *PLoS One*, *7*, e49781.

Van Emmerik-van Oortmerssen, K., van de Glind, G., van den Brink, W., Smit, F., Crunell, C.L., Swets, M., & Schoevers, R.A. (2012). Prevalence of attention-deficit hyperactivity disorder in substance use disorder patients: A meta-analysis and meta-regression analysis. *Drug and Alcohol Dependence*, *122*, 11–19.

Van Ewijk, H. (2012). Diffusion tensor imaging in attention-deficit/hyperactivity disorder: a systematic review and meta-analysis. *Neuroscience and Biobehavioral Reviews*, *36*, 1093–1106.

Van Mil, N.H., Steegers-Theunissen, R.P., Bouwland-Both, M.I., Verbiest, M.M., Rijlaarsdam, J., Hofman, A., . . . Stolk, L. (2014). DNA methylation profiles at birth and child ADHD symptoms. *Journal of Psychiatric Research*, *49*, 51–59.

Vannest, K.J., Davis, J.L., Davis, C.R., Mason, B.A., & Burke, M.D. (2010). Effective intervention for behavior with a daily behavior report card: A meta-analysis. *School Psychology Review*, *39*, 654–672.

Van Veen, M.M., Kooij, J.S., Boonstra, A.M., Gordijn, M C., & Van Someren, E.J. (2010). Delayed circadian rhythm in adults with attention-deficit/hyperactivity disorder and chronic sleep-onset insomnia. *Biological Psychiatry*, *67*, 1091–1096.

Verdejo-Garcia, A., Lawrence, A.J., & Clark, L. (2008). Impulsivity as a vulnerability marker for substance-use disorders: Review of findings from high-risk research, problem gamblers and genetic association studies. *Neuroscience and Biobehavioral Reviews*, *32*, 777–810.

Vgontzas, A.N., Bixler, E.O., & Chrousos, G.P. (2006). Obesity-related sleepiness and fatigue. *Annals of the New York Academy of Sciences*, *1083*, 329–344.

Villodas, M.T., McBurnett, K., Kaiser, N., Rooney, M., Pfiffner, L.J. (2014). Additive effects of parent adherence on social and behavioral outcomes of a collaborative school—home behavioral intervention for ADHD. *Child Psychiatry and Human Development*, *45*, 348–360.

Visscher, P.M., Hill, W.G., & Wray, N.R. (2008). Heritability in the genomics era—concepts and misconceptions. *Nature Reviews. Genetics*, *9*, 255–266.

Visser, J. (2003). Developmental coordination disorder: A review of research on subtypes and comorbidities. *Human Movement Science*, *22*, 479–493.

Visser, J., & Jehan, Z. (2009). ADHD: a scientific fact or a factual opinion? A critique of the veracity of Attention Deficit Hyperactivity Disorder. *Emotional and Behavioural Difficulties*, *14*, 127–140.

Visser, S.N., Bitsko, R.H., Danielson, M.L., & Perou, R. (2010). Increasing prevalence of parent reported attention deficit hyperactivity disorder among children—United States 2003 and 2007. *Morbidity and Mortality Weekly Report*, *59*, 1439–1443.

Vitaro, F., Arseneault, L., & Tremblay, R.E. (1997). Dispositional predictors of problem gambling in male adolescents. *American Journal of Psychiatry*, *154*, 1769–1770.

Vitola, E.S., Salgado, C.A., Silva, K.L., Karam, R.G., Victor, M.M., Mota, N.R., . . . Grevet, E.H. (2012). The role of a lifetime history of oppositional defiant and conduct disorders in adults with ADHD: Implications for clinical practice. *CNS Spectrums*, *17*, 94–99.

Vloet, T.D., Konrad, K., Herpetz-Dahlmann, B., Polier, G.G., & Gunther, T. (2010). Impact of anxiety disorders on attentional functions in children with ADHD. *Journal of Affective Disorders*, *124*, 283–290.

Voigt, R.G., Barbaresi, W.J., Colligan, R.C., Weaver, A.L., & Katusic, S.K. (2006). Developmental dissociation, deviance, and delay: occurrence of attention deficit hyperactivity disorder in individuals with and without borderline to mild intellectual disability. *Journal of Developmental Medicine & Child Neurology*, *48*, 831–835.

Volkow, N.D., Fowler, J.S., Wang, G.J., Baler, R., & Telang, F. (2009). Imaging dopamine's role in drug abuse and addiction. *Neuropharmacology*, *56*, 3–8.

Volkow, N.D., Wang, G.J., Fowler, J.S., & Telang, F. (2008). Overlapping neuronal circuits in addiction and obesity: evidence of systems pathology. *Philosophical Transactions of the Royal Society of London B: Biological Sciences*, *363*, 3191–3200.

Volkow, N.D., Wang, G.J., Ma, Y., Fowler, J.S., Zhu, W., Maynard, L., . . . Swanson, J.M. (2003). Expectation enhances the regional brain metabolic and the reinforcing effects of stimulants in cocaine abusers. *Journal of Neuroscience*, *23*, 11461–11468.

Volkow, N.D., Wang, G., Newcom, J.H., Kollins, S.H., Wiga, T.L., Telang, F., . . . Swanson, J.M. (2011). Motivation deficit in ADHD is associated with dysfunction of the dopamine reward pathway. *Molecular Psychiatry*, *16*, 1147–1154.

Volpe, R.J., DuPaul, G.J., DiPerna, J.C., Jitendra, A.K., Lutz, J.G., Tresco, K., & Junod, R.V. (2006). Attention deficit hyperactivity disorder and scholastic achievement: A model of mediation via academic enablers. *School Psychology Review*, *35*, 47–61.

Volpe, R. J., DuPaul, G. J., Loney, J., & Salisbury, H. (1999). Alternative selection criteria for identifying children with ADHD: Observed behavior and self-reported internalizing symptoms. *Journal of Behavioral Disorders*, *7*, 103–109.

Von Stauffenberg, C., & Campbell, S. B. (2007). Predicting the early developmental course of symptoms of attention deficit hyperactivity disorder. *Journal of Applied Developmental Psychology*, *28*, 536–552.

Von Suchodoletz, A., Trommsdorff, G., Heikamp, T., Wieber, F., & Gollwitzer, P. M. (2009). Transition to school: The role of kindergarten children's behavior regulation. *Learning and Individual Differences*, *19*, 561–566.

Vorspan, F., Mehtelli, W., Dupuy, G., Bloch, V., & Lépine, J. P. (2015). Anxiety and substance use disorders: Co-occurrence and clinical issues. *Current Psychiatry Reports*, *17*, 4. https://doi.org/10.1007/s11920-014-0544-y

Vukovic, R. K., & Lesaux, N. K. (2013). The relationship between linguistic skills and arithmetic knowledge. *Learning and Individual Differences*, *23*, 87–91.

Vuksic, M., Rados, M., & Kostovic, I. (2008). Structural basis of development plasticity in the corticostriatal system. *Collegium Antropologicum*, *32*, 155–159.

Vygotsky, L. S. (1967). Play and its role in the mental development of the child. *Soviet Psychology*, *5*, 6–18.

Wacharasin, C., Barnard, K. E., & Spieker, S. J. (2003). Factors affecting toddler cognitive development in low income families: Implications for practitioners. *Infants & Young Children*, *16*, 175–181.

Wahlstedt, C., Thorell, L. B., & Bohlin, G. (2009). Heterogeneity in ADHD: Neuropsychological pathways, comorbidity and symptom domains. *Journal of Abnormal Child Psychology*, *37*, 551–564.

Wakschlag, L. S., Leventhal, B. L., Thomas, J. M., & Pine, D. (2007). Disruptive Behavior Disorders & ADHD in preschool children: characterizing heterotypic continuities for a developmentally informed nosology for DSM-V. In D. Regier, M. First, & W. Narrow (Eds.) *Age and gender considerations in psychiatric diagnosis: A research agenda for DSM-V* (pp. 243–257). Washington, DC: American Psychiatric.

Waldman, I. D., & Faraone, S. V. (2002). A meta-analysis of linkage and association between the dopamine transporter gene (DAT1) and childhood ADHD. *Behavior Genetics*, *32*, 487–487.

Waldon, J., Vriend, J., Davidson, F., & Corkum, P. (2015). Sleep and attention in children with ADHD and typically developing peers. *Journal of Attention Disorders*. https://doi.org/1087054715575064

Walitza, S., Zellmann, H., Irblich, B., Lange, K. W., Tucha, O., Hemminger, U., . . . Warnke, A. (2008). Children and adolescents with obsessive-compulsive disorder and comorbid attention-deficit/hyperactivity disorder: Preliminary results of a prospective follow-up study. *Journal of Neural Transmission*, *115*, 187–190.

Walker, M. P. (2009). Sleep, memory and emotion. *Progress in Brain Research*, *185*, 49–68.

Walters, A. S., Mandelbaum, D. E., Lewin, D S., Kugler, S., England, S. J., Miller, M., & Dopaminergic Therapy Study Group. (2000). Dopaminergic therapy in children with restless legs/periodic limb movements in sleep and ADHD. *Pediatric Neurology*, *22*, 182–186.

Walther, C. A., Cheong, J., Molina, B. S., Pelham, W. E., Jr., Wymbs, B. T., Belendiuk, K. A., & Pedersen, S. L. (2012). Substance use and delinquency among adolescents with childhood ADHD: The protective role of parenting. *Psychology of Addictive Behaviors*, *26*, 585–598.

Wampold, B. E. (2001). *The great psychotherapy debate: Models, methods and findings*. Mahwah, NJ: Lawrence Erlbaum.

Wang, G. J., Boraud, T., Volkow, N. D., Wigal, T., Kollins, S. H., Newcorn, J. H., . . . Swanson, J. M. (2013). Long-term stimulant treatment affects brain dopamine transporter level in patients with attention deficit hyperactive disorder. *PloS One*, *8*, e63023.

Wang, G. J., Volkow, N. D., Logan, J., Pappas, N. R., Wong, C. T., Zhu, W., . . . Fowler, J. S. (2001). Brain dopamine and obesity. *Lancet*, *357*, 354–357.

Wang, G. J., Volkow, N. D., Telang, F., Jayne, M., Ma, J., Rao, M., . . . Fowler, J. S. (2004). Exposure to appetitive food stimuli markedly activates the human brain. *Neuroimage*, *21*, 1790–1797.

Ward, M.F., Wender, P.H., & Reimherr, F.W. (1993). The Wender Utah Rating Scale: An aid in the retrospective diagnosis of childhood attention deficit hyperactivity disorder. *American Journal of Psychiatry, 150*, 885–890.

Waring, M.E., & Lapane, K.L. (2008). Overweight in children and adolescents in relation to attention-deficit/hyperactivity disorder: Results from a national sample. *Pediatrics, 122*, e1–e6.

Waschbusch, D.A. (2002). A meta-analytic examination of comorbid hyperactive-impulsive-attention problems and conduct problems. *Psychological Bulletin, 128*, 118–150.

Waschbusch, D.A., & Hill, G.P. (2003). Empirically supported, promising, and unsupported treatments for children with Attention-Deficit/Hyperactivity Disorder. In S.O. Lilienfield, S. Jay Lynn, & J.M. Lohr (Eds.), *Science and pseudoscience in clinical psychology*. New York: Guilford Press.

Waschbusch, D.A., & King, S. (2006). Should sex-specific norms be used to assess attention-deficit/hyperactivity disorder or oppositional defiant disorder? *Journal of Consulting and Clinical Psychology, 74*, 179–185.

Wassenberg, R., Hendriksen, J.G.M., Hurks, P.P.M., Feron, F.J.M., Vles, J.S.H., & Jolles, J. (2010). Speed of language comprehension is impaired in ADHD. *Journal of Attention Disorders, 13*, 374–385.

Wasserman, R.C., Diblasio, C.M., Bond, L.A., Young, P.C., & Colletti, R.B. (1990). Infant temperament and school age behavior: Six year longitudinal study in a pediatric practice. *Pediatrics, 85*, 801–807.

Watemberg, N., Waiserberg, N., & Lerman-Sagie, T. (2007). Developmental coordination disorder in children with attention-deficit—hyperactivity disorder and physical therapy intervention. *Developmental Medicine & Child Neurology, 49*, 920–925.

Watson, S.M., Richels, C., Michalek, A.P., & Raymer, A. (2015). Psychosocial treatments for ADHD: A systematic appraisal of the evidence. *Journal of Attention Disorders, 19*, 3–10.

Webster-Stratton, C.H., Reid, M.J., & Beauchaine, T. (2011) Combining parent and child training for young children with ADHD. *Journal of Clinical Child and Adolescent Psychology, 40*, 191–203.

Wehmeier, P.M., Schacht, A., & Barkley, R. (2010). Social and emotional impairment in children and adolescents with ADHD and the impact on quality of life. *Journal of Adolescent Health, 46*, 209–217.

Weiner, B. (1993). On sin versus sickness: A theory of perceived responsibility and social motivation. *American Psychologist, 48*, 957–965.

Weis, R. (2014). *Introduction to abnormal child and adolescent psychology*. USA: Sage.

Weiss, G., & Hechtman, L. (1993). *Hyperactive children grown up* (2nd ed.). New York: Guilford Press.

Weiss, M.D., Craig, S.G., Davies, G., Schibuk, L., & Stein, M. (2015). New research on the complex interaction of sleep and ADHD. *Current Sleep Medicine Reports, 1*, 114–121.

Weiss, M.D. & Murray, C. (2003). Assessment and management of attention-deficit hyperactivity disorder in adults. *Canadian Medical Association Journal, 168*, 715–722.

Weiss, M.D., Wasdell, M.B., Bomben, M.M., Rea, K.J., & Freeman, R.D. (2006). Sleep hygiene and melatonin treatment for children and adolescents with ADHD and initial insomnia. *Journal of the American Academy of Child and Adolescent Psychiatry, 45*, 512–519.

Weissman, D.H., Roberts, K.C., Visscher, K.M., Woldorff, M.G. (2006). The neural bases of momentary lapses in attention. *Nature Neuroscience, 9*, 971–978.

Weisz, J.R., Chorpita, B.F., Palinkas, L.A., Schoenwalk, S.K., Miranda, J., Bearman, S.K., . . . Gibbons, R.D. (2012). Testing standard and modular designs for psychotherapy treating depression, anxiety and conduct problems in youth: A randomized effectiveness trial. *Archives of General Psychiatry, 69*, 274–282.

Weller, E.B., Weller, R.A., Fristad, M.A., Rooney, M.T., & Schecter, J. (2000). Children's interview for psychiatric syndromes (ChIPS). *American Academy of Child and Adolescent Psychiatry, 39*, 76–84.

Welsh, M.C., & Pennington, B.F. (1988). Assessing frontal lobe functioning in children: Views from developmental psychology. *Developmental Neuropsychology, 4*, 199–230.

Wender, E.H. (1986). The food-additive free diet in the treatment of behavior disorders: A review. *Developmental and Behavioral Pediatrics, 7*, 35–42.

Wender, P.H. (1971). *Minimal brain dysfunction in children.* New York: Wiley.

Wender, P.H. (1973). Some speculations concerning a possible biochemical basis of minimal brain dysfunction. *Annals of the New York Academy of Sciences, 205*, 18–28.

Wermter, A.K., Laucht, M., Schimmelmann, B.G., Banaschweski, T., Sonuga-Barke, E.J.S., Rietschel, M., & Becker, K. (2010). From nature versus nurture, via nature and nurture, to gene×environment interaction in mental disorders. *European Child & Adolescent Psychiatry, 19*, 199–210.

Wernicke, J.F., Faries, D., Girod, D., Brown, J., Gao, H., Kelsey, D., . . . Heiligenstein, J. (2003). Cardiovascular effects of atomoxetine in children, adolescents, and adults. *Drug Safety, 26*, 729–740.

Werry, J.S. (1997). Discussion of: "Attention-deficit hyperactivity disorder with bipolar disorder: A familial subtype?" *Journal of the American Academy of Child and Adolescent Psychiatry, 36*, 1388–1390.

Werry, J.S., & Sprague, R. (1970). Hyperactivity. In G. Costello (Ed.), *Symptoms of psychopathology* (pp. 397–417). New York: Wiley.

Weyandt, L.L., & DuPaul, G. (2006). ADHD in college students. *Journal of Attention Disorders, 10*, 9–19.

Weyandt, L.L., & DuPaul, G.J. (2013). *College students with ADHD: Current issues and future directions.* New York: Springer Science & Business Media.

Whalen, C.K., Jamner, L.D., Henker, B., Gehricke, J.G., & King, P.S. (2003). Is there a link between adolescent cigarette smoking and pharmacotherapy for ADHD? *Psychology of Addictive Behaviors, 17*, 332–335.

Whalen, C.K., Henker, B., Janner, L.D., Ishikawa, Sh. S., Floro, J.N., Swindle, R., . . . Johnston, J.A. (2006). Toward mapping daily challenges of living with ADHD: Maternal and child perspectives using electronic diaries. *Journal of Abnormal Child Psychology, 34*, 115–130.

White, S., Milne, E., Rosen, S., Hansen, P., Swettenham, J., Frith, U., & Ramus, F. (2006). The role of sensorimotor impairments in dyslexia: A multiple case study of dyslexic children. *Developmental Science, 9*, 237–226.

Wichstrom, L., Berg-Nielsen, T.S., Angold, A., Egger, H.L., Solheim, E., & Sveen, T.H. (2012). Prevalence of psychiatric disorders in preschoolers. *Journal of Child Psychology and Psychiatry, 53*, 695–705.

Wiersema, R., van der Meere, Roeyers, H., Van Coster, R., & Baeyens, D. (2006). Event rate and event-related potentials in ADHD. *Journal of Child Psychology and Psychiatry, 47*, 560–567.

Wigal, S.B., & Wigal, T.L. (2007). Special considerations in diagnosing and treating attention-deficit/hyperactivity disorder. *CNS Spectrums, 12*(S9), 1–16.

Wigal, T.I.M., Greenhill, L., Chuang, S., McGough, J., Vitiello, B., Skrobala, A., . . . Stehli, A. (2006). Safety and tolerability of methylphenidate in preschool children with ADHD. *Journal of the American Academy of Child and Adolescent Psychiatry, 45*, 1294–1303.

Wiggs, L., Montgomery, P., & Stores, G. (2005). Actigraphic and parent reports of sleep patterns and sleep disorders in children with attention deficit hyperactivity disorder. *Sleep, 28*, 1437–1445.

Wightman, R.M., & Robinson, D.L. (2002). Transient changes in mesolimbic dopamine and their association with 'reward'. *Journal of Neurochemistry, 82*, 721–735.

Wilens, T.E. (2004). Attention-deficit/hyperactivity disorder and the substance use disorders: The nature of the relationship, subtypes at risk, and treatment issues. *Psychiatric Clinics of North America, 27*, 283–301.

Wilens, T.E. (2009). ADHD with substance use disorders. In. T. Brown (Ed.) *ADHD Comorbidities. Handbook for ADHD complications in children and adults* (pp. 249–263). Washington, DC: American Psychiatric.

Wilens, T.E., Biederman, J., Brown, S., Monuteaux, M., Prince, J., & Spencer, T.J. (2002). Patterns of psychopathology and dysfunction in clinically referred preschoolers. *Journal of Developmental & Behavioral Pediatrics, 23*(Suppl.), S31-S36.

Wilens, T.E., Biederman, J., Faraone, S., Martelon, M.K., Westerberg, D., & Spencer, T.J. (2009). Presenting ADHD symptoms, subtypes and comorbid disorders in clinically referred adults with ADHD. *Journal of Clinical Psychiatry, 70*, 1557–1562.

Wilens, T. E., Faraone, S. V., Biederman, J., & Gunawardene, S. (2003). Does stimulant therapy of attention-deficit/hyperactivity disorder beget later substance abuse? A meta-analytic review of the literature. *Pediatrics*, *111*, 179–185.

Wilens, T. E., & Fusillo, S. (2007). When ADHD and substance use disorders inter-sect: Relationship and treatment implications. *Current Psychiatry Reports*, *9*, 408–414.

Wilens, T. E., Kwon, A., Tanguay, S., Chase, R., Moore, H., Faraone, S. V., & Biederman, J. (2005). Characteristics of adults with attention deficit hyperactivity disorder plus substance use disorder: The role of psychiatric comorbidity. *American Journal of Addictions*, *14*, 319–327.

Wilens, T. E., Nierenberg, A. A., Rostain, A., & Spencer, T. J. (2008). Adult attention-deficit hyperactivity disorder and the role of depression. *CNS Spectrums*, *13*, 2–17.

Wilens, T. E., Prince, J. B., Spencer, T., Van Patten, S. L., Doyle, R., Girard, K., . . . Biederman, J. (2003). An open trail of bupropion for the treatment of adults with attention-deficit/hyperactivity disorder and bipolar disorder. *Biological Psychiatry*, *54*, 9–16.

Wilens, T. E., Spencer, T. J., Biederman, J., Brown, S., Tanguay, S., Monuteaux, M. C., & Blake, C. (2002). A review of the pharmacotherapy of adults with attention-deficit/hyperactivity disorder. *Journal of Attentional Disorders*, *5*, 189–202.

Wilkes-Gillan, S., Bundy, A., Cordier, R., Lincoln, M., & Chen, Y. W. (2016). A randomised controlled trial of a play-based intervention to improve the social play skills of children with Attention Deficit Hyperactivity Disorder (ADHD). *PloS One*, *11*(8), e0160558.

Willcutt, E. G. (2006). The etiology of ADHD: Behavioral and molecular genetic approaches. In D. Barch (Ed.), *Cognitive and affective neuroscience of psychopathology*. New York: Oxford University Press.

Willcutt, E. G. (2012). The prevalence of DSM-IV attention-deficit/hyperactivity disorder: a meta-analytic review. *Neurotherapeutics*, *9*, 490–499.

Willcutt, E. G. (2015). Theories of ADHD. In R. A. Barkley (Ed.) *Attention-Deficit Hyperactivity Disorder* (4th ed., pp. 391–404). New York: Guilford Press.

Willcutt, E. G., Betjemann, R. S., McGrath, L. M., Chhabildas, N. A., Olson, R. K., DeFries, J. C., & Pennington, B. F. (2010). Etiology and neuropsychology of comorbidity between RD and ADHD: The case for multiple-deficit models. *Cortex*, *46*, 1345–1361.

Willcutt, E. G., Betjemann, R. S., Wadsworth, S. J., Samuelsson, S., Corley, R., DeFries, J. C., . . . Olson, R. K. (2007a). Preschool twin study of the relation between attention-deficit/hyperactivity disorder and prereading skills. *Reading and Writing*, *20*, 103–125.

Willcutt, E. G., Doyle, A. E., Nigg, J. T., Faraone S. V., & Pennington, B. F. (2005). Validity of the executive function theory of attention-deficit/hyperactivity disorder: A meta-analytic review. *Biological Psychiatry*, *57*, 1336–1346.

Willcutt, E. G., Nigg, J. T., Pennington, B. F., Solanto, M. V., Rohde, L. A., Tannock, R., . . . Lahey, B. B. (2012). Validity of DSM-IV attention deficit/hyperactivity disorder symptom dimensions and subtypes. *Journal of Abnormal Psychology*, *121*, 991–1010.

Willcutt, E. G., & Pennington, B. F. (2000). Psychiatric Comorbidity in children and adolescents with reading disability. *Journal of Child Psychology and Psychiatry*, *41*, 1039–1048.

Willcutt, E. G., Pennington, B. F., Boada, R., Ogline, J. S., Tunick, R. A., Chhabildas, N. A., & Olson, R. K. (2001). A comparison of the cognitive deficits in reading disability and attention-deficit/hyperactivity disorder. *Journal of Abnormal Psychology*, *110*, 157–172.

Willcutt, E. G., Pennington, B. F., Olson, R. K., Chhabildas, N., & Hulslander, J. (2005). Neuropsychological analyses of comorbidity between reading disability and attention deficit hyperactivity disorder: In search of the common deficit. *Developmental Neuropsychology*, *27*, 35–78.

Willcutt, E. G., Sonuga-Barke, E.J.S., Nigg, J. T., & Sergeant, J. A. (2008). Recent developments in neuropsychological models of childhood psychiatric disorders. In T. Banaschewski & L. A. Rhode (Eds.), *Biological child psychiatry. Recent trends and developments. Advances in biological psychiatry*. Basel: Karger.

Williams, D., Tijssen, M., van Bruggen, G., Bosch, A., Insola, A., Di Lazzaro, V., . . . Brown, P. (2002). Dopamine-dependent changes in the functional connectivity between basal ganglia and cerebral cortex in humans. *Brain*, *125*, 1558–1569.

Williams, J., & Dayan, P. (2005). Dopamine, learning, and impulsivity: A biological account of Attention-Deficit/Hyperactivity Disorder. *Journal of Child & Adolescent Psychopharmacology, 15*, 160–179.

Williams, N.M., Franke, B., Mick, E., Anney, R., Freitag, C., Gill, M., . . . Faraone, S.V. (2012). Gennome-wide analysis of copy number variants in attention deficit hyperactivity disorder: Confirms the role of rare variants and duplications at 15q13.3. *American Journal of Psychiatry, 169*, 195–204.

Williams, N.M., Zaharieva, I., Martin, A., Langley, K., Mantripragada, K., Fossdal, R., & Thapar, A. (2010). Rare chromosomal deletions and duplications in attention-deficit/hyperactivity disorder: A genome-wide analysis. *Lancet, 376*, 1401–1408.

Willis, T.J., & Lovaas, I. (1977). A behavioral approach to treating hyperactive children: The parent's role. In J.B. Millichap (Ed.), *Learning disabilities and related disorders* (pp. 119–140). Chicago: Yearbook Medical.

Willoughby, M.T., Curran, P.J., Costello, E.J., & Angold, A. (2000). Implications of early versus late onset of attention-deficit/hyperactivity disorder symptoms. *Journal of the American Academy of Child and Adolescent Psychiatry, 39*, 1512–1519.

Wilson, H.W., & Donenberg, G. (2004). Quality of parent communication about sex and its relationship to risky sexual behavior among youth in psychiatric care: A pilot study. *Journal of Child Psychology & Psychiatry, 45*, 387–395.

Wilson, P.H., & McKenzie, B.E. (1998). Information processing deficits associated with developmental coordination disorder: A meta-analysis of research findings. *Journal of Child Psychology and Psychiatry, 39*, 829–840.

Wingo, A.P., & Ghaemi, S.N., (2007). A systematic review of rates and diagnostic validity of comorbid adult attention-deficit/hyperactivity disorder and bipolar disorder. *Journal of Clinical Psychiatry, 68*, 1776–1784.

Winters, N.C., Collett, B.R., & Myers, K.M. (2005). Ten-year review of rating scales, VII: Scales assessing functional impairment. *Journal of the American Academy of Child and Adolescent Psychiatry, 44*, 309–338.

Wolff, P.H. (1969). The natural history of crying and other vocalizations in early infancy. In B.M. Foss (Ed.), *Determinants of infant behavior* (Vol. 4). London: Methuen.

Wolraich, M.L. (2003). *Vanderbilt ADHD Teacher Rating Scale (VADTRS) and the Vanderbilt ADHD Parent Rating Scale (VADPRS)*. Oklahoma City: University of Oklahoma Health Sciences Centre: Available online at: www.nichq.org.

Wolraich, M.L., & DuPaul, G.J. (2010). *ADHD diagnosis and management: A practical guide for the clinic and the classroom*. Baltimore: Brookes.

Wolraich, M.L., Feurer, I.D., Hannah, J.N., Baumgaertel, A., & Pinnock, T.Y. (1998). Obtaining systematic teacher reports of disruptive behavior disorders utilizing DSM-IV. *Journal of Abnormal Child Psychology, 26*, 141–152.

Wolraich, M., Lindgren, S.D., Stumbo, P.J., Stegink, L.D., Applebaum, M.I., & Kiritsy, M.C. (1994). Journal article reviews: Effects of diets high in sucrose or aspartame on the behavior and cognitive performance of children. *Developmental and Behavioral Pediatrics, 15*, 23–27.

Wood, J., Crager, J., Delap, C., & Heiskell, K. (2007). Beyond methylphenidate: Nonstimulant medications for youth with ADHD. *Journal of Attention Disorders, 11*, 341–350.

Wooltorton, E. (2005). Suicidal ideation among children taking atomoxetine (Strattera). *Canadian Medical Association Journal, 173*, 1447.

World Health Organization. (1978). *International classification of diseases* (9th ed.). Geneva: Author.

World Health Organization. (1992). *International classification of diseases* (10th ed.). Geneva: Author.

Wu, J., Xiao, H., Sun, H., Zou, L., & Zhu, L-Q. (2012). Role of dopamine receptors in ADHD: A systematic meta-analysis. *Molecular Neurobiology, 45*, 605–620.

Wymbs, B., Molina, B., Pelham, W., Cheong, J., Gnagy, E., Belendiuk, K., . . . Waschbusch, D. (2012). Risk of intimate partner violence among young adult males with childhood ADHD. *Journal of Attention Disorders, 16*, 373–383.

Xu, M., & Zhang, J. (2004). Molecular genetic probing of dopamine receptors in drug addiction. *Current Opinion in Drug Discovery & Development*, *7*, 703–708.

Yeh, M., & Weisz, J.R. (2001). Why are we here at the clinic? Parent-child (dis)agreement on referral problems at outpatient treatment entry. *Journal of Consulting and Clinical Psychology*, *69*, 1018–1025.

Yerys, B.E., Wallace, G.L., Sokoloff, J.L., Shook, D.A., James, J.D., & Kenworthy, L. (2009). Attention deficit/hyperactivity disorder symptoms moderate cognition and behavior in children with autism spectrum disorders. *Autism Research*, *2*, 322–333.

Yochman, A., Ornoy, A., & Parush, S. (2006). Co-occurrence of developmental delays among preschool children with attention-deficit—hyperactivity disorder.*Developmental Medicine & Child Neurology*, *48*(06), 483–488.

Yochman, A., Parush, S., & Ornoy, S. (2004). Responses of pre-school children with and without ADHD to sensory events in daily life. *American Journal of Occupational Therapy*, *58*, 294–302.

Yoder, P.J., & Warren, S.F. (1993). Can developmentally delayed children's language development be enhanced through prelinguistic intervention? In: A.P. Kaiser, D.B. Gray (Eds.), *Enhancing children's communication: Research foundations for intervention* (pp. 35–63). Baltimore: Brookes.

Yoon, S.Y.R., Jain, U., & Shapiro, C. (2012). Sleep in attention-deficit/hyperactivity disorder in children and adults: past, present, and future. *Sleep Medicine Reviews*, *16*, 371–388.

Yoshimasu, K., Barbaresi, W.J., Colligan, R.C., Killian, J.M., Voigt, R.G., Weaver A.L., & Katusic, S.K. (2011). Written-language disorder among children with and without ADHD in a population-based birth cohort. *Pediatrics*, *128*, e605–12.

Young, A.R., Beitchman, J.H., Johnson, C., Douglas, L., Atkinson, L., Escobar, M., & Wilson, B. (2002). Young adult academic outcomes in a longitudinal sample of early identified language impaired and control children. *Journal of Child Psychology and Psychiatry*, *43*, 635–645.

Young, S., & Amarasinghe, J.M. (2010). Practitioner review: Non-pharmacological treatments for ADHD: a lifespan approach. *Journal of Child Psychology and Psychiatry*, *51*, 116–133.

Young, S., Bramham, J., Gray, K., & Rose, E. (2008). The experience of receiving a diagnosis and treatment of ADHD in adulthood: A qualitative study of clinically referred patients using interpretative phenomenological analysis. *Journal of Attention Disorders*, *11*, 493–503.

Young, S.L., Taylor, M., & Lawrie, S.M. (2015). "First do no harm". A systematic review of the prevalence and management of antipsychotic adverse effects. *Journal of Psychopharmacology*, *29*, 353–362.

Youngstrom, E. A., Arnold, L.E., & Frazier, T.W. (2010). Bipolar and ADHD comorbidity: Both artifact and outgrowth of shared mechanisms. *Clinical Psychology*, *17*, 350–359.

Zachor, D.A., Roberts, A.W., Hodgens, J.B., Isaacs, J.S., & Merrick, J. (2006). Effects of long-term psychostimulant medication on growth of children with ADHD. *Research in Developmental Disabilities*, *27*, 162–174.

Zahn-Waxler, C. (2001). The development of empathy, guilt, and internalization of distress: Implications for gender differences in internalizing and externalizing problems. In R. Davidson (Ed.), *Anxiety, depression, and emotion: Wisconsin symposium on emotion* (Vol. I, pp. 222–265). New York: Oxford Press.

Zametkin, A.J., Nordahl, T.E., Gross, M., King, A. C., Semple, W.E., Rumsey, J., . . . Cohen, R.M. (1990). Cerebral glucose metabolism in adults with hyperactivity of childhood onset. *New England Journal of Medicine*, *323*, 1361–1366.

Zentall, S.S. (1985). A context for hyperactivity. In K.D. Gadow & I. Bialer (Eds.), *Advances in learning and behavioral disabilities* (Vol. 4, pp. 273–343). Greenwich, CT: JAI Press.

Zito, J.M., Safer, D.J., Dos Reis, S., Gardner, J.F., Boles, M., & Lynch, F. (2000). Trends in the prescribing of psychotropic medications in preschoolers. *Journal of the American Medical Association*, *283*, 1025–1030.

Zito, J. M., Safer, D.J., Dos Reis, S., Gardner, J.F., Magder, L., Soeken, K., . . . Riddle, M.A. (2003). Psychotropic practice patterns for youth: a 10-year perspective. *Archives of Pediatric and Adolescent Medicine*, *157*, 17–25.

Zucker, R.A. (2006a). Alcohol use and the alcohol use disorders: A developmental-biopsychosocial systems formulation covering the life course. In D. Cicchetti & D.J. Cohen (Eds.), *Developmental psychopathology* (2nd ed., pp. 620–656). New York: Wiley.
Zucker, R.A. (2006b). The developmental behavior genetics of drug involvement: Overview and comments. *Behavior Genetics*, *36*, 616–625.
Zucker, R.A., Donovan, J.E., Masten, A.S., Mattson, M.E., & Moss, H.B. (2008). Early developmental processes and the continuity of risk for underage drinking and problem drinking. *Pediatrics*, *121*(Suppl. 4), S252–S272.
Zuvekas, S.H., & Vitiello, B. (2012). Stimulant medication use in children: A 12-year perspective. *American Journal of Psychiatry*, *169*, 160–166.
Zwart, L.M., & Kallemyn, L.M. (2001). Peer-based coaching for college students with ADHD and learning disabilities. *Journal of Postsecondary Education and Disability*, *15*, 1–15.
Zwicker, J.G., Missiuna, C., & Boyd, L.A. (2009). Neural correlates of developmental coordination disorder: A review of hypotheses. *Journal of Child Neurology*, *24*, 1273–1281.
Zwirs, B.W., Burger, H., Buitelaar, J.K., & Schulpen, T.W. (2006). Ethnic differences in parental detection of externalizing disorders. *European Child and Adolescent Psychiatry*, *15*, 418–426.

Index

Preface

This book is a complete and comprehensive guide to ADHD, which is the most commonly diagnosed neurodevelopmental disorder and most researched area in child and adolescent mental health. On the one hand, thousands of empirical studies have been carried out on ADHD, and several theoretical models have been proposed for its understanding. Theoretical knowledge and research evidence are indispensable in order to guide clinical decisions. On the other hand, thousands of parents, teachers, and mental health professionals put enormous effort on a daily basis to address this disorder and provide the best care, education, and treatment to individuals with ADHD who struggle to keep up behaviorally, emotionally, and academically. Evidence-based interventions are needed in order to help them and provide generalizable, long-lasting results.

The decision to write this book was driven by our continuous critical conceptual thinking on the best way to help children and adolescents with ADHD and their families. Along the way, this need extended to adults with ADHD. This book represents an attempt to cover two needs: the first one for sound and solid theoretical knowledge based on up-to-date research, and the second one for effective interventions. It compiles information gathered from research, as well as clinical insights developed over our years of working with children, adolescents, and adults with ADHD and their families. First, a critical presentation of the current scientific knowledge regarding the nature, etiology, theories, diagnosis, and treatment of the disorder is attempted. To this end, we have effectuated a thorough and exhaustive bibliographic research whose results are critically presented from a clinical scientist's perspective. Second, we propose a new framework for the diagnosis and treatment of ADHD, the multilevel approach. This approach is based on cognitive-behavioral theory and the developmental paradigm in psychopathology and has evolved from our extensive research and clinical practice. We aim to bring together high-level research with the latest scholarship and apply them to practice.

We expect this book to reach several types of readership. We believe that we have written a monograph covering all aspects of ADHD (first part), followed by a professional guide (second and third parts) that presents the clinical implications of the theoretical first part in a comprehensive and systematic manner. Therefore, this book can be used primarily as a professional reference. It is addressed to clinicians and scholars of different disciplines who are faced with the task of assessment and management of ADHD in various settings: psychologists (clinical, developmental, and educational), psychiatrists, speech therapists, occupational therapists, clinical social workers, and special educators. We wanted to offer them a comprehensive book, providing research-based conceptualization of ADHD, structured description of assessment, and a complete and integrative early intervention and treatment program from infancy to adulthood. It is therefore our hope that this book plays an important role in clinical care and educational settings.

Secondarily, this book can be used as a niche textbook, written to be one of several books used in a course, or a book for reference usage. It can be mainly used in courses of both developmental psychopathology and special education either at an advanced undergraduate level or in master's programs.

Finally, this book could serve as a scientific source of information for highly motivated educators who need specialized knowledge in order to manage ADHD at both a behavioral and an educational level.

Although there are numerous excellent books on ADHD, this one provides a unique and innovative perspective. To the best of our knowledge, there is no published work with the key features that characterize this book, as follows.

First, the book provides a summary and critical synthesis of the most up-to-date scientific knowledge and research evidence about ADHD, based on nearly 2,000 scientific papers and books published until 2017, with special focus on the last decade. The substantial scientific literature we read spans that of developmental psychopathology, development psychology, social psychology, cognitive psychology, theories and empirical research on ADHD, neurobiology, and readings in the field of other disciplines.

Second, the book uses a developmental perspective and covers ADHD throughout the life span from infancy to adulthood. Therefore, it places ADHD within the context of developmental challenges.

Third, the presentation of comorbidities holds a central place in the first part of the book and uses an original approach. On the one hand, it covers the whole range of possible comorbidities. On the other hand, it offers interpretations regarding the nature of the relationship of ADHD with each one of the comorbid disorders. As it is clear that none of these comorbidities can be attributed to chance, the factors that may contribute to the co-occurrence of ADHD with each disorder are highlighted and their complex interplay is discussed.

Fourth, this book is written in such a way that each chapter leads harmoniously and smoothly to the next one, forming a coherent body of knowledge with a beginning and an end, contrasting with most edited books. Furthermore, the interconnection between theory and practice is highlighted throughout the book as we attempt to bridge the gap between research evidence and clinical application. To this purpose, we propose a complete and coherent approach to diagnosis and treatment, the multilevel approach, which relies on central aspects of the most influential theories of ADHD and combines elements of the most effective evidence-based treatments. Furthermore, it presents a number of innovations in an attempt to overcome several of the shortcomings of the existent interventions, and it focuses specifically on early identification and intervention, based on data relevant to brain neuroplasticity, epigenome, and other genetic and neurological research findings.

Fifth, this book is largely based on the long experience of the authors at both the theoretical and clinical levels. Both authors are professors of developmental psychopathology—researchers but, above all, active clinicians on a daily basis, over the last 25 years. This combination of profound theoretical knowledge and extant clinical experience can lead to a richer, deeper, and global understanding of the disorder. As a result, this book is illustrated with a variety of clinical examples that accompany descriptions, and it closes with seven clinical cases that combine the main theoretical and clinical ideas of the whole book in coherent stories.

In order to achieve the completion of this work, we were called upon to put forth an extensive amount of work, but it has been well worth it! The collaborative process of writing this book has been a source of immense pleasure and invaluable satisfaction. We have spent long hours of idea exchange, joint thinking, writing, and rewriting in order to clarify issues and provide a text that would satisfy the most demanding readership. It is time to share this unique experience of exploring the world of ADHD with you. We now invite you to join us, and welcome you all to the pages ahead.

Katerina Maniadaki & Efthymios Kakouros

Acknowledgments

This book represents the culmination of nearly 25 years of clinical practice with children and adolescents with ADHD and their families. Everything began with them and nothing could have happened without them. We feel honored that parents, now numbering several thousands, have entrusted their children's present and future to us. We are genuinely grateful for the opportunity to learn so many things from them. We cordially thank them.

We especially acknowledge all those teachers who have collaborated with us over the years toward a common goal: to provide support and assistance to children struggling to cope in mainstream unfriendly educational settings. We are thankful to them.

Our colleagues in the Psychological Center "ARSI" have also been a source of knowledge and support, a small part of which is condensed in the final chapter of this book. We gratefully acknowledge their contribution.

Mrs. Antonia Psarou, psychologist and English teacher, has translated one of our Greek books, *The Management of ADHD*, on which the current book is largely based. We are grateful for her enormous help.

Last but not least, our thanks are extended to our editors at Routledge Taylor & Francis for their continuous and genuine support in order to bring this work to fruition.

Finally, we wish to thank each other for a wonderful 20-year journey of scientific collaboration during which we shared the same passion toward deeply understanding developmental psychopathology, and constantly improving our services to children and families seeking our assistance. As long as this collaboration goes on, inspiration for future scientific destinations will not cease to exist.

Abbreviations

ADs	Anxiety Disorders
ADD	Attention Deficit Disorder
AMP	Amphetamine
APA	American Psychiatric Association
ASD	Autism Spectrum Disorder
ATX	Atomoxetine
BDs	Bipolar Disorders
BMI	Body Mass Index
CBT	Cognitive-Behavioral Therapy
CD	Conduct Disorder
CNS	Central Nervous System
CPs	Conduct Problems
DBT	Dialectical Behavior Therapy
DCD	Developmental Coordination Disorder
DDs	Depressive Disorders
DMDD	Disruptive Mood Dysregulation Disorder
EEG	Electroencephalograph
FDA	Federal Drug Administration
FEDs	Feeding and Eating Disorders
GD	Gambling Disorder
GWAS	Genome-Wide Association Study
ICD	International Classification of Diseases
ID	Intellectual Disability
IQ	Intelligence Quotient
MBD	Minimal Brain Damage
MD	Mathematics Disorder
MPH	Methylphenidate
MRI	Magnetic Resonance Imaging
NIMH	National Institute of Mental Health
NREM	Non-Rapid Eye Movement
OCD	Obsessive-Compulsive Disorder
ODD	Oppositional Defiant Disorder
RD	Reading Disorder
REM	Rapid Eye Movement
SLD	Specific Learning Disorder
SLPs	Speech and Language Problems
SUD	Substance Use Disorder
SWD	Sleep-Wake Disorders
TDs	Tic Disorders

Introduction

ADHD is a neurodevelopmental disorder with a great impact on the individual, the family, and the society throughout the life span. Individuals with ADHD experience continuing impairment in multiple domains of functioning. ADHD puts an individual at greater risk for developing a wide range of psychiatric disorders, experiencing academic failure, manifesting delinquent behavior, and having a disturbed social life, decreased success at work, and a lower quality of life in general. It is also associated with higher health care and societal costs. Moreover, nowadays it is well-known that ADHD is a chronic disorder that does not disappear by adolescence. As a consequence, referrals of adults for ADHD are increasing at a rapid pace.

During the last decade, scientific knowledge regarding etiology and treatment of ADHD has expanded. New theoretical models have been formulated, leading to a better understanding and conceptualization of the disorder. Medication and psychosocial interventions have moved forward as well. However, to date, there has been no treatment claiming to produce stable and long-lasting results, leading to the "normalization" of the pathophysiological substrate of the disorder.

In order to encompass all important aspects of ADHD, this book is structured in three parts. Part I provides the reader with all the basic information about ADHD, and aims to lead to the profound understanding of its multifaceted nature according to the latest research findings and the most prominent theoretical models. The overall focus is on providing information about the history of ADHD, its clinical presentation across the life span, epidemiology, theoretical models, and comorbidities, so that the readership can be acquainted with all aspects of ADHD.

Chapter 1 presents an overview of ADHD's history from 1750 until nowadays. In this chapter, the most important theories that have shaped the current conceptualization of the disorder are presented, along with the social circumstances that may have influenced them. The aim of this chapter is to help the reader comprehend the scientific trajectory of the disorder, and to clarify the impact of the scientific views of each era on the conceptualization and management of ADHD. The paramount question to be addressed by this chapter is the debate regarding ADHD being a 'real' disorder or a political/cultural construct, artificially constructed to serve financial purposes.

Chapter 2 begins with the clinical presentation of children with ADHD, and describes two clinical case vignettes, one of a boy and one of a girl, in order to highlight the primary and secondary symptoms of the disorder and illustrate the heterogeneity that characterizes this population. Afterward, the basic differences between a child with ADHD and a child with developmentally appropriate overactivity and impulsivity levels are reviewed. In addition, gender differences in ADHD are explored, and some distinctive features of ADHD in girls are mentioned, as girls with the disorder are estimated to be an understudied and underdiagnosed population. We review gender differences in clinical manifestation, comorbidity, and response to treatment. Finally, ADHD is considered in the context of the family.

Chapter 3 discusses the developmental course and outcome of ADHD across the life span, from infancy to adulthood. The differences in the manifestation of ADHD in each developmental stage are outlined and the primary difficulties of the individual over time are highlighted. Finally, we review risk and protective factors that appear to be associated with the functioning of individuals with ADHD and with outcomes.

Chapter 4 presents epidemiological data regarding the prevalence of ADHD worldwide. It also seeks to explain differences in prevalence depending on gender, nationality, and culture. Factors associated with the wide range of differences between studies are discussed, and methodology issues are revealed.

Chapter 5 focuses on the extensive presentation of the main scientific views regarding the etiology of ADHD, based on genetic, neuroimaging, neurophysiological, and neurochemical studies. For this purpose, it reviews the most important findings on genetic, neurobiological, and environmental factors that interact in complex and dynamic ways, and contribute to the phenotypic occurrence of the disorder. This chapter also seeks to explain the pathway through which all these factors lead to the behavioral manifestations of ADHD, and to reveal the importance of the early experiences of a genetically vulnerable child for the behavioral occurrence of the disorder.

Chapter 6 aims to present the most influential theories of ADHD, which attempt the integration of research findings in comprehensive models in order to conceptualize the disorder. Four theoretical models have been chosen for this purpose: the Executive Dysfunction theory, the Delay Aversion theory and the Dual Pathway model, the Cognitive-Energetic model, and the Dynamic Developmental theory. These four models enable the clinician to associate ADHD behaviors with their potential causes and design personalized interventions based on solid knowledge of both theoretical and research evidence.

Chapter 7 focuses on each of the 13 major comorbid disorders with ADHD. It reviews a number of basic issues regarding the definition and the concept of comorbidity in developmental psychopathology. This chapter has been influenced by the growing awareness of the interrelatedness of many psychiatric disorders. Specific attention has been given to the description of the nature of the relationship between ADHD and each one of the comorbid disorders described. In each section, epidemiological data on comorbidity are reviewed, the basic characteristics of each disorder according to DSM-5 are presented, and in-depth understanding of the reasons that underlie this comorbidity is attempted. In this way, we aim to capture the complex and heterogeneous nature of ADHD, and to elucidate epigenetic environmental factors and common neurological features that can lead to comorbidities. We also express and substantiate the tentative view that several of these disorders may be better considered within the ADHD spectrum as different manifestations of the disorder at different developmental stages.

Part II of the book provides a detailed review of the procedure through which a thorough clinical assessment can be conducted with children, adolescents, and adults, leading eventually to the diagnosis of ADHD. Clinicians are provided with the core concepts underlying diagnosis. A critical view of the current taxonomic systems is expressed.

Chapter 8 introduces the readers to the concepts and goals of assessment and diagnosis in the framework of developmental psychopathology. Moreover, several issues that merit consideration are presented regarding both the diagnostic criteria themselves and their use by clinicians. Finally, the basic principles and the diagnostic procedure within the multilevel approach, which is a clinical approach formulated and proposed by the authors, are described. This approach incorporates multiple assessment methods relying on several informants across multiple settings. It focuses not only on the child but on their family and school environment as well. Maladaptive cognitions are also assessed. Implicit in the discussion is the notion that diagnosis is a dynamic ongoing process that leads to the choice of the best intervention strategies, and continues throughout treatment.

Chapter 9 presents the DSM-5 diagnostic criteria for ADHD along with the shortcomings of the previous version, which led to their revision. The associated features supporting diagnosis of ADHD in DSM-5 are also highlighted. A summary of the changes made is given and their possible implications in clinical practice are discussed. This chapter also presents the diagnostic criteria of ADHD in ICD-10, and discusses the suggested revisions in the forthcoming ICD-11.

Chapter 10 synthesizes the major topics and reviews the essential components of a comprehensive diagnostic assessment for ADHD. Moreover, it recommends several methods that could be used for the diagnosis of ADHD as well as comorbid conditions. The issue of differential diagnosis is briefly summarized. General guidelines are given, and the importance of the impairment criterion is discussed. A wide range of measures for the diagnosis of ADHD is proposed and their properties are described. Particular attention is being paid to methods for establishing an understanding of the child's personality and their main strengths and weaknesses. We adopt a whole-child ecological approach rather than a symptom-focused viewpoint, and we argue in favor of an interdisciplinary approach. The basic principles of the feedback session to the family are delineated. Furthermore, the specificities of the diagnosis of ADHD in adults are extensively analyzed, and the most frequent difficulties and complications are discussed.

Part III of the book covers the treatment of ADHD, reviews available information until today, and presents the latest developments on this issue. In addition, it provides the clinician with a comprehensive guide to the implementation of a complete treatment program in children and adolescents, adopting a developmental perspective on the basis of the multilevel approach.

Chapter 11 provides an overview and presents issues concerning the current state of major treatments for ADHD. The information presented draws heavily on the growing literature on evidence-based treatments for this disorder. Pharmacotherapies, psychosocial interventions, combined treatments, and several complementary and alternative interventions are reviewed. We provide an update on empirical findings, and we offer a critical view regarding the efficacy of each one and a comparison of their strengths and limitations. Furthermore, we present novel treatment choices and future research directions. Finally, we review recent findings regarding the neuroplasticity of the developing brain in the framework of the bio-psycho-social model of ADHD, and we argue in favor of early intervention that may lead to its secondary prevention. The evolving literature on the efficacy of early intervention programs is summarized.

Chapter 12 presents the theoretical background and the clinical framework of the multilevel approach for the treatment of ADHD in children and adolescents. This approach offers multiple treatment modalities to deal with the multifaceted problems that this population experiences. It stems from cognitive-behavior theory, and it uses the developmental paradigm in psychopathology, but it also borrows principles from systemic approach and social psychology. It is argued that this approach has the potential to overcome many of the shortcomings of the existent interventions, and can lead to optimal long-term outcomes. In this chapter, the basic techniques that can be used for ADHD management are presented and a step-by-step approach regarding the clinical work with parents, teachers, and children, according to their developmental level, is suggested. The clinician is described as the coordinator of the implementation of the intervention at school, at home, and in the clinical setting. Guidelines and recommendations are delineated for parents and teachers as well. One of the novel contributions of this chapter is the intervention proposed for preschoolers, which has the potential to lead to the secondary prevention of the disorder. Treatment is described as a completely personalized procedure, tailored to each child's needs. In the framework of the multilevel approach, treatment is not conceptualized as addressing ADHD per se but each child's specific difficulties, as they emerge from the combination of the various factors that make the phenotype of ADHD unique for each child.

Chapter 13 presents the basic characteristics of contemporary interventions for ADHD in adults. Each one is evaluated on the basis of the most recent empirical evidence. Pharmacotherapies and cognitive-behavioral interventions are thoroughly reviewed. Our aim is to provide clinicians with the core principles supporting the implementation of Cognitive-Behavioral Therapy (CBT) in adults with ADHD. We also cover the research available relevant to coaching and specific interventions designed for college and university students with ADHD.

Chapter 14 presents six clinical cases by experienced clinicians. These cases have been chosen to represent the whole range of ADHD spectrum, across the two sexes, different developmental stages, and comorbid disorders. Our purpose is to illustrate the way of implementing the multilevel approach in the treatment of ADHD in children, adolescents, and adults. In this chapter, we aim to show the manner in which the basic principles of theories of ADHD are integrated in treatment and turned into practice to result in effective management of the disorder. Finally, we aim to point out that clinicians with complete, coherent, integrated, and multifaceted theoretical knowledge, relevant clinical experience, and certain personality characteristics may make the difference between effective and ineffective use of methods and strategies.

Part I

The Nature of ADHD

1 The History of ADHD

1.1 Introduction

Knowledge of the historical background of a disorder is essential for any scientist who wishes to study it in depth and gain a global understanding of the factors that have influenced the current conceptualization of the disorder. In clinical practice, history taking, which informs on the evolution of an individual, is indispensable for the establishment of a diagnosis. Similarly, knowledge on the evolution of scientific thought regarding a specific disorder over time is vital for better understanding the disorder.

The study of the appearance of ADHD as a diagnostic category contributes to a better comprehension of prevalent cognitions in different eras, on the basis of which different kinds of interventions have been proposed for its treatment. The importance of this study is also reinforced by the fact that over the course of a century of scientific research, many views of the pioneers in the investigation of the disorder reappear in the forefront and have a direct impact on the formulation of contemporary theories of ADHD.

Since the first reports on symptoms currently considered typical of ADHD, there has been ongoing controversy over its nosological structure and empirical validity (Insel, 2013). Various terms have been used to describe the range of symptoms that appear under the umbrella of the disorder. In some cases, this range was extended to include more symptoms while, in other cases, it was shortened on the grounds that some of the symptoms were considered as more relevant to other disorders. These changes in nomenclature were closely associated with the symptoms that were regarded as predominant in each era, as well as with the theories that prevailed regarding the etiology of the disorder.

1.2 The Historical Roots of ADHD: The Period Until 1900

Sporadic references to individuals with characteristics currently attributed to ADHD can be found even in ancient times. For instance, the Greek physician Galen often used to prescribe opium for restless, hyperactive children (Goodman & Gilman, 1975). Furthermore, relevant reports are also encountered in literature. For example, Shakespeare made reference to a malady of attention experienced by one of the characters of his play, *Henry VIII* (Barkley, 1996). In medical and broader scientific literature, however, the history of the disorder spans two and a half centuries.

For many years, the first scientific reports on symptoms of this disorder were accredited to the British physician George Still (1902) and, particularly, to the lectures he delivered at the beginning of the 20th century. These reports will be thoroughly discussed in Section 1.3.1.

Recently, however, Barkley and Peters (2012) discovered a medical textbook dated back to 1775, a century prior to Still's descriptions, under the authorship of the German physician

Melchior Adam Weikard. This discovery was made owing to a report by the Australian chemist John Gould, and is believed to be the first known scientific reference to ADHD symptoms. In this book, there was a chapter on "Attention Deficits" (*Attentio Volubilis*) as part of a wider section on "Sicknesses of the Spirit" (*Geisteskrankheiten*). This chapter described adults and children who were inattentive, hyperactive, and impulsive, also characterized by poor effort and low persistence. According to Barkley and Peters, most of Weikard's descriptions show considerable overlap with attention problems believed to exist in ADHD, as it is currently conceptualized in contemporary diagnostic manuals. Weikard implied that the aforementioned difficulties could result from poor upbringing or child-rearing, but he also accepted biological predisposition. For their treatment, he recommended sour milk, steel powder, horse riding, and even seclusion for severe cases.

The next known reference to symptoms associated with ADHD appears in a book of the Scottish physician Alexander Crichton, dealing with an inquiry into the nature of mental disorders (Crichton, 1798). This textbook included a chapter on 'attention disorders' and was discovered by Palmer and Finger (2001). In this book, Crichton claimed that attentional problems were a consequence of either hereditary factors or accidental diseases to which the person has been exposed. These diseases affect the nerves and the brain. Crichton argued that early education of children could serve to enhance attention, especially if tailored to individual variation in personal interests and motivation.

In 1809, John Haslam provided a case history of a 10-year-old boy who was indulged, mischievous, and uncontrollable. He was considered "the terror of the family" (p. 199). Three years later, the famous American physician Benjamin Rush (1962/1812) described a syndrome involving the inability to focus attention and speculated on the "defective organization in those parts of the body which are occupied by the moral faculties of the mind" (p. 339).

In the middle of the 19th century, the German pediatrician Heinrich Hoffman (1865) published a children's book of didactic poems based on his clinical observations, and described various psychological conditions among children (see Stewart, 1970). In this book, there is a poem titled *Fidgety Philip*, which seems to portray the case of a child with disruptive behavioral problems. Presently, this child could easily be diagnosed as having ADHD, Hyperactive/Impulsive Presentation, using DSM-5 criteria (Martinez-Badía & Martinez-Raga, 2015). There is also a second one, titled *Johnny-Head-in-Air*, which describes a boy who is constantly distracted by external stimuli and is highly inattentive over a broad range of activities. However, these descriptions cannot be acknowledged as medical descriptions. As Taylor (2011) notes, Hoffman "presents an interesting and influential picture of children as active agents, making their own lives, and as complex beings, in contrast to the age's contradictory and polarized views of children as angels or as savages" (p. 71). Fidgety Phil has nevertheless become a commonly used allegory for ADHD.

Representative excerpts of these two poems are cited below:

The story of Fidgety Philip

"Let me see if Philip can
Be a little gentleman;
Let me see if he is able
To sit still for once at table."
Thus spoke, in earnest tone,
The father to his son;
And the mother looked very grave
To see Philip so misbehave.

But Philip he did not mind
His father who was so kind.
He wriggled
And giggled,
And then, I declare,
Swung backward and forward
And tilted his chair,
Just like any rocking horse;—
"Philip! I am getting cross!"

The Story of Johnny Head-in-the-Air

As he trudged along to school,
It was always Johnny's rule
To be looking at the sky
And the clouds that floated by;
But what just before him lay,
In his way,
Johnny never thought about;
So that everyone cried out,
"Look at little Johnny there,
Little Johnny Head-in-Air!"

Running just in Johnny's way
Came a little dog one day;
Johnny's eyes were still astray
Up on high,
In the sky;
And he never heard them cry
"Johnny, mind, the dog is nigh!"
Bump!
Dump!
Down they fell, with such a thump,
Dog and Johnny in a lump!

Two years later, in 1867, the British psychiatrist Henry Maudsley published his book *The Physiology and Pathology of the Mind*, where he described the case of a child who manifested strong impulsivity and destructive behavior. In the United States, the American philosopher, psychologist, and physician William James (1890/1950) described a normal variant of character—which he called "explosive will"—in his textbook *Principles of Psychology*. This variant was characterized by difficulties similar to those observed in individuals with ADHD. In 1899, the Scottish psychiatrist Sir Thomas Clouston reported three cases of children who presented hyperexcitability, hypersensitiveness, mental explosiveness, and learning difficulties.

In France, the concept of ADHD has its roots in the description of children and adults with attention problems by Jean-Etienne Dominique Esquirol (1845). Furthermore, Désiré-Magloire Bourneville (1895) noted that some children and adolescents who were treated at the Bicêtre Hospital in Paris suffered from attention and behavioral problems. Finally, according to Bourneville (1895), one of his students, Charles Baker, provided in his 1892 thesis a clinical description of four children with symptoms of hyperactivity and impulsivity.

1.3 The Period 1900–1960

1.3.1 George Still's Descriptions and Viewpoints

In 1902, George Still, the founder of pediatrics in England, presented a series of three lectures to the Royal College of Physicians under the name *Goulstonian lectures.* The same year, these lectures were published in the *Lancet.* This is considered as the scientific starting point of the history of ADHD (Lange, Reichl, Lange, Tucha & Tucha, 2010). In this seminal paper, Still described 43 children who presented with severely impaired sustained attention and self-regulation. Most of these children were also hyperactive and impulsive. Many were often aggressive, defiant, resistant to discipline, and excessively emotional. They seemed to be entirely driven by emotion and not at all by intellect. They had difficulty controlling their behavior, and one of their main characteristics was their proneness to immediate gratification. This problem resulted in the children's inability to internalize rules and boundaries. Therefore, they seemed to be insensitive to punishment, even physical, and unable to learn from the consequences of their actions. Intellectual ability of this population varied from mental retardation to normal levels.

According to Still, these children displayed a major defect in "inhibitory volition" and "moral control." In fact, this view is consistent with James (1890), the prominent American philosopher, psychologist, and physician who supported that sustained attention constitutes an important part of the moral control of behavior. James indicated that "effort of the attention is the essential phenomenon of will." This view might have provided the philosophical foundation of current ADHD conceptualization (Martinez-Badía & Martinez-Raga, 2015). Still (1902) believed that moral control derives from a cognitive comparison between a person's action and an action that conforms to "the idea of the good of all" (p. 1008). Therefore, these children have great difficulty inhibiting a behavior that is inappropriate with reference to moral rules due to deficits in this cognitive mechanism of comparison that Still called "moral consciousness."

According to Barkley (1998a), this idea of comparing an individual action to a general rule involves two capacities: first, understanding the long-term consequences of one's actions and, second, keeping in mind information about oneself and one's actions along with information about the moral rule against which these actions must be compared. These views are closely associated with the contemporary concepts of self-awareness, working memory, and rule-governed behavior, which constitute central concepts in contemporary theories of ADHD.

Still considered that volition and moral control of behavior develop gradually in children, hence these mechanisms are less developed in younger children. He proposed the use of age-referenced criteria in order to determine if these mechanisms are adequately developed in a child. During this assessment, we should take into account individual differences in development, which are influenced by both environmental and inherent factors. Still was the first to suggest a developmental approach to the diagnosis of this disorder.

In Still's opinion, the causes of the disorder were biological. In accord with James's theory, he assumed that there is a causal relationship among inhibitory volition, moral control, and sustained attention and that their insufficient or deficient development is the result of the same underlying neurological impairment. He contended that the disorder could be either the result of hereditary predisposition or of prenatal or postnatal injury. In some cases, this behavior was secondary to an acute brain disease that had caused some type of brain dysfunction and was likely to improve upon recovery from the disease. However, this pattern of behavior could also lead to chronic impairment, thus raising the risk for manifestation of criminal acts during adulthood. Therefore, Still believed that any biological dysfunction that could cause significant brain damage might, in its milder form, lead to deficient development of moral control.

Although many of the children described by Still came from a chaotic family environment, others came from families who provided a seemingly proper upbringing. Still believed that children growing up in dysfunctional families should be exempt from the category of lack of moral control; he reserved it for children who displayed failure of moral control despite the positive impact of a favorable family environment (Barkley, 2015a).

Still's descriptions constitute a significant milestone in the conceptualization of the constellation of symptoms that are nowadays identified as ADHD. Although Still's work did not seem to have any influence at the time, several of his observations were corroborated 50 years later (Taylor, 2011). Still was the first to observe that in most cases the disorder occurred before 8 years of age, with a ratio of 3:1 in favor of males.

Additionally, he noted that conditions like alcoholism, criminality, and affective disorders were more commonly present among the biological relatives of these children. According to Still's reports, some of these children manifested Tic Disorders (TDs). This was perhaps the first time that comorbidity between ADHD and TDs had been recognized. The preceding observations were bolstered by numerous subsequent studies (see Chapter 7). Finally, Still's demonstration of a connection between brain damage and deviant behavior was highly influential. However, Still did not refer exclusively to children who would receive an ADHD diagnosis nowadays, but he included the full range of current externalizing disorders in his descriptions (Conners, 2000a).

Later, Tredgold (1908) and Pasamanick, Rogers, and Lilienfeld (1956) would return to Still's views, supporting that learning and behavioral problems may be caused by some form of mild undiagnosed brain damage. Both Still and Tredgold concluded that medications or alterations in the environment could lead to temporary improvement in the symptoms of the disorder. However, they considered them as developmentally static conditions. The need for special education environments for these children was specifically emphasized at the time.

Around the same time period, in Spain, the physician Rodriguez-Lafora (1917) described a group of children with psychopathic constitutions whom he called "the unstables." These children presented with intense inconstancy of attention, excessive activity, impulsive behavior, and the tendency to get carried away by their "adventurous temperament."

To conclude, the origins of many current notions about ADHD, Oppositional Defiant Disorder (ODD), Conduct Disorder (CD), and Specific Learning Disorder (SLD), diagnoses that would probably be given today to the children described by Still and Tredgold, can be traced in the relevant scientific views that developed at the beginning of the 20th century. However, it took the scientific community almost 70 years to return to some of them. One of the main reasons for this delay was the prevalence of the psychodynamic views, which emphasized the role of upbringing in the development of behavioral problems in children (Barkley, 2015a).

1.3.2 Minimal Brain Damage (MBD)

In 1917–1918, following a world outbreak of encephalitis epidemic, clinicians were called in to deal with the numerous cases of children who had survived but exhibited remarkably abnormal behavior with major cognitive and behavioral deficits (Cantwell, 1981; Kessler, 1980). These deficits included impaired attention, impulsivity, excessive motor activity, learning difficulties, impairment in cognitive functions (including memory), emotional instability, and antisocial behavior (Ebaugh, 1923; Stryker, 1925). This pattern of behavior, which has notable similarities with the current notion of ADHD, was clearly the result of brain damage, and was described as *postencephalitic behavior disorder*. The prognosis of these children was rather pessimistic. However, interventions developed on the basis of simple behavioral techniques reported significant improvement (Bender, 1942; Bond & Appel, 1931).

The assumption of a causal connection between brain damage and deviant behavior led researchers to study other potential causes of brain injury in children, including birth trauma (Shirley, 1939), epilepsy (Levin, 1938), and exposure to toxic substances (Byers & Lord, 1943). These conditions were associated with a great number of cognitive and behavioral impairments. Many of these children also had mental retardation and more severe behavioral problems compared to children diagnosed with ADHD today. During this era, however, researchers did not attempt to differentiate the impact of mental retardation, learning disabilities, or other neuropsychological disorders from the impact of behavioral problems on the maladjustment of these children (Barkley, 2015a).

Other researchers (Blau, 1936; Levin, 1938) noted a resemblance in behavior between hyperactive children and monkeys with a frontal lobe ablation. Some researchers relied on this similarity to postulate that severe hyperactivity in children might be the result of frontal lobe damage, even if this could not be demonstrated neurologically (Levin, 1938). Such evidence was, however, provided by subsequent studies (Chelune, Ferguson, Koon, & Dickey, 1986; Lou, Henriksen, & Bruhn, 1984; Lou, Henriksen, Bruhn, Borner, & Nielsen, 1989). On the other hand, milder forms of hyperactivity were attributed to psychological causes, such as negative child-rearing practices and pathogenic family structures.

The Second World War also gave many researchers the opportunity to study a vast number of people with head traumas, among other wounds. It was discovered that injury to any part of the brain often resulted in hyperactivity, restlessness, and overaroused behavior (Goldstein, 1942).

Under these circumstances, the theory of MBD was born (Strauss & Lehtinen, 1947). This diagnosis was given to children on the basis of their behavioral characteristics, even when neurological evidence of such damage was insufficient or even absent (Dolphin & Cruickshank, 1951). However, the most notable contribution of this approach to understanding psychopathology lies in the fact that it prompted researchers to realize that at least some disorders might be associated with organic causes.

As far as intervention is concerned, in their influential paper, Strauss and Lehtinen (1947) recommended alterations in the educational environment of these children and placement in smaller, better controlled classrooms, with limited distracting stimuli such as bright colors and pictures on the walls. As a result, strikingly austere classrooms were developed in the United States. Teachers were instructed to avoid jewelry or colorful clothes, and walls did not have any posters or pictures, despite the fact that scientific proof of the efficacy of this practice has never been provided (Zentall, 1985).

Around this time period (1937–1941), a series of clinical reports were published concerning medical treatment of child psychopathology in general and behavior disorders in particular (Bradley, 1937; Bradley & Bowen, 1940). In 1937, Charles Bradley, a Rhode Island psychiatrist, reported a positive effect of stimulant medication in 30 children with various behavior disorders and learning difficulties. This discovery was based on a chance finding while he was trying to treat headaches by using *Benzedrine* (D,L-amphetamine, the racemic form of amphetamine), which was "the most potent stimulant available at the time" (Gross, 1995). This medication did not treat the headaches but caused a striking improvement in behavior and school performance in some of the children, along with some decrease in motor activity. Subsequent studies (Laufer, Denhoff, & Solomons, 1957) confirmed a positive response to this kind of treatment in a high percentage of children. Since then, stimulant medications have become a first-line treatment for ADHD.

By the end of the 1950s, hyperactivity was interpreted as the result of some brain damage even when it was not evident or clearly specified through neurological examination. It came to be common practice to accept the behavior pattern alone as evidence of brain damage (Conners, 2015). Intervention for these children was restricted to stimulant medication and reduced stimulation in the educational setting.

In the 1950s, a shift in research interest regarding the etiological mechanisms underlying this disorder became apparent. A series of studies on possible neurological alterations were conducted. Specific credit should be given to Laufer and colleagues (1957), who claimed that *hyperkinetic impulse disorder*, their new appellation, was caused by defective filtering of external stimuli by the diencephalon, resulting in an excess of stimulation at the cerebral cortex. Their results suggested a functional disturbance rather than damage to the brain as the cause of this syndrome (Conners, 2000a). They also suggested that the disrupted interaction between infants and their parents probably precipitated the emotional problems that would arise later in life. Although this study was never replicated, it is considered to be a milestone in the history of the disorder because it was the first time that a specific neurological mechanism had been proposed as an etiological factor.

1.4 The Period 1961–1980

1.4.1 The Questioning of MBD

In the 1960s, many researchers seriously questioned the existence of a unitary syndrome of brain damage in children, and challenged the argument that every child displaying abnormal behavior, without further evidence, was to have MBD (Birch, 1964; Rapin, 1964). It should be pointed out that a diagnosis of brain damage was given only to 5% of the children who manifested pertinent behaviors (Rutter, 1977). According to some researchers (Rie & Rie, 1980; Rutter, 1977; 1982), the symptoms of this syndrome did not reveal strong correlation among them, as they did not have a clearly specified etiology and did not follow a similar course, nor did they lead to similar outcomes. Furthermore, MBD symptoms were so numerous that they virtually covered the whole spectrum of psychopathology.

In 1963, the Oxford International Study Group of Child Neurology (Bax & MacKeith, 1963) held a conference and stated that brain damage should not be inferred from problematic behavior signs alone. They therefore advocated a shift in terminology by replacing the term Minimal Brain Damage with *Minimal Brain Dysfunction* (Ross & Ross, 1976; Kessler, 1980). This term denoted a type of neurological dysfunction without serious brain damage, indicating that the organic substrate of the disorder was milder than it was believed.

In 1963, the official definition of Minimal Brain Dysfunction was formulated as follows (Clements, 1966a):

> The term minimal brain dysfunction refers to children of near average, average or above average general intelligence with certain learning or behavioral disabilities ranging from mild to severe, which are associated with deviations of function of the central nervous system. These deviations may manifest themselves by various combinations of impairment in perception, conceptualization, language, memory and control of attention, impulse or motor function.
>
> (pp. 9 f.)

This definition is certainly better, compared to the vague term of MBD. It clearly depicts the three main symptoms of inattention, impulsivity, and hyperactivity characterizing the current notion of ADHD (Lange et al., 2010). Furthermore, the importance that this approach attributed to neurological mechanisms over environmental ones was critical at that time because psychoanalytic theory held parents and the family environment responsible for these symptoms in children (Kessler, 1980; Taylor, 1983).

However, the concept of Minimal Brain Dysfunction syndrome started to gradually fade, as it was considered to be vague, ambiguous, and with no meaningful contribution to treatment (Kirk, 1963). In fact, in the 1970s, this term was definitively abandoned and replaced by more concrete and descriptive labels, such as *hyperactivity, learning disability*, and *dyslexia* (Barkley, 2015a). These labels referred to more homogeneous populations with specific cognitive and behavioral problems rather than to a speculative, unrecognizable neurological etiological mechanism. It is argued, however, that despite the criticisms of the Minimal Brain Dysfunction concept, once new brain imaging tools became available, researchers would eventually return to neurological explanations (Conners, 2015).

1.4.2 The Hyperactivity Syndrome and the Publication of DSM-I and DSM-II

As the concept of Minimal Brain Dysfunction began to fade, investigators shifted their attention to the symptom thought to be more typical of this disorder, namely that of hyperactivity. Therefore, the concept of hyperactivity syndrome was generated. Laufer, Denhoff, and Solomons (1957) are usually credited with the first behavioral description of this syndrome, which anticipated by more than three decades a very similar symptom list in DSM and its revisions.

However, this idea originated in the reports of the German physicians Franz Kramer and Hans Pollnow (1932) titled "On a Hyperkinetic Disease of Infancy." The most characteristic symptom of affected children was a marked motor restlessness, characterized by a conspicuous lack of purposefulness (Kramer & Pollnow, 1932, p. 1). In summary, Kramer and Pollnow established a concept of the hyperkinetic disease that closely resembles later concepts of ADHD.

Chess (1960) defined the hyperactive child as follows: "The hyperactive child is one who carries out activities at a higher than normal rate of speed than the average child, or who is constantly in motion, or both" (p. 2379). Chess decisively contributed to the advancement of scientific research through the views that he expounded in his classic article for a number of reasons: (a) he considered motor activity as the main feature of the disorder; (b) he emphasized the need for objective assessment of the symptoms beyond parents' and teachers' subjective reports; (c) he exonerated parents from blame for their children's symptoms; and (d) he separated the hyperactivity syndrome from the brain damage syndrome. Furthermore, in line with current recommendations, he proposed a multimodal treatment approach, incorporating parent counseling, behavior modification, psychotherapy, medication, and special education (Barkley, 2015a).

Other investigators during this era (Werry & Sprague, 1970) concurred with Chess's views and regarded hyperactivity as an extreme form of motor activity, albeit within the boundaries of "normal" child behavior. In fact, in contrast to Still's views, prognosis for these children was believed to be more benign (Laufer & Denhoff, 1957; Solomons, 1965). This suggestion fostered the widely held belief that ADHD concerns children exclusively and is outgrown by adolescence. This erroneous belief prevailed for many decades.

During the 1950s, formal diagnosis for ADHD evolved at a very slow pace. In the first edition of DSM (DSM-I), published by the American Psychiatric Association (APA, 1952), almost all childhood disorders were ignored. At the same time, the concept of "immaturity" was widely used in various studies of this period to explain children's hyperactive and impulsive behavior. DSM did not explicitly cite any references evidencing validity (or reliability) of these diagnostic categories, but it seems to have relied on four separate studies and reviews (Mallett, Natarajan, & Hoy, 2014).

It should be noted that DSM and its modification processes have been characterized by a long history of controversies and disputed diagnostic criteria (Kirk & Kutchins, 1992). Some years later, a definition of the concept of hyperactivity was incorporated in the official diagnostic nomenclature. In the second edition of DSM (DSM-II; APA, 1968), the syndrome appears by the name *Hyperkinetic Reaction of Childhood* and is described in a sentence: "The disorder is characterized by overactivity, restlessness, distractibility, and short attention span, especially in young children; the behavior usually diminishes by adolescence" (p. 50). This description reflected a shift in perspective during this era, given that a term associated with a potential etiological mechanism had changed into a descriptive term that was behavior-oriented and focused on the predominant symptom of the syndrome (Braswell & Bloomquist, 1991).

In the 1960s, the prevailing view in North America was that hyperactivity constitutes a common disorder, mainly caused by some kind of brain dysfunction, yet less severe than it was previously believed. The disorder was described as a homogeneous syndrome that is outgrown to a great degree by adolescence, with excessive motor activity being the predominant feature. Stimulant medication and psychotherapy, combined with reduced stimulation in classrooms, was the treatment of choice by the 1970s.

While these were the prevailing views in North America, hyperactivity was still regarded in Europe, and particularly in England, as a highly uncommon condition, often accompanied by other indicators of brain damage, including epilepsy, hemiplegia, and mental retardation, or by a history of brain injury or infection (Taylor, 1988). These contrasting views and interpretations of the disorder between North America and Europe led to dissimilar estimations in respect of the prevalence of the disorder, diagnostic criteria, and treatment by the 1980s (Rutter, 1989; Taylor, 1988).

1.4.3 From Hyperactivity to Attention Deficits

From 1970 to 1980, the number of studies on the hyperactivity syndrome rose dramatically. Over 2,000 studies were published by the end of the decade, and a series of scientific textbooks appeared. This syndrome became the subject of meticulous and systematic research. At the same time, both the scientific community and the public showed increased interest in it.

At the beginning of the decade, the defining features of the syndrome were broadened to encompass symptoms such as impulsivity, short attention span, distractibility, low frustration tolerance, and aggressiveness, which had been considered merely associated characteristics since then. Heterogeneity of the syndrome gradually became noticeable. Contrary to theories of the past 25 years, the prevailing view during this decade was that hyperactivity was not an indispensable symptom among individuals with brain damage. Children with brain damage did not manifest a homogeneous pattern of behavioral deficits. On the other hand, children with hyperactivity seldom had some clearly identified neurological damage (Rutter, 1989). As a result, in the 1970s, the predominant focus on hyperactivity was shifted toward the attention deficit of affected children.

Dykman, Ackerman, Clements, and Peters (1971), who were part of a remarkable group of researchers at the University of Arkansas, formulated MBD as a disorder of attention, emphasizing poor performance, increased reaction time, and decreased physiological reactivity. They suggested that *Specific Learning Disability* along with its associated behavioral characteristics constituted an *Attentional Deficit Syndrome*. Although others are often given credit for the reintroduction of attention in the discourse for ADHD, the Arkansas Group was actually the first to provide this insight (Conners, 2015). However, the two prevailing theories of this era were the ones of Wender and Douglas.

1.4.3.1 Wender's Theory

Wender (1971) maintained the term Minimal Brain Dysfunction, and investigated the main psychological characteristics of children with this syndrome in six domains: (a) motor behavior; (b) perceptual-cognitive functioning; (c) learning; (d) impulse-control; (e) interpersonal relations; and (f) emotion. Many of the characteristics reported by Still reappear in Wender's theory, and are summarized by Barkley (2015a) as follows.

Regarding motor behavior, Wender argued that the main characteristics of these children were hyperactivity and poor motor coordination. He also claimed that excessive speech, colic, and sleep disturbances were associated with the syndrome. He expressed the opinion that some hypoactive children who did not display hyperactivity but presented with attention problems should also receive the diagnosis of Minimal Brain Dysfunction, as they manifested many of the other characteristics related to the syndrome.

As far as the perceptual-cognitive domain is concerned, Wender described short attention span, daydreaming, distractibility, and poor organization of ideas as core elements. Furthermore, he observed that the majority of these children also had learning difficulties. Other grave difficulties were poor self-control, low frustration tolerance, inability to delay gratification, antisocial behavior, difficulties in planning, and poor sphincter control, leading to enuresis and encopresis.

In the domain of interpersonal relations, Wender highlighted the unresponsiveness of these children to social demands as a profound weakness. Stubbornness, excessive independence, disobedience, noncompliance, and imperviousness to discipline were some of the characteristics that denoted the effect of the disorder on interpersonal relations.

Finally, in the emotional domain, Wender described increased anger, aggressiveness, and temper outbursts, as well as dysphoria. Dysphoria involved anhedonia, low self-esteem, anxiety, and depression.

According to Wender's theory, children with Minimal Brain Dysfunction have difficulties in the aforementioned domains for the following reasons:

1. They fail to experience adequately both pleasure and pain. As a consequence, they display reduced sensitivity to reward and punishment, leading to decreased susceptibility to social norms.
2. They display high and poorly modulated level of activation, which is related to problems with auto-regulation of behavior. Furthermore, secondarily to their high level of activation, they have a short attention span, and are more easily distracted than other children.
3. They show excessive extraversion as a result of their poor modulated activation, leading to low frustration tolerance and frequent anger outbursts.

Wender's theory is of interest, yet leaves a lot of questions unanswered. Terms such as "activation" and "extraversion" are ambiguous and abstract. Moreover, the pathway leading from the causes of the syndrome, as thought by Wender, to its primary deficits and behavioral symptoms remains obscure. Furthermore, his theory does not seem to differentiate symptoms of ADHD from those of ODD. This is understandable because his observations were based on clinic-referred cases, and it is well-known that comorbidity among clinic-referred cases seems to be the rule rather than the exception (Gillberg, 2010).

1.4.3.2 Douglas's Theory

In an article based on her presidential address to the Canadian Psychological Association, Virginia Douglas (1972) claimed that the main cause of the impairment of hyperactive children is not hyperactivity per se but deficits in sustained attention and impulse control. These cognitive functions are responsible for organizing, recording, and processing information. She also noted that these are the areas that are positively affected by stimulant medications.

According to her model, which Douglas further elaborated and substantiated during the next decade (1980a,b; 1983), symptoms of ADHD are caused by deficits in four main areas: (a) organization and maintenance of attention and effort; (b) inhibition of impulsive responding; (c) modulation of arousal levels to meet situational demands; and (d) unusually strong tendency toward seeking immediate reinforcement.

Douglas's theory and subsequent studies by herself and her colleagues exerted substantial influence on scientific research and triggered a great number of studies with a focus on attention disorders. The significance of her theory principally lies in the fact that she defined many of the characteristics of children with ADHD using objective measures. Furthermore, she proved that hyperactive children can have "normal" or "near-normal" performance on tasks assessing sustained attention under conditions of continuous and immediate reinforcement, but their performance drastically decreases when reinforcement is partial (Freibergs & Douglas, 1969; Parry & Douglas, 1976). Along with Susan Campbell (1973), they showed that deficits in sustained attention can be present even in circumstances where significant distractions are absent.

Furthermore, Douglas's colleague, Gabrielle Weiss, based on her follow-up studies, demonstrated that although hyperactivity of these children often declined in adolescence, their problems with sustained attention and impulsivity persisted. These impairments were exposing them to greater risk for school failure and social maladjustment (Weiss & Hechtman, 1993). These findings were confirmed by studies of the following decade (Barkley, Fischer et al., 1990; Brown & Borden, 1986).

However, subsequent studies questioned the fact that attention deficits can account for the varied behavioral deficits manifested by children with ADHD (Prior & Sanson, 1986). Moreover, this theory could not explain the way in which the aforementioned deficits eventuate in the clinical manifestations of ADHD symptoms.

Nevertheless, Douglas's theory was so influential that seems to have played a pivotal role in the reconceptualization of the disorder in DSM-II (APA, 1980), where a new diagnostic label was adopted, and the disorder was renamed *Attention Deficit Disorder (ADD, with or without hyperactivity)*. In this edition, deficits in sustained attention and impulse control were officially recognized as more critical than hyperactivity in establishing a diagnosis.

This shift of focus from hyperactivity to impaired attention was important at the time because there was considerable evidence that (a) hyperactivity was not specific to this particular disorder but was a symptom of other psychiatric disorders as well (anxiety, mania, autism, etc.); (b) there was no clear delimitation between "normal" and "abnormal" levels of motor activity; (c) the term "activity" was actually a multidimensional construct; and (d) in many children hyperactivity was situational in nature (Barkley, 2015a). In fact, a decade thereafter, similar concerns were raised about the construct of attention.

1.4.4 Theories of Environmental Causes

During the 1970s, the impact of stimulant medication on school-aged hyperactive children was investigated more thoroughly, and its use spread at a rapid rate. Nonetheless, the inappropriate or excessive use of these drugs attracted the attention of the mass media in the United States, creating a scandal over the pharmacological treatment for ADHD. It was argued that ADHD was not a real disorder but a "myth" fostered in Western societies by intolerant teachers and parents in combination with an inadequate educational system (see Section 1.8.2; Anderson, 1996; Conrad, 1975; Schrag & Divoky, 1976). Meanwhile, it was claimed that hyperactivity in children was the consequence of environmental causes.

At the same time, healthy diet and the improvement of the quality of life via environmental manipulations was excessively emphasized. Within this framework, a new theory on ADHD emerged, suggesting that hyperactive behavior was the result of an allergic or toxic reaction to some food substances, such as color additives or preservatives (Feingold, 1975). It was claimed that poor diet could account for problematic behavior in half of the cases of hyperactive children. This view became so popular that parent groups were formed with the aim of promoting Feingold's diet. In California, legislation was proposed requiring that "harmful" foods be removed from school cafeterias. Eventually, the National Advisory Committee on Hyperkinesis and Food Additives (1980), which was convened for this purpose, concluded that there was no sufficient evidence to support Feingold's theory. Nevertheless, almost ten years had passed by before the popularity of this theory waned among the public.

Another theory concerning the role of the environment in the development of hyperactive behavior in children was proposed by Block (1977), who postulated that technological advancement and the hectic pace of cultural changes cause increased excitation and stimulation. These environmental factors interact with a predisposition in some children to produce the manifestation of hyperactive and impulsive behavior. Block presumed that the increasing incidence of hyperactivity in Western developed societies buttressed the validity of his theory.

Block's view was criticized by Ross & Ross (1982), who concluded that it was not sufficiently corroborated by research data. Undoubtedly, ADHD is closely related to social and cultural factors, not with reference to etiology but relatively to its impact on the individual's socialization process. In the context of an increasingly competitive world economy where particular emphasis is placed on self-control, completion of duties, and discipline, children who struggle to respond to these demands find themselves in a disadvantageous position to conform to educational and societal expectations. In a society or era with less intense pressures for achievement and performance, however, individuals with this disorder might not be confronted with these adaptation challenges (Hinshaw & Scheffler, 2014).

Another widespread theory suggested that hyperactivity is the result of inappropriate childrearing and ineffective parenting strategies (Barkley, 2015a). This perspective was adopted by both psychoanalysts and behaviorists, although each part viewed the etiological mechanisms involved differently. On the one hand, psychoanalysts (Bettelheim, 1973; Hartocollis, 1968) contended that parents who are intolerant of their infants' increased motor activity may react with extremely negative and demanding responses, giving rise to clinical levels of hyperactivity. On the other hand, behaviorists (Willis & Lovaas, 1977) highlighted that poor conditioning of children to stimulus control by commands and instructions leads to noncompliant and antisocial behavior.

Both psychoanalysts and behaviorists held mothers mainly responsible for the development of the disorder in children. This point of view found some support in studies reporting that negative mother-child interactions in preschool years are associated with the persistence of hyperactivity into subsequent developmental stages (Campbell, 1987). However, it is common knowledge that correlational data do not prove causal connections between the variables that are investigated. Therefore, these studies did not prove that negative interactions between parents and children *cause* hyperactivity but that they are *associated* with its persistence and course over time. In general, scientific research did not provide any support for theories on mothers' responsibility for the development of hyperactivity in children for reasons that are discussed in Section 5.4.2. Nevertheless, parenting practices still constitute a decisive factor for the outcome of the disorder.

1.5 The Period 1981–2000

1.5.1 The Publication of DSM-III and DSM-III-R

A radical change in the conceptualization of ADHD occurred in 1980, with the publication of the third edition of DSM (DSM-III; APA, 1980). This edition added a new perspective on the diagnosis of mental disorders. It came as a complete turnaround to the tradition of utilizing psychoanalytic reasoning for the explanation of symptoms and justification of diagnoses, and incorporated an approach based on a descriptive (symptom-based) multiaxial diagnosis (Kirk & Kutchins, 1992). DSM-III included a much broader definition for its previous hyperkinetic reaction of childhood, which was renamed ADD.

Three categories of symptoms were presented: attention deficit, impulsivity, and hyperactivity. The symptoms referring to attention deficit and impulsivity were described as the predominant characteristics of the syndrome. Hyperactivity was no longer an essential diagnostic criterion for the disorder as it occurred in two types, *with or without hyperactivity* (ADD+H/-H). In this respect, DSM-III departed from the International Classification of Diseases (ICD-9) by the World Health Organization (1978), which continued to focus on hyperactivity as indicator of the disorder.

Moreover, at that time there was not sufficient research data to justify this subtyping, and to point to the usefulness and validity of the second type. It was not evident if the attention deficit of the subtype of ADD-H was qualitatively similar to that of the subtype with hyperactivity, or if the two types had to be considered as two separate psychiatric disorders (Barkley, 2006b). Only during the next decade, research showed that children of these groups differed in many aspects. Children with ADD-H were described as being daydreaming and less aggressive, with more learning difficulties, and with fewer peer rejection experiences relative to children with ADD+H (Barkley, Grodzinsky, & DuPaul, 1992).

DSM-III did provide a landmark definition for ADD+H/-H. The new diagnostic criteria defined symptoms more explicitly, provided guidelines for a diagnosis based on age of onset and duration of symptoms, and considered the exclusion of other childhood psychiatric disorders to be a prerequisite for the diagnosis. It also energized the application of neuroscience techniques (Taylor & Sonuga-Barke, 2008). However, it continued to carry many of the overtones of the MBD that it replaced. According to Taylor (2011), the nature of this concept also led to limitations, among which he included (a) the assumption of "deficit"; (b) the focus on "attention" at the expense of other cognitive changes; (c) the lack of operational definitions of the behavioral criteria; (d) the "universal" approaches to psychological treatment; (e) the confounding of behavioral attention with cognitive function; and (f) the scarcity of work on the determinants of course, cultural effects on prevalence, or metacognitive and self-perception changes.

During the next years, the creation of subtypes of ADD on the basis of the presence or absence of hyperactivity continued to be discussed controversially (Barkley, 2006b). In order to further improve the diagnostic criteria, in particular with respect to empirical validation, the revision of the third edition of DSM (DSM-III-R; APA, 1987) removed the concept of two subtypes, incorporated once again hyperactivity into the name of the disorder, and renamed it *Attention Deficit-Hyperactivity Disorder* (ADHD).

The revisions suggested in DSM-III-R were fundamental for many reasons. The symptoms of inattention, impulsivity, and hyperactivity were collapsed into a single list of symptoms with a single cutoff score. This list included 14 criteria, four of which were new ones and nine of which had been reworded (Quay, 1999). Emphasis was placed on the necessity of assessing ADHD symptoms with reference to the child's mental age. The exclusion of affective disorders was no longer a prerequisite for the diagnosis of ADHD. In addition, there was now a criterion for onset before age 7 and a mild-to-severe rating scale. These changes were reportedly empirically derived through rating scales and a field trial (Conners, 2000a).

The most important revision, however, was the removal of the category "ADD-H" and its replacement by a residual category, named ***undifferentiated attention deficit disorder***. It was mentioned that this revision was made due to lack of empirical data to support the presence of this category. However, this change received sharp criticisms by authors claiming that ADHD with and without hyperactivity are very different disorders in children (Edelbrock et al., 1984; Lahey et al., 1987). Finally, ADHD was classified with two other behavioral disorders (ODD and CD) in a broader category named ***disruptive behavioral disorders***, owing to their frequent symptom overlap and comorbidity.

1.5.2 Toward the Publication of DSM-IV

In the latter half of the 1980s, some doubts arose as to the central role of a deficit in attention in ADHD. Findings of some studies conducted during this period failed to verify the existence of attention deficits in hyperactive children under all experimental conditions (van der Meere & Sergeant, 1988). Furthermore, given that attention involves the perception, filtering, and processing of information, researchers did not report deficits in these areas. To the contrary, some of them observed that motivational factors significantly affected the presence and degree of ADHD symptoms during an experiment (Glow & Glow, 1979; Rosenthal & Allen, 1978).

Following these observations, a new scientific view began to emerge that motivational factors and deficits in reinforcement mechanisms were of major importance (Barkley, 2006b). This perspective was grounded on the view that the main difficulty of children with ADHD lies in self-regulation and rule-governed behavior, as well as in impairments in their responses to behavioral consequences (Barkley, 1981a; Benninger, 1989; Quay, 1988). This reduced sensitivity to consequences was considered to be of neurological nature. This idea was not innovative. In fact, at the beginning of the century, Still (1902) discussed deficits in "inhibitory volition" (self-regulation) and "moral control of behavior" (rule-governed behavior). Comparable ideas had also been supported by Wender (1971) and the Australian scientists Glow and Glow (1979). In the 1980s, however, these views were more clearly expounded and substantiated by empirical data.

According to Barkley (2015a), this new scientific approach could explain the situational variability in ADHD symptoms. Moreover, it was congruent with neuroanatomical studies that indicated decreased activation of brain reward centers (Lou, Henriksen, & Bruhn, 1984), as well as with studies of the functions of dopamine pathways in regulating motivation (Benninger, 1989). More important, the theoretical framework of such a model could form a more solid basis for the development of effective treatments.

During the 1980s, plenty of new diagnostic tools for ADHD were developed. The development of direct behavioral observation measures was also of paramount importance, as they could be more objective and useful in assessment in conjunction with parent and teacher rating scales (Abikoff, Gittelman-Klein, & Klein, 1977).

During the 1990s, one of the most noteworthy developments was the occurrence of studies investigating the neurological and genetic basis of ADHD. In 1990, a landmark study was conducted at the National Institute of Mental Health (NIMH) (Zametkin et al., 1990). The researchers investigated brain metabolic activity in 25 adults with ADHD who also had children with ADHD. For the purposes of the study, they used Positron Emission Tomography (PET), an exquisitely sensitive technique for detecting various states of brain activity and their localization within the cerebral hemispheres.

At the same time, other researchers used Magnetic Resonance Imaging (MRI) to evaluate brain structures in children with ADHD (Hynd et al., 1990). Additionally, a series of studies, particularly those conducted by Biederman and colleagues (1995), clarified and verified the hereditary nature of ADHD. Finally, some researchers began to employ molecular genetic techniques to analyze DNA taken from children with ADHD and their family members, in order to identify genes that may be associated with the disorder (Blum, Cull, Braverman, & Comings, 1996; Comings et al., 1991). This field of research continues to be an intriguing and fruitful area of research endeavor.

1.5.3 The Publication of DSM-IV and DSM-IV-TR

The task force on DSM-IV began its work soon after the publication of DSM-III-R to comply with the expected publication of ICD-10 in 1993 (Frances, Pincus, Widiger, & Davis, 1989). Before the fourth edition of DSM was outlined in 1994, a number of more comprehensive and better structured field trials were conducted (Lahey et al., 1994). In general, the revisions made were more extensively and more systematically based on empirical data and provided better substantiation. Consequently, they rendered DSM-IV (APA, 1994) the main guide for the diagnosis of mental disorders, including ADHD, until it was superseded by its recent 5th revision (Beauchaine, Klein, Erickson, & Norris, 2013).

DSM-IV criteria for ADHD reveal several novelties, including being noticeably longer and more detailed. ADHD is classified with CD and ODD in the category *attention-deficit and disruptive behavior disorders* and in the broader category *disorders usually first diagnosed in infancy, childhood, or adolescence*. In order for a diagnosis to be established, some symptoms must be first presented prior to age 7, have persisted for at least six months, be inconsistent with the individual's developmental level, and cause clinically significant impairment in two or more settings.

The single list of symptoms that was given in DSM-III-R is replaced by two groups of criteria, and it is stated that in each of these groups six out of the nine criteria must be met. Consequently, the previously heterogeneous category of ADHD is subdivided into three subtypes: a predominantly inattentive type, a predominantly hyperactive-impulsive type, and a combined type with symptoms of both dimensions. By using this categorization, the concept of the two separate dimensions of attention deficit and hyperactivity-impulsivity was reverted (Conners, 2000a), and the possibility of a diagnosis of a purely inattentive form of the disorder was reintroduced (Barkley, 2006b). Therefore, the DSM-IV diagnostic criteria moved forward in order to correct the mistaken idea that ADHD represents a unipolar disorder (Goldstein & Goldstein, 1998).

In order to bridge the span between DSM-IV and DSM-5, a text revision was undertaken in 2000 (DSM-TR; APA, 2000). In this revision, there were no alterations in the diagnostic categories and their criteria, yet additional sections were included with supplementary information about diagnosis.

In the late 1990s, it was clear that ADHD was a disorder of neurological and genetic background and not the outcome of familial or social effects. Furthermore, it was widely argued among scientists that the primary feature differentiating ADHD from other mental and developmental disorders was behavioral disinhibition, leading to impaired self-regulation. In addition, it became evident that ADHD is a chronic disorder that does not subside in adolescence.

As far as treatment is concerned, multidimensional models were recommended, including medication, intervention for the child (training in self-control and social skills, behavior modification, etc.), and also parent and teacher training. Moreover, a significant longitudinal study was undertaken by the NIMH (MTA Cooperative Group, 1999), which focused on investigating the efficacy of various treatments. This study will be presented in depth in Section 11.4.

1.6 The Period 2000 to the Present

1.6.1 International Recognition of ADHD and the Publication of DSM-5

Since 2000, there has been an explosion in the scientific ADHD literature, which has doubled in 2013 alone. New candidate genes for the understanding of the disorder have been identified, apart from those that are involved in the regulation of dopamine and norepinephrine networks in the brain. These new genes are involved in brain cell growth and neuronal sprouting.

Moreover, comorbidity in ADHD and the impact of various types of comorbidity on the individual's functioning were further investigated. In this period, sustained-release stimulants were introduced as well as two new nonstimulants for treating ADHD. Finally, the need for a multidimensional approach of the disorder, combining various interventions, became imperative. New psychosocial methods were suggested for the treatment of the numerous difficulties experienced by these children in various domains of functioning.

In the 21st century, ADHD gained international recognition and acceptance as a chronic neurodevelopmental disorder. Scientific societies for ADHD were established, and conferences were held throughout the world with the aim of sharing and managing new knowledge. Associations were formed by parents of children with ADHD as well as by adults with the disorder with a view to raising awareness and supporting individuals with ADHD and their families.

One of the recent scientific developments is the latest revision of DSM, which started in 1999 and led to the publication of DSM-5 in May 2013 (APA, 2013).

In this latest revision of DSM, ADHD is classified in the supraordinate category of neurodevelopmental disorders and bears the same name without considerable changes in the diagnostic criteria. However, the three subtypes of ADHD are removed and are replaced by three different *presentations*, depending on the current symptom pattern of the disorder during assessment. The age-of-onset criterion also changes from 7 to 12, and the number of symptoms that are required for diagnosis in older adolescents and adults changes from six to five. Additionally, three severity specifiers of the disorder are added, and comorbidity with Autism Spectrum Disorder (ASD) is now accepted. All major changes in DSM-5 as well as the current diagnostic criteria for ADHD are presented in detail in Section 9.2.

1.6.2 Questioning the Existence of ADHD

1.6.2.1 ADHD as "an Invention of the Pharmaceutical Industry"

Although research regarding ADHD has led to the prevailing view that it is a chronic neurodevelopmental disorder with a neurophysiological and genetic background, its conceptualization remains a controversial issue. There is still ongoing and wide-ranging dispute over the nature of ADHD, which is considered ambiguous by a minority of the scientific community. In other words, there are scientists who question the fact that it is a real disorder. Some critics go as far as to completely reject the notion of ADHD, and call it "a scandalous fraud" (Breggin, 2007). This issue has been known as the *ADHD debate*.

The controversy over the true existence of ADHD arose in the 1970s and escalated in the 1990s, on the grounds of the fact that the diagnosis of ADHD and subsequent medical prescription for its treatment increased by almost five times in the United States (Olfson, Gameroff, Marcus, & Jensen, 2003). As a result, many claimed that ADHD was a fabrication that promoted the interests of the pharmaceutical industry (Timimi, 2002). In fact, it was reported that among the work group advisors of DSM-5, 78% received grants for their research from pharmaceutical companies (Cosgrove & Krimsky, 2012).

However, the fact that medication is excessively or wrongly prescribed in some cases does not negate the existence of ADHD but discloses malpractices followed by some clinicians (Timimi & Taylor, 2004). Excessive use of medication for the treatment of ADHD is a serious issue, but the existence of ADHD per se is an entirely different matter.

1.6.2.2 ADHD as "a Cultural or Political Construct"

Some authorities suggest that ADHD is a "cultural construct" that derives from poor and improper child-rearing and an inefficient education system (Hallahan & Kauffman, 2005; Timimi & Taylor, 2004). However, according to relevant meta-analyses, epidemiological studies that took place in less developed countries reported similar findings to those of the Western world, thus corroborating the cross-cultural validity of ADHD (Polanczyk, De Lima, Horta, Biederman, & Rohde, 2007; Rohde et al., 2005). Furthermore, as Taylor notes (Timimi & Taylor, 2004), if ADHD was a social construct based on the excessive demands made by society and school on children, then it would affect *all* the children and not just a part of them. Besides, it has been confirmed that ADHD is seen in all social classes. Undoubtedly, cultural factors can influence the degree to which ADHD is considered a problem by a certain society, but this does not challenge its existence.

Others dispute that ADHD is a real disorder, claiming that its etiology is not clearly defined, that diagnosis is based on subjective assessments and not on laboratory measures or medical examinations, and that the long-term effects of treatment are not well-established (Mayes, Bagwell, & Erkulwater, 2008; Visser & Jehan, 2009). Furman (2008), for instance, argues that because evidence for the genetic or neuroanatomical causes of ADHD is inconclusive, we cannot acknowledge it as a disorder. However, at this point, we should stress the fact that these limitations do not refer only to ADHD but to almost all the disorders within the realm of psychopathology. Thus, according to this line of reasoning, the whole psychopathology should be called into question as well.

Szasz (2001), who has been widely known for his anti-psychiatry stance, contends that ADHD has been created as a nosology by psychiatrists with the aim of putting a medical interpretation on antisocial features of people. In fact, he declares that ADHD "was invented and not discovered" (p. 212).

Another standpoint, within the framework of social constructivism, is that ADHD, like many other disorders, is part of governmental plans. More specifically, it is suggested that the subdivision of the population into an exponentially increasing number of categories renders manipulation of people's conduct a much simpler task (Tait, 2005). In other words, it is claimed that both diagnosis and treatment for ADHD are an attempt to exercise "social control for deviant behavior" (Conrad, 2007).

1.6.2.3 ADHD and the Hunter Versus Farmer Hypothesis

One of the most controversial theories about ADHD is the *hunter versus farmer* hypothesis, which was formulated by Thom Hartmann (1995) and is based on the theory of evolution.

The theory states that ADHD has its origins in an adaptation of members of hunter-gatherer societies in response to the rise of farming societies.

Hartmann argued that people with ADHD seem to have retained some of the characteristics that were necessary for survival at the time when people were hunter-gatherers. For example, impulsive behavior, increased motor activity, novelty seeking, rapid shift of attention, and frequent risk-taking were critical aspects of human behavior at a time when our ancestors struggled to survive in adverse and unforeseen environmental circumstances before the advent of agriculture. Hunters had to be aware of signs of their prey and of dangers. They were also supposed to make quick decisions. This was a stimulating experience, where impulsivity and hyperactivity, two symptoms of ADHD, seemed beneficial.

With the evolution to farming as a way of life, and later to industrialization, different characteristics became better adapted for survival. Farmers had to work linearly. For the farmer to have a successful crop, things had to happen at certain times, in a certain way, interspersed with a lot of waiting. To organize the crops in order to maximize their yield, farmers had to develop more linear thinking.

Over many years, most humans adapted to farming cultures. However, Hartmann speculates that people with ADHD retained some of the older hunter characteristics that are no longer conducive to successfully adapting to the environment. Therefore, the hunter versus farmer hypothesis proposes that the high frequency of ADHD in the contemporary world represents otherwise normal behavioral patterns that become maladaptive in such evolutionarily novel environments as the formal school classroom.

There are some sporadic research findings consistent with Hartmann's theory (Arcos-Burgos & Acosta, 2007). For example, a genetic variation associated with ADHD was found with increased frequency among nomadic populations and populations that migrated often (Chen, Burton, Greenberger, & Dmitrieva, 1999). According to these data, it appears that ADHD characteristics might offer an advantage to certain cultural groups.

Evidence for this theory is also provided by the study of Eisenberg, Campbell, Gray, and Sorenson (2008) on an isolated tribe in Northern Kenya, the Ariaal. About 40 years ago, this tribe was divided. Some members, who had been leading a nomadic lifestyle until then, permanently settled in a place and adopted an agricultural lifestyle. The two groups of the tribe were tested for carrying the DRD4/7R allele, which is associated with ADHD. It was revealed that members of the group who maintained a nomadic lifestyle and had this allele were generally healthier than the members who did not have it. On the contrary, the presence of this allele in members who had turned to an agricultural lifestyle produced an adverse effect, as the members who carried it exhibited worse outcomes. According to this study, the ADHD associated allele of the DRD4 gene promotes behavioral/psychological traits that are helpful in some social and ecological contexts but detrimental in others.

Building on this theory, Jensen and colleagues (1997) regard ADHD as a "disorder of adaptation" and suggest that many emotional and behavioral responses may not just be "symptoms" of a disorder, but they might reflect adaptive responses of an individual to environmental demands. The same view is adopted by Gallagher, who suggests that ADHD constitutes an evolutionary mechanism that enhances creativity and inventiveness of the population. Therefore, it does not constitute a neurological "defect" but rather a variant temperament that has a detrimental impact on the individual due to a lack of social tolerance for individual differences (http://borntoexplore.org).

To conclude, these evolutionary theories do not offer any substantial evidence in order to become widely accepted. They provide, however, an interesting theoretical framework for understanding the way in which the interaction between the individual's genetic characteristics and environmental demands or expectations can lead to adaptation or dysfunction.

1.7 Conclusion

As Thapar, Langley, & Muñoz-Solomando (2013) note, when issues with major social, clinical, and practical implications are investigated, including ADHD, it is important to start with a hypothesis concerning the nature of the problem. However, it is of equal importance for researchers "not to fall in love" with their hypotheses but to empirically test and substantiate them. Therefore, it is crucial that mental health practitioners remain informed about the latest scientific developments, refresh and update their knowledge, and ensure that they provide the best possible services to people who seek their help. As Thapar, Cooper Eyre, and Langley (2013) state, "we might not like genetics but when evidence emerges we need to understand and appraise it so that we are able to communicate and clarify findings to families who ask" (p. 221).

First, some of the views that have been discussed so far and question the existence of ADHD imply a false dichotomy between social/nonbiological and biological interpretations. However, these two aspects cannot be separated (Rutter, 2007). Psychosocial adversity can lead to biological changes, affecting the human brain (Hackman, Farah, & Meaney, 2010). Such changes can in turn result in psychosocial adversity or exacerbate the psychosocial stressors an individual is met with. Most mental health problems—as well as normal patterns of behavior—constitute a complex amalgam of inherited and environmental factors that coact and interact in a dynamic way (Thapar, Harold, Rice, Langley, & O'Donovan, 2007). Causality in these cases is circular or cyclical, not purely linear. Besides, most contemporary theories for the causality of ADHD have moved away from one-dimensional biological models and emphasize the role of early experiences in shaping the developing brain (see Section 5.5).

Second, the debate on whether ADHD should be recognized as a true disorder or not is primarily focused on medication, ignoring other treatments. At this point, a methodological error is committed. The acceptance of a disorder should be differentiated from the nature of interventions that clinical scientists, families, social policy, and the education system chose to employ for its management. The use of medication in children undoubtedly arouses many reservations and concerns. Overdiagnosis of the disorder on the grounds of financial interests and concomitant excessive prescription for medication is unethical and strongly disapproved. However, the way in which scientific findings are used is a different matter from the findings themselves. By the end of this book, we aim to reveal that available research data definitively prove the existence of ADHD as a true neurodevelopmental disorder.

Third, respect for individual differences is a basic and fundamental principle among mental health professionals. On the basis of this principle, children have the right to be given the opportunity to develop their personal skills, follow their inclinations, and cultivate their talents. Such an endeavor is futile if children face difficulties that prevent them from fully developing their personality, acquiring knowledge, and effectively applying it. Respect for individual differences does not mean eliminating differences and ignoring difficulties in the name of a philosophical approach that promotes the children's right to develop freely and follow their own developmental rate. Respect for differences means acknowledging them, exploiting strengths, and addressing weaknesses.

According to our clinical experience, many parents who have difficulty managing their emotions and accepting the diagnosis of ADHD for their child try to deny the existence of the disorder, using the following common arguments:

"Isn't a child allowed to be naughty or overactive?"
"Why should a child always obey rules?"
"Is it bad for a child to be spontaneous?"
"Doesn't everyone get distracted from time to time?"
"No child likes school."

And the most impressive: "If impulsivity, hyperactivity, and inattention represent a disorder, then all children have ADHD."

In our opinion, such viewpoints questioning ADHD provide a solid alibi for parents in order not to admit that their child faces a problem because this problem might undermine their own emotional integrity and dignity. We believe that the aforementioned generalizations and dogmatic views are not realistic. Through the pages of this book, we hope to give satisfactory and substantiated answers to each one of these questions and, at the same time, disprove oversimplistic and superficial views, including the one that "then all children have ADHD."

We strongly believe that individuals who simply manifest symptoms of the disorder but can easily adapt to their environment without facing any impairment in their daily functioning should not receive the diagnosis of ADHD. In cases, however, where ADHD symptomatology seriously limits daily functioning and creates difficulties in people's responses to environmental demands, the establishment of a diagnosis and the provision of evidence-based treatment is an obligation, not a choice. Lack of support to these individuals may have devastating effects on their development and progress. In addition, we should be aware that as societal expectations and demands increase, the number of people that fail to respond to them will increase as well.

In the end, regardless of whether critics of the notion of ADHD are right or wrong, what really matters is whether such attitudes help these people—who struggle and suffer—to cope with their difficulties. We know for certain that in cases where the presence of ADHD is recognized early and the opportunity for treatment is offered, the benefit that is gained is enormous. Besides, a diagnosis does not define the person. Diagnosis simply serves as a tool that offers a framework for evaluating evidence, applying it, and communicating to people who seek help for themselves or for their children.

If we take into account the professional backgrounds of the supporters of the dispute of ADHD, we will better understand their perspective, which guides the way they approach this issue. Gordon Tait is a sociologist. Thomas Szasz is a psychoanalyst. Thom Hartmann is a radio host, author, and entrepreneur. We believe that it is easy to make a philosophical analysis from the perspective of a sociologist, an author, and even a psychoanalyst concerning the existence of ADHD and the devastating role that demanding societies and bad education systems play in children's learning and behavior. However, people who have not closely experienced the agony that parents of children with ADHD go through can perpetually contemplate whether ADHD is a real or a fictitious disorder.

Mary's daughter is a pupil in the first grade of elementary school, who spends endless hours every afternoon doing her homework. Peter's son has no friends because he teases and hits other children in his attempt to play with them and attract attention. Helen is summoned to school every week to receive complaints concerning her daughter's disruptive behavior both by her teacher and by other mothers, who hold her responsible. David's son dropped out of school at age 15, and is frequently taken to the juvenile detention center. Emily's 30-year-old daughter is not able to maintain a relationship or keep a job. All of us, who have met Mary, Peter, Helen, David, Emily, and their children, do not wonder whether ADHD exists or not because *we know* it does, as we are confronted with it on a daily basis and recognize its implications.

In addition, as clinicians, we are often the receptors of the expression of gratitude by people who received effective treatment as children following the diagnosis of ADHD. Many of these grown-up children have experienced important positive outcomes in their lives, including studying at university, pursuing a successful career, or becoming good parents. At these moments, we feel grateful in our turn that science has progressed to such an extent that we can now *recognize* and *diagnose* ADHD and intervene early enough in order to *prevent* its adverse effects on functioning and quality of life of people with the disorder.

2 Clinical Presentation of Children With ADHD

2.1 Heterogeneity in the Phenotype of Children With ADHD

ADHD is mainly characterized by a persistent and developmentally inappropriate pattern of three continuum symptom dimensions of inattention, impulsivity, and hyperactivity. Due to these core deficits, individuals with ADHD display impairments in concentration and sustained attention, along with difficulties with impulse control and rule-governed behavior (Barkley, 1990). These primary symptoms of ADHD are mainly displayed during structured activities that require mental effort, have a repetitive pattern, do not stimulate the child's interest, and are not accompanied by strong intrinsic or extrinsic motivation.

Recent theoretical formulations have emphasized that ADHD is not a unitary construct but is characterized by substantial clinical heterogeneity, because each child's presentation is unique (Castellanos, Sonuga-Barke, Milham, & Tannock, 2006; Nigg, 2006). The way in which symptoms are manifested is influenced by a wide range of factors, such as child's sex and age, predominant symptoms, parental responses, and situational factors. Moreover, it is widely acknowledged that ADHD is a multifactorial disorder with complex etiology. Therefore, its phenotype is also defined by a combination of genetic, environmental, neuropsychological, and other variables. In light of this evidence, we are in favor of the view that ADHD should be treated as a spectrum disorder (Swanson, Wigal, Lakes, & Volkow, 2011).

Furthermore, depending on the severity of the core symptoms of inattention or impulsivity-hyperactivity, this phenotype might diversify even further. To illustrate the heterogeneity in the phenotype of ADHD, two clinical case vignettes, the first describing 8-year-old John with ADHD, combined presentation, and the second referring to 5-year-old Helen, with ADHD, predominantly inattentive presentation, will be presented below.

2.2 Illustrative Cases

2.2.1 The Case of John, 8 Years

John is a lively child who always rushes around without getting tired. He often gives the impression that he is under considerable pressure in situations when he has to remain still. At home, he seems restless, as he is jumping, running, and climbing all the time. Sometimes, he does dangerous stunts without getting scared. He finds it particularly difficult to remain seated for a long time, for instance during meals or study time. John is clumsy, stumbles and falls frequently, and bumps into objects and people while walking. As a result, he often causes damage and is highly prone to accidents. In general, John displays intense and vigorous motor activity in situations in which it is inappropriate to do so.

John is an extremely impatient and impulsive child. He has difficulty waiting his turn in games, and he often rushes into activities before full instructions are given. Moreover, he often blurts out answers before questions are completed. He is stubborn and cannot tolerate delay in the fulfillment of his desires. He often interrupts others' discussions and speaks without permission in class. He often acts carelessly. At home, he gets easily bored of his toys and he shifts from one activity to another without completing any of them.

John often gives the impression that he does not listen when he is spoken to. He has difficulty remaining focused on a task and frequently shifts his attention from one task to another. He often fails to finish his work, particularly when it requires mental effort and sustained attention, or when it is not highly intriguing. He usually repeats the same mistakes, even though he can tell the corresponding rules by heart. His parents feel puzzled by John's difficulty in sustained attention as far as homework is concerned, as opposed to his high level of concentration when he is engaged in electronic games or when anticipating a reward. In addition, he is constantly losing things. His mother complains that he never tidies up his room on his own initiative, and she describes him as "messy and disorganized."

John is often rude, abrupt, disobedient, and unruly. He usually talks back to his parents. He tells lies and sometimes becomes aggressive toward other children. He often does "stupid" things and his parents say that he is "immature." Other children avoid playing with him because he does not always follow game rules, cheats, and gets angry when he loses. John expresses his feelings with great intensity and it is difficult for him to calm down. His mother often avoids taking him to social events with her in order to prevent his unpredictable reactions, as the child is constantly in a "state of alarm." Furthermore, he seems indifferent to the consequences of his behavior on others or even on himself. As a result, he mainly acts according to his impulses. Past experiences do not seem to influence his future behavior. John does not seem to learn from his mistakes, even when he has been repeatedly punished for them.

John has learning difficulties and is hard to motivate. However, he manages to retain some information during the lesson and he responds to the demands of his class to a satisfactory degree. In fact, his teacher is often impressed by his clever answers and she describes him as an "intelligent but lazy child." At home, study time is exhausting both for John and his mother. John refuses to sit at his desk. When he is eventually convinced to do so, he is interrupting all the time by asking irrelevant questions, or walking across the room. Therefore, study time is usually a time-consuming process. His mother sometimes feels that John is fooling her and that he is trying to "get on her nerves." What she finds particularly annoying is that he barely tries to be careful and behave properly and that he actually gives the impression that he does this on purpose. As a result, John gets constantly scolded and punished.

Overall, John is a very hard-to-manage child. He is always at the center of attention, as his behavior is defiant and highly annoying to others. On the one hand, everybody complains about him. On the other hand, John feels that he is treated unfairly, as everybody reprimands him. John is a child who causes trouble to the people around him and at the same time causes trouble to himself as well. He is a child with low self-esteem, who often experiences negative criticism and rejection both at home and at school.

We will now describe more clearly this child's presentation and performance at school, according to his teacher's description.

John is a restless child who rarely stays in the same place for a long time. He is constantly standing up, walking across the classroom, teasing his classmates, and disrupting the lesson. In addition, he drops his books and pencils all the time or he asks to go to the toilet very often, thus upsetting the class. In the classroom, he taps his hands on the desk or makes other kinds of noises. Even when he is forced to sit down, for example when performing an activity, he squirms in his seat, fidgets with his hands or feet, and appears to be feeling extremely uncomfortable. Oftentimes, he destroys objects that may either belong to him or to his classmates. Around his desk there are torn notebooks, books, pencils, and the like all over the place.

He has a short attention span and he is easily distracted. When he succeeds in a task or a test, he gets overly excited. However, when activities require persistence and sustained interest, particularly written ones, John gets frustrated and quits after a while. In general, he has trouble getting started and persevering in tasks or projects.

Sometimes, John seems not to listen to what he is told. He gives the impression that he is lazy. Other times, he may act as a bully toward his classmates. He is easily aroused emotionally, and he moves to the extreme of his emotions with great speed and intensity. He is irritable, and has intense outbursts of anger. He hardly complies. He often quits team games because he argues with his classmates, mainly when he loses.

John has difficulty with reading, especially when he is not familiar with the text. He also has difficulty with auditory discrimination. Sometimes, he confuses small words such as *at* and *to*, or *does* and *goes*. He also makes word reversals such as *tip* for *pit*. Inversions such as *m* and *w*, *b* and *d*, or *u* and *n*, as well as transpositions such as *felt* and *left*, are frequent in both his reading and writing. He often leaves words incomplete while writing. His spelling is poor and he may spell the same word differently on the same page. He does not pay attention to details, and he often makes careless mistakes. He has particular difficulty with language exercises, which he usually completes only when the teacher explains to him what to do step-by-step.

2.2.2 *The Case of Helen, 5 Years*

Helen is a quiet 5-year-old girl, attending nursery school. Her parents were never concerned with her behavior because Helen never caused trouble either at home or in the preschool setting, which she attended when she was 3 years old.

Helen had a delayed speech onset. She said her first words when she was 20 months old, and formed her first complete sentences when she was 3 years old. Her parents did not worry about this delay, as Helen seemed to fully understand speech, carried out orders, and seemed a "smart child," according to her family. Besides, both her pediatrician and her nursery teacher told Helen's parents not to worry because many children have a delayed speech onset. They also said that every child has their own rate and that, once they begin talking, they continue to develop speech very rapidly.

At age 4 years, Helen was able to communicate verbally with ease. However, she could not pronounce clearly all the consonants (particularly /r/, /s/, /z/, /x/, /ts/, /tz/, and /θ/). Moreover, she substituted some phonemes with others (such as /r/ with /l/, /f/ with /θ/, /v/ with /ð/), and often omitted consonants in words with consonant clusters (*boken* for *broken* or *poon* for *spoon*). Helen omitted syllables in multisyllable words (e.g., *nana* for *banana*), and she often reversed syllables in words. As a result, she frequently mispronounced frequently occurring words.

Now, at age 5 years, her articulation has improved, but her phonemic awareness remains impaired so that her speech is not entirely clear yet. Therefore, she avoids speaking much at school and to people with whom she is not very familiar. At home, however, she speaks ceaselessly. Her parents describe her as a talkative child, or to be more specific, "a chatterbox." They complain that she often becomes annoying, as she is constantly interrupting their conversations, and always wants to be at the center of attention. In nursery school, her teacher notes that Helen does not participate willingly in verbal activities and, when she is forced to do so, she gives one-word answers, and her speech is deprived of the complexity expected for her developmental level.

Although Helen walked normally at age 12 months, her parents describe her as a "clumsy" child. It took her a long time to learn how to pedal a bike, and she finds it difficult to throw and catch a ball. She seems unable to learn how to hopscotch and skip. She frequently falls due to her poor balance. Her parents enrolled her in ballet classes, but she does not seem to do well. Overall, she avoids activities that require coordination of complex movements. At the playground, she usually plays on the swings, and does not get involved in games that require more intense physical activity. She does not alternate feet when going down the stairs. Her father considers that Helen is simply not a "sports person," whereas her mother claims that the reason why their child faces such difficulties is because they have not dedicated enough time to acquaint her with these kinds of activities.

Helen does not like drawing, and avoids playing jigsaw games. Her teacher notes that Helen has particular difficulty staying inside the lines when coloring an image in outline, and that she has poor fine motor skills and difficulties in performing subtle movements. She does not hold the pencil correctly, namely she does not use a tripod grasp. Furthermore, she cannot make precise cuts with scissors, even when the picture is simple, and she has particular difficulty with prewriting exercises. Her parents believe that she will eventually learn all these later, and hold the opinion that "children do not have to know how to write when they go to nursery school because they will be bored in the first grade." Therefore, they do not understand why the teacher "pushes" the child to do such activities despite the child's unwillingness to do so.

Helen is often absent-minded and does not always answer questions that are addressed to her. She gives the impression that "her mind is somewhere else," and that she is daydreaming. Additionally, she finds it difficult to follow the rules of a conversation, as she jumps from one topic to another, interrupts the interlocutor, and does not easily keep the conversation flowing.

Furthermore, she can hardly concentrate for more than a few minutes on any table play at nursery school. In addition, she often gives up on difficult tasks, and leaves everything unfinished and messy.

Helen seems to have difficulty with time management. For instance, she gets carried away when she has to get ready quickly in order to go somewhere. Her attention is easily distracted by other stimuli during daily routines, such as getting dressed, taking a shower, or eating. Therefore, these activities become time-consuming and often exhausting, both for her and her mother.

At some point, the nursery school teacher suggested that Helen's parents should seek professional help so that the child could go through an assessment and be evaluated for the presence of ADHD. The teacher was particularly worried about issues of school readiness. She was afraid that the child might not be ready to respond to the demands of elementary school. Helen's parents said: "The child is simply a bit immature. Besides, she is highly unlikely to have ADHD because she is very quiet and not at all naughty!"

The truth is that both 8-year-old John and 5-year-old Helen have ADHD, but the clinical presentation and the degree of severity of the disorder differ considerably between the two children. These differences are mainly due to the fact that the children belong to opposite sexes, are at different developmental stages, and display different presentations of ADHD. However, both of them need professional help after a thorough assessment and the establishment of the correct diagnosis.

2.3 Distinguishing Between the Overactive Child and the Child With ADHD

A reasonable question that is often raised mainly by parents and teachers is how a child with ADHD can be distinguished from a child that is simply overactive and more inattentive than same-age peers but does not have a disorder. This question reflects a wider theoretical issue in psychopathology concerning the boundaries between normal and abnormal behavior. To be more specific, this issue refers to the appropriateness of categorical or dimensional classification taxonomies, and can be simply put as follows: do developmental disorders constitute categories or dimensions of behavior?

Contemporary diagnostic manuals adopt a categorical classification of disorders. However, future research trends point to the need for a shift toward a dimensional approach. Dimensions assume continuity between normality and psychopathology, whereas categories suppose discontinuity (Rutter, 2011). Kinsbourne (1977) was the first to suggest that temperament falls on a continuum of characteristics such as impulsivity and hyperactivity. Consequently, it is assumed that everyone exhibits the core symptoms of ADHD, from a minimal to a maximal degree. Differences among individuals represent differences in frequency, persistence, and severity of symptoms. Consequently, a dimensional classification has the potential to help us better differentiate the "simply overactive child" from "the child with ADHD." Children receiving the diagnosis of ADHD represent the upper end of the temperamental continuum. To answer the question raised previously, we can additionally use the impairment criterion, which plays a central role in the theoretical formulation of diagnostic manuals.

Hyperactivity, impulsivity, and inattention observed in a child should be of concern mainly when (a) they are manifested with significantly increased frequency, persistence, and severity; and (b) they cause impairment in the child's daily functioning in major domains, including school performance, interpersonal relationships, and social interactions.

Regarding the first criterion, developmental psychology describes the milestones that should be reached by developmental level in each domain. Therefore, knowledge of the basic principles of developmental psychology is essential for the identification of possible deviances from developmentally appropriate behavior, with reference to severity, persistence, and frequency of this behavior.

Regarding the second criterion, parents and teachers can usually correctly identify a child's impairment in daily functioning. For example, a child who is extremely energetic to such a degree that requires increased parental supervision does not raise any concern in terms of psychopathology as long as there are no particular problems in the parent–child relationship, proneness to accidents, or obstacles in the child's general well-being. Similarly, a child who often gets distracted but manages to redirect attention to the topic of conversation or to the task at hand, finishes activities—even if taking a little longer—and fully exploits their capabilities at school and in other contexts, is not characterized as a child with a disorder. Finally, if a child tends to interrupt conversations, talks too much, and is impatient, but gets along well with peers and does not get involved in rule violation or illegal activity, no worries should be raised.

Building on the preceding examples, two inferences can be made. First, a child's functioning does not depend only on their own strengths and weaknesses, but also on familial and societal expectations and demands as well as on adults' level of tolerance toward the child's behavior. In fact, some researchers claim that increasing demands for higher academic and professional performance have led to the increased incidence of ADHD as revealed in epidemiological studies (Hinshaw & Scheffler, 2014).

This finding gives prominence to a major shortcoming of the contemporary classification systems, which consider the symptoms as inherent in the individual and not as the outcome of the interplay between the individual and the environment (Rutter, 2011). However, it is widely acknowledged that the demands posed on children for sustained attention, control of motor activity, and compliance with complex rule systems differ according to family, social, or cultural parameters.

Children who face difficulties in the aforementioned areas and live in highly demanding environments are more likely to exhibit functional impairment and, therefore, be given the diagnosis of ADHD. In contrast, children with ADHD symptoms who live in environments with opportunities for engaging in increased motor activity, along with a less complex rule system and fewer educational demands, are likely to respond more effectively and thus never receive any diagnosis. This line of reasoning can explain why children with ADHD-like behaviors could respond effectively to environmental demands 50 years ago, but need professional help in order to cope with these demands nowadays.

Second, the current diagnostic criteria for ADHD do not seem to assume equal significance with reference to their impact on children's functioning. To be more specific, behaviors that are included in the hyperactivity list may not pose any difficulty to the child but mainly cause disturbance to the child's environment. In contrast, we consider that behaviors that are included in the inattention list, as well as one of the criteria referring to impulsivity ("acts before thinking"), may impair the child's functioning more severely.

As a consequence, we suggest that the most important question is not whether a child is simply overactive or has ADHD but whether they face difficulties of such kind and severity that place them in need of professional help. Clinicians are qualified to answer this question, based on their deep knowledge on psychopathology and diagnostic criteria, their theoretical approach, their personal judgment, and their clinical experience. However, a child's assessment is usually preceded by the fact that parents, teachers, or any adult who is closely associated with the child are concerned about their behavior. Some qualitative differences in various areas of development between children with ADHD and their peers will be described below. These differences may serve as indices for the need for professional evaluation.

In the area of motor development, a key difference between a child with ADHD and an overactive child lies in the ability to control motor activity in situations when this is required. Overactive children are capable of easily controlling their motor activity to a satisfactory degree when such activity is inappropriate and may lead to negative consequences. In contrast, children with ADHD usually have enormous difficulty keeping quiet even in circumstances where they know that this is obligatory. In cases where overactive behavior might lead to punishment, for example walking across the classroom, children with ADHD, especially at younger ages, struggle to remain seated, and might fidget or squirm in an attempt to satisfy their need for movement. When they are allowed to move freely, they will probably display signs of exhaustion due to the effort made in order to restrain from standing up for a long time. For example, they might be blushed, sweaty, or sighing with relief. Therefore, the fundamental difference is not whether a child manifests increased motor activity or not because even a child with ADHD is able to control it, if highly motivated, but the amount of effort put into it and the fatigue that usually results from this effort.

Another crucial difference concerns the quality of motor activity of children with ADHD in relation to their peers. Children with ADHD are often clumsy in terms of both gross and fine motor skills (Carte, Nigg, & Hinshaw, 1996; Seidman, Biederman, Faraone, Weber, & Ouellette, 1997). Consequently, children with ADHD often fall down, cause accidents, and have difficulty with some activities, including buttoning, drawing, and so forth. In contrast, children who are merely overactive do not usually have such difficulties. In fact, they can be very dexterous.

Increased motor activity in children with ADHD can often be evident even during sleep. Mothers of these children often report that their children sleep poorly and face sleep disturbances (Ball, Tiernan, Janusz, & Furr, 1997). They may toss and turn all the time, even kick when they are asleep. In contrast, overactive children do not display such behaviors during sleep.

Speech and Language Problems (SLPs) are often comorbid conditions in children with ADHD (Kim & Kaiser, 2000). In fact, they often constitute the first worrying signs for parents, and are a common reason for referral to child mental health services. A high rate of children with ADHD have delayed speech onset and, when they eventually talk, they might have problems both in articulation and syntax, even in the first years of elementary school (Agapitou & Andreou, 2008). Such difficulties are not usually detected in the cases of overactive children.

The attention span of children with ADHD is short by definition. However, this does not mean that these children cannot concentrate at all. Many of them can concentrate to a satisfactory degree and for a quite long time if they are highly motivated to do so and the activity they have to do stimulates their interest (Luman, Oosterlaan & Sergeant, 2005). In contrast, an overactive child can concentrate more easily, without needing strong motivation.

Children with ADHD are often irritable and excitable. Their inability to respond satisfactorily to several of the demands of their environment, combined with the fact that they are often reprimanded, usually trigger defiant and oppositional behaviors (Barkley, 1990). Consequently, these children display various behavioral problems more frequently relative to merely overactive children.

2.4 ADHD Manifestations in Girls

Although extensive research has been conducted on boys with ADHD, comparable studies of girls are scarce, possibly due to the challenges of recruiting sufficient samples of girls with the disorder (Hinshaw & Blachman, 2005). Even in studies where girls were included, they have been lumped with their more numerous male counterparts, thus making it difficult to draw firm conclusions regarding the nature of ADHD in females. Consequently, female manifestations of the disorder have been relatively neglected in ADHD research until recent years.

However, over the last years, research on girls with ADHD has generated increasing interest, as it has been shown that they exhibit significant functional impairments in various areas across development (Hinshaw, 2002). Their difficulties are evident both in childhood and adolescence (Biederman, Monuteaux, Mick, Spencer, Wilens et al., 2006; Hinshaw, Owens, Sami & Fargeon, 2006), as well as in adulthood (Babinski et al., 2010). As a generality, females may have fewer symptoms as measured by the DSM-IV-TR criteria, but are just as impaired as males by these symptoms (Quinn & Madhoo, 2014).

Compared to typically developing girls, those with ADHD are at greater risk for displaying delinquent behavior in adolescence (Biederman, Monuteaux, Mick, Spencer, Wilens, Klein et al., 2006; Molina et al., 2007). Furthermore, girls with ADHD have impaired peer relation ships. Findings suggest that school-aged girls with ADHD have fewer friends relative to girls without ADHD (Blachman & Hinshaw, 2002), whereas women with ADHD have reduced chances of getting married relative to women without ADHD, as well as relative to men with ADHD (Barkley, 2006a). It has also been reported that although peer problems are clearly detrimental for boys' and girls' functioning, their negative impact may be particularly evident among girls with ADHD, mainly through their association with negative self-image and internalizing disorders (Mikami & Lorenzi, 2011).

The preceding findings can be easily explained according to the gender appropriateness hypothesis (Kerr, Lambert, Stattin, & Klackenberg-Larsson, 1994). Culturally defined stereotypes of masculinity and femininity set the rules for boys' and girls' gender appropriate behavior. When children do not comply with these cultural rules, their behavior is perceived as gender inappropriate, and is less well-tolerated. Stereotypes of femininity are directly opposed to ADHD characteristics. This fact makes the social environment less favorably disposed toward these characteristics when exhibited by girls (Diamantopoulou, Henricsson, & Rydell, 2005;

Maniadaki, 2003). It has been found that girls with ADHD need to make considerable effort in order to respond to social expectations regarding typical female behaviors (Quinn, 2005). As Hope Langner (2002) notes about women with ADHD, "If they make a great effort to respond to social expectations associated with femininity, then their self-worth ends up being dependent on others. Creating a false self is a risk, even if it secures provisional acceptance" (p. 72). This interpretation is consistent with the view that a disorder has a more negative impact on the individual when gender stereotypes are broken (Kerr, Lambert, Stattin, & Klackenberg-Larsson, 1994).

The findings relating to sex differences in ADHD among males and females are variable and inconsistent, probably due to dissimilar subject selection processes and criteria used to define the disorder. Meta-analyses of gender and ADHD (e.g., Gaub & Carlson, 1997; Gershon, 2002) have revealed a subset of studies showing no substantial sex differences on measures of impulsivity, academic achievement, and social functioning (Biederman et al., 2005; Blachman & Hinshaw, 2002; Breen & Altepeter, 1990; Seidman et al., 1997; Sharp et al., 1999). In a more recent longitudinal study based on a sample of 1,478 children with ADHD in ten European countries, no sex differences were found on these measures (Novik et al., 2006). A recent meta-analysis reported no significant sex effects on a continuous performance task assessing attention (Hasson & Fine, 2012).

However, other studies demonstrated significant differences in areas such as intellectual impairment as well as ratings of internalizing and externalizing behavior. A key finding is that boys with ADHD display behavioral problems more frequently than their female counterparts (Biederman, Faraone et al., 1999; Gordon & Mettelman, 1994). According to findings based both on observational studies in natural settings (Abikoff et al., 2002) and on behavioral rating scales, boys with ADHD display defiant, disruptive, and aggressive behavior more often than girls (Gaub & Carlson, 1997). Moreover, comorbidity rates between ADHD and CD are higher among boys (Biederman, Faraone et al., 1999). These findings may explain the fact that a family is usually more negatively affected and more heavily burdened when the child with ADHD is a boy rather than a girl (Thorell & Rydell, 2008).

On the other hand, girls with ADHD are at great risk for developing depression, mainly in adolescence and adulthood, relative to boys (Biederman, Ball et al., 2008; Hinshaw et al., 2006; Rasmussen & Levander, 2009). A study confirmed that 14% of teenage girls with ADHD had taken antidepressant medication before receiving the diagnosis of ADHD (Quinn, 2005). In addition, girls usually experience more stress (Gadow & Sprafkin, 1997; Lahey et al., 2007), have a higher rate of enuresis (Berry, Shaywitz, & Shaywitz, 1985; Sharp et al., 1997), and are more likely to suffer peer rejection relative to boys (Rucklidge & Tannock, 2001). Furthermore, low self-esteem is more prominent in females with ADHD than in males with ADHD or non-ADHD female controls (Ek, Westerlund, Holmberg, & Fernell, 2008; Rucklidge & Tannock, 2001). Poorer self-esteem may persist past childhood, and self-esteem among adults with ADHD has been reported to be lower in women than in men.

Comorbidity with Depressive Disorders (DDs) and Anxiety Disorders (ADs) in childhood has been reported to persist in adolescence and adulthood more often in girls than in boys (Biederman et al., 2012; Monuteaux, Mick, Faraone, & Biederman, 2010). This might explain why women with ADHD are 2.4 times more likely to receive psychiatric help relative to men with ADHD (Dalsgaard, Mortensen, Frydenberg, & Thomsen, 2002).

Girls with ADHD have been found to display more severe cognitive deficits, especially in the areas of speech development and cognitive function, as well as poorer academic achievement relative to boys (Berry et al., 1985; Gordon & Mettelman, 1994). These findings have led several researchers to suggest that different kinds of impairments may contribute to the identification of ADHD across genders. Behavioral problems may increase the likelihood of detecting boys with ADHD, whereas cognitive deficits may have a more prominent role in the identification of girls (Babinski et al., 2010; Gaub & Carlson, 1997). Clinically, boys are more commonly diagnosed with the combined subtype and show a greater preponderance of hyperactive/impulsive symptoms, whereas girls with ADHD are more often diagnosed with the inattentive subtype (Hinshaw et al., 2006; Willcutt, 2012). Moreover, several differences have been demonstrated relative to executive function profiles of boys and girls with ADHD (Dirlikov et al., 2015), although previous research had yielded more similarities than differences between the two sexes in this area (Rucklidge, 2010; Seidman et al., 2005).

Regarding the age of referral for boys and girls with ADHD, the findings are inconsistent. Berry and colleagues (1985) found that hyperactive girls were younger than boys at the time of referral for medical attention, whereas inattentive girls where older than inattentive boys at referral. Silverthorn and colleagues (1996) found that girls with ADHD were younger at the time of referral despite the fact that their parents reported the onset of symptoms no earlier in girls than in boys with ADHD. This finding has led these authors to suggest that parents seem to have a lower tolerance for ADHD symptoms in girls, and thus refer them at an earlier age.

In contrast, other authors have found that there was a trend for girls with ADHD to be older at the time of referral (Brown, Madan-Swain, & Baldwin, 1991; Nussbaum, 2012). This finding could reflect either insensitivity to early signs of the disorder in girls or an actual difference in the life course of the disorder in boys and girls. For example, it may reflect a buffering effect of girls' earlier developmental maturity (Simon, Czobor, Bálint, Mészáros, & Bitter, 2009).

Boys and girls with ADHD have also been compared on family variables. Regarding the quality of their interactions with their mothers, it has been found that hyperactive boys receive more direction and praise. They also elicit greater maternal concern about their adjustment than hyperactive girls (Befera & Barkley, 1985). Moreover, mothers have been found to be more critical of daughters than of sons with ADHD (Barkley, 2006b). Regarding the psychiatric status of parents, it has been found that mothers of hyperactive boys have higher levels of marital discord than mothers of hyperactive girls (Befera & Barkley, 1985). It has also been reported that girls with ADHD tend to come from families with lower socioeconomic status (Berry et al., 1985).

Finally, minor differences have been detected with respect to boys' and girls' response to various kinds of treatment, either medication or psychosocial (Nussbaum, 2012).

McGee and Feehan (1991) suggest that the source of information may be an important determinant of the magnitude of observed sex differences. For example, teacher ratings of inattention and hyperactivity show more pronounced sex differences than parent ratings of the same behaviors, with teachers reporting more hyperactive/impulsive symptoms than parents (Kakouros, Maniadaki, & Karaba, 2005; Ullebø et al., 2012). It is therefore hypothesized that inattentive behaviors are at least partly underrecognized in girls because girls do not present with management problems in the classroom to the extent that boys do.

This view is also supported by Schachar and colleagues (2002), who showed that aggressive and defiant behavior in children exerts a negative *halo effect* on ratings of inattention. Negative halo effects occur when undesirable behaviors in one area lead to assumptions of undesirable behaviors in other domains. The presence of oppositionality in children seems to increase the likelihood of inattentive or hyperactive ratings even in the absence of these symptoms. In other words, when a child with ADHD displays disruptive behavior, the teacher is more likely to notice other difficulties as well, including inattention. To the contrary, when a child with ADHD does not exhibit disruptive behavior, the teacher may ignore other difficulties. The first case is usually true for boys with ADHD, whereas the second case applies more to girls. Therefore, studies based on rating scales may detect more boys with ADHD than girls.

This view is further substantiated by the finding that the severity of problems in girls with ADHD is differentiated depending on the sample of the study (Gaub & Carlson, 1997). Specifically, in studies based on community samples, girls appear to have fewer difficulties relative to boys. In contrast, in clinic-referred populations, boys and girls appear similarly impaired. It can be inferred, therefore, that clinic-referred girls are not representative of girls with ADHD in general. Consequently, it may be that the more severe impairment observed in girls with ADHD compared to boys may be restricted to clinic-referred populations. Presumably, the relative lack of sex differences in symptoms within referred samples may indicate that only the most impaired girls are being referred (Arcia & Conners, 1998; Gaub & Carlson, 1997; Gershon, 2002).

An area that has not received sufficient attention yet is sex differences in symptom manifestation and impairment in adults with ADHD (Fedele, Lefler, Hartung, & Canu, 2012). It appears that sex differences found in child and adolescent samples are smaller or nonexistent in adults. Adult men and women do not seem to differ in phenotypic expression of ADHD, in neither lifetime inattentive, hyperactive, or total ADHD symptom scores nor current hyperactive or total ADHD symptom scores (Biederman et al., 2005; Rasmussen & Levander, 2009). However, there is some evidence that ADHD-related impairment impacts adult men and women differently, in that women with ADHD report higher levels of impairment than men in several areas of functioning (Fedele et al., 2012).

2.5 ADHD in the Family Context

ADHD is a disorder that adversely affects not only the individual but the whole family as well. It should be conceptualized within the family context as it is actually a family affair. ADHD may disrupt family functioning in many ways.

Parenting a child with ADHD is an arduous process that poses a variety of challenges for parents, and sometimes exceeds their coping capacities. Parents of these children not only have to deal with the core symptoms of the disorder, but also with a series of associated problems and comorbid conditions. In order to handle these issues effectively, they are required to show great patience, tolerance, and consistency. Furthermore, parents usually have considerable difficulty in accurately differentiating undesirable behaviors deriving from ADHD from those that fall within the realm of normal child development. Making sense of the disorder is an ongoing activity because ADHD does not have evident biological markers and is characterized by variability in its presentation. For these reasons, parents of children with ADHD sometimes expect that their child's behavior will become "normalized" and "more mature" as they grow up. Therefore, they may have greater difficulty accepting the diagnosis than parents of children with other developmental disorders (Kendall, 1998).

Behaviors exhibited by children with ADHD are full of challenges because these children are usually more demanding and less cooperative. They are more often in a negative mood, and require more intensive parental supervision relative to typically developing children. They fail to follow rules without repeated reminders. Parents have to cope with the child's tendency to avoid effortful tasks, and to deal with repeated complaints and negative comments by teachers regarding their child's inappropriate behavior at school. They are often in the embarrassing position of explaining their child's behavior to other parents, and accept the fact that their child is not invited to parties. They may spend long hours helping their child with homework, which is rather frustrating given that their child seems to have good potential but cannot fully exploit it. Other times, they feel angry and extremely tired because their child does not seem to understand despite their great patience to explain everything. They are constantly pressed for time in order to fulfill their parenting duties. They strive to make daily routines run smoothly, including dressing, eating, studying, taking a shower, and sleeping, because the child often gets carried away and procrastinates. As a result, valuable time is wasted, and tension is caused, particularly at the end of the day. Parents often have to deal with the child's defiant and oppositional behavior, even in front of others. Therefore, it is extremely difficult for parents to always remain calm and handle things properly.

To illustrate the burden that ADHD may pose on the family, the case of Paul is described. Paul is an 8-year-old student in the second grade of elementary school. His mother keeps a diary, upon our request, describing his morning routine before he goes to school. The emotions that she expresses and the impact of the child's behavior on his parents are typical in families of children with ADHD.

> It is Tuesday, 2nd of April. Paul wakes up on his own quite well. He starts to get dressed. I say to him: "Darling, get dressed and revise for your spelling test because we did not have time to do that yesterday." He retorts: "No!" He starts to fool around as he is getting dressed. Although he has only put on his trousers, he starts to play with our puppy. The time is 7.45, and he has not got dressed yet. I call out to him to come and drink his milk. He again answers: "No, I don't want to." I ask him what snack he would like for school, and he answers: "Nothing." "But will your stomach be empty all day?" I ask him. "Yes" he answers. Although he woke up in a good mood, suddenly he became extremely bad-tempered. Even though I have explained to him a thousand times what he needs to do in order to be on time for the school bus, most of the days he leaves home in a hurry. He remembers that he wants a toy, and he takes an hour to find it; he nags or cries for no reason. He has many times left for school without having washed himself because, when the bus was coming, he was searching for something or he was crying.
>
> This annoys us and we often shout at him. In the end, I argue with my husband. "Don't yell at him," one of us says. "But can't you see what he's doing?" the other answers. I don't know how to react anymore. I don't know when we should be angry with him and when we shouldn't. I don't understand what we are doing wrong. Living with him is very difficult not only because of his school homework but also because of his behavior in general. It is true that we have been yelling a lot at him all these years because of his inappropriate behavior. Now we are trying to control each other, but sometimes it is very difficult. We are very tired. There is never peace and quiet in our home.
>
> I have realized that he wants a lot of love and he needs us to dedicate a lot of time to him. Whatever we start doing with him, though, ends up being a disaster; we feel disappointed. When we read him a story, he stands up and runs. When we play a board game, he does not accept the rules and cries. When he plays football with his dad, he keeps the ball to himself all the time and does not let his dad score a goal. When we go on a trip, we come back home irritated. When he goes to a party, he plays so aggressively that adults do not want to invite him anymore and children ask him to leave. I feel so sad and embarrassed because of this! I love my child very much and I want to do what is best for him, but sometimes I would like him to disappear for a while so that I can have a few peaceful moments.
>
> When I take him to the theatre, he won't sit to watch the play. I have been taking him to the track for four years, and he has driven me crazy. Sometimes he is very willing and sometimes he obstinately refuses to go. His grandparents cannot stand him and refuse to keep him so that his dad and I can go for a walk. I know that all these describe Paul's negative side and for sure he has a lot of positive aspects, as well. But I have been struggling to raise him over these years and this is the side of him that sticks in my mind.

Kendall and Shelton (2003) developed a typology that applied the general concept of family management style to families with children and adolescents with ADHD. This typology may add useful information to the conceptualization and treatment of ADHD as well as affect family functioning on a global level (Conlon, Strassle, Vinh, & Trout, 2008). These authors suggested a hierarchical model to rank four family management styles, depending on the way families deal with the disorder. The first category represents the lowest functioning family, and the fourth one the highest functioning family in the typology.

1. *The chaotic family* is characterized by extreme stress, receives little external support, maintains very little internal structure (e.g., there might be spousal violence or financial instability), and experiences a lack of responsiveness alternating with extreme rigid parenting strategies in response to the child's behaviors resulting from ADHD.
2. *The ADHD-controlled family* centralizes the child's disorder, for example through reinforcement of the child's negative behaviors by ignoring, justifying, or excusing them on account of familial exhaustion. Such a family is both powerless and hopeless as a result of the child's ADHD symptoms.
3. *The surviving family* moves beyond ADHD and focuses on other aspects of family life by receiving social support and counseling and using diverse parenting strategies. This family manages ADHD symptoms by using various parenting strategies.
4. *The reinvested family* expresses a renewed sense of energy in successfully managing the child's difficulties. Through familial reinvestment, the parents use adaptive coping strategies that allow the family to feel restored and in control rather than merely surviving the child's negative behavior. A family usually reaches that point when they have received effective counseling or treatment.

A prominent finding regarding families of children with ADHD is that parents experience greater stress in their role as caretakers than parents of typically developing children do (Deault, 2010; Johnston & Mash, 2001; Theule, Wiener, Tannock, & Jenkins, 2013). The stress is lower in the case of parents of girls with ADHD relative to parents of boys with the disorder, probably due to the fact that girls with ADHD do not have so many behavioral problems (Reader, Stewart, & Johnson, 2009). Furthermore, mothers experience heightened stress relative to fathers (Kendall, Leo, Perrin, & Hatton, 2005). Because of mothers' caregiving role in families and because much of the ADHD parenting work is left to them, mothers carry primary responsibility for the exceedingly difficult work of these children's care while simultaneously organizing home and family life and acting as the child's advocate and liaison with the school, health care system, extended family, and neighborhood (Kendall, 1998).

This stress appears to be multifaceted. The degree of severity of primary ADHD symptoms (McCleary, 2002; Morgan, Robinson, & Aldridge, 2002) and associated behavioral problems (Costa, Weems, Pellerin, & Dalton, 2006; Goldstein, Harvey, & Friedman-Weieneth, 2007) are closely associated with the level of stress among the parents of these children. Fathers of children with ADHD and comorbid CD are reported to have increased drinking problems (Chronis et al., 2003). In general, the amount of stress that parents of children with ADHD undergo seems to remain high through adolescence (Deault, 2010).

Parental stress arises when a parent's perceptions of the demands of parenting outstrip his or her resources for dealing with them (Deater-Deckard, 1998). The dominant model of parenting stress delineates two major components: a child domain, arising directly from child characteristics, and a parent domain that is more affected by parental functioning (Abidin, 1995). Consequently, how parents experience stress is closely associated with feelings of parenting self-efficacy, namely the estimation of the degree to which they feel capable of performing the varied tasks associated with their highly demanding parenting role (Mash & Johnston, 1990; McCleary, 2002; Morgan et al., 2002).

Parents of children with ADHD report lower levels of parenting self-efficacy (Hoza et al., 2000; Johnston, 1996) and less satisfaction in their parenting role (Podolski & Nigg, 2001). They often internalize negative beliefs about themselves as parents. In a study that we carried out on a sample of 118 mothers of preschool-aged children, we presented them with a vignette that described a 5-year-old child with ADHD symptoms. In half of the sample, the child was presented as a girl, and in the other half as a boy. Mothers reported low self-efficacy to cope with such a child, especially in the case of the boy (Maniadaki, Sonuga-Barke, Kakouros, & Karaba, 2005). It is obvious that when parents feel inadequate at coping with the challenges that stem from their child's behavior, and when they do not believe that they have the ability to influence this behavior, they tend to abandon effort (Gerdes et al., 2007).

Other research (Chronis et al., 2003; Nigg & Hinshaw, 1998) suggests that both mothers and fathers of children with ADHD experience elevated rates of depression and anxiety compared with parents of normal controls. It has been suggested that parental depression in this population may be related to an underlying genetic predisposition, and may result from common factors with the child's ADHD (Biederman, Faraone, & Lapey, 1992; Fischer, 1990; Johnston & Mash, 2001). Alternatively, as Harrison and Sofronoff (2002) point out, depressive symptoms in parents of children with ADHD may be associated with feelings of *learned helplessness*, as a result of their inability to change their children's behavior in spite of all their efforts.

Recognizing symptoms of depression in mothers of children with ADHD is highly significant because depression has a negative effect on the way in which mothers perceive, interpret, and handle their child's behavior (Chi & Hinshaw, 2002). Depressed mothers tend to display significantly higher levels of negative and disengaged behavior and significantly lower levels of positive social interactions (Lovejoy, Graczyk, O'Hare, & Neuman, 2000). Maternal depression emerged as a significant predictor of CD among children with ADHD in the subsequent 2–8 years following the initial evaluation (Chronis et al., 2007).

Mothers of children with ADHD often report that they have feelings of anger and rejection toward their child. They also report decreased parental warmth and reduced positive involvement. These mothers consider that their quality of life has deteriorated and that they have fewer positive family experiences due to their child's difficulties (Whalen et al., 2006). In the study mentioned earlier (Maniadaki, Sonuga-Barke, Kakouros et al., 2005), mothers were asked to record the emotions that the behaviors described in the vignette evoked in them. Discomfort, sadness, embarrassment, and worry were reported as predominant emotions.

Overall, it appears that a child's ADHD can have a considerable impact on the level of parental and family stress, as well as on the way parents view their competency in managing their child's difficulties and dealing with the daily challenges resulting from these difficulties. These aspects inevitably establish a framework within which the child develops, along with their difficulties. Mental health and well-being in parents play a substantial role in the child's developmental course and long-term outcome. Similarly, caregiving strain, quality of life decrements, and marital relations are of equal importance (Whalen et al., 2006). These factors can color the contact between parent and child, altering both the affective tone and the behavioral content of their interactions.

For example, increased parental stress was found to negatively influence parent–child relationships, via its influence on parenting strategies (Morgan et al., 2002; Rodgers, 1998). Maladaptive coping strategies are associated with less constructive discipline practices, such as permissive and authoritarian parenting styles (McKee, Harvey, Danforth, Ulaszek, & Friedman, 2004), which may contribute to more disruptive and less compliant behavior in children with ADHD (DuPaul, McGoey, Eckert, & VanBrakle, 2001). Parents with elevated stress levels are less supportive toward their children regarding their learning, less rewarding, and less encouraging (Rogers, Wiener, Marton, & Tannock, 2009a). Parents of children with ADHD tend to be more directive and punitive, and they express disapproval more often than do mothers of typically developing children (McKee et al., 2004). Given the self-regulation deficits of children with ADHD, these practices may serve to maintain or exacerbate the child's poor self-regulatory behavior (Johnston & Mash, 2001). If parents withdraw affect as a result of their child's problematic behavior and, at the same time, make negative comments in the absence of positive comments, the child may internalize a negative self-image that will probably result in the development of conduct problems (Kaminski, Jones, & Harshaw, 2004).

In general, it has been demonstrated that the ongoing and persistent difficulties caused by ADHD symptoms may trigger parental stress and lead to maladaptive parenting practices, which in turn usually increase child disruptive behavior, thus creating a vicious circle of negative interactions between parents and children (Barkley, 1998a; Gerdes et al., 2007). Consequently, not only can the child's ADHD characteristics affect parental behavior but, conversely, parenting and family behavior can affect the course of the child's ADHD symptoms (Johnston & Mash, 2001).

Negative parent–child interactions may aggravate in cases where ADHD or other psychopathology is present in the parent as well, which is a common phenomenon (Chronis et al., 2003). In these cases, even more dysfunctional interactions between parents and children are observed, along with less consistent discipline, less effective parenting, and more stress (Barkley, Murphy, & Fisher, 2008). Parenting is mediated by parents' own psychopathology. The presence of ADHD in parents puts them at risk for engaging in harsh or lax parenting practices. Lax parenting mostly characterizes mothers with predominant symptoms of inattention (Harvey, Danforth, McKee, Ulaszek, & Friedman, 2003).

In addition, parents of children with ADHD who experience psychological maladjustment are less able to employ effective strategies in order to modify their child's behavior following parent training (Kazdin, 1995). Consequently, they abandon this effort more easily and drop out more frequently (Chacko et al., 2008; Friars & Mellor, 2007).

Disrupted family interactions and conflicts between spouses are often reported in families of children with ADHD (Johnston & Mash, 2001). Marital dissatisfaction and increased marital conflict are often reported. On the whole, it seems that ADHD adversely influences the quality of interparental interactions, leading to marital discord (Deault, 2010; McCleary, 2002). This influence seems to be less significant in case the child displays predominantly symptoms of inattention (Theule, Wiener, Tannock, & Jenkins, 2013).

It seems likely that children with ADHD demonstrate similar problems with inhibition and self-regulation when interacting with siblings, and that these behaviors will contribute to higher conflict and less warmth in sibling relationships (Mikami & Pfiffner, 2008). Children with ADHD seem to express more anger, aggressiveness, negative feelings, and a lack of cooperation toward their siblings relative to their typically developing counterparts (Mash & Johnston, 1983a). These problems seem to be more common in cases where oppositional and defiant behaviors are also present among children with ADHD (Smith, Brown, Bunke, Blount, & Christophersen, 2002).

In a qualitative study based on a sample of 11 families of boys with ADHD, their siblings systematically described their relationship as "chaotic, conflictual and exhausting" (Kendall, 1999). Furthermore, they reported that they often get "victimized" by their sibling with ADHD and that their family underestimates their needs because family life is centered around the child with ADHD. A predominant emotion reported was bitterness, due to the fact that family life is defined by and revolves around the presence of ADHD.

In other studies, siblings of children with ADHD also reported being angry at their parents because they often hold them to different rules and standards than their sibling with ADHD (Kendall, 1999; Singer, 1997). Complaints about parents further accumulate, as siblings of children with ADHD often report that they do not feel that their emotional needs are adequately met and that they would like to receive more attention (Singer, 1997).

Furthermore, siblings of children with ADHD have more emotional and behavioral problems, according to their parents' reports (Listug-Lunde, Zevenbergen, & Petros, 2008; Smith et al., 2002). In a longitudinal study, it was found that siblings of children with ADHD are at higher risk for psychopathology and impairment in social functioning than matched control children (Faraone, Biederman, Mennin, Gershon, & Tsuang, 1996). Not surprisingly, all of these add to the stress that parents already experience and parenting becomes even more challenging and overwhelming. Other problems that families of children of ADHD often encounter are social isolation and low social adjustment. Parents of these children are more often exposed to social criticism for their children's inappropriate behavior. They often receive direct or indirect accusations from their social environment, and are held responsible for their children's behavior. Such criticism further influences their already reduced self-perceived parenting efficacy. As a result, some parents may feel the need to avoid some social situations, including inviting or visiting friends, organizing family outings, or attending events where the child is expected to have self-control and display prosocial behavior (Miranda, Marco, & Grau, 2007). In addition, parents of children with ADHD often report feeling trapped because their parenting role places many restrictions on their personal time (Miranda et al., 2007).

Taking the aforementioned discussion into consideration, psychoeducation and counseling for ADHD are necessary for parents of these children but may not always be enough. It becomes clear that they also need emotional support and, sometimes, psychotherapy in order to manage their stress more effectively and process those negative feelings that might serve as a barrier to successfully implementing new parenting techniques (Miranda et al., 2007; Treacy, Tripp, & Baird, 2005). Indeed, parental psychological maladjustment is related to a lower likelihood that parents will complete behavioral management training programs for ADHD (Chacko et al., 2008). Professionals who work with children with developmental difficulties and their families can confirm that simple knowledge of a strategy does not guarantee its effective implementation as well.

Moreover, in order to achieve the best possible outcomes, it is essential that both parents participate in psychosocial interventions for ADHD. It has been found that when parents get actively involved in treatment, not only does the child's behavior improve but also parents' overall functioning and the quality of family interactions (Gerdes, Haack, & Schneider, 2012; Pelham & Fabiano, 2008). Negative parenting practices (e.g., inconsistent discipline and physical punishment) seem to be employed less, and fathers are more actively and positively involved in their child's daily routine, which has a beneficial influence on family interactions in general.

3 Developmental Course and Outcome of ADHD

3.1 Introduction

There is a growing consensus that knowledge of normal developmental processes is essential for understanding the nature of childhood behavior disorders and providing effective treatments (Cicchetti & Cohen, 2006; Sameroff, 2000). Professionals who work with children and adolescents must be able to interpret symptom expression that takes into account normal development in order to accurately distinguish symptoms from normative misbehavior. For example, toddlers hopping around while their mother is talking to them might be considered cute, but adolescents hopping around in class when addressed to by their teacher are not considered cute anymore!

The presentation of ADHD changes over time—and perhaps across genders—due to developmental maturation (Biederman, 2011). As a typically developing child is completely different at age 4 years compared to age 8 years, similarly, a child with ADHD has a completely different clinical presentation at age 4 years compared to age 8 years. Furthermore, knowledge on the rapid rate that development follows, especially during infancy and early childhood, is indispensable for the comprehension of the child's behavior and avoidance of misinterpretations. For example, sustained attention deficits are one of the main features of ADHD. If we define sustained attention as the time the child spends engaged with a specific object, we need to take into account that there is a 98% increase in the child's ability for sustained attention between 2.5 and 3.5 years of age (Ruff & Lawson, 1990). Therefore, there are marked developmental changes in the control of attention during the preschool years.

Besides, apprehension of both capabilities and limitations at each developmental stage determines adults' demands and expectations from children. Overestimation or underestimation of children's abilities can have equally detrimental effects on their developmental trajectory. The way in which adults interpret and evaluate the child's behavior is of the utmost importance for the quality of the relationship that will be developed between them, which is bidirectional in nature.

Consequently, proficient knowledge of the diagnostic criteria that define a disorder is not enough for its recognition and the establishment of a valid diagnosis. More important, it is not enough for the holistic comprehension of the difficulties and impairments of the individual who presents it. A child with ADHD bears some genetic and neurobiological deficits by birth. However, the translation of these deficits into symptoms and impairments during development, their effect on different developmental domains, and the overall developmental course of the child, are not merely determined by the quality and severity of the underlying biological background. Some of the factors that may considerably affect the child's developmental course are described in Section 3.8.

For all these reasons, the use of a developmental approach and sound knowledge on the course of ADHD across the life span are essential. A central tenet of this approach is that consideration of normal developmental processes is necessary in understanding the emergence of disorder, associated impairments, and accumulating comorbidities over the life course (Cicchetti & Cohen, 2006). Knowledge regarding the development and typical course of ADHD may help the clinician to identify critical periods for intervention, to describe behavioral profiles that predict risk for specific outcomes, and to plan effective interventions (Davis & Kollins, 2012).

3.2 Persistence of ADHD Symptomatology

Although historically considered a disorder of childhood, long-term follow-up studies of children and retrospective studies of adults with ADHD since the 1980s have shown that the disorder often persists into late adolescence and adulthood (Barbaresi et al., 2013). Overall, it is estimated that in 30% to 60% of children with ADHD, symptoms persist into adolescence or even adulthood (Bagwell, Molina, Pelham, & Hoza, 2001; Mannuzza & Klein, 2000; Mannuzza, Klein, & Moulton, 2003). ADHD persistence can be described at three levels: *syndromatic*, referring to stability of the full diagnostic status; *symptomatic*, referring to stability of partial diagnostic status; and *functional*, referring to stability of partial diagnostic status plus functional impairment (Biederman, Mick, & Faraone, 2000). Estimates of syndromatic persistence range from 33% to 48%, and estimates of symptomatic persistence range from 36% to 85% (Holbrook et al., 2016).

Stability of diagnosis in a 3-year predictive validity study in children diagnosed with ADHD at 3.8 to 7 years of age has been found at a rate of 79% (Lahey et al., 2004). Likewise, in a follow-up of the Preschool ADHD Treatment Study, it was found that 76% and 77.2% of children diagnosed with ADHD at 4 years of age still met the criteria of diagnosis at 3- and 6-year follow-up, respectively (Riddle et al., 2013).

In a recent report of ADHD persistence, based on a clinical sample of boys followed over 10 years into young adulthood, it was found that 45% of baseline cases continued to meet full DSM-IV criteria, and 78% met at least one of the study's persistence definitions, as described earlier (Biederman, Petty, Clarke, Lomedico, & Faraone, 2011). ADHD symptomatology seems to be highly persistent in case ADHD symptoms are accompanied by associated behavioral problems during preschool years (Campbell, 2002).

ADHD persistence has also been studied in samples consisting exclusively of girls. In a 5-year prospective follow-up study of 123 girls with ADHD and normal controls, the disorder was persistent at 71% by age 16 (Mick et al., 2011). This estimate is consistent with findings reported by Hinshaw and colleagues (2006).

However, ADHD symptomatology may present considerable variability throughout development. Individuals with ADHD can fluctuate in the degree and type of symptoms they experience over time (Von Stauffenberg, & Campbell, 2007). In many cases, these fluctuations are likely to be associated with the subjective view of the professional who makes the assessment. In other cases, however, they may represent a clear differentiation in the individual's behavior depending on current developmental stage.

ADHD persistence studies recognize inattention and hyperactive/impulsive trajectories separately, as differing developmental patterns have been suggested for these behavioral dimensions (Holbrook et al., 2016). First, it seems that symptoms of hyperactivity/impulsivity appear in development a few years before inattentive symptoms (Loeber, Green, Lahey, Christ, & Frick, 1992). Second, overt signs of hyperactivity/impulsivity tend to decline with increasing age, whereas inattentive symptoms remain relatively stable or decline at a very modest rate (Biederman et al., 2000; Holbrook et al., 2016; Rohde, Barbosa et al., 2001; Todd et al., 2008).

However, it has been suggested that the apparent decline of hyperactive symptoms may be attributed to the fact that the symptom descriptors used in DSM-IV generally did not apply to adolescent and adult behaviors (Holbrook et al., 2016). As this has been addressed in DSM-5 with additional examples to illustrate behaviors more representative for adolescents and adults with ADHD, future studies are expected to further clarify this issue. It is also worth noting that even if hyperactive/impulsive symptoms decline with age, they do not normalize (Biederman et al., 1998). In addition, associated problems in individuals with ADHD seem to be stable and persistent over time (Lavigne et al., 1998; Mathiesen & Sanson, 2000).

Lahey, Pelham, Loney, Lee, and Willcutt (2005) have also shown that approximately 39% of children with ADHD may change from one subtype to another at least once during an 8-year period. Therefore, it becomes clear that there is considerable intragroup variability in the stability of the ADHD diagnosis. On the basis of these findings, ADHD subtypes have been replaced in DSM-5 with course specifiers that summarize clinical presentation of the individual at the time of evaluation. This issue is discussed in detail in Chapter 9.

Furthermore, it is worth mentioning that adolescents and adults may display certain ADHD symptoms in a different way from children. For example, adolescents or adults with ADHD may experience internalized hyperactivity, marked by feelings of internal restlessness, inability to relax, and dysphoria when inactive, instead of overt hyperactivity (Asherson et al., 2012). In addition, ADHD may affect adults' functioning in various domains differently, as discussed in Section 3.7 (Barkley, 2002a; Barkley, Fischer, Smallish, & Fletcher, 2006).

3.3 ADHD in Infancy

Identification of early markers predictive of the development of ADHD has the potential to facilitate early diagnosis and enable intervention at a period of critical changes in the rapidly developing brain so that the trajectory of the disorder can be significantly altered. Although empirical data regarding precursors of ADHD in infancy are extremely limited, significant progress has been noted over the last years.

Most theoretical conceptualizations of early signs or precursors of ADHD focus partly on infant temperament, especially high levels of reactivity (approach, negative emotionality, activity level), and low levels of regulation (impulsivity, attentional control), as potential risk factors for later ADHD (Campbell, Halperin, & Sonuga-Barke, 2014).

Turecki (1989) popularized the term ***difficult child*** to describe infants with temperamental characteristics that present a significant challenge to their caregivers during routine care activities. He considered that difficult infants demonstrate high activity levels, intense and unpredictable reactions, difficulty adapting to new situations, and generally negative mood. Thomas and Chess (1977) argued that approximately 10% of infants have a ***difficult temperament***. These infants are characterized by some innate qualities that negatively affect their ability to accommodate and meet the environment's expectations as well as the manner in which the environment responds to them.

Difficult infants have been referred to as children *at risk* (Ross & Ross, 1982). They usually cry more, relative to other infants, and present a high-pitched monotonic cry or scream without obvious reason (Wolff, 1969). They may be restless and overactive in their sleep, and they have difficulty establishing a sleep routine. Their pattern of sleep is irregular and they may wake up repeatedly (Nichamin, 1972).

Approximately 25% of children with severe sleep problems in infancy will later qualify for the diagnosis of ADHD (Döpfner, Rothenberger, & Sonuga-Barke, 2004).

Their irregularities often extend to their eating habits. They are obstinate and obstructive feeders, often having difficulty making the transition from milk to solid food (Ross & Ross, 1982). Furthermore, some adverse prenatal and perinatal factors are often recorded in the history of these infants, including poor maternal health during pregnancy, toxemia or eclampsia, low birth weight, and longer labor (Hartsough & Lambert, 1985; Robson & Pederson, 1997).

Finally, these infants are often described as experiencing excessive colic, although what seems like colic to parents might merely represent excessive irritability (Goldstein & Goldstein, 1998). However, even in cases when infants experience colic indeed, mothers' beliefs do not always correspond to the infants' actual temperament. In a prospective study, 59 mothers of infants with frequent colic were asked to evaluate their child's temperament. Twenty-three percent of these mothers regarded their children as more difficult and more active at age 12 months compared to 5% of controls. However, researchers evaluated the infants with the use of standardized temperamental scales and did not confirm mothers' beliefs (Lehtonen, Korhonen & Korvenranta, 1994).

Our clinical experience is in line with the research findings reported so far. Oftentimes, when we ask mothers when they first noticed their child's hyperactive behavior, they respond that their child had been hyperactive even during pregnancy and very difficult to manage since birth. Obviously, such a statement is more indicative of mothers' subjective belief than actual child behavior. Because of these children's difficult behavior and the challenge it poses to parenting skills, mothers may feel that these difficulties extend to the period of pregnancy. Lehtonen and colleagues (1994) argue that various biological, interpersonal, and environmental factors may combine to impact parents' cognitions and subsequently children's behavior.

The developmental course of these difficult infants is frequently characterized by several impairments. In a retrospective study, Wasserman, Diblasio, Bond, Young, and Colletti (1990) assessed parent ratings of temperament at age 4 months to behavior problems at age 6 years in a sample of 129 children. High correlation has been found between parent-rated temperamental difficulty and subsequent behavior problems. It seems that interaction between child factors and parental attitudes about typical infant behavior eventually contribute to the longitudinal outcome.

Apparently, difficult infant temperament has a significant negative impact on the relationship parents develop with their child. New parents may feel guilty or inadequate because of their inability to calm their baby down, therefore exhibiting overly permissive or solicitous behavior toward their child (Goldstein & Goldstein, 1998). These responses impede the development of a healthy interpersonal relationship and increase the chances for the occurrence of several difficulties throughout development.

Furthermore, mothers of young children with ADHD often report experiencing a higher level of stress in parenting and lower self-esteem. Mash and Johnston (1983b) reported that the greater the levels of these two variables, the more distorted were mothers' cognitions about their child's problem. Besides, due to the hereditary nature of ADHD, parents of these children often face similar problems themselves. This pairing of similar deficits in parent and child often places the child in cumulative negative experiences within familial environment, thus leading to exacerbation of existing difficulties.

Early behavioral markers are usually nonspecific; that is, they are indicative of risk for psychopathology, but cannot determine which type of pathology will develop in later childhood. Therefore, a specific behavior pattern during infancy that directly leads to the diagnosis of ADHD has yet to be found. However, there are certain early signs that render some infants vulnerable to manifesting several developmental deficits, including those characterizing ADHD. These include neurodevelopmental immaturity, increased activity level, emotional dysregulation, overresponsivity to environmental stimulation, and lower cognitive functioning (Sonuga-Barke, Auerbach, Campbell, Daley, & Thompson, 2005).

Identifying markers of ADHD liability before 2 or 3 years of age is difficult. Over the last years, some studies have tried to detect infant behaviors that are more likely to be associated specifically with the diagnosis of ADHD. Studies conducted on infants at familial risk for ADHD have revealed that behavioral markers of vulnerability to ADHD may be present even in the neonatal period. In a prospective study carried out on a neonatal sample of 158 male infants whose fathers had elevated symptoms of ADHD, it was found that the infants displayed poorer motor maturity and autonomic stability relative to controls (Auerbach et al., 2005).

Another study based on a sample of 78 infants, aged 8 to 12 months, whose mothers met the criteria for the diagnosis of ADHD, revealed poor sustained attention and increased levels of motor activity relative to the control group (Ninowski, 2010). Furthermore, according to laboratory and parent ratings, a positive association was found between low levels of inhibitory control at age 2 years and ADHD behaviors (Gagne, Saudino, & Asherson, 2011).

A large prospective study on a sample of 1,106 infants who were followed from 1 month of age through sixth grade, has shown that children with high- versus low-ADHD symptomatology at third grade could be distinguished using cognitive and behavioral measures as early as 15 months (females) and 24 months (males) (Arnett, MacDonald, & Pennington, 2013).

However, the biggest prospective study that has been conducted so far regarding early detection of ADHD in infancy was based on a sample of 2,057 children, followed from age 5 months to 8 years in Quebec, Canada (Galéra et al., 2011). According to the results, a host of prenatal and early postnatal factors that have been linked to the development of ADHD at age 5 months were positively associated with the emergence of core ADHD symptoms by early school years. It seems that developmental trajectories that are associated with certain risk factors and lead to the manifestation of ADHD can be identified early on, even during the first semester of life. These findings are of paramount importance because many of these risk factors are reversible or modifiable and therefore can be early intervention targets, as discussed in Section 11.7.

Furthermore, disharmony in the early mother–child relationship of children later diagnosed with ADHD has been reported in longitudinal studies (Battle & Lacy, 1972). Infants who had a disorganized attachment with their mother were found to display teacher-rated ADHD symptoms at age 6 to 8 years (Pinto Turton, Hughues, White & Gillberg, 2006). Disorganized attachment can be theoretically linked to ADHD through neonatal irritability and high temperamental emotionality that are frequent features of ADHD and also predispose to disorganization (Green & Goldwyn, 2002).

In a more recent study, preliminary evidence has been reported that negative emotionality, specifically infant anger/irritability at 6 months of age may identify infants with familial history of ADHD, providing an early indicator of ADHD liability (Sullivan et al., 2015). Negative emotionality and irritability have consistently been linked to ADHD (Karalunas et al., 2014; Shaw, Stringaris, Nigg, & Leibenluft, 2014). Furthermore, the evolution of effortful control depends in part on the degree to which negative emotionality is present in early life (Posner, Rothbart, & Rueda, 2014; Rothbart et al., 2011). Thus, negative emotionality in the first year may disrupt subsequent development of effortful control and, by extension, contribute as an early marker of risk for ADHD. Infants in the study of Sullivan and colleagues (2015) were indeed found to exhibit reduced self-regulation strategies.

In conclusion, due to the paucity of available empirical data concerning this age group in relation to ADHD, the predominant view is that infants who show early signs like the ones described so far belong to a general high-risk group and are vulnerable to exhibit several neurodevelopmental disorders. However, the type of disorder they will finally manifest depends both on their genetic predisposition and the quality of their early interactions with their caregivers.

3.4 ADHD in Preschool Years

Historically, the majority of research on ADHD has involved school-aged children. However, over the last years, researchers have begun to systematically study the validity of ADHD diagnosis in preschoolers. As a result, a growing scientific literature on this subject has emerged (Posner et al., 2007). In fact, there has been an important increase in the number of preschool children being diagnosed with ADHD and subsequently treated with stimulants (Zito et al., 2000).

Prevalence of ADHD during preschool years is estimated at 3.3%, which is the minimum rate usually reported for older children. However, it is noted that barely a quarter of these children are being referred to mental health services for evaluation and treatment (Egger et al., 2006). Research evidence supports the existence of a relation between preschool behavioral difficulty and later adjustment problems in adolescence and adulthood, which indicates the stability of the disorder over time (Barkley et al., 2006; Lee, Lahey, Owens, & Hinshaw, 2008). Preschool ADHD persists into school age in 60% to 80% of cases, with the combined subtype showing most persistence (Lahey et al., 2004; von Stauffenberg & Campbell, 2007). At age 4 years, severity of hyperactivity and presence of conduct problems is a particularly significant indicator of persistence (Riddle et al., 2013; Sonuga-Barke et al., 2005).

It has been shown that an overactive, temperamental infant frequently turns into a hyperactive, oppositional toddler (Barkley, 1990). However, clinical assessment of preschool ADHD is particularly subtle and complex (Wakschlag et al., 2007). An important issue is how to differentiate clinical from normative transient disruptive behaviors within the preschool age, as most preschoolers exhibit at least some of the behaviors that fall under the rubric of ADHD (Bunte, Schoemaker, Hessen, van der Heijden, & Matthys, 2014). At this age, it is natural for children to be more active, impulsive, and inattentive, but also vigorous and unrestrained, in an effort to learn about the world, explore their abilities, and test adults' limits (Campbell, 1985).

Difficulty in distinguishing ADHD symptoms from normative preschool characteristics is also attributed to the fact that higher order cognitive abilities that are important in ADHD, such as executive functioning and reward discounting, are not yet sufficiently developed until the second or third year of life (Sullivan et al., 2015). Control over motor activity, impulsivity, negative emotions, attention shifting, and attention focusing evolve rapidly during this developmental period (Campbell, 2002; Jones, Rothbart, & Posner, 2003).

Martin (2009) referred to this issue as the "zone of diagnostic ambiguity," suggesting that this zone is rather wide in disorders like ADHD, leading to significant variability among clinicians regarding diagnosis and subsequent treatment. Therefore, the diagnosis of ADHD in young children usually relies on the extent to which reported symptoms are more pronounced or prevalent than in other children of the same age (Biederman, 2011).

The way adults interpret behaviors indicative of ADHD plays a significant role in the identification of the disorder during preschool years. As Campbell notes (1985), "Differences in knowledge attribution and tolerance levels influence how the child's behavior is construed and whether typical behavior is defined by parents as problematic or problematic behavior is seen acceptable" (p. 408).

There is a scientific consensus over the reliability and predictive validity of ADHD as early as 4 years of age (Egger, Kondo & Angold, 2006; Lahey et al., 2004). However, as it has been already discussed, some early signs can be reliably detected in infancy and are associated with subsequent functional impairment in various domains (Egger et al., 2006). More recently, it has been suggested that the diagnosis of ADHD can be reliably made as early as age 3 years (Pauli-Pott & Becker, 2011), which is in line with our own clinical view. In addition, studies suggest that 60% to 70% of children later diagnosed with ADHD were identifiable during their preschool years (Barkley, 1981b). Taking into account this evidence, it is of surprise that some clinicians still avoid diagnosing ADHD prior to age 6, potentially delaying much-needed treatment and certainly losing the chance for early intervention (Curchack-Lichtin, Chacko, & Halperin, 2014).

During preschool years, the combined and the hyperactive-impulsive subtypes of ADHD are more commonly observed compared to the inattentive subtype (Galéra et al., 2011). This finding might be associated with the difficulty evaluating attention deficits during this developmental stage as opposed to externalizing hyperactive and impulsive behavior. As a result, the difficulties of children with this subtype are not often discernible by parents until school entry.

ADHD at preschool age shares many of the characteristics of its school-aged counterpart, as psychosocial impairment on a range of variables is already present. Preschoolers with ADHD are often impulsive, disobedient, and particularly daring. As a result, they are more likely to encounter accidental injuries (Barkley, 2002b). In addition, they seem to have inexhaustible energy resources, and their motor activity is particularly increased. They are very demanding and prone to temper tantrums when they get angry or frustrated, mainly in the face of parental prohibitions (Campbell et al., 2014; Kakouros et al., 2005). More than half of the parents of preschoolers with ADHD state that they are unwilling to take their child out to a store or a restaurant due to inappropriate behavior (Egger et al., 2006). This attitude may result from the young children's inability to modulate their behavior in response to different situational demands.

Preschool children with ADHD usually present with deficits in multiple developmental domains over and above the core symptoms of ADHD (Yochman, Ornoy, & Parush, 2006). Toddlers with ADHD often delay in language development and have SLPs at a higher rate relative to typically developing toddlers (Kim & Kaiser, 2000; Tirosh & Cohen, 1998) (see Section 7.2). These difficulties concern both receptive and expressive language (Agapitou & Andreou, 2008; Gilliam & Demesquita, 2000). Moreover, it seems that many toddlers with ADHD have difficulties in pragmatics. They may use more stereotyped ways of conversation and face difficulties in the functional and effective use of language within the framework of communication (Bishop & Baird, 2001; Geurts & Embrechts, 2008; Papaeliou, Maniadaki, & Kakouros, 2015). It is argued that delayed speech onset is probably one of the earliest clinical indicators of risk for the presence of ADHD (Ornoy, Uriel, & Tennenbaum, 1993). Our clinical experience corroborates this argument.

It has been repeatedly noted that children experiencing language problems are at a greater risk for a wide range of behavioral and academic problems (Cunningham & Boyle, 2002; Gremillion & Martel, 2014). Preschoolers with ADHD may enter kindergarten significantly behind typically developing children in basic math and prereading skills (Spira & Fischel, 2005). This is explained by these children's poor experiences with early literacy activities, such as those that increase phonemic awareness and early numeracy activities (DuPaul & Langberg, 2015). Phonemic awareness is a component of phonological awareness and reflects children's awareness of individual sounds in words and their ability to manipulate these sounds (Ehri, 2005). Phonological awareness is the general child sensitivity to several phonological units that make up spoken speech (Justice, 2006). As a result, these children are approximately one standard deviation below typically developing children with respect to school readiness skills and behaviors (DuPaul et al., 2001). More important, the educational impairments exhibited by these children in preschool years are associated with chronic underachievement in the main academic domains throughout the school years (Massetti et al., 2008).

Another important developmental problem in preschool children with ADHD is motor performance (see Section 7.9). Qualitative behavioral motor aspects seem to be predictive of ADHD in 5- to 7-year-old children (Kroes et al., 2002). Also, 5- to 6-year-old children later diagnosed with ADHD were less accurate and more variable in an executive motor control task than their peers without ADHD (Kalff et al., 2003). Thus, young children with ADHD often exhibit difficulties that lead to higher rates of utilization of remedial services, such as speech and language, occupational, and physical therapy, and they are more likely to be placed in special education programs (Marks et al., 2009).

Typically developing preschoolers acquire basic foundational social skills during this developmental stage. This process is usually disrupted for toddlers with ADHD. Although they have not developed well-set, negative patterns of social interaction yet, they are more aggressive, less compromising, and less cooperative with peers during group activities (Kakouros et al., 2005). Generally, it has been reported that toddlers with ADHD exhibit a significantly higher frequency of negative social behaviors, especially in free play settings, and have greater social skills deficits relative to normal controls (DuPaul et al., 2001; Handen & Valdes, 2007).

On a neuropsychological level, it has been reported that toddlers with ADHD have similar difficulties to older children with reference to executive functions, such as working memory, planning, organizational skills, attentional flexibility, and behavioral inhibition (Sonuga-Barke et al., 2005). A meta-analysis of 25 studies has revealed that such deficits in executive functions may effectively differentiate these children from their typically developing counterparts (Pauli-Pott & Becker, 2011).

In a recent longitudinal study, it was found that a wide range of neuropsychological deficits at preschool, including reaction time variability, emotional reactivity, and working memory, were significantly related to inattention measured 13 years later (Sjöwall, Bohlin, Rydell, & Thorell, 2017). In addition, regulation of happiness/exuberance and anger reactivity was significantly related to hyperactivity/impulsivity. Working memory and reaction time variability in preschool have been significantly related to academic achievement in late adolescence beyond the influence of early ADHD symptoms. Based on these findings, the authors suggest that early neuropsychological deficits have a true predictive value not only for the development of ADHD, but also for functional impairments associated with the disorder, such as academic underachievement.

Nowadays new instruments have been developed for screening ADHD in preschool years, including both checklists and structured interviews, and many behavioral signs have been revealed for identifying these children before formal school entry (Carlson, 2005; Davis & Williams, 2011). The diagnostic challenge and primary area of concern for the clinician is to understand the fine line between appropriate early identification and overdiagnosis. In other words, it is crucial to avoid pathologizing developmentally aberrant but time-limited manifestations of dysfunction, but also underestimating the clinical significance of early signs for the later onset of a full-blown disorder (Sonuga-Barke et al., 2005).

3.5 ADHD in Middle Childhood

Most research studies on ADHD are based on samples of school-aged children. Although ADHD is manifested early in preschool years, children are mainly referred for assessment between the ages 5 and 8 (Campbell et al., 2014). Despite evidence for early signs, ADHD is identified by schoolteachers more often than by parents or physicians, indicating that diagnoses are unlikely to occur prior to entrance into a formal school setting (Sax & Kautz, 2003). Unfortunately, parents of preschoolers are still frequently advised that their child's problems are transient and will be outgrown.

School entry represents a major life transition for children. The introduction of the child to new, potentially more demanding and structured environments may aggravate existing difficulties of preschool ADHD (Sonuga-Barke et al., 2005). Various abilities are essential for a successful school trajectory, including sustained attention, adherence to rules, following through on instructions, engagement in classroom activities, exhibiting self-regulated behavior, as well as some cognitive abilities that are involved in the process of learning to read and write. Children with ADHD, however, usually have deficits in the aforementioned domains that become more apparent in middle childhood because they pose great obstacles in successfully adapting to new situational demands. During this period, learning difficulties and conduct problems are often added to the difficulties already experienced by children with ADHD. Therefore, their clinical presentation becomes even more complicated.

Academic performance of children with ADHD is lower compared to that of their peers by 30%. Furthermore, their school performance is by 80% lower than expected with reference to their intellectual ability (DuPaul & Volpe, 2009). Specifically, their skill levels are around two-thirds of a standard deviation below their peers in reading, mathematics, and spelling (Frazier, Youngstrom, Glutting, & Watkins, 2007). At least 56% of these children will need professional help, and 30% to 50% may qualify for special education services (Barkley, Fischer et al., 1990; Faraone et al., 1993). Furthermore, students with ADHD are three times more likely to repeat a grade during elementary school (Barry, Lyman, & Grofer Klinger, 2002).

Educational impairment is one of the main reasons individuals with ADHD are referred for assessment and treatment (Loe & Feldman, 2007). These children are often identified because they are struggling to learn to read. They may also exhibit difficulties acquiring math skills, such as learning addition and subtraction, and understanding concepts like measurement (Anderson, 2010; DuPaul & Langberg, 2015). Educational impairment is one of the major consequences of ADHD as it affects future personal finances, access and ability to pursue higher education, employment, and health (Sjöwall et al., 2017). Furthermore, the long-term connection between ADHD and juvenile delinquency is largely mediated by academic underachievement (Defoe, Farrington, & Loeber, 2013; Maniadaki & Kakouros, 2011; Maniadaki, Kakouros, & Karaba, 2010).

Rapport, Scanlan, and Denney (1999) postulated that there are both cognitive and behavioral pathways from ADHD to academic underachievement: the cognitive pathway mediates the impact of ADHD on achievement via deficits in executive functions, and the behavioral pathway through its influence on classroom behavior. For example, due to their deficits in sustained attention, which interferes with lesson attendance and effortful control, these children may slowly fall behind in academic tasks requiring practice for proficiency (Pfiffner & Barkley, 1990). Furthermore, they may fail to pay attention to instructions, rush through assignments, and forget to check the accuracy of their work (DuPaul & Langberg, 2015). In a substantial number of cases, academic underachievement may also be attributed to the frequent comorbidity of ADHD with SLD (see Section 7.3).

Besides, a number of student variables, such as motivation, study skills, interpersonal skills, and engagement, which have been called *academic enablers*, have been found to mediate the relationship between ADHD symptoms and academic achievement (DiPerna, Volpe, & Elliott, 2005; Volpe et al., 2006). Such deficits predict the academic outcomes of children with ADHD, above and beyond the traditional symptoms of the disorder (Langberg et al., 2011). Poor organizational skills, such as misplacing, losing, or forgetting materials, failing to record homework assignments, and not completing or handing in assignments may also hinder academic performance (Power, Werba, Watkins, Angelucci, & Eiraldi, 2006). In addition, students with ADHD often lack persistence and quit significantly more often than typically developing children, especially when they encounter difficulties with a task and experience frustration (Johnson & Reid, 2011; Scime & Norvilitis, 2006).

Such academic difficulties are not limited to the school setting, as ADHD symptoms contribute to functional impairments in homework as well, including low engagement, poor productivity, avoidance, noncompliance, off-task behavior, problematic time management, and procrastination (Gureasko-Moore, DuPaul, & White, 2007; Rogers et al., 2009a). Consequently, students with ADHD usually result in attending class unprepared. In addition, parents of children with ADHD often report that they feel less efficacious at helping their children with their homework relative to parents of typically developing children. Especially fathers of these children report being more disengaged from their children's learning and using more coercive and punitive interactions regarding their children's achievement (Rogers, Wiener, Marton & Tannock, 2009b).

Students with ADHD may often disrupt classroom activities. They have difficulty remaining seated for a long time and exhibiting on-task behavior during instruction, particularly when passive classroom activities are required. Other times, they may leave their seat without permission and walk around disturbing their classmates. Even when they are seated, they often fidget in their chair, play with inappropriate objects, or repetitively tap hands and feet (DuPaul & Stoner, 2003). Furthermore, they call out without permission, interrupt the teacher and their classmates at inappropriate times, and get very angry when confronted with reprimands (DuPaul & Stoner, 2003). In an attempt to set boundaries for these children, teachers often enter a coercive cycle. A pattern of negative reinforcement usually develops as the teacher may interrupt the lesson to focus on misbehavior. As a result, teacher behavior brings children with ADHD to the center of attention of the whole class, which reinforces the behavior that led to the interruption of the lesson.

In the elementary classroom setting, children with ADHD are usually described as daydreaming and absent-minded. However, careful examination suggests that daydreaming may result from lack of interest in some of the activities that teachers suggest, especially when these activities do not involve the child's active participation, such as listening to the teacher's lecture or reading silently (DuPaul & Volpe, 2009). Difficulty of children with ADHD in investing in tasks that do not motivate them often ends up in the engagement of significantly nonproductive activity during work. According to Barkley (1997a), difficulties that seem to be associated with inattention are actually associated with poor self-control and dysfunction in the reward processing. In other words, poor sustained attention of children with ADHD may represent impairments in task-directed persistence and interference control. As a result, these children cannot persist in effort toward tasks that provide little immediate reward and flit from one uncompleted activity to another. In addition, these children frequently prefer to engage in immediately rewarding behaviors, such as watching TV or playing on the computer, over work completion, which is associated with delayed award such as the teacher's praise (DuPaul & Langberg, 2015).

Behavior of children with ADHD is often unpredictable and distressing to teachers, because they may successfully complete a task one day but fail in a similar task the next day. Although these children seem to know the rules, they do not follow them systematically (Lougy & Rosenthal, 2002). Therefore, they do not have difficulty learning rules, but applying them consistently. Teachers often interpret this inconsistency in performance as laziness and poor effort, which may lead them to exert increased pressure and make constant reprimands. Nonetheless, for children with ADHD this inconsistency is the outcome of their impulsive behavior and the degree of motivation for a certain activity. The teacher's misinterpretation and subsequent negative response may result in a heightened degree of frustration for both teacher and child (Goldstein & Goldstein, 1998).

At this age, most children are capable of recognizing that they have control over their behavior and that contingencies of their actions depend on them. However, children with ADHD usually have an external locus of control. In other words, they tend to place responsibility for their actions on others, and hold the belief that they have little control over their life. This lack of self-confidence further increases the tendency of these children to give up on tasks easily, because they believe that success does not depend mainly on their own effort but on extrinsic factors (Milich & Okazaki, 1991). Recurring experiences of failure in conjunction with constant negative comments made by adults expose these children to a greater risk for developing low self-esteem, which in turn constitutes a negative predictor of outcome (Patterson, Reid, & Dishion, 1992).

Difficulties of children with ADHD also extend to the domain of peer relationships. Studies employing sociometric measures have found high rates of peer rejection for children with ADHD, ranging from 52% to 82% (Hoza et al., 2005). In addition, these children are rarely chosen by peers for social interaction (Pelham & Milich, 1984). The degree of severity of impulsivity symptoms is closely related to the degree of aggression that they express as well as with the frequency of involvement into fights (Halperin et al., 1995). This behavior often leads to the marginalization of children with ADHD by their peers. Furthermore, their friendships are characterized by less stability and duration, and more conflicts (Blachman & Hinshaw, 2002).

Peer problems can be attributed to their poor social skills, including abilities to initiate and structure interactions, listen carefully to their partner, perspective-taking abilities, wait their turn in games, inhibit their impulsive responses for the sake of the group's well-being, manage anger and frustration, and come up with alternative ways of solving problems that arise in their personal relationships (Murray-Close et al., 2010). Difficulties of children with ADHD in their social interactions seem to exacerbate when ADHD co-occurs with learning difficulties (Flicek, 1992).

Therefore, school-age years constitute a period when several factors will determine the quality of developmental progression in adolescence and adulthood, and set the foundations for the outcome of the disorder. These factors include the quality of interactions between the child with ADHD and their environment, number and severity of comorbid disorders and associated difficulties, as well as implementation of effective interventions.

3.6 ADHD in Adolescence

ADHD is currently viewed as a lifelong developmental disorder that does not remit by adolescence, as it was previously believed (Barkley, Fischer et al., 1990; Mick et al., 2011). As children enter adolescence, the presentation of ADHD symptoms appears to change. ADHD symptoms of hyperactivity and impulsivity may decline, whereas symptoms of inattention usually do not (Fischer, Barkley, Fletcher, & Smallish, 1993; Hart, Lahey, Loeber, Applegate, & Frick, 1995). However, all three core symptoms generally remain much higher in adolescents with ADHD relative to typically developing peers (Biederman et al., 1998).

Furthermore, it seems that the overall adjustment across multiple domains, including academic achievement, prosocial behavior, and interpersonal relationships, is lower among adolescents with ADHD, whereas comorbidity rates with other psychopathological conditions is increased (Lee et al., 2008). Besides, most empirical evidence points to the conclusion that disruptive behavior disorders, into which ADHD was classified in DSM-IV, demonstrate the greatest persistence of all childhood disorders throughout development (Campbell & Ewing, 1990; Moffitt, 1990).

Many of the problems that children with ADHD experience during school-age years persist into adolescence. In addition, new problems are added, leading to concerns about the safety and health of adolescents with ADHD. For example, use of drugs and alcohol is particularly increased among adolescents with ADHD (Molina, Bukstein, & Lynch, 2002) (see Section 7.12.1). Moreover, ADHD is positively associated with cigarette use during adolescence at an earlier age than controls (Molina et al., 2013; Molina & Pelham, 2003). Some studies suggest that the risk for adolescent substance use among children with ADHD is heightened only among those who had comorbid externalizing problems, even if those problems remitted by adolescence (Realmuto et al., 2009; Nigg, 2013a). However, given the complex nature of ADHD with CD (see Section 7.11.2), the risk incurred by CD does not absolve the risk for substance use among children with ADHD because in many cases ADHD leads to CD (Owens, Cardoos, & Hinshaw, 2015).

Adolescents with ADHD are reported to display an early onset of first sexual intercourse, as well as risky sexual behavior (Flory, Molina, Pelham, Gnagy, & Smith, 2006). Barkley, Fischer, Smallish, and Fletcher (2006) have found that adolescents and young adults with ADHD had more lifetime sexual partners, higher rates of pregnancy/impregnation, and higher rates of lifetime sexually transmitted infections. Affiliation with peers whose attitudes favor involvement in nonconventional activities is strongly related to risky sexual behavior (Marshal, Molina, & Pelham, 2003). In addition, low levels of perceived parental monitoring and trust, conflictual relationships with parents, and poor quality of parent–teen communication regarding safe sex are all associated with engagement in risky sexual behavior (Wilson & Donenberg, 2004).

The transition of children with ADHD from primary to high school brings new developmental challenges, one of which is the adjustment to the increased demands of the school environment. On the one hand, there are new subjects in the school curriculum that require extensive use of operational thinking. On the other hand, there are increased expectations related to management of classwork and homework for multiple teachers, better organization of school material, effective time management, development of study and note-taking skills, and so forth (Evans, Langberg, Raggi, Allen, & Buvinger, 2005). At the same time, adolescents are expected to function with more independence, and self-regulate their own goal-directed organization and planning behaviors, without needing constant monitoring from their parents (Steinberg, 2005).

Adolescents with ADHD usually display impairments in these domains. As a result, academic and educational attainment problems continue through high school (Kent et al., 2011). These adolescents continue to display significant deficits in reading, math, and spelling in comparison to their peers (Frazier et al., 2007). In addition, they frequently display problems with academic performance related to examination completion, studying for tests, homework completion, and note-taking in the classroom (Evans et al., 2001).

Academic impairment, difficulties in peer relationships, and deviant behaviors constitute the most common reasons for referral of adolescents with ADHD to mental health services (Edwards, Barkley, Laneri, Fletcher, & Metevia, 2001). Adolescents with ADHD have higher rates of expulsion, absenteeism, grade retention, course failure, and school dropout (Molina et al., 2009; Robb et al., 2011). They also have a greater chance of obtaining a lower-level diploma and failing to graduate from secondary school (Galéra et al., 2009). Furthermore, they are much more likely to display delinquent behavior and get involved in the juvenile justice system relative to their peers (Maniadaki & Kakouros, 2008; Maniadaki, Kakouros & Karaba, 2009; 2010; Mannuzza, Klein, Konig, & Giampino, 1989).

Adolescents with ADHD usually report a negative self-image and low self-esteem (Brook & Boaz, 2005; Kruger & Kendell, 2001; Treuting & Hinshaw, 2001). They also consider that their parents and teachers do not understand them and that they receive constant criticism for lack of motivation and poor effort. As a consequence, interactions between these adolescents and their parents are often conflictual. Furthermore, they often experience heightened levels of stress, especially with respect to school (Brook & Boaz, 2005). Due to their low self-esteem, their poor self-control, and their strong need for acceptance, these adolescents might be particularly vulnerable to affiliate with deviant peers and engage in law-breaking activities.

Therefore, it seems that adolescence is a period during which the problems of children with ADHD may magnify, unless they have been dealt with earlier. These problems may also exaggerate due to the particular nature of this developmental stage. Typically developing adolescents seek their personal identity, usually dispute figures of status and authority, experience mood fluctuations, and often like to get involved into risky situations. The interplay of these normative developmental characteristics with core and associated features of ADHD may create a pathway toward social marginalization, use of drugs, resignation from academic learning, school dropout, and manifestation of antisocial and delinquent behavior.

It is evident that the developmental progression of children with ADHD into adolescence is to a great extent related to their experiences and course during school-age years. From our point of view, the prerequisites for a healthy transition from middle childhood to adolescence for youth with ADHD are the following:

1. The diagnosis must have been established early.
2. Teachers and parents must have understood the nature of the child's difficulties and have been trained to effectively address them.
3. The child must have received professional help.
4. The child must have been supported to shape a positive self-image, high self-esteem, and healthy interpersonal relationships.

However, in case diagnosis has not been established early, learning difficulties and behavioral problems are present during school-age years, and the child and family have not received effective help, adolescence often aggravates existing problems and facilitates the adolescent to gravitate toward deviant pathways.

3.7 ADHD in Adulthood

Worldwide prevalence studies of ADHD in adults estimate rates to be between 2.5% and 4.3% (Fayyad et al., 2007; Simon et al., 2009), indicating that this is one of the most common adult mental health conditions. Almost 50% to 70% of individuals diagnosed with ADHD in childhood continue to meet diagnostic criteria for the disorder as they achieve adulthood (Kaplan & Stevens, 2002; Lie, 1992; Tamam, Karaku, & Ozpoyraz, 2008). However, it has been found that when ADHD is not identified during childhood, it usually remains undiagnosed in adulthood as well (Weiss & Murray, 2003). Consequently, there is a compelling need to understand the presentation and impact of ADHD symptoms in adults.

The ADHD symptoms that seem to be more persistent over time are attention deficits and impulse disinhibition (Barkley, 1990; Weiss & Hechtman, 1993). For this reason, a great number of children who were diagnosed with ADHD, combined type, may progress into adults with predominantly inattentive type, according to DSM-IV criteria (McGough & Barkley, 2004). Symptomatology of these individuals in adulthood gives mainly the impression of irresponsibility, because they have low self-esteem, often face difficulty making decisions and taking initiatives, and are frequently dismissed from their jobs (Achenbach, Howell, McConaughy, & Stanger, 1995).

Brown (2009) describes six clusters of cognitive functions that tend to be impaired in adults with ADHD:

1. Activation (organizing, prioritizing, and activating to work)
2. Focus (focusing, sustaining, and shifting attention to tasks)
3. Effort (regulating alertness, sustaining effort, and processing speed)
4. Emotion (managing frustration and regulating emotions)
5. Memory (utilizing working memory and accessing recall)
6. Action (monitoring and self-regulating action).

Deficits in activation lead adults with ADHD to excessive procrastination. Deficits in focus make these individuals get easily distracted not only by external but also internal stimuli, such as tangential thoughts, remembering another task, or an internal sense of restlessness (Ramsey, 2015). Deficits in effort may lead to inability to finish long-term projects. Difficulty regulating alertness may result in sleep disturbances. Deficits in emotion regulation create chronic difficulties managing frustration, anger, worry, disappointment, desire, and other emotions. Deficits in memory impede effective implementation of acquired knowledge. Finally, deficits in self-regulating action lead to poor self-control, impulsive behavior, and disturbed relationships.

The transition into young adulthood is a unique period marked by increases in available choices (due to the end of formal schooling) and decreases in structure and support (Schulenberg, Sameroff, & Cicchetti, 2004). Prospective longitudinal studies that have followed children with ADHD into adulthood find evidence of continuing impairment in multiple domains of daily functioning (Klein et al., 2012; Barkley, Fischer et al., 2006). These problems were often discernible in late adolescence and continued into adulthood.

Given the frequency, severity, and persistence of academic problems of youth with ADHD, it is expected that they will continue to have difficulties when they pursue higher education. Indeed, adults with ADHD are far less likely to enroll in higher education upon the completion of high school (DuPaul & Weyandt, 2009; Kuriyan et al., 2013). Even those who become college students, continue to be impaired academically, complete fewer years of college, and fail to graduate (Weyandt & DuPaul, 2013). Frequently, they evidence lower grade point averages, poorer study skills, fewer academic coping behaviors, and poorer time management compared with peers without ADHD (Blase et al., 2009; Weyandt & DuPaul, 2006). They also describe losing focus when working on tasks that require a measure of persistence, such as household chores (Ramsey, 2015).

This fact is expected to have an adverse impact on their job prospects. In addition, a professional career requires skilled labor, independence of supervision, and acceptance of responsibility. Adults with ADHD tend to be impulsive and inattentive and may lack persistence in attending to work-related tasks (Biederman & Faraone, 2006; Kessler et al., 2005). Moreover, they face difficulties in maintenance of motivation and self-discipline (Barkley & Murphy, 2010).

As a result, the quality of the work adjustment of adults with ADHD differs significantly from that of normal controls. It seems that adults with ADHD experience an unstable employment situation and frequent job changes (Barkley, Fischer et al., 2006). There is also some evidence that they attain lower status employment (Barkley, Murphy, & Fischer, 2008; Kuriyan et al., 2013) and receive lower work performance ratings from employers relative to their colleagues without ADHD (Barkley, Fischer, Smallish, & Fletcher, 2002). It appears that young adults with ADHD may contribute to their own job instability by quitting more frequently than their peers (Kuriyan et al., 2013).

Consequently, their income is often low, which makes them experience heightened stress regarding their financial situation (Brook, Brook, Zhang, Seltzer, & Finch, 2013). However, even in case they do not have a low income, financial stress is particularly increased among adults with ADHD, probably due to their difficulty planning and maintaining control over their financial resources.

Despite the poor outcomes noted above, there is evidence that a subgroup of children diagnosed with ADHD are successful after high school, attending and completing college, and achieving high status employment (Hechtman, 1999). Therefore, understanding of variables that may predict adulthood occupational and educational achievement is very important (see Section 3.8).

Adults with ADHD also encounter difficulties in developing and maintaining positive interpersonal relations, similarly to children and adolescents. They seem to have fewer friends and greater difficulty managing tension that is sometimes generated in friendly or romantic relations (Barkley et al., 2008; Babinski et al., 2010). As a result, they may blow up inconsistently and spark discord in their relationships. Men with ADHD, especially those with conduct problems persisting from childhood, have been found to be verbally aggressive and violent toward their partner five to nine times more often than controls (Wymbs et al., 2012). Furthermore, adults with ADHD commonly report being in less satisfying intimate relationships and a threefold higher rate of divorce (Biederman, Faraone et al., 2006; Kessler et al., 2006; Klein et al., 2012).

According to a recent review, adults with ADHD also experience difficulties in their parenting role (Johnston, Lui, & Williamson, 2014). These difficulties usually concern monitoring child behavior, controlling or managing child misbehavior, organizing issues regarding their child's everyday routine, and problem solving in parenting situations. Furthermore, parents of children with ADHD are often more inconsistent toward their child, present increased variability in emotional responsiveness, and employ more overreactive and harsh discipline strategies (Johnston, Mash, Miller, & Ninowski, 2012). These deficits in parenting are particularly important, given the highly heritable nature of ADHD, which makes the co-occurrence of ADHD in child and parent relatively common. From a developmental psychopathology perspective, deficits in parenting contribute critical variance in determining trajectories of child development as they are reciprocally related to child vulnerabilities (Johnston, Mash, Miller, & Ninowski, 2012).

Adults with ADHD are consistently found to be overrepresented in jails and prisons worldwide. A review of nine studies of ADHD rates among adult male prison inmates found rates ranging from 24% to 67% (Gudjonsson, Sigurddsson, Young, Newton, & Peersen, 2009). These rates were estimated at 40% in Sweden (Ginsberg, Hirvikoski, & Lindefors, 2010), 45% in Germany (Rösler et al., 2004), and over 50% in Finland (Haapasalo & Hämäläinen, 1996). The study conducted in Sweden highlighted that only 2 out of the 30 prison inmates confirmed with ADHD had received the diagnosis in their childhood, despite the fact that most of them had used mental health services and received educational support in the past. Rates of ADHD in imprisoned women seem lower (around 10%), but more increased relative to the general population (Rösler, Retz, Yaqoobi, Burg, & Retz-Yunginger, 2008). According to Faraone and Biederman (2004), adults with ADHD are twice as likely as the general population to be arrested for an offense. However, as noted by Sibley and colleagues (2011), "individuals with childhood ADHD are at an earlier and unremitting risk for offending at all delinquency severity levels and across a wider variety of crimes" (p. 29).

The limited prospective studies available lead to similar conclusions. Based on official arrest records of clinic-referred children with ADHD at mean age 21, Barkley, Fischer, Smallish, and Fletcher (2004) found significantly more arrests and felonies in probands than in normal comparisons. Mannuzza, Klein and Moulton (2008) followed 207 boys with ADHD aged 6 to 12 until 38 years. It has been found that significantly more ADHD probands than comparisons had been arrested (47% vs. 24%), convicted (42% vs. 14%), and incarcerated (15% vs. 1%). Similar results have been reported by Satterfield and colleagues (2007), who concluded that a substantial subgroup of children with ADHD became serious adult offenders. However, these individuals had been exhibiting behavioral problems since childhood. Children with ADHD without similar problems in childhood did not exceed the control group in rates of adult antisocial behavior.

Mannuzza, Klein, and Moulton (2008) highlight that even children with ADHD who did not have CD in childhood have increased chances of getting involved in delinquent acts in adulthood, if they develop CD or SUD in adolescence. However, even without any comorbidity, it seems that individuals with ADHD are more likely to exhibit delinquent behavior at some point in their life (Dalsgaard, Mortensen, Frydenberg, & Thomsen, 2013; Sibley et al., 2011).

Car accidents as well as leisure time accidents are particularly increased in adults with ADHD (Kaya et al., 2008). Drivers with ADHD seem to have more risky behavior, violate traffic laws more often, drive without a license, drive under the influence of alcohol, and receive more fines for speeding compared to drivers without ADHD (Barkley, Murphy, DuPaul, & Bush, 2002; Jerome, Habinski, & Segal, 2006). However, according to a recent meta-analysis, these behaviors mainly concern adults with ADHD and comorbid CD (Vaa, 2014).

In the Milwaukee Young Adult Outcome Study, Barkley (2002a) reported that the rate of sexual transmitted infections among young adults with ADHD aged 19 to 25 (87% males) exceeded the rate of the control group fourfold. In addition, the ADHD group was also more likely to report unplanned pregnancies. It has been found that high-quality mother–child relationship moderates risk for risky sexual behavior among college students with ADHD (Huggins, Rooney, & Chronis-Tuscano, 2015). Furthermore, risky sexual behavior is closely related to alcohol use, which is increased among young adults with ADHD (Rooney, Chronis-Tuscano, & Yoon, 2012).

Furthermore, it has been shown that nearly 80% of adults with ADHD present with at least one comorbid mental disorder (Sobanski et al., 2007; Torgersen, Gjervan, & Rasmussen, 2006). Generally, adults with ADHD report significantly poorer quality of life relative to adults without ADHD (Brod, Johnston, Able, & Swindle, 2006; Mick, Faraone, Spencer, Zhang, & Biederman, 2008).

Despite the relatively high prevalence of ADHD in adults and subsequent impairment, it has been shown that only 11% of them are likely to receive some kind of treatment (Stephen & Kevin, 2008). Prescription of medication in adults with ADHD generally follows the same principles as in children, and high rates of positive outcomes are reported (approximately 50% to 80%), mainly with respect to reduction of the core symptoms of the disorder (Wilens, Prince et al., 2003) (see Section 13.2).

However, it has been found that work and interpersonal impairments in adults with ADHD seem to extend to those who are treated with medications (Safren, Sprich, Cooper-Vince, Knouse, & Lerner, 2010). This finding provides a continued justification for the importance of additional approaches in reducing not only core ADHD symptoms, but also associated functional impairments. As medication does not equip people with coping strategies and skills, psychosocial interventions are considered highly important in the treatment of impairments experienced by adults with ADHD (see Section 13.3).

Before closing this section, a provocative novel point of view should be noted. Recently, Moffitt and colleagues (2015) examined the assumed continuity of ADHD from childhood to adulthood in the Dunedin representative birth cohort of 1,037 individuals followed to age 38. An unexpected finding was the emergence of a substantial group of individuals who met all

DSM-5 criteria for ADHD except that of onset by age 12. About 90% of these individuals were de novo cases that had not met childhood criteria. As the authors write, there is an "intriguing possibility that adult ADHD is a bona fide disorder that has unfortunately been mistaken for the neurodevelopmental disorder of ADHD because of surface similarities, and given the wrong name." Castellanos (2015) notes that acceptance of such a novel entity needs independent replication in order for a new syndrome to be revealed.

3.8 Moderators and Mediators of Outcome

The presence of ADHD constitutes a risk factor for a series of negative outcomes in the individual's life. However, there is a wide range of developmental trajectories that a child with ADHD may follow. According to our clinical experience, we may encounter people with ADHD in prisons and in universities as well. There are adults with ADHD who have difficulty keeping a job or a relationship, and others who are happy in their personal life and successful in their professional career. Some children with ADHD manage to control their symptoms and reap the benefits of treatment, and others struggle to function effectively within the contexts of their family and school. It is clear that the presence of the disorder is not the sole determiner of the individual's developmental course. The outcome of ADHD is influenced by a series of risk and resilience factors that interact throughout development.

An important research question concerns the identification of predictive factors in childhood that lead to persistence or remittance of ADHD and associated impairments in adolescence and adulthood. From a clinical point of view, the ability to differentiate persisting from remitting ADHD in early childhood is meaningful, as it may lead to the identification of those children with the greatest need for early intervention services and, subsequently, to the prevention of long-term negative outcomes (Chacko et al., 2009; Sonuga-Barke et al., 2006). As noted in a recent meta-analysis, the current knowledge about risk markers of the course of ADHD is still unsatisfactory to guide clinical practice (Caye et al., 2016). However, several predictive factors have been revealed.

Predictive factors may be moderators or mediators. Moderator variables reflect baseline characteristics that predict change in ADHD symptoms over development. Mediator variables reflect effects that explain the change in ADHD symptoms such that change in a mediator would predict change in ADHD (Cheung et al., 2016).

Convergent findings emphasize the role of the individual's intellectual ability in moderating the developmental course of ADHD (Cheung et al., 2016; Hechtman, 1999). Children with ADHD and high intelligence have better academic performance, which has a positive impact on their self-esteem as well as on the development of adaptive skills (Barkley, 2006b). Furthermore, these children often come up with ways to manage their difficulties more effectively on their own. Finally, longitudinal treatment studies report positive associations between childhood IQ in ADHD and treatment response (Owens et al., 2003).

Furthermore, in some cases, certain personality traits are more likely to affect the individual's psychosocial functioning than the symptomatology of the disorder per se because individual differences in personality structure are often related to the level of functioning (Pelkonen, Martunnen, Laippala, Lonngvist, & Aro, 1997). It has been found that the longitudinal course of ADHD is related to late adolescent personality structure. Individuals with persistent ADHD have lower Conscientiousness and Agreeableness, and increased Neuroticism, with respect to the Five-Factor Model of personality (Miller, Miller, Newcorn, & Halperin, 2008).

It has been hypothesized that elevated rates of unsuccessful relationships among adults with persistent ADHD may be due to the fact that they are emotional labile and disagreeable. Accordingly, low Conscientiousness may be particularly important in considering poor educational and employment outcomes in individuals with persistent ADHD (Miller et al., 2008). However, the direction of the relationship between ADHD and personality is not clear yet, as the presence of ADHD might influence personality structure or personality factors may influence the persistence/remission of ADHD. The way in which these constructs influence and interact with each other over the course of development remains to be elucidated.

Severity of symptomatology alone does not seem enough for understanding the heterogeneity observed in the course of ADHD (Gordon et al., 2006). However, the total number of ADHD symptoms as a marker of severity is associated with persistence in adulthood (Karam et al., 2015; Lara et al., 2009) and has also been linked to future antisocial outcomes (Thapar, van den Bree, Fowler, Langley, & Whittinger, 2006). In addition, there are longitudinal findings that severity of ADHD symptoms predicts later adolescent functioning (Molina et al., 2009).

Psychiatric comorbidity with ODD, DDs, and ADs in ADHD probands at baseline predicts not only more impaired outcome (Biederman et al., 2010) but also persistence of the disorder over time (Biederman et al., 2011). Furthermore, comorbid CD in childhood has been significantly associated with persistence of ADHD, particularly if the onset of CD is before age 10 years (Harvard Mental Health Letter, 2011; Jones & Foster, 2009). The degree to which children exhibit aggressive behavior is a strong predictive sign for the involvement of individuals with ADHD in delinquent acts in adolescence and adulthood (Lochman & Wayland, 1994). Especially girls with ADHD and additional behavior problems seem to be at the greatest risk for both persistent ADHD symptoms and associated functional impairments as they transition through adolescence and into early adulthood (Mick et al., 2011).

A mediating factor between ADHD and delinquent behavior seems to be school failure (Rösler et al., 2004). It has also been suggested that a strong tendency to lie in childhood is closely associated with delinquent behavior in adolescence (Satterfield & Schell, 1977) and in adulthood (Satterfield et al., 2007), because delinquents often need to verbally conceal their criminal behavior.

Individuals with ADHD often ignore danger, seek adventure, and get involved in high-risk actions, violating social norms and exposing both themselves and others to danger. Adolescents with ADHD can easily turn to delinquency when they live in environments that favor the development of these characteristics, as for example in neighborhoods with less informal social control and high criminality rates, or in a family where parental monitoring is absent (Jones & Lynam, 2009). In case interactions between the adolescent with ADHD and their parents are conflictual, the adolescents' tendency to dispute institutions and authority figures increases even further. Consequently, the chance of being involved with the law is also increased (Mukolo & Hefilnger, 2011).

Family factors such as maternal psychopathology and psychosocial adversity, including increased family conflict, decreased family cohesion, and poor quality of parent–child relationships significantly predict persistence of ADHD in adolescence and adulthood (Biederman et al., 2011), and may account for the link between early ADHD and antisocial behavior (Thapar et al., 2006). These factors are also closely associated with harsh parenting practices (Pfiffner, McBurnett, Rathouz, & Judice, 2005), which may lead to a greater risk for physical abuse. Indeed, children with ADHD are at increased risk for maltreatment (Briscoe-Smith & Hinshaw, 2006; Cicchetti & Manly, 2001). In turn, maltreatment is associated with future delinquent behavior. It has been found that childhood maltreatment increases the risk of adolescent/young adult arrest over and above the risk associated with childhood CD. ADHD youth classified as maltreated are three and a half times more likely to be arrested when compared to ADHD youth without a maltreatment history (De Sanctis, Nomura, Newcorn, & Halperin, 2012).

Parenting practices also serve as a significant mediator of the relation between ADHD severity and child social outcome (Kaiser, McBurnett, & Pfiffner, 2011). Lower levels of paternal sensitivity and maternal positive regard in early childhood are uniquely predictive of higher levels of inattentiveness in middle childhood (Keown, 2012). Furthermore, intrusive paternal behaviors during father–son interactions are predictive of hyperactive-impulsive behaviors at school (Keown, 2012). Fathers who fail to synchronize their actions to the child's cues and adapting their behavior accordingly may compromise the development of attentional and self-organizing skills in children showing early signs of ADHD (Johnston & Mash, 2001; Sonuga-Barke et al., 2006).

Ineffective parenting is also related to poor development of social skills in children, which in turn leads to difficulties in peer relations. Poor peer relations constitute an independent negative predictive factor in the course of the disorder (Bagwell, 2001; Hurt, Hoza, & Pelham, 2007). Children with ADHD and serious difficulties in their friendly interactions with peers are more susceptible to the development of associated mental health problems, substance use in adolescence, and overall impairment in their psychosocial functioning (Mrug et al., 2012). In a longitudinal study, peer rejection was found to partially mediate the predictive relationship between early ADHD symptoms and subsequent antisocial behavior (Miller-Johnson, Coie, Maumary-Gremaud, & Bierman, 2002). To the contrary, children with ADHD who succeed in developing and maintaining friendships with high quality and high degree of intimacy during school-age years have better social interactions later in their life (Becker, Fite, Luebbe, Stoppelbein, & Greening, 2013).

It has been suggested that neurocognitive deficits act as intermediate factors between genetic factors and ADHD symptoms (Castellanos & Tannock, 2002; Uebel et al., 2010). Initial evidence suggests that several neurocognitive functions in childhood have predictive value for ADHD persistence (Cheung et al., 2015). However, these results are mixed and inconclusive. It seems that the cognitive and neurobiological processes relating to the developmental pathways toward persistence or remission of ADHD are scarcely investigated and that the true moderating effect of neurocognitive deficits is not yet established.

To conclude, the outcome of ADHD over time appears to follow a number of possible pathways with biological and environmental factors interacting in a multitude of ways. These developmental pathways involve transactional processes whereby the child, their parents, peers, and teachers reciprocally shape each other's behavior over the course of time (Johnston & Mash, 2001; Sonuga-Barke et al., 2005).

The socioeconomic level of the family, the existence of ADHD and other mental health problems in parents, the kind of communication between the parents and their "difficult" child, timely or not diagnosis of the disorder, and the way in which parents perceive and interpret the child's behavior are some of the factors that will affect the child's self-perception and self-esteem, their ability to develop and maintain healthy social relationships, as well as the extent to which they will learn to manage their difficulties. All these will determine the presence of several comorbid conditions including CD, which in turn will affect the development of behaviors such as school dropout, substance abuse, and involvement in antisocial and criminal acts.

4 Epidemiology of ADHD

4.1 Prevalence

Despite decades of research, the prevalence of ADHD has been difficult to estimate. Prevalence rates of ADHD have been reported with great variability among different studies, mainly due to methodological reasons.

The observed variations result partially from differences in the definition of ADHD and the diagnostic criteria that are used across studies. For example, it has been shown that prevalence rates based on DSM-IV are higher than those based on ICD-10 (Goodman, Ford, Richards, Gatward, & Meltzer, 2000; Polanczyk et al., 2007).

Some of the discrepancies can also be attributed to demographic characteristics of the population (gender, age, ethnicity, clinical, or community sample) and the source of information for the evaluation of symptoms (Skounti, Philalithis, & Galanakis, 2007). For example, parent and teacher reports are not always congruent. This happens either because symptom occurrence may be dependent on the setting or because parents and teachers may value symptoms differently (Polanczyk & Rohde, 2007). Prevalence estimates may also differ depending on how data from different sources are combined (Rowland et al., 2015). Finally, ADHD prevalence may be culture dependent, as what is considering abnormal in one culture may be more acceptable in another, affecting therefore the informants' reports. Consequently, the results of studies based on different methodology or different diagnostic criteria are hardly comparable.

However, accurate prevalence data are needed in order to evaluate the needs of individuals with ADHD, design social policy, and plan the allocation of funds. Improved estimates are also needed to address whether ADHD is underrecognized or overidentified and to determine whether the incidence of the disorder is actually increasing or merely being detected more effectively (Rowland et al., 2015). Finally, valid prevalence data may also establish the existence of ADHD as a bona fide mental disorder as opposed to a social construction (Moffitt & Melchior, 2007). The higher prevalence rates that have been reported in North America compared to Europe (Anderson, 1996; Timimi & Taylor, 2004) have led to a debate whether ADHD is a real disorder or a fabrication of the Western civilization (see Section 1.8.2). Valid explanations for inconsistencies in the cross-national prevalence of ADHD can stand against assertions that ADHD is not a real disorder.

The most common method of estimating the prevalence of ADHD relies on behavioral rating scales completed by parents and teachers rather than on a clinical evaluation. These rating scales measure a constellation of behaviors typical of ADHD profile. This is an easy and fast way to collect epidemiological data for large samples of children. Optimally, the population prevalence should reflect the total population, but in practice, it has been difficult to establish a level of study participation that makes the sample representative (Ullebø, Posserud, Heiervang, Obel, & Gillberg, 2012).

In studies using this methodology, it is highly possible that the prevalence of ADHD is overestimated because the mere presence of ADHD symptomatology in a person is not enough for the establishment of a diagnosis. This approach does not incorporate important criteria relevant to the diagnosis of ADHD, such as the functional impairment criterion. In a study evaluating the DSM-IV ADHD prevalence with and without the requirement of impairment for the diagnosis, prevalence rates varied from 3.7% to 8.9%, with lower rates associated with more rigorous impairment criterion (Canino et al., 2004).

Initial prevalence estimates of ADHD among school-aged children varied from 1% to 20% (DuPaul, 1991; Ross & Ross, 1982). Nowadays, there is a scientific consensus that prevalence rates range between 3% and 7% of the child population (APA, 2000). In DSM-5 (APA, 2013), this prevalence is estimated at 5%, practically meaning that in every classroom with 25 to 30 students there should be at least one student with ADHD. In studies that are not exclusively based on assessment scales but on the full use of the diagnostic criteria of DSM-IV, the mean prevalence rate ranges from 4.9% to 6.2% (Barkley, 1998b; Neuman et al., 2005).

The first comprehensive review of the literature on the prevalence of ADHD was published in 2007 (Polanczyk et al., 2007). It included 102 studies conducted over the last 25 years across the world with a total community sample of 171,756 children. Meta-analysis resulted in an overall combined prevalence estimate of 5.29%, associated with significant heterogeneity. Furthermore, the initial differences in prevalence rates between North America and Europe were not confirmed. In 2012, a second comprehensive review was published, focusing only on studies using DSM-IV diagnostic criteria. Meta-analytical results generated estimates ranging from 5.9% to 7.1% (Willcutt, 2012).

The most recent relevant review is the result of the joint effort of the two research teams involved in these previous studies, including 135 studies published between 1985 and 2012 (Polanczyk, Willcutt, Salum, Kieling, & Rohde, 2014). In this review, a meta-regression analysis was conducted to test the effect of time on prevalence estimates of ADHD generated by standardized diagnostic procedures. It was concluded that, in the past three decades, there has been no evidence to suggest an increase in the number of children in the community who meet criteria for ADHD when standardized diagnostic procedures are followed. In other words, when controlling for study methods, prevalence estimates did not vary as a function of year of study. The authors argue that the increase in the rates of diagnosis of ADHD reported in several studies (Brault & Lacourse, 2012; Robinson, Sclar, Skaer, & Galin, 2004) may not represent true increase of the prevalence of the disorder as these studies rely on parent and teacher reports and not on the study of representative samples in the community.

With respect to the prevalence of ADHD in adults, it is estimated at 4% to 5% (Tamam, Karaku, & Ozpoyraz, 2008; Wingo & Ghaemi, 2007), whereas recent data mention 2.5% (APA, 2013). According to the results of a nationally representative survey in the United States on a sample of 3,199 individuals aged 18 to 44 years, the estimated prevalence of ADHD in adults was 4.4% (Kessler et al., 2006). This is considered the most comprehensive study to date. A meta-analysis that examined the cross-national prevalence of adult ADHD demonstrated that it is relatively similar across cultures (Fayyad et al., 2007).

4.2 Sex Ratio

The predominant idea in ADHD research for many years was that this disorder was manifested mainly in the population of boys. George Still (1902) was possibly the first to describe the sex discrepancy of ADHD. Since then, the disproportionate occurrence of ADHD in males has been noted in a plethora of studies.

Sex differences in the rates of ADHD are well-documented in the literature, as boys outnumber girls in both community and clinical samples. According to the APA, this ratio is almost 2:1 in children and 1.6:1 in adults (APA, 2013; Kessler et al., 2006). Meta-analyses in population-based samples from Europe and the United States show that males are two to four times more likely to meet full DSM-IV ADHD criteria than females (Catalá-López et al., 2012; Willcutt, 2012). In clinical samples, the prevalence of ADHD is on average six times higher in boys. Boys diagnosed with ADHD outnumber girls by up to 10:1 (Biederman et al., 2002).

It seems that sex differences in prevalence are more pronounced during childhood and become less obvious with increased age (Davies, 2014; Swanson et al., 2013). It has been found that the prevalence rate for ADHD among boys appears to decline between the ages of 10 and 20 years, whereas the prevalence among girls remains relatively constant across these same ages (Cohen et al., 1993). A possible explanation is that adults' self-referral is usually precipitated by comorbid internalizing problems that tend to be more frequent in women with ADHD than in men (Rucklidge, 2010). A fact of interest is that from 2001 until 2009, there was a much bigger increase in the prescription of ADHD medication to women relative to men. This fact may indicate that there are different mechanisms that lead women and men to seek help (Nussbaum, 2012; Swanson et al., 2013).

Multiple hypotheses have been put forth in an attempt to explain the reported sex difference in the prevalence of ADHD. These hypotheses can be grouped in two broad categories: (a) bias hypotheses and (b) true difference hypotheses (Hartung, Van Pelt, Armendariz, & Knight, 2006).

Hypotheses included in the first category refer to the view that this difference is not a real phenomenon but reflects contextual bias. Specifically, it has been suggested that it can be attributed to selection bias in clinically referred samples, possibly due to the nature of the associated problems and the *expression* of ADHD in the two sexes (Gershon, 2002). Boys exhibit higher levels of hyperactivity, conduct problems, aggressiveness, and other externalizing symptoms compared to girls, whose ADHD symptoms are more covert. Such disruptive behaviors are usually perceived by parents and teachers as more stressful (Gaub & Carlson, 1997; Gershon, 2002).

In addition, it has been found that the presence of oppositionality increases the likelihood of inattentive or hyperactive ratings even in the absence of these symptoms (Abikoff, Courtney, Pelham, & Koplewicz, 1993; Hartung et al., 2006). The more frequent manifestation of disruptive behavior in boys with ADHD than girls and the subsequent negative halo effects that this behavior elicits make it more likely for these boys to be noticed, seen as treatment priority, and be referred to child mental health services (Biederman, Faraone et al., 1999; Gaub & Carlson, 1997; Kakouros, Maniadaki, & Papaeliou, 2004). Thus, disruptiveness may predict service use for ADHD and account for the reported sex difference in clinical samples (Breen & Barkley, 1988; Maniadaki et al., 2006a).

This interpretation is corroborated by empirical data, according to which, in the group of children with ADHD that do not receive any kind of therapy, the percentage of girls is higher (18.7%) compared to that of boys (13.9%) (Robinson, Sclar, Skaer, & Gallin, 2004). It has been suggested that sex is a bigger risk factor for failing to access ADHD services than poverty, rural living, and access to medical insurance combined (Ohan & Visser, 2009).

Another relevant hypothesis refers to lack of measurement invariance. This means that ADHD rating scales are not psychometrically equivalent for females and males, such that the measure differs in internal or external validity by sex (Arnett, Pennington, Willcutt, DeFries, & Olson, 2015). In a similar vein, it has been suggested that the DSM diagnostic criteria are not sensitive to the difficulties of girls with ADHD, thus leading to the underdiagnosis of the disorder in girls (Hudziak, Achenbach, Althoff, & Pine, 2007; Regier,

First, & Narrow, 2007; Waschbusch & King, 2006). This view is corroborated by research findings suggesting that, when diagnosis is made according to dimensional and not categorical criteria, the difference in the ratio of boys to girls is three times smaller (Swanson et al., 2013). However, this concern was eventually not taken into account in DSM-5 (see Sections 9.1 and 9.2).

Finally, there is some evidence that reported sex difference in the prevalence of ADHD may be influenced by the identity of the informant, with teachers reporting more hyperactive/impulsive behaviors in boys than parents (Ullebø et al., 2012). In addition, parent and teacher attitudes seem to play a significant role in their referral decisions.

A study that we conducted on a sample of 115 educators and 118 mothers of preschool children revealed that their self-efficacy beliefs regarding management of child disruptive behavior was more closely related to their referral decision than the severity of the disruptive behavior itself (Maniadaki, Sonuga-Barke, & Kakouros, 2006; Maniadaki, Sonuga-Barke, Kakouros et al., 2005). Furthermore, although the vignette presented was identical for boys and girls, participants felt that it would be easier for them to control girls' behavior than boys'. Consequently, they were more willing to seek professional help for boys than girls.

Moreover, in a study that was conducted on 200 teachers of elementary school, a hypothetical scenario was presented describing a child with ADHD, and teachers were asked if they would refer this child to a mental health service. According to the results, teachers appeared more likely to refer boys than girls, even when all other aspects of symptom expression were similar (Sciutto, Nolfi, & Bluhm, 2004).

Another study found that teachers held sex-specific expectations about treatment. Specifically, they rated medication more favorably as treatment for boys than girls and nonpharmacological interventions as more beneficial for girls than boys (Pisecco, Huzinee, & Curtis, 2001). Based on these results, the authors suggest that teachers might refer boys with ADHD more often than girls because they expect that medication, which needs prescription, is more beneficial for boys, whereas girls may be sufficiently treated within classroom. Ohan and Visser (2009) have also found that parents' and teachers' beliefs in the efficacy of treatment mediate the relationship between child sex and service seeking, especially their belief that learning assistance would benefit boys more than girls.

The second broad category of hypotheses suggests that there are actual differences between boys and girls and is based on the higher prevalence of ADHD in boys relative to girls in community samples. Within this category, both biological and psychosocial theories are included. Biological theories suggest that there are differences in the neurological substrate of ADHD in boys and girls (Hermens, Kohn, Clarke, Gordon, & Williams, 2005; James & Taylor, 1990; Smalley et al., 2000). Within this framework, two competing models prevail.

The constitutional variability model suggests that boys with ADHD have greater genetic variability because they are slower to develop and transcribe genomic information (James & Taylor, 1990; Taylor & Ounsted, 1972). In other words, ADHD in males shares the same etiology with individual differences in motor activity and attention in the general population. As a result, boys with ADHD are at the end of the continuum of individual differences. In contrast, it is claimed that ADHD in girls is attributed to a discrete pathological event, such as brain damage.

According to the polygenic multiple threshold model, girls have a higher threshold for the level of liability needed to manifest ADHD and, therefore, are less frequently affected by the disorder (Faraone et al., 1995; Rhee, Waldman, Hay, & Levy, 1999; Smalley et al., 2000). It has also been suggested that low birth weight is a stronger predisposing factor for the development of ADHD in boys relative to girls (Martel, Lucia, & Nigg, 2007). This finding has been explained on the basis of behavioral genetic data suggesting that girls may be endowed with more protective factors that keep them from developing ADHD, perhaps reducing the impact of risks such as low birth weight (Rhee, Waldman, Hay, & Levy, 2001).

However, empirical data regarding these two models yield inconclusive results (Eme, 1992; Seidman et al., 2005; Silverthorn, Frick, Kuper, & Ott, 1996). Most studies lead to the conclusion that the neurological background of ADHD does not differ in the two sexes neither qualitatively nor quantitatively. Boys and girls with ADHD have similar performance in executive function tasks (Castellanos et al., 2000), and respond similarly to stimulant drugs (Pelham, Walker, Sturges, & Hoza, 1989). These findings also extend to adolescents with ADHD (Rucklidge & Tannock, 2002).

Some more recent neuroimaging studies have demonstrated, however, that males with ADHD showed reduced activation relative to male controls in several brain regions during a working memory task, whereas females with and without ADHD showed equivalent activation (Valera et al., 2009). Several differences in EEG measures have been reported as well, possibly indicating a more extensive neurodevelopmental phenotype in males with ADHD (Barry et al., 2006; Hermens et al., 2005).

Within the category of psychosocial theories, the most prominent is the differential socialization hypothesis, which suggests that, despite similar predisposition to the disorder, girls are less likely to display ADHD symptoms due to differential socialization practices to which they have been exposed in relation to boys (Keenan & Shaw, 1997). Numerous studies indicate that parents encourage girls in dependent behavior and in feminine, especially nurturant, play. In contrast, parents encourage boys to be independent and to engage in active, physical behavior. Girls receive closer adult supervision and control. In general, girls grow up in a more structured and directed world than boys. Boys are left to play alone more, allowed to work independently, and encouraged to become more self-reliant (Brody & Hall, 2000).

In addition, socialization pressures orient girls and boys to adopt different cultural gender roles in life regarding emotion expression (Brody & Hall, 2000; Shields, 2002; Zahn-Waxler, 2001). Boys and girls may have different expectations concerning what their emotion expressions will achieve, leading to different interpersonal goals and different motives for regulating their emotions. Girls tend to be more likely than boys to convey submissive emotions, such as sadness and anxiety. Boys tend to be more willing to express disharmonious emotions, such as anger and laughing at another (Chaplin, Cole, & Zahn-Waxler, 2005). Girls are encouraged to suppress assertiveness and aggression for the sake of communion, whereas boys are allowed to remain agentic (the tendency to be individualistic, self-assertive, and expansive) and be even overtly aggressive if needed (Brody & Hall, 2000). One result of these differential social experiences is that girls may expect negative consequences for themselves when expressing negative emotions such as anger and rage (Timmers et al., 1998).

Therefore, gender may moderate the relation between social information processing and behavior through cognitions that are more interpersonally related for girls and more instrumentally related for boys (Maniadaki, 2003). If girls are encouraged to hide the expression of intense emotions and refrain from the manifestation of behaviors that may be part of ADHD symptomatology, the detection of the disorder is more difficult. Common treatment goals for ADHD include the development of self-control skills, auto-regulation of behavior, and adherence to rules. It seems, however, that these domains generally constitute common goals of socialization for the female sex in general. Therefore, the way in which girls usually socialize seems to assist girls with ADHD in hiding their difficulties and covering up their weaknesses in a way that they are more difficult to notice (Maniadaki, 2003; Maniadaki & Kakouros, 2008).

Research findings provide some evidence for this hypothesis. Chaplin, Cole, and Zahn-Waxler (2005) examined sex differences in children's submissive and disharmonious emotions and parental attention to these emotions. Sixty children and their mothers and fathers participated when children were 4 and 6 years old. It was found that girls expressed more submissive emotions than boys, and fathers attended more to this kind of behavior when expressed by girls than boys. Parental attention at preschool age predicted later submissive expression level, and child disharmonious emotion predicted later externalizing symptoms.

To conclude, the literature is largely inconclusive as to whether any or several of the hypotheses presented so far can account completely for the sex differences in the prevalence of ADHD. It is also unclear whether they can account for the full magnitude of differences in prevalence between referred and nonreferred samples. Considerably more research is needed on this topic, particularly studies of population-based samples that are free of referral biases (Hartung et al., 2006).

4.3 Cultural Considerations

Even though ADHD is one of the most extensively researched issues in developmental psychopathology, most studies have been carried out on white middle-class males or were not powered to analyze the impact of baseline characteristics such as ethnic background. ADHD issues to date continue to be based on assumptions of universality of the American mainstream experience. Therefore, the effect of cultural/ethnicity factors on the manifestation and assessment of ADHD has not been adequately investigated and diversity variables have been largely ignored (Franc & Purper-Ouakil, 2009). Consequences of this research deficit may include under- and over-diagnosis based on cultural insensitivity and diagnostic bias, misinterpretation of prevalence data, and misjudgments of appropriate treatment modalities (Gingerich, Turnock, Litfin, & Rosen, 1998).

Cultural context influences not only the structure of the environment in which an individual with ADHD functions, but also the way such an individual is understood. Cultural factors are particularly significant in the evaluation of psychopathology because similar behaviors are likely to be interpreted differently across social and cultural environments. As a result, the understanding of what is "normal" and "abnormal" is different as well. In most cultures, some children display disruptive behavior that is considered unacceptable by adults. However, the kind of behavior that is considered unacceptable in one culture may be acceptable in another and vice versa (Gingerich et al., 1998). Thus, there is considerable difference across cultures in tolerance of behaviors that do not conform to societal rules.

Furthermore, cultural background may impact the way child symptoms are perceived by adults. In a study carried out by Mann and colleagues (1992), experienced clinicians from four different countries were asked to rate the videotaped behavior of 8-year-old boys in terms of ADHD symptomatology. Considerable intercultural differences in raters' attitudes were noted, even though identical rating criteria were applied and identical behaviors were evaluated. For example, clinicians from China and Indonesia rated the children as more hyperactive and disruptive than clinicians from Japan and North America. In a similar study, teachers from China provided significant higher ratings compared to teachers of the United Kingdom and Hong Kong (Alban-Metcalfe, Cheng-Lai, & Ma, 2002). This finding can be easily understood once Chinese school culture is taken into account, given that children in China are expected to remain still and on-task for long hours in large, structured, quiet classrooms (Hinshaw et al., 2011).

It is obvious that cross-cultural prevalence rates of ADHD may not be comparable due to lack of homogeneity in the diagnostic criteria as well as in sampling methodology and sample characteristics. However, ADHD has been observed in all the countries where relevant studies have been carried out so far, and it is worthwhile to examine variations in prevalence rates of

ADHD in different cultures. In China, ADHD rates range from 1.3% to 13.6%. In Japan, a rate of 7.7% is reported, in Israel 5%, in Brazil 5.8%, and in Germany 10.9% (Dwivedi & Banhatti, 2005). The prevalence of ADHD among schoolchildren in Africa ranges between 5.4% and 8.7% (Bakare, 2012). In India, the prevalence of ADHD was found to reach 29% (Bhatia, Nigam, Bohra, & Mallik, 1991), whereas in New Zealand it barely touched 3% (Fergusson, Horwood, & Lynskey, 1993).

The prevalence of ADHD also varies across ethnicities in countries with ethnic minorities. In the United States, African American children have the highest rate of ADHD, and Asian Americans have the lowest (APA, 2000). Reid, Casat, Norton, Anastopoulos, and Temple (2001) found that teachers considered African American boys 2.5 times more likely than Caucasian males to have ADHD and African American girls 3.5 times more likely to have the disorder. However, we are uncertain whether these differences are due to real behavioral differences among the groups, rater bias due to ethnicity, instrument bias, or other confounding factors (Hartnett, Nelson, & Rinn, 2004; Reid et al., 2000).

Evidence for rater bias has been inconclusive. Sonuga-Barke, Minocha, Taylor, and Sandberg (1993) compared teacher reports with direct observations on student behavior in analog and natural classroom settings in the United Kingdom. Teacher ratings of Asian children overestimated observed symptom levels. However, a similar study in the United States showed similar correlations between teacher ratings and direct observations across ethnic groups, indicating that elevated teacher ratings of African American students may reflect true variations in behavior levels (Epstein et al., 2005).

In contrast, in studies that were based on parental reports, rates of ADHD were lower in African American children compared with Caucasians (Pastor & Reuben, 2005). Studies that were conducted on minority ethnic groups that live in Holland yielded similar results (Zwirs, Burger, Buitelaar, & Schulpen, 2006). This low detection rate in parental reports of ADHD symptoms may be related to a higher tolerance of children's externalized behavior, differences in educational goals and expectations, and fear of stigmatization in families from certain ethnic groups (Livingston, 1999). In addition, lower rates of ADHD recognition by parents of African American children have been conceptualized as differences in explanatory models of ADHD (Bussing, Schoenberg, Rogers, Zima, & Angus, 1998).

Rater's country of origin may also influence ADHD ratings. In the study of Reid and colleagues (2001), African American children were more likely to be assessed as children with ADHD if the teacher was Caucasian rather than African American. African American teachers tended to perceive less difference between African American and Caucasian students than did Caucasian teachers. In a similar vein, de Ramírez and Shapiro (2005) found that teacher ethnicity significantly mediated Hispanic teachers' ratings of Hispanic students. However, no influence of teacher ethnicity was found in the ratings generated by Caucasian teachers.

It is also of interest that even though African American children seem to be assessed as children with ADHD by their teachers at much higher rates, they receive official diagnosis and treatment only by two-thirds compared to Caucasians (Arnold et al., 2003; Bussing et al., 1998; Miller, Nigg, & Miller, 2009). African American and Asian/Pacific Islanders are only half as likely as Caucasians to receive any mental health services (Garland et al., 2005). On the other hand, half of the children with ADHD who do not receive any kind of treatment in the United States are African American (Maddox & Wilson, 2004). This discrepancy has been linked to cultural variations in help-seeking behaviors of parents, limited accessibility to mental health services, and parent distrust of the biomedical explanatory model of ADHD and medication treatments (Bussing, Gary, Mills, & Garvan, 2007; Franc & Purper-Ouakil, 2009). Poor treatment of ADHD in children of ethnic minorities is one more factor that can justify the increased detection of these problems by teachers (Miller et al., 2009).

An alternative interpretation involves a mediating variable, low socioeconomic status, which has been identified as a precipitating factor for the development of ADHD in high-risk children (Reid et al., 2001). Given that minorities are more likely to have lower socioeconomic status, it is possible that ethnic differences in the prevalence of ADHD may partially be associated with financial differences, as these are reflected in the people's quality of life (Barbarin & Soler, 1993).

The National Survey of Children's Health in 2007 revealed elevated regional variability in the prevalence of ADHD in the United States (Visser et al., 2010). For example, it was found that children in North Carolina were 2.5 times more likely to receive the diagnosis of ADHD relative to children in California. For boys in North Carolina aged 9 and over, the probability of an ADHD diagnosis ranged between 25% and 30%. Another study found lower diagnostic prevalence in the West versus the Midwest regions of the United States (Schneider & Eisenberg, 2006). Regional variability has been reported in other countries as well, including Australia and Israel. In the case of Israel, much lower rates of ADHD have been reported in the population of Arabs relative to the population of Jews (Hinshaw et al., 2011).

Careful examination of the causes of regional variability may contribute to a better understanding of the epidemiology of ADHD. According to Hinshaw & Scheffler (2014), this variability may be associated with some of the following factors:

1. Differentiation of the population of children in each region (e.g., boys versus girls, different racial and ethnic compositions) or the socioeducational and financial status of the parents.
2. Differences in the patterns of health care policies and providers, access to mental health services, training of the clinicians, or other practice-style effects.
3. Differences in cultural values that prevail in each region and determine social expectations related to child appropriate behavior and academic achievement.
4. Differences between school settings and school practices across regions.

Furthermore, the specific diagnostic system used by a given region or country may also contribute to the reported regional or international differences. For example, it is more difficult to receive a diagnosis of *hyperkinetic disorder* in ICD than a diagnosis of ADHD in DSM. Up to date, there is no equivalent in ICD to the DSM's inattentive type. Furthermore, more symptoms are required for the diagnosis of hyperkinetic disorder than ADHD. This more stringent definition of hyperkinetic disorder may explain the lower rates of diagnosis in the United Kingdom relative to the United States (Hinshaw & Scheffler, 2014). Many children with impulsive and overactive behavior patterns who would receive the diagnosis of ADHD in the United States were instead judged to have "conduct problems" in the United Kingdom. We appreciate that these differences will considerably be eliminated with the next revision of ICD, as serious efforts are now being made so that ICD and DSM converge as much as possible (see Section 9.6).

To conclude, culturally sensitive research is urgently needed in order to enhance understanding of both across-nation and within-nation variability. In addition, the increasing awareness of cultural biases in both parents' and health care providers' attitudes toward ADHD emphasizes the need for culturally competent interventions. It is particularly important that social cognitions, parents' expectations, and the school system's demands are taken into consideration in order to understand the context in which the child with ADHD is asked to perform. When ethnic minority children attend schools embedded within the majority culture, behavioral differences are likely to be better understood by viewing them through a cultural lens (Livingston, 1999).

In addition, over the last years, contemporary Western societies are becoming more and more multicultural, and ethnic diversity is increasing. Therefore, schools and mental health providers face the challenge of delivering services to evolving and diverse populations. Careful choice of assessment measures, adequate parent information, training for health care providers, and community education are particularly important (Franc & Purper-Ouakil, 2009). Finally, as Rohde and colleagues (2005) state, diagnosis must incorporate the influences of ethnicity and values in order for it to be both comprehensive and culturally valid.

5 Causality of ADHD

5.1 Introduction

Early scientific reports made reference to hereditary factors and abnormalities in brain structure and function as etiological underpinnings of ADHD. During the 20th century, researchers repeatedly noted similarities between symptoms of ADHD and those produced by lesions or injuries to the frontal lobes and the prefrontal cortex specifically (Benton, 1991; Heilman, Voeller, & Nadeau, 1991; Mattes, 1980). Individuals suffering such injuries have been known to demonstrate deficits in sustained attention, inhibition, emotion regulation, motivation, and the capacity to organize behavior across time (Grattan & Eslinger, 1991; Stuss & Benson, 1986).

The neurobiological substrate of ADHD was supported by other evidence as well, including early onset of symptoms, persistence over time, frequent co-occurrence with other developmental disorders with a neurobiological substrate (e.g., SLD, ASD, DCD, etc.), and the substantial reduction of primary symptoms following medication. However, the scientific community had not explicitly acknowledged the neurobiological underpinnings of ADHD until recently with the classification of ADHD into neurodevelopmental disorders in DSM-5 (see Section 9.2).

Over the last decade, research into the field of ADHD causality has made rapid progress. Currently, we know with certainty that ADHD is a neurodevelopmental disorder of multifactorial causality with genetic basis. Its manifestation is the outcome of the interplay between genetic predisposition and a series of environmental factors that affects the structure and function of many different regions of the brain. ADHD is often referred to as "the final common pathway" of the combination of various kinds of predisposing factors and conditions (Sonuga-Barke, Wiersema, van der Meere, & Roeyers, 2010). However, the exact causes, processes, and etiological mechanisms leading to its manifestation are not yet fully understood (Cortese, 2012).

Contemporary research investigates thoroughly a wide range of factors associated with ADHD using sophisticated and highly advanced techniques. Studies have begun to combine findings from molecular genetics with those from neurophysiology, neuroimaging, and neurochemistry, in an effort to better understand the impact of genetic factors on the development, structure, and functioning of several brain networks (Barkley, 2013). A further advance is that studies also place particular emphasis associating research findings with the predominant theories of ADHD (see Chapter 6). In some cases, ADHD emerges as the result of interactions between genetically at-risk children and environmental adversities (Barkley, 2015c). In a few cases, ADHD may be caused or exacerbated through exposure to various biohazardous events during pregnancy or early infancy. All of the preceding factors can give rise to ADHD through some disturbance in the integrity of the prefrontal-cortical-cerebellar network.

5.2 Genetic Factors

5.2.1 Behavioral Genetics

The influence of genes on behavior is quantified by estimating heritability, the proportion of the total phenotypic variance in a trait that is attributable to genetic influences (Willcutt, 2006). ADHD is considered one of the most hereditable disorders, with an estimated mean heritability of 75% (Faraone, 2005). In fact, it is often said that ADHD is "a family affair." Researchers have always noted the significantly higher prevalence of psychopathology in the parents and other relatives of children with ADHD, in particular CD, DDs, and SUD (Thapar, O'Donovan, & Owen, 2005).

Family studies systematically confirm the high incidence of ADHD among the family members of the individual with the disorder. ADHD shows familial clustering both within and across generations. The risk of ADHD among first degree relatives of individuals with ADHD is increased by between twofold and eightfold from the base rate of ADHD in the population (Biederman, Faraone, Keenan, Knee, & Tsuang, 1990; Faraone et al., 2005). Strongly increased risk for ADHD (40% to 60%) among the offspring of adults with ADHD has been reported (Biederman, Faraone et al., 1995; Coghill & Banaschewski, 2009). These rates are similar to those reported about the genetic predisposition associated with height, and higher than those reported about intelligence (Coghill & Banaschewski, 2009).

The impact of heredity on the development of ADHD is also confirmed by adoption studies, which allow separation of inherited and postnatal environmental effects by examining the degree of concordance between individuals with ADHD and their biological and adoptive parents. All five relevant published studies are consistent in showing a strong inherited contribution (Thapar, Cooper et al., 2013). Thus, adoption studies have shown that ADHD is transmitted only to biological relatives, which strongly implicates genetic factors as the main causal influences on familial risk for the disorder (Franke et al., 2012).

Twin studies also show high heritability rates for ADHD, estimated to be around 70% to 90% (Faraone et al., 2005). However, it is worth mentioning that heritability estimates not only include genetic influences but also the effects of gene-environment interplay (Thapar, Cooper et al., 2013) (see Section 5.5). This view is corroborated by the fact that the monozygotic concordance was less than 100% in all studies.

5.2.2 Molecular Genetics

The tremendous progress of molecular genetics has made it possible for scientists to gain insight into potential predictive risk factors for the manifestation of ADHD. The earliest studies involved testing for associations between disorder and variants in candidate genes that were selected because they were thought likely to be involved in the pathophysiology of ADHD (Gizer, Ficks, & Waldman, 2009).

Initial investigation of the genetic underpinnings of ADHD used the candidate genes approach. This approach investigates the role of a specific gene identified because it is part of a biological system that is associated with the disorder, for example, genes that are associated with the dopamine pathway. By comparing the frequency of the different alleles at the candidate locus among individuals with and without ADHD, it is possible to test if any of the alleles are associated with increased risk for ADHD (Willcutt, 2006).

At least 27 potential susceptibility genes in relation to ADHD have been studied so far. Recent meta-analyses report that at least eight gene variants have been reliably linked to ADHD, mainly in children. These include the D4 and D5 dopamine receptor genes (DRD4,

DRD5), the dopamine transporter gene (DAT1), the serotonin transporter gene (5HTT), the serotonin 1B receptor gene (HTR1B), and the SNAP-25 gene (Faraone et al., 2005; Gizer, Ficks, & Waldman, 2009; Kaplan & Stevens, 2002). The important role of dopamine receptors seems to be confirmed by recent meta-analyses as well (Li, Sham, Owen, & He, 2006; Wu, Xiao, Sun, Zou, & Zhu, 2012). However, meta-analyses of candidate genes for susceptibility to ADHD have shown small genetic effects (Faraone et al., 2005). All these genes combined explain only 1% of the phenotypic variance of ADHD (Nigg, 2013b). Thus, they are not likely to be sufficient to cause ADHD, they have small predictive value, and they do not highlight novel biological mechanisms (Thapar et al., 2013).

Another approach of localizing genes that might be associated with a given disorder is family-based linkage analysis, which is used to screen broad sections of the genome to identify regions that may contain additional genes that increase susceptibility to the disorder (Willcutt, 2006). Linkage is the tendency for genes and other genetic markers to be inherited together because of their location near one another on the same chromosome. Isolated linkage studies that have been carried out on adults with ADHD have led to the identification of some novel genes (e.g., LPHN3, BAIAP 2, CLOCK, and NOS1) associated with ADHD across the life span (Franke et al., 2012). It has been suggested that the genetic component of ADHD in adults is partly different from the one observed in children, which may constitute a significant predictive index for the differentiation of persisters from desisters in the future (Franke et al., 2012).

A particularly interesting finding refers to the detection of a variant of the COMT gene, which has been repeatedly found to be associated with CD in the presence of ADHD but not with CD alone (Caspi et al., 2008; Langley, Heron, O'Donovan, Owen & Thapar, 2010; Monuteaux, Biederman, Doyle, Mick, & Faraone, 2010; Thapar et al., 2005). This specific variant (COMTvall58met), which differentiates the function of the dopamine system in the prefrontal cortex, is associated with performance on executive function measures, emotional regulation, and social understanding. Social cognition mediates the association between the COMT gene and antisocial behavior in ADHD. In other words, there is no evidence that the COMT gene increases the risk of the disorder itself, but it could have a modifying effect on the ADHD phenotype through its association with antisocial behavior in individuals with ADHD (Thapar et al., 2005). This finding might be considered as one of the very few examples that explain the mechanism through which a gene leads to the manifestation of a certain symptom of a disorder via its effect on a specific brain function (Franke et al., 2012).

A different approach is adopted by Genome-Wide Association Studies (GWAS). This is a highly advanced approach that is not based on a hypothesis concerning certain genes (*hypothesis-free*), but refers to the comprehensive scan of the whole genome in many individuals, to potentially identify common genetic polymorphisms and their thresholds in order to find certain polymorphisms that are associated with a pathological feature. These polymorphisms usually refer to a nucleotide (Single Nucleotide Polymorphisms; SNPs) in various positions of the genome and might be involved in the presence of complex disorders such as ADHD (Franke, Neale, & Faraone, 2009; Stergiakouli & Thapar, 2010).

However, none of these studies has revealed any gene variant that passes the statistical threshold for genome-wide significance, suggesting that any gene variant for ADHD must have a very small individual effect or include multiple rare alleles (Franke et al., 2012). Limited results may be due to the fact that GWAS require thousands of individuals with ADHD to detect statistically significant effects (Nigg, 2013b). However, this is a promising field of future research because sufficiently large samples may reveal the nature of the genes implicated in ADHD. Furthermore, in light of current advances in epigenetics, future GWAS need to consider both genetic and epigenetic loci (Mathews & Janusek, 2011).

A more recent approach goes beyond seeking individual genes and suggests organizing common genetic variants into chemical and neurophysiological groups, called pathways. Two studies have used this approach so far and offered interesting results. Poelmans, Pauls, Buitelaar, and Franke (2011) identified a coherent network related to nicotinic receptors and to neural growth. Stergiakouli and colleagues (2012) also identified relevant genetic pathways in these metabolic systems that are related to the CNS and cholesterol metabolism, which is essential for neural development. These findings are still preliminary, but they point toward a very promising future field of study in genetic research.

The fourth approach of genetic research concerns seeking rare structural genetic variants, including duplications or chromosome deletions. It has long been recognized that rare chromosomal microdeletion syndromes, such as 22q11 microdeletion syndrome (velocardiofacial syndrome), which involve a deletion encompassing many genes, can lead to increased risk of ADHD (Antshel, Philips, Gordon, Barkley, & Faraone, 2006). Two other specific chromosomal regions have been detected as possibly being associated with ADHD: one on chromosome 16p13.11 (Williams et al., 2010) and the other on chromosome 15q11–13 (Stergiakouli et al., 2012; Williams et al., 2012). Structural variants in these areas are present in less than 1% of the general population and double the risk for ADHD (Williams et al., 2010). This method is expected to produce very important outcomes in genetic research on ADHD in the next decades.

In conclusion, even though genetic research on ADHD has made enormous progress, its findings explain a very small part of the heterogeneity in the clinical manifestation of the disorder. Genetic influences do not directly alter the phenotype but are complex in nature, such that a large network of small genetic variations may add and interact to produce the disruption of neural architecture that is behaviorally expressed as ADHD (Konrad & Eickhoff, 2010). It seems that no individual genes that contain mutations have been directly associated with the disorder. The genes that have been found to provide susceptibility to ADHD are normal allelic variations that are very common among the general population. This fact may partly explain the high prevalence of ADHD (Rutter, 2006b). These alleles do not have a direct genetic impact but function within the context of a multifactorial etiology that also includes environmental factors. Furthermore, gene-environment interplay should be taken into account because high heritability does not equal genetic determination (Visscher, Hill, & Wray, 2008). When heritability is lower than 100%, room for environmental influences is implied.

5.3 Factors Associated to Brain Structure and Function

5.3.1 Neuroimaging Studies

Over the past few decades, the pathophysiology of ADHD has been studied with the use of various sophisticated neuroimaging approaches by searching for abnormalities in brain regions and their connections that are involved in attention, executive function, motor control, response inhibition, and working memory, even during rest. Commonly used structural MRI measures include volume and density of the gray or white matter of the whole brain or subregions, as well as the brain cortical gray matter thickness (Vaidya, 2011). Several neuronal deficits in attention and executive function processing networks have been frequently reported. These abnormalities in the brain have been associated with impaired cognitive, affective, and motor behaviors seen in ADHD.

Initial volumetric studies have consistently shown an overall reduction in total cerebral volume of about 3% to 8% both in children and adults with ADHD, particularly in the frontostriatal circuitry (Carmona et al., 2005; Castellanos et al., 2002). Findings regarding more specific lobar or regional volume reductions have so far been inconsistent for the temporal and parietal lobe (Castellanos et al., 2002; Filipek, 1999), whereas occipital and frontal lobe volumes have more consistently been reported to be smaller in individuals with ADHD (Durston et al., 2004; Seidman et al., 2005; 2006; Sowell et al., 2003).

A meta-analysis of whole-brain voxel-based morphometry studies in children with ADHD found consistent regional gray matter reduction in ADHD individuals in right putamen and globus pallidus (Ellison-Wright et al., 2008). The most recent meta-analysis, which used the newer meta-analytic technique of signed differential mapping, demonstrated substantial global reduction in gray matter volumes in the prefrontal cortex, most prominently in the right nucleus lentiformis up to the caudate nucleus (Nakao, Radua, Rubia, & Metaix-Cols, 2011). The prefrontal cortex is the region of the brain that regulates higher cognitive processes and serves in decision making, impulse control, planning, goal achievement, and the consideration of future consequences. In a recent study, significantly lower gray matter volume was found in participants with ADHD relative to controls in several brain regions, such as the anterior cingulate cortex, the occipital cortex, and the hippocampus/amygdala complex, as well as in widespread cerebellar regions (Bonath, Tegelbeckers, Wilke, Flechtner, & Krauel, 2016).

Similar findings of smaller extent have also been detected in healthy siblings of boys with ADHD, indicating the genetic background of the disorder (Durston et al., 2004). Findings confirm an association between a variant of the DRD4 gene, which encodes the dopamine receptor D4, and the reduced prefrontal gray matter volume in individuals with ADHD (Durston et al., 2005). Such converging findings associate genetic factors with pathological findings in the brain structure of individuals with ADHD, leading to a better understanding of the etiological mechanisms of the disorder.

Recently, scientific interest shifted from oncometric measures to the detection of other morphological differences (Shaw & Robin, 2009). Studies focusing on architectural alterations have reported global thinning of the cortex in individuals with ADHD (Narr et al., 2009; Shaw et al., 2006), reductions in the density of the dorsolateral prefrontal cortex, and decreased cortical folding (Sowell et al., 2003).

These abnormalities may be due to a delay in structural maturation. The peak of cortical thickness maturation was found to be delayed in children with ADHD relative to their counterparts by an average of 3 years across all cortical regions, with up to 4–5 years delay in frontal and temporal areas, respectively (Shaw et al., 2007). The median age by which 50% of the cortical points attained peak thickness in children with ADHD was 10.5 years, whereas in typically developing controls it was 7.5 years. The rate of cortical thinning in these regions has been correlated with severity of hyperactivity and impulsivity in children with ADHD and those without (Shaw et al., 2011). This delay is mainly detected in regions of the prefrontal cortex that are important in the control of cognitive processes, including attention and organization of behavior. Furthermore, this finding is also associated with genetic factors, as an association between the thinner cerebral cortex of the individuals with ADHD and the presence of the allele 7R of the DRD4 gene has been found (Shaw et al., 2007). According to Barkley (2015c), these findings underscore a dimensional view of ADHD, given that thinning is linked to the number of ADHD symptoms even in control children.

Recently, morphological differences in other cerebral structures have been reported, including the amygdala (Plessen et al., 2006) and the thalamus (Ivanov et al., 2010), thus providing neurobiological evidence for the emotional and attentional disturbances frequently manifested in ADHD (Li et al., 2012). By now, most replicated findings have suggested significant decrease of the whole brain gray matter and white matter volumes and significant regional underdevelopment in the prefrontal cortex, basal ganglia substructures, and cerebellum in individuals with ADHD (Frodl and Skokauskas, 2012; Kaplan & Stevens, 2002; Valera,

Faraone, Murray, & Seidman, 2007). These findings are associated with the poor neurophysiological performance among children with ADHD on tasks that required response inhibition and goal-oriented behavior (Qiu et al., 2009).

Another neuroimaging technique that has been used to gain insights into the pathophysiology of ADHD is functional MRI (fMRI). Both *task-based* and *resting-state* fMRI have been used. Task-based fMRI provides a measure of the activity of neural regions involved in particular tasks, whereas resting-state fMRI investigates the function of those neuronal networks that are activated at rest, that is, without a specific task (Castellanos & Proal, 2012; Castellanos et al., 2008; Fair et al., 2010).

With respect to the results from studies using this technique, two perspectives have been developed. A series of studies have demonstrated significant hypoactivity in frontal, temporal, parietal lobes, and cerebellar regions of individuals with ADHD (Hale, Bookheimer, McGough, Phillips, & MacCracken, 2007; Rubia et al., 2000; Schneider et al., 2010). These findings generally mirror brain regions that are implicated by studies of structural imaging and are related to behavioral inhibition, planning, working memory, and attentional processes (Bush, 2010; 2011). Among other regions, the anterior cingulate cortex has been implicated repeatedly in the lack of attentional control usually displayed by individuals with ADHD.

In some cases, however, the opposite was observed in studies using resting-state fMRI. These studies focus on the Default Mode Network, which is the most studied intrinsic functional connectivity system. This is a distributed network of brain regions, comprising midline structures including the posterior cingulate cortex and the ventromedial prefrontal cortex (Buckner, Andrews-Hanna, & Schacter, 2008). This network normally shows highly correlated brain activity during rest and a reduced level of activation during performance of sensory and cognitive demanding tasks. Deactivation of this network has been associated with increased task difficulty (Singh & Fawcett, 2008).

This network seems to work conversely in individuals with ADHD, as it is not activated during rest but during performance of cognitive tasks (Dickstein, Bannon, Castellanos, & Milham, 2006). Sonuga-Barke and Castellanos (2007) suggested that ADHD could be considered a default network disorder because this network in ADHD might be refractory to regulation by other neural systems. As a result, it would produce intrusions into ongoing cognition and behavior, which would manifest as periodic lapses in on-task performance and spontaneous fluctuations in attention, a hallmark of ADHD. In others words, it may compete with task-specific neural processing and contribute to distractibility (Eichele et al., 2008; Li, Yan, Bergquist, & Sinha, 2007; Weissman, Roberts, Visscher, & Woldorff, 2006). This hypothesis is supported by research findings that focus on the interregional functional connectivity within this network during the resting-state and show dysfunctional connectivity among individuals with ADHD (Fair et al., 2010).

Another advance in the field has been the study of abnormalities in the microstructure of the white matter fibers that connect gray matter regions (Nagel, 2011). On this purpose, Diffusion Tensor Imaging (DTI) is used. DTI is an imaging technique that has emerged as a valuable tool in ADHD research. It is based on the random diffusion of water molecules and provides in vivo quantitative information relating to the white matter microstructure, which can reveal microscopic details about tissue architecture. With the use of this technique, numerous micro-structural abnormalities in the white matter among children with ADHD have been found (Favuluri et al., 2009; Hamilton et al., 2008; Konrad & Eickhoff, 2010). These abnormalities, which were detected in children with ADHD as early as age 7 years, may lead to disrupted functional connectivity between brain regions, ultimately resulting in the manifestation of ADHD symptoms (Nagel, 2011). The neural pathways that are associated with the areas of abnormal white matter are the pathways connecting the cortical regions, cortical-striatum and cortical-cerebellum (De La Fuente et al., 2013). Even though the findings of these studies require further investigation, they are consistent with previous research using other neuroimaging modalities. Consequently, this technique is considered very promising in investigating the neurobiological underpinnings of ADHD and provides us with new prospects for future research (Cortese, 2012; van Ewijk, 2012).

In conclusion, it seems that structural imaging studies gradually shifted from the investigation of the morphology of a few discrete brain regions to the study of multifaceted morphological alterations in a complex network organization (Sergeant, Geurts, Huijbregts, Scheres, & Oosterlaan, 2003). In addition, they now focus on altered connectivity and communication between several cortical and subcortical regions. Structural connectivity refers to the presence of an axonal connection between two brain regions. Functional connectivity is defined as the temporal correlation or coherence of spatially remote neurophysiological events (Konrad & Eickhoff, 2010). Results suggest that the structural and functional connectivity deficits and the ADHD symptoms might arise incidentally from a common etiologic mechanism, involving altered modulation of synaptic potentiating and pruning by dopamine and other factors during development (Liston et al., 2011). This progress is in line with the shift in the conceptualization of ADHD from simple causal models based on simple deficits to more complex theoretical frameworks that take into consideration the clinical heterogeneity of ADHD (Sonuga-Barke, 2005; 2011) (see Chapter 6).

It seems that many of the early neurodevelopmental processes that are deficient in individuals with ADHD and are associated with brain structure, organization, and function are controlled by genetic mechanisms (Koten et al., 2009; Lenroot et al., 2009). An extensive network of small genetic variants interact with each other and with environmental factors, leading to the disruption of the neuronal architecture that is behaviorally expressed with ADHD symptoms (Konrad & Eickhoff, 2010). However, the mechanism through which these factors affect the development and interconnection of neurons is still under examination.

Currently, there are no accepted uses of neuroimaging techniques either for diagnosing ADHD or for predicting clinical outcome, because no neuroimaging test has been shown to provide adequate diagnostic accuracy and reliability at the individual level, given that relevant studies are based on group-averaged brain data (Bush, 2008; Cortese, 2012). However, a negative magnetic tomography in a person with some kind of mental disorder does not necessarily mean that this person does not have any brain dysfunction; rather, it means that we need to improve our imaging tools in order to detect even minimum abnormalities in the structure and function of the brain (Agarwal, Port, Bazzocchi, & Renshaw, 2010). Consequently, further technological development is expected to strengthen the power of neuroimaging tools.

5.3.2 Neurophysiological Studies

The quantitative analysis of the electroencephalograph (EEG) for the neurophysiological study of ADHD has been used for about 40 years. Early studies found abnormalities in the EEG of children with ADHD, including excess slow-wave activity and increased epileptiform spike and wave activity (Satterfield, Cantwell, & Satterfield, 1974). These findings were thought to suggest underarousal and maturational delay as underlying pathophysiologies in ADHD.

Technological advancements allowed more accurate measures of brain electrical activity. It has been found that the majority of people with ADHD have increased slow wave (theta) activity by 32%, mainly during resting state. This fact is associated with poor brain activity (Snyder & Hall, 2006). However, elevated theta power may be a nonspecific marker of cortical dysfunction, common to other disorders, such as epilepsy, BDs, and SUD (Coutin-Churchman et al., 2003).

The most stable finding among studies is that 90% of the individuals with ADHD exhibit elevated theta/beta power ratios over frontal and central midline cortical regions (Monastra, 2008). This finding seems to remain stable throughout development and suggests a "developmental deviation" in ADHD, which would result from a neurodevelopmentally immature cortical underarousal.

Some isolated studies have reported other differences as well, but their findings need replication (De La Fuente et al., 2013; Kuperman et al., 1996). Furthermore, it is highlighted that considerable heterogeneity has been observed in EEG characteristics of individuals with ADHD, illustrating the heterogeneity that generally characterizes this disorder (Loo & Makeig, 2012). In conclusion, the predominant findings from the use of EEG are combined with the findings from the use of neuroimaging techniques to a satisfactory degree.

Thorough meta-analysis of relevant studies has shown that the use of EEG can discriminate between individuals with ADHD and normal controls in approximately 94% of cases (Snyder & Hall, 2006). Although the use of EEG is very useful for research purposes, this method is not used in clinical practice for the diagnosis of ADHD because it is diagnostically inferior to clinical assessment (Millichap, Millichap, & Stack, 2011). Additionally, it has been emphasized that, on a clinical level, the EEG of children with ADHD does not show abnormalities in approximately 24% of the cases. As a result, it has very little to contribute to the diagnostic process (Loo & Barkley, 2005).

5.3.3 Neurochemical Factors

Response of individuals with ADHD to medications that affect certain neurochemical systems of the brain stimulated the investigation of the neurochemical background of the disorder. Specifically, it has been found that stimulant medications and atomoxetine (ATX) function either via synthesis and release of catecholamines (dopamine, epinephrine, and norepinephrine) in the synapses or via their inhibition and reuptake. Specifically, stimulants block the reuptake of dopamine and norepinephrine into the presynaptic neuron, and amphetamines also promote the release of dopamine and norepinephrine into the extraneuronal space. ATX blocks the norepinephrine transporter, which also takes up dopamine in the prefrontal cortex, thus increasing concentration of both dopamine and norepinephrine (Prince, 2008).

Studies from different fields have converged on the catecholamine neurotransmitter system, which includes the noradrenergic and dopaminergic system, as contributing to the impairments seen in ADHD. Dopamine and noradrenaline are intrinsically linked via chemical pathways. Through neuromodulation of fronto-striato-cerebellar circuits, they play a critical role in prefrontal-dependent executive functions, often reported to be deficient in individuals with ADHD (del Campo, Chamberlain, Sahakian, & Robbins, 2011).

Recent PET imaging data demonstrate a diminished availability of the D2/D3 subtypes of the DA receptor in adults with ADHD, as well as significantly increased DAT binding in the right caudate, compared with matched controls (Prince, 2008). The dysfunction of the dopaminergic system has been associated with the deficits of individuals with ADHD in the domains of motivation and processing, reward, and reinforcement (Volkow et al., 2011), whereas dysregulation of the noradrenergic system is associated with inattention (Arnsten & Li, 2005). Furthermore, the role of the serotoninergic system, which is associated with the regulation of emotions, has recently aroused scientific interest (Arnsten, Berridge, & McCracken, 2009). Serotonin fluctuations have been associated with delay aversion (Sonuga-Barke et al., 2011). Furthermore, a review of relevant studies confirmed that dopaminergic and serotoninergic genotypes interact with psychosocial factors in influencing severity of ADHD symptoms in childhood (Nigg et al., 2010).

However, it seems that alterations in any single neurotransmitter system are unlikely to explain the complexity of ADHD neurobiology. Future studies should investigate the interplay between several dysfunctional neurotransmitter systems (Cortese, 2012).

5.4 Environmental Factors

5.4.1 Prenatal and Perinatal Factors

The proportion of variance due to environmental factors can be subdivided into shared and nonshared environmental influences. Shared environmental influences are those that increase the similarity of individuals within a family in comparison to unrelated individuals in the population. In contrast, nonshared environmental influences are those that lead to differences among individuals in a family (Willcutt, 2006).

It has been estimated that approximately 20% to 25% of the heterogeneity in the etiology of ADHD can be explained by specific individual nonshared environmental factors. ADHD has been associated with a series of environmental factors, but it is particularly difficult to identify causality because many of the available research findings are based on correlational data. These factors may act in an additive or interactive manner with genetic influences to increase risk for ADHD, or may even represent an alternative etiological pathway that is sufficient to cause the later development of ADHD in a subset of cases (Swanson, Oosterlaan et al., 2000). It should be noted that these environmental adversities usually involve biological events, not just psychosocial influences (Barkley, 2015c). Moreover, it can be claimed that people often shape their own environment, influenced by their genetic origins as well. Consequently, distinguishing environmental factors from genetic ones becomes even more perplexing (Thapar & Rutter, 2009).

Additionally, any selected putative risk factor is likely to be correlated with other social measures, such as low socioeconomic status, poor diet, low birth weight, maternal smoking, poor parenting, and so on. It is uncertain whether the measured predictor is indeed the 'true' environmental risk involved, or merely a *proxy marker* of the true causal factor (Shanahan & Hofer, 2005). A proxy risk factor refers to any correlate of a strong risk factor that may also appear to be a risk factor for the same outcome, even though the only connection between that correlate and the outcome lies in the strong risk factor correlated with both (Kraemer, Stice, Kazdin, Offord, & Kupfer, 2001).

One of the most thoroughly studied prenatal risks that have been associated with ADHD is exposure to maternal smoking during pregnancy. It seems that the risk for ADHD in a child whose mother smoked during pregnancy increases in proportion with the frequency and extent of maternal smoking (Langley et al., 2005). However, in observational designs it is difficult to adequately control for familial and social confounds. In addition, recent studies showed that the effect of maternal smoking during pregnancy on offspring ADHD is much lower than it was suggested, and it seems to be associated more with behavioral problems rather than ADHD (Gatzke-Kopp & Beauchaine, 2007).

Thapar and her colleagues (2009) compared the chances of manifesting ADHD in children of two groups of women who had conceived through assisted reproduction: in the first group, women had a genetic relation with the child, whereas in the second group they did not. It was concluded that association between smoking and the presence of ADHD was stronger in the group of women who had a genetic relation with the child, indicating that smoking alone does not seem to be etiologically associated with ADHD. To sum up, it seems that the association between maternal smoking during pregnancy and ADHD may wholly or substantially represent familial and inherited confounds, that is gene-environment correlation (D'Onofrio et al., 2008; Thapar et al., 2009).

Other prenatal factors that have been associated with offspring ADHD is maternal stress during pregnancy (Glover, 2011), moderate alcohol or drug use, and exposure to illicit substances (Linnet et al., 2003). However, these children seem to have a different neuropsychological profile from the typical cases of children with ADHD (Mick, Biederman, Faraone, Sayer, & Kleinman, 2002). Recent neuroimaging studies have shown that fetal exposure to smoking and alcohol is associated with reduced brain volume in children with ADHD, especially in the cerebellum (de Zeeuw et al., 2012). It seems that far more evidence is required to confirm and understand the nature of these potential relationships. For example, it has been suggested that maternal smoking and alcohol consumption may be proxies for elevated ADHD in the parents that conveys a genetic ADHD risk to offspring (Langley, Heron, Smith, & Thapar, 2012).

ADHD, especially the inattentive subtype, has also been found to be associated with low birth weight (< 2.5 kg) and prematurity (Bhutta, Cleves, Casey, Cradock, & Anand, 2002). It has been found that low birth weight was three times more common in children with ADHD than in normal controls, perhaps accounting for 14% of all ADHD cases (Mick et al., 2002). However, both low birth weight and prematurity are determined by other factors, such as maternal health and nutrition, low socioeconomic status, stress, and so on, making identification of specific biological mechanisms particularly difficult (Nigg, 2013b).

Another group of environmental risk factors for ADHD includes environmental toxins, such as pesticides, polychlorinated biphenyls (PCBs), and lead, which may damage the neural networks implicated in the disorder (Polanska, Jurewicz, & Hanke, 2013). Lead is the most studied toxic element. Studies in this field provide evidence that low levels of lead in the blood are associated with ADHD or ADHD-related symptoms (Polanska et al., 2013). Data obtained from the 1999–2002 National Health and Nutrition Examination Survey found higher blood lead concentrations in mothers of children with ADHD, with lead exposure accounting for 290,000 excess cases of ADHD in U.S. children, equal to the number of cases related to prenatal tobacco exposure (Braun, Kahn, Froehlich, Auinger, & Lanphear, 2006).

However, overall findings have been inconsistent because some studies confirm a link between environmental toxins and ADHD symptoms (Bouchard, Bellinger, Wright, & Weisskopf, 2010; Eubig, Aguiar, & Schantz, 2010), whereas others do not (Eskenazi et al., 2007; Lee, Jacobs, & Porta, 2007). There is considerable evidence for the negative impact of environmental toxins on neurodevelopment, but this issue requires further investigation. Nevertheless, public health policies aimed at reducing exposure of children to toxins is a desirable way forward (Thapar et al., 2013).

Finally, another risk factor for ADHD is nutrition. This idea originated in the 1980s, when Feingold's (1975) views spread widely (see Section 1.4.4). Feingold claimed that ADHD symptoms constitute an allergic or toxic reaction of some children to artificial food colorings and preservatives in their diet. Even though in the beginning Feingold affirmed that these ingredients affect behavior, he later expanded his theory claiming that these ingredients are responsible for a wide range of learning difficulties and attention problems. Another substance that was held responsible during that period for the development of ADHD symptoms in children was sugar (Smith, 1975). These theories, however, did not receive scientific verification and were abandoned (Wender, 1986; Wolraich et al., 1994). However, some more recent studies have confirmed that food additives increase hyperactive behavior in children that have already developed the disorder (Schab & Trinh, 2004).

Recently, interest in the possible association between diet and ADHD has been revived, but contemporary studies approach this issue from the perspective of nutritional deficiencies in children with ADHD, including magnesium, iron, potassium, zinc, and polyunsaturated fatty acids (Nigg, Lewis, Edinger, & Falk, 2012).

It has been suggested that the implication of iron and zinc in ADHD makes biological sense because both are essential cofactors of enzymes necessary in the production of monoaminergic neurotransmitters, which are implicated in the pathophysiology of ADHD (Scassellati, Bonvicini, Faraone, & Gennarelli, 2012). Cortese and colleagues (2011) found significantly lower thalamic iron levels in children with ADHD compared to normal controls. The authors suggest that the supposed impairment of thalamus functioning, associated with iron deficiency, might contribute to ADHD symptoms via its impact on alertness, at least in a subsample of children.

Overall, the value of studies looking at diet and ADHD is limited by small-sized trials, subjective measures of outcome, and varied protocols for intervention (Ballard, Hall, & Kaufmann, 2010). Besides, any possible associations can be interpreted as the outcome of ADHD, which may cause the need for the consumption of larger amount of some dietary constituents for the improvement of brain function (Nigg, 2013b). Therefore, there is not consistent evidence to support the notion that dietary factors play a major causal role in ADHD.

In conclusion, it seems that the association of some environmental factors that affect the child either during pregnancy or early during infancy with higher chances of developing ADHD has been statistically confirmed. However, the way in which the effect of these factors leads to neurochemical alterations that will later be phenotypically expressed through ADHD symptoms has not yet been understood. These factors are speculated to change the patterns of gene expression during pregnancy, but the specific molecular processes involved in this chain of events have yet to be investigated (Mill & Petronis, 2008).

5.4.2 Psychosocial Factors

ADHD has been associated with multiple indicators of psychosocial adversity, including parental mental illness, family adversity, low socioeconomic status, peer victimization, and child abuse, among others (Ouyang, Fang, Mercy, Perou, & Grosse, 2008; Pheula, Rohde, & Schmitz, 2011; Taylor & Sonuga-Barke, 2008). However, the direction of these associations has been questioned: does psychosocial adversity lead to ADHD, or does ADHD cause psychosocial adversity? Noting adverse circumstances is clearly clinically important, but care is needed in ascribing direction of effects, causality, and potential blame (Thapar et al., 2013).

Efforts exclusively focusing on seeking ADHD etiology in psychosocial factors were scarce and did not receive much support. Some researchers claimed that hyperactive behavior in children is the outcome of parental malpractices (Silverman & Ragusa, 1992; Willis και Lovaas, 1977). This view was based on findings from longitudinal studies that showed a positive correlation between negative mother-child interactions during preschool years and persistence of hyperactive behavior in childhood (Campbell, 1987) and adolescence (Barkley, Fischer et al., 1990). However, this correlation does not prove causal relationship. Besides, it could be argued that persistence of ADHD symptoms and mother's negative responses are both mediated by the severity of ADHD symptoms, as longitudinal studies highlight that the severity of symptoms constitutes a predictive factor for their persistence in time (Campbell & Ewing, 1990).

This point of view is also corroborated by studies that investigated the effects of stimulant medication and placebo on mother–child interactions. It was consistently found that medications led to reduction of hyperactivity and increase of obedience and compliance in children, and to a corresponding reduction in maternal negative responses toward their children (Barkley, Karlsson, Pollard, & Murphy, 1985; Danforth, Barkley, & Stokes, 1991). These findings suggest that it is the child's difficult behavior that may result in mother–child hostility rather than the opposite (Barkley & Cunningham, 1979; Barkley et al., 1985). Furthermore, this view about parental responsibility for the development of ADHD in the child does not answer basic questions about the multiple deficits associated with the disorder.

Twin studies have also demonstrated very little impact of psychosocial factors on the development of ADHD. Social status, educational level, parental occupation, and child-rearing practices may affect individual differences in ADHD symptoms at a rate of only 0% to 6% (Levy, Hay, McStephen, Wood, & Waldman, 1997; Sherman, Iacono, & McGue, 1997).

In addition, family variables, like the ones mentioned before, have been termed environmental even though they are partly under genetic influence themselves (Nigg, Nikolas & Burt, 2010). Inherited risks may influence the likelihood of exposure to environmental adversity and alter sensitivity to environmental risk factors. A relevant example is negative parenting in families of children with ADHD. Parents of these children often have ADHD themselves and, therefore, it is this genetic contribution that further disrupts family interactions and may account for the largest degree of risk for ADHD (Plomin, 1995; Pressman et al., 2006).

At present, there is no convincing evidence that psychosocial adversity has a causal relationship with ADHD. Psychosocial explanations have not proven to be consistent with the scientific findings on the disorder. As Barkley (2015c) notes,

> We are now able to conclude unequivocally that ADHD cannot and does not arise from purely main effects of social factors, such as child-rearing, family conflict, marital difficulties, insecure infant attachment, television or video games, the pace of modern life, or interactions with peers.
>
> (p. 357)

However, we should highlight that both family and school environment may strongly influence the outcome of ADHD. There is no doubt that psychosocial factors may modify the severity of ADHD symptoms, their persistence in time, their expression, and the emergence of secondary adverse outcomes (Langley et al., 2010).

Over the last years, the study of psychosocial factors associated with ADHD has reignited research interest regarding their contribution to the development of the disorder as a result of their interaction with neurological and genetic factors. This issue will be thoroughly presented in the next section.

5.5 Gene-by-Environment Interaction

As it has become apparent so far, ADHD cannot be exclusively attributed to any isolated causal factor. Clinical manifestations of ADHD cannot be sufficiently explained by the dysfunction of just one gene, neurotransmitter system, or brain region. It is certain that various genes, brain regions, and neurotransmitters are involved in the development of ADHD. Consequently, the biomedical model of ADHD, which promotes the investigation of brain regions where lies the common primary dysfunction that causes ADHD, tends to become abandoned nowadays for a number of reasons (Sonuga-Barke & Halperin, 2010).

First, the precise genes that lead to increased risk for ADHD remain elusive. Research has merely identified various genes that are often—but not always—involved in the development of the disorder. However, the way in which these genes affect behavior is not entirely clear. Even genes that have been systematically associated with the development of ADHD hardly explain the heterogeneity that describes this disorder. Second, some environmental factors have a negative impact only on individuals with a certain genotype, given that not all people who are exposed to some of the aforementioned risk factors develop the disorder. Third, individuals with similar genetic predisposition for the development of ADHD may manifest symptoms of different severity and in different combinations, resulting in different clinical presentations depending on the environment to which the individual will be exposed (Nigg et al., 2010). Finally, the biomedical model does not explain comorbidity or how it is possible for different groups of individuals to present different patterns of brain alterations and neurocognitive deficits and yet still receive the diagnosis of ADHD (Halperin, Trampush, Miller, Marks, & Newcorn, 2008; Sonuga-Barke, 2005). For these reasons, scientific interest has shifted the search from simple and one-dimensional interpretation models of ADHD to models that take complex developmental processes into account.

ADHD is currently conceptualized through a bio-psycho-social epigenetic model (Singh, 2008) as the outcome of the dynamic interplay among genetic, neurophysiological, neurochemical, and environmental factors, affecting brain structure and function early in the process of development. As such, its causal architecture seems to be characterized by complexity and heterogeneity (Sonuga-Barke, 2010). The brain is considered as the main organ of integration between genes and environment (Johnson, Jones, & Gliga, 2015).

This is a dynamic conception of cause, which postulates that there is a developmental pathway from risk to disorder. ADHD might be originated in genes, but its emergence depends on the way in which genes affect the individual's response to the environment. Gene-by-environment interaction refers to the fact that environments can modify the expression of individuals' genetic background by either strengthening or weakening the effect of genes on phenotypes (Rutter, 2006a). In other words, gene-by-environment interactions lead on the possible ways in which environments "get under the skin" (Rutter, 2010, p. 3). It seems that environmental shaping of the expression of genes affects the emergence of psychopathology even in highly heritable disorders. Therefore, the initiating neurobiological causes that underpin ADHD operate as nondeterministic risk factors and allow for alterations that will eventually determine the course of the disorder (Sonuga-Barke & Halperin, 2010).

Gene-by-environment interactions may take various forms. Genetic predisposition may affect a person's vulnerability by differentiating the possibility of being exposed to certain environmental risk factors (Nigg et al., 2010). It may also alter individual sensitivity to particular environmental effects or actively evoke negative response from others (Coghill & Banaschewski, 2009; Daley, Sonuga-Barke, Thompson, & Chen, 2008). Children exposed to environment stressors known to increase risk for certain disorders are at higher risk if they carry particular gene variants that render them more susceptible to those stressors. Alternatively, environmental factors may contribute to the manifestation of genetic effects that would otherwise remain silent or modify the way genes are expressed (Mill & Petronis, 2008). In other words, children carrying a genotype known to increase susceptibility for a specific mental disorder may only develop that disorder if they are exposed to specific environmental risk factors (Wermter et al., 2010).

In the last decade, studies that focus on epigenetics have multiplied. This term refers to a variety of processes that affect gene expression without any direct modification of the nucleotide sequence in the DNA (Schuch, Utsumi, Costa, Kulikowski, & Muszkat, 2015). Therefore, epigenetic modifications do not alter the sequence composition of the genome, but regulate its operation. According to the epigenetic paradigm, even structural conditions determined by genes might be modulated, inhibited, or expressed by environmental adversities or influences (Schuch et al., 2015). Epigenetic information provides instruction on how, where, and when genetic information will be used. Therefore, environmental factors may modulate gene expression and influence behavior.

At the molecular level, the classic epigenetic alteration is that of *DNA methylation*, namely modification of chromatin structure. Chromatin is the mixture of DNA and proteins that synthesizes chromosomes and constitutes an indispensable part of the mechanism of regulating genetic expression. In other words, chromatin can inform the cell about which genes must silence and which must be released for action, because the structure of a gene may alternatively be in an "active" or "inactive" state (Mill & Petronis, 2008). Through DNA methylation, histone modifications, and small regulatory RNAs, the epigenome systematically controls gene expression during development, both in utero and throughout life (Archer, Oscar-Berman, & Blum, 2011).

Therefore, the expression of a great part of human variability does not only depend on DNA structure, but also on regulatory markings that control whether and how a gene is expressed (Rutter, 2008). Furthermore, a gene may have different effects on different domains through epigenetics (Rutter, 2006b). This process possibly plays a pivotal role in the fact that ADHD characteristics are not often expressed in the same way in monozygotic twins, as could be expected given their common genome (Lehn et al., 2007). This interpretation is buttressed by the finding that one-third of monozygotic twins have a common genome but different epigenomes (Fraga et al., 2005).

The epigenome is the result of the epigenetic process. It refers to a network of chemical "switches" that regulate the activation of human genes, determining the degree to which their activity will be reinforced or reduced. The epigenome is altered due to extrinsic factors, because it basically functions as a mediating link between the environment and the cell. In other words, a dynamic epigenome transduces psychosocial stimuli to the genome (Mathews & Janusek, 2011). Therefore, parts of the epigenome are modified throughout our lifetime, depending on the environmental conditions, changing in turn the expression of genes. These changes either protect the cell or lead to diseases. Furthermore, it has been suggested that epigenetic effects can be transmitted across generations. This process is of paramount importance because there is significant evidence that these chemical processes might be susceptible to change, even reversible, and as such allow for intervention and modification (Mill & Petronis, 2008; Rutter, 2007).

In the past decade, it became increasingly clear that epigenetic processes play crucial roles in the modulation of neurodevelopment. In a prospective study seeking to investigate whether the methylation patterns of neuronal genes observed at birth were associated with the occurrence of ADHD symptoms at age 6 years, it has been found that lower DNA methylation levels were associated with higher ADHD symptom scores (van Mil et al., 2014).

A series of studies provides examples of the interaction between genetic and environmental factors, including prenatal and perinatal as well as psychosocial factors. Most studies have focused on prenatal exposure to maternal risk factors. The impact of maternal smoking and alcohol consumption during pregnancy on the development of ADHD in the offspring has already been discussed. However, studies have identified some interactions between exposure to smoke in the prenatal period and specific genotypic variants, particularly affecting DAT1, DRD4, and neuronal acetylcholine receptor subunit alpha-4 (CHRNA4) (Becker, El-Faddagh, Schmidt, Esser, & Laucht, 2008; Brookes et al., 2006). For instance, children with two copies of a DAT polymorphism exhibited greater risk of ADHD, but only if they were exposed to prenatal maternal smoking (Kahn, Khoury, Nichols, & Lanphear, 2003). Similarly, the association between maternal alcohol use during pregnancy and offspring ADHD seems to be moderated by the 30-bp VNTR polymorphism in intron 8 of DAT1. Children with the 10/3-repeat haplotype who were exposed prenatally to alcohol are at increased risk for ADHD compared to children without the haplotype (Brookes et al., 2006).

There are similar findings about the interaction of genes with other environmental factors as well. For example, there is evidence suggesting that the impact of exposure to pesticides during pregnancy is associated with negative effects on the cognitive development of the child depending on the genotype (Engel et al., 2011). Moreover, it seems that some food additives may aggravate ADHD symptoms in children who have already developed the disorder but only if they carry a certain genotype, namely polymorphisms in the HNMT gene (Stevenson et al., 2010).

The postnatal social environment has received less research attention in gene-by-environment studies. However, according to the diathesis-stress model, ADHD is more heritable in a risk environment. The basic premise of this model is that environmental stressors activate a diathesis, transforming the potential of personal predisposition into the presence of psychopathology (Pennington et al., 2009).

A recent study suggested that child maltreatment constitutes a risk factor for ADHD only in girls and particularly in those who have the 10R allele of the DAT1 gene (Li & Lee, 2012). Furthermore, children homozygous for this allele have been found to be at increased risk of developing ADHD symptoms when exposed to social adversity (Laucht et al., 2007). These findings are not surprising given that individuals with this specific genotype are generally more susceptible to psychosocial stress (Caspi, Hariri, Holmes, Uher & Moffitt, 2010). Additionally, it appears that children with DRD4 7-repeat risk alleles have a greater vulnerability to poor parenting (Bakermans-Kranenburg, Van IJzendoorn, Pijlman, Mesman, & Juffer, 2008).

Another relevant example concerns studies that were conducted on Romanian orphans who had been exposed to severe deprivation very early in infancy and had increased rates of ADHD relative to the general population (Rutter et al., 2007). First of all, it should be noted that many of these children developed not only symptoms of ADHD but also symptoms of ASD and ID, indicating that exposure to such circumstances generally has detrimental effects on the child's neurodevelopment (Beckett et al., 2006).

Stevens and colleagues (2009) investigated the moderating effect of DRD4 and DAT1 functional polymorphisms on deprivational influences following institutionalization upon ADHD. It has been found that severe institutional deprivation was an ADHD risk factor only among children with specific polymorphisms in the DAT1 gene but not the DRD4 genotype. The authors offer two possible explanations regarding the underlying neurobiological mechanism responsible for this interaction. One possibility is that the presence of the DAT1 10R-6R haplotype alters dopaminergic functioning in such a way to make the child differentially susceptible to the influence of the environment. A second possibility is that extended environmental adversity has epigenetic effects leading to differential expression of the DAT1 gene within those brain regions involved in the regulation of attention, activity, and impulse control through dopaminergic mechanisms.

In a similar vein, Lahey and colleagues (2011) carried out a 9-year longitudinal study of 4- to 6-year-old children with ADHD in order to test interactions between maternal parenting and the VNTR polymorphism in the 3′ untranslated region of the dopamine transporter gene of children. The researchers obtained a significant inverse relation between levels of both positive and negative parenting at 4 to 6 years and the number of later symptoms of CD, but mainly among children with two copies of the 9-repeat allele of the VNTR.

It has been suggested that the same genes may interact with different environmental risk factors, affecting, therefore, different aspects of the disorder in different developmental periods. There is evidence that interaction of genes with prenatal and perinatal risk factors mainly affects the development of hyperactivity, whereas their interaction with psychosocial factors at a subsequent developmental stage may be mainly associated with inattention (Nigg et al., 2010).

In conclusion, it seems that the development of ADHD depends on extremely complex and multifactorial etiological mechanisms, the understanding of which may have multiple effects in clinical practice. The prenatal and early postnatal environment can "program" stable changes in gene expression through epigenetic processes. These processes lead to changes in the structure and function of the brain and affect its biochemistry, resulting in the development of ADHD in the individual. Therefore, epigenetic modifications serve as the molecular basis for environmental signals that influence behavioral outcomes and, as such, provide a bridge between the psychosocial and the biological world (Mathews & Janusek, 2011).

This understanding may facilitate the early detection of children who have a genetic predisposition to develop ADHD and the implementation of early intervention programs (see Section 11.7). It can lead to the improvement of methods of classification and diagnosis of the disorder. It can assist in understanding its heterogeneity. It can also lead to the development of more effective treatments. It can explain the different response of many individuals with ADHD to different kinds of medications. On a macro-social level, it can affect the social policy with reference to environmental toxins, diet, and other related factors.

Most importantly, it seems that epigenetics render secondary prevention of ADHD possible in high-risk children. On the one hand, DNA is an active target for remodeling by cellular signals that are activated by environmental events (Meaney, 2010). On the other hand, the developing brain is malleable and more readily affected by environmental factors, as significant neurobiological development takes place during early life. It seems plausible, then, that early life experiences, involving primary affective-regulatory processes, may become embedded in the circuitry of the developing brain through epigenetic modifications and lead to long-term changes in neurobiology and behavior (Schuch et al., 2015). Consequently, the developing brain may be more susceptible to environmentally induced epigenetic modification through early intervention, which, in turn, may alter these children's adverse developmental course and intercept the course of the disorder itself.

6 Theories of ADHD

6.1 Introduction

The progress of science is shaped by the assumptions held by scientists about the nature of the phenomena under investigation. These assumptions provide a common theoretical basis that allows communication among them (Sonuga-Barke, 1998). In addition, theoretical models are a systematic guide in clinical research aiming at a better understanding of psychopathology.

Neuropsychological theories of ADHD etiology have become the norm in past years, following up on a nearly century-long tradition. The goal of neuropsychological research was initially to detect single core deficits that provide parsimonious causal explanations of the diversity of behavioral symptoms found in ADHD (Pennington, 2005; Sonuga-Barke, 1998). This idea dominated the conceptual landscape for many years and has been one of the major constraints on scientific progress in the field of ADHD (Sonuga-Barke & Coghill, 2014).

However, there is no theoretical model that can explain all deficits that are associated with ADHD or account for all cases of the disorder (Nigg, Willcutt, Doyle, & Sonuga-Barke, 2005). ADHD is neuropsychologically heterogeneous, with different individuals being affected to different degrees and in different domains. Transition from models that attempt to identify a unique core deficit to models that incorporate multiple neurocognitive deficits and pathways shows a reconceptualization of ADHD toward recognition of its complexity and heterogeneity. In these models, ADHD is regarded as an umbrella construct that includes multiple potentially dissociable but overlapping neuropsychological profiles (Castellanos, Sonuga-Barke, Milham, & Tannock, 2006).

Some researchers postulate that ADHD may be the common outcome of different etiological pathways with different pathophysiological substrates resulting in different neuropsychological types of the disorder (Nigg, Blaskey, Stawicki, & Sachek, 2004; Sonuga-Barke, 2005). Others suggest that ADHD can be attributed to dysfunction of multiple neuronal networks within the individual (Sergeant et al., 2003).

Over the last decade, ADHD is not seen as a disorder of attention but as a disorder in key aspects of self-regulation, particularly in the effective use of mechanisms that enable behavior to be adapted appropriately to a changing context (Johnstone, Barry, & Clarke, 2012; Nigg, 2005a). Furthermore, most current models suggest that ADHD is associated with motivational factors and altered reinforcement sensitivity (Luman, Trip & Scheres, 2010).

We will present briefly four influential theories of ADHD. Each of them has undergone transformations over the last decade in order to include new data that have arisen from genetic and neuropsychological studies. Some of these additions are components of the other leading theories, and all of them can be conceived as varying along a continuum of explanatory power (Johnson, Wiersema, & Kuntsi, 2009). These theories contribute substantially to the deeper understanding of the neuropsychological processes that lead to the clinical manifestation of ADHD.

Beyond these four predominant theories, it should be mentioned that other models also exist, mainly referring to reinforcement sensitivity in ADHD. Tripp and Wickens (2008) proposed a neurochemical deficit model and discussed altered reinforcement sensitivity in ADHD in relation to neurotransmitter functioning. Nigg and Casey (2005) proposed a brain-pathway deficit model and discussed ADHD in relation to neuroanatomical pathway functioning. Frank (2005), and Williams and Dayan (2005) approached ADHD from a neurocomputational perspective. However, detailed presentation of these models is beyond the scope of the present chapter.

6.2 Executive Dysfunction Theory

The *Executive Dysfunction theory*, which was suggested by Russell Barkley in an especially influential paper (1997c), is the most well-researched theoretical conceptualization of ADHD. Its main idea is that symptoms of ADHD arise from a general weakness in executive functioning, with poor inhibitory control being a core deficit.

Typically developing individuals regulate their behavior through internal processing of information related to the present context, past events, and anticipated future events (Barry & Kelly, 2006). Therefore, typically developing individuals usually display rule-governed behavior, which is controlled by verbally mediated rules that describe the contingency between a behavior and a consequence without either of them being necessarily present. However, behavior of individuals with ADHD is governed more by temporal factors, such as immediate reinforcement, rather than internally driven processes. Consequently, individuals with ADHD have difficulty exhibiting appropriate behaviors when external consequences are removed, exhibiting deficits in self-regulation, namely rule-governed and goal-oriented behavior (Barkley, 2012a).

In order to better understand the concept of self-regulation, we will borrow an example from Barkley (http://adhdlectures.com/pdf/ADHD_EF_and_SR.pdf). Let's imagine that we enter a coffee shop while we are on a diet and see a display counter filled with pastries. An option is to give in to the temptation and buy some. Alternatively, we may decide to resist. In order to deal with temptation while waiting for our coffee to be prepared, we may avert our eyes from the counter, walk to a different section of the shop, engage in internal speech concerning the necessity of buying these pastries, or even visualize an image of the new slenderer version of ourselves we expect to achieve in the near future.

These actions require a number of distinct yet interacting mental abilities: (a) we have to realize that a dilemma has arisen when we entered the shop (self-awareness); (b) we have to restrain our urge to buy the pastries (behavioral inhibition); and (c) we have to redirect our attention away from the tempting objects (attentional management), either by talking to ourselves (verbal self-instruction) or by visualizing an image of our goal (nonverbal working memory). These mental activities may lead to self-regulation for the achievement of a goal.

According to the Executive Dysfunction theory, the essential impairment in ADHD is an early appearing core deficit in response inhibition, a superordinate cognitive function within the larger system of executive functioning components. Response inhibition sets the occasion for the occurrence of the other executive functions and refers to three distinct processes: (a) inhibiting the initial prepotent response[1] to an event so as to create a delay in responding; (b) interrupting an ongoing response that is proving ineffective, thereby permitting a delay in the decision to continue responding; and (c) protecting the self-directed responses that will occur within the delay, as well as the goal-directed behavior they generate, from disruption by competing events and responses (interference control or resistance to distraction) (Barkley, 1997a). Response inhibition constitutes a prerequisite for the development of self-control

(Muraven & Baumeister, 2000), regulation of emotions (Eisenberg, 2002), and cognitive flexibility (Arbuthnott & Frank, 2000).

Deficits in inhibitory control lead to secondary impairments in other executive functions that are partially dependent on inhibition for their effective execution. According to Barkley (2012), the basis for the concept of executive functioning arose in the 1840s, in an effort to understand the functions of the frontal lobes generally and the prefrontal cortex specifically. Several attempts to operationalize components of this umbrella term have been made since then, but the construct of executive functioning is still criticized for conceptual underspecification (Nigg, 2005a).

One of the most popular definitions appearing in the literature refers to executive functioning as "the ability to maintain an appropriate problem-solving set for attainment of a future goal" (Welsh & Pennington, 1988, pp. 201–202). Executive functions are "higher-order" neurocognitive processes that are necessary for mature adult goal-directed behavior, such as conflict detection, set-shifting and set maintenance, higher level attention, interference control, integration across space and time, decision making, temporal foresight, and working memory (Stuss and Alexander, 2000). They also include planning, sequencing, reasoning, sustained attention, inhibition of inappropriate and selection of appropriate responses, and regulation of response via alertness or allocation of effort (Castellanos et al., 2006). These processes facilitate decision making by maintaining information about possible choices in working memory and integrating it with information about the current context, in order to opt for the optimal response.

Barkley (1997a) postulates that deficits are observed in four cognitive mechanisms of executive functioning: (a) nonverbal working memory (sensing to the self); (b) verbal working memory (internalization of speech); (c) self-regulation of affect, motivation, and arousal (self-directed appraisal); and (d) reconstitution (self-play). These four functions share a common characteristic:

> They all represent private, covert behaviors that at one time in development were entirely public and outer- or other-directed in form. They have become turned on the self to control behavior, and have become covert or internalized in form as maturation proceeds.
>
> (Barkley, 1997a, pp. 154–155)

Recently, Barkley (2012a) revised the definition of executive functioning by including emotional and social (apart from cognitive) aspects. Emotion regulation and self-motivation are now included as important components of executive functioning. In this more recent version, Barkley broadened his model by separating out self-awareness (or self-direction of attention), which was originally placed within the nonverbal working memory system. He has also incorporated the concept of *genetic phenotype*, defined as genetic effects at a distance that are of consequence to the survival and welfare of the organism. He argues that inhibition, self-awareness, and self-directed sensory-motor actions codevelop as a unity to form the executive functioning as it likely evolved in human evolution. Subsequently, executive functioning has been expanded to include self-directed speech, emotion/motivation, and play (planning/problem solving) (Antshel, Hier, & Barkley, 2014). Therefore, the initial instrumental cognitive level of executive functioning expands over time to link up with methodical, self-reliant behavior and the next higher level in a hierarchy of executive functioning in daily life. This linkage between instrumental and self-reliant levels of executive functioning is part of what Barkley argues as an *extended phenotype* of executive functioning into daily and lifelong effective social functioning (Antshel, Hier, & Barkley, 2014).

Deficits in executive functions are associated with a great array of behavioral manifestations in ADHD. For example, deficiency in nonverbal working memory may interfere with children's capacity to use imitation effectively in order to acquire new knowledge and to learn from other people's experiences in the formulation of their own behavior. This happens because the ability to mentally represent information is necessary in order to apply past acquired information in the formulation of current and future directed behavior. Deficiency in internalization of speech weakens the control of behavior by verbal thought and the application of rules and instructions given by others. Deficiency in self-regulation may diminish the individual's capacity to regulate negative affect, delay gratification, and persist in goal-directed actions. Reconstitution refers to the capacity for analyzing and synthesizing internal information in order to generate behaviors in response to new events. Deficiency in reconstitution may negatively impact behavioral flexibility and creativity of the individual.

From a neurological standpoint, executive functioning involves the operation of multiple neural circuits that connect the prefrontal cortex with the basal ganglia, the thalamus, and the parietal cortex, which present structural abnormalities and poor activation among individuals with ADHD (Bradshaw & Sheppard, 2000). Furthermore, the dopaminergic and noradrenergic neurotransmitter systems, which dysfunction in individuals with ADHD, are particularly important for the functioning of the aforementioned brain regions (Nieoullon & Coquerel, 2003). It should be noted that the use of these neural circuits in the conceptualization of ADHD is not specific to the Executive Dysfunction theory but extends to other models as well.

This model is supported by a plethora of neuropsychological studies that have found deficits in executive functions among individuals with ADHD (Bitsakou, Psychogiou, Thompson, & Sonuga-Barke, 2008; Nigg, 2005a; Pennington & Ozonoff, 1996). Meta-analyses of over 250 studies provide strong support for the theory that ADHD is due in part to weaknesses in inhibitory control and other aspects of executive functioning (Willcutt, 2015).

However, several research findings question the capacity of this theory to explain the full complexity of symptoms of ADHD (Sergeant et al., 2003; Willcutt, Doyle, Nigg, Faraone, & Pennington, 2005). The overall effect sizes from relevant meta-analyses indicate that each specific executive functioning deficit accounts for no more than 10% of the variance in ADHD symptoms (Willcutt, 2015). Therefore, although deficits in executive functioning are clearly associated with ADHD, they are neither necessary nor sufficient to cause ADHD in isolation. Furthermore, these deficits are not exclusively associated with ADHD, but they seem to be present in other disorders as well, including CD (Morgan & Lilienfeld, 2000) and ASD (Geurts, Verte, Oosterlaan, Roeyers, & Sergeant, 2004; Happe, Booth, Charlton, & Hughes, 2006).

It has been found that executive dysfunction is not present in all individuals with ADHD (Wahlstedt, Thorell, & Bohlin, 2009). For instance, Nigg and colleagues have demonstrated in a combined analysis of more than 1,000 ADHD cases that only approximately half of children with ADHD show a deficit in inhibitory control as measured on an extensive battery of neuropsychological tasks. It has been suggested that ADHD caused by executive dysfunction could be considered as a distinct subtype with difficulties of greater severity for a subgroup of individuals (Nigg et al., 2005). Furthermore, deficits in executive functioning seem to be primarily associated with inattention symptoms rather than hyperactivity/impulsivity symptoms (Chhabildas, Pennington, & Willcutt, 2001; Wahlstedt et al., 2009; Willcutt et al., 2005).

Finally, neuropsychological tests are often quite complex and involve a number of different executive functions. Performance of individuals with ADHD on neuropsychological tests is context-dependent because executive functions are not fixed core deficits but dynamic processes (Nigg & Casey, 2005; Sonuga-Barke et al., 2010). Factors such as motivation and arousal also influence performance, making it difficult to locate the root of dysfunction (Willcutt et al.,

2005). For example, response inhibition, as measured by the *Stop Signal* task,[2] is the summation of cognitive functions, including sustained attention, goal-oriented behavior, and target detection, as well as control of the primed motor response (Castellanos et al., 2006). Therefore, it is not clear to what degree deficits in each of these processes contribute to the poor performance of individuals with ADHD on this task.

However, regardless of its weaknesses, this seminal model is of indisputable value. It is currently the most fully articulated cognitive model of ADHD, providing a sophisticated account of the development of executive functions and regulatory control. This model has considerably contributed to the understanding of ADHD and has prompted numerous studies that led to the development of alternative theoretical models of ADHD.

6.3 The Delay Aversion Theory and the Dual Pathway Model

The *Delay Aversion theory* has been described by Edmund Sonuga-Barke and colleagues (Sonuga-Barke, Taylor, Sembi, & Smith, 1992) and belongs to the theories that focus on the role of motivation and reinforcement sensitivity in the conceptualization of ADHD. This theory is based on the assumption that ADHD behaviors are functional expressions of an underlying motivational style, termed delay aversion. Initial empirical data showed that poor performance of children with ADHD on tasks that require behavioral inhibition may not be due to inability to withhold responding but to their attempt to reduce the trial length (Sonuga-Barke, Houlberg, & Hall, 1994).

Individuals differ in their tolerance for boredom and their intrinsic motivation by a particular task (Sonuga-Barke & Castellanos, 2007). It is suggested that children with ADHD have a negative emotional reaction to delay, expressed in different ways under different settings and circumstances. When faced with a choice between immediacy and delay, they will choose immediacy, exhibiting impulsivity. They will also choose small immediate over large delayed rewards only in circumstances where this leads to a shorter overall delay (Tripp & Alsop, 2001; Willcutt et al., 2008). In situations where there is no choice and delay cannot be avoided, children with ADHD systematically try to reduce their perception of length of delay by either creating or attending to nontemporal features of the environment that may serve as immediate reinforcers. Consequently, children with ADHD often shift their attention to aspects of the environment that stimulate their interest or act on this environment to increase arousal. It has been demonstrated that subjective perception of time during delay is modified when attention is directed toward nontemporal features of the environment (Gautier & Droit-Volet, 2002), or when the environment provides stimulation through activity (Sonuga-Barke, 2003).

From a psychopathologic perspective, behaviors that create nontemporal stimulation, such as fidgeting, could be characterized as hyperactivity. Attention to nontemporal stimuli that may take children off task could be characterized as inattentiveness and is expected to increase during long and boring tasks and lead to poor performance. An increase in children's hyperactivity and inattention during delay periods has been empirically confirmed (Antrop et al., 2002). Children with ADHD display patterns of vigilance to delay-related cues similar to those exhibited by anxious children in situations of physical and social threat (Sonuga-Barke, De Houwer, De Ruiter, Azensten, & Holland, 2004). However, it has been argued that delay aversion should be more strongly associated with hyperactivity than with inattention (Castellanos et al., 2006). Support for this claim has been found in two studies of community-based samples (Scheres, Lee, & Sumiya, 2008; Thorell, 2007).

This model posits that ADHD may be the outcome of a process of classical conditioning, which is based on the interaction of a genetically susceptible child with their environment (Sonuga-Barke, 2002; 2005). Parental practices play a moderating role in this process. A child genetically predisposed to delay aversion, who prefers small and immediate rewards instead of bigger and delayed ones, often fails to effectively respond to contextual demands related to waiting and delay. Parents who set unrealistically high standards and do not forgive failures to wait are more likely to create the context for the emergence of ADHD. Furthermore, parental failure to follow through on promised rewards may lead the child to distrust future events and be unwilling to wait. Under certain circumstances, the child's delay aversion and impulsive response may elicit negative or punitive responses from adults. Gradually, delay settings acquire negative connotations for the child due to their association with the unpleasant experience of failure and disappointment, from which the child tries to escape (Sonuga-Barke, 2005).

The Delay Aversion theory has been extended and refined to provide an integrated model for the conceptualization of ADHD, which is referred to as the *Dual Pathway model.* This model has incorporated aspects of the Executive Dysfunction theory within a single psycho-pathophysiological framework (Sonuga-Barke, 2003; 2005; Sonuga-Barke et al., 2010). As Sonuga-Barke (2002) states, "at a more abstract level, the model represents a reconciliation of two philosophically distinct views of behavioral disorder—one that seeks to identify the site of dysfunction in disorder while the other seeks to explore the role of function" (p. 31). This model challenges the Delay Aversion theory, in which delay-related processes in ADHD are seen as a single overarching construct, and recognizes two distinct pathways between originating causes and clinical expression.

The first pathway is cognitive, includes diminished inhibitory control, is linked to the meso-cortical dopamine branch of the dopamine system projecting into the prefrontal cortex, and is categorical in nature. Children who follow this pathway differ qualitatively from their typically developing peers. On a neuropsychological level, they exhibit difficulties in planning, emotion regulation, and generally self-regulation.

The second pathway is related to motivation and delay aversion, is associated with fundamental alterations in reward mechanisms, is linked to the meso-limbic dopamine branch associated with the reward circuits, and is dimensional in nature. Children on this pathway have continuously distributed traits and differ quantitatively from their typically developing peers. They may manifest ADHD primary symptomatology only in delay-rich environments or in case of high social expectations about impulse control.

This model was based on empirical data from studies both on school-aged (Solanto et al., 2001) and preschool children (Sonuga-Barke, Dalen, & Remington, 2003). More recent studies revealed similar findings (Karalunas & Huang-Pollock, 2011; Thorell, 2007). These studies compared performance of children with ADHD and normal controls both on response inhibition and delay aversion tasks. It has been found that measures of inhibitory deficit and delay aversion were not correlated with each other but were both moderately associated with ADHD.

Initially, the two pathways were presented as independent factors acting additively to account for ADHD symptomatology. However, other studies found that a significant subset of individuals with ADHD exhibit deficits in both processes, suggesting that these pathways may not be entirely independent but may interact synergistically (Marco et al., 2009; Sonuga-Barke, Sergeant, Nigg, & Willcutt, 2008). Furthermore, on a neuro-biological level, these two pathways can be understood as the interplay between cortical and subcortical brain regions in the regulation of action, cognition, and motivation (Haber, 2004; Sonuga-Barke, 2003).

This theory has further evolved to an integrated motivational framework whereby the preference of immediate over delayed rewards in ADHD is just one expression of a broader motivational style (Sonuga-Barke et al., 2008). According to the most recent accounts, delay aversion is grounded in the neurocircuitry of catecholamine-modulated brain reward circuits. This circuit is specifically implicated in signaling rewards and regulating the maintenance of responding under conditions of delayed rewards (Cardinal, Pennicott, Lakmali, Robbins, & Everitt, 2001). Fundamental impairments in the neural signaling of delayed reward lead to discounting of this kind of reward and to failures to choose future rewards.[3] During development, the delay-impaired child learns to associate delay settings with social censure and failure and becomes motivated to escape or avoid delay. Therefore, delay escape becomes an especially potent reinforcer for individuals with ADHD.

This acquired secondary motivational attitude, combined with a preference for immediacy, linked to deficits in signaling future rewards, finally leads to a marked tendency for delay avoidance. This attitude is expressed in different ways as a function of whether delay can be escaped or must be tolerated. In the first case, individuals with ADHD may exhibit impulsivity by choosing an immediate reward. In the second case, they may exhibit either inattention, by allocating their attention to aspects of the environment that reduce the subjective perception of time, or hyperactivity, by acting on their environment to create nontemporal stimulation.

This delay-averse motivational style constrains the normal acquisition of organizational skills by reducing the demands for self-organization and limiting the experience required for the development of such skills (Sonuga-Barke, 2003). By this mechanism, a fundamentally motivational disorder acquires specific cognitive characteristics in the areas of everyday self-organizational skills, and eventually takes the clinical form of ADHD (Sonuga-Barke, 2005).

This model was further extended and refined to include temporal processing deficits in ADHD as a dissociable third neuropsychological pathway, leading to the proposal of a triple pathway model (Sonuga-Barke, Bitsakou, & Thompson, 2010).

From a clinical perspective, the usefulness of this model is evident in terms of both diagnosis and treatment. First, it stresses the importance of specifying the neuropsychological subtype of ADHD in clinical assessment. Second, it supports the potential value of personalized approaches to treatment, and may lead to novel putative treatment targets. For instance, in the case of the delay aversion subtype, introduction of delay restructuring through training is proposed (Sonuga-Barke, 2004). With the use of the operant technique of delay fading, children can be presented with repeated exposure to rewarded predictable delay periods of gradually increasing length in order to increase their tolerance to delay and, thereby, reduce ADHD symptoms. Finally, this model places particular emphasis on the investigation of environmental factors that trigger and reinforce symptom manifestation to be used as targets in parent training programs.

6.4 The Cognitive-Energetic Model

The *Cognitive-Energetic model* was originally proposed by Sanders (1983) and was later applied to individuals with ADHD by Joe Sergeant and colleagues (Sergeant, Oosterlaan, & van der Meere, 1999), in order to offer an alternative conceptual framework for ADHD by differentiating it from other developmental disorders. This model combined aspects of several models of ADHD and was grounded in an information processing framework. It has been claimed that both the Executive Dysfunction theory and the Delay Aversion theory have been incorporated in the Cognitive-Energetic model in terms of how the ventro-medial frontal cortex influences executive functions (Sergeant et al., 2003).

The Cognitive-Energetic model suggests that information processing efficiency can be explained in terms of three ordered levels and their energy distribution. The first level is *process* and refers to the activation of four computational mechanisms of attention: (a) stimulus encoding, (b) memory search, (c) binary decision, and (d) motor organization.

The second level is *state* and encompasses three distinct energetic pools: (a) arousal, (b) activation, and (c) effort. Arousal is defined as phasic responding, which is time-locked to stimulus processing and is influenced by signal intensity and novelty. The arousal pool is associated with the mesencephalic reticular formation and the amygdala (Sergeant, 2005). Activation is a tonic change of physiological activity that is associated with readiness to respond (Pribram & McGuinness, 1975). In this respect, activation is related to the concept of sustained attention (Posner & Peterson, 1990). The activation pool is associated with the basal ganglia and striatum. Effort is the necessary energy to meet the demands of a task (Sergeant, 2000). The effort pool is located within the hippocampus.

Finally, the third level is *management*, which includes executive functions such as planning, monitoring, error detection, and error correction. These functions lead to the evaluation of the energetic state and regulate the effort that is required for the execution of a certain task. Management is associated with the prefrontal cortex.

Sanders (1983; 1998) showed that both process and energetic state may be affected by the modification of the tasks that the individual is asked to perform. For example, arousal state may be affected by the repetitiousness of the stimulus, whereas activation may be affected by the vagueness of the stimulus. Effective cognitive function lies in an optimal energetic state, in which arousal and activation are adapted as successfully as possible to the demands of a given situation.

The concept of state regulation is central to this model. When a suboptimal state of arousal for the demands of a task is identified by the evaluation mechanism, effort is required in order to counterbalance it by either activating or inhibiting the arousal and activation states. The association between arousal/activation and performance is considered to take the form of an inverted U, which means that any deviation from the optimal energetic state, either extremely low or extremely high activation, leads to performance decrements (Metin et al., 2016; van der Meere, Gunning, & Stemerdink, 1995).

Sergeant and colleagues (2003) embrace Barkley's view that ADHD symptoms reflect executive control dysfunction, but they suggest that the hypothesized inhibition deficit in ADHD is dependent upon the state of the subject and the allocation of energy to the tasks at hand. Consequently, inhibition deficits in ADHD may, at least in part, be due to energetic dysfunction.

The concept of poor arousal and activation in individuals with ADHD is also buttressed by some neurochemical and neurophysiological studies that showed that arousal is associated with the noradrenergic system and activation with the dopaminergic system (Borger & van der Meere, 2000; Wiersema, van der Meere, Roeyers, Van Coster, & Baeyens, 2006). Furthermore, the elevated theta/beta power ratios that have been found in the EEGs of individuals with ADHD have been related to cortical underarousal (Barry, Johnstone, & Clarke, 2003).

This model postulates that event rate, the speed with which stimuli are presented, is an important determinant of performance and has its locus at the activation pool. The association between ADHD and reaction time variability as a function of event rate has been consistently demonstrated in studies using both clinical (Johnson et al., 2007; Klein, Wendling, Huettner, Ruder, & Peper, 2006) and community samples (Berwid et al., 2005; Kuntsi, Andreou, Ma, Borger, van der Meere, 2005).

According to the Cognitive-Energetic model, event rates alter the motor activation state. When event rates speed up or slow down appropriately, performance of individuals with ADHD can worsen or significantly improve. A recent meta-analysis confirmed that low event rate may induce underactivation, resulting in slow and inaccurate responses, whereas high event rate may induce overactivation, resulting in fast and inaccurate responses (Metin, Roeyers, Wiersema, van Der Meere, & Sonuga-Barke, 2012). In general, children with ADHD perform more poorly in conditions of relatively slow event rates as compared with fast and moderate event rates. It has also been proposed that best performance is obtained at medium event rates (Sonuga-Barke, 2002; van der Meere et al., 1995). Therefore, the optimal event rate for some tasks might simply be different for individuals with ADHD compared to individuals without ADHD.

In order to compensate for a suboptimal activation state, extra effort allocation is necessary during difficult and challenging conditions. Effort allocation is closely associated with the individual's motivation as well as with reward anticipation (Sergeant, 2005). It has been confirmed that high motivation and reward anticipation significantly improve task performance by optimizing the energetic state of individuals with ADHD (Andreou, Agapitou, & Karapetsas, 2005; Luman et al., 2005). Therefore, according to this model, the sensitivity for reinforcement contingencies in individuals with ADHD is explained as evidence for a lack of effort allocation. Encouragement and reward improve arousal and activation state and induce the necessary energy to meet the task demands, leading to better performance. Therefore, differences between individuals with ADHD and typically developing individuals are minimized when individuals with ADHD are at an optimal state of arousal, activation, and effort.

The Cognitive-Energetic model integrates cognitive and motivational factors into a comprehensive interactive model, which is corroborated by a plethora of research data. However, it has some weaknesses. First, it is difficult to specify the optimal energetic state, which may depend on the context and differ among individuals (Johnson et al., 2009; Luman et al., 2005). Second, empirical evaluation of various components of this model is difficult, although on a neurobiological level recent research findings clarify the concept of energetic state, which is fundamental in this model (Killeen, Russell, & Sergeant, 2013).

6.5 Dynamic Developmental Theory

The *Dynamic Developmental theory* has been developed by Sagvolden and colleagues (Sagvolden, Johansen, Aase, & Russell, 2005) on the basis of behavioral analysis. It incorporates many aspects of previous models and broadens the conceptualization of ADHD by including developmental, social/environmental, and neurobiological aspects. It mainly refers to the hyperactive-impulsive and the combined type. Much of the data supporting this theory are based on animal data.

The Dynamic Developmental theory suggests that ADHD is the result of fundamental alterations in basic reinforcement learning processes via two behavioral mechanisms: altered *reinforcement* of novel behaviors and deficient *extinction* of maladaptive behaviors.

The efficacy of reinforcement is highly dependent on its temporal immediacy. In ADHD, rewards become abnormally low in reinforcing power as they become distant in time due to a shorter and steeper delay-of-reinforcement gradient, which abbreviates the time period in which learning could take place between behaviors and consequences. The delay gradient describes the effect of the reinforcer and the time interval between response and reinforcer (Luman et al., 2005). A steep gradient indicates that a reinforcer loses its value relatively quickly when the delay between the desired behavior and the reinforcer increases, resulting in impulsive behavior (Johansen, Aase, Meyer, & Sagvolden, 2002). Consequently, it seems that only responses in proximity to a reinforcer will be conditioned in children with ADHD, and only short sequences of responses can be reinforced. However, when reinforcers are powerful, frequent, and immediate, the differences in behavior between children with ADHD and their typically developing peers are expected to be minimal.

Extinction of a behavior generally occurs when reinforcement is no longer provided and subsequently the response is not elicited. It is suggested that the extinction process is faulty in ADHD, thereby perpetuating the exhibition of socially inappropriate behaviors.

Dysfunction of these mechanisms is attributed to a hypofunctioning mesolimbic dopamine system, which is considered to be the ***brain reward circuitry*** (Johansen et al., 2002; Wightman & Robinson, 2002). A large body of evidence shows the importance of increased activity of the mesolimbic dopamine system, particularly in the nucleus accumbens, during reinforcement (Johansen, Sagvolden, Aase, & Russell, 2005; Knutson, Adams, Fong, & Hommer, 2002). Hypofunction of this system among individuals with ADHD when anticipating reward has been corroborated by neuroimaging studies (Plichta et al., 2009; Stark et al., 2011). Dopamine hypofunction might be caused by a combination of insufficient glutamate input from the prefrontal cortex to dopamine neurons and faulty regulation of dopamine release (Sagvolden et al., 2005).

Dopamine neuron activity has the function of constantly reprogramming neuronal connections by strengthening connections associated with reinforced behavior, while at the same time weakening other neuronal connections associated with nonreinforced behavior. These synapses created by dopamine release in early developmental periods determine, to a great extent, the way in which we perceive reinforcement through the life span. Consequently, behavior is guided by neuronal representations of previous experience, namely by our encoded memories in neuronal networks. The hypofunction of dopamine systems limits the time available for associating behavior with its consequences in individuals with ADHD, resulting in altered reinforcement and extinction signals (Johansen et al., 2005).

Within this model, the short-term effects of the interactions between child predispositions and environmental social factors produce predictable behavioral outcomes as a child develops a history of behaviors and consequences. The inability to associate behaviors with consequences would inhibit learning in the social contexts where emerging behaviors are rewarded, punished, or extinguished, depending on their appropriateness (Barry & Kelly, 2006). The symptoms of ADHD would emerge over time as the child adjusts neurologically to dopamine activity (Sagvolden, Johansen et al., 2005). Furthermore, these altered learning processes may affect language development and the cognitive functions controlled by language, such as rule-governed behavior and self-control.

This model explains many of the clinical manifestations of ADHD, such as delay aversion, hyperactivity, poor sustained attention, behavioral variability, and poor response inhibition (Johansen et al., 2009). For example, hyperactivity may be attributed to a combination of factors, including failure in extinction, resulting in too many responses, and a short delay-of-reinforcement gradient, resulting in poor reinforcement of appropriate behavior. Impulsivity may also be explained by a short delay-of-reinforcement gradient, due to which the significance of the immediate reinforcer is much stronger than the delayed reinforcer, which remains unlinked to the original response. Delayed learning of complete and functional behaviors may be causing the frequent shifts from activities, noncompletion of tasks, lack of long-term planning, and other behaviors that are considered as resulting from impulsivity (Aase & Sagvolden, 2005). Therefore, children with ADHD need stronger and more salient reinforcers to produce the desired behavior compared with typically developing children.

The dopamine system also regulates selective attention toward a stimulus depending on its reinforcing power for the individual relative to other available stimuli (Johansen et al., 2009). The power of a given reinforcer differs from person to person. For example, a child with ADHD who plays a computer game, which is perceived as a highly reinforcing process, experiences heightened levels of dopamine release and the ensuing positive emotions, resulting in the increase of sustained attention and performance on this game. In contrast, studying a school subject, which is not usually perceived as a reinforcing process, does not lead to increase of dopamine release, thus resulting possibly in the child's poor attention and performance. Therefore, it has been suggested that attention problems may result from changed motivational processes, as they are evident mainly when the task is unwelcome or uninteresting (Johansen et al., 2002).

Sagvolden and colleagues (2005) distinguish between *motor impulsiveness* and *cognitive impulsiveness.* Motor impulsiveness is defined as "bursts of responses with short inter-response times" (p. 399). Cognitive impulsiveness implies that "private events like thoughts and plans are dealt with for short sequences of time with rapid shifts, resulting in problems with generating and following plans, problems with organizing own behavior, forgetfulness, and inefficient use of time" (p. 399). In that sense, problems like off-task behaviors or reduced length of time spent on a task, usually linked to inattention, are viewed as aspects of cognitive impulsiveness within this model (Johansen et al., 2002).

According to this model, ADHD is not considered a pathological condition that represents a distinct entity, qualitatively different from "normal" behavior, but rather a case in which the function of the Central Nervous System (CNS) exceeds the limits of normal variability and adaptation. The two key mechanisms of this theory have been empirically tested mainly with animals (Johansen, Killeen, & Sagvolden, 2007; Johansen, Sagvolden, & Kvande, 2005) and less with children with ADHD (Aase, Meyer, & Sagvolden, 2006; Aase & Sagvolden, 2006; Sagvolden, Aase, Zeiner, & Berger, 1998).

One of the main points of criticism of this theory is that it cannot explain the whole set of difficulties experienced by children with ADHD, including increased motor activity during sleep and other sleep disturbances, which cannot be interpreted by altered reward sensitivity and poor extinction of inappropriate behavior (Karatekin, 2005; Rothenberger & Kirov, 2005). Similarly, these mechanisms cannot explain attention deficits that seem to be associated with certain cognitive deficits (Carrasco, Lopez & Aboitiz, 2005). Another point of criticism refers to the fact that this theory is mainly based on animal models, thus giving oversimplistic explanations to behaviors that are more complex in humans (Rubia, 2005).

However, it is a theoretical model with substantial appeal for ADHD. It integrates a plethora of research findings into a comprehensive model, taking into account both neurobiological and social factors. It incorporates development and socialization as critical factors in the conceptualization of ADHD across the life span (Barry & Kelly, 2006). Moreover, it suggests clear research hypotheses that can be empirically tested (Levy, 2005) and uses the theory of social learning in the attempt to understand the course of ADHD throughout development (Nigg, 2005b). On a clinical level, it facilitates prediction of the behavior of individuals with ADHD in certain circumstances and, therefore, allows better control of this behavior (Moderato & Presti, 2005). It also provides a theoretical framework for several behavioral interventions in which reinforcement contingencies are used (Luman et al., 2005).

6.6 Summary

The four theories of ADHD reviewed in this chapter are powerful in accounting for a wide range of ADHD symptoms. Although they have significant differences among them, they share a lot of common aspects. They build upon each other and incorporate previously proposed narrower views within larger models (Barry & Kelly, 2006). Current multiple-deficit models suggest that ADHD arises from the additive and interactive combination of several neuropsychological deficits, none of which is necessary or sufficient to cause the disorder when it occurs in isolation (Willcutt, 2015). These deficits are mediated by neural networks distributed across many locations of the brain.

Poor inhibitory control and altered response to reinforcement are recognized as fundamental aspects of ADHD, whether they are considered as causal or symptomatic. Furthermore, all theories pinpoint dysfunction in related neural systems, mainly located in the prefrontal cortex of the brain. Finally, the importance of dopamine as the main neuromodulator implicated in signaling of rewards is acknowledged almost unanimously (Williams et al., 2002).

A crucial advance is to confirm the validity of different neuropsychological profiles, and to clarify the relationships among them. It is important to determine what proportion of individuals with ADHD have each profile, what proportion have combinations of these deficits, and what proportion have difficulties that remain unexplained by any of these models, taken singly or in combination (Pennington, 2005). Furthermore, it is important for neuropsychological theories to integrate cognitive and motivational processes and their interaction, which is definitely a hallmark of both adaptive and maladaptive behavior (Pennington, 2005).

Over the last years, many researchers have made an attempt to compare the predominant theoretical models of ADHD, so that they can incorporate their common aspects into an integrated model, with the aim of a comprehensive multidimensional conceptualization of the disorder. Such an example is the formulation of the Dual Pathway model, which also incorporates aspects from the Executive Dysfunction theory. The same theory attempts to be connected with the Cognitive-Energetic model. For example, a question is raised about whether the concepts of delay aversion and suboptimal energetic state constitute clearly distinct concepts or refer to the same concept put in different words because of the different theoretical background they come from (Sonuga-Barke et al., 2010). These two theories highlight the dynamic nature of ADHD and its contextual dependence, and suggest that differences between individuals with ADHD and typically developing individuals are minimized under certain circumstances. Furthermore, both the Dual Pathway model and the Dynamic Developmental theory stress the importance of immediate and frequent reward for the improvement of performance of individuals with ADHD.

Consequently, researchers coming from different theoretical positions may be describing the same phenomena using different words and concepts. They may also be defining the same phenomena from a different temporal or anatomical perspective. For example, an arousal deficit among people with ADHD may influence their motivation to complete a task (Cognitive-Energetic model) or their ability to sustain attention to a task (Executive Dysfunction theory), which behaviorally may manifest as delay aversion and poor performance on some executive function tasks. This behavior may be reinforced inappropriately and, due to dysfunction of the dopaminergic system, extinction of the socially inappropriate behavior may not occur (Dynamic Developmental theory) (Johnson et al., 2009).

In conclusion, each theory has significantly contributed to the better understanding of ADHD, but there is a long way toward a comprehensive model that will effectively integrate all the currently available empirical data on ADHD and will thoroughly explain the pathway from genes to pathological behavior for all individuals who manifest this exceptionally heterogeneous disorder. Future models need to fully integrate temperament, neuropsychology, genetics, and developmental interpersonal processes. Humans are not at the mercy of the dopaminergic function of their brain. Their behavior is not shaped merely by skillful manipulations of rewards and punishments. We believe that understanding the mechanisms that differentiate the way that each person perceives and interprets their personal experience may constitute the missing link from the chain that links genes, brain anatomy, environment, psychosocial factors, and clinical manifestation of ADHD symptoms.

Notes

1 The prepotent response is that response for which immediate reinforcement is available within a particular context or which has been previously associated with that response in that context (Barkley, 1997a).
2 This test presents equally probable stimuli on a computer screen (e.g., different letters) with the instruction to press a corresponding key as fast as possible, depending on which letter appears, creating a prepotent tendency to respond on most trials. In a minority of trials, a signal (e.g., a punctuation mark) indicates that the child should not respond but inhibit their prepotent response.
3 This view is more thoroughly discussed in the presentation of the Dynamic Developmental theory (Sagvolden et al., 2005, see Section 6.5), an alternative but related model, acknowledged by the Dual Pathway model.

7 Comorbidity

7.1 Conceptualization and Kinds of Comorbidity in the Case of ADHD

7.1.1 The Issue of Comorbidity in Developmental Psychopathology

In psychopathology, comorbidity refers to the co-occurrence of two or more supposedly different disorders in the same person at above chance levels (Caron & Rutter, 1991). The prevalence and extent of the comorbidity phenomenon has led to a very large literature documenting comorbidity across the range of psychopathology (Krueger & Markon, 2006). Over the last years, the comorbidity issue has been studied extensively, mainly for three reasons. First, comorbidity can yield considerable insight into the causal pathways that lead to mental disorders. Understanding how comorbidity arises is an important step toward understanding the development of psychopathology. Second, understanding comorbidity contributes to the advancement of nosology and the improvement of diagnostic classification systems (Tomblin & Mueller, 2012). Third, increasing knowledge regarding the etiology of comorbidity between two disorders may lead to more rational treatment decisions and, eventually, to more effective interventions (Rhee, Willcutt, Hartman, Pennington, & DeFries, 2008).

Different conceptualizations of comorbidity have been proposed in order to explain the reasons for joint occurrence of mental disorders. Some of them consider comorbidity as a genuine phenomenon, and others view it as an artifact of the structure of the classification systems. A comprehensive description of possible comorbidity models has been provided by Klein and Riso (1993) and quantified by Neale and Kendler (1995).

A possible explanation offered is that co-occurring disorders share common etiology or risk factors. A further explanation is that a disorder may lead to the occurrence of another through the process of epigenesis, or that one disorder may create an increased risk for the emergence of the other. Alternatively, one disorder may constitute an early manifestation of another (Caron & Rutter, 1991). In other words, two disorders may represent different stages in the course of the same underlying condition. Finally, another possible basis for observed comorbidity is that the comorbid condition is not simply a co-occurrence of two separate disorders but rather represents a meaningfully different condition that is distinctive from the two disorders when they occur separately (Rutter, 1997). In most cases, however, it is acknowledged that comorbidity refers to similarities in the pathogenic processes of the co-occurring disorders (Tomblin & Mueller, 2012). This possibility arises from the fact that most developmental disorders are multifactorial in origin and that many causal factors are not diagnosis-specific.

A radically different interpretation of comorbidity is offered by Cramer, Waldorp, van der Maas, & Borsboom (2010), in their conceptualization of mental disorders and their symptoms as a network. Under the assumption of such an approach, a mental disorder is a network of symptoms that stand in direct, possibly causal, relations to one another. Comorbidity between mental disorders is then conceptualized as direct relations between symptoms of multiple disorders.

Nevertheless, comorbidity still remains a controversial issue. In conventional medicine, for example, physical diseases usually refer to distinct clinical entities with clearly defined boundaries and structured pathology. Therefore, potential co-occurrence of some physical diseases cannot be disputed. In developmental psychopathology, however, the rarity of cases that are described as meeting criteria for a single disorder signals the need for fundamental changes in the way we think about classifying developmental disorders. Therefore, some developmental disorders, including ADHD, are better viewed as existing along a dimension of severity and differing not in kind but in degree (Angold, 1988).

This view is consistent with the concept of *spectrum* in developmental psychopathology, which suggests a continuum of clinical conditions with similar phenotypes but different levels of severity (Kaplan, Dewy, Crawford, & Wilson, 2001). Therefore, there is a range in variability across developmental dimensions, with some individuals displaying more severe features than others. According to this line of reasoning, there may be a continuum of severity in terms of the number of diagnoses. In other words, children identified with two or more developmental disorders may present in fact *only one* clinical condition but *of greater severity* relative to children who receive a diagnosis without comorbid disorders.

To illustrate the concept of the continuum, the case of Jim will be presented briefly.

> Jim is a 7-year-old boy with normal intellectual capacity who displays symptoms of hyperactivity, impulsivity, and inattention to a degree that is inconsistent with his developmental level. At the same time, he has difficulties in most areas of language development, including articulation, auditory discrimination, oral expression, and pragmatics. He is also clumsy, has poor fine and gross motor skills, along with serious difficulties in main academic domains, namely in reading, writing, and mathematics. This child is particularly defiant and disobedient and has difficulty with social interactions which may stem, among other reasons, from his difficulties in pragmatics.

This mixed clinical presentation is very commonly seen by clinicians who work in the field of child psychopathology and principally indicates the presence of ADHD. However, if we want to establish a diagnosis for Jim, we will find ourselves in the awkward position of having to give seven (!) different diagnoses according to DSM-5: (a) ADHD; (b) language disorder; (c) speech-sound disorder; (d) SLD with impairment in writing, reading, and mathematics; (e) Developmental Coordination Disorder (DCD); (f) ODD; and (g) social (pragmatic) communication disorder. Additionally, in case the child experiences heightened stress because of his inability to respond to developmental challenges and environmental demands, which is quite common, then he might also meet the criteria for the diagnosis of one or more ADs.

The case of Jim could be better described as a case of *multimorbidity*, because "comorbidity" does not explicitly refer to more than two diagnoses and patterns of association among mental disorders (Batstra et al., 2002). This term is gaining wide acceptance in the literature of medical disease, but it appears rarely in the literature of mental disorders (Krueger & Markon, 2006). However, if we consider this situation as simply multimorbid, we are unable to comprehend what is really happening to Jim. In reality, it is highly unlikely that the child truly has seven different and entirely distinct disorders. Thus, it can be inferred that the use of comorbidity in everyday clinical practice raises several concerns. As Kaplan and colleagues note (2001), few children represent prototypical cases of specific disorders, yet describing a child as